The MMPI: A Contemporary Normative Study of Adolescents

Developments in Clinical Psychology

Glen R. Caddy, series editor
Nova University

MMPI-168 Codebook, by Ken R. Vincent, Iliana Castillo, Robert I. Hauser, H. James Stuart, Javier A. Zapata, Cal K. Cohn, and Gregory O'Shanick, 1984

Integrated Clinical and Fiscal Management in Mental Health: A Guidebook, by Fred Newman and James Sorensen, 1986

The Professional Practice of Psychology, edited by Georgiana Shick Tryon, 1986

Clinical Applications of Hypnosis, edited by Frank A. DePiano and Herman C. Salzberg, 1986

Full Battery Codebook, by Ken R. Vincent, 1987

Developments in the Assessment and Treatment of Addictive Behaviors, edited by Ted D. Nirenberg, 1987

Feminist Psychotherapies, edited by Mary Ann Douglas and Lenore E. Walker, 1988

Child Multimodal Therapy, by Donald B. Keat II, 1990

Psychophysiology for Clinical Psychologists, by Walter W. Surwillo, 1990

Strategic Health Planning: Methods and Techniques Applied to Marketing and Management, by Allen D. Spiegel and Herbert H. Hyman, 1991

Behavioral Medicine: International Perspectives (Vol. 1–3), edited by D.G. Byrne and Glenn R. Caddy, 1992

The MMPI: A Contemporary Normative Study of Adolescents, by Robert C. Colligan and Kenneth P. Offord, 1992

In Preparation:

Language and Psychopathology, by Stephen Schwartz

The MMPI: A Contemporary Normative Study of Adolescents

Adolescent Norms for Basic Validity, Clinical, and Selected Research/Supplemental Scales with Commentary on the MMPI-2 and MMPI-A

Robert C. Colligan, Ph.D.

Head, Section of Psychology, Mayo Clinic and Mayo Foundation;
Professor of Psychology, Mayo Medical School; Rochester, MN

Kenneth P. Offord, M.S.

Consultant, Section of Biostatistics, Mayo Clinic
and Mayo Foundation; Assistant Professor of Biostatistics,
Mayo Medical School; Rochester, MN

ABLEX PUBLISHING CORPORATION
NORWOOD, NEW JERSEY

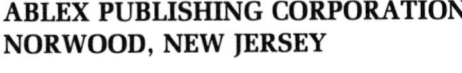

Printed in the United States of America.

Library of Congress Cataloging-in-Publication Data

Colligan, Robert C.
    The MMPI: a contemporary normative study of adolescents/Robert
C. Colligan, Kenneth P. Offord.
        p. cm.
    "Adolescent norms for basic validity, clinical, and selected research/
supplemental scales with commentary on the MMPI-2 and MMPI-A."
    Includes bibliographical references and index.
    ISBN 0-89391-872-5 (cloth); 0-89391-985-3 (paper)
    1. Minnesota Multiphasic Personality Inventory.   2. Minnesota
Multiphasic Personality Inventory for Adolescents.   I. Offord,
Kenneth P.   II. Title
BF698.8.M5C65   1992
155.2'83—dc20   92-24378
                                                                        CIP

Ablex Publishing Corporation
355 Chestnut Street
Norwood, New Jersey 07648

TABLE OF CONTENTS

LIST OF TABLES

LIST OF FIGURES

Dedication

To the memory of Virginia (Jinny) Riddle Hathaway, who for more than 30 years was a school psychologist and later chief psychologist for the Child Study Department of the Minneapolis Public Schools, whose skills, sensitivity, concern, understanding, and caring about children, adolescents, and co-workers contributed so much to their lives.

Foreword

Psychological tests, like most wines, are not expected to improve with age. Yet in each situation there are some that do gain richness as they age. Hathaway observed, not long after the MMPI had achieved its final profile format, that the instrument appeared adequately promising and warranted a full-scale revision, which he thought should address many of its already recognized limitations. Those remarks were made (in 1952) before the MMPI had become the standard resource for objective evaluation of personality. It is also significant that these remarks were made before the development and introduction of psychotropic medications into the practice of psychiatry. Years later, Hathaway looked back upon the instrument that he had developed and, considering the challenge of revising it, concluded that the two factors mentioned above, the vast body of information tied to the original form and the virtual absence of unmedicated criteria cases, made revision virtually impossible. As though to validate Hathaway's decision, the authors of the new edition of the test, the MMPI-2, neither used new criteria cases nor provided norms that were tied to the existing literature for the MMPI.

The pressures to revise an old instrument come from the promise that a revision will provide an improved and more valid estimate of the true score. In the area of intelligence testing, new tests provided real improvements. In the case of the Binet, the revision done by Terman was a natural derivative of the old scale and a clear improvement. Devising an intelligence scale, however, requires a set of appropriate items, a bunch of kids, and a sharp pencil. From the items administered to children of known age, items may be selected or discarded depending upon their interrelationships. They are age weighted. Scores may be derived from accumulated item responses, and ratios provided. If one chooses, a normal distribution may be derived. The great wonder of the efficiency of this process is the natural relationship between age and intellectual development, which allows for the selection of items. As long as items relate to age, and as long as their content relates to school performance, the results are assured.

Criteria groups such as in the MMPI provide an analagous function for the MMPI scales.

By 1953 psychiatry ceased to be a static field, just as the MMPI was becoming established. Electroshock treatments and psychotropic medications were to sweep through the diagnostic and treatment facilities of the nation. With these changes it became increasingly difficult to find cases in any way comparable to those that had appeared in the original criteria groups for the MMPI. More important, perhaps, was that traditional descriptive psychiatry was on the wane, and with it, the ability to locate homogeneous groups of cases.

Thus, as we survey the research on the MMPI, we are still left with the problem that the original scales (those based upon diagnostic groups) have not been replaced. The old scales are the scales currently available. Even the most recent efforts to develop a new test have neither succeeded in providing meaningful new clinical scales nor improved scales based upon criteria groups. The original clinical scales, based as they were on a few cases, are still the heart of the test. That they work as well as they do affirms how carefully the original item selection and case selection work was done.

If not scale revision, is it possible that a better selection of normative material would enhance the validity of the test? It is interesting to note that, while Hathaway once revised the normal sample, he showed little interest or conviction that other normative materials would add to the usefulness of the test. Starke was well aware of the rapidly expanding body of information concerning the MMPI and that the test's postpublication validation rested on these data. Just as to change the item format or item content threatened the data base, so he realized that changing the normative material would make it exceedingly difficult to get access to that rapidly expanding amount of information.

It should have been noted from the earliest uses of test scores that the scores obtained could not have been from normal distribution scores. (Obtaining as many very high T scores as occurred would have exhausted the world's population many times over.) Hathaway also must have been aware that the inclusion of the normal contrast group from which items were derived into the norm group accentuated any contrast between the norm group and other test takers. Even when his extensive studies of ninth graders showed that a number of the scales were distributed differently among adolescents, Hathaway showed little interest in the development of adolescent norms for the test. Never having had children, Starke thought of adolescents as essentially pathological adults.

For a careful methodologist and a sound scientist to have ignored these obvious difficulties with the parameters that were attached to the normal group seems quizzical. Yet a parametric shift had occurred in the methods that were developing for the interpretation of the MMPI. These appeared to make the norm group a less significant matter (especially as contrasted with the place of the norm group in the intelligence test).

It was recognized at the outset that the function of the scale items was to provide a measure of the degree to which a subject (responding to those items) was like the criteria group. Each item answered in the positive direction could be interpreted as evidence of the presence of a greater number of symptoms that were characteristic of the criteria group. The more items, the more symptoms. But what was recognized beyond this was that the discriminant validity of the test (its multiphasic power, if you will) depended upon the competition between elevations on the different scales, which were measured simultaneously in the administration of the test. While elevation represents the severity of symptomatology, *pattern* is the index to underlying psychopathology and its organization.

Work with adults had sped along rapidly as the test gained acceptance in the Veterans' Administration after World War II. Test interpretation had become a task of pattern recognition. Use of the MMPI for adolescents lagged considerably. Among adolescents, the most powerful research studies focused upon normal populations. Clinical studies followed. Thus, it was possible for Marks, and others, to promote a set of adolescent norms that had time to gain acceptance before such a large body of clinical information had been derived from adult norms.

One might note that Hathaway was never impressed with the importance of statistical elegance for its own sake, just as he was not impressed with the concept of social desirability as a necessary sanitizing concept in the selection of items. Starke recognized that the MMPI was functioning better than he had ever dreamed, flawed as it might be, and he was not apt to go into a revision that would be driven simply by statistical elegance. Thus he did not address some of the more subtle questions that are now being raised.

A look at raw data from large populations shows how differently the raw scores for the scales are distributed. When the available options concerning a new norm group are reviewed, the first question is, how *should* these data be distributed? Some are almost normal in distribution, and some show very distinct positive skewness. In a revision of the norms, should the scales be transformed so they all have the same shape? Some writers strongly argue "yes" and provide elegant distributions to convert raw scores. Others maintain that the naturally occurring different distributions are themselves important. It is argued that, with respect to the highly skewed distributions, they are different from the more normally occurring distributions in ways that should not be altered. Possibly one of the reasons that pattern recognition analysis works with the MMPI profile is that existing distributions accentuate fundamental pathology.

Tied as we are to the past and to the process of pattern recognition, absent so far as I know of any standardization materials that could be used to develop new patterns to be recognized to supplant the old ones, it seems to me that a leap away from the old test is a leap away from the database that supports the use of the test. This is an argument that is driven by the clinical use of the test in the study of clinical symptomatology and its underlying pathology. These clinical practices seem to depend on access to the old system of scoring and interpretation.

Other uses of the test include cross-cultural contrasts, age-group comparisons, studies of ethnicity, and personnel selection. All of these applications are better addressed if the test materials available have a kind of currency and recognized generality in their normative representations.

If the psychologist is faced with the problem of determining (a) how a particular subject contrasts with the background group, and (b) what is known about the personality of that subject, it seems as though it is necessary to have both kinds of normative material available. A defense of the use of the test in either context, personnel or cross-cultural work on the one hand, or clinical personality work on the other hand, requires the basic reference material upon which descriptive (comparative) statements can be made.

In these two tasks, the user can select the appropriate normative materials from those available. The user is not restricted to justifying the use of a simple norm group decision for all uses of the test. Colligan and Offord provide the reader with an additional set of normative data, representing a new and valuable resource to address specific interpretive application of the MMPI.

Peter F. Briggs, Ph.D.
San Diego 1991

Preface

This work describes the adolescent MMPI research project done as a companion to the contemporary normative MMPI study of adults completed by members of the Section of Psychology and Section of Biostatistics at the Mayo Clinic in 1983. In the adolescent study, we wanted to study changes that might have occurred in the way contemporary normal adolescents in junior and senior high school respond to the items of the MMPI. Because of the many significant changes that we observed when MMPI responses from our contemporary normal adult sample were compared with the original adult MMPI norms, and that later were noted by the authors of the MMPI-2, we believed that it was necessary to investigate the possibility that similar changes had occurred among adolescents ages 13 to 17 years during the 25 years since Marks and Briggs established their normal adolescent samples.

This research report also presents the procedures used to develop contemporary adolescent norms and is intended to serve as a manual for their use. Just as with the contemporary norms developed for adults, the adolescent T-score tables were constructed by raw score conversion procedures that yield *normalized* T scores. This is a departure from the original Hathaway standard scores, which were based on linear scaling procedures that have been used in the past, and also is different from the linear transformations used in developing the "uniform" T scores for the adult norms of the MMPI-2. These procedures, by design, maintain the skewness in the underlying distribution of raw scores and the spikiness of the MMPI profile (Ben-Porath, 1990). The procedures are difficult to understand and represent a departure from the manner in which contemporary psychological test scores are usually reported. Normalized T scores also differ significantly from the "uniform" T scores (a variation of the traditional linear T score) in that the "uniform" T scores do not follow the gaussian (normal) curve. If the underlying distribution of raw scores does not follow a gaussian form, use of normalized T scores provides more accurate estimates of target percentile ranks than do linear scaling procedures. Thus, clinicians who use these normalized T scores, which have the traditional mean of 50 and the traditional standard deviation of 10, can be confident that a raw score falling at T score 60 will be very close to the 85th percentile and that a raw score at 70 will be very close to the 98th percentile for all of the 13 basic validity and clinical scales. This condition was not always true for the standard T scores of the MMPI that were derived using linear scaling procedures, and for the MMPI-2 it is true only for the eight scales on which uniform T scores were calculated.

Not surprisingly, given the restricted age range in our contemporary normal adolescent sample—13 through 17 years—no age-related changes of significance to practitioners were found on the clinical scales. Those observed on scales 5 (Mf) and 0 (Si) accounted for such a small proportion of the variance that it was not believed necessary to develop age-specific tables as done by Marks and Briggs.

We also have included detailed information about the manner in which the study was performed so that (a) readers will be able to understand how these findings were obtained and what they represent, and (b) other researchers will be able to replicate our procedures and findings.

Finally, because the MMPI is being used with increasing frequency among adolescents other than the medical and psychiatric patients for whom it was originally intended, it is essential that clinicians, researchers, and students be keenly aware of the differences in response patterns between adolescents of the past and contemporary teenagers. Interpretive statements based on profile configuration and elevation are likely to remain the same, but clinical accuracy and usefulness are likely to be increased and the results of greater relevance in understanding our adolescent patients when these contemporary norms are used.

Acknowledgments

Only persons who have conducted similar research projects can appreciate the dependence of the principal investigators on the various contributions of other people in bringing such research efforts to fruition. The acknowledgments that follow convey only in part the appreciation we feel for the assistance and persistence of the people who helped us at different points throughout the study.

First, we express gratitude to the Mayo Clinic and Mayo Foundation for the intramural funds that made this research project possible.

Just as with the contemporary normative study of adults, we again found the assistance of Dr. Harold Baker, who consulted with us during the subject selection process, and Ms. Toni Genalo, both from the statistical laboratory at Iowa State University, to be invaluable during the 3 years that it took to complete this normative study.

In chronologic order of the tasks of the study, our project was initiated by my secretary, Ms. Jacquelyn D. Keller, who assisted in managing the nearly 12,000 introductory letters and the other items that made up the study packet. She was assisted by the supervisor and assistant supervisor of the Mayo Clinic Typing Service, Ms. Barbara S. Pickett and Ms. Rebecca M. E. Valentine, and by Ms. Barbara (Barcy) Jones, our primary packet assembler. Later, Ms. Lois Falk served as study coordinator, beginning with the process of organizing the telephone interview schedule for the members of nearly 7,000 households. Our 11 telephone interviewers were outstanding in their persistence and quality of work, both of which contributed significantly to the gratifying response rate from our households and from the teenagers themselves. Thus, we owe a very special thank-you to Ms. Marie Ivnik, Ms. Evelyn Rasmussen, Ms. Karen Osborne, Ms. Kay Fritsch, Ms. Linda Malec, Ms. Maggie Bartels, Ms. Eva Colligan, Ms. Lois Rink, Ms. Barb Kirschling, Ms. Jane VanNorstrand, and Ms. Carol Bailey. Their work began with a full-day training session on telephone interviewing and record-keeping procedures in January of 1985 and ended approximately 6 months later as the school year drew to a close for our teenage subjects.

The massive amounts of data were ably managed by Ms. Christine Tjossem and Mr. Jeffrey J. Larson-Keller from the Section of Biostatistics, and by Mr. Glenn A. Augustine, from the Section of User Systems and Analysis; Ms. Marilyn K. Nelson was primarily responsible for preparing the results in tabular form.

Mrs. Rose M. Barry was responsible for typing the first drafts, but the manuscript itself could not have been prepared without the assistance of Ms. Patricia J. Erwin, our reference librarian, who willingly expedited our efforts at obtaining archival material from various sources. In addition, members of the Section of Publications, Ms. Maurine T. Wulf, Mrs. Roberta J. Schwartz, Ms. Virginia A. Dunt, Ms. Barbara A. Golenzer, Mrs. Dorothy L. Tienter, and Dr. Bernard K. Forscher, Head of the Section of Publications, were all instrumental in preparing the manuscript component of the project, with Ms. LeAnn M. Stee being most directly involved in the editorial process. We also thank Ms. Leslie L. Litwiller and Ms. Marcia W. Blackburn from computer graphics, Mr. Robert C. Benassi, Head of the Section of Medical Graphics, Mr. Thomas F. Flood in Photographic Production, and Mr. James S. Martin, Head of the Section of Photographic/Audiovisual/Video Communications for their willingness to participate and the creativity that they brought to their efforts.

We have also appreciated the assistance of Dr. Harriet Blodgett in preparing the dedication and the comments we received from Roger Greene, Ph.D., Robert Archer, Ph.D., and David Nichols, Ph.D., pertaining to the supplemental MMPI scales selected for inclusion. We thank Dr. Glenn R. Caddy, editor of the *Developments in Clinical Psychology* series, Ms. Barbara Bernstein, acquisitions manager, Ms. Carol Davidson, production manager, Mr. Walter J. Johnson, President, and the production staff at Ablex for their energy and support in bringing this project to its completion as a manual for clinicians.

Robert C. Colligan, Ph.D.
Kenneth P. Offord, M.S.
Mayo Clinic and Mayo Foundation
Rochester, Minnesota

Biographical Notes

Starke Rosecrans Hathaway was born in Central Lake, Michigan, on August 22, 1903. He described himself as "intensely curious about the way things worked" during childhood and adolescence and had a great interest in mechanical matters and electronics—he earned his ham radio operator's license at age 13 years. He subsequently enrolled in the electrical engineering program at Ohio University. During his junior year, after discovering that the textbook for a course in electricity was one he had studied independently during high school, he changed his major to psychology, initiating his studies with courses in advanced mental measurement and an advanced seminar in psychology. He never enrolled in the introductory psychology courses, and after completing a minor in mathematics he earned his bachelor's degree in psychology in 1927. During these years he maintained a campus workshop where he developed a vacuum tube psychogalvanometer. He received a patent for this device, which was a forerunner of later polygraph equipment. He also taught physiology and introductory psychology courses. His master's degree in psychology, with a minor in statistics, was obtained at Ohio State University in 1928. In 1930 he began his doctoral research in physiology with a minor in anatomy at the University of Minnesota. He was awarded the Ph.D. degree in 1932 for his thesis, "An Action Potential Study of Neuromuscular Relations." For the next 5 years he pursued postgraduate studies in gross and microscopic anatomy, continued to use his own electromechanical devices to perform myographic studies of voluntary motions and nerve conduction, taught courses in laboratory psychology and statistics, and, since he had but a few courses left, also considered finishing an M.D. degree. Although he stated that he never regretted not earning his M.D. degree, he also admitted that there were times when his life would have been easier had he done so. Later, he wrote that he continued to do these things ". . . until 1937, the year I really began my career as a 'medical-psychologist' . . ." (Krawiec, 1978, p. 109). For the next 40 years he provided strong leadership in the field of medical psychology. Dr. Hathaway died at his Minneapolis home on July 4, 1984.

John Charnley McKinley was born in Duluth, Minnesota, on November 8, 1891. He received his bachelor's degree at the University of Minnesota in 1915, his M.A. degree in 1917, and his M.D. degree in 1919. Dr. McKinley was trained as a neuropsychiatrist and neuropathologist but also was interested in research and earned his Ph.D. degree in 1921 at the University of Minnesota with a doctoral dissertation entitled, "The Intraneural Plexus of Fasciculi and Fibers in the Sciatic Nerve." After psychiatric training at the New York City Psychiatric Institute, Dr. McKinley returned to the University of Minnesota as an instructor and later became assistant professor of neuropathology. Subsequently, he became a professor of neuropsychiatry and was head of the department of medicine and neuropsychiatry until his retirement in 1946. He died in January 1950.

The collaboration between Drs. McKinley and Hathaway began early and was fruitful. McKinley was the head of the division of neuropsychiatry at the University of Minnesota at the time Hathaway began his doctoral studies. McKinley was interested in using the electromyographic apparatus and vacuum-tube amplifiers developed by Hathaway for physiologic investigations. Six articles in this area were published by Hathaway before his work in personality assessment. In addition, and before the collaboration that led to the development of the MMPI, McKinley and Hathaway, with three other members of the department of neuropsychiatry, joined in reviewing the literature of the day, a project that yielded a medical textbook, *An Outline of Neuropsychiatry* (1944), edited by McKinley.

SOURCES

American men and women of science (the social and behavioral sciences). (1973). 12th ed. Edited by Jaques Cattel Press. New York: J.C. Press/R.R. Bowker.

Hathaway, S. R. (1978). Through psychology my way. In T. S. Krawiec (Ed.), *The psychologists: Autobiographies of distinguished living psychologists* (Vol. 3, pp. 105–123). Brandon, VT: Clinical Psychology Publishing Company.

Krawiec, T. S. (Ed.). (1978). *The psychologists: Autobiographies of distinguished living psychologists* (Vol. 3). Brandon, VT: Clinical Psychology Publishing Company.

McKinley, J. C. (1944). *An outline of neuropsychiatry* (4th ed.). Dubuque, IA: William C. Brown.

New York Academy of Medicine. (1969). *Author catalog of the library* (Vol. 24). Boston: G.K. Hall.

Who was who in America. (1960). Vol. 3.

AN OVERVIEW:
MMPI RESPONSE PATTERNS
FROM CONTEMPORARY NORMAL
ADOLESCENTS AND ADULTS

Proficiency in use of the Minnesota Multiphasic Personality Inventory (MMPI) with adolescents requires a thorough grounding in basic MMPI knowledge and in the interpretive procedures in use today. This work is not intended as an interpretive manual because several such contemporary texts are available, such as those for use with adolescents (Archer, 1987) and adults (Friedman, Webb, & Lewak, 1989; Graham, 1990; Greene, 1991), those presented specifically for the supplemental/research scales (Caldwell, 1988; Levitt, 1989), and the guide for providing specific interpretive feedback to the client or patient (Lewak, Marks, & Nelson, 1990).

Hathaway initiated work on the MMPI more than 50 years ago, in 1937; his goal was to assist physicians in screening medical patients for psychological problems related to the presenting medical symptoms (McKinley & Hathaway, 1943). Although Hathaway and McKinley stated that they had difficulty finding a publisher, the University of Minnesota Press finally agreed to publish it, and thus the MMPI became generally available to clinicians about 1943. The acceptance and successful application of the new instrument were gratifying, and the MMPI rapidly gained popularity among medical and mental health professionals. Researchers and clinicians alike expended great amounts of energy on develop- ment and use of the new instrument with a wide variety of patients with medical or mental health problems, greatly expanded its use among adolescents, and increasingly applied it to normal people as part of job-screening procedures and to other populations outside the medical and mental health practice, for which it had been originally intended. In 1983, a team of Mayo Clinic psychologists and a biostatistician (Colligan, Osborne, Swenson, & Offord, 1984c) developed new adult norms that complemented the MMPI data on 50,000 medical patients published in 1973 (Swenson, Pearson, & Osborne). However, although there has truly been a proliferation of new scales and shortened forms of the MMPI have been developed, little attention was given to revision-oriented research until

1

recently. In 1989, a virtually new instrument, the MMPI-2, was published specifically for adults, but the authors of the MMPI-2 manual state, "we recommend that you use the original MMPI for adolescents" (Butcher, Dahlstrom, Graham, Tellegen, & Kaemmer, 1989, p. 15).

Although Hathaway and McKinley had originally intended that nonworking items from the MMPI pool would be deleted and new ones would be added— indeed, they commented on the ease with which this task could be done because the original MMPI was presented to the patient as a card-sorting task with one MMPI item printed on each card—once the MMPI had been copyrighted and published as a booklet of items, this activity ceased (Hathaway & McKinley, 1940). It was unfortunate that the experimental version (that is, the card form) was not maintained, because it would have allowed new items to be developed and evaluated empirically. Furthermore, given copyright constraints, researchers had no opportunities to deal with problems such as reading level, the definitions of difficult words, modification of phraseology to conform to contemporary nonsexist standards, and the alteration of colloquial terms from the past.

However, of greatest concern to clinicians and researchers alike was the lack of contemporary norms for both adolescents and adults. The original normative base was established during the late 1930s and the early 1940s. The 1943 manual indicated that the sample was "fairly adequate for the ages 16 to 55" (Hathaway & McKinley, 1943, p. 3) and reported that 19 women and 13 men were in the age range from 56 to 65 years, but no adolescents younger than 16 years and no geriatric subjects older than 65 years were included. At that time, a typical Minnesota normal adult was about 35 years old, had about 8 years of education, lived in a small town or a rural area, worked at a skilled or semiskilled trade, and was married; women tended to have a somewhat higher level of education than men, typically near the 10th-grade level (Dahlstrom, Welsh, & Dahlstrom, 1972).

The MMPI was used with adolescents from its beginning. Initially, however, Hathaway did not believe that separate norms for adolescents were necessary or desirable. In the manuals, the adolescents and young adults were typically grouped in the age range of 16 to 25 years, comparable to the current age range of high school and college students. Later, starting in 1947, Hathaway undertook with Monachesi (Hathaway & Monachesi, 1953), a sociologist, a large-scale study related to juvenile delinquency that included more than 15,000 ninth-grade students throughout the state of Minnesota with a follow-up of 12th-grade students completed in 1957. On the basis of data from their ninth-grade sample, they subsequently supported the practice of drawing two additional lines on MMPI profiles obtained from adolescent patients to provide another reference point for understanding and interpreting the profile (Hathaway & Monachesi, 1963).

Although Hathaway and his associates were aware of age-related changes, both among older adults and younger adolescents, insufficient numbers were available for the purpose of developing age-specific norms. However, with the gradually increasing age of our society, geriatric norms are essential. Conversely, because the MMPI is being used with increasing frequency among younger adolescents, norms for this group are equally desirable. Clinicians have commented for years on the informal adjustments they found necessary to make in interpreting MMPI profiles for contemporary young people (for example, scale 5 [Mf]) and for geriatric clients (for example, on scales 1 [Hs] and 2 [D]). However, aside from a refinement of the original Minnesota normal sample by Hathaway and Briggs

(1957) and the adolescent data provided by Marks and Briggs (1967), no contemporary normative standards were ever published. A provocative doctoral thesis by Diehl (1977) specifically drew attention to the obvious changes in expected MMPI response patterns based on a large community sample over a wide age range, but unfortunately the results of this study were never made available to clinicians.[1]

It is obvious that there have been dramatic changes for adolescents and adults in our society since 1937. Our higher educational level; the changes brought about by the feminist movement; an improved standard of living; liberalization of moral, religious, and ethical views; the increased divorce rate; greater family mobility; changes in the nuclear family; and the shift from an agrarian economic base to present-day technology have had an impact on everyone in the United States.

To evaluate the degree to which such changes in our society might have affected the MMPI response patterns of normal adolescents and adults, two contemporary normative studies were undertaken.

To develop contemporary norms for adults, we randomly selected 1,919 households and during a structured telephone interview gathered information about age, sex, education, ethnic group membership, and potentially significant mentally or physically handicapping conditions among potential respondents. This yielded a sample of 1,408 subjects who completed the MMPI (86% response rate). They ranged in age from 18 to 99 years and were comparable to the original Minnesota normative sample in terms of selection criteria and the geographic area in which they lived. We then randomly selected a subset of subjects to match the age and sex distribution of the white adult population as determined by the 1980 census. Results showed, not surprisingly, that our contemporary normal sample was somewhat older than the original Hathaway database (mean age, 45 years for women, 43 years for men) and more educated (mean level of 13 years of education for both men and women). MMPI data from this group were then compared with the Hathaway-Briggs sample, the only remaining pool of data still available from the original Minnesota normal sample.

Again, not surprisingly, significant changes were evident in MMPI response patterns for both men and women, yielding a more elevated mean profile in comparison with the Hathaway-Briggs data. The changes were more apparent for men than for women and suggested that a more conservative approach should be taken for profile interpretation. Significant age-related changes also were found, present to a degree suggesting that more careful consideration be given to the impact of both age and sex. Therefore, tables of normalized T scores were prepared separately for each sex and for adults in general (Colligan, Osborne, Swenson, & Offord, 1983), and subsequently age-specific norms for both the basic clinical and the supplemental/research scales were published (Colligan, Osborne, Swenson, & Offord, 1989).

A very different approach was undertaken by the University of Minnesota Press. Six years after our normative study of adults was published, the University of Minnesota Press in 1989 released the MMPI-2, a revised version of the MMPI. In the MMPI-2, 107 new items were added to supplement the original item pool. In addition, 15 new homogeneous content scales intended to replace those

---

[1]Diehl's work was subsequently presented as a chapter describing differences in MMPI response patterns between normal black and white adults (Dahlstrom et al., 1986).

developed by Wiggins (1966; Wiggins, Goldberg, & Appelbaum, 1971) and to provide measures of personality factors of importance to contemporary clinicians (such as type A behavior patterns) were developed. To add the new items without excessively lengthening the MMPI, 106 items from the original item pool (19% of the total item pool), including the 16 duplicated items, were deleted. However, nearly all of the items from the 13 basic validity and clinical scales were included in the MMPI-2, although items were dropped from scales F, 1 (Hs), 2 (D), 5 (Mf), and 0 (Si). Exclusion criteria for those dropped items included outmoded content, items referring to religion, bowel or bladder function, or sexual preference, and items believed to be objectionable or offensive. In addition, many items were reworded to improve readability, eliminate sexist language, and improve clarity. Nearly all of the items were reordered, with items for the original 13 basic validity and clinical scales being placed first in the booklet so they could be scored from the first 370 items of the MMPI-2.

Thus, the MMPI-2 is, essentially, an instrument consisting of (a) the original 13 basic validity and clinical scales, and (b) 15 content scales[2] specifically developed for it from the original item pool, supplemented by 107 newly written items. Normative standards were derived from a sample of 1,462 females and 1,138 males ranging in age from 18 to 84 years drawn from seven states (California, Minnesota, North Carolina, Ohio, Pennsylvania, Virginia, and Washington) supplemented by small samples from military bases and Indian reservations. The four major ethnic groups of the United States (blacks, Native Americans, Hispanics, Asians) are represented proportionately according to the 1980 census. The sample was well educated; 49% of the males and 42% of the females were college graduates or had also obtained postgraduate degrees. It is not clear whether random selection procedures were used; the manual states that "subjects . . . were contacted through a variety of methods, most by direct mail from directories and advertising lists . . . by advertisements and special appeals, as well as by follow-up contacts with subjects listed in stratified catchment area rolls" (Butcher et al., 1989, p. 4). Response rates were not reported. Apparently no screening criteria for inclusion were applied with regard to normality; however, incomplete records, those having 41 or more items left blank, a raw score on scale F of 20 or greater, or a raw score of 20 or greater on the F_B scale (a new F scale, "Back F," comprised of items from the second half of the MMPI-2 booklet) were excluded.

In addition to a new normative sample, new procedures were used in transforming raw scores on the various scales into standard scores. The new procedure resulted in a "uniform T score," with the term *uniform* referring to the

---

[2]Both rational and statistical means (item-scale correlations; Cronbach alpha coefficients) were used to develop 15 new content scales, using for each "only those items that were obviously homogeneous in content with the rest of the items . . ." (Butcher et al., 1989, p. 42). The new scales include the content dimensions of Anxiety (ANX), Fears (FRS), Obsessiveness (OBS), Depression (DEP), Health Concerns (HEA), Bizarre Mentation (BIZ), Anger (ANG), Cynicism (CYN), Antisocial Practices (ASP), Type A (TPA), Low Self-Esteem (LSE), Social Discomfort (SOD), Family Problems (FAM), Work Interference (WRK), and Negative Treatment Indicators (TRT). As noted earlier, no criterion groups, independently established as having these characteristics, were used in the development of these new scales. Thus, for example, no sample of patients with a formal psychiatric diagnosis of depression or patients diagnosed as having somatoform disorder were used in the development of the Depression (DEP) or Health Concerns (HEA) scales, respectively, or for any of the others. Observations of each spouse by the other were used to provide preliminary validity data. The profile of response patterns on the new content scales was developed using the authors' "uniform" T scores.

comparability of scale elevation, in terms of percentile rank, on the eight selected scales for which the uniform T scores were calculated. Basically, the "uniform T score" appears to be a modification of the traditional linear T scores used on the MMPI but has a correction factor to equalize skewness in the underlying distribution of raw scores. The differences between the uniform T score on the MMPI-2 and the normalized T scores we chose for our work are aptly illustrated by the observation of typical percentile ranks. For example, a uniform T score of 50 is at the 55th percentile, and a uniform T score of 75 is at the 98th percentile (Ben-Porath, 1990). A new heavy line on the MMPI-2 profile form representing the point of clinical/interpretive significance (analogous to the heavy line set at a T score of 70 on the original MMPI profile forms) now is set at a uniform T score of 65, falling at the 92.1 percentile. Using normalized T scores, a T score of 50 is at the 50th percentile, a score of 60 is at the 84.1 percentile, and a T score of 70 is at the 97.7 percentile, as would be expected from use of the traditional gaussian normal curve. We used normalized T scores for all 13 of the basic validity and clinical scales of the MMPI, but in the MMPI-2 the uniform T scores were not applied to the three validity scales or to scale 5 (Mf) or 0 (Si).

In general, clinicians who are anticipating use of the MMPI-2, at least on a trial basis, might consider thinking of the new instrument as being comprised of two sets of items. First, the first 370 items are actually the updated or reworded MMPI items from which the 13 basic validity and clinical scales are formed, although 13 items were deleted because they were believed to have content that was objectionable to some respondents. Second, the MMPI-2 is comprised of 107 new items written especially to supplement the original item pool for the 15 new content scales. The clinical lore from the original MMPI is believed to transfer satisfactorily to the MMPI-2, because the first 370 items of the MMPI-2 carry the basic clinical and validity scales of the original MMPI. Virtually no clinical data or research reports are available on the 15 new content scales that make up the remainder of the MMPI-2, although some information and behavioral correlates for their interpretation have been derived from the normative sample itself.

Will there be an MMPI-2 for adolescents? An effort to revise and shorten the original MMPI to make it more appropriate for adolescents has been described at a preliminary level by the University of Minnesota Press (Archer, 1990).

The changes in our society have had no less impact on the role of contemporary adolescents. Therefore, a companion study of contemporary normal adolescents was also done (Colligan & Offord, 1989). The basic procedures were similar to those used for the adult study. Thus, a random sample of 11,930 households within the 8,000+ square miles encompassed by a 50-mile radius around Rochester, Minnesota, was obtained. As with the adult sample, telephone interviewers obtained demographic information and determined whether potential respondents had physically or mentally handicapping conditions that could bias MMPI responses. Only one subject of each sex, regardless of age, from each household was obtained because of the possibility of the confounding effects of heredity. Just as with the adults, adolescents with chronic diseases were excluded, as were those receiving treatment for cancer, reported as being in counseling or psychotherapy, recovering from chemical dependence, or having mental retardation or a learning disability. These procedures yielded a sample of MMPIs from 691 girls and 624 boys ranging in age from 13 to 17 years. The response rates were excellent—83% for girls and 71% for boys.

When the MMPI response patterns of this group were compared with the standards suggested by Hathaway and Monachesi (1963), significant differences were found. However, the data from Hathaway and Monachesi were not intended to be used for normative purposes but rather as a reference or standard. Therefore, the data from our contemporary normal adolescents also were compared with the norms provided by Marks and Briggs (1967). Marks and Briggs had developed tables that currently remain the most widely used for evaluating and interpreting adolescent MMPI profiles. Of their normative base, about 40% was established by drawing cases from the data set obtained by Hathaway and Monachesi in 1947, 1954, and 1957 and about 60% was drawn from adolescents during the 1964–1965 school year. Thus, the most recent of those data are about 25 years old, and the remainder are about 35 to 40 years old.

Results showed, again not surprisingly, significant changes among the response patterns of our contemporary normal adolescents compared with those obtained from the Marks and Briggs data, with girls showing more changes than boys. Therefore, we used our data to develop contemporary norms for adolescents, separately by sex. No dramatic age-related changes among the relatively narrow age range were found, so separate norms for each age were not pursued.

We also found that, in general, adolescents of today differ from contemporary adults, at least in MMPI terms, in much the same way as adolescents of the past differed from adults of the past. Therefore, it remains equally clear that separate norms for adolescents continue to be needed.

In addition to the development of contemporary normative standards for adolescents and adults, the manner in which the tables were calculated also differs significantly from the past. It is widely believed that the standard scores plotted on the MMPI profile sheet using the original normative tables are normalized T scores. This assumption means that a score, on any scale, falling at a value of T 70 would be at (approximately) the 98th percentile for the normative sample. However, the so-called T-score tables in the original MMPI manuals are not T scores by the usual definition of being derived from probabilities related to the normal curve. Rather, these T scores are simply a linear transformation of the raw scores, to a mean of 50 and a standard deviation of 10. This procedure, unfortunately, preserves the marked skewness in the underlying distributions of raw scores. Thus, scale elevations of similar degree in terms of linear T scores, unfortunately, do not have equivalent meanings in terms of percentile rank or deviation from the mean. Therefore, power transformations, a procedure that compensates for the underlying skewness in the underlying distribution of raw scores, were used to calculate normalized T scores for both the adolescent and the adult tables.

This monograph is divided into five sections. The first provides a brief overview of the history and development of the MMPI, and the second part summarizes the contemporary normative study of adults. The third part describes the normative data that are currently available for adolescents, the fourth part describes our adolescent study, and the fifth part provides information about use of the new normative tables. Extensive appendices are provided for clinicians and researchers regarding item-response frequencies, normative data for several research and supplemental scales, correlation matrices, and mean profiles for various groups.

PART I

THE MINNESOTA MULTIPHASIC PERSONALITY INVENTORY (MMPI): A BRIEF HISTORICAL REVIEW

UNDERPINNINGS

Work on the Medical and Psychiatric Inventory,[3] as the Minnesota Multiphasic Personality Inventory (MMPI) was originally known, began in 1937 at the University of Minnesota hospitals (Hathaway & McKinley, 1943). The project was a collaborative undertaking by Starke R. Hathaway, a young medical psychologist, and John Charnley McKinley,[4] a professor of neuropsychiatry who was also head of the Department of Medicine and Neuropsychiatry. Both men had strong research interests. Hathaway began his training in a program of electrical engineering at Ohio University, but he subsequently changed his major, earning his bachelor's and master's degrees in psychology. However, he continued to be interested in electronics, developing a vacuum-tube psychogalvanometer for which he received a patent. Using this type of equipment, he completed his Ph.D. degree in physiology. In addition to being a physician (neurologist), McKinley also had earned a Ph.D. degree for research in physiology and neuroanatomy, and he used the electromyographic apparatus and vacuum-tube amplifiers developed by Hathaway in his own research.

The primary motivation for initiating their MMPI project stemmed from an important and practical question: how can one assess the psychological factors associated with the diseases or physical problems seen in medical practice? This was not an idle question but a vexing problem.

---

[3]Later it was called the Multiphasic Personality Schedule and finally the Minnesota Multiphasic Personality Inventory; frequently, however, it was simply known affectionately as the "Mult."

[4]Because another physician named John McKinley was practicing medicine in the Minneapolis area at the same time, Dr. Hathaway's collaborator identified himself as J. Charnley McKinley (Mrs. Starke [Virginia] Hathaway, personal communication, May 1983).

Indeed, McKinley and Hathaway (1943) noted that

> competent internists have estimated variously that from 30 to 70 per cent of the ambulatory patients who appear for medical attention come primarily because of one or more complaints that turn out to be psychoneurotic in nature. . . . a considerable proportion of medical patients are beset by and wish for relief from emotional states rather than from bodily disease. . . . often these patients are as much influenced for the better by reassurance, suggestion and encouragement as by those measures directed at the organic state. (p. 161)

It was believed that a self-report questionnaire would reduce the need for time-consuming clinical interviews to evaluate a patient's mental health status and would help identify patients who might be able to profit from psychological interventions.

In addition, the new tool was viewed as potentially helpful for assessing treatment outcomes. Specifically, it was believed that the new questionnaire would help to match patients for severity or comparable emotional impairment, so that new treatments (such as insulin shock therapy, a popular approach during the late 1930s) could be evaluated fairly.

In addition, results of such a self-report questionnaire were anticipated to be helpful for establishing a psychiatric diagnosis by virtue of the pattern of symptoms reported by the patient.

Research on self-report questionnaires had been carried out for about 50 years prior to the research efforts mounted by Hathaway and McKinley. However, although apparently being of some value for personality screening during World War I, self-report measures were found to have little value for clinicians who attempted to use them for evaluating patients during peacetime (Bell, 1934; Bernreuter, 1933; Ellis, 1946; Ellis & Conrad, 1948). The virtually fatal weakness of these early inventories was primarily due to an excessive dependence on the face validity and rational construction of the test items. Typically, items were deliberately written for the assessment of a particular facet of personality on the basis of an abstract construct, theory, or clinical experience. There was also a belief that the greater the number of items endorsed by the patient, the greater was the strength of that trait in the individual responding to the items. However, these interpretations of test scores were not verified by interview or by any other independent method of classification to establish their validity. Furthermore, authors of these early inventories tended to assume that the items would be answered by the respondent just as if the question had been asked by an interviewer. This assumption could not be supported either, because it quickly became apparent that there were significant contradictions between the self-report given through the answers to the items and the subject's actual behavior or interview responses.

Later, efforts were undertaken to improve the sophistication of these early self-report inventories. For example, in an effort to describe one potential source of bias, the Humm-Wadsworth Temperament Scale (Humm & Wadsworth, 1935) contained some items that were said to be able to differentiate patients identified by psychiatric study as having different types of temperaments. Clinicians also obtained a "no count" score by determining the number of symptoms that were denied by the patient. If the "no count" score was high, excessive defensiveness or denial was hypothesized, and if the "no count" score was very low, a tendency to overreport symptoms was suggested.

Thus, at the time development of the MMPI was initiated, self-report personality-functioning questionnaires were held in low repute. Indeed, members of clinical psychology training programs were so disillusioned that course work with such instruments was not provided since "it was so widely accepted that personality inventories were valueless" (Hathaway, 1965, p. 461).

Hathaway and McKinley were keenly aware of the problems associated with these early personality inventories. However, they were also positively influenced by researchers who had used criterion groups as part of item selection procedures, an approach followed by Binet and Simon (1916) in the development of their intelligence scale and by Strong for the Vocational Interest Blank (1927, 1943). Therefore, Hathaway and McKinley believed that a patient's responses to self-report items might not necessarily represent accurate historical fact, or even a patient's current beliefs, but rather be an indication of similarity to other persons who had answered the same items in the same way as the patient.

Because their approach to item selection and scale construction exemplified an empirical approach, Hathaway and McKinley were able to counter the prevailing and negative beliefs about such instruments held by most clinicians of that era (Hathaway, 1964). Apparently, these adverse views were often strongly stated, but Hathaway was undaunted: "I was never particularly threatened by the unpopularity of the MMPI with the psychology establishment. In the early days, the opposition to it was outspoken" (Hathaway, 1978, p. 117).

Nevertheless, the departure to rational empiricism was a difficult decision to make, to implement, and, even more, to market. As Hathaway stated, "It was difficult to persuade a publisher to accept the MMPI in 1941. Dr. McKinley and I had faith sufficient to carry us through several rejections before the University of Minnesota Press finally undertook publication" (Dahlstrom & Welsh, 1960, p. vii); and later he stated,

We ran into considerable difficulty publishing the MMPI. The Psychological Corporation was not interested in it because they already had some personality tests and were advised by some psychologist, whose letter I later read, that the MMPI had nothing new in it and was unduly awkward and impractical. At least two other test publishers were not interested enough to support it either. Finally, the University of Minnesota Press contributed $300 and . . . University Hospitals, contributed $300 more . . . and the first limited edition of the MMPI was published . . . production . . . soon outran the facilities . . . they were doing nothing but turning out the MMPI . . . the University of Minnesota continued to hold the copyright . . . McKinley and I chose never to own the rights. (Hathaway, 1978, p. 117)

To summarize Hathaway's basic philosophy regarding scale construction,

The break from the face validity approach to item selection for a scale was the result of a conscious decision. No item was ever eliminated from a scale because its manifest content seemed to have no relation to the syndrome in question; conversely no item was arbitrarily accepted if the validating evidence for the item was not strong. (Hathaway, 1956, p. 106) . . . all the items were empirically selected by contrast of criterion groups with other clinical groups and with various normal groups. All scales were tested by one or more cross-validation samples. Frequency distributions of the cross-validation samples were constructed to show the separation of the criterion abnormal type from normals, from patients who were physically ill (but not obviously with mental symptoms), and finally from miscellaneous psychiatric cases having diagnoses other than the one being studied. This multiple checking of items and scales is probably the most characteristic general procedure relative to the derivation. Beyond this, specific steps in scale development were so varied that they cannot be completely described. (Hathaway, 1956, p. 104)

DEVELOPMENT

Although the work was undertaken in 1937 (McKinley & Hathaway, 1943), the first report describing the initial steps of its construction did not appear until 1940. This research report also had a different title for the instrument, the Multiphasic Personality Schedule (Minnesota), and described the steps Hathaway and McKinley used to develop the item pool (Hathaway & McKinley, 1940).

Some of the items apparently were written by the authors (for example, perhaps some of those eventually included on scale L), but generally they came from portions of textbooks in psychiatry, psychology, medicine, and neurology dealing with mental status examination. It also seems that prior scales of personal and social attitudes and personality functioning were reviewed.

Apparently some items from these other instruments were adapted and included for use. For example, item 16 from the Humm-Wadsworth Temperament Scale (Humm & Wadsworth, 1933; Humm & Wadsworth, 1935, p. 192)—"Do you frequently find yourself worrying about something?"—appears to have become item 217 in the original MMPI booklet—"I frequently find myself worrying about something"—and item 9 from the Humm-Wadsworth Temperament Scale— "Have you encountered some problems that are so full of possibilities that you have been unable to make up your mind about them?"—appears to have been transposed to become item 100 in the original MMPI booklet form—"I have met problems so full of possibilities that I have been unable to make up my mind about them." Indeed, the Humm-Wadsworth Temperament Scale appears to have been a rich source of stimulation for the MMPI item pool in that 151 of the 318 items on the Scale were among the MMPI items (D. S. Nichols, personal communication, 1989). Stated another way, between 25% and 30% of the items in the final MMPI item pool clearly have their roots in the item pool of the Humm-Wadsworth Temperament Scale.

This work yielded a pool of about a thousand items. These were reduced to 504 items through procedures only partially defined (such as eliminating duplicates). They covered the 25 content categories listed in Table 1 and are reflective of the sources from which the items had been drawn. Later, it appears that 9 items were dropped and 55 items primarily related to patterns of masculine-feminine interest were added; thus, the total number was brought to the current item pool of 550 unique items. A list of the items in each content category, identifying the items that have been deleted from the MMPI-2, is available from the authors.

The original MPI (Medical and Psychiatric Inventory) or MPS (Multiphasic Personality Schedule) was composed of a deck of 3- by 5-inch cards, each with one item. The cards were randomized by shuffling and then were presented to the patient, who was asked to sort the cards into piles marked "true," "false," and "cannot say."

Much later, with the advent of computer scoring, it was found that, if 16 items were repeated on the back of the 8½ by 11-inch answer sheet, the test could be

Table 1
Content Categories of the Original MMPI Item Pool

1. General health (9 items)
2. General neurologic (19 items)
3. Cranial nerves (11 items)
4. Motility and coordination (6 items)
5. Sensibility (5 items)
6. Vasomotor, trophic, speech, secretory (10 items)
7. Cardiorespiratory (5 items)
8. Gastrointestinal (11 items)
9. Genitourinary (6 items)
10. Habits (20 items)
11. Family and marital (29 items)
12. Occupational (18 items)
13. Educational (12 items)
14. Sexual attitudes (19 items)
15. Religious attitudes (20 items)
16. Political attitudes—law and order (46 items)
17. Social attitudes (72 items)
18. Affect, depressive (32 items)
19. Affect, manic (24 items)
20. Obsessive, compulsive (15 items)
21. Delusions, hallucinations, illusions, ideas of reference (31 items)
22. Phobias (29 items)
23. Sadistic, masochistic (7 items)
24. Morale (33 items)
25. Items to "indicate whether the individual is trying to place himself in an improbably acceptable or unacceptable light (15 items)"[a]

[a]Later, 55 items relating to masculinity–femininity were added as category 25; category 25 in this table, subsequently called the "Lie" scale, was then renumbered as category 26.

scored with a significant reduction of time, because fewer passes through the pencil-mark[5] sensing device were required for scoring the true and false answers. Thus, the patient responded to a total of 566 statements. A list of the items found on various research/supplemental scales is provided in Appendix A.

No information was reported regarding the manner in which these 16 items were selected, nor are we informed of the manner in which the items from the total pool—originally randomized by shuffling—were placed into the order in which they occurred at the time the MMPI was published in a booklet form by the University of Minnesota Press in 1943. We are told only that "the order that Hathaway and McKinley used . . . places the items that appear on the main clinical and validity scales early in the test" (Dahlstrom & Welsh, 1960, p. 31) and that, of the 357 items needed for the 3 validity and 10 clinical scales, "the first items are generally not psychologically disturbing . . . ." (Dahlstrom & Welsh, 1960, p. 5), a consideration that appears to have been done deliberately in order to "give an opportunity for judging the person's ability to read and respond to the rest of the test appropriately" (p. 5).

[5]The "electrographic" pencils of that time contained a metallic (iron) substance, carried by the graphite in the pencil lead, that was detected by fine wire brushes as the cards passed through the machine.

As for scoring of the individual item responses, the scales are directionally constructed so that higher scores reflect abnormality and items are more often endorsed by members of the criterion samples. Originally, because the items were printed on index cards and placed in a box marked "true," "false," or "cannot say," there was little room for confusing the direction of response. Currently, however, with mark-sense computer scoring, the subject's response can be read as true, false, neither true nor false marked, or both true and false marked. Items in the last two categories are read as unscorable and increase the patient's score on the ?/Question scale. Items left unanswered or read by the computer as unscorable reduce the raw score for the scale on which such items fall.

NORMAL AND CRITERION SAMPLES

Hathaway and McKinley did not presume to understand or predict how patients with different types of psychological problems or psychiatric diagnoses would respond to items from the MMPI pool, an approach very different from that of prior personality-inventory construction efforts. Rather, using an empirical approach, they decided to let the patients themselves provide this information using the medium of their card-sorted, true-false responses to the newly constructed item pool. It was believed that certain patterns of attitudes, beliefs, feelings, and symptoms would appear. It was further expected that such patterns of responses would characterize patients having certain types of mental problems, and also that establishing a patient's pattern of responses would aid clinicians in establishing a psychiatric diagnosis. Therefore, it was essential to develop criterion groups of patients, each carefully diagnosed and having known attributes of social, behavioral, and emotional functioning that could be used as the standard against which to evaluate the response patterns of other patients undergoing assessment. Furthermore, the manner in which normal people and medical patients without mental health problems responded to the MMPI item pool also needed to be established.

The following section briefly reviews the procedures through which the normal and psychiatric criterion groups were established.

The Original Minnesota Normal Sample

The first group of 724 normal subjects—the "Minnesota Normals," as the data set later came to be called—was comprised of friends and relatives of hospitalized patients at the University of Minnesota. More specifically, "These are individuals who themselves are not ill but are bringing relatives or friends to the clinic. They constitute the bulk of our so-called normal cases" (Hathaway & McKinley, 1940, p. 252). In general, "The subjects were approached in the halls and waiting rooms of the hospital and invited to participate in the research project" (Dahlstrom & Welsh, 1960, p. 44).

What types of bias might have entered the subject pool with such an approach? Dahlstrom, Welsh, and Dahlstrom (1975) noted that "not every visitor was approached and since not everyone who was asked was able or willing to comply with the request, there were many opportunities for biases to enter" (p. 109). How does one further define normality of functioning under such circumstances?

Dahlstrom et al. (1975) went on to present several important and related points, as follows:

> most of the general criticism of the MMPI and its reliance upon hospital visitors for the normal subject sample has emphasized the likelihood of biases in a pathological direction (anxiety and depression about the possible death of close relatives who are seriously ill, preoccupation with sickness and physical complaints in a medical setting, emotional and financial insecurities arising from extended health crises, etc.) and the possible distortions that such factors could introduce into the basic scales . . . these effects, if . . . sizeable, will work against the successful construction of diagnostic scales . . . the fact that useful scales did emerge is itself evidence that the pathological bias was not seriously deleterious. (p. 109)

Later on, they also noted, with regard to volunteers who participate in psychological research, that "the little evidence that is available in the research on volunteering . . . indicates that only the more emotionally stable and psychological healthy hospital visitors may have felt free to accept the offer to serve science and humanity" (p. 109). Their conclusion, almost as a harbinger of our findings more than 40 years later, was as follows: "then it is possible that the Minnesota test norms may be set a little too low for use with the general population" (p. 109)—an implication that the potential effects of the two factors discussed above do not equally cancel each other.

However, two other samples of normal people also were included. Many clinicians are unaware of these additional two groups. The first of these was described as "a normal group from the University Testing Bureau (265 cases). These are mainly pre-college high school graduates who came to the Testing Bureau for pre-college guidance, but there are a number of representatives from various college classes as well" (Hathaway & McKinley, 1940, p. 252).

Finally, to provide some control for urban background and socioeconomic status, the third sample was described as "a group of normals whom we were able to contact through the courtesy of the local WPA Administration (265 cases)"; they were skilled white-collar workers from local projects (Hathaway & McKinley, 1940, p. 252).

These three groups constituted a total sample of 1,254 married and single men and women ranging in age from 16 through 65 years. During scale development and later cross validation, various subsamples of these three groups were used, but the total sample, in entirety, does not seem to have been used at any one point.

A minimal amount of descriptive information about the subjects was provided. Overall, the samples were described as corresponding well to the 1930 census data for Minnesota regarding age, sex, and marital status. More specifically, in the group of 724 normal subjects, 66% of the women and 74% of the men were married, none of the subjects in the precollege/college-class sample were married, and no information regarding age or marital status was reported for the WPA group. The average age of adults in our contemporary society has been increasing gradually. The original Minnesota Normals may therefore have been somewhat younger by contemporary standards. Thus, among the original Minnesota normals there were 107 men and 98 women ages 16 through 25 years, 233 men and 149 women ages 26 through 43 years, 69 men and 43 women ages 44 through 54 years, and only 16 men and 9 women ages 55 through 65 years. Apparently, no subjects older than 65 years were included, although, as stated above, no information regarding age was reported for the WPA group. All of the subjects from the college testing bureau were adolescents and young adults ages 16 to 25 years old.

Defining "Normality."   Basic demographic information was obtained from each subject, although participants were not required to state their name. The information included age, sex, education, occupational level, marital status, number of children, and information about any family history of mental illness or mental retardation. Aside from this, however, to determine specifically whether these respondents would be included in the normal sample, an additional determination was made. Thus,

> the assumption is made, of course, that these people are in good health, which may not always be the case. To help establish them as real normals we asked them whether or not they are receiving treatment for any illness. Only those who say they are not under a physician's care are accepted in this group. (Hathaway & McKinley, 1940, p. 252)

The significance of the Minnesota Normals simply cannot be overemphasized. It is obvious that such a group is necessary, in the criterion sense, for scale development, but these people also contributed significantly in another way. It was the mean response pattern of the members of this normal group that served as the metric (standard) used to develop the numbers used for plotting the profiles of patients. With the exception of persons using the MMPI-2, this standard continues to remain the one primarily in use today. Thus, whether one is evaluating an airline pilot with a degree in aeronautical engineering, a business executive, a high school dropout, or a court referral, it is the pattern of responses from the original Minnesota normal sample that serves as the basis for comparison. How appropriate are such comparisons for members of contemporary society? Described earlier as being comparable to the 1930 census data for Minnesota, we also are told more specifically,

> In 1940, such a Minnesota normal adult was about thirty-five years old, was married, lived in a small town or rural area, had had eight years of general schooling, and worked at a skilled or semi-skilled trade (or was married to a man with such an occupational level). (Dahlstrom et al., 1972, pp. 7–8)

Unfortunately, data from the total sample of original Minnesota normal subjects are no longer available. The data that remain available,[6] however, were reported later as a subsample from the original normative group in an article providing norms for several new MMPI scales (such as Ego Strength). This "improved" sample was based on cases that had been

---

[6]These data were from Dr. Grant Dahlstrom and Dr. Mark Appelbaum, L. D. Thurstone Psychometric Laboratory, Davie Hall 013-A, University of North Carolina, Chapel Hill, North Carolina 27514.

drawn from the general Minnesota normal sample described in the MMPI Manual. . . . To make up these samples the old norms were improved by re-examination of every one of the records to discard incomplete ones or any others that looked defective; other records from among the originals were substituted for defective ones and some attempt was made to select cases so as to improve the representativeness of the sampling. (Hathaway & Briggs, 1957, p. 364)

The normative sample for the MMPI-2 is as important to this new instrument as the original Minnesota normals were to the original MMPI. Early reviews and clinicians raised questions about the new instrument and the representativeness of the new normative sample. Concern has been expressed, for example, about the increased reading level that is required for the MMPI-2; the manual indicates that a reading comprehension at the eighth-grade level is required (Butcher et al., 1989, pp. 1, 14), in contrast to the fifth- to sixth-grade reading level required for the original MMPI item pool. Although many of the original items were rewritten, the manual notes that response patterns for the original MMPI items and for the updated, reworded MMPI items were not significantly different in most cases, and that, when there were significant changes, no appreciable differences were found with regard to the psychometric properties of the updated, reworded items. Thus, clinicians who have been concerned about the impact of items in the original pool whose wording was apparently awkward can now be reassured about their use, because contemporary persons are apparently able to deal satisfactorily with their format and content.

The concern about the high academic educational level achieved in the MMPI-2 normative sample has already been mentioned (that is, 45% of the total sample was made up of people who were college graduates or had postgraduate degrees). In addition, it should be noted that 42% of the men and 40% of the women came from "professional" occupational groups; these are in contrast to the 16% expected for both men and women according to data from the 1980 census. Further, among the men, about 18% were in the occupational groups of clerical and skilled workers, compared with 50% expected from census data; for the women, about 26% were in the categories of clerical or skilled workers, whereas 55% of U.S. adults were in this category according to the 1980 census data.

Although our data clearly demonstrated strong age relationships for many scales, particularly among older age groups, unfortunately no specific age norms have been provided for the MMPI-2. The impact of ethnic group membership is not presented in the manual. Although Dahlstrom, Diehl, and Lachar (1986) have provided data minimizing the importance of such variables after age, sex, educational level, and socioeconomic status have been partialed out, it is questionable whether clinicians who work primarily with black clients will be entirely comfortable without such data for the MMPI-2. Even though the MMPI-2 includes an appropriate proportion of blacks, based on the 1980 census, it should be kept in mind that this number is insufficient (n = 126 males and 188 females) for normative purposes, although ethnic-specific mean raw scores are provided in the manual for the 13 basic scales (Butcher et al., 1989, p. 105).

The manual also uses the term *national norms*, although users should keep in mind that only seven states were represented. Indeed, 22% of the sample came from Minnesota, 18% from North Carolina, 17% from Ohio, 12% from Pennsylvania, 10% from Virginia, 10% from the state of Washington, and 9% from California. Clinicians have speculated for years about the impact of rural-urban status on MMPI response patterns, but no breakdown of scores in this manner is provided.

Finally, it does not appear that any type of screening was done to determine mentally or physically handicapping conditions that might have induced a response bias. Apparently no criteria for "normality" were applied, even in the sense used by Hathaway and McKinley. It was our belief that enough is already known about the MMPIs obtained from medical patients, psychiatric patients, and other important classifications; thus, it would be important to determine how people without such potentially biasing characteristics would respond to the MMPI items.

Contrast Samples

The questionnaire had initially been called the MPI (Medical and Psychiatric Inventory); as such, it was necessary to determine the pattern of responses that might be expected from medical patients. Therefore, a sample of 254 medical patients, also from the University of Minnesota Hospital and screened to exclude those having concomitant psychiatric problems, was obtained. No information regarding age, sex, marital status, or socioeconomic level was reported, although the authors stated that these patients were

> mainly on the medical service but also in lesser numbers from other services of the hospital. . . . most of these patients are in the hospital for one or another physical disease. Some of these were suffering acute illnesses such as upper respiratory infections, jaundice and the like; others were chronically ill with carcinoma, gastric ulcer, leukemia, and a variety of other conditions. (Hathaway & McKinley, 1940, p. 252)

It should be noted that no general sample of psychiatric or medical patients was used in the construction of the new MMPI-2 norms. However, implicitly, the authors did not want to cross validate the original validity and clinical scales of the MMPI but rather wanted simply to provide new contemporary normative standards for the 13 original scales, just as we had done in 1983. Nevertheless, because most of the subjects in the MMPI-2 normative sample were married and because both partners were encouraged to complete the MMPI-2 (through financial reimbursement), partner ratings were obtained. Results supported the traditional interpretation of the basic scales, at least from the data obtained from these normative subjects. As a separate endeavor, however, 15 new content scales were constructed. Partner ratings were again used to provide some preliminary support for their validity.

Criterion Samples

In addition to the hospitalized medical patients and the visitors, white-collar WPA workers, and college students, all of whom had been screened for normality by the definition given above, criterion samples of patients with a diversity of mental health problems also were required. These consisted of carefully studied psychiatric patients who had been hospitalized for various reasons. Members of the criterion groups, diagnosed by the psychiatric procedures and nomenclature of the 1940s, provided the response patterns that constituted the data used to derive each of the basic clinical scales of the MMPI. For an item to be retained on the final version of the various MMPI scales, the endorsement patterns for each item had to differentiate among members of the normal sample, the medical patients, and the psychiatric patients who did not have the diagnosis of the patients who were being used as the criterion group for that clinical scale.

It should be noted that the new MMPI-2 content scales, developed from the original MMPI item pool and supplemented by 107 new items written specifically for this purpose, did not make use of criterion groups either. Rather, the 15 new content scales were derived by a combination of rational and statistical procedures to ensure scale homogeneity (Butcher, Graham, Williams, & Ben-Porath, 1990). As an example, even though the new content scale "TPA" (for type A behavior pattern) is believed to assess characteristics of type A personality, no criterion group of individuals diagnosed as having type A personality features was assessed with the scale as part of its derivation or cross validation. Nevertheless, the MMPI-2 manual (p. 43) states, rather definitively, that persons who obtain high scores on TPA "are hard-driving, fast-moving, and work-oriented . . . who frequently become impatient, irritable, and annoyed. They do not like to wait or be interrupted. There is never enough time in a day for them to complete their tasks. They are direct and may be overbearing" (Butcher et al., 1989).

Thus, although we are provided with an interpretive characterization and norms for this scale and for 14 other content scales, as yet there has been no published research about the manner in which individuals already known to have, in this example, the type A personality style, respond to the items of the scale bearing that name. Therefore, it appears that the charges leveled at the early researchers and their self-report questionnaire construction and their excessive reliance on rational construction may hold true for these new MMPI-2 content scales as well, until further research supports or refutes their usefulness.

Indeed, Hathaway's comments in this regard are as pertinent now as they were when he summarized them later in his career. It is widely known that the earliest objective personality assessment instruments suffered from excessive dependence on rational construction and face validity of the items composing the measure. However, Hathaway noted that this approach was typical for that era, because "personality inventory items were all supposed to ask an obvious and unmistakable question that was pertinent to the aspect of personality the scale was designed to measure" (Hathaway, 1965, p. 456). Although, in discussing one of the "most successful" (Hathaway, 1965, p. 458) personality tests developed during that era, the Bernreuter Personality Inventory, Hathaway noted the "devastating critiques" that subsequently were published. With regard to the Bernreuter Inventory, "The validity of the scales depended first upon the face validity of the items assigned to the scales . . ." (Hathaway, 1965, p. 458) and second on weighted scores from groups of criterion cases—who actually had obtained only extremely high or low scores on other similar paper-and-pencil tests. It is of great significance to note that "These criterion cases were not verified by interviews or any other validation method independent of the tests" (Hathaway, 1965, p. 458). This latter point was central to Hathaway's concept of empirical validity.

Hathaway viewed empirical validity as being "determined in the relationship of the items and test to criterion groups of subjects or to ratings that are applied to persons separately from the application of the test. Validity is suggested in the correlation or overlap statistics that tell how closely the test scores come to the independent criteria" (Hathaway, 1965, p. 456). Although Burisch (1984) commented on this point in his article on approaches to personality inventory construction, he appeared to view it somewhat casually. Nevertheless, under the label of "Multiple Act Criteria," referring to relatively observable patterns of behavior, he stated that, "the approach holds great promise" but, while supporting the method, he also noted that "The data-gathering procedure is extremely cumbersome" (Burisch, 1984, p. 217). Epstein (1987) decried the MMPI scales for not measuring a single construct, a feature that, since they do not, allows different patients to obtain the same scores for very different reasons on the same scale. Thus, two patients may have a significant clinical depression, even though their MMPI elevation on scale 2 (D) was obtained by endorsement of different item sets. Although this observation may be more of a problem for theory construction, as Epstein noted, he suggested that specific items endorsed by the patient be reviewed, although he also complained that "this would make the test similar to a standardized interview" (Epstein, 1987, p. 104). Knowledgeable MMPI users will be aware that one of Hathaway's original goals for the MMPI was to reduce the "use of the time consuming interview technic that is conventional in the psychiatric approach" (McKinley & Hathaway, 1943, p. 161).

Beyond this, current clinical practice encourages the use of profile subscale analysis, the use of supplemental scales, and a review of the statements viewed as "critical items" for the clinician's typical clientele. In an early report on the validity of personality questionnaires, Landis and Katz (1934) noted that

> There is a need for a questionnaire type of scale which is based not on preconceived notions of what does or does not constitute undesirable personality traits, but which will make use of the analysis of many questions which may or may not seem to be immediately relevant. (p. 355)

It is noteworthy to recall that, in Gough's work in developing the F minus K index, he found that "Relatively skilled persons are unable to simulate either a psychoneurotic or psychotic condition on the MMPI in such a way as to avoid detection" (Gough, 1947, p. 223).

Finally, Hathaway also raised the important issue of assessing conscious or unconscious response style that will require attention from persons working with the new homogeneous, face-valid MMPI-2 content scales. Hathaway noted that "face-valid questions worked fine when the respondent was motivated to admit to the way he felt, but it seemed that he could usually recognize and avoid any item that he chose to avoid" (Hathaway, 1965, p. 468). Because of recognition of the influence of both conscious, deliberate response bias as well as unconscious determinants of response set or item-endorsement proclivity, the susceptibility of the MMPI to yield both false-negative and false-positive profiles was investigated. As a result of this thinking, work was initiated toward the development of a single bipolar scale for discrimination of fake good at one pole and fake bad at the other. This scale or factor of test-taking attitude was ultimately made available as the K scale of the MMPI. . . . the development of K was in the main devoted to the attempt to eliminate the false negative and false positive cases when the test profiles were near the borderline. (Hathaway, 1965, pp. 469–470)

The term *borderline* referred to "the conventional normal-abnormal borderline value where the score is two standard deviations above the mean" (Hathaway, 1965, p. 470).

A supplement to the existing validity scales (F_B) was created by the authors of the MMPI-2; the F_B (Back F) was developed by collecting the items having "extremely low endorsement frequencies" and combining them into a scale, with the majority of the 40 items appearing after the items on the original F scale. Thus, the F_B scale is intended to identify profiles in which the patient has "shifted to an essentially random pattern of responding" (Butcher et al., 1989, p. 27) during the latter half of the MMPI-2 booklet. In addition, two new scales addressing response inconsistency (VRIN, Variable Response Inconsistency; TRIN, True Response Inconsistency) may be helpful to clinicians also. Unfortunately, however, the manual currently notes that "The use of VRIN and TRIN is experimental at this stage and require. caution until more empirical evidence has been accumulated" (Butcher et al., 1989, p. 28).

These three new scales may be helpful to clinicians in identifying profiles obtained from patients who were randomly inconsistent in their response pattern. However, no new scales sensitive to response bias were developed for the MMPI-2, nor were K-weighting procedures applied to any of the new content scales. Thus, until clinical data accumulate, elevations on the content scales should be most appropriately viewed as suggestive in nature, and the absence of an elevation should not be construed as indicating a lack of the characteristic purported to be measured by that scale. A review of the basic clinical profile, with particular attention to K, as well as some of the other supplemental scales dealing with response bias (such as F minus K, Pm, Dn, Ad), may assist the clinician, in much the same fashion that K was used on an intuitive basis with the basic profile before the formalized K-weighting procedure was developed.

A brief description of each of the basic validity and clinical scales of the MMPI, and the rationale for their development, listed by the order in which they appear on the standard MMPI profile sheet, follows.

VALIDITY SCALES

Obviously, patients can exert considerable influence over their MMPI item responses and resulting MMPI profile configuration.

The earlier personality questionnaires had not dealt sufficiently with the issue of test-response bias. Hathaway and McKinley thought that it was important to assume that such bias existed (for example, defensiveness extending to faking good, and plus-getting tendencies extending to faking bad in order to appear psychiatrically abnormal), and then to assess the degree and direction of the conscious or unconscious distortion present, and, finally, to assign a compensatory correction value.

Table 2
MMPI Scale L (The Lie Score)

True: (none)

False:

15. Once in a while I think of things too bad to talk about.
30. At times I feel like swearing.
45. I do not always tell the truth.
60. I do not read every editorial in the newspaper every day.
75. I get angry sometimes.
90. Once in a while I put off until tomorrow what I ought to do today.
105. Sometimes when I am not feeling well I am cross.
120. My table manners are not quite as good at home as when I am out in company.
135. If I could get into a movie without paying and be sure I was not seen I would probably do it.
150. I would rather win than lose in a game.
165. I like to know some important people because it makes me feel important.
195. I do not like everyone I know.
225. I gossip a little at times.
255. Sometimes at elections I vote for men about whom I know very little.
285. Once in a while I laugh at a dirty joke.

Note. No items were deleted from scale L on the MMPI-2.

Scale ? (Question Score, Cannot Say, Q)[7]

As the number of nonscorable items increases (that is, items answered both true and false and items that have not been answered at all), scale scores will be lower and probably so on several scales because of overlapping items on different scales. The T scores assigned to the ? score were selected arbitrarily. Thus, a raw score of 30 or less earned a T score of 50, and a raw score of 55 was assigned a T score of 57. About 3% of the Minnesota normal sample had a T score exceeding 70, corresponding to a raw score of approximately 103 (Hathaway & McKinley, 1943).

Among the women in our contemporary normal sample, 41% had a raw question/Q of 0; 17% had a Q/? of 1; 11% had a Q/? of 2; 80% had a Q/? of 5 or less; and 90% had a Q/? of 21 or less. Among the men, the results were comparable; 41% had a raw Q/? of 0; 18% had a Q/? of 1; 9% had a Q/? of 2; 80% had a Q/? of 5 or less; and 90% had a Q/? score of 21 or less.

No data on Q/? are provided in the MMPI-2 manual, although the authors stated that, if 31 or more items are left unanswered, "the test record must be considered highly suspect if not completely invalid" (Butcher et al., 1989, p. 22).

In general, these figures reflect the increased emphasis that clinicians have conveyed to patients about the importance of responding to all of the MMPI items.

Scale L (Lie Score; 15 Items)

The L scale (Table 2) was composed of items describing "extremely good and rare human qualities which it is statistically absurd to suppose will all or in large part

---

[7]In the Mayo Clinic automated MMPI scoring and interpretive system, we use the designations "Q" and "NABA" (not answered or both true and false answered) for the total number of items left blank plus those answered both true and false.

be his [sic the patients]" (Meehl & Hathaway, 1946, p. 530) and were described as "a fairly subtle trap for anyone who wanted to give an unusually good impression of himself" (Meehl & Hathaway, 1946, p. 538). Again, the T score values for this scale were assigned arbitrarily, apparently on the basis of observed scores: "very few individuals obtained raw scores of seven or more, and the two or three percent level is at about ten. These values were arbitrarily called the 60 and 70 T-score points respectively" (Meehl & Hathaway, 1946, p. 538); later, however, after experience, a raw L score of 7 was changed to a T score of 70.

Scale F (Validity, Frequency, Infrequency; 64 Items)

Items for the F scale (Table 3) were chosen in part "to include a variety of content" and were selected empirically "because they were answered with a relatively low frequency . . . by the main normal group; the scored direction . . . is the one which is rarely made by unselected normals" (Meehl & Hathaway, 1946, p. 535). With regard to interpretation of the F score, if it was high, "the other scales are likely to be invalid either because the subject was careless or unable to comprehend the items, or because someone made extensive errors in entering the items on the record sheet," whereas a low F score was viewed as "a reliable indication that the subject's responses were rational and relatively pertinent" (Hathaway & McKinley, 1943, p. 4). A raw F score of 16 was arbitrarily assigned a T score of 70. This value later was used by Hathaway and Monachesi (1963) to define F-invalid adolescent MMPI profiles that were excluded from analysis. However, their comments indicate that many "high-F" profiles (that is, those having raw F scores of 16 to 21, inclusive) "would probably be acceptable for inclusion" (p. 27). Higher F values, called "ultra high-F" or "UHF" profiles, were scores of 22 or higher and were not acceptable to Hathaway because of the great likelihood of uncooperativeness on the part of the adolescent respondent.

Factors believed to increase F included malingering, noncooperation, random responding, poor reading ability, and decreased language comprehension; persons with impaired reality testing or schizoid mentation also were found to obtain elevated scores.

On the MMPI-2, the following four items were deleted from scale F:

14. I have diarrhea once a month or more.
53. A minister can cure disease by praying and putting his hand on your head.
206. I am very religious (more than most people).
258. I believe there is a God.

Scale K (Correction; 30 Items)

The items for the K scale (Table 4), originally called L6, were selected by experimental work that included both normal and psychiatric cases. Two different lines of research were pursued. First, subjects were asked to complete the MMPI under two different circumstances. Thus, subjects were required deliberately to assume certain mental attitudes and deliberately seek to obtain desirable or undesirable scores on the MMPI. Then they were asked to complete

Table 3
MMPI Scale F (Validity, Frequency, Infrequency)

True:
- [a]14. I have diarrhea once a month or more.
- 23. I am troubled by attacks of nausea and vomiting.
- 27. Evil spirits possess me at times.
- 31. I have nightmares every few nights.
- 34. I have a cough most of the time.
- 35. If people had not had it in for me I would have been much more successful.
- 40. Most any time I would rather sit and daydream than to do anything else.
- 42. My family does not like the work I have chosen (or the work I intend to choose for my life work).
- 48. When I am with people, I am bothered by hearing very queer things.
- 49. It would be better if almost all laws were thrown away.
- 50. My soul sometimes leaves my body.
- [a]53. A minister can cure disease by praying and putting his hand on your head.
- 56. As a youngster I was suspended from school one or more times for cutting up.
- 66. I see things or animals or people around me that others do not see.
- 85. Sometimes I am strongly attracted by the personal articles of others such as shoes, gloves, etc., so that I want to handle or steal them though I have no use for them.
- 121. I believe I am being plotted against.
- 123. I believe I am being followed.
- 139. Sometimes I feel as if I must injure either myself or someone else.
- 146. I have the wanderlust and am never happy unless I am roaming or traveling about.
- 151. Someone has been trying to poison me.
- 156. I have had periods in which I carried on activities without knowing later what I had been doing.
- 168. There is something wrong with my mind.
- 184. I commonly hear voices without knowing where they come from.
- 197. Someone has been trying to rob me.
- 200. There are persons who are trying to steal my thoughts and ideas.
- 202. I believe I am a condemned person.
- 205. At times it has been impossible for me to keep from stealing or shoplifting something.
- [a]206. I am very religious (more than most people).
- 209. I believe my sins are unpardonable.
- 210. Everything tastes the same.
- 211. I can sleep during the day but not at night.
- 215. I have used alcohol excessively.
- 218. It does not bother me particularly to see animals suffer.
- 227. I have been told that I walk during sleep.
- 245. My parents and family find more fault with me than they should.
- 246. My neck spots with red often.
- 247. I have reason for feeling jealous of one or more members of my family.
- 252. No one cares much what happens to you.
- 256. The only interesting part of newspapers is the "funnies."
- 269. I can easily make other people afraid of me, and sometimes do for the fun of it.
- 275. Someone has control over my mind.
- 286. I am never happier than when alone.
- 291. At one or more times in my life I felt that someone was making me do things by hypnotizing me.
- 293. Someone has been trying to influence my mind.

22

Table 3 *(continued)*

False:
17. My father was a good man.
20. My sex life is satisfactory.
54. I am liked by most people who know me.
65. I loved my father.
75. I get angry sometimes.
83. Any man who is able and willing to work hard has a good chance of succeeding.
112. I frequently find it necessary to stand up for what I think is right.
113. I believe in law enforcement.
115. I believe in a life hereafter.
164. I like to study and read about things that I am working at.
169. I am not afraid to handle money.
177. My mother was a good woman.
185. My hearing is apparently as good as that of most people.
196. I like to visit places where I have never been before.
199. Children should be taught all the main facts of sex.
220. I loved my mother.
257. I usually expect to succeed in things I do.
[a]258. I believe there is a God.
272. At times I am all full of energy.
276. I enjoy children.

[a]These items were deleted from scale F on the MMPI-2.

the MMPI under standard administration for comparative purposes. The shifts in item-response patterns then were used as an index of faking good or faking bad.

The second approach used MMPI response patterns obtained from normally functioning individuals who obtained atypical or abnormal MMPI profiles. Response patterns from members of this group were compared with MMPI profiles that (a) fell within the expected normal range of scores but (b) had been obtained from hospitalized psychiatric patients. The 22 items initially composing L6 appeared useful for identifying patients prone to either defensiveness or its converse, plus-getting. However, scores on the clinical scales from patients diagnosed as having schizophrenia or depression were also low. Therefore, eight additional correction items were added. The value of the K score was immediately evident, although the "original method of using K was admittedly vague and inspectional" (McKinley, Hathaway, & Meehl, 1948, p. 20), with a profile of borderline pathology being underinterpreted if the K score was low because of the assumption of a plus-getting tendency. If the same profile had an elevated K score, the profile would be overinterpreted because of the assumed degree of defensiveness associated with elevated K scores. Aside from the empirical approach just described, the content of the K items seemed "to suggest an attitude of denying worries, inferiority feelings, and psychiatrically unhealthy symptoms, together with a disposition to see only good in others as well as oneself" (Meehl & Hathaway, 1946, p. 541).

Later, the clinical utility of five of the clinical scales—1 (Hs), 4 (Pd), 7 (Pt), 8 (Sc), and 9 (Ma)—was improved by a formal, proportional weighting system rather than by using the inspectional, clinical, intuitive approach that was used initially. In addition, it was found that K scores increased systematically with socioeconomic status, with persons having a college education obtaining scores approximately 1 to 1.5 standard deviations above the mean for the Minnesota normal sample. Among the members of our adult sample, this relationship

Table 4
MMPI Scale K (Correction)

True:

   96. I have very few quarrels with members of my family.

False:

   [a]30. At times I feel like swearing.

   39. At times I feel like smashing things.

   [a]71. I think a great many people exaggerate their misfortunes in order to gain the sympathy and help of others.

   89. It takes a lot of argument to convince most people of the truth.

   124. Most people will use somewhat unfair means to gain profit or an advantage rather than to lose it.

   129. Often I can't understand why I have been so cross and grouchy.

   134. At times my thoughts have raced ahead faster than I could speak them.

   138. Criticism or scolding hurts me terribly.

   142. I certainly feel useless at times.

   148. It makes me impatient to have people ask my advice or otherwise interrupt me when I am working on something important.

   [a]160. I have never felt better in my life than I do now.

   [a]170. What others think of me does not bother me.

   171. It makes me uncomfortable to put on a stunt at a party even when others are doing the same sort of things.

   180. I find it hard to make talk when I meet new people.

   [a]183. I am against giving money to beggars.

   217. I frequently find myself worrying about something.

   234. I get mad easily and then get over it soon.

   267. When in a group of people I have trouble thinking of the right things to talk about.

   [a]272. At times I am all full of energy.

   296. I have periods in which I feel unusually cheerful without any special reason.

   316. I think nearly anyone would tell a lie to keep out of trouble.

   322. I worry over money and business.

   374. At periods my mind seems to work more slowly than usual.

   383. People often disappoint me.

   397. I have sometimes felt that difficulties were piling up so high that I could not overcome them.

   398. I often think, "I wish I were a child again."

   406. I have often met people who were supposed to be experts who were no better than I.

   [a]461. I find it hard to set aside a task that I have undertaken even for a short time.

   [a]502. I like to let people know where I stand on things.

Note. No items were deleted from scale K on the MMPI-2.

[a]These items were used as a correction factor within the K scale.

between scores on scale K and educational level continues to be very significant ($r = 0.18$ for women; 0.16 for men).

Although Hathaway always used raw scores with K correction for plotting adolescent MMPI profiles, subsequent researchers believed there was insufficient support for its use. Therefore, adolescent profiles typically are plotted without K correction (Marks, Seeman, & Haller, 1974).

Nevertheless, clinicians and researchers should be reminded that in their original work Marks et al. (1974) mentioned only two studies (one was an abstract—Berry & Marks, 1972—and the other was a brief one-page report—Marks & Seeman, 1962) bearing on this issue. Unfortunately, because they did not provide K-corrected T-score tables, it was not possible for further research efforts to be undertaken. Therefore, no subsequent research to support or refute this position has been done since the practice was initiated. Recently, however, to encourage such investigation, and to determine whether traditional K-weighting (Meehl & Hathaway, 1946) would be useful in some settings, we have developed and presented such norms (Colligan & Offord, 1989), and these tables are reprinted in this volume (see Appendix I). From a clinical perspective, although most adolescents earn low scores on K, some do not. Adolescents with a more adultlike pattern of scores on the validity scales may require K-corrected profiles for accurate interpretation. This view suggests that adolescent K-weighting may therefore fulfill the original purpose for which K was intended—compensating for adolescent cautiousness or defensiveness in response style (Heilbrun, 1963; Nakamura, 1960; Tyler & Michaelis, 1953; Wooten, 1984; Yonge, 1966). Nevertheless, this is an empirical question that requires further study, and we are eager to have clinicians in other settings pursue such clinical and research efforts.

CLINICAL SCALES

Scale 1 (Hs, Hypochondriasis; 33 Items)

Scale 1 (Table 5), initially entitled H-C$_H$, was based on a sample of 50 patients described as being from the "somewhat unprivileged classes" and having "only pure, uncomplicated hypochondriasis" (defined as an "abnormal psychoneurotic concern over bodily health") (McKinley & Hathaway, 1940, p. 255). They also were described as showing an

> abnormal concern for their bodily functions. Their worries and preoccupations with physical symptoms typically persist in the face of strong evidence against any valid physical infirmity or defect. This worry over their health dominates their life and often seriously restricts the range of their activities and interpersonal relations. The classic picture of hypochondriacs also includes egocentricity, immaturity, and lack of insight. (Dahlstrom & Welsh, 1960, p. 53)

The age and sex compositions of this sample were not stated, but patients with personality disorders, psychoses, or organic problems were excluded.

In the MMPI-2, one item from the original MMPI item pool was deleted from scale 1 (Hs), as follows:

63. I have had no difficulty in starting or holding my bowel movement.

Scale 2 (D, Depression; 60 Items)

The depression items (Table 6) were obtained from a group of 50 psychiatric patients described as being "in the depressed phase of a manic-depressive psychosis" (Hathaway & McKinley, 1942, p. 75) and characterized by symptoms including "poor morale, lack of hope in the future, and dissatisfaction with the patient's own status generally" (Hathaway & McKinley, 1942, p. 74).

In addition to this criterion group, 50 other patients who had relatively high scores on the experimental version of the depression scale but who had no observable signs of depression, and also 40 people from the normal sample who obtained a high depression score on the preliminary scale, were included.

Table 5
MMPI Scale 1 (Hs, Hypochondriasis)

True:
23. I am troubled by attacks of nausea and vomiting.
29. I am bothered by acid stomach several times a week.
43. My sleep is fitful and disturbed.
62. Parts of my body often have feelings like burning, tingling, crawling, or like "going to sleep."
72. I am troubled by discomfort in the pit of my stomach every few days or oftener.
108. There seems to be a fullness in my head or nose most of the time.
114. Often I feel as if there were a tight band about my head.
125. I have a great deal of stomach trouble.
161. The top of my head sometimes feels tender.
189. I feel weak all over much of the time.
273. I have numbness in one or more regions of my skin.

False:
2. I have a good appetite.
3. I wake up fresh and rested most mornings.
7. My hands and feet are usually warm enough.
9. I am about as able to work as I ever was.
18. I am very seldom troubled by constipation.
51. I am in just as good physical health as most of my friends.
55. I am almost never bothered by pains over the heart or in my chest.
[a]63. I have had no difficulty in starting or holding my bowel movement.
68. I hardly ever feel pain in the back of the neck.
103. I have little or no trouble with my muscles twitching or jumping.
130. I have never vomited blood or coughed up blood.
153. During the past few years I have been well most of the time.
155. I am neither gaining nor losing weight.
163. I do not tire quickly.
175. I seldom or never have dizzy spells.
188. I can read a long while without tiring my eyes.
190. I have very few headaches.
192. I have had no difficulty in keeping my balance in walking.
230. I hardly ever notice my heart pounding and I am seldom short of breath.
243. I have few or no pains.
274. My eyesight is as good as it has been for years.
281. I do not often notice my ears ringing or buzzing.

[a]This item was deleted from scale 1 (Hs) on the MMPI-2.

In the MMPI-2, the following three items from scale 2 (D) were deleted:

58. Everything is turning out just like the prophets of the Bible said it would.
95. I go to church almost every week.
98. I believe in the second coming of Christ.

Scale 3 (Hy, Hysteria; 60 Items)

For scale 3 (Table 7), the criterion group of 50 cases had each received a diagnosis of "psychoneurosis, hysteria" or had been described as having "characteristic hysterical components" believed to account for the conversion symptoms that were present. Descriptively, these patients were viewed as "less obviously neurotic and to have during disabled periods, a more specific set of physical symptoms" (McKinley & Hathaway, 1944, p. 162).

Table 6
MMPI Scale 2 (D, Depression)

True:
- 5. I am easily awakened by noise.
- 13. I work under a great deal of tension.
- 23. I am troubled by attacks of nausea and vomiting.
- 32. I find it hard to keep my mind on a task or job.
- 41. I have had periods of days, weeks, or months when I couldn't take care of things because I couldn't "get going."
- 43. My sleep is fitful and disturbed.
- 52. I prefer to pass by school friends, or people I know but have not seen for a long time, unless they speak to me first.
- 67. I wish I could be as happy as others seem to be.
- 86. I am certainly lacking in self-confidence.
- 104. I don't seem to care what happens to me.
- [b]130. I have never vomited blood or coughed up blood.
- 138. Criticism or scolding hurts me terribly.
- 142. I certainly feel useless at times.
- 158. I cry easily.
- 159. I cannot understand what I read as well as I used to.
- 182. I am afraid of losing my mind.
- 189. I feel weak all over much of the time.
- [b]193. I do not have spells of hay fever or asthma.
- 236. I brood a great deal.
- 259. I have difficulty in starting to do things.

False:
- 2. I have a good appetite.
- 8. My daily life is full of things that keep me interested.
- 9. I am about as able to work as I ever was.
- 18. I am very seldom troubled by constipation.
- 30. At times I feel like swearing.
- 36. I seldom worry about my health.
- 39. At times I feel like smashing things.
- 46. My judgment is better than it ever was.
- 51. I am in just as good physical health as most of my friends.
- 57. I am a good mixer.
- [a,b]58. Everything is turning out just like the prophets of the Bible said it would.
- [b]64. I sometimes keep on at a thing until others lose their patience with me.
- [b]80. I sometimes tease animals.
- 88. I usually feel that life is worthwhile.
- 89. It takes a lot of argument to convince most people of the truth.
- [a,b]95. I go to church almost every week.
- [a,b]98. I believe in the second coming of Christ.
- 107. I am happy most of the time.
- 122. I seem to be about as capable and smart as most others around me.
- 131. I do not worry about catching diseases.
- 145. At times I feel like picking a fist fight with someone.
- 152. Most nights I go to sleep without thoughts or ideas bothering me.
- 153. During the past few years I have been well most of the time.
- [b]154. I have never had a fit or convulsion.
- 155. I am neither gaining nor losing weight.
- 160. I have never felt better in my life than I do now.
- 178. My memory seems to be all right.
- [b]191. Sometimes, when embarrassed, I break out in a sweat which annoys me greatly.
- 207. I enjoy many different kinds of play and recreation.
- 208. I like to flirt.

(continued on next page)

Table 6 *(continued)*

---

233. I have at times stood in the way of people who were trying to do something, not because it amounted to much but because of the principle of the thing.
241. I dream frequently about things that are best kept to myself.
242. I believe I am no more nervous than most others.
248. Sometimes without any reason or even when things are going wrong I feel excitedly happy, "on top of the world."
[b]263. I sweat very easily even on cool days.
[b]270. When I leave home I do not worry about whether the door is locked and the windows closed.
271. I do not blame a person for taking advantage of someone who lays himself open to it.
272. At times I am all full of energy.
285. Once in a while I laugh at a dirty joke.
296. I have periods in which I feel unusually cheerful without any special reason.

---

[a]These items were deleted from scale 2 (D) on the MMPI-2.

[b]These statements were described as "primarily correction items and not especially indicative of depression" (Hathaway & McKinley, 1942, p. 77).

No demographic information was provided for these cases.

Clinicians soon noted that, when scale 1 (Hs) was higher than scale 3 (Hy), physical complaints were likely to be more diffuse and psychological factors were established more easily. However, when scale 3 (Hy) was higher than scale 1 (Hs), the patient was likely to present a relatively normal psychological appearance—to which clinicians sometimes referred as a "sweet-smelling persona" because of the initially good impression made by such patients—with physical symptoms more likely to mimic those of common physical syndromes.

Scale 4 (Pd, Psychopathic Deviate; 50 Items)

The number of patients in the criterion sample for scale 4 (Table 8) was not stated. However, we are told that it included both sexes, there were more females than males, and all patients were 17 to 22 years old.

The group was characterized by "stealing, lying, truancy, sexual promiscuity, alcoholic overindulgence, forgery and similar delinquencies. There were no major criminal types. . . . All of the criterion cases had long histories of minor delinquency" (McKinley & Hathaway, 1944, p. 167) and also were described as having "repeated and flagrant disregard for social customs and mores, an inability to profit from punishing experiences . . . and an emotional shallowness in relation to others, particularly in sexual and affectional display" (Dahlstrom & Welsh, 1960, p. 60).

Scale 5 (Mf, Masculinity-Femininity; 60 Items)

For scale 5 (Table 9), the original research plan apparently was "to collect relatively large samples of homosexual invert males and of homosexual females. . . . [but] the plan went awry because it became apparent that the homosexual samples were too heterogeneous" (Hathaway, 1956, p. 110). No demographic information was reported for the criterion group of 13 homosexual men. They were selected "for their relative freedom from neurosis. . . . for

Table 7
MMPI Scale 3 (Hy, Hysteria)

True:
- 10. There seems to be a lump in my throat much of the time.
- 23. I am troubled by attacks of nausea and vomiting.
- 32. I find it hard to keep my mind on a task or job.
- 43. My sleep is fitful and disturbed.
- 44. Much of the time my head seems to hurt all over.
- 47. Once a week or oftener I feel suddenly hot all over, without apparent cause.
- 76. Most of the time I feel blue.
- 114. Often I feel as if there were a tight band about my head.
- 179. I am worried about sex matters.
- 186. I frequently notice my hand shakes when I try to do something.
- 189. I feel weak all over much of the time.
- 238. I have periods of such great restlessness that I cannot sit long in a chair.
- 253. I can be friendly with people who do things which I consider wrong.

False:
- 2. I have a good appetite.
- 3. I wake up fresh and rested most mornings.
- 6. I like to read newspaper articles on crime.
- 7. My hands and feet are usually warm enough.
- 8. My daily life is full of things that keep me interested.
- 9. I am about as able to work as I ever was.
- 12. I enjoy detective or mystery stories.
- 26. I feel that it is certainly best to keep my mouth shut when I'm in trouble.
- 30. At times I feel like swearing.
- 51. I am in just as good physical health as most of my friends.
- 55. I am almost never bothered by pains over the heart or in my chest.
- 71. I think a great many people exaggerate their misfortunes in order to gain the sympathy and help of others.
- 89. It takes a lot of argument to convince most people of the truth.
- 93. I think most people would lie to get ahead.
- 103. I have little or no trouble with my muscles twitching or jumping.
- 107. I am happy most of the time.
- 109. Some people are so bossy that I feel like doing the opposite of what they request even though I know they are right.
- 124. Most people will use somewhat unfair means to gain profit or an advantage rather than to lose it.
- 128. The sight of blood neither frightens me nor makes me sick.
- 129. Often I can't understand why I have been so cross and grouchy.
- 136. I commonly wonder what hidden reason another person may have for doing something nice for me.
- 137. I believe that my home life is as pleasant as that of most people I know.
- 141. My conduct is largely controlled by the customs of those about me.
- 147. I have often lost out on things because I couldn't make up my mind soon enough.
- 153. During the past few years I have been well most of the time.
- 160. I have never felt better in my life than I do now.
- 162. I resent having anyone take me in so cleverly that I have had to admit that it was one on me.
- 163. I do not tire quickly.
- 170. What others think of me does not bother me.
- 172. I frequently have to fight against showing that I am bashful.
- 174. I have never had a fainting spell.
- 175. I seldom or never have dizzy spells.
- 180. I find it hard to make talk when I meet new people.
- 188. I can read a long while without tiring my eyes.

(continued on next page)

Table 7 *(continued)*

---

190. I have very few headaches.
192. I have had no difficulty in keeping my balance in walking.
201. I wish I were not so shy.
213. In walking I am very careful to step over sidewalk cracks.
230. I hardly ever notice my heart pounding and I am seldom short of breath.
234. I get mad easily and then get over it soon.
243. I have few or no pains.
265. It is safer to trust nobody.
267. When in a group of people I have trouble thinking of the right things to talk about.
274. My eyesight is as good as it has been for years.
279. I drink an unusually large amount of water every day.
289. I am always disgusted with the law when a criminal is freed through the arguments of a smart lawyer.
292. I am likely not to speak to people until they speak to me.

Note. No items were deleted from scale 3 (Hy) on the MMPI-2.

psychotic disorders. . . . [and] psychopathic tendencies'' (Dahlstrom & Welsh, 1960, p. 64).

Procedures for this scale varied considerably from those used in developing the other clinical scales. First, 55 new items ''primarily related to masculinity-femininity'' (Hathaway & McKinley, 1943, p. 162) had been added to the item pool, apparently before 1943. Thus, response frequencies for these 55 items were not available from the original Minnesota normal group; as a result, 54 soldiers (men) and 67 airline employees (women) composed a supplemental group of normal people. Furthermore, the normative data provided in the 1943 MMPI manual were based on a sample of engineers of various ages and unselected army noncommissioned men.

Item selection procedures were not presented clearly. However, first the items were evaluated by differences in response frequency between the sexes. Second, comparisons were made with the new male normal sample obtained specifically for this scale. Finally, comparisons were made with a group of men (number not specified) selected on the basis of ''invert'' scores—response patterns consistent with those obtained by a group of passive homosexual men—on a test of masculine-feminine interests (Terman & Miles, 1936). Thus, for the first time, a test-related criterion group was used as part of the selection procedures, differing from the earlier criterion groups that had been established by psychiatric diagnosis.

It should be noted that 37 of the 60 items on the Mf scale actually were derived from the original MMPI item pool (indicated with a ''c'' on Table 9), and the remaining 23 items came from the 55 items that had been added later.

Interpretation of scores on scale 5 thus remained a problem, with the scale basically providing a measure of the tendency toward masculinity or femininity of interest pattern, even though the original intent had been to identify a homosexual orientation. Later, in the handbook for military clinical psychologists, Hathaway and Meehl (1951) emphatically stated that

> T scores of 60 to 75 are not uncommon among males in literary and artistic lines of work. *One would never be justified in assuming an identity between high scores on this scale and the existence of homosexual practices.* . . . Naturally, unusual caution should be used in the clinical interpretation of high scores. (p. 81; emphasis in original)

Table 8
MMPI Scale 4 (Pd, Psychopathic Deviate)

True:

16. I am sure I get a raw deal from life.
21. At times I have very much wanted to leave home.
24. No one seems to understand me.
32. I find it hard to keep my mind on a task or job.
33. I have had very peculiar and strange experiences.
35. If people had not had it in for me I would have been much more successful.
38. During one period when I was a youngster I engaged in petty thievery.
42. My family does not like the work I have chosen (or the work I intend to choose for my life work).
61. I have not lived the right kind of life.
67. I wish I could be as happy as others seem to be.
84. These days I find it hard not to give up hope of amounting to something.
94. I do many things which I regret afterwards (I regret things more or more often than others seem to).
102. My hardest battles are with myself.
106. Much of the time I feel as if I have done something wrong or evil.
110. Someone has it in for me.
118. In school I was sometimes sent to the principal for cutting up.
127. I know who is responsible for most of my troubles.
215. I have used alcohol excessively.
216. There is very little love and companionship in my family as compared to other homes.
224. My parents have often objected to the kind of people I went around with.
239. I have been disappointed in love.
244. My way of doing things is apt to be misunderstood by others.
245. My parents and family find more fault with me than they should.
284. I am sure I am being talked about.

False:

8. My daily life is full of things that keep me interested.
20. My sex life is satisfactory.
37. I have never been in trouble because of my sex behavior.
82. I am easily downed in an argument.
91. I do not mind being made fun of.
96. I have very few quarrels with members of my family.
107. I am happy most of the time.
134. At times my thoughts have raced ahead faster than I could speak them.
137. I believe that my home life is as pleasant as that of most people I know.
141. My conduct is largely controlled by the customs of those about me.
155. I am neither gaining nor losing weight.
170. What others think of me does not bother me.
171. It makes me uncomfortable to put on a stunt at a party even when others are doing the same sort of things.
173. I liked school.
180. I find it hard to make talk when I meet new people.
183. I am against giving money to beggars.
201. I wish I were not so shy.
231. I like to talk about sex.
235. I have been quite independent and free from family rule.
237. My relatives are nearly all in sympathy with me.
248. Sometimes without any reason or even when things are going wrong I feel excitedly happy, "on top of the world."
267. When in a group of people I have trouble thinking of the right things to talk about.
287. I have very few fears compared to my friends.
289. I am always disgusted with the law when a criminal is freed through the arguments of a smart lawyer.
294. I have never been in trouble with the law.
296. I have periods in which I feel unusually cheerful without any special reason.

Note. No items were deleted from scale 4 (Pd) on the MMPI-2.

Table 9
Table 9
MMPI Scale 5 (Mf, Masculinity-Femininity)

True:

    4. I think I would like the work of a librarian.

    25. I would like to be a singer.

a,b,c69. I am very strongly attracted by members of my own sex.

a70. I used to like drop-the-handkerchief.

    74. I have often wished I were a girl. (Or if you are a girl) I have never been sorry that I am a girl.

c77. I enjoy reading love stories.

    78. I like poetry.

    87. I would like to be a florist.

    92. I would like to be a nurse.

  126. I like dramatics.

  132. I like collecting flowers or growing house plants.

c134. At times my thoughts have raced ahead faster than I could speak them.

  140. I like to cook.

  149. I used to keep a diary.

b,c179. I am worried about sex matters.

c187. My hands have not become clumsy or awkward.

  203. If I were a reporter I would very much like to report news of the theater.

  204. I would like to be a journalist.

c217. I frequently find myself worrying about something.

c226. Some of my family have habits that bother and annoy me very much.

b,c231. I like to talk about sex.

c239. I have been disappointed in love.

  261. If I were an artist I would like to draw flowers.

c278. I have often felt that strangers were looking at me critically.

c282. Once in a while I feel hate toward members of my family whom I usually love.

a295. I liked "Alice in Wonderland" by Lewis Carroll.

b,c297. I wish I were not bothered by thoughts about sex.

c299. I think that I feel more intensely than most people do.

False:

    1. I like mechanics magazines.

c19. When I take a new job, I like to be tipped off on who should be gotten next to.

c26. I feel that it is certainly best to keep my mouth shut when I'm in trouble.

c28. When someone does me a wrong, I feel I should pay him back if I can just for the principle of the thing.

c79. My feelings are not easily hurt.

c80. I sometimes tease animals.

  81. I think I would like the kind of work a forest ranger does.

c89. It takes a lot of argument to convince most people of the truth.

c99. I like to go to parties and other affairs where there is lots of loud fun.

c112. I frequently find it necessary to stand up for what I think is right.

c115. I believe in a life hereafter.

c116. I enjoy a race or game better when I bet on it.

c117. Most people are honest chiefly through fear of being caught.

c120. My table manners are not quite as good at home as when I am out in company.

b,c133. I have never indulged in any unusual sex practices.

  144. I would like to be a soldier.

c176. I do not have a great fear of snakes.

c198. I daydream very little.

c213. In walking I am very careful to step over sidewalk cracks.

c214. I have never had any breaking out on my skin that has worried me.

  219. I think I would like the work of a building contractor.

  221. I like science.

  223. I very much like hunting.

Table 9 (continued)

[c]229.   I should like to belong to several clubs or lodges.
[a,c]249.   I believe there is a Devil and a Hell in afterlife.
[c]254.   I like to be with a crowd who play jokes on one another.
[c]260.   I was a slow learner in school.
[c]262.   It does not bother me that I am not better looking.
[c]264.   I am entirely self-confident.
[c]280.   Most people make friends because friends are likely to be useful to them.
283.   If I were a reporter I would very much like to report sporting news.
300.   There never was a time in my life when I liked to play with dolls.

[a]These items were deleted from scale 5 (Mf) on the MMPI-2.
[b]These items are scored in the opposite direction for females (that is, one raw score point is added to the Mf score for a woman who answers "false" to item 69, 179, 231, or 297 or who responds "true" to item 133); the other items are scored in the same direction for both men and women.
[c]These items were derived from the original MMPI item pool.

It should also be noted that one attempt was made to develop a comparable scale for women (Fm) derived from a sample of homosexual women. However, it was abandoned because of its high correlation (0.78 to 0.95) with scale 5 (Mf), and cross validation was unfavorable for the identification of female homosexuality.

In the MMPI-2, four items were deleted from scale 5 (Mf), as follows:

69.   I am very strongly attracted by members of my own sex.
70.   I used to like drop-the-handkerchief.
295.   I liked "Alice in Wonderland" by Lewis Carroll.
249.   I believe there is a Devil and a Hell in afterlife.

Scale 6 (Pa, Paranoia; 40 Items)

Demographic information and the sample size of the criterion group were not reported for scale 6 (Table 10). However, the most common diagnoses reported among members of this group were

> paranoid state, paranoid condition, and paranoid schizophrenia. Symptomatically they tended to have ideas of references, to feel that they were persecuted by individuals or groups, and to have grandiose self-concepts. . . . suspiciousness, an excess of interpersonal sensitivity, and an underlying rigidity of opinions and attitudes. (Hathaway, 1956, p. 109)

Apparently Hathaway was reluctant to publish this scale because the preliminary form could not be improved; however, the value of this "temporary scale. . . . was that there were a few false positives. When a person had a high score, he tended to be diagnosed as paranoid or at least he was felt to be sensitive and rigid in personal relationships" (Hathaway, 1956, p. 110).

Scale 7 (Pt, Psychasthenia; 48 Items)

For scale 7 (Table 11), the 20 psychiatric inpatients—proportions of age and sex were not reported—were characterized

Table 10
MMPI Scale 6 (Pa, Paranoia)

True:
15. Once in a while I think of things too bad to talk about.
16. I am sure I get a raw deal from life.
22. At times I have fits of laughing and crying that I cannot control.
24. No one seems to understand me.
27. Evil spirits possess me at times.
35. If people had not had it in for me I would have been much more successful.
110. Someone has it in for me.
121. I believe I am being plotted against.
123. I believe I am being followed.
127. I know who is responsible for most of my troubles.
151. Someone has been trying to poison me.
157. I feel that I have often been punished without cause.
158. I cry easily.
202. I believe I am a condemned person.
275. Someone has control over my mind.
284. I am sure I am being talked about.
291. At one or more times in my life I felt that someone was making me do things by hypnotizing me.
293. Someone has been trying to influence my mind.
299. I think that I feel more intensely than most people do.
305. Even when I am with people I feel lonely much of the time.
317. I am more sensitive than most other people.
338. I have certainly had more than my share of things to worry about.
341. At times I hear so well it bothers me.
364. People say insulting and vulgar things about me.
365. I feel uneasy indoors.

False:
93. I think most people would lie to get ahead.
107. I am happy most of the time.
109. Some people are so bossy that I feel like doing the opposite of what they request even though I know they are right.
111. I have never done anything dangerous for the thrill of it.
117. Most people are honest chiefly through fear of being caught.
124. Most people will use somewhat unfair means to gain profit or an advantage rather than to lose it.
268. Something exciting will almost always pull me out of it when I am feeling low.
281. I do not often notice my ears ringing or buzzing.
294. I have never been in trouble with the law.
313. The man who provides temptation by leaving valuable property unprotected is about as much to blame for its theft as the one who steals it.
316. I think nearly anyone would tell a lie to keep out of trouble.
319. Most people inwardly dislike putting themselves out to help other people.
327. My mother or father often made me obey even when I thought that it was unreasonable.
347. I have no enemies who really wish to harm me.
348. I tend to be on my guard with people who are somewhat more friendly than I had expected.

Note. No items were deleted from scale 6 (Pa) on the MMPI-2.

by excessive doubt, by compulsions, obsessions, and unreasonable fears. . . . not so much by well-marked fears of individual things or acts as by great doubts as to the meaning of his reactions in what seems to be a hostile environment. In other cases . . . he is forced through fear to compulsively perform needless, disturbing or personally destructive acts or to dwell obsessively upon lines of thought which have no significance for his normal activities. (McKinley & Hathaway, 1942, p. 615)

Table 11
MMPI Scale 7 (Pt, Psychasthenia)

True:

10. There seems to be a lump in my throat much of the time.
15. Once in a while I think of things too bad to talk about.
22. At times I have fits of laughing and crying that I cannot control.
32. I find it hard to keep my mind on a task or job.
41. I have had periods of days, weeks, or months when I couldn't take care of things because I couldn't "get going."
67. I wish I could be as happy as others seem to be.
76. Most of the time I feel blue.
86. I am certainly lacking in self-confidence.
94. I do many things which I regret afterwards (I regret things more or more often than others seem to).
102. My hardest battles are with myself.
106. Much of the time I feel as if I have done something wrong or evil.
142. I certainly feel useless at times.
159. I cannot understand what I read as well as I used to.
182. I am afraid of losing my mind.
189. I feel weak all over much of the time.
217. I frequently find myself worrying about something.
238. I have periods of such great restlessness that I cannot sit long in a chair.
266. Once a week or oftener I become very excited.
301. Life is a strain for me much of the time.
304. In school I found it very hard to talk before the class.
305. Even when I am with people I feel lonely much of the time.
317. I am more sensitive than most other people.
321. I am easily embarrassed.
336. I easily become impatient with people.
337. I feel anxiety about something or someone almost all the time.
340. Sometimes I become so excited that I find it hard to get to sleep.
342. I forget right away what people say to me.
343. I usually have to stop and think before I act even in trifling matters.
344. Often I cross the street in order not to meet someone I see.
346. I have a habit of counting things that are not important such as bulbs on electric signs, and so forth.
349. I have strange and peculiar thoughts.
351. I get anxious and upset when I have to make a short trip away from home.
352. I have been afraid of things or people that I knew could not hurt me.
356. I have more trouble concentrating than others seem to have.
357. I have several times given up doing a thing because I thought too little of my ability.
358. Bad words, often terrible words, come into my mind and I cannot get rid of them.
359. Sometimes some unimportant thought will run through my mind and bother me for days.
360. Almost every day something happens to frighten me.
361. I am inclined to take things hard.

False:

3. I wake up fresh and rested most mornings.
8. My daily life is full of things that keep me interested.
36. I seldom worry about my health.
122. I seem to be about as capable and smart as most others around me.
152. Most nights I go to sleep without thoughts or ideas bothering me.
164. I like to study and read about things that I am working at.
178. My memory seems to be all right.
329. I almost never dream.
353. I have no dread of going into a room by myself where other people have already gathered and are talking.

Note. No items were deleted from scale 7 (Pt) on the MMPI-2.

The authors also noted that, although carefully diagnosed, two of the subjects, both teenagers, were probably included erroneously: "For example. . . . One of these was not at all similar in item responses to the remainder of the criterion group. It is probable that this 16-year-old boy was wrongly diagnosed" (McKinley & Hathaway, 1942, p. 617).

Scale 8 (Sc, Schizophrenia; 78 Items)

About 60% of the criterion group of 50 patients for scale 8 (Table 12) were women (their ages were not reported) who had assorted subtypes of schizophrenia. They were characterized as

> constrained, cold, and apathetic or indifferent. . . . remote and inaccessible, often seemingly sufficient unto themselves. Delusions of varying degrees of organization, hallucinations, either fleeting or persistent and compelling, and disorientation may appear in various combinations. Inactivity, or endless stereotypy, may accompany the withdrawal of interest from other people or external objects and relationships. These persons frequently perform below the levels expected of them on the basis of their training and ability. (Dahlstrom & Welsh, 1960, p. 71)

None of the efforts to develop scales related to differential diagnostic categories (such as paranoid schizophrenia) were successful, and Sc4—the fourth preliminary scale to be developed—was chosen as the final version of the schizophrenia scale. Unfortunately, it identified only about 50% to 60% of the diagnosed cases, with a false-positive rate of about 10% to 15%. After scale K was developed and applied to scale 8 (Sc), the number of high-scoring normal subjects was significantly decreased, although Hathaway remained dissatisfied with the scale because "even with the correction, a considerable number of the cross-validation cases managed to stay below the T score 61" (Hathaway, 1956, p. 109).

Scale 9 (Ma, Hypomania; 46 Items)

The 24 inpatients composing the criterion group for scale 9 (Table 13)—no demographic data were reported—were characterized by

> the milder degrees of manic excitement occurring typically in the manic depressive psychoses. The cardinal symptoms of maniacal conditions are generally stated to be an elated but unstable mood, psychomotor excitement and flight of ideas. Hypomanic trends follow the same pattern in general, but in lesser degrees that may be at times so unobtrusive as not to impress even an expert. . . . only manic patients of moderate or light degree were usable, since the more severe cases could not cooperate adequately in sorting the inventory items. (McKinley & Hathaway, 1944, p. 162)

Patients who were confused, delirious, or schizophrenic or who had agitated depressions also were excluded. Two factors appeared to be measured by the scale: the first was described as "ebullient optimism," and the second was believed to account for the hypomanic state.

Table 12
MMPI Scale 8 (Sc, Schizophrenia)

True:
15. Once in a while I think of things too bad to talk about.
16. I am sure I get a raw deal from life.
21. At times I have very much wanted to leave home.
22. At times I have fits of laughing and crying that I cannot control.
24. No one seems to understand me.
32. I find it hard to keep my mind on a task or job.
33. I have had very peculiar and strange experiences.
35. If people had not had it in for me I would have been much more successful.
38. During one period when I was a youngster I engaged in petty thievery.
40. Most any time I would rather sit and daydream than to do anything else.
41. I have had periods of days, weeks, or months when I couldn't take care of things because I couldn't "get going."
47. Once a week or oftener I feel suddenly hot all over, without apparent cause.
52. I prefer to pass by school friends, or people I know but have not seen for a long time, unless they speak to me first.
76. Most of the time I feel blue.
97. At times I have a strong urge to do something harmful or shocking.
104. I don't seem to care what happens to me.
121. I believe I am being plotted against.
156. I have had periods in which I carried on activities without knowing later what I had been doing.
157. I feel that I have often been punished without cause.
159. I cannot understand what I read as well as I used to.
168. There is something wrong with my mind.
179. I am worried about sex matters.
182. I am afraid of losing my mind.
194. I have had attacks in which I could not control my movements or speech but in which I knew what was going on around me.
202. I believe I am a condemned person.
210. Everything tastes the same.
212. My people treat me more like a child than a grown-up.
238. I have periods of such great restlessness that I cannot sit long in a chair.
241. I dream frequently about things that are best kept to myself.
251. I have had blank spells in which my activities were interrupted and I did not know what was going on around me.
259. I have difficulty in starting to do things.
266. Once a week or oftener I become very excited.
273. I have numbness in one or more regions of my skin.
282. Once in a while I feel hate toward members of my family whom I usually love.
291. At one or more times in my life I felt that someone was making me do things by hypnotizing me.
297. I wish I were not bothered by thoughts about sex.
301. Life is a strain for me much of the time.
303. I am so touchy on some subjects that I can't talk about them.
305. Even when I am with people I feel lonely much of the time.
307. I refuse to play some games because I am not good at them.
312. I dislike having people about me.
320. Many of my dreams are about sex matters.
324. I have never been in love with anyone.
325. The things that some of my family have done have frightened me.
332. Sometimes my voice leaves me or changes even though I have no cold.
334. Peculiar odors come to me at times.
335. I cannot keep my mind on one thing.
339. Most of the time I wish I were dead.

(continued on next page)

Table 12 (continued)

341. At times I hear so well it bothers me.
345. I often feel as if things were not real.
349. I have strange and peculiar thoughts.
350. I hear strange things when I am alone.
352. I have been afraid of things or people that I knew could not hurt me.
354. I am afraid of using a knife or anything very sharp or pointed.
355. Sometimes I enjoy hurting persons I love.
356. I have more trouble concentrating than others seem to have.
360. Almost every day something happens to frighten me.
363. At times I have enjoyed being hurt by someone I loved.
364. People say insulting and vulgar things about me.

False:
8. My daily life is full of things that keep me interested.
17. My father was a good man.
20. My sex life is satisfactory.
37. I have never been in trouble because of my sex behavior.
65. I loved my father.
103. I have little or no trouble with my muscles twitching or jumping.
119. My speech is the same as always (not faster or slower, or slurring; no hoarseness).
177. My mother was a good woman.
178. My memory seems to be all right.
187. My hands have not become clumsy or awkward.
192. I have had no difficulty in keeping my balance in walking.
196. I like to visit places where I have never been before.
220. I loved my mother.
276. I enjoy children.
281. I do not often notice my ears ringing or buzzing.
306. I get all the sympathy I should.
309. I seem to make friends about as quickly as others do.
322. I worry over money and business.
330. I have never been paralyzed or had any unusual weakness of any of my muscles.

Note. No items were deleted from scale 8 (Sc) on the MMPI-2.

Scale 0 (Si, Social IE, Introversion–Extroversion; 70 Items)

Scale 0 (Table 14) was the only scale to be developed by someone outside Hathaway's original research group and was the last of the scales to be added to the basic clinical profile. Furthermore, of the basic clinical scales, scale 0 (Si) is the second scale having its roots in test-related criterion groups, and the only one for which the criterion sample was not obtained from psychiatric diagnosis (Drake, 1946).

The T-S-E Inventory (thinking, social, emotional) was a scale rooted in the tenets of Jung (Evans & McConnell, 1941). Because the T-S-E Inventory had been found useful for counseling college students, and because many of its items resembled those of the MMPI, it was decided to use the social section of the T-S-E Inventory to ascertain students to compose a criterion group for a comparable scale to be developed on MMPI items. Thus, because the T-S-E Inventory differentiated students who varied in their degree of participation in campus activities, the criterion sample for high social participation scored at or above the 65th percentile (n = 50 college women), and those in the criterion group for being low in campus social participation scored below the 35th percentile (n = 50 college women). Initially, men were not included because the study was

Table 13
MMPI Scale 9 (Ma, Hypomania)

True:

11. A person should try to understand his dreams and be guided by or take warning from them.
13. I work under a great deal of tension.
21. At times I have very much wanted to leave home.
22. At times I have fits of laughing and crying that I cannot control.
59. I have often had to take orders from someone who did not know as much as I did.
64. I sometimes keep on at a thing until others lose their patience with me.
73. I am an important person.
97. At times I have a strong urge to do something harmful or shocking.
100. I have met problems so full of possibilities that I have been unable to make up my mind about them.
109. Some people are so bossy that I feel like doing the opposite of what they request even though I know they are right.
127. I know who is responsible for most of my troubles.
134. At times my thoughts have raced ahead faster than I could speak them.
143. When I was a child, I belonged to a crowd or gang that tried to stick together through thick and thin.
156. I have had periods in which I carried on activities without knowing later what I had been doing.
157. I feel that I have often been punished without cause.
167. It wouldn't make me nervous if any members of my family got into trouble with the law.
181. When I get bored I like to stir up some excitement.
194. I have had attacks in which I could not control my movements or speech but in which I knew what was going on around me.
212. My people treat me more like a child than a grown-up.
222. It is not hard for me to ask help from my friends even though I cannot return the favor.
226. Some of my family have habits that bother and annoy me very much.
228. At times I feel that I can make up my mind with unusually great ease.
232. I have been inspired to a program of life based on duty which I have since carefully followed.
233. I have at times stood in the way of people who were trying to do something, not because it amounted to much but because of the principle of the thing.
238. I have periods of such great restlessness that I cannot sit long in a chair.
240. I never worry about my looks.
250. I don't blame anyone for trying to grab everything he can get in this world.
251. I have had blank spells in which my activities were interrupted and I did not know what was going on around me.
263. I sweat very easily even on cool days.
266. Once a week or oftener I become very excited.
268. Something exciting will almost always pull me out of it when I am feeling low.
271. I do not blame a person for taking advantage of someone who lays himself open to it.
277. At times I have been so entertained by the cleverness of a crook that I have hoped he would get by with it.
279. I drink an unusually large amount of water every day.
298. If several people find themselves in trouble, the best thing for them to do is to agree upon a story and stick to it.

False:

101. I believe women ought to have as much sexual freedom as men.
105. Sometimes when I am not feeling well I am cross.
111. I have never done anything dangerous for the thrill of it.
119. My speech is the same as always (not faster or slower, or slurring; no hoarseness).
120. My table manners are not quite as good at home as when I am out in company.
148. It makes me impatient to have people ask my advice or otherwise interrupt me when I am working on something important.

(continued on next page)

Table 13 *(continued)*

---

166. I am afraid when I look down from a high place.
171. It makes me uncomfortable to put on a stunt at a party even when others are doing the same sort of things.
180. I find it hard to make talk when I meet new people.
267. When in a group of people I have trouble thinking of the right things to talk about.
289. I am always disgusted with the law when a criminal is freed through the arguments of a smart lawyer.

Note. No items were deleted from scale 9 (Ma) on the MMPI-2.

conducted during World War II and it was believed that the military draft would have resulted in an atypical group of male college students. Subsequently, however, cross validation was performed with 81 college men and 87 college women, with final norms being developed from 358 college women and 193 college men. Because the scores were so similar, the original tables developed separately for each sex later were combined.

Additional cross validation was provided by participation in high school and college extracurricular activities (Drake & Thiede, 1948; Gough, 1949).

In the MMPI-2, one item was deleted from scale 0 (Si), as follows:

462. I have had no difficulty starting or holding my urine.

Table 14
MMPI Scale 0 (Si, Social Introversion)

True:
32. I find it hard to keep my mind on a task or job.
67. I wish I could be as happy as others seem to be.
82. I am easily downed in an argument.
111. I have never done anything dangerous for the thrill of it.
117. Most people are honest chiefly through fear of being caught.
124. Most people will use somewhat unfair means to gain profit or an advantage rather than to lose it.
138. Criticism or scolding hurts me terribly.
147. I have often lost out on things because I couldn't make up my mind soon enough.
171. It makes me uncomfortable to put on a stunt at a party even when others are doing the same sort of things.
172. I frequently have to fight against showing that I am bashful.
180. I find it hard to make talk when I meet new people.
201. I wish I were not so shy.
236. I brood a great deal.
267. When in a group of people I have trouble thinking of the right things to talk about.
278. I have often felt that strangers were looking at me critically.
292. I am likely not to speak to people until they speak to me.
304. In school I found it very hard to talk before the class.
316. I think nearly anyone would tell a lie to keep out of trouble.
321. I am easily embarrassed.
332. Sometimes my voice leaves me or changes even though I have no cold.
336. I easily become impatient with people.
342. I forget right away what people say to me.
357. I have several times given up doing a thing because I thought too little of my ability.
377. At parties I am more likely to sit by myself or with just one other person than to join in with the crowd.

Table 14 (continued)

383. People often disappoint me.
398. I often think, "I wish I were a child again."
411. It makes me feel like a failure when I hear of the success of someone I know well.
427. I am embarrassed by dirty stories.
436. People generally demand more respect for their own rights than they are willing to allow for others.
455. I am quite often not in on the gossip and talk of the group I belong to.
473. Whenever possible I avoid being in a crowd.
487. I feel like giving up quickly when things go wrong.
549. I shrink from facing a crisis or difficulty.
564. I am apt to pass up something I want to do when others feel that it isn't worth doing.

False:

25. I would like to be a singer.
33. I have had very peculiar and strange experiences.
57. I am a good mixer.
91. I do not mind being made fun of.
99. I like to go to parties and other affairs where there is lots of loud fun.
119. My speech is the same as always (not faster or slower, or slurring; no hoarseness).
126. I like dramatics.
143. When I was a child, I belonged to a crowd or gang that tried to stick together through thick and thin.
193. I do not have spells of hay fever or asthma.
208. I like to flirt.
229. I should like to belong to several clubs or lodges.
231. I like to talk about sex.
254. I like to be with a crowd who play jokes on one another.
262. It does not bother me that I am not better looking.
281. I do not often notice my ears ringing or buzzing.
296. I have periods in which I feel unusually cheerful without any special reason.
309. I seem to make friends about as quickly as others do.
353. I have no dread of going into a room by myself where other people have already gathered and are talking.
359. Sometimes some unimportant thought will run through my mind and bother me for days.
371. I am not unusually self-conscious.
391. I love to go to dances.
400. If given the chance I could do some things that would be of great benefit to the world.
415. If given the chance I would make a good leader of people.
440. I try to remember good stories to pass them on to other people.
446. I enjoy gambling for small stakes.
449. I enjoy social gatherings just to be with people.
450. I enjoy the excitement of a crowd.
451. My worries seem to disappear when I get into a crowd of lively friends.
[a]462. I have had no difficulty starting or holding my urine.
469. I have often found people jealous of my good ideas, just because they had not thought of them first.
479. I do not mind meeting strangers.
481. I can remember "playing sick" to get out of something.
482. While in trains, busses, etc., I often talk to strangers.
505. I have had periods when I felt so full of pep that sleep did not seem necessary for days at a time.
521. In a group of people I would not be embarrassed to be called upon to start a discussion or give an opinion about something I know well.
547. I like parties and socials.

[a]This item was deleted from scale 0 (Si) on the MMPI-2.

PART II

THE CONTEMPORARY NORMATIVE STUDY OF ADULTS: A SUMMARY

THE NEED FOR CONTEMPORARY MMPI NORMS FOR ADULTS

The MMPI clearly has demonstrated its clinical and research usefulness in that it remains the most frequently used and thoroughly researched of the objective personality assessment tools (Lubin, Larsen, & Matarazzo, 1984; Lubin, Larsen, Matarazzo, & Seever, 1985; Piotrowski & Keller, 1989), even among clinicians with a strong behavioral orientation (Piotrowski & Keller, 1984, 1989; Piotrowski & Lubin, 1989), neuropsychologists (Guilmette, Faust, Hart, & Arkes, 1990; Sellers & Nadler, 1990), and investigators in the field of health psychology (Piotrowski & Lubin, 1989, 1990). It also holds an important place in training programs (More- land & Dahlstrom, 1983; Watkins, Campbell, & McGregor, 1988; Watkins, Campbell, McGregor, & Godin, 1989), currently a very different position from that held by clinicians at the time Hathaway and McKinley were beginning their work on MMPI development. More specifically, commenting on this issue, Hathaway (1965) noted,

> applied psychologists become so disillusioned that when the new clinical psychology training programs were being developed, it was so widely accepted that personality inventories were valueless that some program directors did not feel that any course work in their nature and interpretation was worth the effort. Students dismissed the paper-and-pencil inventories out of hand. (p. 461)

However, the need for contemporary norms is as obvious as the changes in our society that have occurred during the 50 years since the MMPI was first conceived. In addition, age-related MMPI changes were apparent in the original sample and have long been recognized by clinicians, particularly those working with adolescent or geriatric populations, but in the original derivation research "the numbers of subjects at each age level, however, were too few to give very stable estimates of any systematic age changes. Accordingly, no special age norms were proposed

43

. . . one standard reference group was used for all adult age levels'' (Dahlstrom, et al., 1975, p. 151). Finally, the MMPI is being used with increased frequency among groups of people who are far different from the medical and psychiatric patients for whom it was originally intended. Therefore, it is essential that users of the MMPI be aware of MMPI response patterns from contemporary normal people.

However, until 1983 there had not been a systematic reexamination of the original adult norms to determine their validity for contemporary use. At that time, Mayo Clinic researchers published MMPI data obtained from a random sample of 1,919 households within a 50-mile radius of Rochester, Minnesota (Colligan et al., 1983). After these households had received an informational and invitational letter, telephone interviewers screened potential respondents from each of the household units for significant mentally or physically handicapping conditions. A sample of 1,408 participants ranging in age from 18 through 99 years was obtained according to a carefully documented outline of procedures (Figure 1). Because we wanted to make comparisons with the original Minnesota normal sample, it was important that the subjects be from the same geographic area as the original Minnesota group, and, as in the Hathaway and McKinley sample, that they not be under the care of a physician or any other health care professional for any illness or handicapping condition.

Although it was desirable to develop a new normal reference sample comparable to the original Minnesota normal sample, the mean educational level of 13 years for both men and women in the contemporary sample was significantly higher than the 8th- and 10th-grade levels for men and women, respectively, in the original Minnesota normal group. Furthermore, the age of our contemporary normal sample was somewhat older (mean age, 45 years for women and 43 years for men) and their age range was noticeably broader because Hathaway and McKinley had not included persons older than 65 years in their sample.

For specific comparative purposes, a randomly selected subset of subjects was identified from the total pool of respondents. They were selected to match the age and sex distribution of the white adult population of the United States according to the 1980 census. The MMPI data from this sample of 335 women (age, 18 through 99 years) and 305 men (age, 18 through 85 years) were then compared with the data of Hathaway and Briggs, the only remaining pool of MMPI information remaining from the original Minnesota normal sample (Hathaway & Briggs, 1957).

Not surprisingly, when these comparisons were made, contemporary normal people scored significantly higher on all of the clinical scales of the MMPI, with men showing greater degrees of change than women (Colligan, Osborne, Swenson, & Offord, 1984b, c). The changes in mean profile were clinically relevant as well as statistically significant, as shown in Figure 2. In these figures, had there been no change in MMPI response patterns, the mean for our contemporary normal sample would have fallen at a T score of 50 and the mean score + 2 SD would have fallen at a T score of 70 because both profiles are based on, and have been plotted using, norms from the original Minnesota normal sample.[8] More specifically, Tables 15 and 16 provide the means and standard deviations for the

---

[8]In the original computerized scoring and interpretive system for the MMPI developed at the Mayo Clinic, the T scores were calculated by mathematical equation; the system does not use a table look-up function. At times, this method may produce a difference of 1 to 2 T-score points from those obtained by using rounded raw scores, mean raw scores, or interpolated T-score values from the adult normative tables presented by Dahlstrom and Welsh (1960, pp. 437–438).

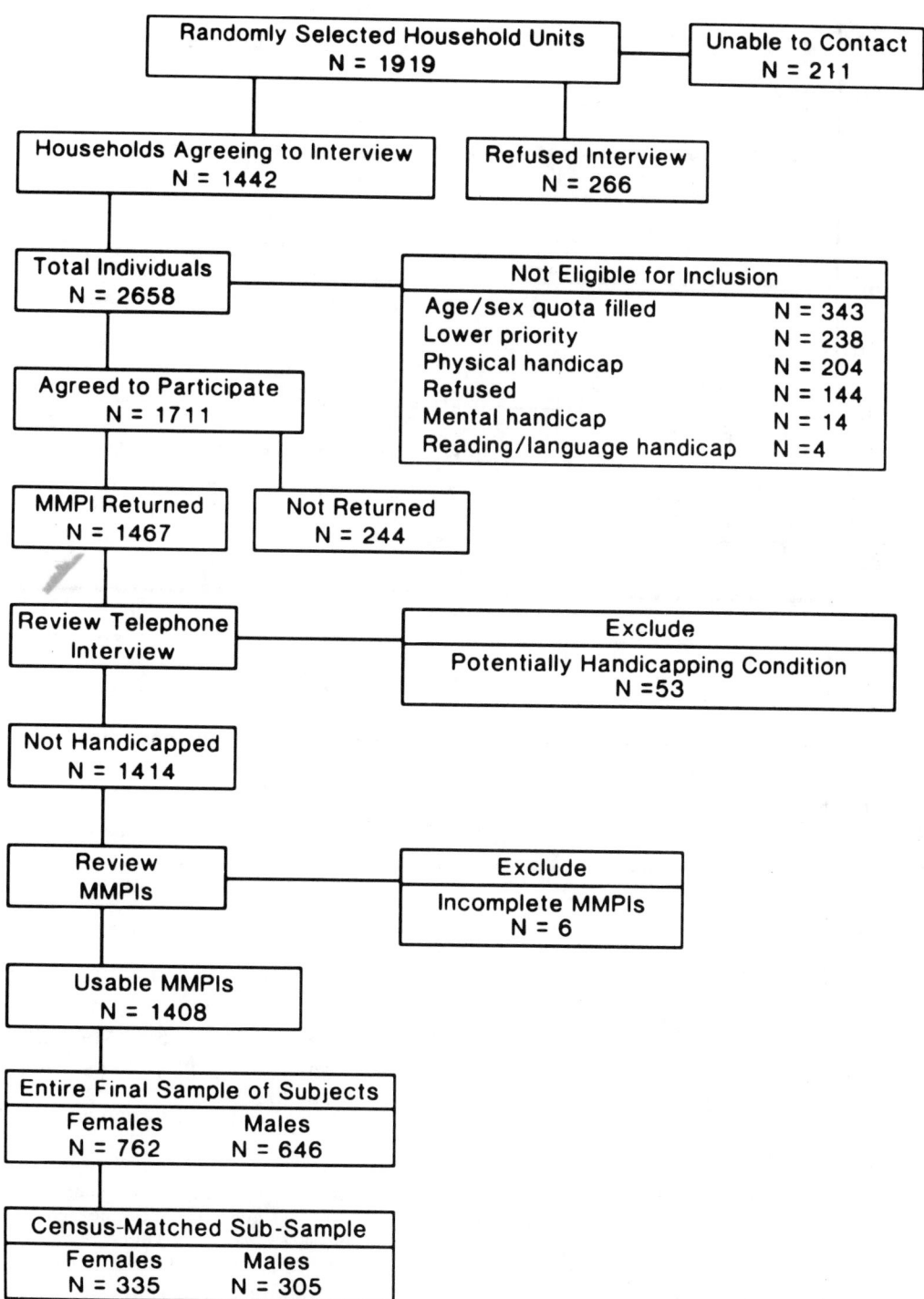

Figure 1. Steps in the MMPI contemporary normative study of adults. *Note.* From Colligan, R. C., Osborne, D., Swenson, W. M., & Offord, K. P. (1983). *The MMPI: A contemporary normative study.* New York: Praeger Publishers. By permission of Mayo Foundation.

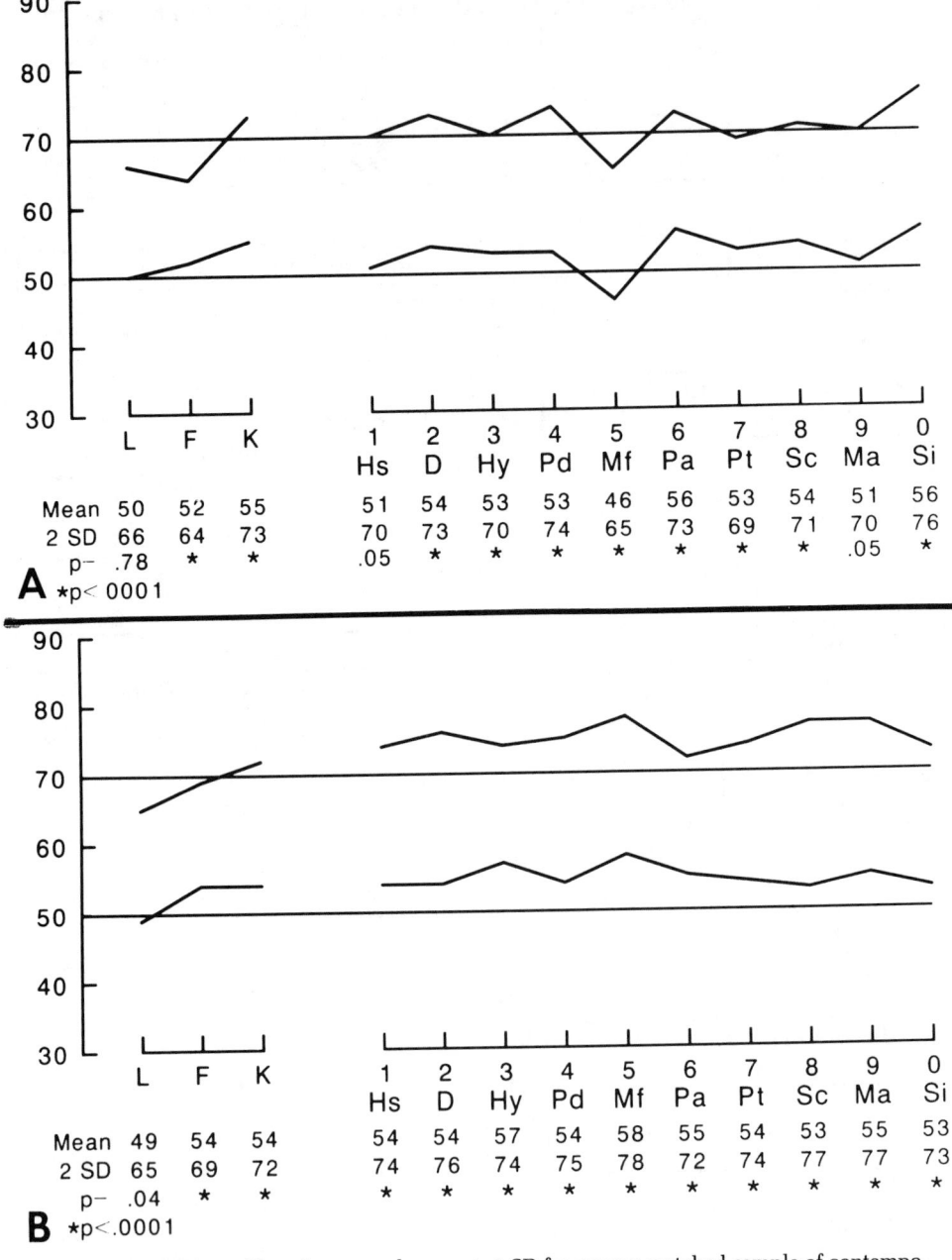

Figure 2. MMPI profiles of mean and mean + 2 SD for census-matched sample of contemporary normal women (A, n = 335) and men (B, n = 305). See text for explanation of validity and clinical scales. Note. From Colligan, R. C., Osborne, D., Swenson, W. M., & Offord, K. P. (1983). *The MMPI: A contemporary normative study*. New York: Praeger Publishers. By permission of Mayo Foundation.

Table 15 A

Mean Raw Scores With K Correction for Basic MMPI Scales by Age Group and for Census-Matched Sample, Normal Contemporary Women

Age group, yr	N	L	F	K	1 (Hs) + .5 K	2 (D)	3 (Hy)	4 (Pd) + .4 K	5 (Mf)	6 (Pa)	7 (Pt) + 1 K	8 (Sc) + 1 K	9 (Ma) + .2 K	0 (Si)
18–19	42	2.9(2.0)	4.2(3.1)	14.1(4.2)	13.0(3.4)	19.4(4.4)	21.1(4.1)	21.7(3.6)	37.6(4.0)	9.9(3.7)	27.2(4.2)	26.6(4.5)	20.3(4.1)	25.3(8.0)
20–29	128	3.0(2.0)	3.4(2.6)	14.7(5.1)	12.5(3.3)	20.3(4.3)	20.6(4.0)	21.2(4.2)	38.7(4.6)	10.0(3.0)	27.4(4.4)	24.9(5.5)	18.3(4.3)	28.2(10.0)
30–39	147	3.2(1.9)	3.1(2.7)	15.3(4.6)	12.6(4.2)	20.2(5.5)	21.2(4.9)	21.1(4.4)	39.1(4.3)	10.1(2.8)	26.5(5.5)	24.1(6.3)	17.4(3.8)	28.3(9.2)
40–49	110	3.7(1.7)	3.3(2.4)	14.9(4.6)	13.5(3.8)	20.5(4.4)	21.2(4.3)	20.2(4.6)	38.8(4.1)	10.1(2.6)	26.5(4.6)	24.1(5.0)	17.1(4.3)	30.4(9.0)
50–59	130	4.3(2.1)	3.6(2.5)	15.1(4.7)	14.7(4.6)	21.6(5.1)	22.2(5.1)	20.3(4.6)	38.0(4.5)	9.3(2.6)	26.4(5.9)	24.1(5.9)	16.5(3.9)	30.4(9.7)
60–69	117	5.2(2.4)	3.2(2.0)	15.4(4.5)	14.2(4.6)	21.7(4.4)	21.0(5.0)	18.8(3.7)	37.0(4.0)	8.6(3.0)	26.1(4.9)	23.7(4.9)	15.1(4.0)	33.0(9.0)
70+	88	5.9(2.5)	4.5(3.5)	13.2(4.5)	15.9(5.7)	23.3(5.5)	22.0(5.4)	18.4(4.1)	35.8(3.9)	9.2(3.0)	27.1(5.6)	24.2(6.1)	16.2(3.8)	32.0(8.8)
Census-matched	335	4.1(2.4)	3.6(2.7)	14.8(4.6)	13.6(4.5)	21.2(4.9)	21.4(4.8)	20.3(4.4)	38.3(4.5)	9.8(2.9)	26.9(4.9)	24.4(5.4)	17.1(3.9)	30.1(9.3)

Note. Values are reported as mean (SD).

Table 15 B

Mean Raw Scores With K Correction for Basic MMPI Scales by Age Group and for Census-Matched Sample, Normal Contemporary Men

Age group, yr	N	L	F	K	1 (Hs) + .5 K	2 (D)	3 (Hy)	4 (Pd) + .4 K	5 (Mf)	6 (Pa)	7 (Pt) + 1 K	8 (Sc) + 1 K	9 (Ma) + .2 K	0 (Si)
18–19	16	3.3(2.5)	5.2(2.3)	11.9(4.5)	12.3(4.5)	18.3(4.7)	19.6(4.2)	23.8(4.6)	25.2(5.1)	10.2(2.8)	27.6(5.0)	26.6(6.1)	22.1(4.2)	28.9(9.2)
20–29	101	2.8(1.6)	5.1(3.8)	13.5(4.6)	11.7(3.1)	17.7(4.5)	18.8(4.0)	21.6(4.2)	24.8(5.3)	9.9(3.1)	25.8(4.7)	25.9(5.8)	20.7(4.2)	26.7(10.3)
30–39	133	3.3(1.9)	4.8(3.5)	14.4(4.5)	12.1(3.6)	18.9(4.9)	20.7(4.5)	22.1(4.9)	25.2(5.1)	10.4(2.8)	25.9(5.3)	25.0(6.3)	19.1(4.3)	27.2(9.7)
40–49	98	3.6(2.1)	3.9(2.7)	15.7(4.3)	12.5(3.4)	18.4(4.4)	20.1(4.4)	20.9(4.1)	24.9(5.3)	9.3(2.7)	24.7(4.3)	23.7(4.5)	18.0(3.7)	26.5(8.7)
50–59	111	4.1(2.1)	4.1(2.9)	14.6(4.8)	13.7(4.4)	19.5(4.5)	21.3(5.0)	20.1(4.3)	24.5(4.7)	9.3(3.0)	24.8(4.1)	23.2(6.1)	16.6(3.8)	28.7(9.0)
60–69	113	5.0(2.5)	4.0(3.3)	15.0(4.5)	13.5(4.3)	20.2(4.5)	20.1(4.8)	19.4(4.2)	23.3(4.4)	8.6(3.3)	24.8(4.7)	23.1(5.3)	16.5(3.9)	28.9(8.7)
70+	74	6.0(2.7)	4.3(2.9)	15.0(4.6)	15.0(4.0)	21.1(4.6)	20.1(4.8)	19.0(3.8)	21.9(4.3)	8.8(2.9)	24.4(4.2)	23.6(4.4)	16.2(3.7)	29.7(7.6)
Census-matched	305	3.8(2.4)	4.5(3.3)	14.2(4.8)	12.9(3.9)	18.9(4.6)	20.0(4.7)	20.8(4.5)	24.4(5.0)	9.5(3.0)	25.6(4.9)	24.6(6.3)	18.7(4.4)	27.8(9.4)

Note. Values are reported as mean (SD).

Table 16 A

Mean Raw Scores Without K Correction for Selected Basic MMPI Scales by Age Group and for Census-Matched Sample, Normal Contemporary Women

Age group, yr	N	1 (Hs)	4 (Pd)	7 (Pt)	8 (Sc)	9 (Ma)
18–19	42	5.7 (4.0)	16.0 (3.5)	13.1 (6.4)	12.5 (7.2)	17.6 (4.2)
20–29	128	4.9 (4.0)	15.3 (4.3)	12.7 (7.4)	10.2 (7.5)	15.4 (4.6)
30–39	147	4.7 (4.6)	15.0 (4.6)	11.2 (7.7)	8.9 (7.6)	14.3 (4.0)
40–49	110	5.8 (4.0)	14.3 (4.6)	11.6 (6.6)	9.2 (6.4)	14.1 (4.3)
50–59	130	6.9 (4.7)	14.3 (4.5)	11.3 (7.3)	9.1 (6.6)	13.5 (4.0)
60–69	117	6.3 (4.8)	12.7 (3.5)	10.7 (6.4)	8.3 (5.6)	12.0 (4.1)
70+	88	9.1 (5.8)	13.2 (4.3)	13.9 (7.6)	11.0 (7.4)	13.5 (3.9)
Census-matched	335	5.9 (4.7)	14.4 (4.4)	12.1 (7.2)	9.6 (7.0)	14.1 (4.0)

Note. Values are reported as mean (SD).

Table 16 B

Mean Raw Scores Without K Correction for Selected Basic MMPI Scales by Age Group and for Census-Matched Sample, Normal Contemporary Men

Age group, yr	N	1 (Hs)	4 (Pd)	7 (Pt)	8 (Sc)	9 (Ma)
18–19	16	6.0 (4.6)	18.9 (4.8)	15.8 (7.2)	14.8 (7.4)	19.8 (4.1)
20–29	101	4.7 (3.7)	16.2 (4.6)	12.3 (6.8)	12.4 (7.7)	18.0 (4.6)
30–39	133	4.6 (4.0)	16.3 (5.2)	11.5 (7.4)	10.5 (8.3)	16.2 (4.6)
40–49	98	4.4 (3.9)	14.6 (4.2)	9.0 (6.2)	8.0 (6.0)	14.9 (3.9)
50–59	111	6.1 (4.7)	14.3 (4.3)	10.2 (6.1)	8.6 (7.0)	13.8 (3.9)
60–69	113	5.8 (4.0)	13.4 (4.0)	9.8 (6.2)	8.1 (5.8)	13.5 (3.9)
70+	74	7.2 (4.1)	13.1 (3.6)	9.4 (6.0)	8.7 (5.1)	13.2 (4.0)
Census-matched	305	5.5 (4.1)	15.2 (4.7)	11.3 (7.1)	10.4 (7.8)	15.8 (4.6)

Note. Values are reported as mean (SD).

age groups in the total normal adult sample using raw scores with and without K correction.

Age-Related Changes

In addition, and again not surprisingly, numerous and significant relationships with age were apparent for most MMPI scales for both men and women (Table 17).

Three figures illustrate the implications of these changes. Figures 3, 4, and 5 represent the mean T score from the original Minnesota normal sample for scales 2 (D), 4 (Pd), and 9 (Ma) plotted over the seven age groups of the adult study. The line at T score 50 is included as a reference point for the expected response pattern had their been no age-related changes. In the first example (Figure 3), there is a systematic increase in scores on scale 2 (D) for both women and men as age increases. In the second and third examples (Figures 4 and 5), a systematic decrease in scores on scales 4 (Pd) and 9 (Ma) for both women and men is apparent with increasing age. An awareness of these changes is essential to the understanding and interpretation of scores at both ends of the age continuum. Appendix B provides similar information for eight age ranges, including our new sample of contemporary adolescents.

Table 17
Linear Correlation Coefficients Between Chronologic Age and Selected MMPI Scales Among Contemporary Normal Adults, Ages 18 to 99 Years

MMPI scale	Females (n = 762)		Males (n = 646)	
	Raw score[a]	T score[b]	Raw score[a]	T score[b]
L	.44***	.44***	.42***	.42***
F	.07	.07	-.11**	-.11**
K	-.04	-.04	.11**	.11**
1 (Hs)	.24***	.24***	.18***	.25***
2 (D)	.20***	.20***	.21***	.21***
3 (Hy)	.08*	.08*	.07	.07
4 (Pd)	-.22***	-.24***	-.30***	-.27***
5 (Mf)	-.19***	.19***	-.17***	-.17***
6 (Pa)	-.16***	-.15***	-.19***	-.19***
7 (Pt)	-.01	-.04	-.16***	-.13***
8 (Sc)	-.03	-.07	-.20***	-.16***
9 (Ma)	-.25***	-.26***	-.38***	-.38***
0 (Si)	.19***	.19***	.11**	.11**

[a]Raw scores without K correction.
[b]K-corrected T scores (old norms).
Asterisks indicate p values: *0.01 $<p \le$ 0.05; **0.001 $<p \le p$ 0.01; *** $p \le$ 0.001.
Note. From Colligan, R. C., Osborne, D., Swenson, W. M., & Offord, K. P. (1983). *The MMPI: A contemporary normative study.* New York: Praeger Publishers. By permission of Mayo Foundation.

Because of these age-related changes, two types of adult normative tables were developed. The first was a set of general adult norms, calculated separately for women and men, and based on the response patterns from the census-matched age samples mentioned earlier. The second set was composed of age-specific norms intended primarily for use among geriatric patients (Colligan et al., 1983, 1989). It is important that clinicians be aware of such changes among the geriatric age groups because they are very noticeable. As an example, Figure 6 illustrates the mean profile for normal women and men ages 70 years or older.

DEVELOPING NEW ADULT MMPI NORMS

For interpretation of the raw scores that a patient earns across the various MMPI scales, they must be transformed into some type of standard unit. Because the MMPI scales have different numbers of items, contain different proportions of subtle and obvious items, and yield different average scores and standard deviations, all require that transformation to a standardized unit be made. Transforming the raw scores to standard units allows comparisons to be made across the different MMPI scales, so that the same standard score value will represent the same relative degree of deviation from the normative mean, in standard units, regardless of the scale under consideration. The convention for MMPI scales has been to standardize the T scores so that, in the normative group, they have a mean of 50 and a standard deviation of 10. In a normal (gaussian) distribution, a score falling at the mean is at the 50th percentile, and a value falling 2 standard deviations above the mean is at the 97.7 percentile.

In addition, many people believe that T scores of equivalent value, from

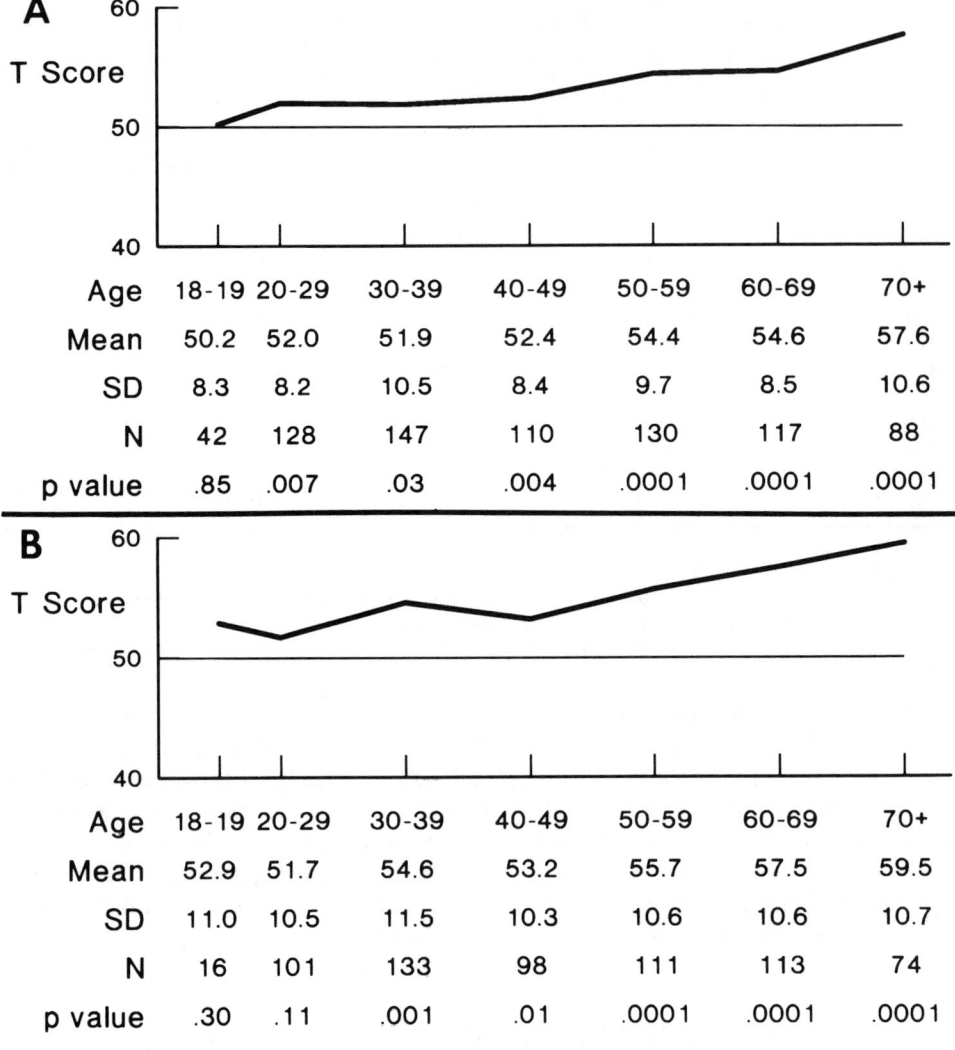

A	18-19	20-29	30-39	40-49	50-59	60-69	70+
Age	18-19	20-29	30-39	40-49	50-59	60-69	70+
Mean	50.2	52.0	51.9	52.4	54.4	54.6	57.6
SD	8.3	8.2	10.5	8.4	9.7	8.5	10.6
N	42	128	147	110	130	117	88
p value	.85	.007	.03	.004	.0001	.0001	.0001

B	18-19	20-29	30-39	40-49	50-59	60-69	70+
Age	18-19	20-29	30-39	40-49	50-59	60-69	70+
Mean	52.9	51.7	54.6	53.2	55.7	57.5	59.5
SD	11.0	10.5	11.5	10.3	10.6	10.6	10.7
N	16	101	133	98	111	113	74
p value	.30	.11	.001	.01	.0001	.0001	.0001

Figure 3.   Mean MMPI T scores for scale 2 (D, Depression) among contemporary normal adults for seven age groups, using original Hathaway norms and K-corrected scores. A, Women. B, Men. Note. From Colligan, R. C., Osborne, D., Swenson, W. M., & Offord, K. P. (1983). The MMPI: A contemporary normative study. New York: Praeger Publishers. By permission of Mayo Foundation.

different MMPI scales and obtained from the original MMPI tables, can be interpreted as having equivalent percentile ranks; however, they cannot be interpreted as such because of skewness in the underlying distribution of raw scores. This issue (the impact of skewness) was evaluated in the original normative sample and was found to be of considerable, but unrecognized, significance for most of the basic MMPI scales (Colligan, Osborne, & Offord, 1980). The standard scores used in the original MMPI tables are not T scores by the usual statistical definition. Rather, a linear transformation of raw-to-standard scores was used. The transformation simply made the mean for each scale 50 and the standard deviation 10, on the basis of responses from the Minnesota normal

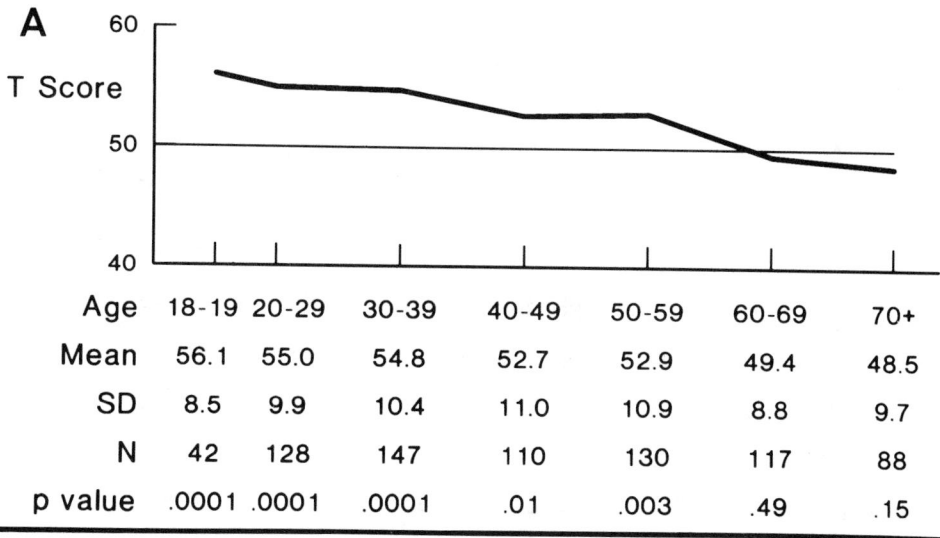

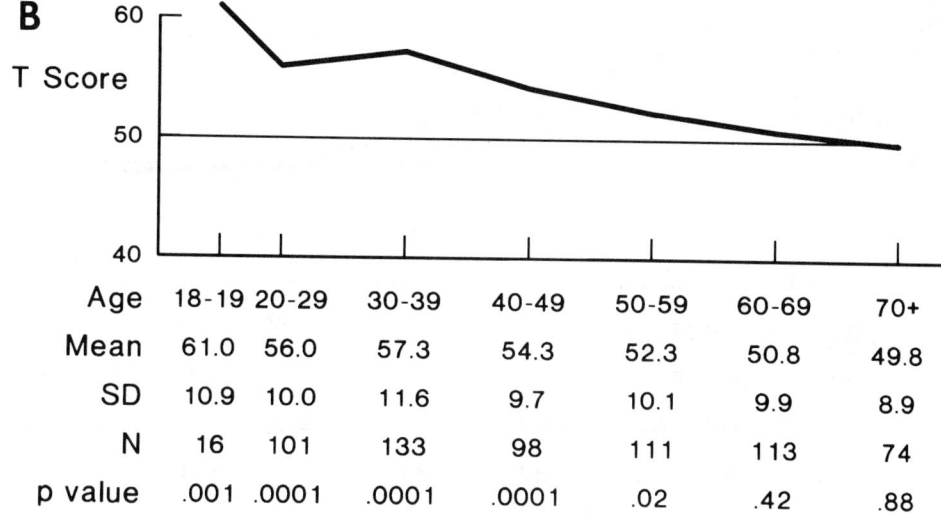

Figure 4.   Mean MMPI T scores for scale 4 (Pd, Psychopathic Deviate) among contemporary normal adults for seven age groups, using original Hathaway norms and K-corrected scores. A, Women. B, Men. Note. From Colligan, R. C., Osborne, D., Swenson, W. M., & Offord, K. P. (1983). The MMPI: A contemporary normative study. New York: Praeger Publishers. By permission of Mayo Foundation.

sample. However, when linear transformations are used, T scores of equal numerical size may represent markedly different percentile ranks when the underlying raw scores are not normally distributed. Furthermore, it should be noted that, if the distribution of raw scores for the various MMPI scales carried a common pattern of distribution (that is, skewness, kurtosis), then the percentile ranks for the T scores derived from a linear transformation would also be comparable across the various MMPI scales (essentially, the procedure carried out during the development of "uniform T scores" for the MMPI-2; that is, the term uniform refers to the relatively uniform degree of skewness in the distribution of the scores on the eight clinical scales selected for such transformations). How-

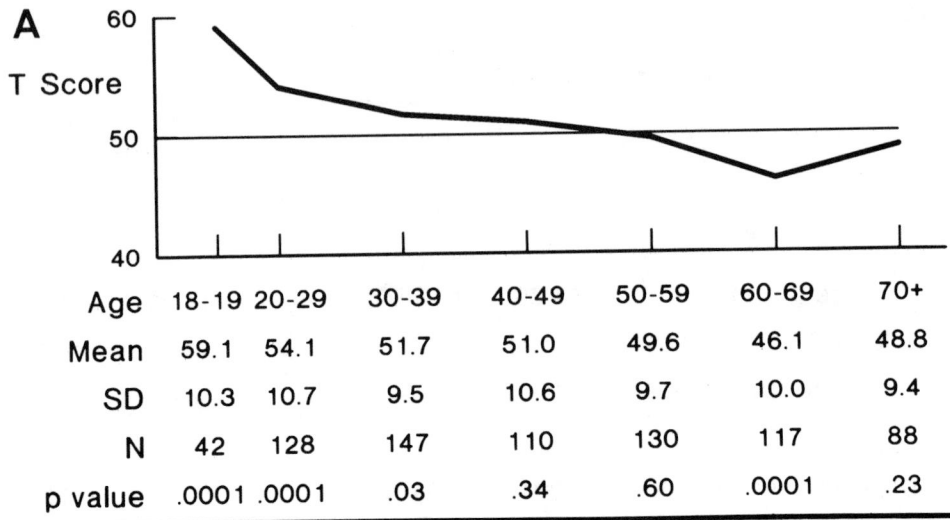

Age	18-19	20-29	30-39	40-49	50-59	60-69	70+
Mean	59.1	54.1	51.7	51.0	49.6	46.1	48.8
SD	10.3	10.7	9.5	10.6	9.7	10.0	9.4
N	42	128	147	110	130	117	88
p value	.0001	.0001	.03	.34	.60	.0001	.23

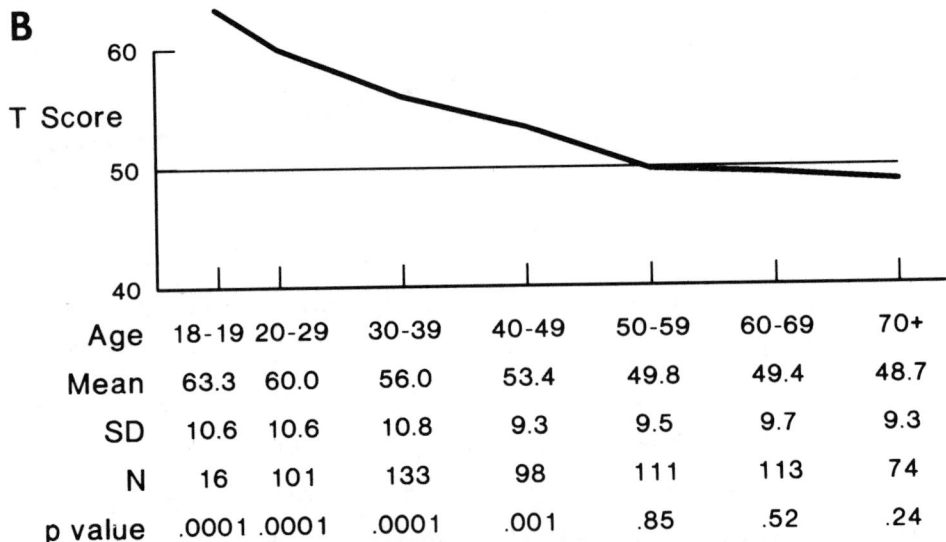

Age	18-19	20-29	30-39	40-49	50-59	60-69	70+
Mean	63.3	60.0	56.0	53.4	49.8	49.4	48.7
SD	10.6	10.6	10.8	9.3	9.5	9.7	9.3
N	16	101	133	98	111	113	74
p value	.0001	.0001	.0001	.001	.85	.52	.24

Figure 5. Mean MMPI T scores for scale 9 (Ma, Hypomania) among contemporary normal adults for seven age groups, using original Hathaway norms and K-corrected scores. A, Women. B, Men. Note. From Colligan, R. C., Osborne, D., Swenson, W. M., & Offord, K. P. (1983). The MMPI: A contemporary normative study. New York: Praeger Publishers. By permission of Mayo Foundation.

ever, unfortunately, such values still would not fall at the percentile ranks we have come to expect from experience with the normal (gaussian) curve typically used in other common psychometric instruments.

As one might expect from the nature of the scales and the manner in which they were developed, almost all of the MMPI scales, for both men and women, are significantly skewed to the right, based on an analysis of the refined Hathaway-Briggs Minnesota normal sample (Colligan et al., 1980).

A T score of 70 traditionally has been viewed as a point of particular significance because it falls 2 standard deviations above the mean. However, a T

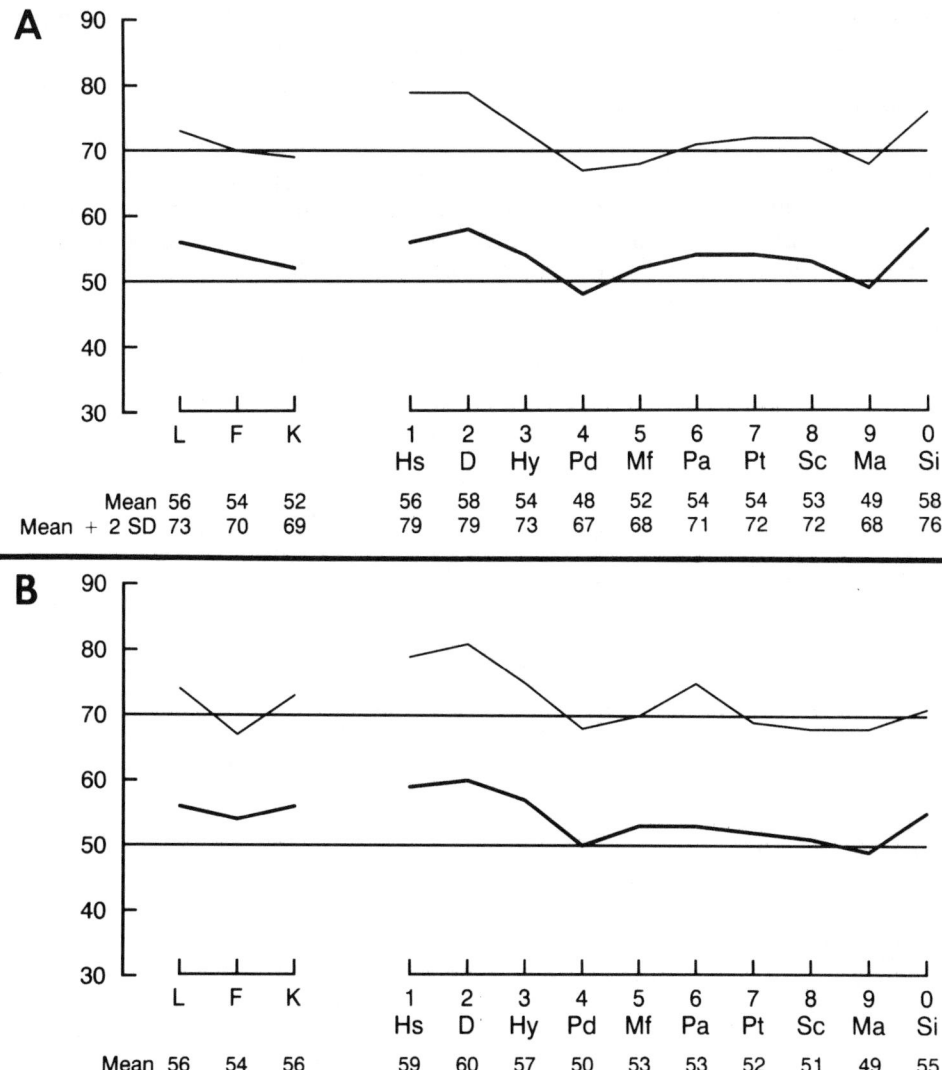

Figure 6. MMPI profiles of mean and mean + 2 SD for normal geriatric subjects, using original Hathaway norms and K-corrected scores. A, For 88 women ages 70 to 99 years. B, For 74 men ages 70 to 91 years.

score of 70, derived from a linear transformation of raw scores that are skewed, may not represent the 97.7 percentile. For example, a moderately depressed patient with a T score of 70 on scale 2 (D), according to the original MMPI norms, would not be in a relatively small and exclusive group of approximately 2% of the population. Rather, this person is among a relatively large group of 8% of the normal population who would be categorized at this value because the raw scores, and the T scores obtained by linear transformation, on scale 2 are substantially skewed (Colligan et al., 1980).

To correct this deficiency, we selected raw score transformation equations that would yield transformed standard score values—normalized T scores—that approach a normal (gaussian) distribution. The Box-Cox power transformation technique was used (Box & Cox, 1964). This process also allowed the expression of raw scores much higher than the ones actually observed in our normal sample, in terms of units of standard deviations from the mean of the normal reference sample.

These new normalized T scores for the general adult population, for all possible K-corrected raw scores, are presented in Tables 18 and 19 for women and men. Tables of normalized T scores also have been prepared for raw scores without K correction, separately by sex (Colligan et al., 1983, 1989).

Table 18
Normalized T Scores for K-Corrected Raw Scores in Contemporary Normal Women, Ages 18 to 99 Years

K-Corrected Raw Score	L	F	K	1(Hs) + .5K	2(D)	3(Hy)	4(Pd) + .4K	5(Mf)	6(Pa)	7(Pt) + 1K	8(Sc) + 1K	9(Ma) + .2K	0(Si)	K-Corrected Raw Score
0	27	28	18	-38	-91	-38	-97	135	-15	-141	-103	-38	-13	0
1	35	39	20	-15	-59	-19	-64	133	6	-101	-70	-16	-1	1
2	41	46	22	-1	-41	-11	-44	131	15	-77	-51	-7	4	2
3	46	51	25	8	-28	-5	-30	128	21	-61	-37	-1	7	3
4	51	54	27	16	-17	0	-19	126	27	-48	-26	5	10	4
5	55	57	29	22	-9	5	-10	124	32	-37	-18	10	13	5
6	59	60	31	27	-2	9	-3	122	36	-29	-10	15	16	6
7	62	62	33	32	4	13	4	119	41	-21	-4	19	18	7
8	65	64	35	35	10	16	9	117	44	-14	2	23	20	8
9	68	66	38	39	14	19	14	115	48	-8	7	26	22	9
10	71	67	40	42	19	23	19	113	52	-3	11	30	24	10
11	74	69	42	45	23	26	23	111	55	2	15	33	26	11
12	77	70	44	48	26	28	27	108	58	7	19	36	27	12
13	79	71	46	50	30	31	31	106	61	11	23	39	29	13
14	82	73	48	52	33	34	34	104	64	15	26	42	31	14
15	84	74	50	55	36	36	37	102	67	19	29	45	32	15
16		75	53	57	39	39	40	100	69	22	32	48	34	16
17		76	55	59	41	41	43	97	72	26	35	50	35	17
18		77	57	60	44	43	45	95	74	29	37	53	36	18
19		77	59	62	46	45	48	93	77	32	40	55	38	19
20		78	61	64	48	48	50	91	79	35	42	58	39	20
21		79	63	65	51	50	53	88	82	37	44	60	40	21
22		80	66	67	53	52	55	86	84	40	46	62	42	22
23		80	68	68	55	54	57	84	86	42	48	65	43	23
24		81	70	69	56	56	59	82	88	45	50	67	44	24
25		82	72	71	58	58	61	80	90	47	52	69	45	25
26		82	74	72	60	60	63	77	93	49	54	71	46	26
27		83	76	73	62	61	64	75	95	51	56	73	47	27
28		84	78	74	63	63	66	73	97	53	57	75	49	28
29		84	81	76	65	65	68	71	99	55	59	77	50	29
30		85	83	77	66	67	69	68	101	57	61	79	51	30
31		85		78	68	69	71	66	102	59	62	81	52	31
32		86		79	69	70	72	64	104	61	64	83	53	32
33		86		80	71	72	74	62	106	62	65	85	54	33
34		87		81	72	74	75	60	108	64	66	87	55	34
35		87		82	73	75	76	57	110	66	68	88	56	35
36		88		83	74	77	78	55	112	67	69	90	57	36
37		88		83	76	78	79	53	113	69	70	92	58	37
38		89		84	77	80	80	51	115	70	72	94	59	38
39		89		85	78	82	82	49	117	72	73	95	60	39
40		89		86	79	83	83	46	118	73	74	97	61	40
41		90		87	80	85	84	44		74	75	99	61	41
42		90		88	81	86	85	42		76	76	100	62	42
43		91		88	82	88	86	40		77	77	102	63	43
44		91		89	83	89	87	37		78	78	104	64	44
45		91		90	84	90	88	35		80	79	105	65	45
46		92		91	85	92	89	33		81	80	107	66	46
47		92		91	86	93	90	31		82	81	108	67	47
48		92		92	87	95	91	29		83	82	110	68	48
49		93			88	96	92	26		84	83	112	68	49
50		93			89	97	93	24		86	84	113	69	50

(continued on next page)

Table 18 (continued)

K-Corrected Raw Score	L	F	K	1(Hs) +.5K	2(D)	3(Hy)	4(Pd) +.4K	5(Mf)	6(Pa)	7(Pt) +1K	8(Sc) +1K	9(Ma) +.2K	0(Si)	K-Corrected Raw Score
51		93			90	99	94	22		87	85	115	70	51
52		94			91	100	95	20		88	86	116	71	52
53		94			92	101	96	17		89	87		72	53
54		94			93	103	97	15		90	88		72	54
55		95			93	104	98	13		91	89		73	55
56		95			94	105	99	11		92	90		74	56
57		95			95	107	100	9		93	90		75	57
58		95			96	108	100	6		94	91		76	58
59		96			97	109	101	4		95	92		76	59
60		96			97	110	102	2		96	93		77	60
61		96					103			97	94		78	61
62		97					104			98	94		79	62
63		97								99	95		79	63
64		97								100	96		80	64
65										100	97		81	65
66										101	97		81	66
67										102	98		82	67
68										103	99		83	68
69										104	99		84	69
70										105	100		84	70
71										105	101			71
72										106	101			72
73										107	102			73
74										108	103			74
75										109	103			75
76										109	104			76
77										110	105			77
78										111	105			78
80											106			80
81											107			81
83											108			83
85											109			85
87											110			87
89											111			89
91											112			91
93											113			93
95											114			95
97											115			97
99											116			99
101											117			101
103											118			103
105											119			105
107											120			107
108											121			108

Note. Professionals obtaining raw scores over 78 which are not shown in the table should use the next higher value to determine the appropriate T score.

Note. From Colligan, R. C., Osborne, D., Swenson, W. M., & Offord, K. P. (1983). *The MMPI: A contemporary normative study.* New York: Praeger Publishers. By permission of Mayo Foundation.

Table 19

Normalized T Scores for K-Corrected Raw Scores in Contemporary Normal Men, Ages 18 to 85 Years

K-Corrected Raw Score	L	F	K	1(Hs) + .5K	2(D)	3(Hy)	4(Pd) + .4K	5(Mf)	6(Pa)	7(Pt) + 1K	8(Sc) + 1K	9(Ma) + .2K	0(Si)	K-Corrected Raw Score
0	29	23	20	-43	-76	-36	-97	1	-12	-127	-87	-34	-7	0
1	37	35	22	-18	-46	-17	-64	3	9	-89	-57	-15	4	1
2	43	42	24	-3	-29	-9	-44	5	17	-67	-40	-6	9	2
3	48	47	26	7	-17	-2	-30	7	23	-52	-28	-0	12	3
4	52	51	29	15	-8	3	-20	9	29	-40	-18	5	15	4
5	56	54	31	21	0	7	-11	11	34	-30	-10	10	18	5
6	59	57	33	27	7	11	-4	13	38	-21	-4	14	20	6
7	63	59	35	32	12	15	3	15	42	-14	2	18	22	7
8	66	61	37	36	17	19	8	17	46	-8	7	21	24	8
9	69	63	39	40	22	22	14	19	49	-2	11	25	26	9
10	72	65	41	43	26	25	18	21	52	3	15	28	28	10
11	74	66	43	46	30	28	22	23	56	8	19	31	29	11
12	77	68	45	49	33	31	26	25	59	12	22	34	31	12
13	80	69	47	52	36	34	30	27	61	16	25	37	33	13
14	82	70	49	54	39	36	33	29	64	20	28	39	34	14
15	84	71	52	56	42	39	36	31	67	23	31	42	36	15
16		72	54	59	44	41	39	33	69	27	34	44	37	16
17		73	56	61	47	44	42	35	72	30	36	47	38	17
18		74	58	63	49	46	44	37	74	33	38	49	40	18
19		75	60	64	51	48	47	39	77	35	41	51	41	19
20		76	62	66	53	50	49	41	79	38	43	54	42	20
21		77	64	68	55	53	51	43	81	41	45	56	43	21
22		78	66	69	57	55	54	45	84	43	47	58	44	22
23		78	68	71	59	57	56	47	86	45	48	60	46	23
24		79	70	72	61	59	58	49	88	48	50	62	47	24
25		80	73	74	62	61	59	51	90	50	52	64	48	25
26		80	75	75	64	63	61	53	92	52	53	66	49	26
27		81	77	77	66	64	63	55	94	54	55	68	50	27
28		82	79	78	67	66	65	57	96	56	56	70	51	28
29		82	81	79	69	68	66	59	98	57	58	71	52	29
30		83	83	80	70	70	68	61	99	59	59	73	53	30
31		83		81	71	72	69	63	101	61	61	75	54	31
32		84		82	73	73	71	65	103	63	62	77	55	32
33		84		83	74	75	72	67	105	64	63	79	56	33
34		85		85	75	77	74	69	107	66	64	80	57	34
35		85		86	76	78	75	71	108	67	66	82	58	35
36		86		86	77	80	76	73	110	69	67	84	59	36
37		86		87	79	82	78	75	112	70	68	85	60	37
38		87		88	80	83	79	77	113	72	69	87	61	38
39		87		89	81	85	80	79	115	73	70	88	61	39
40		87		90	82	86	81	81	117	74	71	90	62	40
41		88		91	83	88	82	83		76	72	91	63	41
42		88		92	84	89	84	85		77	73	93	64	42
43		89		93	85	91	85	87		78	74	94	65	43
44		89		94	86	92	86	89		79	75	96	66	44
45		89		94	87	94	87	91		81	76	97	67	45

(continued on next page)

Table 19 (continued)

K-Corrected Raw Score	L	F	K	1(Hs) +.5K	2(D)	3(Hy)	4(Pd) +.4K	5(Mf)	6(Pa)	7(Pt) +1K	8(Sc) +1K	9(Ma) +.2K	0(Si)	K-Corrected Raw Score
46		90	95	88	95	88	94			82	77	99	67	46
47		90	96	89	97	89	96			83	78	100	68	47
48		91	97	89	98	90	98			84	79	102	69	48
49		91		90	99	91	100			85	80	103	70	49
50		91		91	101	92	102			86	80	105	71	50
51		92		92	102	93	104			87	81	106	71	51
52		92		93	103	94	106			88	82	107	72	52
53		92		94	105	94	108			89	83		73	53
54		93		94	106	95	110			90	84		74	54
55		93		95	107	96	112			91	84		74	55
56		93		96	109	97	114			92	85		75	56
57		93		97	110	98	116			93	86		76	57
58		94		97	111	99	118			94	87		76	58
59		94		98	112	100	120			95	87		77	59
60		94		99	114	100	122			96	88		78	60
61		95				101				97	89		79	61
62		95				102				98	89		79	62
63		95								99	90		80	63
64		95								99	91		81	64
65										100	91		81	65
66										101	92		82	66
67										102	93		83	67
68										103	93		83	68
69										103	94		84	69
70										104	94		85	70
71										105	95			71
72										106	96			72
73										106	96			73
74										107	97			74
75										108	97			75
76										109	98			76
77										109	98			77
78										110	99			78
80											100			80
82											101			82
84											102			84
86											103			86
88											104			88
91											105			91
93											106			93
95											107			95
97											108			97
100											109			100
102											110			102
105											111			105
107											112			107
108											113			108

Note: Professionals obtaining raw scores over 78 which are not shown in the table should use the next higher value to determine the appropriate T score.

Note. From Colligan, R. C., Osborne, D., Swenson, W. M., & Offord, K. P. (1983). *The MMPI: A contemporary normative study*. New York: Praeger Publishers. By permission of Mayo Foundation.

PART III

ADOLESCENTS, ADULTS, AND THE MMPI

The importance of carefully assessing personality factors among adolescents with emotional, behavioral, learning, or medical problems is obvious. The MMPI can be read by persons with a sixth-grade reading level, and a tape-recorded version is available for disabled readers.

Readers may wonder why so much space has been given to the contemporary adult normative study when this is a manual of norms for clinicians using the MMPI with adolescents. There are several reasons.

First, Hathaway initially did not believe that it was necessary or even desirable to have special MMPI norms for adolescents. In all of his research work with adolescents he used the T-score tables developed from the Minnesota normal sample. In addition, all of the raw scores were K corrected.

Hathaway's rationale was very straightforward. He believed that, because adult beliefs and mores make up the culture of our society, adolescents need to be understood and viewed in the context of likenesses to and differences from adult expectations. Therefore he stated,

> We do not advocate the use of special juvenile norms with the MMPI, since to do so would arbitrarily erase much of the contrast between adolescents and adults. . . . When test results are under study, use of adult norms keeps the amount and nature of the contrast always in view. (Hathaway & Monachesi, 1963, p. 39)

And elsewhere (during the study of Minnesota 9th- and 12th-grade students), it was stated that,

> It might be maintained that such a contrast of the scores for youth with those for adults is not fair and that scale norms should be considered in relation to adolescence and not to the average adult. There are, however, adequate arguments against this adjustment of norms. The culture only partially accepts the differences between

youths and adults. As an example, when young people express or use their energy in ways that are acceptable to society, any differences implied in their behavior are not censured or may be passed off by an attitude exemplified in the statement "Kids will be kids!" If, however, the exuberance of youth produces acts that run counter to the interests or more of the adult, then such acts are regarded as evidence of a tendency to delinquency and are labeled amoral or asocial. Essentially, this culturally determined attitude can be summed up by saying that it is understood that young people are in need of excitement and are likely to be rebellious, but they are expected to hold these tendencies in check and express them within the limits considered proper by their parents or other adults.

In the light of this attitude, the application of adult norms to young people is proper and adjustment of the norms would obscure the very real fact that there is a significant, almost universal, quality in young people that makes them prone to socially unacceptable behavior. We want our scales to show behavior differences that are significant to society even if the implied personalities are "normal" for the age level. Since the core of society is the early adult and middle-aged pattern of mores, the use of MMPI norms based chiefly on middle-aged married persons can be justified even for young people. (Hathaway & Monachesi, 1953, pp. 24–25)

Adult MMPI response patterns were also compared with those of juvenile delinquents, and Monachesi noted,

All four of the delinquent groups show clearly significant differences from average adult norms. If we are interested in establishing the existence of measurable differences between the average adult and the nondelinquent adolescent or the average adult and the delinquent adolescent, then these differences seem clear on most of the scales; the more marked differences are those between the adult and the adolescent delinquent, with the nondelinquent youngster in the middle. (Monachesi, 1953, pp. 44–45)

Second, the Minnesota normal sample contained a significant proportion of adolescents and young adults. Indeed, 28% of the first normal sample were age 16 to 25 years, and all of the members of the second normal sample of college students were 16 to 25 years old. No data regarding age were provided for the third normal sample. Unfortunately, no further age breakdown was provided in the original work (Hathaway & McKinley, 1940). Data from the "improved" Minnesota normal sample of adults and adolescents did not provide this information either (Hathaway & Briggs, 1957).

Why are normative data for both adolescents and adults being presented in the same manual? Again, there are several reasons.

Hathaway later modified his views regarding the use of adolescent norms. In part this may have been due to the influence of his wife. Virginia Riddle Hathaway was a skillful clinician in her own right, a child and adolescent psychologist experienced with the MMPI, who was involved in providing psychological services to students in the Minneapolis public school system for nearly 30 years.[9] Thus, from both clinical and research use, it quickly became apparent that adolescent MMPI response patterns were remarkably different from

---

[9]Mrs. Hathaway died at her Minneapolis home on October 4, 1987.

those obtained from adults. Indeed, some of the early descriptions of adolescent and adult differences were strongly stated; for example:

> Adolescents are not easy to absorb into our culture. A large number of them get test profiles suggesting that they are resisting their environmental restraints, and many other test profiles give the impression that these youngsters are suffering from some mental disturbance. . . . there are clear similarities to the averaged data from adult patients who have been classed as having a schizophrenic or a sociopathic disorder. . . teen-agers more often have sociopathic or psychotic types of profile patterns than do adults. (Hathaway & Monachesi, 1963, p. 39)

Yet it was also apparent that "when contrasted to the data on the neurotic scales . . . symptoms of depression, physical complaint, and psychasthenia are less common in the adolescent" (Hathaway & Monachesi, 1963, p. 39).

Therefore, in order to balance the comparison of the social functioning of adolescents among their peers with adult culture, in MMPI terms, clinicians were encouraged not only to use the mean adult profile but also to consider the mean response patterns of normal adolescents. Hathaway proposed that a sample of normal Minnesota ninth-grade students be used for comparative purposes, as a standard or baseline of expected adolescent MMPI values. The adolescent's MMPI response pattern could then be compared with reference points derived from separate samples of normal adults and normal adolescents. More specifically, clinicians were encouraged to use the standard MMPI profile sheet of adult norms and add to it a second set of lines representing the expected values for normal adolescents:

> We do provide normative data giving means . . . . A good practice for those working with juvenile cases is to overprint the regular MMPI profile charts with dotted lines showing the juvenile means and the juvenile means with 2 S.D.s added. For example, on scale 4 the mean would show a T score 59 and the corresponding 2 S.D. T score, comparable to the adult norm of 70, would be at 59 plus 21, which is T score 80. (Hathaway & Monachesi, 1963, p. 39)

ORIGINAL MINNESOTA ADOLESCENT NORMS

To what "normative data" was Hathaway referring? The samples that he suggested for use in establishing adolescent standards actually were derived from two large samples of Minnesota adolescents being studied as part of a major longitudinal project on juvenile delinquency. For this reason, profiles believed to be invalid were systematically excluded. Therefore, the "juvenile norms" actually were based on a subset of MMPI profiles that were believed to be valid according to a specific set of rules for the validity scales, and they were not based on responses from the entire data set. The samples used in the study of juvenile delinquency and for Hathaway's adolescent norms are described below.

The Minneapolis Sample

In 1947, the MMPI was administered to 3,971 (87%) of the 4,572 ninth-grade students enrolled in the 16 public high schools of Minneapolis, Minnesota

(Hathaway & Monachesi, 1963). Their ages ranged from 13 through 18 years (mean, 14.8 years for girls and 15.1 years for boys), although all were in the ninth grade. However, because "a crucial aspect of the study . . . was the search for early symptoms of a variety of subsequent psychological adjustment problems" (Hathaway & Monachesi, 1963, p. 16), it quickly became apparent that the size of the Minneapolis sample was inadequate. Therefore, additional data were gathered.

The Minnesota Statewide Sample

The database was enlarged by administering the MMPI to a Minnesota statewide sample of 11,329 ninth-grade students in 1954. Participants were obtained from 92 schools in 86 different communities, they were from 47 of the 87 counties in Minnesota, and they constituted 28% of the students enrolled in ninth-grade public school classrooms in Minnesota for that year. The ages of the subjects ranged from 13 through 18 years (mean, 14.4 years for girls and 14.6 years for boys). Approximately 48% of the students were from the cities of Duluth, Minneapolis/St. Paul, and surrounding suburban areas, and the remainder were from the farms and small towns of rural Minnesota.

The father's educational level was used as an index of socioeconomic status: about 2% had both undergraduate- and graduate-level training, about 5% were 4-year college graduates, about 20% had a high school education and some additional training, approximately 23% were semiskilled (they had completed grade school and some high school), about 17% had completed grade school and were described as slightly skilled, approximately 8% were described as having a grade school education and as being day laborers, and 4% were not classified (total is not exactly 100% because of rounding). Also, about 22% of the sample was comprised of three categories of "farmer," ranging from above-average to submarginal income, and no specific levels of education were provided.

Determination of living arrangements found that about 86% of the adolescents lived with both of their parents and about 10% lived with a single parent (about 8% with their mother, 2% with their father); about 6% were living in single-parent households due to separation or divorce. About 2% of the sample lived with step-parents, and 2% lived with neither parent.

Considerable effort was exerted to obtain MMPI responses from these students in a professional manner, and "every effort was made to develop really cooperative interest and participation" with school personnel and parents (Hathaway & Monachesi, 1963, p. 33).

Trained field workers established contact with the superintendent or principal who had received a prior letter of information. All MMPIs were completed during school hours. In some schools the entire ninth grade was assembled in one room while the MMPI was administered; in others it was carried out by sections. The following directions were paraphrased to the students, and time was allowed for questions:

> This is a test to study personality. The study is being made by people at the university and your records will be kept by them. No one will look at your answers to individual questions because the grades depend on counting up the marks only. The test has a great many statements about people, what they like, and what they think. It is used to aid in advising men and women about jobs and other problems.

We want to see if it will be a help when taken by persons who are younger. So we are asking you to do it. You may find that some of the statements don't fit you at all, or they won't fit you until you are older. If you find any of these, answer them the best you can or leave them blank, but try to answer every statement. Work quickly but don't be careless. Some of the statements will be in the past tense; for example: "My father was a good man." Answer as though in the present if your father is living and you are with him. (Hathaway & Monachesi, 1963, p. 107)

During the session students were encouraged to "answer just as you feel" or to "leave it blank if you wish, but try to decide on an answer even if you are not sure it really describes you" (Hathaway & Monachesi, 1963, p. 34).

Other specific management guidelines for gathering the data in a standardized manner also were provided to field workers.

Exclusion Criteria

After the MMPIs were scored, profiles believed to be invalid were excluded. Decisions about validity were based on the raw scores earned on scales L and F. For scale L, a raw score of 0 through 9 was considered valid, and a score of 10 or more was described as a "high-L" profile. When scale L alone was used as the criterion, 2.3% of the profiles from the girls and 2.5% of the profiles from the boys were excluded.

For scale F, MMPI profiles with raw scores ranging from 0 through 15 were considered valid. Those with raw F scores ranging from 16 through 21 were called "high-F" profiles. In addition, those with F scores of 22 or higher were labeled "ultra high-F" (UHF). With these criteria for scale F, 3.4% of the girls' profiles were considered invalid because of elevated F scores (2.8%, high F; 0.6%, UHF), and 8.4% of the boys' profiles were considered invalid (5.5%, high F; 2.9%, UHF).

Thus, to summarize, approximately 6% of the MMPI profiles from the girls were excluded because they were believed to be invalid from the raw scores earned by these students on scale L or F. Approximately 11% of the MMPIs obtained from the adolescent boys were excluded for the same reason.

Subsequently, the T-score data comprising the sample of valid MMPIs (4,944 males and 5,207 females) were presented in tabular form, using raw scores with K correction. However, these T scores were based on the original Minnesota normal sample of adults (Hathaway & Monachesi, 1963). The mean profiles for these adolescent boys and girls are shown in Figure 7. They illustrate the differences between adolescent and adult response patterns and demonstrate the "impression that these youngsters are suffering from some mental disturbance" (Hathaway & Monachesi, 1963, p. 39).

However, as noted earlier, these data from the delinquency project were never used to develop specific adolescent normative tables. Rather, Hathaway suggested they were to be used as a comparative standard in conjunction with the norms from the Minnesota normal adult sample, which also had included a significant proportion of adolescents and young adults.

Grade 12 Follow-Up Sample

The reliability and stability of response patterns were evaluated by administering the MMPI again to a substantial proportion of the ninth-grade students 4 years

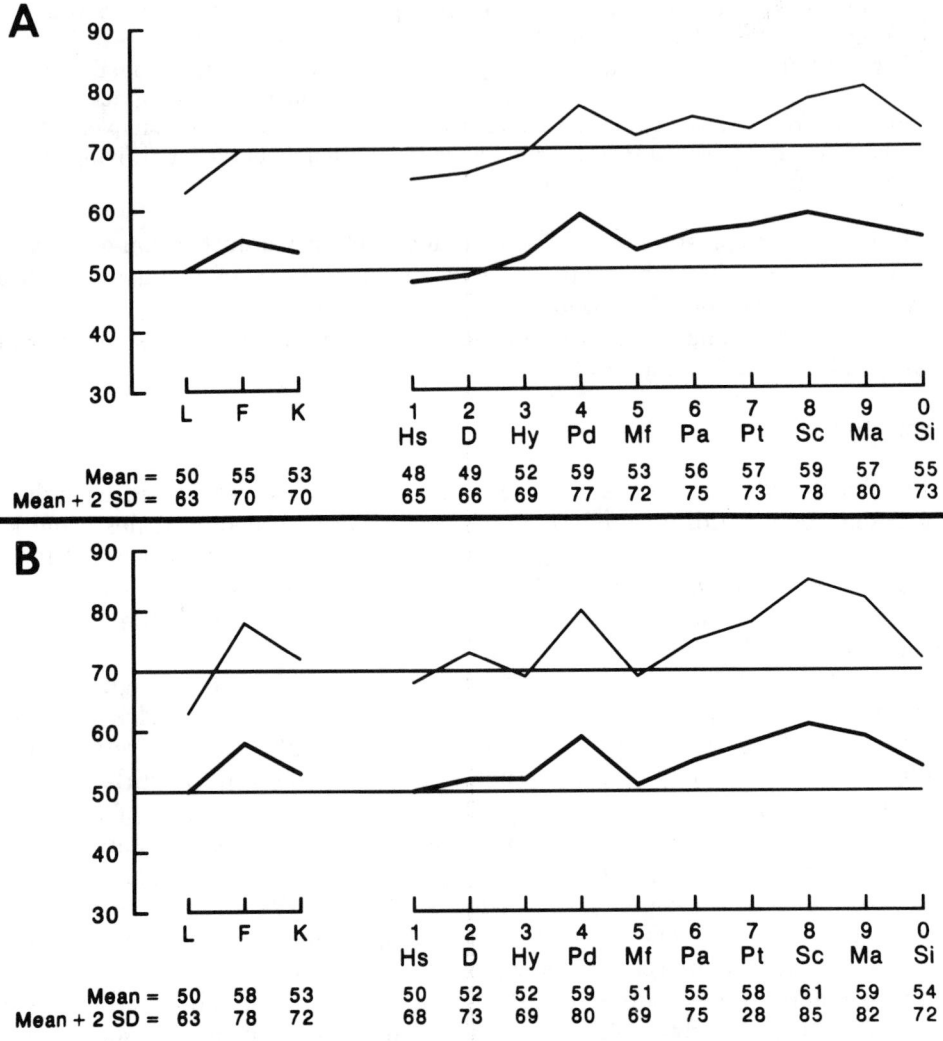

Figure 7.   Mean and mean + 2 SD MMPI profiles for the 1954 Minnesota statewide sample of ninth-grade students obtained by Hathaway and Monachesi, using original adult norms and K-corrected scores. A, Girls (n = 5,?07; mean age, 14.4 years). B, Boys (n = 4,944; mean age, 14.6 years).

later, during grade 12. The specific manner in which these cases were selected was not described, although the students came only from the sample obtaining valid profiles during the ninth-grade study. The follow-up sample was comprised of 1,922 (39%) of the adolescent boys and 2,054 (39%) of the adolescent girls from the original ninth-grade sample. For comparative purposes, the mean profiles from these data are presented in Figure 8 (Hathaway & Monachesi, 1963, derived from Table 76, p. 155); raw scores with K correction and the norms derived from the original Minnesota normal adult sample were used.

Summary

Hathaway believed that it was important to evaluate MMPIs from adolescents in the context of adult MMPI response patterns. Later, he considered it equally

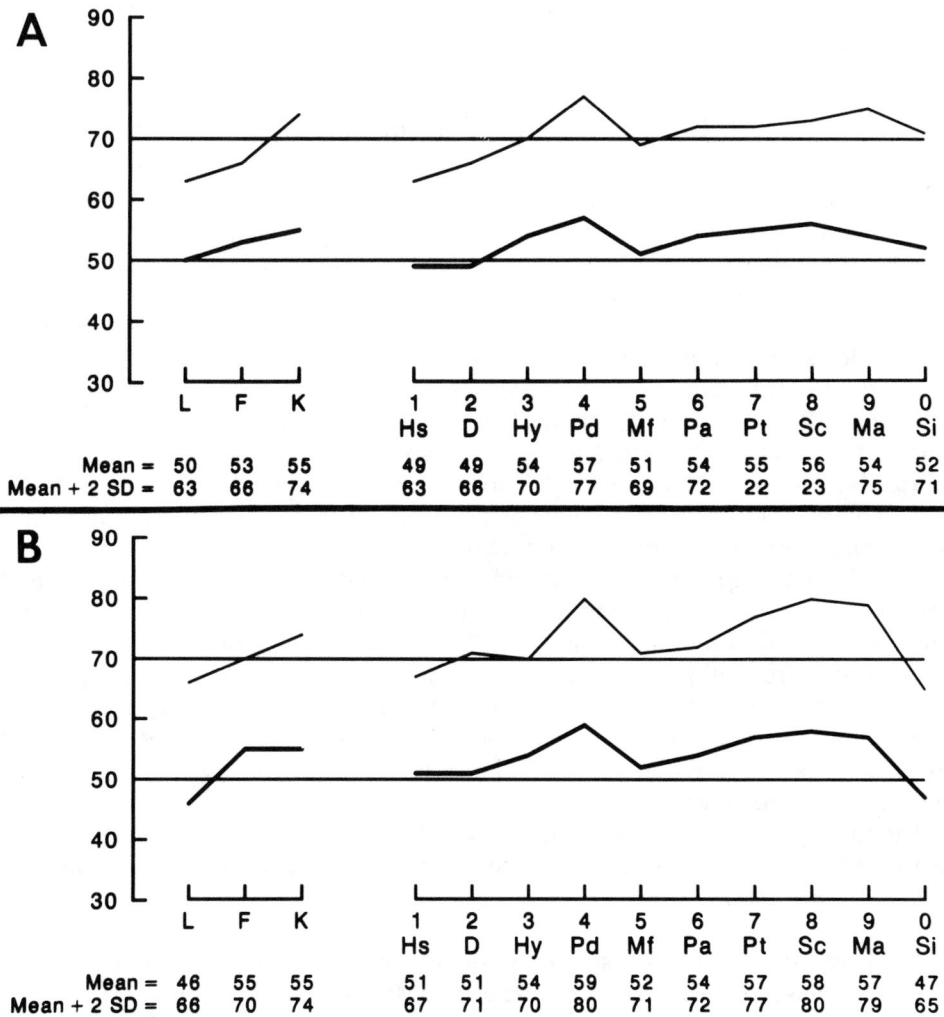

Figure 8. Mean and mean + 2 SD MMPI profiles for the 1957 Minnesota statewide sample of 12th-grade students obtained by Hathaway and Monachesi, using original adult norms and K-corrected scores. A, Girls (n = 2,054). B, Boys (n = 1,922).

important to consider the MMPI response patterns of normal adolescents as well (Hathaway & Monachesi, 1961). However, he never developed specific adolescent norms. Rather, valid MMPI profiles from a sample of more than 15,300 MMPIs obtained from ninth-grade students ranging in age from 13 to 18 years were used to establish reference points for normal adolescents for the basic validity and clinical scales of the MMPI. However, about 6% of the MMPIs obtained from girls and about 11% of those obtained from boys were excluded, because they were believed to be invalid on the basis of raw scores earned on scale L or F.

These data[10] are no longer used in this manner, because they were superseded

---

[10]Researchers and clinicians should be aware that data from selected samples of 9th- and 12th-grade subjects from 1948, 1954, and 1957 obtained by Hathaway and Monachesi recently have been reported (Gottesman et al., 1987).

by the development of a new normative sample and the subsequent development of specific adolescent norms by other researchers.

MARKS AND BRIGGS COMBINED SAMPLE

The adolescent norms most frequently used by clinicians today are those first presented in mimeographed form by Marks and Briggs (1967, 1987). These tables were first published in Volume I of the revised MMPI Handbook (Dahlstrom et al., 1972). However, although the two volumes of the Handbook thoroughly covered clinical and research applications among adults, no information was provided about adolescents or the derivation procedures for the adolescent norms prepared by Marks and Briggs. Shortly thereafter, as part of a reference work on adolescent and adult MMPI code types, Marks et al. (1974) described the procedures used to obtain the sample of normal adolescents specifically intended for normative purposes. The normative tables developed from this sample provided separate norms for adolescents ages 14 years or younger, 15 years, 16 years, 17 years, and 18 years, separately for females and males.

The Marks and Briggs tables differed from the data provided by Hathaway and Monachesi in three important ways. First, separate norms were provided for adolescents of different ages. Second, "It is important to note that these norms were derived from all profiles regardless of L, F, or K scale elevations. No profiles were eliminated from analysis because of *any* scale values" (Marks et al., 1974, p. 134; emphasis in original). Third, "we should also note that all adolescent profiles . . . are scored and plotted *without* the K correction" (Marks et al., 1974, p. 134; emphasis in original).

The third point also represented a significant departure from the earlier work done by Hathaway and Monachesi (1963), and it was justified by the following reasons (Marks et al., 1974):

1. "K was developed on a small sample of adults . . . hence its applicability to adolescents is at best questionable" (Marks et al., 1974, p. 134).
2. The major MMPI handbooks (Dahlstrom et al., 1972; Welsh & Dahlstrom, 1956) "have repeatedly cautioned against its use with samples different from those from which K was developed" (Marks et al., 1974, p. 134).
3. Much earlier, Marks and Seeman (1962) reported "a negative correlation (-0.53, p = 0.05) between validity coefficients (based on psychotherapist descriptions) and K score magnitude for an adolescent sample" (Marks et al., 1974, p. 134).
4. Finally, in a doctoral dissertation, Berry (1971) "examined the efficiency of five multivariate classification methods in identifying discriminable subgroups of adolescent MMPI profiles with and without K, and reported superior results for the cluster of profiles scored *without* the K correction" (Marks et al., 1974, p. 134, 137; emphasis in original).

Although they differed from Hathaway in these procedural respects, Marks et al. (1974) also believed that it was important to be aware of likenesses and differences in response patterns of adults and adolescents. More specifically, they stated

We are in basic agreement with the recommendation by Hathaway and Monachesi (1963) that one should view adolescent MMPI scores against an adult norm background. Nevertheless, it still appears to us that the meaning "disturbed" or "abnormal" adolescents is established against an adolescent normative view. We do not find these two sets of norms mutually exclusive. (Marks et al., 1974, p. 137)

This is a point with which we concur.

The normative sample constructed by Marks and Briggs was obtained in two stages. First, the Minneapolis and Minnesota statewide samples described above were used. From this pool of MMPIs, "Briggs selected from these profiles, samples of 100 boys and 100 girls 14, 15, and 16 years of age and 80 boys and 40 girls, 17 years of age" (Marks et al., 1974, p. 134). In order to obtain sufficient numbers of adolescents ages 17 and 18 years, data from the 1957 follow-up study (Hathaway & Monachesi, 1963) were probably used as well. The numbers just reported yield a sample of 380 boys and 340 girls. Criteria for selecting these profiles from the total sample were not specified.[11] During the second stage of the study,

In order to obtain a larger and more nationally representative sample, 1,046 additional profiles were collected in 1964 and 1965 from both rural and urban, public and private school youngsters living in Alabama (N = 129), California (N = 189), Kansas (N = 230), Missouri (N = 108), North Carolina (N = 225), and Ohio (N = 165). (Marks et al., 1974, p. 134)

Apparently, responses to individual items were not obtained, and only the total raw scores for the basic clinical and validity scales were used.

The specific circumstances under which the MMPIs were obtained from this second-stage subsample were not specified, although the authors stated,

to the best of our knowledge, all profiles were obtained from white boys and girls who, at the time of testing, were neither institutionalized, nor being treated for an emotional disturbance. . . . some unknown small percentage of the sample were subjects who had dropped out of school prior to the time of testing; in some instances they were siblings of youngsters involved in treatment who themselves were not emotionally disturbed. (Marks et al., 1974, pp. 134, 137)

Combining the samples obtained during these two stages of construction (that is, the cases that Briggs selected from the 1947, 1954, and 1957 Minneapolis and Minnesota statewide sample and from the six-state sample of 1964 to 1965) yielded a total sample of 952 adolescent boys and 854 adolescent girls whose scores on the validity and clinical scales of the MMPI were used to develop normative tables across four age groups.[12]

---

[11]The reference work by Marks et al. (1974) does not specify the nature of the selection procedures used by Briggs, but we had assumed that profiles deemed invalid by scale L or F had been excluded, a point that was not substantiated on inquiry (P. F. Briggs, personal communication, September 1985). Recently, however, published information suggests that this may not be the case, because "a large proportion (40%) of the adolescent males and females for the Marks et al. norms were provided by one of us (P.F.B.) in an unsystematic manner from the entire Hathaway-Monachesi cohort before any of the profiles were excluded for any reason including age, F, L, and omitted items." (Gottesman et al., 1987, p. 245)

[12]From the values presented (Marks et al., 1974, p. 134), it appears that 1,046 profiles were obtained during 1964–1965. This number, when combined with the cases selected by Briggs, described as 380

However, among the 271 boys and 280 girls composing the sample used in developing the table for age 14 or younger, the authors noted that "about 20% of the cases in the 14 year-old group are as young as 9 years of age" (Marks et al., 1974, p. 137). In addition, among the 166 boys and 139 girls used in the development of the normative tables for ages 17 and 18, the authors also stated that "approximately 10% of the subjects in the 17 year-old group are actually 18 years of age. However, we included an 18 year-old *only* if the youngster was still living in his or her parental home" (Marks et al., 1974, p. 137; emphasis in original).

Although the means for both sexes varied little over age, no overall summary table for adolescents in general was provided. However, mean profiles for the total group, separately by sex, were reported. These mean profiles, estimated from Marks et al. (1974, p. 137), are presented in Figure 9. Remember that, because no profile was omitted because of elevated scores on validity scales L and F and about 60% of the sample was obtained from 1964 to 1965, the norms presented by Marks and Briggs differ from the data reported by Hathaway and Monachesi (1963).

COMMENTS ON CURRENTLY AVAILABLE ADOLESCENT MMPI NORMS

Is there a need for new adolescent norms for the MMPI?

Hathaway originally was opposed to the use of separate adolescent (or juvenile) norms, believing that response patterns from adolescents should always be contrasted with those of adults. However, it should be kept in mind that the original Minnesota normal sample for the MMPI contained normal subjects as young as 16 years of age, although the exact proportion of adolescents remains unknown.

While advocating that adolescent profiles be contrasted with adult response patterns, Hathaway also encouraged clinicians to plot two additional lines from his normal adolescent sample representing the mean and the mean plus 2 standard deviations for comparative purposes. These values were derived from 4,944 boys and 5,207 girls who met criteria for valid MMPI profiles on the basis of scales L and F, and they were obtained from the 1954 Minnesota statewide sample of ninth-grade students. All values were calculated using raw scores with K correction.

However, these data are now more than 35 years old, and their value as a standard for comparison with contemporary adolescent MMPIs is questionable.

The adolescent norms subsequently presented by Marks and Briggs (1967) and more widely disseminated in their reference work on adolescent and adult MMPI code types (Marks et al., 1974) are based on a two-stage construction process. During the first stage, 40% of the adolescent sample was drawn from the MMPIs

boys and 340 girls, yields a sum of 1,766 subjects, 40 less than the 1,806 actually presented in their tables (Marks et al., 1974, pp. 135 and 136). Although no explanation for this discrepancy was reported, Briggs actually may have selected 80 girls 17 years of age, instead of the 40 reported in the text (p. 134); thus, the 40 may have been a typographical error.

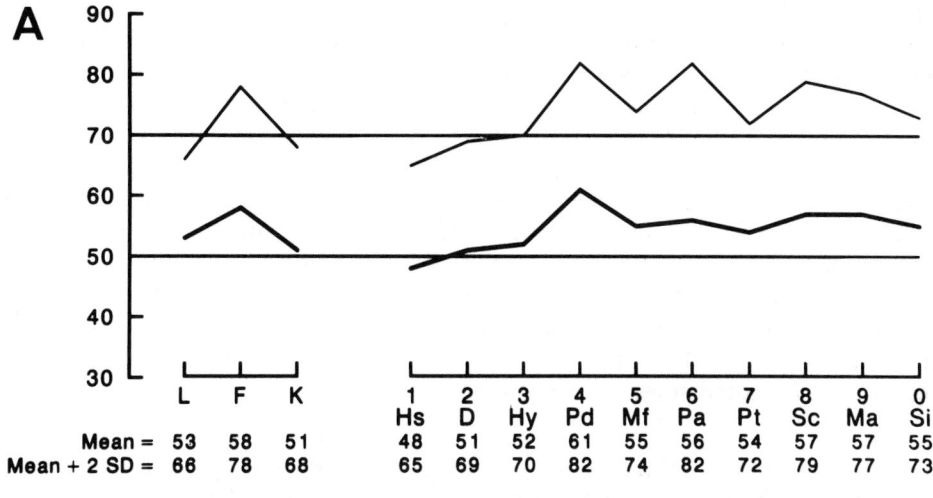

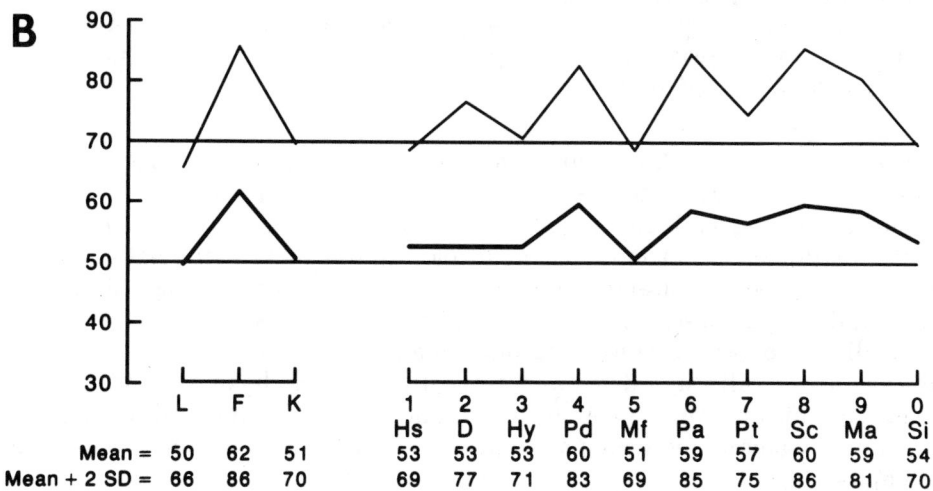

Figure 9.   Mean and mean + 2 SD MMPI profiles from Marks and Briggs' sample of normal adolescents ages 9 to 18 years, using original adult norms and scores without K correction. *A*, Girls (n = 854). *B*, Boys (n = 952).

gathered in the 1947, 1954, and 1957 Minnesota samples that had been originally obtained by Hathaway and Monachesi (1963) for their study of juvenile delinquency. Subsequently, a six-state sample of MMPIs, accounting for the remaining 60% of the total sample, was obtained during the school year for 1964 to 1965. Although this portion of the data is a newer sample of adolescents, it is now more than 25 years old.

Is there any evidence that MMPI response patterns among adolescents have changed? The changing role of adolescents in our society during the 50 years since development of the MMPI was initiated—the beatniks of the late 1940s, the happy days of the 1950s, the turmoil of the 1960s with flower children and hippies and the Kent State demonstrations and the Viet Nam War era—and the increasing divorce rate during this span of time, and all of the other changes in the typical American family, would lead one to suspect that adolescent attitudes and their expression may very well have changed.

Several sources of objective evidence are already available. A longitudinal study comparing the scores earned by entering freshmen at the University of Minnesota over a 14-year period, from 1948 to 1962, found significant changes (Loper, Robertson, & Swanson, 1968). Generally speaking, during this time entering students were described as having become more independent, sensitive, energetic, socially outgoing, and optimistic. These changes were present to a degree that led the authors to recommend changes in normative data.

Some changes have been reported more specifically. It was interesting to learn that, when Marks et al. (1974) were completing their adolescent code-type research, they noted several differences also:

> In studying adolescents during recent years, we have noticed sharp increases in the frequencies of certain behaviors which were not at all prevalent at the time we collected our original data. To take some outstanding examples, drug use and abuse, premarital sex, pregnancy, and violence appear much more often in the case histories of youth seen in psychotherapy in the 1970's than they did for those seen during the 1960's. (Marks et al., 1974, p. 138)

Somewhat later, a 10-year longitudinal study interpreted changes in MMPI response patterns as being descriptive of greater feelings of alienation and role confusion among college students, in part because of the major changes in societal attitudes associated with the turmoil of the 1960s (Schubert & Wagner, 1975). These adverse trends showed some improvement among college men studied during a subsequent 5-year period (Schneider, 1976).

Finally, response patterns from our contemporary sample of normal adults showed statistically significant and clinically relevant changes on nearly every scale. Significant age changes were present on most of the scales also, most prominently among the young adult ages (18 to 25 years) and the geriatric ages (65 to 99 years).

For all of these reasons, we planned an investigation of normal adolescents; it was intended to be a companion research project to complement the prior MMPI study of normal adults. Thus, we intended to locate, and obtain MMPI responses from, normal adolescents who reported no physically or mentally handicapping conditions that might bias response patterns.

Following Hathaway's suggestion, these data would then be compared with contemporary MMPI response patterns obtained from normal adults. Next, for historical purposes, comparisons would be made with the data reported by Hathaway and Monachesi (1963). Finally, these contemporary data would be evaluated against the most widely used adolescent norms currently available, those disseminated by Marks and Briggs (1967, 1987).[13]

---

[13]Clinicians should be aware that the Marks and Briggs (1967) norms have been reprinted recently by Marks and Briggs (1987): Adolescent norms for males and females at ages 17, 16, 15, and 14 and below. See Archer (1987), pp. 197–213.

PART IV

THE CONTEMPORARY NORMATIVE STUDY OF ADOLESCENTS

PURPOSE

Because it had been clearly demonstrated that MMPI response patterns from normal adults had changed significantly during the past 50 years, we were interested in determining whether comparable changes had occurred among normal adolescents.

Therefore, the general intent of the adolescent MMPI research project can be stated simply: Are the MMPI norms currently available for adolescents, which are based on MMPIs obtained from adolescents during the years 1947, 1954, 1957, and 1964 to 1965, data that are now 25 to 45 years old, outdated for use with adolescents from contemporary society?

To permit a meaningful response to this question, we believed that it would be necessary to obtain MMPIs from a large contemporary sample of normal adolescents who met criteria similar to those participating in the original Minnesota normal sample of adults developed by Hathaway and McKinley (1940) and who also were comparable to the subjects used in the Marks and Briggs (1967) norms. The MMPI responses obtained from the contemporary normal adolescent sample then would be systematically compared with the responses from subjects in the Marks and Briggs sample. In actuality, our comparisons could be made only with the mean raw scores for the basic validity and clinical scales of the MMPI, because responses to individual items from the 1964 to 1965 portion of their sample were apparently not made available to Marks and Briggs.

In addition, because Hathaway originally believed that adult norms should be used in evaluating adolescent MMPIs, the MMPI response patterns of our contemporary normal adolescents also would be compared with the patterns of our contemporary normal adults.

Finally, because Hathaway later suggested that a second set of profile lines be drawn to represent the expected range of scores for adolescents, this group and our contemporary normal sample of adolescents also would be compared.

To conduct the research that would address the questions posed above and allow these comparisons to be made, the following procedures were outlined.

1. Preliminary investigations were made.
2. The geographic area to be sampled was delineated.
3. Household units were selected randomly.
4. Letters of information and invitation were sent to selected household units.
5. Structured telephone interviews were completed.
6. Subject selection procedures were applied.
7. MMPI study packets and consent forms were sent to selected subjects.
8. Flowcharts of each subject's status were maintained.
9. Follow-up and thank-you letters were sent.
10. MMPIs were inspected and processed after being returned.
11. Telephone interview data were reviewed.
12. MMPI protocols were screened for completeness.
13. Demographic data were coded, keypunched, and verified.
14. Data were analyzed and summarized separately by age and sex.
15. Comparisons were made with:
    a. data from the original Minnesota normal adult sample (Hathaway & Briggs, 1957)
    b. Hathaway's ninth-grade statewide adolescent reference sample (Hathaway & Monachesi, 1963)
    c. contemporary normal adults (Colligan et al., 1983)
    d. the Marks and Briggs (1967, 1987) normative tables for adolescents.
16. New normative tables were developed:
    a. normalized T-score tables using raw scores, without K correction, separately by sex, for the total sample
    b. T-score tables using raw scores, with K correction, separately by sex, for the total sample
    c. norms were developed for selected supplemental and research scales using the new adolescent normal sample.

PRELIMINARY INVESTIGATIONS

Initially we believed that normal subjects could be identified from medical records in which the statement summarizing the patient's physical examination, or the summary diagnosis, was "normal" or "negative." We thought that using such a plan would ensure a truly well-documented index of mental and physical functioning. However, evaluation of MMPIs obtained from a large sample of adolescent medical outpatients ranging in age from 15 through 19 years (534 males and 659 females) showed that these profiles were significantly different from the norms provided by Marks and Briggs (1967) and also from Hathaway's (Hathaway & Monachesi, 1963) ninth-grade reference sample, primarily by significant elevations on scales 1 (Hs), 2 (D), and 3 (Hy) (Colligan & Osborne, 1977). These differences paralleled the results of a preliminary investigation carried out later with a large adolescent and adult sample of such "normal" medical outpatients (903 males and 810 females). The mean profile for both of these samples was characterized by the "psychosomatic V" or "conversion V" profile configuration reported in a much earlier study of adults with no physical findings on their general medical examination (Polley, Swenson, & Steinhilber, 1970).

In general, it seemed to us that adolescent medical outpatients differed from the normal adolescents in the Marks and Briggs norms and in the Hathaway and Monachesi sample in much the same way that adult medical outpatients, described as having normal or negative physical examinations, differed from the original Minnesota normal sample of adults.

Therefore, following the outline used for the adult normative study, we planned to obtain an entirely new, randomly selected, population-based sample of normal adolescents.

GEOGRAPHIC LOCATION

All of the subjects included in Hathaway's original Minnesota normal sample of adolescents and adult subjects were drawn primarily from the small towns and rural areas of Minnesota and were described as corresponding well to the 1930 census data regarding age, sex, and marital status.

Hathaway's Minnesota statewide ninth-grade reference sample was drawn entirely from Minnesota and was composed of about 28% of the ninth-grade students in the public schools of Minnesota.

It should be recalled that about 40% of the cases of the Marks and Briggs norms were drawn from the Minnesota statewide ninth-grade reference sample. The remaining 60% of cases were obtained during the school year 1964 to 1965 from a six-state supplemental sample (Alabama, North Carolina, Missouri, Ohio, Kansas, and California).

Marks and Briggs did not report any systematic differences among these regional groups, but a large proportion of their data came from Minnesota. For our study, it was decided that the contemporary normal adolescent sample would be drawn from the same three-state area of Minnesota, Iowa, and Wisconsin that had been used in our earlier study of contemporary normal adults.

More specifically, the household units from which we drew our adolescent subjects came from a roughly circular 8,000-square-mile area with a radius of approximately 50 miles surrounding Rochester, Minnesota. Furthermore, we believed that the positive impact of the Mayo Clinic would be significant within this area and likely to increase the possibility that selected subjects, and their parents, would be willing to give consent to participate in the study.

HOUSEHOLD SELECTION PROCEDURES

Telephone company representatives indicated that more than 99% of the households in this geographic area of the Midwest had telephone service. Therefore, just as with the adult study, telephone directories for the 177 Minnesota, 14

Wisconsin, and 7 Iowa cities, towns, and villages within the sampling area described above were used as the primary source of household units.

More exactly, this area included one city (Rochester, Minnesota) with a population in the 50,000 to 100,000 range, two cities (Austin and Winona, Minnesota) with populations from 25,000 to 50,000, and six cities with populations from 5,000 to 25,000; the remainder of the area included rural communities and villages with populations less than 5,000.

Because we planned to study adolescents whose ages ranged from 13 through 17 years, it was decided that at least 100 subjects for each year of age, separately for each sex, would be needed. With a sample of this size, age-specific norms could be developed if needed (for example, by using regression models on age). Thus, a total sample of 1,000 adolescent subjects or more would provide sufficient numbers for accurate estimates of the mean, median, selected percentiles, and other points of clinical and statistical interest.

The Marks and Briggs tables provide separate norms for four age groups—14 years and younger, 15 years, 16 years, and 17 and 18 years—separately for each sex. We believed that having samples of at least 100 subjects for each sex and each year of age from 13 through 17 years would allow us to evaluate the need for age-specific norms.

To compensate for the anticipated frequency of families without adolescents in our catchment area, anticipated refusal rates, potentially handicapping conditions, and attrition rates among participants, we randomly selected 11,930 household units from the combined telephone listings covering the geographic area described above. These randomly selected household units were spread proportionately by population density over the entire geographic area.

INITIAL MAIL CONTACT

Subject selection was carried out in two steps. In the first step, a carefully drafted letter of information was sent to the person whose household had been randomly chosen from the telephone directory listings. The letter briefly stated the purpose of the study, encouraged participation, described the task of completing the MMPI, indicated the value of the project, and, of greatest importance, prepared household members for the structured telephone interview that might follow. The letter also allowed the household to refuse further participation in the study.

A stamped, self-addressed return envelope also was provided. If the household unit did not have any adolescents in the age range from 13 through 17 years, people were asked to place a check mark by the statement so indicating and return the information to us. A second, alternative statement that could be marked indicated that the household contained adolescents in the age range from 13 through 17 years, but that they or their parents did not want to participate in the study. This procedure was used to identify the households not requiring a subsequent telephone call and hence reduce the number of such follow-up contacts.

TELEPHONE INTERVIEW

Eleven telephone interviewers were trained to do a standardized interview developed specifically for this research project. Because all of our subjects were

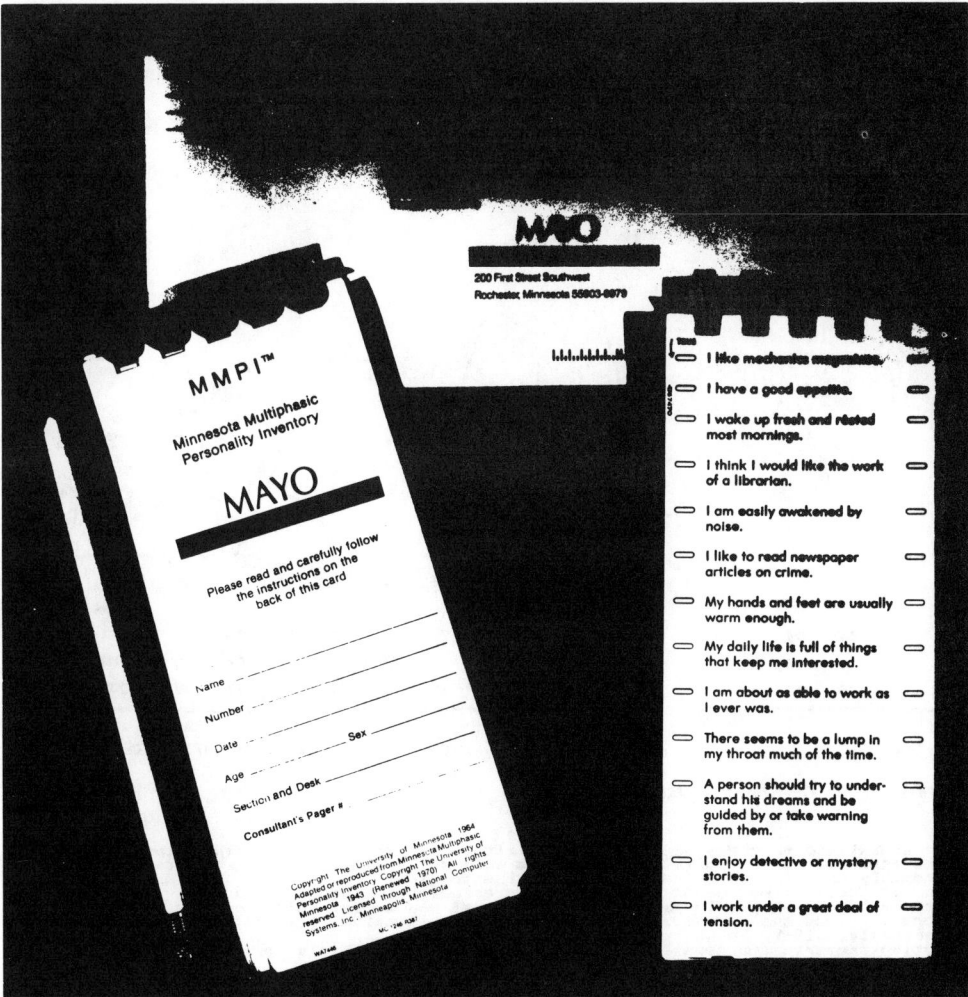

Figure 10.   Data card decklet for Mayo Clinic computerized scoring and interpretative system for the MMPI. *Note.* From Colligan, R. C., & Offord, K. P. (1989). The aging MMPI: Contemporary norms for contemporary teenagers. *Mayo Clinic Proceedings, 64,* 3–27. By permission of Mayo Foundation.

FOLLOW-UP

Each adolescent subject who returned an MMPI was sent a short thank-you letter. Because our return rate was very high (83% for girls and 71% for boys), it was unnecessary to send many letters of encouragement. We received 103 inquiries from adolescents or responsible adults requesting information about the outcome of the study. These individuals were sent a short letter summarizing the project and outlining the results.

INSPECTION AND SCORING OF MMPI DECKLET

Later, before processing, each MMPI decklet was inspected to verify each subject's identification number, age, and sex. In addition, because the marks

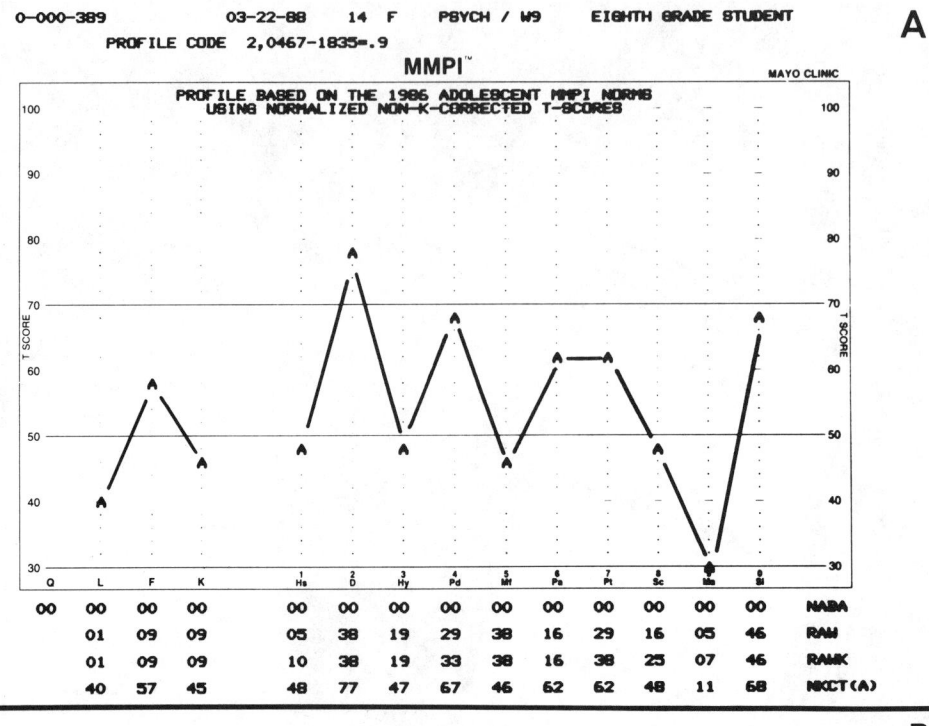

Figure 11. Typical MMPI printout for adolescent (eighth-grade student) from the Mayo Clinic computerized scoring and interpretative system. *Note.* From Colligan, R. C., & Offord, K. P. (1989). The aging MMPI: Contemporary norms for contemporary teenagers. *Mayo Clinic Proceedings, 64,* 3–27. By permission of Mayo Foundation.

indicating a subject's true or false responses in the MMPI decklet were read by an optical scanning device, the clarity of the response marks also was evaluated. In some cases answers had been marked with a felt-tip pen or some other writing instrument, in which case the answers had to be re-marked. Incomplete MMPIs were excluded. Incomplete MMPIs were defined as those having 75 or more unscorable items; only 30 of the 690 girls who were included and 41 of the boys who were in the final sample had scores in the range of 20 to 74.

Responses to each of the MMPI items were recorded automatically to disk storage as the MMPIs were processed.

REVIEW OF TELEPHONE INTERVIEW DATA

Before the final MMPI data sets were established, information from the structured interview was reviewed to verify the eligibility or exclusion status for each subject. Adolescents in whom the presence of a handicapping condition was questionable were included if the telephone interviewer and the independent reviewer agreed on inclusion. In some cases it was necessary to recontact the household to obtain further information about an adolescent's condition.

CODING OF DEMOGRAPHIC DATA

Basic demographic data subsequently were coded, keypunched, verified, and then merged with the MMPI data.

TIME LINE FOR COMPLETION

The study protocol was prepared in the fall of 1984 and received approval from the Mayo Institutional Review Board later that year. Letters of invitation were sent in batches beginning in January 1985. Our telephone interviewers and their coordinator also were trained in January 1985, and the telephone follow-up calls were initiated late in the month. The process of mailing, calling, and data management continued for the next 6 months until June 1985, as the school year drew to a close for our adolescent participants.

Data processing was initiated and preliminary analyses were completed in 1986; by 1987, plans were made to incorporate the results of the study into the Mayo Clinic computerized scoring and interpretive system for the MMPI, where it has been in use since.

DATA ANALYSIS

All of the data reported herein were analyzed separately by sex, because the body of MMPI research literature clearly documents the differential response patterns obtained from males and females.

In addition, data initially were analyzed separately for each of the five age groups (13, 14, 15, 16, and 17 years), as well as separately by sex, because we wanted to compare our data with those reported by Marks and Briggs (1967). These comparisons were based on raw scores without K correction following the convention endorsed by Marks et al. (1974).

However, because we also wanted to make comparisons with Hathaway's original adolescent data (Hathaway & Monachesi, 1963) and also with the original Minnesota normal sample of adults and adolescents (Hathaway & Briggs, 1957), K-corrected raw scores also were calculated.

Finally, comparisons were made with the census-matched contemporary normal adult sample, the study we had completed earlier (Colligan et al., 1983, 1984b, 1989; Colligan, Osborne, Swenson, Offord, & Davis, 1984d).

RESULTS

The outcomes of each of the research procedures are outlined below and in Figure 12.

Outcome of Sampling Procedures

With telephone listings as the source of household units for potential subjects, 11,930 households, distributed by relative population density, were randomly

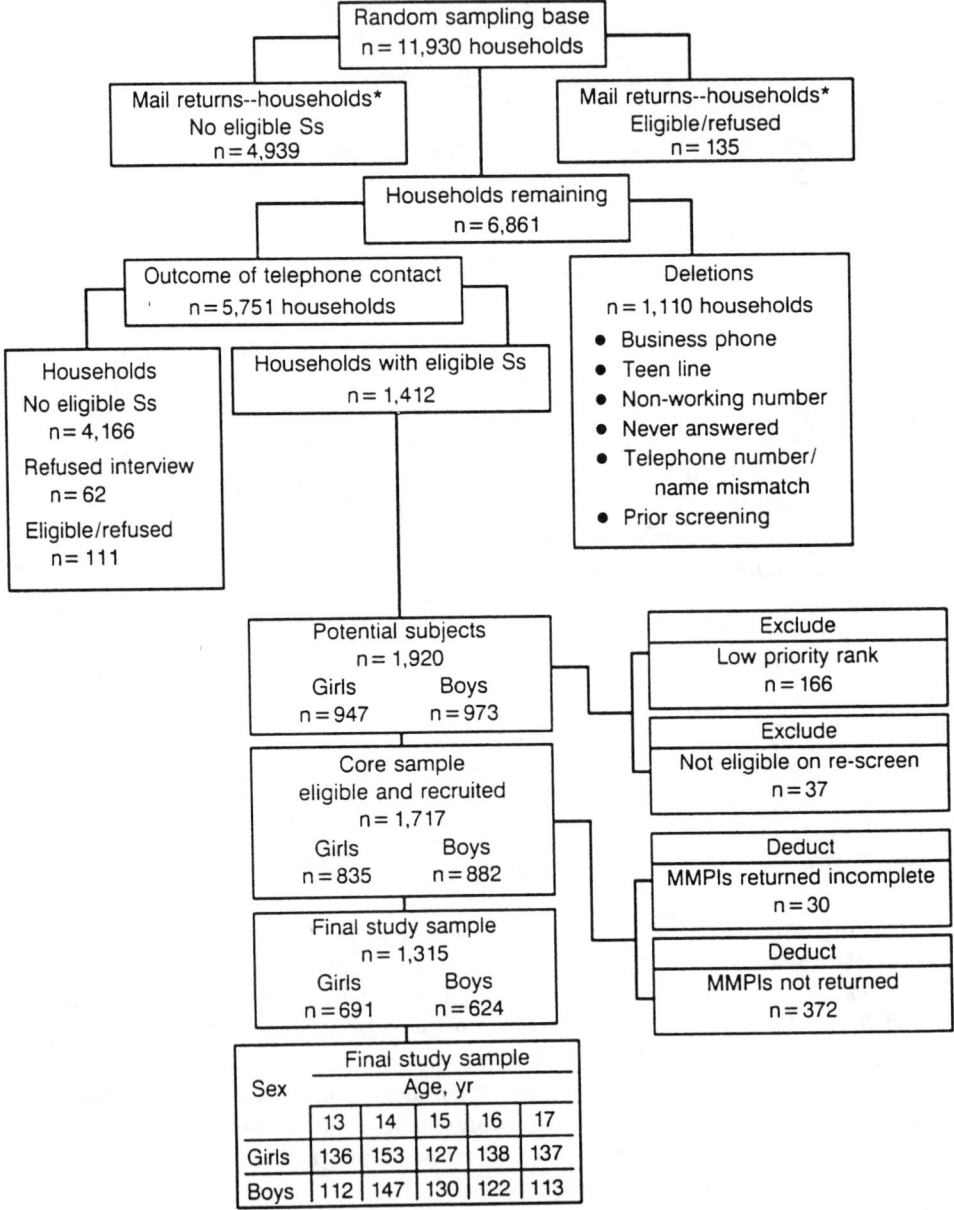

Figure 12. Procedures used for selection of adolescent subjects for MMPI contemporary normative study. Ss, subjects; *, five household units were inadvertently deleted from the pool. Note. From Colligan, R. C., & Offord, K. P. (1989). The aging MMPI: Contemporary norms for contemporary teenagers. *Mayo Clinic Proceedings, 64*, 3–27. By permission of Mayo Foundation.

selected; letters of introduction and invitation were sent to families in the 8,000 square miles encompassed by a 50-mile radius around Rochester, Minnesota.

Of these households, 5,074 (43%) responded by returning the checklist enclosed with the informational/invitational letter. Nearly all of those returning the checklist (n = 4,939 households, 97% of those returning the checklist) indicated that they had no adolescents in the age range from 13 to 17 years. However, 135 households (3% of those returning the checklist) stated that their household contained adolescents in this age range but that they did not want to participate in the study.

Subsequently, efforts were made to contact all of the 6,861 remaining household units by telephone. During this process, 1,110 household units had to be deleted from the study sample for various reasons not related to the study. The single greatest source of deleted household units (652 units, 59% of those deleted) was a nonworking telephone number, usually because the family had moved from the area. The second greatest source of deleted household units (312 units, 28% of those deleted) was a mismatch between the resident's name and the telephone number for that household unit. These reasons seem to reflect the mobility of the Midwest population; the mismatches occurred because a new family moving into the area had been assigned the telephone number of a prior resident. We also encountered a small proportion of telephones being used in the home for business purposes, "teen-lines," and telephones in households that already had been screened under a different telephone number.

Thus, 5,751 households were of interest and received telephone calls to enumerate potentially eligible candidates. Needless to say, of greatest concern to us was not the category of teen-lines or business telephones but rather that of straightforward refusals. Fortunately, only a very small number (62 of the 5,751, 1%) refused our interviewer's call. Unfortunately, this refusal gave us absolutely no information about the nature of that household unit. However, in a second group of household units (111 of the 5,751, 2%) the responsible party conversed with our interviewer long enough for us to determine that the household contained adolescent subjects in the desired age range of 13 through 17 years but that either the potential subject or the responsible adult (or both) did not want to participate in the study.

Just as with the mail returns, however, we learned during the course of the telephone interview that most of our household units (4,166, 72% of the households called) did not contain adolescents in the desired age range. Interestingly, many of these households expressed disappointment that they were unable to participate and offered to enroll nieces, nephews, or other relatives who they were sure would be interested in the study; this course of action was not pursued.

Thus, we accumulated 1,412 household units containing one or more adolescents in the age range of 13 through 17 years, and it was from this base of household units that our subjects were drawn.

Thus, to summarize, 11,930 informational/invitational letters were sent to randomly selected household units. However, only 10,820 were potentially viable households, because 1,110 had to be deleted because they had nonworking telephone numbers, business telephones, and other categories of nonresidence telephones. Of the potentially viable households (10,820), 246 households refused participation even though they indicated that they had eligible subjects (135 refused by mail, 3%; 111 refused during telephone interview, 2%).

Stated another way, most (87%) of our randomly selected Midwest household units (11,930) did not contain adolescents in the desired age range of 13 through 17 years. Of the 1,658 remaining households (13%) that contained potential subjects, we were refused participation by 14% (246). It should also be recalled that we had absolutely no information about the status of the 1% of our households who did not reply to our letter and also refused our telephone call (62, 1% of the 5,751 households receiving a telephone interview call). Thus, 1,412 households had potential study subjects.

These 1,412 households—which were randomly selected and whose potentially eligible residents and their parent, guardian, or responsible adult indicated their willingness to participate—yielded 1,920 eligible subjects.

Remember that the telephone interviewers first ascertained the number of persons in the household who ranged in age from 13 through 17 years and subsequently determined whether each eligible participant had a potentially physically or mentally handicapping condition. Only those whose interview results indicated that they were free from such potentially biasing conditions were included in the final sample. In addition, because of anticipated attrition through incomplete or nonreturned MMPIs, subjects who also met the eligibility criteria but who were not ranked as the primary subject in the household also were sent an MMPI research packet. Hence, the person in the household who had been selected as the first choice for the study could be replaced with someone else from the same household who had the next highest priority rating, should the first-chosen subject of that sex fail to complete or to return the MMPI.

Among the subjects who were sent MMPI research packets, the response rates were excellent, ranging from 81% to 85% for the girls over the five age ranges and from 68% to 79% for the boys. Nevertheless, 15% of the girls (138) and 24% of the boys (234) did not return the MMPI at all, and 1% of the girls (6) and 2% (24) of the boys returned MMPIs that were incomplete and not usable. After deleting these subjects, 1,518 remained; from these it was necessary to deduct 166 MMPIs because they were potential substitute subjects who were unused because a subject with a higher priority rating was included instead. Thus, 1,352 subjects remained in the total pool.

At this point, information from the telephone interviews was reviewed and 37 subjects (17 female and 20 male) were excluded because it was believed that their MMPI responses might be biased because of a potentially physically or mentally handicapping condition.

After these deletions, a total group of 1,315 adolescents remained in the final sample. The age and sex distribution of this group is presented in Table 20, as are the return rates for the eligible subjects (excluding potential substitute subjects).

Handicapping Conditions

Potentially physically or mentally handicapping conditions were divided into the same 20 categories outlining the systems of the body (Lyght, 1966) that had been used for the adult study. These categories included cardiovascular, dermatologic, endocrine, gastrointestinal, hematologic, hepatic and biliary, immunologic, infectious, musculoskeletal and connective tissue, neurologic, nutritional and metabolic, gynecologic, ophthalmologic, otorhinolaryngologic,

Table 20
Sample Sizes and Return Rates for MMPIs Sent to Normal Adolescents Agreeing to Participate in the Adolescent Normative Study

	Female subjects			Male subjects		
	Sent	Returned		Sent	Returned	
Age, yr	No.	No.	%	No.	No.	%
13	168	136	81	165	112	68
14	182	153	84	186	147	79
15	150	127	85	185	130	70
16	169	138	82	183	122	67
17	166	137	83	163	113	69
Total	835	691	83	882	624	71

Note. From Colligan, R. C., & Offord, K. P. (1989). The aging MMPI: Contemporary norms for contemporary teenagers. *Mayo Clinic Proceedings, 64,* 3-27. By permission of Mayo Foundation.

pediatric/genetic/congenital, psychiatric, pulmonary, renal and urologic, malignant disorders, and also a miscellaneous category that covered multiple-system involvement such as injuries that might have been sustained from a motorcycle accident.

As noted above, about 2% of the subjects were eliminated from the final sample when telephone interview data regarding potentially handicapping conditions were reevaluated. No single category predominated the reasons for exclusion, although among the girls the three main categories were limited intellectual abilities or significant learning disabilities (three subjects), participation in regular counseling/therapy sessions (three subjects), and musculoskeletal problems of significance (four subjects).

Among the boys, the three main categories were learning disability or mild intellectual impairment (six subjects), asthmatic or allergic conditions (three subjects), and neurologic conditions (three subjects).

However, because some potentially handicapping conditions were found not to interfere significantly in the adolescent's life, some subjects with diagnosable problems were included. Nevertheless, of our final sample, 97% of the girls and 96% of the boys described themselves as having no handicapping conditions at all. Of the 3% of the girls (24 girls) and the 4% of the boys (26 boys) with such conditions, the three most prominent categories were respiratory conditions such as asthma or allergy-related seasonal conditions, dermatologic conditions such as acne, and temporary musculoskeletal conditions such as a sprained wrist or sport-related injured knee.

Racial/Ethnic Background

Although a diversity of ethnic and racial cultures is found in the Midwest, no effort was made to selectively sample these groups specifically. About 1% (17 subjects) in our final sample described themselves as non-white. The largest proportion was composed of persons of Southeast Asian descent, followed by those describing themselves as Oriental, having a Hispanic background, and blacks; no Native Americans were represented.

Therefore, with the exception of these 17 subjects, all of our subjects were white.

Education

With the exception of three subjects (two girls and one boy who had dropped out of school during grades 8, 9, and 10), all of our subjects were still in school. These subjects were enrolled in grades 7 through 12, with two exceptions: one boy was still in grade 6 and one 17-year-old girl was enrolled in her first year of college.

Family Status

Three pieces of information were obtained to describe the nature of the household from which the subject had been drawn. These included the type of living arrangements of the family, the education of the person identified as "head of the household," and finally education of the spouse or companion of the head of the household.

Nearly all of our subjects came from two-parent families (90% of the girls and 91% of the boys), although we did not identify whether this was a first or subsequent marriage for the couple. Most of the single parents were mothers (7% for subjects of both sexes), and 1% of the subjects lived with their father as the single parent. Six of the subjects (two girls, four boys) were living with guardians or other family relatives, and five (all girls) were living outside the typical family unit.

These data compare favorably with Hathaway's data. As reported earlier, 86% of his ninth-grade sample were living with both parents.

With regard to educational status, 44% of the persons in our sample who were in the head-of-household category were high school graduates, 5% had 1 or 2 years of vocational school education, 17% had 1 to 3 years of college education, 15% were college graduates, and 11% had completed advanced, graduate-level degrees. The remainder (9%) had completed 11 years or less of education. (The total is 101% because of rounding.)

In Hathaway's data, only 5% of the fathers of his ninth-grade sample had a 4-year college degree, and 2% had graduate-level work; the largest proportion (22%) had a partial high-school education.

In our sample, the highest level of education that had been completed by the spouse of the head of the household was high school for 49%, 1 or 2 years of vocational/technical school training for 6%, 1 to 3 years of college for 22%, 4 years of college for 15%, and advanced, graduate-level degrees for 3%. Of the remainder, 5% had 11 years or less of education.

No comparable information was obtained for Hathaway's ninth-grade study.

In summary, just as with the contemporary sample of normal adults, the parents of our normal adolescents were comparable to, but slightly more educated than, the white population of the United States in general. More specifically, census data indicate that 37% of our national population has completed 4 years of high school, 15% have 1 to 3 years of education beyond high school, and 18% have completed 4 years of college.

VALIDITY SCALE CHARACTERISTICS OF THE MMPIs THAT WERE INCLUDED IN THE FINAL SAMPLE

When the MMPIs were reviewed for completeness, 30 subjects had left 75 or more items blank, and these subjects were excluded. All other MMPIs were included. For our female adolescents, the raw Q/? score ranged from 0 to 72 (mean raw score, 4.8; standard deviation, 7.9; median, 2). The raw Q/? score was 0 in 25% of the sample, 1 in 17%, and 2 in 11%; 72% had a raw score of 5 or less, and 90% had a raw score of 11 or less.

For the male adolescents, the raw Q/? score ranged from 0 to 74 (mean raw score, 6.5; standard deviation, 10.1; median, 3). The raw Q/? score was 0 in 17% of the sample, 1 in 14%, and 2 in 11%; 66% had a raw score of 5 or less, and 90% had a raw score of 14 or less.

Just as with the adult study, these scores may be slightly inflated because of an artifact associated with MMPI format for the data card decklet used at the Mayo Clinic. If the subject inadvertently forgets to complete one side of the data card or turns over two of the cards at the same time, the Q/? score will be elevated by the 12 or 13 MMPI items for each side of the MMPI data card decklet that has not been completed.

Because this was a normative study, it is important to reiterate that no MMPI profile was excluded on the basis of scores on scale L, F, or K, nor on the basis of the F minus K dissimulation index or any other index of response bias.

For the adolescent girls, the mean raw score on L was 2.7 (standard deviation, 1.6); values ranged from 0 to 11. For the boys, the mean raw score on L was 3.1 (standard deviation, 1.9); values ranged from 0 to 11.

Among the girls, raw scores on scale F varied from 0 to 34 (mean, 6.9; SD, 5.1); 93% of the sample had a raw F score of 15 or less. For the boys, raw scores on scale F ranged from 0 to 29 (mean, 7.8; SD, 5.3); 90% of the sample had a raw F score of 15 or less.

Raw scores on scale K ranged from 1 to 25 for the girls (mean, 11.8; SD, 4.5) and from 1 to 26 for the boys (mean, 12.0; SD, 4.9).

ANALYSIS OF CONTEMPORARY ADOLESCENT MMPI DATA

The databases established by the MMPI responses from the contemporary normal adolescents were used to address three basic questions.

First, have adolescent MMPI response patterns changed in comparison with adult response patterns? Recall that Hathaway had initially questioned the need for separate adolescent norms, believing that the most primary comparison should be made with adult MMPI response patterns so that the differences between adolescents and adults would always be apparent.

Second, have there been significant changes in contemporary adolescent MMPI response patterns in comparison with the data reported by Marks and Briggs (the only adolescent norms currently available)? In this regard it should be remembered that Marks et al. (1974) had noted the significant changes in the types of problems that brought adolescents to the attention of mental health professionals over the span of time involved in their derivation study of adolescent MMPI code types.

Third, are significant age-related changes in response patterns apparent over this span of adolescent ages? Clear age-related trends were noted across ages among the contemporary normal adults, but ages in that study ranged from 18 through 99 years, whereas the age range among the adolescents was relatively restricted, extending only from age 13 through 17 years.

We believed that the answers to these three questions would determine whether new MMPI normative tables for adolescents should be developed.

Historical Comparisons

The first historical comparison needs to be made with the original Minnesota normal sample of adults whose ages ranged from 16 to 65 years. Figure 7 presented the mean profiles for the 5,207 ninth-grade girls and 4,944 ninth-grade boys that Hathaway had suggested be used for comparative purposes. Remember that these scores were based on the original adult norms and used raw scores with K correction.

For a contemporary comparison, the mean profiles for our contemporary normal sample of adolescents who were 14 years old are presented in Figure 13, using the same metric—namely, the original Hathaway adult normative tables and raw scores with K correction. Appendix C provides the same information for the other adolescent ages in our normal sample, separately by sex, and for the total sample, by sex.

It is apparent that our contemporary normal adolescents of age 14 years, when compared with Hathaway's ninth-grade sample, obtained higher mean scale scores and a noticeably elevated profile. However, it should be kept in mind that profiles believed to be invalid on the basis of scores on scales L and F were systematically excluded from the Hathaway data, a procedure not used for the contemporary normal sample.

Comparisons Between Contemporary Normal Adolescents and Contemporary Normal Adults

Figure 14 illustrates the need for separate adolescent norms for both sexes. The mean profile for our total sample of normal adolescent males and females was calculated using contemporary adult norms, following Hathaway's original suggestion. If there were no differences in response patterns between contemporary normal adolescents and contemporary normal adults, the mean profile would fall on the horizontal line representing a T score of 50, the mean for contemporary adults on each scale. The second line, the mean + 2 SD, would fall on the horizontal line representing a T score of 70, the mean + 2 SD for contemporary adults on each scale. Appendix D provides the same information for the other adolescent ages in our normal sample and for the total sample, separately by sex.

The configuration of the profile for both sexes suggests that contemporary adolescents do not see the world in such conservative or conforming ways as our

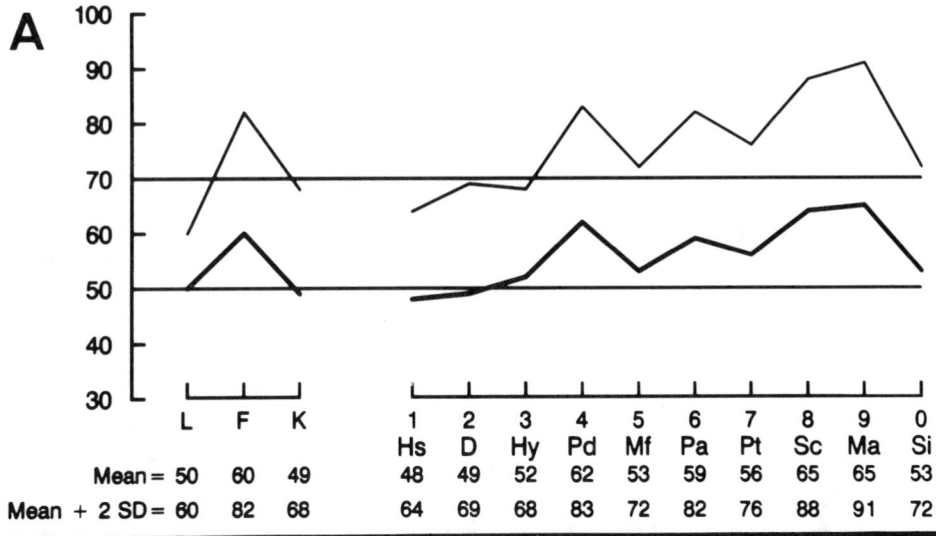

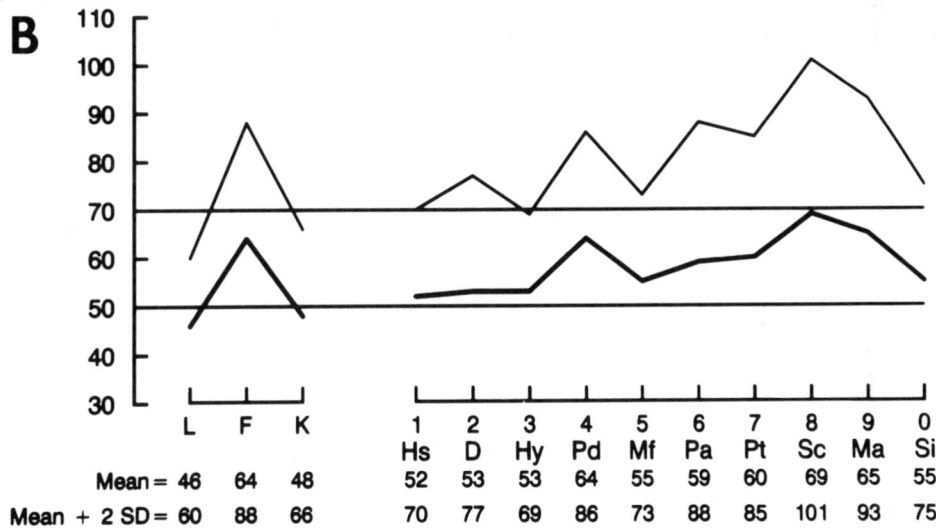

Figure 13.   Mean and mean + 2 SD MMPI profiles for contemporary normal adolescents, age 14 years, using original Hathaway adult norms and K-corrected scores. A, Female subjects (n = 153). B, Male subjects (n = 147).

contemporary normal adults (scale F). They do not have the same degree of defensiveness and are more likely to be open, indeed perhaps more self-critical as well, in expressing their feelings and views (scale K). As a group they report relatively few physical or somatic symptoms, and equally little in the way of a dysphoric or pessimistic mood (scales 1, 2, and 3). However, the slope of the profile indicates significant feelings of independence and antiestablishment views (scale 4)—which may reflect family opinions as well—accompanied by a relatively high degree of psychological energy and a greater activity level than usually found among adults (scale 9). Their social interests seem to be consistent with those of our contemporary normal adults (scale 0), but there are indications for considerable sensitivity—indeed, perhaps oversensitivity—to the thoughts,

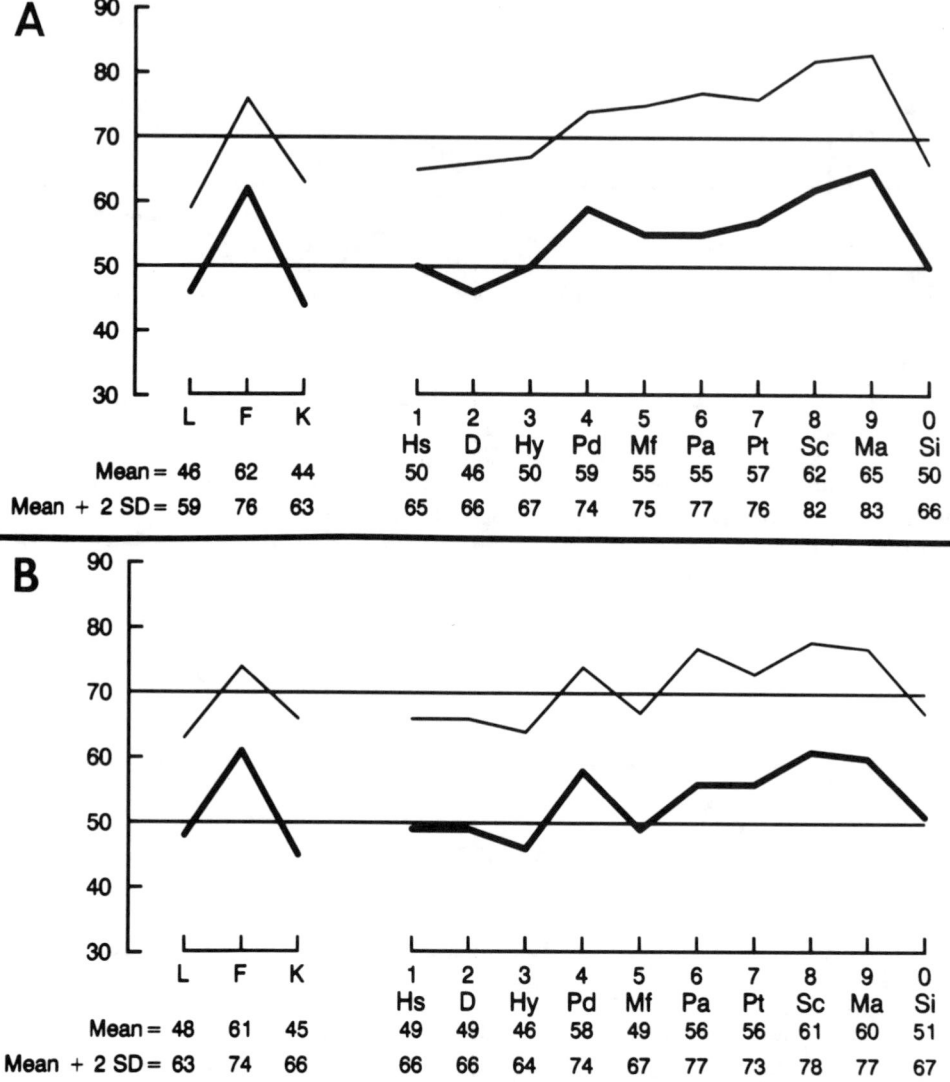

Figure 14.   Mean and mean + 2 SD profiles for contemporary normal adolescents, ages 13 through 17 years, using contemporary adult norms and K-corrected scores. *A*, Female subjects (n = 691). *B*, Male subjects (n = 624).

motives, and behavior of others (scale 6), accompanied by feelings of anxiousness and expressions of difficulty in developing and maintaining close personal relationships (scales 7 and 8).

Needless to say, these significant differences and atypical-from-adult response patterns are of considerable import to clinicians who work with adolescents and their families. Hathaway originally expressed the opinion that it was important to highlight adolescent differences through the use of adult norms, but the current data support his later suggestion to apply adolescent values for comparative purposes and also that of Marks et al. (1974) regarding the need for separate adolescent norms.

Thus, in response to the first question we posed—whether adolescent MMPI response patterns have changed in comparison with adult response patterns—the answer is yes. More specifically, adolescents of the past obtained MMPI response patterns that differed significantly from those of the original adult norms. Contemporary normal adults obtain response patterns significantly different from the original adult norms. Finally, contemporary normal adolescents obtain MMPI response patterns that are significantly different from those of contemporary normal adults.

It is interesting to note, however, that normal adolescents of today differ, in general, from normal adults of today in much the same manner as adolescents of the past differed from adults of that era, at least in terms of the MMPI.

Comparisons With Marks and Briggs Adolescent Norms

Clinicians need to be aware that adolescent MMPI response patterns continue to be different from those of contemporary adults, but they also need to be able to ascertain the degree to which a specific teenage patient's view of the world, or stresses, or emotional/behavioral symptoms are different from those of other adolescents. Therefore, it is equally important to address the second question we posed and determine whether there are significant differences between the response patterns obtained from our contemporary normal adolescents and the normative adolescent data provided by Marks and Briggs (1967).

However, appropriate comparisons with the norms provided by Marks and Briggs are difficult to establish. Recall that about 40% of the MMPIs used in their norms were drawn from the samples originally obtained by Hathaway and Monachesi in 1947, 1954, and 1957 (Hathaway & Monachesi, 1953, 1963). Unfortunately, selection criteria were not specified. The remaining portion of the Marks and Briggs data, about 60%, was obtained during the 1964–1965 school year. However, selection procedures were not clearly specified, and apparently random sampling techniques were not used. Furthermore, the sample was comprised of adolescent MMPIs obtained from six states covering a wide geographic area of the United States. Finally, Marks et al. (1974) noted that about 20% of their 14-year-old subjects were actually as young as 9 years and that about 10% of the subjects in their sample of 17-year-olds were actually 18 years of age, although they were living in their parents' home.

With these caveats in mind, Tables 21 and 22 report the values for each MMPI validity and clinical scale, for each age and for the total sample, separately for each sex, so that the values reported for the Marks and Briggs sample can be directly compared with those of our contemporary normal adolescents. Raw scores with and without K correction are presented for completeness. To summarize the tables, overall, 62% of all scale comparisons for our female adolescents in the five different age groups and 48% of all scale comparisons for our normal male adolescents showed statistically significant differences.

To illustrate the differences for one age group, Figure 15 compares the contemporary 14-year-old samples with the norms for the normal 14-year-old adolescents presented by Marks and Briggs. If there were no differences in response pattern, then the mean profile line would fall at the horizontal line on the MMPI profile sheet representing a T score of 50, the mean for the Marks and Briggs sample of 14-year-old adolescents. Also, the line representing the mean + 2 SD would fall at the horizontal line representing a T score of 70, the mean + 2

Table 21

Raw Scores for Basic MMPI Scales, With and Without K Correction, for Contemporary Normal Female Adolescents at Five Ages

Scale[a]	13 yr[b] (n = 136)		14 yr (n = 153)		15 yr (n = 127)		16 yr (n = 138)		17 yr (n = 137)		Total (n = 691)	
	Mean	SD	Mean	SD	Mean	SD	Mean	SD	Mean	SD	Mean	SD
L	2.9***	1.5	3.0***	2.0	2.5***	1.6	2.3***	1.5	2.7***	1.4	2.7	1.6
F	7.5***	4.9	6.9**	4.8	6.8	5.5	7.6	5.4	5.8**	4.6	6.9	5.1
K	11.4***	4.4	12.3**	4.8	11.6***	4.6	11.1***	4.2	12.3	4.6	11.8	4.5
1 (Hs)	6.4*	3.8	6.0	4.2	6.9*	5.4	7.7*	5.5	6.3**	4.3	6.6	4.7
1 + 0.5K[c]	12.3	3.5	12.4	3.9	13.0	4.6	13.5	4.9	12.7	3.9	12.8	4.2
2 (D)	19.3	4.6	19.0	4.9	19.2	5.2	21.0	5.7	18.9***	4.7	19.5	5.1
3 (Hy)	19.9	4.7	20.2	4.3	20.7	4.8	21.1	5.1	20.9	4.7	20.5	4.7
4 (Pd)	18.3***	5.0	18.6***	5.2	19.1**	5.7	19.8***	5.8	18.5	4.9	18.9	5.3
4 + 0.4K[c]	22.9	4.5	23.5	4.8	23.8	5.1	24.3	5.3	23.5	4.5	23.6	4.8
5 (Mf)	35.1	4.5	35.4	4.7	36.3***	4.6	36.7***	4.4	36.9***	4.1	36.1	4.5
6 (Pa)	10.5	3.4	11.2	4.0	11.4	3.9	11.8*	4.2	11.1*	3.4	11.2	3.8
7 (Pt)	17.9***	8.1	17.2**	8.1	19.1***	9.1	20.3***	8.8	17.1	7.5	18.3	8.4
7 + 1.0K[c]	29.3	5.6	29.4	5.8	30.7	6.3	31.4	6.5	29.4	5.1	30.0	5.9
8 (Sc)	19.9***	10.1	19.5***	10.3	20.6***	10.8	21.5***	11.4	16.7	9.2	19.6	10.5
8 + 1.0K[c]	31.3	7.8	31.8	8.1	32.3	7.9	32.6	9.1	29.0	7.0	31.4	8.1
9 (Ma)	20.1***	5.2	20.5***	5.2	21.2***	4.9	20.7***	5.2	19.5***	5.0	20.4	5.1
9 + 0.2K[c]	22.4	4.8	23.0	5.0	23.5	4.6	22.9	5.0	21.9	4.7	22.7	4.8
0 (Si)	30.0	7.3	28.5	8.4	28.5	8.9	30.9	9.1	26.8***	8.3	28.9	8.5

Note. Notations of significance refer to comparisons with norms of Marks and Briggs (1967). No comparisons were made on the "Total" column or on scales with K correction.

[a]See text for explanation of validity and clinical scales.

[b]Specific norms for age 13 years were not available in data of Marks and Briggs (1967); they were presented simply for age 14 years or younger.

[c]Marks and Briggs (1967) did not provide K-corrected scores, but they are presented here for those who want to plot the profile in accordance with the suggestion of Hathaway and Monachesi (1963).

*$0.01 < p \leq 0.05$. **$0.001 < p \leq 0.01$. ***$p \leq 0.001$.

Note. From Colligan, R. C., & Offord, K. P. (1989). The aging MMPI: Contemporary norms for contemporary teenagers. Mayo Clinic Proceedings, 64, 3-27. By permission of Mayo Foundation.

SD for the 14-year-old adolescent sample reported by Hathaway and Briggs. Following the convention espoused by Marks et al. (1974), the T scores for these profiles are based on raw scores without K correction. The mean profiles for each age group from 13 through 17 years also are presented in Appendix E, using the norms provided by Marks and Briggs for each age and sex. Another perspective on the relative changes in contemporary adolescent MMPI response patterns is illustrated in Figure 16. It summarizes the mean profile from the total sample of contemporary normal adolescents and the total sample of adolescents used for the Marks and Briggs norms and places them on a common metric, the contemporary adult norms, using scores without K correction.

To summarize the clinical implication of the differences between the Marks and Briggs norms and the contemporary MMPI response patterns, it appears that today's adolescents are more assertive, adventurous, and desirous of independence than adolescents from 1947, 1954, 1957, and 1964–1965, the years during which the Marks and Briggs data were obtained. However, there are also indications of increased difficulty in attaining interpersonal intimacy, perhaps because of the greater degree of sensitivity or cautiousness in relating to others,

Table 22

Raw Scores for Basic MMPI Scales, With and Without K Correction, for Contemporary Normal Male Adolescents at Five Ages

Scale[a]	13 yr[b] (n = 112) Mean	SD	14 yr (n = 147) Mean	SD	15 yr (n = 130) Mean	SD	16 yr (n = 122) Mean	SD	17 yr (n = 113) Mean	SD	Total (n = 624) Mean	SD
L	3.2*	1.8	3.2*	2.1	2.8***	1.7	3.1***	2.0	3.0***	1.8	3.1	1.9
F	7.5	4.6	8.8**	5.6	7.1	5.4	8.3	5.7	7.0*	4.9	7.8	5.3
K	12.4	5.0	11.3***	4.8	12.1*	5.0	12.1*	4.6	12.4	4.9	12.0	4.9
1 (Hs)	5.9	4.4	6.3**	3.9	5.6	3.9	6.6	3.9	5.4	4.0	6.0	4.0
1 + 0.5K[c]	12.4	3.9	12.2	3.6	12.0	3.5	12.9	4.0	11.8	3.9	12.3	3.7
2 (D)	18.3	5.2	18.3	4.6	17.8	4.5	18.2	4.6	17.0***	4.8	17.9	4.7
3 (Hy)	17.9	4.3	18.2	4.5	18.2	4.5	18.8	4.5	19.0	5.0	18.4	4.5
4 (Pd)	18.4	4.9	19.9***	5.5	18.9	5.5	19.5*	5.0	18.3	5.0	19.1	5.2
4 + 0.4K[c]	23.4	4.5	24.5	5.2	23.8	5.2	24.3	4.8	23.2	5.0	23.9	5.0
5 (Mf)	22.9***	5.0	23.3***	4.4	23.7***	4.8	23.9***	5.2	23.8***	4.9	23.5	4.8
6 (Pa)	10.9	3.9	11.2*	4.7	11.2	3.5	11.5	3.6	11.1	4.1	11.2	4.0
7 (Pt)	15.0	8.0	16.9***	8.4	15.2	7.8	17.1***	7.7	14.9	8.2	15.9	8.1
7 + 1.0K[c]	27.4	5.2	28.2	5.7	27.3	5.2	29.2	5.5	27.3	5.8	27.9	5.5
8 (Sc)	18.7*	10.5	20.6***	11.1	18.2	9.5	20.5**	10.4	16.9	10.0	19.1	10.4
8 + 1.0K[c]	31.1	7.5	31.9	8.6	30.?	7.3	32.6	8.3	29.3	8.1	31.1	8.1
9 (Ma)	20.3***	4.8	21.1***	5.9	20.2**?	4.4	21.5***	4.3	20.7***	4.5	20.8	4.9
9 + 0.2K[c]	22.8	4.5	23.4	5.5	22.6	4.0	24.0	4.0	23.2	4.1	23.2	4.5
0 (Si)	29.3	8.3	30.0	8.8	27.6	9.0	28.7	8.2	25.7***	8.7	28.3	8.7

Note. Notations of significance refer to comparisons with norms of Marks and Briggs (1967). No comparisons were made on the "Total" column or on scales with K correction.

[a]See text for explanation of validity and clinical scales.

[b]Specific norms for age 13 years were not available in data of Marks and Briggs (1967); they were presented simply for age 14 years or younger.

[c]Marks and Briggs (1967) did not provide K-corrected scores, but they are presented here for those who want to plot the profile in accordance with the suggestion of Hathaway and Monachesi (1963).

*$0.01 < p \leq 0.05$. **$0.001 < p \leq 0.01$. ***$p \leq 0.001$.

Note. From Colligan, R. C., & Offord, K. P. (1989). The aging MMPI: Contemporary norms for contemporary teenagers. Mayo Clinic Proceedings, 64, 3-27. By permission of Mayo Foundation.

as suggested by the profile, even though general expressions of interest in social interaction have remained stable.

AGE-RELATED MMPI CHANGES AMONG CONTEMPORARY ADOLESCENTS

In response to the first two questions posed earlier—regarding contemporary adolescent response patterns in comparison with adolescents and adults of the past—the data reported thus far clearly support the need for developing new MMPI norms for contemporary adolescents. However, Marks and Briggs (1967, 1987) developed their tables to include four age groups: ages 14 years and younger, 15, 16, and 17.[14]

The determination of whether age-specific norms were desirable or whether they were truly needed required a two-stage evaluation strategy. First, the tabular

[14]However, Marks et al. (1974) stated "ages 17 and 18" (pp. 158, 162).

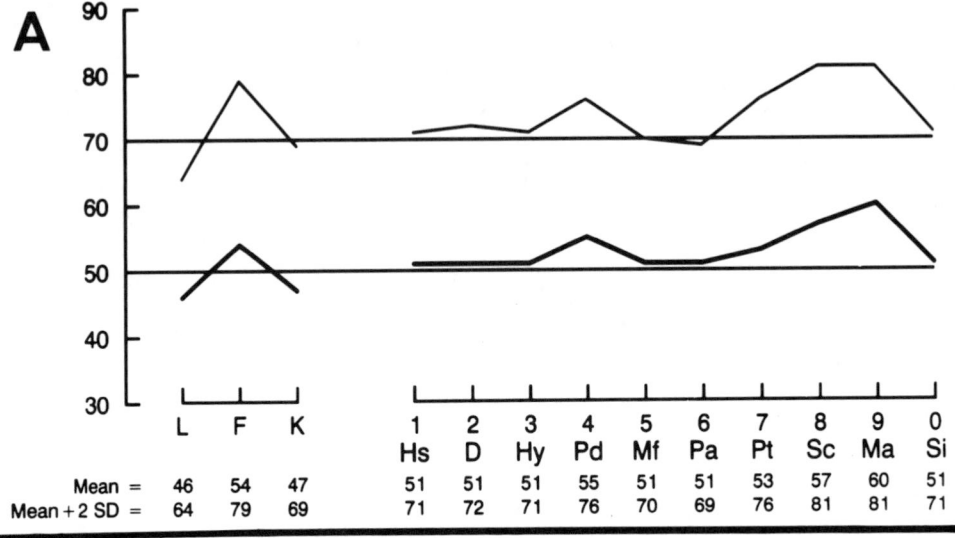

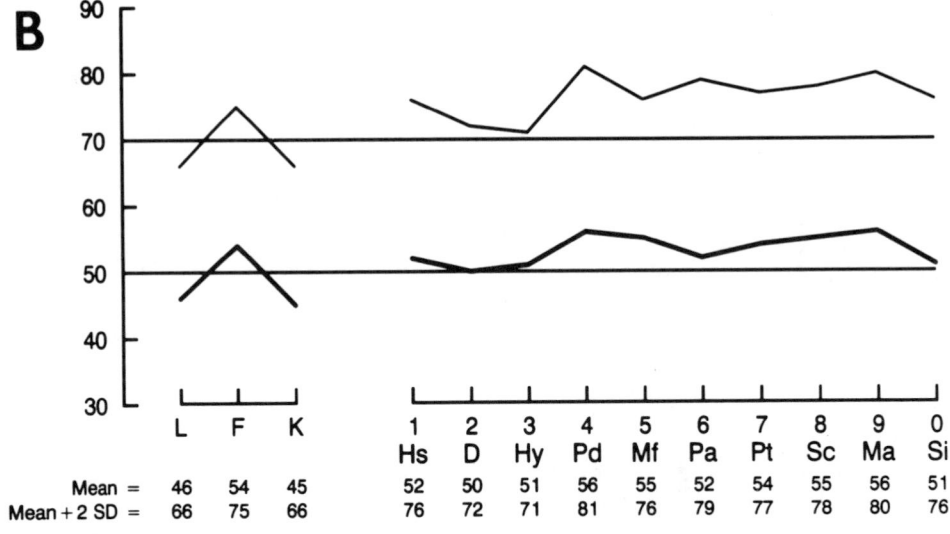

Figure 15.   Mean and mean + 2 SD MMPI profiles for contemporary normal adolescents 14 years of age, using the Marks and Briggs norms (1967) for adolescents of the same age and scores without K correction. A, Female subjects (n = 153). B, Male subjects (n = 147). *Note.* From Colligan, R. C., & Offord, K. P. (1989). The aging MMPI: Contemporary norms for contemporary teenagers. *Mayo Clinic Proceedings, 64,* 3–27. By permission of Mayo Foundation.

data provided by Marks et al. (1974, pp. 135, 136) needed to be reanalyzed to determine whether statistically significant and clinically relevant age-related changes were evident. Second, this analytic procedure also needed to be applied to the data from our contemporary sample of normal adolescents.

Reanalysis of Marks and Briggs Data

A three-step reanalysis of the Marks and Briggs data was undertaken to determine whether there was compelling evidence for the development of age-specific adolescent norms.

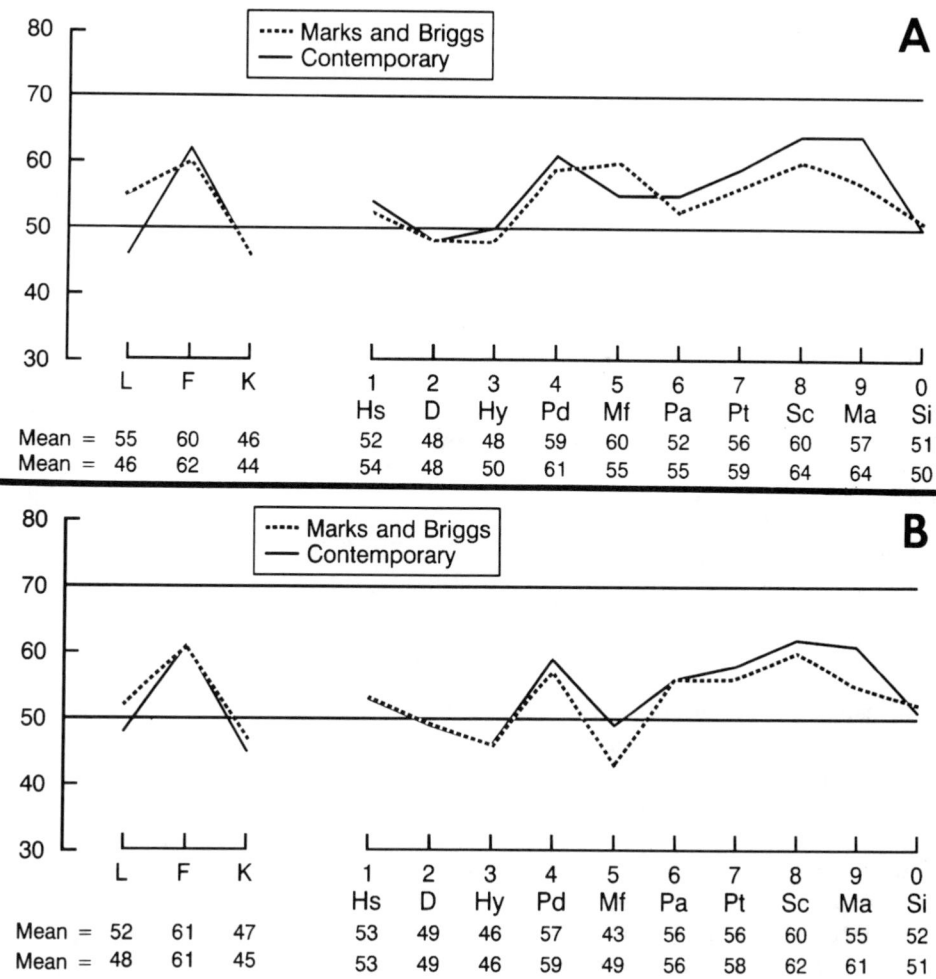

Mean = 55 60 46   52 48 48 59 60 52 56 60 57 51
Mean = 46 62 44   54 48 50 61 55 55 59 64 64 50

Mean = 52 61 47   53 49 46 57 43 56 56 60 55 52
Mean = 48 61 45   53 49 46 59 49 56 58 62 61 51

Figure 16. Mean MMPI profiles for normal adolescents ages 9 through 18 years in Marks and Briggs sample (n = 854 female and 952 male subjects) and for contemporary normal adolescents ages 13 through 17 years (n = 691 female and 624 male subjects), using contemporary adult norms and scores without K correction. A, Female subjects. B, Male subjects.

The first step in the reanalysis process determined whether there were significant variations in mean scores across age in the Marks and Briggs sample, separately for each sex. Therefore, the mean raw score values for each validity and clinical scale over the four age groups, separately for each sex, were tabulated. Next, we computed the P value from a one-way analysis of variance, testing the null hypothesis of equality of the age-group means separately for each sex. The results of this analysis are provided in Tables 23 and 24.

Examination of the data for the female adolescents in the Marks and Briggs sample (Table 23) shows that the change in means of one of the validity scales was not significant (scale K) over the four age groups and that only two of the clinical scales (scale 6, Pa; scale 9, Ma) showed no significant age-related change. Among the validity scales for the boys (Table 24), just as for the girls, scale K showed no

Table 23

Variations in Mean MMPI Raw Scores Across Four Age Groups for Female Adolescents
in Marks and Briggs Sample

| Scale | Mean raw score[a] | | Difference | $F(3,850)$[b] | p value[c] |
	Largest	Smallest			
L	5.1	4.0	1.1	8.9	<0.001
F	7.2	5.5	1.7	6.3	<0.001
K	13.5	12.6	0.9	1.7	NS
1 (Hs)	8.0	5.5	2.5	11.4	<0.001
2 (D)	21.2	18.5	2.7	13.9	<0.001
3 (Hy)	21.4	19.6	1.8	4.4	0.005
4 (Pd)	18.4	16.6	1.8	5.4	0.001
5 (Mf)	35.2	33.5	1.7	5.3	0.001
6 (Pa)	10.9	10.1	0.8	0.9	NS
7 (Pt)	16.8	14.9	1.9	3.6	0.013
8 (Sc)	17.6	14.5	3.1	4.6	0.003
9 (Ma)	17.0	16.2	0.8	1.4	NS
0 (Si)	32.0	28.6	3.4	10.2	<0.001

[a]Largest and smallest over the four age groups.

[b]From one-way analysis of variance testing the simultaneous equality of the means in all four age groups.

[c]Associated two-tailed p value; values were not significant (NS) if $p > 0.05$.

Note. Data from Marks et al. (1974), pp. 135-136, Tables 1 and 2.

significant age-related change, and 7 of the 10 clinical scales showed no significant age-related change. These included scales 1 (Hs), 2 (D), 5 (Mf), 7 (Pt), 8 (Sc), 9 (Ma), and 0 (Si). For scales showing no significant changes, there was no linear relationship nor any other relationship of significance.

Thus, the answer to the initial reanalysis question—whether the means of the validity and clinical scales vary across age and sex in the Marks and Briggs sample—was yes, in general, for the girls and no, in general, for the boys.

The second step in the reanalysis determined whether there were rank-order or linear relationships that could statistically account for the variation among the mean raw scores on the validity and clinical scales. There were 10 such scales among the 13 basic validity and clinical scales for the girls and 5 for the boys. The scales that showed no significant age-related changes based on the results of analysis of variance can be dismissed from consideration, because it has already been determined that they carry no such age relationship of significance; nevertheless, for completeness, data regarding these scales will be included.

For the scales showing significant age-related mean differences according to the results of the analysis of variance, it is important to determine whether systematic rank or linear trends might explain the variation among means.

Because we were using summary data and did not have the individual values available for each subject in the study, it was necessary to use linear correlations between age and mean raw score. Although this method is certainly satisfactory, given the preliminary evaluation by analysis of variance, use of rank correlations with exact ages would have been more sensitive.

Table 25 provides the linear correlations between the raw scores without K correction and age among the Marks and Briggs normal adolescents, separately for each sex. Levels of statistical significance for correlation based on samples of this size are provided in the footnote.

Table 24

Variations in Mean MMPI Raw Scores Across Four Age Groups for Male Adolescents in Marks and Briggs Sample

Scale	Mean raw score[a]		Difference	$F(3,948)$[b]	p value[c]
	Largest	Smallest			
L	4.8	3.7	1.1	9.7	<0.001
F	8.5	7.2	1.3	2.8	0.039
K	13.5	13.2	0.3	0.2	NS
1 (Hs)	5.9	5.3	0.6	1.4	NS
2 (D)	19.1	17.9	1.2	2.3	NS
3 (Hy)	19.3	17.5	1.8	5.3	0.001
4 (Pd)	18.9	17.6	1.3	3.1	0.026
5 (Mf)	21.3	20.8	0.5	0.7	NS
6 (Pa)	11.5	10.3	1.2	3.1	0.026
7 (Pt)	14.9	14.4	0.5	0.2	NS
8 (Sc)	17.8	16.4	1.4	0.9	NS
9 (Ma)	18.5	17.7	0.8	1.4	NS
0 (Si)	29.5	28.9	0.6	0.4	NS

[a]Largest and smallest over the four age groups.
[b]From one-way analysis of variance testing the simultaneous equality of the means in all four age groups.
[c]Associated two-tailed p value; values were not significant (NS) if $p > 0.05$.
Note. Data from Marks et al. (1974), pp. 135-136, Tables 1 and 2.

Table 25

Linear Correlations Between MMPI Raw Scores Without K Correction and Age Among Normal Adolescents in Marks and Briggs Sample

Scale	Females (n = 854)		Males (n = 952)	
	r[a]	r^2	r[a]	r^2
L	0.17	0.03	0.17	0.03
F	0.15	0.02	0.08	0.01
K	-0.07	0.01	0.02	<0.01
1 (Hs)	0.19	0.04	0.06	<0.01
2 (D)	0.21	0.05	0.08	0.01
3 (Hy)	0.12	0.01	0.12	0.01
4 (Pd)	0.13	0.02	0.09	0.01
5 (Mf)	-0.13	0.02	-0.02	<0.01
6 (Pa)	-0.004	<0.01	0.03	<0.01
7 (Pt)	0.11	0.01	0.02	<0.01
8 (Sc)	0.13	0.02	0.05	<0.01
9 (Ma)	<0.01	<0.01	0.04	<0.01
0 (Si)	0.17	0.03	0.01	<0.01

[a]For samples of this size, an r value of 0.09 is significant at $p = 0.05$ and an r value of 0.12 is significant at $p = 0.01$.

However, of greatest importance is the interpretation of the correlation. The second column in Table 25 (r^2) indicates the proportion of variance that is accounted for by a linear trend on age for each of the clinical and validity scales.

The third and final step in our reanalysis of the Marks and Briggs data was to determine whether the relationship between age and scale score was clinically relevant, once it had been determined that such a relationship could not be attributed to chance variation. To assess the practical, clinical significance of such relationships, one can interpret the squared correlation coefficient (r^2) multiplied by 100 as the percentage of variation in the raw score about its mean that is explained by age. It has been our experience that, if 10% or less of the variation cannot be explained by an independent factor, such as age in this case, then there is little utility in using that explanatory factor clinically, or making tables specific to different levels of the explanatory factor (in this situation for example, age). Therefore, as a rule of thumb, it was decided in advance that, if more than 10% of the variance was accounted for by the relationship with age, this finding would be a strong argument for the development of an age-specific normative table for scales so affected.

However, a review of the Marks and Briggs values for the girls in Table 25 indicates that none of the scales approached this level; one scale (2, D, Depression) had a correlation with age ($r = 0.21$) that accounted for 5% of the variance in the scores. For the boys, as might have been anticipated from the results of the analysis of variance and the small size of the correlations, none of the clinical scales had values accounting for more than 1% of the variance by age; the highest value occurred among the validity scales (scale L, $r = 0.17$) and accounted for only 3% of the variance, the same as that noted for the girls on scale L.

As a result of the reanalysis of the data presented by Marks and Briggs, we concluded that there was no compelling evidence that could be used as a precedent for developing age-specific norms. However, the same analyses needed to be applied to the contemporary normal sample of adolescents to determine whether there was sufficient evidence for age-related changes in scale scores to warrant the development of separate and specific normative tables for each age (and sex), as done by Marks and Briggs (1967).

Analysis of Relationships Between Scale Scores and Age in the Contemporary Normal Adolescent Sample

It was unnecessary to evaluate the changes in mean score by age group across our five age groups using the analysis of variance procedure used for the Marks and Briggs sample. Because we had the raw scale score data available for each participating subject, we were able to proceed directly to the correlation analysis.

Therefore, Table 26 presents the rank correlation between raw scores without K correction and age among the members of our normal adolescent sample, separately by sex.

For completeness, linear correlations were also calculated (Table 27) to make it easier for the reader to make direct comparisons between the correlational results presented for the Marks and Briggs sample and the values obtained from our contemporary normal adolescents.

When the rank-correlation relationships between age and scale scores among our normal adolescents were evaluated, no dramatic age-related changes could be found. As with the Marks and Briggs data, no age relationships with any clinical or validity scale approached 10%. Indeed, for the girls the largest rank correlation ($r = 0.14$; scale 5, Mf) explained only 2% of the variance, whereas for the boys the

Table 26

Rank Correlations Between MMPI Raw Scores Without K Correction
and Age Among Contemporary Normal Adolescents

Scale	Females (n = 691)		Males (n = 624)	
	r	p value[a]	r	p value[a]
L	-0.08	0.046	-0.04	NS
F	-0.10	0.007	-0.07	NS
K	0.02	NS	0.03	NS
1 (Hs)	0.03	NS	-0.03	NS
2 (D)	0.03	NS	-0.07	NS
3 (Hy)	0.07	NS	0.09	0.027
4 (Pd)	0.05	NS	-0.001	NS
5 (Mf)	0.14	<0.001	0.06	NS
6 (Pa)	0.07	NS	0.04	NS
7 (Pt)	0.03	NS	-0.003	NS
8 (Sc)	-0.06	NS	-0.05	NS
9 (Ma)	-0.02	NS	0.03	NS
0 (Si)	-0.08	0.03	-0.13	0.001

[a]Two-tailed p value from test of the null hypothesis that the population rank correlation is zero; values were noted as not significant (NS) if $p > 0.05$.

Table 27

Linear Correlations Between MMPI Raw Scores Without K Correction and Age Among
Contemporary Normal Adolescents

Scale	Females (n = 691)			Males (n = 624)		
	r	r^2	p value[a]	r	r^2	p value[a]
L	-0.08	<0.01	0.03	-0.03	<0.01	NS
F	-0.09	<0.01	NS	-0.04	<0.01	NS
K	0.02	<0.01	NS	0.03	<0.01	NS
1 (Hs)	0.03	<0.01	NS	-0.03	<0.01	NS
2 (D)	0.03	<0.01	NS	-0.08	<0.01	0.04
3 (Hy)	0.08	<0.01	0.03	0.08	<0.01	0.04
4 (Pd)	0.04	<0.01	NS	-0.02	<0.01	NS
5 (Mf)	0.15	0.02	<0.001	0.07	<0.01	NS
6 (Pa)	0.07	<0.01	NS	0.04	<0.01	NS
7 (Pt)	0.03	<0.01	NS	-0.001	<0.01	NS
8 (Sc)	-0.06	<0.01	NS	-0.04	<0.01	NS
9 (Ma)	-0.03	<0.01	NS	0.03	<0.01	NS
0 (Si)	-0.07	<0.01	0.05	-0.14	0.02	0.001

[a]Two-tailed p value from the test of the null hypothesis that the population linear correlation is zero; values were noted as not significant (NS) if $p > 0.05$.

largest rank value ($r = -0.13$; scale 0, Si) also accounted for only 2% of the variance related to age (Tables 26 and 27).

Among our normal adolescent girls, validity scales L and F showed a statistically significant inverse rank relationship with age; this was likely a reflection of their gradually attaining an adult reporting style. Among the clinical scales, scores on scale 5 (Mf) increased significantly with age ($p \leq 0.001$), probably because of a broadening range of interests with increasing age and education. Scores on 0 (Si) showed a slight decrease with age decrease with age (p = 0.03), suggesting a greater interest in social contact with increasing age (Table 26).

Among our normal male adolescents, no statistically significant age-related changes were evident among the validity scales. The declining scores on scale 0 (Si), similar to the trend noted among the girls, suggest significantly increasing interest in social contacts and less shyness with increasing age (p = 0.001). In addition, there was a tendency for scores on scale 3 (Hy) to increase with age (p = 0.027), probably reflecting a differential response to the social items of the scale and a gradual approximation of adult reporting style at the older ages (Table 26).

Summary of Analyses of Age-Related Changes

Although the tests of statistical significance and the clinical relevance of age-related changes among our normal adult sample were remarkable, it should be kept in mind that the age range under consideration among members of the adult group extended from age 18 through 99 years for women and age 18 through 85 years for men. Needless to say, given the restricted age range among the members of our contemporary normal sample of adolescents—a 5-year span from 13 through 17 years—it is not surprising that no remarkable changes were evident.

The clinical significance of the correlations representing age-related changes among normal adolescents had little effect on profile configuration because of the small proportion of variance accounted for by age. Therefore, for this reason it was not necessary to establish separate normative tables for each age level, as was done in the past. Instead, the total sample was used to develop general norms for adolescents, although separately for each sex.

DEVELOPMENT OF NEW MMPI NORMS FOR ADOLESCENTS

For interpretation of the raw scores that a patient has earned on the scales of the MMPI, it is useful to transform them into standard units. These transformed scores allow meaningful comparisons to be made across the different scales of the MMPI. Ideally, using transformed scores, the same standard score value could reflect the same degree of deviation from the mean, in standardized units, regardless of the MMPI scale under consideration. The original standard scores, or T scores, of the MMPI are frequently discussed and interpreted as if they were based on the normal curve. However, this is not the case. The T scores that were developed and used for the original MMPI are not T scores by the usual statistical definition. Rather, according to the early manual for the MMPI (Hathaway & McKinley, 1943), standard score equivalents were obtained from the raw scores on the 10 basic clinical scales and were calculated by the following linear transformation:

$$T = 50 + 10 (x_i - \bar{x})/s,$$

in which x_i is the raw score to be transformed, $\bar{x}$ is the mean for the normative sample, and s is the standard deviation of the normative sample. It is important to recall that the standard scores for scales ?/Q, L, and F were assigned arbitrarily.

A T score of 70 traditionally has been viewed as a point of considerable significance to clinicians, because it represents a score falling 2 SD from the mean. However, a T score of 70 that has been obtained from a linear transformation may not represent the 97.7 percentile in a skewed or other nongaussian distribution. Thus, equivalent T-score values may actually represent markedly different percentiles when the raw scores underlying the T scores are not normally distributed. MMPI scales are often discussed and treated by clinicians as though the raw score values were normally distributed, and, regardless of the scale being considered, it is anticipated that the person who received a T score of 70 or above would fall in the 2.3% of the population having atypical scores with regard to deviation from the mean of that MMPI scale. However, when the Hathaway-Briggs data were carefully evaluated to determine the nature of the shape of the distribution of MMPI raw scores, we found this was not so (Colligan et al., 1980).

More specifically, that study assessed the degree of skewness and kurtosis among the raw scores on the various scales of the MMPI. *Skewness* refers to the degree of asymmetry about the mean in the distribution of scores. It may be positive, with the tail of the distribution extending out to the right, or negative, with the tail of the distribution extending to the left. *Kurtosis* is an indication of the degree of flatness or spikiness in the distribution of scores. Analysis of the Hathaway-Briggs data revealed that nearly all of the scales, for both men and women, showed significant skewness to the right, most apparent on scales 1 (Hs), 2 (D), 6 (Pa), 7 (Pt), and 8 (Sc).

In that study, the values of the observed percentiles from the Hathaway-Briggs data were compared with the parametric estimates that were based on the assumption of normality. The assumption that 2.3% of the scores would fall above a T score of 70 was not tenable, as indicated by the discrepancy between the observed percentage above 70 and the expected value of 2.3% (Table 28). Thus, a T score value of 70, a point of considerable clinical significance, does not have equivalent meaning across MMPI scales, and one could be misled into overestimating the degree of psychopathology represented by the score. In addition, a review of the discrepant values also suggests that for the same reason, assignment of profile code types also may be in error.

The findings reported (Table 28) are of clinical as well as statistical significance and suggest that, for females, scales 1 (Hs), 2 (D), 7 (Pt), 8 (Sc), and 9 (Ma) should probably be interpreted more conservatively by clinicians using the original MMPI norms. For men, similar consideration was suggested for scales 1 (Hs), 2 (D), 4 (Pd), 7 (Pt), 8 (Sc), and 9 (Ma).

Furthermore, some computerized interpretive systems are programmed to begin printing a different set of interpretive statements at a T score of 70, a traditional point of clinical significance. Because T scores are dealt with as intergers, this method results in a significant increase in the number of people who receive such statements compared with those who would receive them if the criterion of a T score greater than 70 was used. More specifically, with this procedure, the increase is approximately two percentage points on scales 1 (Hs) and 3 (Hy), and one percentage point on scale 7 (Pt) for women. For men, the increase is approximately one percentage point on scale 7 (Pt).

Thus, the traditional linear transformation of raw scores to standard scores preserves the skewness in the underlying distribution of raw scores. This fact

Table 28
Percentage of Cases With T Scores of More Than 70 in the Hathaway-Briggs Sample

MMPI scale	Percentage of cases with T score > 70	
	Females	Males
1 (Hs)	5.1	7.6
2 (D)	7.3	8.0
3 (Hy)	2.2	3.6
4 (Pd)	3.2	5.4
6 (Pa)	3.8	4.0
7 (Pt)	5.4	5.4
8 (Sc)	4.8	6.3
9 (Ma)	4.8	6.3

Note. Some clinicians, and also some automated systems, make interpretive statements starting at a T score of 70, which results in a significant increase in the number of people who receive such a statement compared with the number who would receive the statement if the criterion of T score *greater than 70* was used. For women, this increase is approximately two percentage points on scales 1 (Hs) and 3 (Hy), and one percentage point on scale 7 (Pt); for males, the difference is approximately one percentage point on scale 7 (Pt).

Note. From Colligan, R. C., Osborne, D., & Offord, K. P. (1980). Linear transformation and the interpretation of MMPI T scores. *Journal of Clinical Psychology, 36,* 162-165. By permission of Clinical Psychology Publishing Company.

contributes to the spikiness of elevated MMPI profiles as well as to the high frequency of MMPI T scores more than 70 and the virtual lack of an equal number of scores deviating to a comparable degree, but in the opposite direction (that is, T scores less than 30).

Normalizing transformations corrects for this underlying skewness and makes the assumption of normality more tenable. Traditionally, this has involved determining the proportion of cases that exceed a given value, plus half of those for that value, and then entering the resulting proportions in a table of the normal curve to find the corresponding Z values.

Aside from correcting the problems associated with linear transformations, what would be the impact of normalized standard scores on MMPI profiles? A review of the MMPI literature found no thorough or systematic evaluation of the changes that might accrue from normalized T scores on MMPI profile configurations, code types, or clinical interpretation.

A tangential study by Weisgerber (1965) used the MMPI to predict dropouts from male applicants to a religious order. Results found that normalized T scores gave essentially the same results as linear T scores but, not surprisingly, that the use of normalized T scores slightly reduced the degree and incidence of deviant profiles.

Unfortunately, Weisgerber's (1965) normalization procedures were not described so the procedure could not be evaluated. (Helmes & Jackson, 1982, have noted that skewness can be altered significantly, depending on the type of normalization procedure that is applied.)

Graham (1990) also expressed concern about the use of normalized T scores, stating that it would lead to an increased rate of false-negative findings among psychiatric patients. However, the cited research, which "demonstrated" the propensity to underdiagnose, was presented only informally and was never published (Graham & Lilly, 1986).

Our clinical experience in using the contemporary norms with our adult medical outpatients had been encouraging (Colligan, Osborne, Swenson, & Offord, 1985). Nevertheless, our departure from tradition did not go on without notice and controversial comment (Hsu, 1984; Hsu & Betman, 1986). Our further work in responding to these concerns and further evaluation of potential changes in code-type frequencies (Colligan et al., 1984a, 1985), and the positive findings described in patients with chronic pain (Ahles, Yunus, Gaulier, Riley, & Masi, 1986) and also in patients with chronic headache (Ahles & Martin, 1989), paralleled our observations of the new norms in women being evaluated for premenstrual syndrome (Chuong, Colligan, Coulam, & Bergstralh, 1988). However, we have continued to maintain that clinicians should plot the MMPI profiles of their patients using both the old and the contemporary norms, a suggestion also supported by others (Miller & Streiner, 1986).

No published literature could be found with regard to normalizing transformations from raw scores to standard scores for adolescent samples. However, this approach was taken by Gottesman, Hanson, Kroeker, and Briggs (1987) in their reanalysis of the Minnesota statewide sample of ninth-grade students originally gathered by Hathaway and Monachesi (1963). Unfortunately, item-level responses to the MMPI from the adolescents used for the Marks and Briggs norms are not available, so we were unable to analyze the degree of skewness and kurtosis among the raw score distributions. However, given the information from Hathaway and Monachesi's research, the degree of skewness among adolescents is likely to be even greater than that within adult samples.

To summarize, from historical review and the results obtained from reanalyzing the Hathaway-Briggs adult data, the following are serious shortcomings in the traditional manner in which MMPI standard scores have been derived, for both adults and adolescents.

1. Scores on all of the basic validity and clinical scales are significantly skewed.
2. The traditional linear transformation of the raw scores to T scores maintains the underlying skewness.
3. When such linear transformations are used, a T score of 70 may represent varying percentiles across the 13 basic MMPI scales, and it is often very different from the expected value of the 97.7 percentile.
4. For the preceding reasons, interpretive statements generated by computer programs may be inaccurate and overstate symptoms or psychopathologic traits.
5. Finally, for the same reason, inaccurate code types may be inadvertently assigned because of the artifact associated with skewness in the distribution of raw scores.

Therefore, just as with the adult study, normalizing procedures were carried out to transform the raw scores, obtained from our adolescent normative sample, to T score tables to be used in plotting adolescent MMPI profiles. This approach also helps to deal with the basic problem encountered when a scale derived from a normal population is used to assess the responses of an atypical sample (for example, psychiatric patients). Although only a few cases had high scores in our normal sample, T scores above 100 are probably meaningful when compared with less elevated scores. Hence, just as with our adult sample, it seemed important to calculate and tabulate normalized T scores for such high raw score values that might be expected from mental health referrals. Such T-score values would be indexed to the responses of our contemporary normal adolescents. This procedure allows the expression of T scores over the entire range of possible raw scores (for example, T scores of 120 or higher), as deviations from the mean for the normal adolescents, in standard deviation units. The standard deviation unit was that obtained from our normal adolescent sample. Therefore, the raw scores from our total adolescent sample were transformed using the Box-Cox power transformation techniques (Box & Cox, 1964). The specific steps undertaken for this procedure have been reported previously (Colligan et al., 1983, 1989).

NEW PROCEDURES FOR TRANSFORMATION OF RAW SCORES TO T SCORES

Raw score transformations were selected that would yield transformed values having a gaussian distribution and allow us to express, as deviations from the mean of the normal sample of adolescents, raw scores that clinicians could expect to be obtained from psychiatric samples, which would be much higher than the ones observed in our normal sample of adolescents. In a normal sample (using $\bar{x}$ = 50, SD = 10), there will rarely be a T score more than 80 (that is, 3 SD or more above the mean) or less than 20 (that is, 3 SD below the mean). For this reason, transformations making use of percentile ranks alone are of limited value when applied to clinical samples that might produce extremely deviant scores.

Tables 29 and 30 summarize the transformations that were used as well as the means and standard deviations of the transformed raw scores. Skewness, if any, is minimal. The calculation of the new normalized T score values is illustrated in the footnotes of these tables. The percentages of cases with normalized T score values of 30 or less and with scores of 70 or more are presented. There is good agreement between the observed and the expected values of 2.3% for T scores of 70 or more.

How will these new transformation procedures and new T-score tables affect the base rate frequency of single and two-point code types? It is likely that there will be changes in the typical appearance and the configuration of the profile, similar to the changes noted when the new normative tables were developed from the contemporary adult sample. However, our investigation of these changes among adult profiles showed them to be easily assimilated by clinicians. First, the general elevation of the adult profile was lowered from 3 to 5 T-score points, depending on the specific scale and the original elevation of the profile; second, there were some changes in code types, although most remained the same, but at a somewhat lower level of elevation. Of the changes in code type, most were represented by a change in the order of the high-point codes (for example, a code originally described as 1-3 might be described as a 3-1 using the contemporary

Table 29

Transformations and Summary Statistics for Female Adolescents (n = 691)

MMPI scale	Transformation[a]			Skewness[b] coefficient	Percentage with T[c]	
(X)	(Y)	$\bar{Y}$	SD of Y	for Y	≤ 30	≥ 70
L	$Y = \sqrt{X}$	1.537	0.564	-0.57***	5.2	1.0
F	$Y = \log_{10}(X + 1)$	0.814	0.281	-0.35***	2.0	1.3
K	$Y = \sqrt{X}$	3.363	0.673	-0.08	2.5	1.3
1 (Hs) + .5K	$Y = \log_{10}(X + 1)$	1.119	0.133	-0.20*	3.8	1.6
2 (D)	$Y = \log_{10}(X + 1)$	1.297	0.109	-0.21*	2.2	2.0
3 (Hy)	$Y = \sqrt{X}$	4.502	0.527	-0.20*	2.3	2.0
4 (Pd) + .4K	$Y = \sqrt{X}$	4.831	0.495	0.14	1.2	3.0
5 (Mf)	$Y = X$	36.056	4.513	-0.13	1.3	3.0
6 (Pa)	$Y = \sqrt{X}$	3.300	0.562	0.20*	1.4	3.3
7 (Pt) + 1K	$Y = \log_{10}(X + 1)$	1.484	0.082	0.00	1.7	2.3
8 (Sc) + 1K	$Y = \log_{10}(X + 1)$	1.498	0.105	0.21*	1.7	3.5
9 (Ma) + .2K	$Y = \sqrt{X}$	4.741	0.511	-0.09	1.6	1.4
0 (Si)	$Y = \sqrt{X}$	5.317	0.806	-0.16	2.3	1.4
1 (Hs)	$Y = \sqrt{X}$	2.391	0.961	-0.11	3.5	2.0
4 (Pd)	$Y = \log_{10}(X + 1)$	1.283	0.118	-0.13	2.7	1.7
7 (Pt)	$Y = \sqrt{X}$	4.147	1.031	-0.24**	3.5	1.2
8 (Sc)	$Y = \sqrt{X}$	4.266	1.197	0.07	1.6	2.2
9 (Ma)	$Y = \sqrt{X}$	4.479	0.576	-0.13	2.6	1.4

[a]Although considered separately, the transformations selected were the same for female and male subjects except for the scores without K correction on 1) scale 5, which is X for females and $\sqrt{X}$ for males; 2) scale 4, which is $\log_{10}(X + 1)$ for females and $\sqrt{X}$ for males; and 3) scale 9, which is $\sqrt{X}$ for females and X for males.

[b]Skewness coefficient $\dfrac{\Sigma(Y_i - \bar{Y})^3 \div \{n/(n - 1)(n - 2)\}}{\{\Sigma(Y_i - \bar{Y})^2 \div (n - 1)\}^{3/2}}$. Some values are significantly different from what would be expected if the underlying distribution was gaussian: *p ≤ 0.05, **p ≤0.01, ***p ≤0.001.

[c]Adolescent T scores are computed as $\left(\dfrac{Y - \bar{Y}}{SD\ of\ Y}\right) \times 10 + 50$, where Y represents the observed, transformed raw score. For females on scale 5 (Mf), because high scores represent a pattern of feminine interest, the numerator is reversed: $\left(\dfrac{\bar{Y} - Y}{SD\ of\ Y}\right) \times 10 + 50$. For example: female, raw score for scale 3 (Hy) of 25 would correspond to a

$$\text{T score} = \left(\dfrac{\sqrt{25} - 4.502}{0.527}\right) \times 10 + 50 = 59.4 \cong 59.$$

Based on an underlying gaussian distribution, the expected percentage with T scores of 30 or less is 2.3% and the percentage with T scores of 70 or more is also 2.3%

norms). A thorough evaluation of these changes has already been reported (Colligan et al., 1985; Hsu & Betman, 1986), and research on patient populations has been reported also (Ahles et al., 1986; Bornstein, Rosenberger, Harkness-Kling, & Suga, 1989; Miller & Streiner, 1986; Munley & Zarantonello, 1989).

Table 31 lists the percentage of cases among our normal adolescents in which each scale is the highest scale of the profile. In addition, the T scores have been further classified by whether the highest T score value is less than 70 or is 70 or higher.

The T scores in Table 31 are based on raw scores without K correction, whereas

Table 30

Transformations and Summary Statistics for Male Adolescents (n = 624)

MMPI scale	Transformation[a]			Skewness[b] coefficient	Percentage with T[c]	
(X)	(Y)	$\overline{Y}$	SD of Y	for Y	≤ 30	≥ 70
L	$Y = \sqrt{X}$	1.633	0.631	-0.63***	5.8	0.8
F	$Y = \log_{10}(X + 1)$	0.868	0.267	-0.27**	4.6	0.8
K	$Y = \sqrt{X}$	3.390	0.722	-0.15	1.6	1.6
1 (Hs) + .5K	$Y = \log_{10}(X + 1)$	1.105	0.124	-0.21*	3.4	2.1
2 (D)	$Y = \log_{10}(X + 1)$	1.264	0.107	0.03	2.9	2.2
3 (Hy)	$Y = \sqrt{X}$	4.257	0.532	-0.01	2.7	2.4
4 (Pd) + .4K	$Y = \sqrt{X}$	4.859	0.511	0.01	2.7	2.4
5 (Mf)	$Y = \sqrt{X}$	4.824	0.498	0.11	1.4	3.4
6 (Pa)	$Y = \sqrt{X}$	3.289	0.609	-0.12	2.6	2.2
7 (Pt) + 1K	$Y = \log_{10}(X + 1)$	1.453	0.082	-0.05	2.1	1.9
8 (Sc) + 1K	$Y = \log_{10}(X + 1)$	1.493	0.106	0.14	2.2	2.9
9 (Ma) + .2K	$Y = \sqrt{X}$	4.794	0.474	-0.19	2.6	2.6
0 (Si)	$Y = \sqrt{X}$	5.257	0.823	0.03	1.8	2.4
1 (Hs)	$Y = \sqrt{X}$	2.297	0.850	-0.04	2.1	2.2
4 (Pd)	$Y = \sqrt{X}$	4.324	0.603	0.01	1.9	2.1
7 (Pt)	$Y = \sqrt{X}$	3.838	1.078	-0.30**	1.6	0.8
8 (Sc)	$Y = \sqrt{X}$	4.194	1.221	-0.01	2.4	1.4
9 (Ma)	$Y = X$	20.792	4.876	0.09	2.4	2.7

[a]Although considered separately, the transformations selected were the same for female and male subjects except for the scores without K correction on 1) scale 5, which is X for females and $\sqrt{X}$ for males; 2) scale 4, which is $\log_{10}(X + 1)$ for females and $\sqrt{X}$ for males; and 3) scale 9, which is $\sqrt{X}$ for females and X for males.

[b]Skewness coefficient $\dfrac{\Sigma(Y_i - \overline{Y})^3 \div \{n/(n - 1)(n - 2)\}}{\{\Sigma(Y_i - \overline{Y})^2 \div (n - 1)\}^{3/2}}$. Some values are significantly different from what would be expected if the underlying distribution was gaussian: *p ≤ 0.05, **p ≤ 0.01, ***p ≤ 0.001.

[c]Adolescent T scores are computed as $\left(\dfrac{Y - \overline{Y}}{SD \text{ of } Y}\right)$ × 10 + 50, where Y represents the observed, transformed raw score.

Based on an underlying gaussian distribution, the expected percentage with T scores of 30 or less is 2.3% and the percentage with T scores of 70 or more is also 2.3%.

those in Table 32 provide the same information for K-corrected values. The entries are percentages representing the number of cases in each scale category. Each subject's profile enters the table only once. The following sections review the data from these tables in comparison with that in other adolescent normative samples.

High Single-Point Code Types

In this section, a single high-point code will refer to the single scale having the highest value among the 10 basic clinical scales. The data first will be considered based on scores without K correction, following the suggestion of Marks et al. (1974), and then based on scores with K-corrected values, as Hathaway advocated (Hathaway & Monachesi, 1953, 1963).

Table 31

Percentage of Single High-Point Codes in the Contemporary Normal Sample of Adolescents by Normalized T Scores (Without K Correction) of Less Than 70 or of 70 or More

High-point MMPI scale	Females (n = 691)			Males (n = 624)		
	T < 70	T ≥ 70	Total	T < 70	T ≥ 70	Total
1 (Hs)	5.50	0.72	6.22	6.57	1.12	7.69
2 (D)	7.09	1.16	8.25	7.85	0.96	8.81
3 (Hy)	12.88	1.88	14.76	13.62	1.44	15.06
4 (Pd)	6.51	0.58	7.09	8.49	1.60	10.09
5 (Mf)	17.80	2.32	20.12	11.70	2.88	14.58
6 (Pa)	5.64	2.03	7.67	6.09	1.28	7.37
7 (Pt)	4.34	0.00	4.34	4.01	0.32	4.33
8 (Sc)	2.75	0.72	3.47	2.40	0.16	2.56
9 (Ma)	12.88	0.87	13.75	13.14	2.40	15.54
0 (Si)	13.17	1.16	14.33	11.86	2.08	13.94

Table 32

Percentage of Single High-Point Codes in the Contemporary Normal Sample of Adolescents by Normalized T Scores (With K Correction) of Less Than 70 or of 70 or More

High-point MMPI scale	Females (n = 691)			Males (n = 624)		
	T < 70	T ≥ 70	Total	T < 70	T ≥ 70	Total
1 (Hs) + .5K	6.51	0.14	6.66	7.69	0.80	8.49
2 (D)	7.24	1.01	8.25	7.05	1.12	8.17
3 (Hy)	10.42	1.30	11.72	10.10	1.28	11.38
4 (Pd) + .4K	6.95	1.59	8.54	7.69	1.92	9.62
5 (Mf)	16.50	2.46	18.96	11.86	2.88	14.74
6 (Pa)	5.07	1.88	6.95	5.77	1.12	6.89
7 (Pt) + 1K	5.07	0.72	5.79	3.53	0.80	4.33
8 (Sc) + 1K	3.47	1.30	4.78	4.49	0.96	5.45
9 (Ma) + .2K	12.30	1.01	13.31	15.06	1.92	16.99
0 (Si)	13.89	1.16	15.05	11.86	2.08	13.94

Female Adolescents. Examination of the data for normalized T scores without K correction shows that for the girls scale 5 (Mf) was the most frequently occurring single high-point code (20%), followed by scale 3 (Hy; 14.8%), scale 0 (Si; 14%), and scale 9 (Ma; 13.8%).

When K-corrected scores are evaluated, scale 5 (Mf) remains the most frequently occurring code (19%), followed by scale 0 (Si; 15.1%). Neither of these scales uses K correction when it is scored for adults. However, the next two highest scales—9 (Ma; 13.3%) and 3 (Hy; 11.7%)—use K correction when scored for adults.

It should be noted, however, that high single-point code types for these four scales—3 (Hy), 5 (Mf), 9 (Ma), 0 (Si)—occur most frequently regardless of whether raw score values with or without K correction are used; only the order of frequency of occurrence is changed.

A review of the comparable data obtained by Hathaway and Monachesi (that is, using K-corrected raw scores) from their ninth-grade sample (5,207 girls and 4,944 boys) indicates noticeable differences.

In the Hathaway and Monachesi data, scale 4 (Pd) was the single high-point code occurring with the greatest frequency (19.9%), followed by scale 9 (Ma; 17.4%) and scales 5 (Mf) and 0 (Si) (12% each) (Hathaway & Monachesi, 1963). Thus, the two scales with K correction have the highest frequency, followed by two that are not K corrected.

Although the samples are roughly comparable, it should be kept in mind that the Hathaway and Monachesi data had been screened for invalid cases on the basis of scales L and F. Also, the data from Hathaway and Monachesi are based on K-corrected T scores derived from the original adult norms. Furthermore, Hathaway used the convention of requiring a T score of 55 or higher before the profile would receive a code for classification purposes. However, among the samples just reported, only 1.6% of the adolescent girls had profiles without a high-point code defined in that fashion.

Hathaway and Briggs did not report code-type data for their normal samples, so no comparisons can be made with their group.

No other normal adolescent normative data are available for comparative purposes. However, among the female adolescent medical patients studied from 1960 to 1965 by Swenson et al. (1973), a sample in which K-corrected scores and the original adult norms also were used, scale 9 (Ma) occurred most frequently as the single high-point code (21.6%), followed by scales 4 (Pd; 18.3%) and 3 (Hy; 11.2%).

Male Adolescents.   Among the boys, the examination of normalized T-score values without K correction showed that scale 9 (Ma) occurred most frequently (15.5%), but it was closely followed by scale 3 (Hy; 15.1%), scale 5 (Mf; 14.6%), and scale 0 (Si; 13.9%).

When normalized K-corrected T scores were used, scale 9 (Ma) occurred with the greatest frequency (17%); for the girls, scale 9 was the third most frequent high-point code. Among the boys, the second most frequent scale was scale 5 (Mf; 14.7%); scale 5 was the most frequent high point among the profiles for the girls. For the boys, the third most frequent scale was scale 0 (Si; 13.9%), and this scale was the second most frequent among the girls. Finally, the fourth most frequent scale for the boys was scale 3 (Hy; 11.4%); this scale was also the fourth most frequent among the girls.

Thus, the same four scales occurred most frequently as high points in both the female and male samples of contemporary normal adolescents, regardless of whether scores with or without K correction were used.

Among the boys in the ninth-grade Minnesota statewide sample reported by Hathaway and Monachesi (1963), using K-corrected T scores, scale 9 (Ma) was the n.ost frequent (21%), the same scale that was highest among boys in our contemporary normal sample (17%). Scale 8 (Sc; 18.6%) was the second most frequent, followed by scale 4 (Pd; 18.2%) and scale 7 (Pt; a distant 7.7%).

As noted above, Hathaway and Briggs provided no data on high-point codes among their normal adolescents.

Among the male adolescent medical patients (Swenson et al., 1973), scale 9 (Ma) also appeared most frequently (19.8%), just as was noted for the adolescent girls, but the second most frequent point for the boys was scale 1 (Hs; 12.3%), followed by scales 4 (Pd; 12%) and 3 (Hy; 10.7%).

Two-Point Code Types

The frequency with which various two-point codes occurred among the contemporary normal adolescents, with use of the same procedures outlined for classifying each case for the high-point codes, also was evaluated using T scores without K correction. K-corrected values also were calculated so comparisons could be made with the data from Hathaway and Monachesi (1963).

Female Adolescents. When T scores without K correction were used, the 5–9/9–5 two-point code occurred most frequently (8.8%), followed by the 5–0/0–5 (6.5%) and the 0–2/2–0 code-type (5.9%) profiles.

With K-corrected T scores, the code types remained the same. The 5–9/9–5 high-point code occurred most frequently (7.8%), followed by the 5–0/0–5 code (7.4%) and the 0–2/2–0 code (7.0%).

By comparison, in the normal adolescent sample of girls described by Hathaway and Monachesi (1963), in which K-corrected T scores also were used, the 4–9/9–4 code was the most frequent (8.0%), followed by the 8–9/9–8 code (6.4%) and the 5–9/9–5 code (4.9%).

Among the adolescent female medical patients described by Swenson et al. (1973), who also used K-corrected T scores, the 1–3/3–1 code type occurred most frequently (11.5%); this finding was not surprising from a sample of medical referrals. This code was followed by the 4–9/9–4 code (9.8%) and the 8–9/9–8 code (5.6%), and the 4–3/3–4 code followed closely (5.5%).

Marks and Briggs provided no two-point code data for their normal adolescent sample.

Male Adolescents. For the contemporary normal boys, when T scores without K correction were used the 3–5/5–3 code occurred most frequently (7.4%), followed by the 3–6/6–3 profile (6.3%) and the 3–4/4–3 and 4–9/9–4 profile codes (both were 5.8%).

When K-corrected scores were used, the 1–3/3–1 code occurred most frequently (7.7%), followed closely by the 2–0/0–2 code (7.5%) and the 4–9/9–4 code (6.4%).

Among the normal male adolescents described by Hathaway and Monachesi (1963), the 8–9/9–8 code occurred most frequently (10.7%), followed by the 4–9/9–4 code (9.2%) and then the 7–8/8–7 code (8.2%).

For the male adolescent medical patients described by Swenson et al. (1973), the 4–9/9–4 code was the most frequent (8.5%), followed by the 1–3/3–1 code (7.3%) and the 3–9/9–3 code (6.6%).

Three-Point Code Types

Female Adolescents. Among the contemporary normal adolescent girls, few three-point codes occurred more than 1% of the time. When these are combined with the inversion of the first two scales, and T scores without K correction are used, the 2–0–7/0–2–7 code was the most frequent (2.2%), followed by the 5–9–3/9–5–3 code (1.9%) and the 5–9–4/9–5–4 and the 5–9–8/9–5–8 codes (1.7% each). When T scores with K correction are used and the same classification scheme is followed, the 3–4–1/4–3–1 code and the 5–0–9/0–5–9 code were the most frequent (1.4% each), followed closely by the 1–3–2/3–1–2 and the 5–9–3/9–5–3 codes (1.3% each). It should be kept in mind that these percentages represent a very small number of cases—10 or fewer subjects—in the total sample of adolescent girls.

Among the adolescent female medical patients described by Swenson et al. (1973), the 4–9–8/9–4–8 profile occurred most frequently (3.7%), followed by the 1–3–2/3–1–2 profile (2.0%) and the 4–9–6/9–4–6 code (1.9%).

Male Adolescents. For the boys, when T scores without K correction are used, the 2–0–7/0–2–7 code occurred most frequently (2.1%), followed by the 3–5–6/5–3–6 code (1.8%) and the 2–3–6/3–2–6 and 3–5–2/5–3–2 codes (1.4% each).

When the same approach is followed but K-corrected values are used, the 3–5–1/5–3–1 code was the most frequent (2.2%), followed by the 1–3–2/3–1–2 and the 2–0–5/0–2–5 codes (1.9% each).

Among the male adolescent medical patients, the 4–9–8/9–4–8 code occurred most frequently (2.9%), followed by the 4–9–3/9–4–3 and 8–9–4/9–8–4 codes (1.8% each) and the 1–3–7/3–1–7 code (1.3%).

Code Types of Low Frequency

The high-point codes allow clinicians to develop base-rate expectations for comparison with the code patterns in their own practice. Although it is important to know the patterns of high-point codes among normal adolescents, it is also useful to know when an atypical pattern appears. Therefore, some information about infrequently appearing elevations is given below.

Thus, conversely, when raw scores without K correction are used, the single scale that is the least likely to occur as a high-point code in our normal sample is the same for both sexes (scale 8, Sc), with a frequency of 3.5% among the girls and 2.6% among the boys.

When K-corrected values are used, scale 8 remains the least frequently occurring high-point code among the girls (4.8%), and scale 7 (Pt) is the least frequent for the boys (4.3%). The next least frequent scale for the boys is scale 8 (Sc; 5.5%), the scale that is least frequent for the girls. Among the girls, the next least frequent code was scale 7 (Pt; 5.8%).

Thus, among normal adolescents, for both boys and girls, the same two scales (7, Pt; 8, Sc) were among the least frequently elevated high-point codes.

Among female adolescent patients (Swenson et al., 1973), the least frequently appearing high-point codes occurred on scales 2 (D; 5.6%), 8 (Sc; 6.3%), and 0 (Si; 6.3%). For male adolescent medical patients, the least frequent high-point codes were scales 6 (Pa; 3.8%), 2 (D; 5.3%), and 0 (Si; 7.1%).

As a historical footnote, although direct comparisons with the tabular data of Hathaway and Monachesi (1963) are not available, among the girls in their sample, scales 2 (D; 16.6%), 1 (Hs; 14.4%), and 5 (Mf; 13.1%) were most often lowest on the profile. For the boys, scales 5 (Mf; 15.4%), 2 (D; 13.4%), and 1 (Hs; 10.3%) were most frequently the lowest on the profile.

CORRELATION MATRICES

Appendix F presents the correlation matrices between raw scores, with and without K correction, and age on the 13 basic scales, and Appendix G presents the correlation matrices between normalized T scores, with and without K correction, and age.

ITEM ANALYSIS

With all the changes already described at the profile level, attention should turn to analyses comparing response patterns in the current and previous normative data at the item level. Unfortunately, although such an analysis was desirable, it was not possible. A data file for the responses to the MMPI items for the Marks and Briggs normative sample is not available. Apparently, the data provided to Marks and Briggs for the school year 1964 to 1965 were conveyed to them by sums of raw scale scores and profile form rather than through individual responses to the 566 items (Marks, 1990).

Comparison with the Minnesota statewide ninth-grade sample of Hathaway and Monachesi (1963) may be of some interest. However, it must be recalled that these data were obtained from MMPIs that had been screened for validity on scales L and F, so some MMPIs were systematically excluded. Furthermore, the item-level data reported by Hathaway and Monachesi regarding responses to individual items are based on a random sample of 100 boys and 100 girls and were not obtained from the entire sample.

Therefore, Appendix H contains the item-response information (percentage responding true) for the contemporary normal adolescent sample, separately by sex and age. The total for all ages is also provided, as is the same information for the Hathaway and Monachesi (1963) sample. A table comparing the percentage responding true between our contemporary normal adolescent females and males is available from the authors.

It should be noted that the item frequencies reported by Hathaway and Monachesi (1963) were not derived from their total sample. Rather, we are told that the information about the percentage responding true to the various MMPI items (Hathaway & Monachesi, 1963, pp. 122–126, Table 26) "were derived from a stratified sample of 100 boys and 100 girls with valid profiles taken from the statewide group. . . . A comparison of these data with other item counts indicates that the values presented are representative and fairly stable" (Hathaway & Monachesi, 1963, pp. 38–39).

Because these data are the only remaining source of information about adolescent response patterns to individual items of the MMPI that have been published—remember, no individual item response frequencies were reported for the Marks and Briggs data—we have presented our item response information in Appendix H in four ways. First, Part 1 lists the numbers of the MMPI items in order, accompanied by the percentage of the contemporary female adolescents who responded true to each item at each age and for the total sample of female adolescents. These data are followed by a separate column reporting the per- centage responding true for that item as obtained from the Hathaway and Monachesi data. Thus, for any MMPI item, the interested clinician or researcher can determine the difference between the ninth-grade adolescent girls in the sample from Hathaway and Monachesi as expressed in 1947 and 1954 and the response patterns of contemporary normal female adolescents ages 13 to 17 years. Part 1 of Appendix H also has the same information for our contemporary male adolescents and the ninth-grade male subjects reported by Hathaway and Monachesi (1963).

Part 2 of Appendix H presents the items in a different order—based on the difference between the percentage responding true to the item from the female adolescents described by Hathaway and Monachesi and our total sample of contemporary normal female adolescents. Some interesting changes in response patterns are evident. For example, the item that showed the single greatest change among these contemporary adolescents—for both sexes—was the same item that also showed the greatest change among our contemporary normal adults, of both sexes. More specifically, item 73 (I am an important person) was answered true (77.1%) to a remarkably greater degree by our contemporary adolescent girls than the adolescent girls in the Hathaway and Monachesi sample (10.0%). Table 33 lists the 20 items showing the greatest proportion of change when the ninth-grade female adolescents from the Hathaway and Monachesi sample are compared with our contemporary normal adolescent girls. Conversely, Table 34 lists the 20 items showing the least change when the sample of ninth-grade female adolescents from the Hathaway and Monachesi sample are compared with our contemporary sample of normal adolescent girls. The first 5 items on the list showed a 0.0% change.

Tables 35 and 36 contain the same comparisons (as Tables 33 and 34) for males. More specifically, Table 35 provides a list of the 20 items showing the greatest percentage point change when the sample of ninth-grade male adolescents are compared with the proportion responding true from our contemporary sample of normal adolescent boys. As noted above, item 73 (I am an important person) was the item showing the most change; 18% of the boys in the Hathaway and Monachesi sample answered true to that item, whereas 80% of the boys in our contemporary normal adolescent male sample endorsed the item true. It should be recalled that this item showed the greatest proportion of change when the responses from the original Minnesota normal sample obtained by Hathaway were compared with the responses from our contemporary normal adult male sample.

Table 36 provides the converse information, listing the 20 MMPI items showing the least change. The first three items on the list showed a 0.0% change from the Hathaway and Monachesi sample to our contemporary normal adolescents.

Table 37 reports the items showing the greatest percentage point difference in those responding true when our contemporary normal adolescent girls are compared with our contemporary normal adolescent boys. This table is analogous therefore to the information by Hathaway and Monachesi (1963, p. 130, Table 31), in which they list the 64 items showing the greatest difference between the "percentages of 'True' responses by boys and girls of the statewide sample."

It was interesting to note that item 1 (I like mechanics magazines), which showed a difference of 72 percentage points in the Hathaway and Monachesi sample (girls, 11% true; boys, 83% true), fell to seventh place in our contemporary normal sample, with a 48 percentage point difference being noted (contemporary female adolescents, 4% true; contemporary male adolescents, 52% true); this change suggests that adolescents of both sexes are less interested in the

Table 33

The 20 MMPI Items Showing the **Greatest** Difference in Percentage Responding True
Between the Hathaway-Monachesi Sample of Ninth-Grade Female Adolescents and
Contemporary Female Adolescents, by the Absolute Difference in Percentage
Responding True

% responding true		
H-M[a]	CNA[b]	MMPI item[c]
10	77	73. I am an important person.
77	28	70. I used to like drop-the-handkerchief.
47	91	101. I believe women ought to have as much sexual freedom as men.
69	28	427. I am embarrassed by dirty stories.
28	63	93. I think most people would lie to get ahead.
20	52	338. I have certainly had more than my share of things to worry about.
81	49	3. I wake up fresh and rested most mornings.
24	55	22. At times I have fits of laughing and crying that I cannot control.
68	38	229. I should like to belong to several clubs or lodges.
47	17	4. I think I would like the work of a librarian.
32	62	442. I have had periods in which I lost sleep over worry.
42	12	457. I believe that a person should never taste an alcoholic drink.
38	8	223. I very much like hunting.
72	42	557. I would like to be a private secretary.
47	17	413. I deserve severe punishment for my sins.
34	4	69. I am very strongly attracted by members of my own sex.
82	52	488. I pray several times every week.
50	79	438. There are certain people whom I dislike so much that I am inwardly pleased when they are catching it for something they have done.
55	27	92. I would like to be a nurse.
30	58	239. I have been disappointed in love.

[a]Hathaway-Monachesi sample, based on a random sample of 100 valid MMPIs from adolescent girls ages 13 to 17 years drawn from the ninth-grade Minnesota statewide sample (n = 5,628) (Hathaway & Monachesi, 1963, pp. 111, 122, Table 26).
[b]Contemporary normal adolescents, based on the total sample of 691 normal female adolescents ages 13 to 17 years.
[c]The 16 duplicated items in the MMPI were considered only once.

topics they expect to find in mechanics magazines. At present, the item showing the greatest difference (item 77, I enjoy reading love stories), a 69 percentage point difference (female adolescents, 81% true; male adolescents, 12% true) was in second place in the Hathaway-Monachesi sample, having a 70 percentage point difference (girls, 87%; boys, 17%). Item 563 (I like adventure stories better than romantic stories) is in second place among our contemporary normal adolescents (female adolescents, 23%; male adolescents, 87%) and was in fourth place in the Hathaway and Monachesi sample (girls, 27% true; boys, 88% true). The item in third place in our contemporary sample (item 74, I have often wished I were a girl. [Or if you are a girl, I have never been sorry that I am a girl]) showed a 63% difference (contemporary female adolescents, 70% true; male adolescents, 7% true) and was also in third place in the Hathaway and Monachesi sample (a 63 percentage point difference), with identical percentages (girls, 70% true; boys, 7% true).

Finally, Table 38 provides the 20 items showing the least percentage point difference in responding true between our female adolescents and male adolescents. The first two items showed a 0.0% difference.

Table 34

*The 20 MMPI Items Showing the **Least** Difference in Percentage Responding True
(When Rounded to the Nearest Whole Percentage) Between the Hathaway-Monachesi
Sample of Ninth-Grade Female Adolescents and Contemporary Female Adolescents, by
Original MMPI Item Number*

% responding true			
H-M[a]	CNA[b]		MMPI item[c]
2	2	56.	As a youngster I was suspended from school one or more times for cutting up.
96	96	60.	I do not read every editorial in the newspaper every day.
75	75	98.	I believe in the second coming of Christ.
81	81	103.	I have little or no trouble with my muscles twitching or jumping.
77	77	112.	I frequently find it necessary to stand up for what I think is right.
7	7	121.	I believe I am being plotted against.
57	57	131.	I do not worry about catching diseases.
19	19	167.	It wouldn't make me nervous if any members of my family got into trouble with the law.
54	54	180.	I find it hard to make talk when I meet new people.
80	80	199.	Children should be taught all the main facts of sex.
76	76	242.	I believe I am no more nervous than most others.
9	9	286.	I am never happier than when alone.
13	13	300.	There never was a time in my life when I liked to play with dolls.
29	29	344.	Often I cross the street in order not to meet someone I see.
1	1	393.	Horses that don't pull should be beaten or kicked.
82	82	449.	I enjoy social gatherings just to be with people.
8	8	471.	In school my marks in deportment were quite regularly bad.
22	22	494.	I am afraid of finding myself in a closet or small closed place.
68	68	528.	I blush no more often than others.
92	92	547.	I like parties and socials.

[a]Hathaway-Monachesi sample, based on a random sample of 100 valid MMPIs from adolescent girls ages 13 to 17 years drawn from the ninth-grade Minnesota statewide sample (n = 5,628) (Hathaway & Monachesi, 1963, pp. 111, 122, Table 26).

[b]Contemporary normal adolescents, based on the total sample of 691 normal female adolescents ages 13 to 17 years.

[c]The 16 duplicated items in the MMPI were considered only once.

For interested readers, tables paralleling the data presented by Hathaway and Monachesi (1963, pp. 126–129, Tables 28 and 29), which provide comparisons between our contemporary normal adult sample and our contemporary normal adolescent sample, are available from the authors. Thus, for each item, separately by sex, the contemporary adult and adolescent samples are listed side by side, in terms of percentage responding true to each item. In addition, these tables present the same information but according to the descending order of the percentage point difference in responding true. As an overview of this information, Table 39 lists the 20 items for the contemporary female adult and adolescent samples that showed the greatest difference, and Table 40 provides the same information for the contemporary male adult and adolescent samples. Tables 41 and 42 list the 20 items showing the smallest difference in percentage responding true for the contemporary adolescent and adult samples, separately for each sex.

MMPI items left unanswered are sometimes evaluated by clinicians. In their Minnesota statewide ninth-grade study, Hathaway and Monachesi (1963) allowed

Table 35

*The 20 MMPI Items Showing the **Greatest** Difference in Percentage Responding True Between the Hathaway-Monachesi Sample of Ninth-Grade Male Adolescents and Contemporary Male Adolescents, by the Absolute Difference in Percentage Responding True*

% responding true		
H-M[a]	CNA[b]	MMPI item[c]
18	80	73. I am an important person.
50	4	69. I am very strongly attracted by members of my own sex.
63	28	537. I would like to hunt lions in Africa.
89	55	223. I very much like hunting.
80	46	561. I very much like horseback riding.
21	55	452. I like to poke fun at people.
47	15	457. I believe that a person should never taste an alcoholic drink.
53	22	548. I never attend a sexy show if I can avoid it.
83	52	1. I like mechanics magazines.
28	58	566. I like movie love scenes.
52	22	329. I almost never dream.
13	43	11. A person should try to understand his dreams and be guided by or take warning from them.
16	45	239. I have been disappointed in love.
49	20	413. I deserve severe punishment for my sins.
22	51	338. I have certainly had more than my share of things to worry about.
51	79	438. There are certain people whom I dislike so much that I am inwardly pleased when they are catching it for something they have done.
38	10	365. I feel uneasy indoors.
48	76	39. At times I feel like smashing things.
28	56	266. Once a week or oftener I become very excited.
24	62	446. I enjoy gambling for small stakes.

[a]Hathaway-Monachesi sample, based on a random sample of 100 valid MMPIs from adolescent boys ages 13 to 18 years drawn from the ninth-grade Minnesota statewide sample ($n = 5,701$) (Hathaway & Monachesi, 1963, pp. 111, 122, Table 26).

[b]Contemporary normal adolescents, based on the total sample of 634 normal male adolescents ages 13 to 17 years.

[c]The 16 duplicated items in the MMPI were considered only once.

their subjects to omit items if they wished, although the students were encouraged to respond to all of the statements if they could. Later, they tabulated the variations in frequency with which the items of the MMPI had been left unanswered. Tables 43 and 44 list the items from their ninth-grade students that were left unanswered by 3% or more of the sample, based on a random sample of 100 girls and 100 boys from the total sample. It was noted that "Religion and sex appear to be the areas which produced the frequent omissions for both boys and girls" (Hathaway & Monachesi, 1963, p. 41).

In comparison with the lists of unanswered items from Hathaway and Monachesi, the girls from our contemporary normal sample shared only three items: 19 (When I take a new job, I like to be tipped off on who should be gotten next to), 20 (My sex life is satisfactory), and 58 (Everything is turning out just like the prophets of the Bible said it would). For the boys, four items were shared: 19 (When I take a new job, I like to be tipped off on who should be gotten next to), 58 (Everything is turning out just like the prophets of the Bible said it would), 236 (I brood a great deal), and 513 (I think Lincoln was greater than Washington).

In general, the five items most frequently left unanswered among the members

Table 36

*The 20 MMPI Items Showing the **Least** Difference in Percentage Responding True (When Rounded to the Nearest Whole Percentage) Between the Hathaway-Monachesi Sample of Ninth-Grade Male Adolescents and Contemporary Male Adolescents, by Original MMPI Item Number*

% responding true			
H-M[a]	CNA[b]		MMPI item[c]
89	89	54.	I am liked by most people who know me.
17	17	61.	I have not lived the right kind of life.
7	7	74.	I have often wished I were a girl. (Or if you are a girl) I have never been sorry that I am a girl.
5	5	123.	I believe I am being followed.
50	50	147.	I have often lost out on things because I couldn't make up my mind soon enough.
5	5	168.	There is something wrong with my mind.
34	34	172.	I frequently have to fight against showing that I am bashful.
88	88	187.	My hands have not become clumsy or awkward.
95	95	220.	I loved my mother.
22	22	249.	I believe there is a Devil and a Hell in afterlife.
2	2	288.	I am troubled by attacks of nausea and vomiting.
8	8	293.	Someone has been trying to influence my mind.
49	49	348.	I tend to be on my guard with people who are somewhat more friendly than I had expected.
71	71	378.	I do not like to see women smoke.
14	14	388.	I am afraid to be alone in the dark.
31	31	432.	I have strong political opinions.
88	88	445.	I was fond of excitement when I was young (or in childhood).
43	43	504.	I do not try to cover up my poor opinion or pity of a person so that he won't know how I feel.
39	39	518.	I have often felt guilty because I have pretended to feel more sorry about something than I really was.
80	80	528.	I blush no more often than others.

[a]Hathaway-Monachesi sample, based on a random sample of 100 valid MMPIs from adolescent boys ages 13 to 18 years drawn from the ninth-grade Minnesota statewide sample (n = 5,701) (Hathaway & Monachesi, 1963, pp. 111, 122, Table 26).

[b]Contemporary normal adolescents, based on the total sample of 634 normal male adolescents ages 13 to 17 years.

[c]The 16 duplicated items in the MMPI were considered only once.

of our contemporary normal adolescents were the same for both female and male subjects, although their order varied somewhat. More specifically, the item most frequently left unanswered (6.9%) by the total group was item 19 (When I take a new job, I like to be tipped off on who should be gotten next to); the second most frequently unanswered item in the total sample (6.8%) was item 236 (I brood a great deal). These were followed by item 70 (I used to like drop-the-handkerchief, 6.3%), item 58 (Everything is turning out just like the prophets of the Bible said it would, 4.9%), and item 471 (In school my marks in deportment were quite regularly bad, 4.7%). A list of the 12 most frequently omitted items is presented in Tables 45 and 46, separately by sex.

Conversely, among our 1,315 contemporary normal adolescents, there were some items that no one left unanswered. Indeed, there were four of these items

Table 37

The 20 MMPI Items Showing the **Greatest** Difference in Percentage Responding True
Between Contemporary Normal Female (n = 691) and Male (n = 634) Adolescents, by
the Difference in Percentage Responding True

% responding true		
Female	Male	MMPI item[a]
81	12	77. I enjoy reading love stories
23	87	563. I like adventure stories better than romantic stories.
70	7	74. I have often wished I were a girl. (Or if you are a girl) I have never been sorry that I am a girl.
85	24	463. I used to like hopscotch.
71	12	149. I used to keep a diary.
13	62	300. There never was a time in my life when I liked to play with dolls.
4	52	1. I like mechanics magazines.
8	55	223. I very much like hunting.
56	13	158. I cry easily.
45	85	539. I am not afraid of mice.
42	4	557. I would like to be a private secretary.
29	65	522. I have no fear of spiders.
62	26	78. I like poetry.
48	13	132. I like collecting flowers or growing house plants.
56	25	295. I liked "Alice in Wonderland" by Lewis Carroll.
33	2	538. I think I would like the work of a dressmaker.
42	11	261. If I were an artist I would like to draw flowers.
13	44	434. I would like to be an auto racer.
55	25	22. At times I have fits of laughing and crying that I cannot control.
61	31	126. I like dramatics.

[a]The 16 duplicated items in the MMPI were considered only once.

among both sexes. These included items 34 (I have a cough most of the time), 125 (I have a great deal of stomach trouble), 196 (I like to visit places where I have never been before), and 197 (Someone has been trying to rob me).

Hathaway and Monachesi provided no information in this regard, so no comparisons with their sample can be made. However, it might be appropriate to view these four items as being relatively "easy" items for adolescents to answer on the MMPI.

Beyond this, a total of 34 items from the original MMPI pool were never left unanswered by our female adolescents; these are listed in Table 47. For our adolescent boys, a total of 28 items were never left unanswered; these are listed in Table 48.

It should be recalled that the K scale was developed to improve the sensitivity and specificity of scales 1 (Hs), 4 (Pd), 7 (Pt), 8 (Sc), and 9 (Ma) when the MMPI was applied to adults (Meehl, 1945; Meehl & Hathaway, 1946). Initially the K scale was scored and then subsequently applied to the "curve" (as the clinical profile was called in the early days) on a subjective or clinical, intuitive basis. Later, specific weights were calculated to maximize the discriminating power of the five scales just mentioned (McKinley, Hathaway, & Meehl, 1948). In general, K weighting appeared to be helpful as a moderator variable for the response bias associated with unconscious defensiveness, a cautious interpersonal style, the tendency to "fake-good," or the tendency to see the world as Pollyanna did, through "rose-colored glasses." Because Marks et al. (1974) calculated their

Table 38

The 20 MMPI Items Showing the **Least** Difference in Percentage Responding True (When Rounded to the Nearest Whole Percentage) Between the Contemporary Normal Female (n = 691) and Male (n = 634) Adolescents, by Original MMPI Item Number

% responding true		
Female	Male	MMPI item[a]
6	6	42. My family does not like the work I have chosen or the work I intend to choose for my life work.
88	88	51. I am in just as good physical health as most of my friends.
89	88	63. I have had no difficulty in starting or holding my bowel movement.
93	93	65. I loved my father.
99	99	75. I get angry sometimes.
98	98	83. Any man who is able and willing to work hard has a good chance of succeeding.
6	6	189. I feel weak all over much of the time.
95	95	220. I loved my mother.
35	35	245. My parents and family find more fault with me than they should.
6	6	273. I have numbness in one or more regions of my skin.
39	38	299. I think that I feel more intensely than most people do.
16	15	342. I forget right away what people say to me.
10	10	351. I get anxious and upset when I have to make a short trip away from home.
38	38	435. Usually I would prefer to work with women.
79	79	438. There are certain people whom I dislike so much that I am inwardly pleased when they are catching it for something they have done.
82	82	451. My worries seem to disappear when I get into a crowd of lively friends.
85	85	474. I have to urinate no more often than others.
95	95	540. My face has never been paralyzed.
13	13	541. My skin seems to be unusually sensitive to touch.
52	52	564. I am apt to pass up something I want to do when others feel that it isn't worth doing.

[a]The 16 duplicated items in the MMPI were considered only once.

tables without K correction, it was not possible to carry out research that would compare the efficacy of scores or profiles calculated with or without K correction. Although one can still find studies of adolescent or young adult subjects using adult norms and K-corrected scores, this is not a desirable practice unless the researcher has carefully considered age in the design or analysis because it has been clearly demonstrated that response patterns of adolescents and adults are different.

From a clinical standpoint, adolescents seldom earn significant scores on scale K, so profiles from such patients are not likely to differ, whether scored with or without K correction. However, for the adolescent who has an adultlike degree of defensiveness or for the sophisticated adolescent patient, we thought that K weighting might be helpful in meeting the original purpose for which K was intended—compensating for the patient's cautiousness and defensive response style.

Therefore, to foster comparisons between the profiles calculated with and without K correction, we also constructed adolescent norms using K-corrected raw scores (Colligan & Offord, 1991) and applying the standard K-weighting procedure described by its authors (Meehl, 1945; Meehl & Hathaway, 1946). As

Table 39

*The 20 MMPI Items Showing the **Greatest** Difference in Percentage Responding True Between Contemporary Normal Female Adolescents and Contemporary Normal Female Adults, by the Decreasing Difference in the Percentage Responding True*

% responding true		
CNS[a]	Adol[b]	MMPI item[c]
38	83	99. I like to go to parties and other affairs where there is lots of loud fun.
44	88	45. I do not always tell the truth.
84	40	96. I have very few quarrels with members of my family.
40	84	181. When I get bored I like to stir up some excitement.
36	79	401. I have no fear of water.
77	34	255. Sometimes at elections I vote for men about whom I know very little.
37	79	438. There are certain people whom I dislike so much that I am inwardly pleased when they are catching it for something they have done.
13	55	22. At times I have fits of laughing and crying that I cannot control.
24	66	266. Once a week or oftener I become very excited.
31	72	39. At times I feel like smashing things.
28	67	241. I dream frequently about things that are best kept to myself.
88	49	132. I like collecting flowers or growing house plants.
8	48	97. At times I have a strong urge to do something harmful or shocking.
43	82	109. Some people are so bossy that I feel like doing the opposite of what they request even though I know they are right.
40	79	282. Once in a while I feel hate toward members of my family whom I usually love.
68	29	70. I used to like drop-the-handkerchief.
41	76	561. I very much like horseback riding.
9	43	157. I feel that I have often been punished without cause.
10	44	40. Most any time I would rather sit and daydream than to do anything else.
20	54	238. I have periods of such great restlessness that I cannot sit long in a chair.

[a]CNS, census-matched sample of contemporary normal adult women (n = 335) ages 18 to 99 years.
[b]Adol, total sample of contemporary normal female adolescents (n = 691) ages 13 to 17 years.
[c]The 16 duplicated items in the MMPI were considered only once.

with our other normative tables, we derived normalized T-score values to allow consistency of comparisons to be made across the 13 validity and clinical scales of the MMPI.

K-CORRECTED RAW SCORE CONVERSION TABLES FOR NORMAL ADOLESCENTS

Because Marks et al. (1974) argued for the use of raw scores without K correction and constructed their normative tables without the use of K-corrected scores, no further research in this regard has been carried out.

However, some implications for profile interpretation and a cogent discussion of the issues related to the use of MMPI scores with and without K correction among young adults (college students, inductees into the military service) and adults have recently been presented (Hsu, 1986). It seems clear that further evidence on these issues needs to be gathered, particularly among MMPIs from adolescents in various referral categories (such as mental health clients, juvenile

Table 40

*The 20 MMPI Items Showing the **Greatest** Difference in Percentage Responding True Between Contemporary Normal Male Adolescents and Contemporary Normal Male Adults, by the Decreasing Difference in the Percentage Responding True*

% responding true		
CNS[a]	Adol[b]	MMPI item[c]
15	60	145. At times I feel like picking a fist fight with someone.
28	70	282. Once in a while I feel hate toward members of my family whom I usually love.
69	29	255. Sometimes at elections I vote for men about whom I know very little.
10	48	157. I feel that I have often been punished without cause.
38	76	39. At times I feel like smashing things.
61	25	428. I like to read newspaper editorials.
24	60	135. If I could get into a movie without paying and be sure I was not seen I would probably do it.
43	78	99. I like to go to parties and other affairs where there is lots of loud fun.
14	49	97. At times I have a strong urge to do something harmful or shocking.
81	46	96. I have very few quarrels with members of my family.
45	79	181. When I get bored I like to stir up some excitement.
25	55	452. I like to poke fun at people.
38	68	416. It bothers me to have someone watch me at work even though I know I can do it well.
46	16	554. If I were an artist I would like to draw children.
77	48	155. I am neither gaining nor losing weight.
56	85	45. I do not always tell the truth.
21	50	469. I have often found people jealous of my good ideas just because they had not thought of them first.
74	45	3. I wake up fresh and rested most mornings.
9	37	358. Bad words, often terrible words, come into my mind and I cannot get rid of them.
45	73	109. Some people are so bossy that I feel like doing the opposite of what they request even though I know they are right.

[a]CNS, census-matched sample of contemporary normal adult men (n = 305) ages 18 to 99 years.
[b]Adol, total sample of contemporary normal male adolescents (n = 624) ages 13 to 17 years.
[c]The 16 duplicated items in the MMPI were considered only once.

delinquents, and substance misusers). It is only through such efforts that the clinical utility of K weighting among adolescent MMPIs can be fairly evaluated for clinical efficacy, with particular attention to the issues of positive and negative predictive power (Glaros & Kline, 1988).

Monachesi (1953) noted that there were variations in the significance of scale-score differences (using critical ratios) between delinquent and nondelinquent adolescents of both sexes that appeared to favor scores without K correction for boys (except on scale 4, Pd) and for girls on scale 9 (Ma). However, he cautioned clinicians and researchers that "One may not conclude from this that the K correction is an improper one" (Monachesi, 1953, p. 47); later, he appeared to be suggesting that comparable studies of adolescents with the same clinical syndromes as the adults used to devise the MMPI scales, which were subsequently K-weighted, would be necessary to establish whether the K correction was appropriate for use (p. 48).

Appendix I presents normative conversion tables for the 13 basic MMPI scales

Table 41

*The 20 MMPI Items Showing the **Least** Difference in Percentage Responding True (When Rounded to the Nearest Whole Percentage) Between Contemporary Normal Female Adolescents and Contemporary Normal Female Adults, by Original MMPI Item Number*

% responding true		MMPI item[c]
CNS[a]	Adol[b]	
5	5	10. There seems to be a lump in my throat much of the time.
12	13	43. My sleep is fitful and disturbed.
81	81	77. I enjoy reading love stories.
0	0	151. Someone has been trying to poison me.
91	91	169. I am not afraid to handle money.
86	86	187. My hands have not become clumsy or awkward.
1	1	197. Someone has been trying to rob me.
2	2	210. Everything tastes the same.
7	7	213. In walking I am very careful to step over sidewalk cracks.
44	44	221. I like science.
8	8	223. I very much like hunting.
81	81	243. I have few or no pains.
3	3	288. I am troubled by attacks of nausea and vomiting.
33	33	292. I am likely not to speak to people until they speak to me.
87	88	294. I have never been in trouble with the law.
6	6	420. I have had some very unusual religious experiences.
43	43	444. I do not try to correct people who express an ignorant belief.
23	24	454. I could be happy living all alone in a cabin in the woods or mountains.
96	96	508. I believe my sense of smell is as good as other people's.
13	13	541. My skin seems to be unusually sensitive to touch.

[a]CNS, census-matched sample of contemporary normal adult women (n = 335) ages 18 to 99 years.
[b]Adol, total sample of contemporary normal female adolescents (n = 691) ages 13 to 17 years.
[c]The 16 duplicated items in the MMPI were considered only once.

using raw scores with K correction on the five scales to which K corrections have traditionally been applied—scales 1 (Hs), 4 (Pd), 7 (Pt), 8 (Sc), and 9 (Ma). The remaining scales, which do not require K correction, also are included for convenience. Clinicians and researchers are encouraged to consider an empirical evaluation of the relative merits of these two approaches for the type of clientele being served, following the suggestion made by Gottesman et al. (1987). Because most MMPIs of adolescents carry little in the way of K anyway, such an approach to K correction might have particular value for settings in which atypically high K values are earned by adolescents.

TOWARD AN ADOLESCENT MMPI

Clinicians working primarily with adolescents may have wondered whether there will be an MMPI-2 for this age group. Indeed, this may eventually be so. However, the time line for such a project is unclear. Thus, in the most recent edition of his interpretive manual, Graham (1990) noted that ''Contemporary normative data for adolescent subjects also have been collected. Although the test

Table 42

*The 20 MMPI Items Showing the **Least** Difference in Percentage Responding True (When Rounded to the Nearest Whole Percentage) Between Contemporary Normal Male Adolescents and Contemporary Normal Male Adults, by Original MMPI Item Number*

% responding true		
CNS[a]	Adol[b]	MMPI item[c]
1	2	23. I am troubled by attacks of nausea and vomiting.
6	6	42. My family does not like the work I have chosen or the work I intend to choose for my life work.
23	23	82. I am easily downed in an argument.
16	17	108. There seems to be a fullness in my head or nose most of the time.
59	59	127. I know who is responsible for most of my troubles.
14	14	158. I cry easily.
65	65	173. I liked school.
79	79	199. Children should be taught all the main facts of sex.
3	3	211. I can sleep during the day but not at night.
70	71	230. I hardly ever notice my heart pounding and I am seldom short of breath.
96	96	285. Once in a while I laugh at a dirty joke.
87	87	302. I have never been in trouble because of my sex behavior.
84	84	330. I have never been paralyzed or had any unusual weakness of any of my muscles.
50	50	348. I tend to be on my guard with people who are somewhat more friendly than I had expected.
77	78	369. Religion gives me no worry.
9	9	420. I have had some very unusual religious experiences.
8	8	470. Sexual things disgust me.
95	96	515. In my home we have always had the ordinary necessities (such as enough food, clothing, etc.).
13	13	541. My skin seems to be unusually sensitive to touch.
87	88	563. I like adventure stories better than romantic stories.

[a]CNS, census-matched sample of contemporary normal adult women (n = 305) ages 18 to 99 years.
[b]Adol, total sample of contemporary normal male adolescents (n = 624) ages 13 to 17 years.
[c]The 16 duplicated items in the MMPI were considered only once.

publisher has indicated that adolescent norms will be published, they are not included in the MMPI-2 manual, and it is not clear whether a separate booklet for adolescents will be made available" (p. 186), with the author noting that the MMPI-2 was intended for subjects 18 years of age or older. As we stated earlier, clinicians have been instructed to continue to use the original MMPI with adolescent patients.

The preliminary steps in developing an MMPI-2 for adolescents were outlined by Williams and Butcher (1989a, b) using 352 girls and 492 boys whose ages ranged from 12 to 18 years and who had been admitted to a treatment facility or special school settings because of emotional or behavioral problems. Most had been involved in substance misuse (about 60%), adolescent inpatient psychiatry units (approximately 24%), day programs (about 8%), and special school programs (approximately 7%). Results of these two investigations offered "reassurance to clinicians and researchers using the MMPI with adolescents that traditional empirical descriptors for most MMPI scales are valid" (Williams & Butcher, 1989a, p. 259), but they raised questions about the validity of a code-type approach for adolescent profiles.

Table 43

MMPI Items Most Frequently Left Unanswered Among the Girls From the Hathaway and Monachesi Minnesota Statewide Sample of Ninth-Grade Students, by Decreasing Order of Frequency in the Hathaway and Monachesi Sample, and the Proportion Left Unanswered Among the Contemporary Normal Adolescents

% left unanswered			
H-M[a]	CNA[b]		MMPI item
9	2.8	255.	Sometimes at elections I vote for men about whom I know very little.
6	5.8	[c]58.	Everything is turning out just like the prophets of the Bible said it would.
6	1.3	101.	I believe women ought to have as much sexual freedom as men.
5	6.4	[c]19.	When I take a new job, I like to be tipped off on who should be gotten next to.
3	1	69.	I am very strongly attracted by members of my own sex.
3	1.6	476.	I am a special agent of God.
3	2.8	232.	I have been inspired to a program of life based on duty which I have since carefully followed.
3	0.4	14.	I have diarrhea once a month or more.
3	0.7	485.	When a man is with a woman he is usually thinking about things related to her sex.
3	3.8	[c]20.	My sex life is satisfactory.
3	0.9	486.	I have never noticed any blood in my urine.
3	0.6	474.	I have to urinate no more often than others.

[a]Hathaway-Monachesi sample, based on a random sample of 100 valid MMPIs from adolescent girls ages 13 to 17 years drawn from the ninth-grade Minnesota statewide sample (n = 5,628) (Hathaway & Monachesi, 1963, pp. 111, 122, Table 26).
[b]Contemporary normal adolescents, based on the total sample of 691 normal female adolescents ages 13 to 17 years.
[c]These items also frequently were left unanswered by the contemporary normal adolescents of the same sex.

In addition to obtaining adolescent responses to the updated MMPI-2 version of the MMPI, Williams (1990a) noted that the experimental form of the MMPI that had been used in gathering adolescent MMPI data included "new items written to evaluate personality and problem areas specific to adolescents. The new MMPI adolescent item content includes areas like peer-group influence, family relations, school and teachers, adolescent sexuality, substance use and abuse, and eating problems" (p. 5).

With regard to this point, Williams went on to note that 16 new content scales intended specifically for adolescents were under development. These 16 new content scales apparently are divided into four general categories (Internal Symptomatic Behaviors, External Aggressive Tendencies, Negative Self-Views, and General Problem Areas), but only 3 of the 16 adolescent content scales are completely new with regard to adolescents. More specifically, the three scales for Adolescent Alienation (aln), Adolescent Low Aspirations (als), and Adolescent School Problems (sch) are entirely new, while the remaining 13 scales were drawn from the new 15 content scales derived for adults. Although the adult content scales of Type A (TPA) and Work Interference (WRK) do not have counterparts among the new adolescent content scales, the remainder apparently translated well to the adolescent age ranges, with relatively few item changes. The convention of lower-case letters has been proposed to distinguish the

Table 44

MMPI Items Most Frequently Left Unanswered Among the Boys From the Hathaway and Monachesi Minnesota Statewide Sample of Ninth-Grade Students, by Decreasing Order of Frequency in the Hathaway and Monachesi Sample, and the Proportion Left Unanswered Among the Contemporary Normal Adolescents

% left unanswered			
H-M[a]	CNA[b]		MMPI item
6	4.3	255.	Sometimes at elections I vote for men about whom I know very little.
5	4	[c]58.	Everything is turning out just like the prophets of the Bible said it would.
4	7.5	[c]19.	When I take a new job, I like to be tipped off on who should be gotten next to.
4	0.3	69.	I am very strongly attracted by members of my own sex.
4	2.1	98.	I believe in the second coming of Christ.
3	1	101.	I believe women ought to have as much sexual freedom as men.
3	1.4	476.	I am a special agent of God.
3	2.6	[c]513.	I think Lincoln was greater than Washington.
3	2.4	232.	I have been inspired to a program of life based on duty which I have since carefully followed.
3	1.1	54.	I am liked by most people who know me.
3	1.4	299.	I think that I feel more intensely than most people do.
3	1.0	57.	I am a good mixer.
3	6.7	[c]236.	I brood a great deal.

[a]Hathaway-Monachesi sample, based on a random sample of 100 valid MMPIs from adolescent boys ages 13 to 18 years drawn from the ninth-grade Minnesota statewide sample (n = 5,701) (Hathaway & Monachesi, 1963, pp. 111, 122, Table 26).

[b]Contemporary normal adolescents, based on the total sample of 634 normal male adolescents ages 13 to 17 years.

[c]These items also frequently were left unanswered by the contemporary normal adolescents of the same sex.

adolescent content scales from those used with adults. Seven adolescent content scales compose a category of "Internal Symptomatic Behaviors" and include Adolescent Anxiety (anx), Adolescent Fears (frs), Adolescent Obsessiveness (obs), Adolescent Depression (dep), Adolescent Health Concerns (hea), Adolescent Alienation (aln), and Adolescent Bizarre Mentation (biz); three scales in the category of "External Aggressive Tendencies" include Adolescent Anger (ang), Adolescent Cynicism (cyn), and Adolescent Conduct Problems (con); the only content scale in the category of Negative Self-Views is Adolescent Low Esteem (lse); and the five content scales in the category of "General Problem Areas" include Adolescent Low Aspirations (las), Adolescent Social Discomfort (sod), Adolescent Family Problems (fam), Adolescent School Problems (sch), and Adolescent Negative Treatment Indicators (trt) (Williams, 1990b).

The new MMPI-2 for adolescents was provisionally entitled the A-MMPI; however, according to information presented more recently (Archer, 1990), it appears that it may finally be called the MMPI-A.

The specific format for the new adolescent MMPI apparently remains in flux, with Graham (1990) noting, "It is not clear whether a separate booklet for adolescents will be made available" (p. 186), while Williams (1990a) was more definite in stating, "not only will there be contemporary age-appropriate norms available for the MMPI, but also a separate booklet with new item content and scales specific to the problems of adolescents" (p. 5).

Table 45

Items From the Original MMPI Item Pool That Were Most Frequently Left Unanswered by Contemporary Normal Female Adolescents (n = 691), by Decreasing Order of Frequency

% left unanswered		MMPI item
CNA[a]	H-M[b]	
6.8	1.0	236. I brood a great deal.
6.4	5	[c]19. When I take a new job, I like to be tipped off on who should be gotten next to.
5.8	6	[c]58. Everything is turning out just like the prophets of the Bible said it would.
5.4	-	70. I used to like drop-the-handkerchief.
4.8	-	471. In school my marks in deportment were quite regularly bad.
3.8	3	[c]20. My sex life is satisfactory.
3.6	-	514. I like mannish women.
3.5	-	202. I believe I am a condemned person.
3.2	-	162. I resent having anyone take me in so cleverly that I have had to admit that it was one on me.
3.2	3	[c]310. My sex life is satisfactory.
3.0	2	513. I think Lincoln was greater than Washington.
2.9	-	299. I think I feel more intensely than most people do.

[a]Hathaway-Monachesi sample, based on a random sample of 100 valid MMPIs from adolescent girls ages 13 to 17 years drawn from the ninth-grade Minnesota statewide sample (n = 5,628) (Hathaway & Monachesi, 1963, pp. 111, 122, Table 26).

[b]Hathaway-Monachesi ninth-grade sample of students of the same sex. -, figure was not available.

[c]These items also frequently were left unanswered by students of the same sex from the Hathaway-Monachesi sample (1963, p. 132, Table 32).

Archer (1990), a member of the Advisory Committee to the University of Minnesota Press, has commented on the emphasis being given to decreasing the total length of the adolescent MMPI. At the time of this writing (February 1991), a goal of 500 items or less was being pursued. To meet this goal, 46 items had been proposed for deletion from the 13 basic validity and clinical scales, primarily from scales F, 5 (Mf), and 0 (Si); this change would allow the basic profile to be scored from the first 349 items of the proposed adolescent MMPI booklet. In addition, 127 items, composed of reworded or revised items from the original item pool and supplemented by new items specific for the social world of adolescents, would be required for the new adolescent content scales.

With regard to supplemental scales (those separate from the 16 proposed adolescent content scales), they are expected to include the items for the Welsh A and R factor scales (Welsh, 1956, 1965), although these will probably be appearing in a revised and shortened form because of the item deletions already noted. The MacAndrew Alcoholism Scale (MacAndrew, 1965) is likely to remain also, given its popularity, if not consensus regarding its usefulness, in the clinical and research literature (Gottesman & Prescott, 1989), but it also will probably have some revisions. Readers should recall that the revised MacAndrew Alcoholism Scale (MAC-R) was developed for the MMPI-2 by deleting four items (58. Everything is turning out just like the prophets of the Bible said it would; 378. I do not like to see women smoke; 483. Christ performed miracles such as changing water into wine; 488. I pray several times every week) and substituting four ''other items known to be associated with alcohol and drug abuse'' (Butcher et al:,

Table 46

Items From the Original MMPI Item Pool That Were Most Frequently Left Unanswered by Contemporary Normal Male Adolescents (n = 624), by Decreasing Order of Frequency

% left unanswered		
CNA[a]	H-M[b]	MMPI item
7.5	4	[c]19. When I take a new job, I like to be tipped off on who should be gotten next to.
7.4	-	70. I used to like drop-the-handkerchief.
6.7	3	[c]236. I brood a great deal.
4.7	-	471. In school my marks in deportment were quite regularly bad.
4.3	-	255. Sometimes at elections I vote for men about whom I know very little.
4.0	5	[c]58. Everything is turning out just like the prophets of the Bible said it would.
2.9	1	20. My sex life is satisfactory.
2.9	-	514. I like mannish women.
2.6	-	432. I have strong political opinions.
2.6	-	433. I used to have imaginary companions.
2.6	-	435. Usually I would prefer to work with women.
2.6	3	[c]513. I think Lincoln was greater than Washington.

[a]Hathaway-Monachesi sample, based on a random sample of 100 valid MMPIs from adolescent boys ages 13 to 18 years drawn from the ninth-grade Minnesota statewide sample (n = 5,701) (Hathaway & Monachesi, 1963, pp. 111, 122, Table 26).

[b]Hathaway-Monachesi ninth-grade sample of students of the same sex. -, figure was not available.

[c]These items also frequently were left unanswered by students of the same sex from the Hathaway-Monachesi sample (1963, p. 132, Table 32).

1989, p. 37), although documentation for this statement was not provided. Because most of the items of the basic profile will be present, it is further anticipated that the Harris and Lingoes (1955) subscales will be available too. Finally, a new scale of maturity/immaturity (Im; Immaturity), derived from both rational and statistical criteria as well as from a theoretical concept of psychological maturation, has been proposed (Archer, 1990). It is believed that adolescents obtaining high scores on the new Im scale are likely to be impulsive, have limited capacity for insight, have difficulty becoming engaged in social relationships, and be characterized by relatively concrete thinking.

In addition to the measures of response inconsistency and the Back F scale (remember, items on F_B comprise a new F scale, made up of items that essentially occurred on the back side of the original MMPI answer sheet and after the last item on scale F on the new MMPI-2 answer sheet format), a new scale of validity, Item-easy/Item-difficult, may be available. This new index is based on a set of 13 items believed to be for a relatively low reading level (from first through fourth grade), entitled the "Item-Easy" group; the adolescent response patterns to these 13 items are compared with 13 other items (Item-Difficult), whose reading level apparently ranges from a seventh grade to an adult level. Should this index prove to be successful, it would help identify adolescents whose MMPI response pattern might be of questionable validity because of their difficulty in reading the items or with reading comprehension.

It should also be noted that there are no current plans for presentation of K-weighted scores or the provision of K-corrected tables, following the precedent set by Marks and Briggs (1967).

Table 47

MMPI Items (n = 34) That Were Answered by Every Member of the Contemporary Normal Sample of Female Adolescents (n = 691)

34.	I have a cough most of the time.
39.	At times I feel like smashing things.
41.	I have had periods of days, weeks, or months when I couldn't take care of things because I couldn't "get going."
48.	When I am with people, I am bothered by hearing very queer things.
49.	It would be better if almost all laws were thrown away.
85.	Sometimes I am strongly attracted by the personal articles of others such as shoes, gloves, etc., so that I want to handle or steal them though I have no use for them.
90.	Once in a while I put off until tomorrow what I ought to do today.
91.	I do not mind being made fun of.
103.	I have little or no trouble with my muscles twitching or jumping.
104.	I don't seem to care what happens to me.
106.	Much of the time I feel as if I have done something wrong or evil.
120.	My table manners are not quite as good at home as when I am out in company.
122.	I seem to be about as capable and smart as most others around me.
125.	I have a great deal of stomach trouble.
128.	The sight of blood neither frightens me nor makes me sick.
129.	Often I can't understand why I have been so cross and grouchy.
142.	I certainly feel useless at times.
144.	I would like to be a soldier.
145.	At times I feel like picking a fist fight with someone.
175.	I seldom or never have dizzy spells.
176.	I do not have a great fear of snakes.
189.	I feel weak all over much of the time.
190.	I have very few headaches.
196.	I like to visit places where I have never been before.
197.	Someone has been trying to rob me.
211.	I can sleep during the day but not at night.
214.	I have never had any breaking out on my skin that has worried me.
218.	It does not bother me particularly to see animals suffer.
263.	I sweat very easily even on cool days.
266.	Once a week or oftener I become very excited.
269.	I can easily make other people afraid of me, and sometimes do for the fun of it.
335.	I cannot keep my mind on one thing.
336.	I easily become impatient with people.
488.	I pray several times every week.

The adolescent normative sample, the method of subject selection, and the like have not as yet been described. However, Butcher (1990a) has indicated that school systems in seven regions of the United States were apparently used to recruit 815 female and 805 male adolescents in junior and senior high school (grades 7 through 12) and ranging in age from 14 to 18 years.

It is also anticipated that uniform T scores will also be used in developing the adolescent norms for the adolescent version of the MMPI-2 and for the new content scales (Tellegen & Ben-Porath, 1990).

Table 48

MMPI Items (n = 28) That Were Answered by Every Member of the Contemporary
Normal Sample of Male Adolescents (n = 624)

---

4.   I think I would like the work of a librarian.
5.   I am easily awakened by noise.
6.   I like to read newspaper articles on crime.
12. I enjoy detective or mystery stories.
27. Evil spirits possess me at times.
29. I am bothered by acid stomach several times a week.
34. I have a cough most of the time.
36. I seldom worry about my health.
51. I am in just as good physical health as most of my friends.
55. I am almost never bothered by pains over the heart or in my chest.
60. I do not read every editorial in the newspaper every day.
119. My speech is the same as always (not faster or slower, or slurring; no hoarseness).
123. I believe I am being followed.
125. I have a great deal of stomach trouble.
132. I like collecting flowers or growing house plants.
186. I frequently notice my hand shakes when I try to do something.
187. My hands have not become clumsy or awkward.
188. I can read a long while without tiring my eyes.
192. I have had no difficulty in keeping my balance in walking.
193. I do not have spells of hay fever or asthma.
194. I have had attacks in which I could not control my movements or speech but in which I
     knew what was going on around me.
196. I like to visit places where I have never been before.
197. Someone has been trying to rob me.
303. I am so touchy on some subjects that I can't talk about them.
306. I get all the sympathy I should.
348. I tend to be on my guard with people who are somewhat more friendly than I had expected.
349. I have strange and peculiar thoughts.
354. I am afraid of using a knife or anything very sharp or pointed.

PART V

A MANUAL FOR USING THE MMPI CONTEMPORARY ADOLESCENT NORMS

CONSTRUCTING ADOLESCENT MMPI PROFILES WITHOUT K CORRECTION

1. Obtain the raw scores, without K correction, for each validity and clinical scale by hand scoring or from a computer scoring service.
2. Enter the sex-appropriate conversion table of the general adolescent norms (Tables 49 and 50). These tables provide the normalized T-score value for all possible raw scores without K correction.
3. Plot the normalized T-score value for each validity and clinical scale on the MMPI profile sheet. Use the T-score values printed at the edge of the profile form as a guide. Disregard the raw score values from the old adult norms or the Marks and Briggs raw score values if they have been preprinted on the profile sheet.
4. To compare the profile based on contemporary adolescent norms with that obtained from the Marks and Briggs data, plot a second profile line, in a different color, using the raw score values that have been preprinted on the adolescent profile form.

CONSTRUCTING ADOLESCENT MMPI PROFILES WITH K CORRECTION

1. Obtain the K-corrected raw score for each validity and clinical scale by hand scoring or from a computer scoring service.
2. Using the table in Appendix I, enter the sex-appropriate conversion table of the general adolescent norms. This appendix provides the normalized T-score value for all possible K-corrected raw scores.

127

Table 49

New Normalized T Scores for Raw Scores Without K Correction in Contemporary Female Adolescents 13 Through 17 Years of Age

Raw score without K correction	Validity scale[a]			Clinical scale[a]										Raw score without K correction
	L	F	K	1 (Hs)	2 (D)	3 (Hy)	4 (Pd)	5 (Mf)	6 (Pa)	7 (Pt)	8 (Sc)	9 (Ma)	0 (Si)	
0	23	21	0	25	-69	-35	-59	130	-9	10	14	-28	-16	0
1	40	32	15	36	-41	-16	-33	128	9	19	23	-10	-4	1
2	48	38	21	40	-25	-9	-18	125	16	23	26	-3	2	2
3	53	42	26	43	-14	-3	-8	123	22	27	29	2	6	3
4	58	46	30	46	-5	3	0	121	27	29	31	7	9	4
5	62	49	33	48	3	7	7	119	31	31	33	11	12	5
6	66	51	36	51	9	11	13	117	35	34	35	15	14	6
7	70	53	39	53	14	15	18	114	38	35	36	18	17	7
8	73	55	42	55	19	18	22	112	42	37	38	21	19	8
9	76	57	45	56	23	22	26	110	45	39	39	24	21	9
10	79	58	47	58	27	25	30	108	48	40	41	27	23	10
11	82	59	49	60	30	28	33	106	50	42	42	30	25	11
12	84	61	51	61	33	30	36	103	53	43	43	32	27	12
13	87	62	54	63	36	33	38	101	55	45	44	35	29	13
14	89	63	56	64	39	36	41	99	58	46	46	37	30	14
15	91	64	58	65	41	38	43	97	60	47	47	39	32	15
16		65	59	67	44	40	46	94	62	49	48	42	34	16
17		66	61	68	46	43	48	92	65	50	49	44	35	17
18		67	63	69	48	45	50	90	67	51	50	46	37	18
19		67	65	70	50	47	52	88	69	52	51	48	38	19
20		68	66	72	52	49	53	86	71	53	52	50	40	20
21		69	68	73	54	52	55	83	73	54	53	52	41	21
22		69	70	74	56	54	57	81	75	55	54	54	42	22
23		70	71	75	58	56	58	79	77	56	54	56	44	23
24		71	73	76	59	58	60	77	78	57	55	57	45	24
25		71	74	77	61	59	61	75	80	58	56	59	46	25
26		72	76	78	62	61	63	72	82	59	57	61	47	26
27		73	77	79	64	63	64	70	84	60	58	62	48	27
28		73	79	80	65	65	65	68	85	61	59	64	50	28

29	74	80	81	66	67	67	66	87	62	59	66	51	29
30	74	81	82	68	68	68	63	89	63	60	67	52	30
31	75		83	69	70	69	61	90	64	61	69	53	31
32	75		84	70	72	70	59	92	65	62	70	54	32
33	76		85	71	74	71	57	94	65	62	72	55	33
34	76			73	75	72	55	95	66	63	73	56	34
35	76			74	77	73	52	97	67	64	75	57	35
36	77			75	78	74	50	98	68	64	76	58	36
37	77			76	80	75	48	100	69	65	78	60	37
38	78			77	82	76	46	101	70	66	79	61	38
39	78			78	83	77	43	102	70	67	81	62	39
40	78			79	85	78	41	104	71	67	82	63	40
41	79			80	86	79	39		72	68	83	63	41
42	79			81	88	80	37		73	68	85	64	42
43	79			82	89	81	35		73	69	86	65	43
44	80			83	90	82	32		74	70	87	66	44
45	80			83	92	82	30		75	70	89	67	45
46	81			84	93	83	28		76	71	90	68	46
47	81			85	95	84	26		76	72		69	47
48	81			86	96	85	24		77	72		70	48
49	81			87	97	85	21			73		71	49
50	82			88	99	86	19			73		72	50
51	82			88	100		17			74		73	51
52	82			89	101		15			75		74	52
53	83			90	103		12			75		74	53
54	83			91	104		10			76		75	54
55	83			91	105		8			76		76	55
56	83			92	107		6			77		77	56
57	84			93	108		4			77		78	57
58	84			93	109		1			78		79	58
59	84			94	110		-1			79		79	59
60	85			95	112		-3			79		80	60
61	85									80		81	61
62	85									80		82	62
63	85									81		83	63
64	86									81		83	64

(continued)

Table 49 (continued)

Raw score without K correction	Validity scale[a]			Clinical scale[a]										Raw score without K correction
	L	F	K	1 (Hs)	2 (D)	3 (Hy)	4 (Pd)	5 (Mf)	6 (Pa)	7 (Pt)	8 (Sc)	9 (Ma)	0 (Si)	
65											82		84	65
66											82		85	66
67											83		86	67
68											83		86	68
69											84		87	69
70											84		88	70
71											85			71
72											85			72
73											86			73
74											86			74
75											87			75
76											87			76
77											88			77
78											88			78

[a]See text (pp. 19-41) for explanation of validity and clinical scales and the number of items in each scale.
Note. Modified from Colligan, R. C., & Offord, K. P. (1989). The aging MMPI: Contemporary norms for contemporary teenagers. *Mayo Clinic Proceedings, 64*, 3-27.

Table 50

New Normalized T Scores for Raw Scores Without K Correction in Contemporary Male Adolescents 13 Through 17 Years of Age

Raw score without K correction	Validity scale[a]			Clinical scale[a]										Raw score without K correction
	L	F	K	1 (Hs)	2 (D)	3 (Hy)	4 (Pd)	5 (Mf)	6 (Pa)	7 (Pt)	8 (Sc)	9 (Ma)	0 (Si)	
0	24	18	3	23	-69	-30	-22	-47	-4	14	16	7	-14	0
1	40	29	17	35	-40	-11	-5	-27	12	24	24	9	-2	1
2	47	35	23	40	-24	-3	2	-18	19	28	27	11	3	2
3	52	40	27	43	-12	3	7	-12	24	30	30	14	7	3
4	56	44	31	47	-3	8	11	-7	29	33	32	16	10	4
5	60	47	34	49	4	12	15	-2	33	35	34	18	13	5
6	63	49	37	52	11	16	19	2	36	37	36	20	16	6
7	66	51	40	54	16	20	22	6	39	39	37	22	18	7
8	69	53	42	56	21	23	25	10	42	41	39	24	20	8
9	72	55	45	58	25	26	28	13	45	42	40	26	23	9
10	74	56	47	60	29	29	31	17	48	44	42	28	25	10
11	77	58	49	62	33	32	33	20	50	45	43	30	26	11
12	79	59	51	64	36	35	36	23	53	47	44	32	28	12
13	81	60	53	65	39	38	38	26	55	48	45	34	30	13
14	83	62	55	67	42	40	40	28	57	49	46	36	32	14
15	85	63	57	69	44	43	43	31	60	50	47	38	33	15
16		64	58	70	47	45	45	33	62	52	48	40	35	16
17		64	60	71	49	47	47	36	64	53	49	42	36	17
18		65	62	73	51	50	49	38	66	54	50	44	38	18
19		66	63	74	53	52	51	41	68	55	51	46	39	19
20		67	65	76	55	54	52	43	69	56	52	48	40	20
21		68	67	77	57	56	54	45	71	57	53	50	42	21
22		68	68	78	59	58	56	47	73	58	54	52	43	22
23		69	69	79	61	60	58	49	75	59	55	55	44	23
24		70	71	81	63	62	60	52	76	60	56	57	46	24
25		70	72	82	64	64	61	54	78	61	57	59	47	25
26		71	74	83	66	66	63	56	80	62	57	61	48	26
27		72	75	84	67	68	64	57	81	63	58	63	49	27
28		72	76	85	69	69	66	59	83	63	59	65	50	28

(continued)

Table 50 (continued)

Raw score without K correction	Validity scale[a]			Clinical scale[a]										Raw score without K correction
	L	F	K	1 (Hs)	2 (D)	3 (Hy)	4 (Pd)	5 (Mf)	6 (Pa)	7 (Pt)	8 (Sc)	9 (Ma)	0 (Si)	
29		73	78	86	70	71	68	61	84	64	60	67	52	29
30		73	79	87	71	73	69	63	86	65	61	69	53	30
31		74		88	73	75	71	65	87	66	61	71	54	31
32		74		90	74	76	72	67	89	67	62	73	55	32
33		75		91	75	78	74	68	90	68	63	75	56	33
34		75			76	80	75	70	92	68	63	77	57	34
35		76			77	81	76	72	93	69	64	79	58	35
36		76			79	83	78	74	95	70	65	81	59	36
37		77			80	84	79	75	96	71	65	83	60	37
38		77			81	86	81	77	97	72	66	85	61	38
39		77			82	87	82	79	99	72	67	87	62	39
40		78			83	89	83	80	100	73	67	89	63	40
41		78			84	90	84	82		74	68	91	64	41
42		79			85	92	86	83		75	69	93	65	42
43		79			86	93	87	85		75	69	96	66	43
44		79			86	95	88	86		76	70	98	67	44
45		80			87	96	90	88		77	71	100	68	45
46		80			88	97	91	89		77	71	102	69	46
47		80			89	99	92	91		78	72		69	47
48		81			90	100	93	92		79	72		70	48
49		81			91	102	94	94			73		71	49
50		81			92	103	96	95			74		72	50
51		82			92	104		97			74		73	51
52		82			93	106		98			75		74	52
53		82			94	107		99			75		75	53
54		83			95	108		101			76		75	54
55		83			95	109		102			76		76	55
56		83			96	111		103			77		77	56
57		83			97	112		105			77		78	57
58		84			98	113		106			78		79	58

132

59	84	98	114	107	79	79	59
60	84	99	116	109	79	80	60
61	85				80	81	61
62	85				80	82	62
63	85				81	83	63
64	85				81	83	64
65					82	84	65
66					82	85	66
67					83	86	67
68					83	86	68
69					84	87	69
70					84	88	70
71					85		71
72					85		72
73					86		73
74					86		74
75					87		75
76					87		76
77					88		77
78					88		78

[a]See text (pp. 19–41) for explanation of validity and clinical scales and the number of items in each scale.

Note. Modified from Colligan, R. C., & Offord, K. P. (1989). The aging MMPI: Contemporary norms for contemporary teenagers. *Mayo Clinic Proceedings, 64*, 3-27.

It should be noted that the T scores that have been calculated without K correction in Appendix I have been reprinted from Tables 49 and 50 for convenience. These scales—2 (D), 3 (Hy), 5 (Mf), 6 (Pa), and 0 (Si)—do not require K correction. Only scales 1 (Hs), 4 (Pd), 7 (Pt), 8 (Sc), and 9 (Ma) require K correction.

3. Plot the normalized T-score value for each validity and clinical scale on the MMPI profile sheet. Use the T-score values printed at the edge of the profile form as a guide. Disregard the raw score values from the old norms or the Marks and Briggs norms if these have been preprinted on the profile sheet.

PART VI

SUMMARY: REMINDERS, RECOMMENDATIONS, SUGGESTIONS, CAVEATS . . .

DEVELOPMENT OF THE MMPI

First, it is important to remember that Hathaway and McKinley originally planned, developed, and utilized the MMPI as a self-report questionnaire to aid physicians in understanding the intertwining of psychological factors and personality traits associated with the presenting medical problems of their patients.

Needless to say, use has broadened remarkably. In addition to being applied to medical and mental health referrals, the MMPI is widely used as part of screening procedures for job applicants: for example, firefighters, police officers, airline pilots, managers, graduate students, and executives. Hence, it is essential for clinicians and researchers to be keenly aware of the MMPI response patterns of normal adults and adolescents.

Second, Hathaway and McKinley also believed that elevations on individual MMPI scales would help establish a psychiatric diagnosis. This expectation was not fulfilled. However, certain response patterns and profile configurations soon became associated with certain patterns of thought and behavior. Hathaway developed a preliminary scheme, refined by others, for classifying these patterns, later known as code types. For example the 4–9/9–4 code type—meaning that scales 4 (Pd) and 9 (Ma) were the highest points of the profile—was found to be associated with an increased risk for antiestablishment behavior among adolescents and, if highly elevated, with juvenile delinquency. Furthermore, research found that certain other scales—such as 2 (D) or 5 (Mf)—could serve as moderators and decrease the likelihood of such behavior, whereas other scales were described as *excitatory*—9 (Ma), for example—increasing the probability of behavioral acting out by the adolescent.

CLINICAL APPLICATION

From the preceding, it is clear that the primary reason for using the MMPI, or any other diagnostic instrument for that matter, is to aid clinicians in developing a

better understanding of the social perceptions, motivations, psychological functioning, and personality characteristics of their patients; the second reason, with
this information as grist for the therapeutic mill, is to help build a closer working
relationship with our patients.

A formal diagnosis will be derived by the clinician who integrates all of the
available information about the patient. Thus, the MMPI is but one source of data
about the patient—or perhaps more accurately, a source of speculations about the
patient's inner life, personality functioning, and psychological characteristics.
These speculations are to be explored and evaluated further through interview or
other objective or projective assessment procedures. Nevertheless, the goals of
these procedures remain the same: namely, to decrease the psychological
distance between the clinician and the patient and to assist the clinician in
understanding the patient's psychological structure and the strategies used in
coping with life stresses.

Unfortunately, the use of computer-generated MMPI reports may have inadvertently contributed to increasing the psychological distance between clinician
and client. Clinicians who are not well educated about the MMPI, or who are
inexperienced in its use, may view the empirically generated phrases, statements,
and paragraphs printed out by the computer as carrying far more weight than
should be ascribed to them. It should be kept in mind that these computer-
generated interpretations do not reflect absolute truth or certainty but are more
appropriately viewed as statements of probability regarding certain facets of the
patient's behavior and personality. Furthermore, the library of statements within
the computer, and the rules used by the computer program to determine which
statements are to be printed, may have been written by clinicians or academicians
whose base of experience may not be a good match with the clientele of the user.

THE AGING MMPI

MMPI response patterns among contemporary normal adults and adolescents
have changed significantly since the original norms were developed. There are
several reasons for these changes.

First, the impact of education and associated changes in our society likely
account for most of the change. Men and women of the late 1930s and early 1940s
who were included in the original adult normative sample had eighth- and
tenth-grade levels of education, respectively, whereas both the men and the
women in our contemporary normal adult sample had a mean level of 13 years of
education.

Second, age may be associated with mean score levels. The original adult
norms were established from persons whose ages ranged from 16 through 65
years, whereas our contemporary normal adult sample was comprised of people
whose ages ranged from 18 through 99 years. Although we selected our
comparative samples by the proportion of age and sex based on the 1980 census,
this method does not adjust for any underlying age-related differences. Unfortunately, information regarding the specific ages of each of the individuals in the
original Hathaway norms is no longer available, so age-related changes cannot be
evaluated in the original work. The fact that the majority of the "Minnesota

Normal Sample'' consisted of volunteers obtained from hospital visitors may also have resulted in unknown response biases.

Third, it has been pointed out that researchers and clinicians were relatively liberal regarding their acceptance of the patient's unanswered MMPI items during the early years of MMPI use. Since then, increasingly stringent requirements for completion of the items have been placed on subjects completing the MMPI. Thus, the original MMPI norms may have had lower values on some scales because of the impact of items that were left blank.

Nevertheless, although the MMPI is aging, the item pool remains viable for use in psychological assessment of medical and psychiatric patients, the groups for which it was originally intended.

USING CONTEMPORARY AND ORIGINAL NORMS

Therefore, for clinicians who are using the old MMPI adult norms, or computer-scoring services that utilize the original Hathaway data, we recommend that a second profile line, based on these contemporary adult norms, be plotted for comparative purposes.

MINNESOTA STATEWIDE NINTH-GRADE SAMPLE

The data provided by Hathaway and Monachesi (1963) should not be used for either normative or comparative purposes. Remember, profiles believed to be invalid were systematically culled from this sample. Furthermore, their study was not intended to provide normative standards, but rather the MMPI data were obtained as part of a large-scale study of juvenile delinquency. These data have been recategorized and recently published in more complete form, including normalized T scores with and without K correction, by Gottesman et al. (1987).

ADOLESCENT NORMS: MARKS AND BRIGGS

Although interesting for historical purposes, the original Hathaway and Monachesi adolescent data that they most fully summarized in 1963 should not be used for plotting MMPI profiles for contemporary adolescents. The data provided by Marks and Briggs in 1967 are more appropriate for use. However, it should be recalled that about 40% of their data came from the Hathaway and Monachesi samples of 1947 to 1957 and therefore are 30 to 40 years old. The remaining 60% of that data pool was gathered during the school year for 1964-1965 and are now more than 25 years old. Therefore, just as with the adult norms, we encourage clinicians who are using the Marks and Briggs norms to plot a second profile line, based on the contemporary adolescent norms presented in this volume, for comparative purposes.

CONTEMPORARY NORMATIVE CHANGES

Because of the combination of changes in response patterns and the normalization procedures used in developing the new T-score tables, MMPI profiles based on these new norms are likely to be somewhat lower in general. Depending on age, sex, and mental health status, a modest proportion of the profiles will change in code type. However, these changes are not likely to be dramatic. For example, we have as yet seen no one with a 4–9/9–4 code type earn a 2–7/7–2 profile code after the profile has been rescored with the contemporary norms. It is more likely that a 2–1–3 profile may change to a 1–3–2 or 3–1–2 code type.

CONTEMPORARY INTERPRETATION

Because of the slight lowering of the profile in general, the interpretive statements generated by the clinician or by the computer program are likely to be more tempered and less pejorative. Thus, computer programs and clinicians typically begin making their strongest statements at or above a T score of 70. Although it is widely believed that a standard T score of 70, using the old norms and the linear transformations used to develop them, falls at the 97.7th percentile, this is not true for nearly all of the MMPI scales. This occurs because a linear transformation maintains the underlying skewness in the distribution of raw scores. Therefore, clinicians may be misled into overstating the degree of psychological stress or psychopathology (that is, by making a statement that is intended to be used with a score falling at the 97.7th percentile) for someone whose score, for example, on the depression scale, actually falls at the 94th percentile, simply because of underlying skewness in the distribution of raw scores. Using the contemporary normative tables, which have been built upon normalized transformations, clinicians can have more confidence that scores, across all scales, fall at the 97.7th percentile when they reach a T score of 70.

In some ways, interpretation using the contemporary adolescent norms is made easier because the T scores from the normalizing transformations fall near their expected percentile ranks, values with which most clinicians are familiar from their use in other contemporary tests and assessment procedures. Therefore, as an example, consider a normalized T-score value of 60, which would fall near the 85th percentile. In general, when considering whether to make a particular interpretive statement, clinicians should remember that someone who is responding in a manner that is different from 85% of normal adolescents requires a statement that has sufficient strength to emphasize this difference.

Furthermore, because of the manner in which percentile ranks change as they approach the tail (for example, the upper extreme) of the distribution, smaller T-score increments beyond this point are likely to be of interpretive significance as well. For example, a normalized T-score value of 65 falls at the 93rd percentile. The same logic may then be applied by the clinician. If this adolescent has obtained a score on a specific scale that is higher than 93% of normal adolescents, then this difference needs to be underscored with the appropriate use of adjectives and other descriptive statements. Thus, it would be unwise for clinicians using the contemporary norms to defer relatively strong interpretive statements until a T score of 70, which falls at the 98th percentile, because differences of lesser magnitude, beginning with T scores near 60, are likely to be meaningful. This normal-value work focuses only on specificity (scores relative to normal adolescents) and not on sensitivity (scores relative to psychopathological criterion groups.)

INTEGRATION OF ADOLESCENT AND ADULT
CONTEMPORARY NORMS

Hathaway's cogent observation regarding the importance of keeping adolescent scores in the context of adult response patterns remains pertinent. This is likely to be particularly helpful when clinicians interpret the results of an adolescent's MMPI to the adolescent or to the adolescent's parents or caregivers. The adolescent who earns T scores having a particular configuration that falls in the range of T score 60 to 65 is reporting scores that differ from 85% to 95% of normal adolescents. The adult family members may be somewhat aware of the behavioral differences between their adolescent and other adolescents of comparable age, but the stresses within the family may be more easily understood when it is pointed out that these adolescent values may differ from the response patterns of more than 98% of normal adults. Thus, while there are moderate but noticeable differences from other adolescents, the MMPI from an adolescent patient is likely to be dramatically different from the adult MMPI standards of contemporary society.

Hence, it is equally important to recall Hathaway's observation regarding the schizophrenic-like appearance of the MMPI profiles from normal adolescents when the responses were plotted using adult standards. This important distinction remains today.

INTERPRETIVE STRATEGIES

Proficiency in using the MMPI with adolescents also requires familiarity with the item content of the scales in general, the item content of the clusters of items within the scales, and the adjectives and descriptive phrases used at different elevations for each of the basic clinical scales. Next, the clinician needs to be conversant with the common two- and three-point code types among adolescents and the interpretations applied to each, at varying levels of elevation. This knowledge must be available for both adolescent and adult MMPI profiles. Also, experienced clinicians need to be aware of the types of profiles most frequently seen among typical referrals to their practice.

Finally, an understanding of the construction and use of selected subscales and supplemental/research scales for the MMPI may also be of value to clinicians in some settings.

The most current work summarizing the use of the MMPI with adolescents has been done by Archer (1984, 1987). A comparable overview of the use of the MMPI with adults, including what is currently known about the MMPI-2, has been provided by Greene (1980, 1991), Graham (1987, 1990), and Butcher (1990b); the application of the MMPI to specific patient populations has also been well summarized in a special volume by Greene (1988).

It is clear from the research literature that MMPI profiles obtained from adolescents should be interpreted with the use of adolescent norms. Profiles and interpretations based on the original Hathaway and McKinley norms for adults from 1943 are particularly inappropriate for adolescents, because they exaggerate symptoms and psychopathology in a grossly inaccurate manner.

In addition, there are some indications that interpretive statements made about adolescent MMPI profiles should use the behavioral correlates and descriptive phrases that have been derived from the experiences of adolescents, rather than simple modifications of interpretations based on adult profiles.

Tradition, as well as the small amount of data available, has suggested that MMPI profiles from adolescents should not be based on K-corrected raw scores. However, no comparative research using K weighting has been done since 1972; given the normative changes we have described, further examination of this proposition needs to be undertaken.

K CORRECTION

Hathaway originally believed that MMPI scale scores for adolescents should be based on raw scores using K correction (Hathaway & Monachesi, 1953, 1961, 1963). However, Marks et al. (1974) found insufficient support for the practice and used raw scores without K correction for all of their work. Since then, this practice has become standard procedure for plotting adolescent profiles.

However, it is important to note that the kind of research that is required to clarify the issue of whether MMPI profiles based on raw scores with K correction are more efficacious than those without K correction has simply not been done. To make it easier for clinicians and researchers to examine this issue, we have included contemporary norms with and without K correction.

Thus, clinicians and researchers who typically deal with a certain type of clientele (such as adolescent psychiatric patients or forensic referrals) should probably plot the profile both ways—using raw scores with and without K correction—to determine which profile appears to be most closely associated with the behavior patterns of such a clientele inside and outside the interview room.

Furthermore, compared with the raw K scores of adults, the raw K scores of adolescents are typically low. Thus, combining this factor with the normalization procedure utilized for transforming raw scores to standard scores should yield profile configurations of the same general shape, although perhaps of slightly different elevation. It was just such differences in elevation that led Meehl and Hathaway (1946) to support the use of K weights among adults, because the procedure improved the discriminating power of the scales to which it was applied.

READING LEVEL

The MMPI is appropriate for adolescents and adults who have at least a sixth-grade level of reading comprehension. However, a few adolescents will not understand some of the item content because of its age or the use of outdated colloquialisms (such as "a good mixer"). Some assistance may need to be provided to adolescents who are unsure of some of the words or their meanings. A tape-recorded version of the MMPI is available and should be used for disabled readers.

MMPI RESEARCH AND AGE-RELATED CHANGES

Because of the considerable amount of variation that exists between general adult and adolescent response patterns, as well as the differences between general adult and geriatric samples, investigators should exercise caution when undertaking MMPI research projects using a sample with a wide range of adolescent-to-geriatric ages, being alert to the possible confounding effects of age and analyzing the data to investigate and evaluate age-related effects (that is, when the study includes both adolescents and adults of various ages).

Conclusion

The MMPI is aging. The research to develop the MMPI was initiated in 1937, and the original normal reference sample for adults was obtained almost 50 years ago. Hathaway and McKinley believed that the MMPI was appropriate for use with adolescents but initially questioned the need for separate adolescent norms. Although it soon became apparent that such adolescent norms were needed, those that have been available are based on MMPIs obtained from adolescents 25 to 40 years ago. Needless to say, for both adolescents and adults, our society has changed dramatically during the 50 years since the MMPI was developed. In 1983, a study of contemporary normal adults found numerous statistically significant and clinically relevant changes in MMPI response patterns, and as a result, contemporary general adult norms for the MMPI were developed. Because of the age-related changes that were also found, specific norms for adults of different ages also were prepared. Subsequently, a companion study of normal adolescents ages 13 through 17 years was completed.

Significant changes were found between the response patterns of contemporary normal adolescents and those from the normative and comparative samples currently available. Therefore, contemporary MMPI norms for adolescents also were developed. However, not surprisingly, given the relatively restricted age range of the new normative sample, no clinically relevant age-related changes in MMPI response patterns were found. Therefore, general adolescent norms, based on our total sample of adolescents, were developed. In the past, linear equations were used to develop normative tables for transforming raw scores to T scores. Unfortunately, however, these procedures maintained any underlying degree of skewness that was present in the underlying distribution of raw scores. As a result, clinicians could not depend on T-score values of similar size having the same meaning from scale to scale, in terms of percentile rank or departure from the mean. Therefore, for both the contemporary adult and the contemporary adolescent studies, transformation equations that generated normalized T scores were used.

These two changes—the use of contemporary samples, and the use of normalized T scores—yield profiles that are somewhat different from those obtained with the old norms and the linear transformations. In general, these contemporary norms yield profiles that are likely to be three to five points lower for adults on all scales, and for the right side of the profile among adolescents, and that do not carry the spiky characteristics associated with the old norms and the use of linear transformations. Nevertheless, the meanings ascribed to each scale, and to the profile configuration, remain the same because they have been supported by years of research. However, the interpretive statements used by clinicians to describe some scale elevations are likely to be applied at lower T-score levels, because clinicians can be more assured that a T score of 60, for example, on a given scale, using normalized T scores and the contemporary norms, falls at a point higher than 85% of the responses of normal adolescents or adults, and a descriptive statement appropriate to that level of difference can safely be made. This was not the case with the original norms because the percentile ranks for these values, across scales, were variable.

We think that these new contemporary norms will contribute to maintaining the MMPI as a viable tool for evaluating the social, emotional, and behavioral functioning of our patients and for clarifying the relationship of such factors to the presenting problem that has brought the patient to our attention.

In 1989, the MMPI-2, a completely revised adult version of the MMPI, was published by the University of Minnesota Press. The new instrument was intended solely for use among adults, and the authors recommended that the original MMPI be used with adolescents. The MMPI-2 can be thought of as being composed of two item pools. First, 370 items, rewritten to conform to current language usage, come from the original Hathaway item pool and contain the 13 basic validity and clinical scales. Some items were deleted from these scales, because they were believed to be offensive to patients or outmoded for contemporary use. Second, the original item pool was supplemented with 107 new items written by the authors of the MMPI-2 to buttress the construction of 15 new content scales that were intended to replace the Wiggins Content Scales. These scales are statistically homogeneous in nature; unfortunately, no criterion groups were used in their development. Some observational data were obtained from spouses within the normative sample, but no clinical data regarding the comparative efficacy of the new scales and the new instrument itself have been published. The authors of the test state in the manual that the original MMPI should continue to be used with adolescents. However, a completely new MMPI-2 for adolescents, provisionally entitled the A-MMPI or MMPI-A, is apparently under development. This new instrument probably will be shorter, will be constructed in the same manner as the MMPI-2, and will include a core of the original MMPI item pool and a new set of items written specifically for adolescent-related content scales.

Finally, it is essential that clinicians who use the MMPI appreciate that it is an adjunct to, and not a substitute for, a carefully completed clinical interview and the development of a psychotherapeutically meaningful relationship with the patient. Although the MMPI and its supplemental scales can potentially provide a wealth of information about our patients, these data should remain speculations until one has become sufficiently acquainted with the patient, and with the parents, teachers, and others who know the patient well, to obtain verification or corroboration. The ultimate purpose of the MMPI is to enable us to become more attuned to the psychological needs and stresses of our patients—an important goal in this age of high technology and computerized assessment, which may actually increase the psychological distance between clinicians and their patients and make a therapeutically useful relationship more difficult to attain.

APPENDIX A

Research/Supplemental Scales for the MMPI

CONTENTS FOR APPENDIX A

Introduction

    d. Social Alienation (Pd4A)
    e. Self-Alienation (Pd4B)
    f. Alienation (Sum of Pd4A and Pd4B) (Pd4)
  Scale 6 (Pa, Paranoia)
    a. Ideas of External Influence (Pa1)
    b. Poignancy (Pa2)
    c. Moral Virtue (Pa3)
  Scale 8 (Sc, Schizophrenia)
    a. Social Alienation (Sc1A)
    b. Emotional Alienation (Sc1B)
    c. Object Loss (Sum of Sc1A and Sc1B) (Sc1)
    d. Lack of Ego Mastery, Cognitive (Sc2A)
    e. Lack of Ego Mastery, Conative (Sc2B)
    f. Lack of Ego Mastery, Defect of Inhibition and Control (Sc2C)
    g. Lack of Ego Mastery, Intrapsychic Autonomy
      (Sum of Sc2A, Sc2B, and Sc2C) (Sc2)
    h. Sensorimotor Dissociation (Sc3)
  Scale 9 (Ma, Hypomania)
    a. Amorality (Ma1)
    b. Psychomotor Acceleration (Ma2)
    c. Imperturbability (Ma3)
    d. Ego Inflation (Ma4)
2. Serkownek Subscales for Scales 5 (Mf) and 0 (Si)
  Scale 5 (Mf, Masculinity-Femininity)
    a. Narcissism-Hypersensitivity (Mf1)
    b. Stereotypic Feminine Interests (Mf2)
    c. Denial of Stereotypic Masculine Interests (Mf3)
    d. Heterosexual Discomfort, Passivity (Mf4)
    e. Introspective, Critical (Mf5)
    f. Socially Retiring (Mf6)
  Scale 0 (Si, Social Introversion-Extroversion)
    a. Inferiority, Personal Discomfort (Si1)
    b. Discomfort With Others (Si2)
    c. Staid, Personal Rigidity (Si3)
    d. Hypersensitivity (Si4)
    e. Distrust (Si5)
    f. Physical-Somatic Concerns (Si6)
3. Wiggins Content Scales
    a. Social Maladjustment (SOC)
    b. Depression (DEP)
    c. Feminine Interests (FEM)
    d. Poor Morale (MOR)
    e. Religious Fundamentalism (REL)
    f. Authority Conflict (AUT)
    g. Psychoticism (PSY)
    h. Organic Symptoms (ORG)
    i. Family Problems (FAM)
    j. Manifest Hostility (HOS)
    k. Phobias (PHO)
    l. Hypomania (HYP)
    m. Poor Health (HEA)
4. TSC Item-Cluster Scales
    a. Cluster I (Social Introversion vs. Interpersonal Poise and Outgoingness) (I)

b. Cluster II (Body Symptoms vs. Lack of Physical Complaints)   (B)
c. Cluster III (Suspicion and Mistrust vs. Absence of Suspicion)   (S)
d. Cluster IV (Depression and Apathy vs. Positive and Optimistic Outlook) (D)
e. Cluster V (Resentment and Aggression vs. Lack of Resentment
   and Aggression)   (R)
f. Cluster VI (Autism and Disruptive Thought vs. Absence
   of Such Disturbance)   (A)
g. Cluster VII (Tension, Worry, and Fears vs.
   Absence of Such Complaints)   (T)

Set 3: State/Trait Personality Characteristics

1. Welsh Factor Dimensions—Scales A and R
   a. First Factor   (A)
   b. Second Factor   (R)
2. College Maladjustment   (MT;Mt)
3. Manifest Anxiety   (MAS;At)
4. Overcontrolled Hostility   (O-H)
5. Control in Psychological Adjustment   (Cn)
6. Ego Strength   (Es)
7. Ego-Resiliency (Alpha Factor—Block) and Ego-Control (Beta Factor—Block)
   a. Ego-Resiliency (Obvious)   (ER-O)
   b. Ego-Resiliency (Subtle)   (ER-S)
   c. Ego-Control—Scale 5   (EC-5)
   d. Ego-Control—Female   (EC-5F)
   e. Ego-Control—Male   (EC-5M)
8. Status   (St)
9. Social Responsibility   (Re)
10. Dominance   (Do)
11. Dependency   (Dy)
12. Prejudice   (Pr)
13. Conversion Low-Back Pain   (Lb)
14. Functional Dorsal Pain   (DOR)
15. Caudality   (Ca)
16. Alcoholism—MacAndrew   (MAC)
17. Substance Abuse Proclivity—MacAndrew   (SAP)
18. Critical Items: Lachar-Wrobel Critical Item Set   (CI)

INTRODUCTION

This section contains normative data for many of the most popular research and supplemental scales for the MMPI.

Of the 550 different items of the MMPI, only 399 are required for scoring the 13 basic validity and clinical scales; thus, 151 items are not used. Early MMPI researchers believed that the unused items of the total pool should not be dropped because they might contribute to scales that would be developed later and, indeed, this has been the case. Because 19% of the original item pool was deleted during construction of the MMPI-2, many such scales will, unfortunately, no longer be available to clinicians and researchers.

Some, such as the Baseball Scale (LaPlace, 1952, 1954), appear to have been used for a single research study and were not greatly applied thereafter. Others, such as the Ego-Strength Scale (Es), also initiated by doctoral-level research, continue to be widely used (Barron, 1953). Some scales have even remained popular without convincing research support for their efficacy. None of the research and supplemental scales currently available for the MMPI, however, have reached the level of acceptance of the Si scale (Introversion-Extroversion). The Si scale (Drake, 1946) was added as scale 0 (Si), becoming the last scale to be incorporated into the basic MMPI profile form and the only scale developed outside of the original Hathaway research team.

SELECTION PROCEDURES

The 29 research and supplemental scales included in this section were selected because of their relatively widespread use among clinicians working with adolescents and the comments made about them in the currently available interpretive manuals for the MMPI. However, users of these scales are cautioned regarding their use for three reasons: sample sizes used in the development of many of these scales frequently were small; in some cases, cross validation at the time of development was not completed; and, for many, substantive research to buttress issues of reliability and validity has not been carried out. Thus, interpretive comments should be speculative in nature and modified by the configuration of the basic validity and clinical scales as well as other information available to the clinician about the patient's age, sex, socioeconomic status, and reason for referral.

Scales were further selected to represent several areas of clinical importance. These include additional measures of profile validity or test-taking attitude and possible response bias, subscales and content clusters that may be helpful in supplementing information gained from the basic clinical profile, and a collection of state-trait related variables covering a wide range of characteristics from somatization proneness and addiction to frank psychopathology. Finally, a set of "critical items," which may require further inquiry through interview when endorsed by the adolescent, are reported.

ORGANIZATIONAL PLAN AND USE OF THE TABLES

Information regarding each of the research and supplemental scales is organized in the same manner.

First, the original article in which the author presented the scale is abstracted. The original citation and occasionally a few concurrent or related articles for that scale are listed.

Second, the items composing the scale and the direction of scoring are given to provide users the opportunity to review item content and to determine whether their own evaluation agrees with the name that has been applied to the scale by others. The raw score for each scale represents the total number of items endorsed in the scorable direction by the patient. Unanswered items and those answered both true and false were omitted from the score. Scores obtained from hand-held templates could differ slightly from those reported here if items marked both true and false are treated as an endorsement.

Third, the normative data are presented separately for female and male adolescents. Each table provides scores from the contemporary normal sample of adolescents, separately by age.

Fourth, it is important to note that the tables do **NOT** contain T-score values. Instead, these sex-specific norms are composed of numbers representing percentile ranks among the five age groups and the total sample of contemporary normal adolescents. The percentile ranks in these tables are defined as the proportion of normal subjects with raw score values that are strictly less than the specified raw score. For example, if the patient's raw score for a specific scale was 11 and the corresponding number in the Total-Sample column was 95, the interpretive statement would indicate that the adolescent patient had earned a raw score having a value higher than 95% of the subjects in the total normal adolescent sample of that sex. Thus, the tabled percentile ranks allow the clinician to state directly that the patient has earned a raw score strictly higher than the stated percentage of subjects in the contemporary normal adolescent sample.

Linear transformations could have been used to develop standard scores for some of these scales. However, for reasons enumerated on page 73 and following, it may not be appropriate to do so. Briefly, such procedures maintain the underlying skewness of the distribution of raw scores. In addition, many of the research and supplemental scales in this Appendix contain such small numbers of items that the use of either linear transformations or normalization procedures would be statistically inappropriate.

Should users of this reference book want to obtain similar normative tables on other special scales, they are encouraged to contact the authors at the Section of Psychology, Mayo Clinic, Rochester, Minnesota, 55905.

REFERENCES

Barron, F. (1953). An ego-strength scale which predicts response to psychotherapy. *Journal of Consulting Psychology, 17,* 327–333.

Drake, L. E. (1946). A social I.E. scale for the Minnesota Multiphasic Personality Inventory. *Journal of Applied Psychology, 30,* 51–54.

LaPlace, J. (1952). *An exploratory study of personality and its relationship to success in professional baseball.* Unpublished doctoral dissertation, Columbia University, New York.

LaPlace, J. P. (1954). Personality and its relationship to success in professional baseball. *Research Quarterly, 25,* 313–319.

APPENDIX A

Set 1: Response Bias, Response Consistency, and General Validity

POSITIVE MALINGERING (Pm;Mp)

Cofer, Chance, and Judson (1949) used three groups of college sophomores (both sexes) in a study of positive and negative malingering on the MMPI. Each sample took the MMPI twice within 2 weeks, once in the faked direction (that is, either positive or negative) and once honestly. The order of administration was counterbalanced. Those who were to "fake good" (positive malingering, 27 subjects) were told to fake the MMPI in the direction of normality. More specifically, "they were asked to imagine themselves as being desirous of entering midshipman training in the Navy and, therefore, as wishing to make the best possible impression through their test scores" (p. 494). Subjects who were to "fake bad" (negative malingering, 28 subjects) were not asked to pretend any specific type of psychiatric disorder but, "to answer the questions as they thought an emotionally disturbed person would answer them. . . . [and] in such a way as to avoid being drafted into the Army" (p. 494). A third group, 26 control subjects, completed the MMPI under standard conditions on both occasions.

The mean K and L scores were found to be significantly ($p < 0.01$) higher under the condition of positive malingering than in the control group.

Beyond this, an item analysis identified 39 items that were sensitive to positive malingering but were not susceptible to negative malingering. These items were left unchanged when the subjects faked bad, but their responses shifted under the fake-good condition. At least half of the subjects answered in a socially undesirable direction when they were responding honestly. Thus, the items appeared to represent characteristics that many people would need to admit about themselves if they were being honest, even though they would be aware of the negative social value of the characteristic. Therefore, the items appeared to be a more subtle version of the already existing L scale.

When the positive malingering scale (Pm) was applied to the records of the students in the three samples, 96% of the honest MMPIs and 86% of the fake-good profiles were correctly identified. To do this, a raw score of 20 or greater on Pm was considered to indicate positive malingering and a raw score of 19 or less on Pm was considered to reflect an honest response style. It should be noted that this cutting point did not classify any negative-malingering profiles inaccurately.

Subsequently, 5 of the 39 items were dropped because of changes noted among members of the control group under the normal-honest test-retest condition. The remaining 34 items contained one pair of the 16 duplicated items on the MMPI (that is, items 21 and 308, "At times I have very much wanted to leave home"); dropping the latter of the pair left a scale of 33 items.

REFERENCE

Cofer, C. N., Chance, J., & Judson, A. J. (1949). A study of malingering on the Minnesota Multiphasic Personality Inventory. *Journal of Psychology, 27,* 491–499.

The following 33 items comprise the positive malingering (Pm;Mp) scale and are listed in order by direction of scoring.

The following items score if answered true:

95.[a]   I go to church almost every week.
143.   When I was a child, I belonged to a crowd or gang that tried to stick together through thick and thin.
144.   I would like to be a soldier.
204.   I would like to be a journalist.
223.   I very much like hunting.
232.   I have been inspired to a program of life based on duty which I have since carefully followed.
264.   I am entirely self-confident.
287.   I have very few fears compared to my friends.
369.[a]   Religion gives me no worry.
373.[a]   I feel sure that there is only one true religion.
400.   If given the chance I could do some things that would be of great benefit to the world.
415.   If given the chance I would make a good leader of people.
434.   I would like to be an auto racer.
461.   I find it hard to set aside a task that I have undertaken even for a short time.
498.[a]   It is always a good thing to be frank.
537.[a]   I would like to hunt lions in Africa.
556.[a]   I am very careful about my manner of dress.

The following items score if answered false:

21.   At times I have very much wanted to leave home.
30.   At times I feel like swearing.
45.   I do not always tell the truth.
102.   My hardest battles are with myself.
105.   Sometimes when I am not feeling well I am cross.
195.   I do not like everyone I know.
208.   I like to flirt.
217.   I frequently find myself worrying about something.
225.   I gossip a little at times.
231.   I like to talk about sex.
255.   Sometimes at elections I vote for men about whom I know very little.
322.   I worry over money and business.
370.[a]   I hate to have to rush when working.

374.   At periods my mind seems to work more slowly than usual.
465.   I have several times had a change of heart about my life work.
499.   I must admit that I have at times been worried beyond reason over something that really did not matter.

---

[a]Items that were deleted from the original MMPI item pool during construction of the MMPI-2.

Research/Supplemental Scales for the MMPI

Females   Positive Malingering   (Pm;Mp)

		Age, yr				
	Total Sample	13	14	15	16	17
N	691	136	153	127	138	137
Median	11	13	12	11	10	11
Mean	11.35	12.49	12.08	10.77	10.45	10.84
SD	3.38	3.16	3.43	3.3	3.09	3.42
Min	1	5	5	1	3	3
Max	25	21	25	20	22	22

	Percentage of Sample with Raw Score < X					
X	Total Sample	13	14	15	16	17
1	0.0	0.0	0.0	0.0	0.0	0.0
2	0.1	0.0	0.0	0.8	0.0	0.0
3	0.1	0.0	0.0	0.8	0.0	0.0
4	0.7	0.0	0.0	0.8	1.4	1.5
5	1.2	0.0	0.0	3.1	1.4	1.5
6	2.9	0.7	1.3	4.7	2.9	5.1
7	6.8	1.5	5.2	9.4	6.5	11.7
8	11.3	5.1	7.8	14.2	14.5	15.3
9	21.0	11.0	15.0	26.0	27.5	26.3
10	29.8	15.4	22.9	35.4	40.6	35.8
11	42.1	29.4	31.4	46.5	58.0	46.7
12	54.3	41.9	44.4	59.1	68.8	58.4
13	63.8	49.3	56.2	70.1	75.4	69.3
14	75.7	64.7	69.3	82.7	83.3	79.6
15	81.8	72.8	77.1	87.4	88.4	83.9
16	88.4	81.6	85.6	91.3	92.8	91.2
17	93.8	88.2	92.2	96.1	97.1	95.6
18	96.4	94.1	93.5	97.6	99.3	97.8
19	97.8	97.8	95.4	98.4	99.3	98.5
20	98.8	98.5	98.7	98.4	99.3	99.3
21	99.3	99.3	98.7	100.0	99.3	99.3
22	99.4	100.0	98.7	100.0	99.3	99.3
23	99.9	100.0	99.3	100.0	100.0	100.0
24	99.9	100.0	99.3	100.0	100.0	100.0
25	99.9	100.0	99.3	100.0	100.0	100.0

Research/Supplemental Scales for the MMPI

Males   Positive Malingering   (Pm;Mp)

		Age, yr				
	Total Sample	13	14	15	16	17
N	624	112	147	130	122	113
Median	14	15	14	14	13	14
Mean	13.89	14.44	14.07	13.87	13.41	13.64
SD	3.59	3.53	3.55	3.67	3.61	3.57
Min	4	7	5	5	4	5
Max	25	22	23	25	23	23

	Percentage of Sample with Raw Score < X					
X	Total Sample	13	14	15	16	17
4	0.0	0.0	0.0	0.0	0.0	0.0
5	0.2	0.0	0.0	0.0	0.8	0.0
6	1.0	0.0	0.7	0.8	0.8	2.7
7	1.6	0.0	2.0	1.5	0.8	3.5
8	3.8	2.7	4.8	3.8	2.5	5.3
9	6.1	6.3	6.1	6.2	4.9	7.1
10	11.9	11.6	8.8	11.5	14.8	13.3
11	17.5	16.1	14.3	16.9	23.0	17.7
12	26.4	21.4	21.1	30.0	36.1	23.9
13	35.6	26.8	34.0	36.2	44.3	36.3
14	45.4	32.1	44.2	46.9	54.9	47.8
15	57.4	49.1	55.8	60.8	60.7	60.2
16	65.9	59.8	66.0	64.6	70.5	68.1
17	76.6	75.0	76.2	74.6	77.0	80.5
18	84.5	83.0	84.4	82.3	85.2	87.6
19	89.7	87.5	89.1	88.5	91.8	92.0
20	93.9	92.0	91.8	95.4	95.9	94.7
21	97.0	95.5	97.3	96.9	97.5	97.3
22	98.2	97.3	98.0	98.5	98.4	99.1
23	99.2	100.0	98.6	99.2	99.2	99.1
24	99.8	100.0	100.0	99.2	100.0	100.0
25	99.8	100.0	100.0	99.2	100.0	100.0

F MINUS K DISSIMULATION INDEX (F – K)

The F minus K dissimulation index (F – K) is calculated by subtracting the raw score earned on scale K from the raw score earned on scale F (that is, raw F – raw K). Many clinicians believe this index to be useful for detecting profiles on which the patient has falsely exaggerated psychopathology.

In Gough's original work (1947), 11 mental health professionals were asked to simulate two types of MMPI patient profiles. The first was the simulation of MMPI responses from a patient having "an acute, severe, anxiety neurosis which would lead to separation from the [military] service, but not to commitment to a mental hospital" (p. 217). The second was the simulation of "a non-deteriorated, acute, paranoid schizophrenic" (p. 217).

These simulated profiles were compared with two criterion groups: 57 severe psychoneurotic patients, and 13 paranoid schizophrenic patients. A cutting score of F – K ≥ +4 successfully identified 9 of the 11 simulated severe psychoneurotic profiles, and a cutting score of F – K ≥ +16 successfully identified 9 of the 11 simulated psychotic profiles.[1]

Later, Gough (1950) reviewed several other research studies on this topic, totalling 2,092 cases, and found that all of the normal and patient samples had mean F – K scores less than 0 and all of the groups of dissemblers or malingerers had mean F – K scores greater than 0.

Examination of the distribution of F – K raw scores (Gough, 1956, p. 324, Table 3) for a sample of 691 normal adults, apparently the 294 normal men and 397 normal women described by McKinley and Hathaway (1944), reveals that 93% of the sample have F – K scores of +1 or less (range, -26 to +1), 4% have F – K scores in the interval +2 to +4, and only 3% have scores in the interval +5 to +25.

Based on the total sample (2,092) of authentic and dissembled cases, Gough recommended a cutting score of ≥ +9. This score earned a Phi coefficient that minimized false-positives and false-negatives and correctly identified 97% of the authentic records and 75% of the dissembled or "fake bad" profiles.

Gough noted that it was more difficult to detect "fake good" profiles, indicating that although an F – K cutting score of -11 would correctly classify 25 of 27 fake-good profiles it also would misidentify 19 of 27 authentic profiles among the studies he reviewed.

REFERENCES

Gough, H. G. (1947). Simulated patterns on the Minnesota Multiphasic Personality Inventory. *Journal of Abnormal and Social Psychology, 42,* 215–225.

Gough, H. G. (1950). The F minus K Dissimulation Index for the Minnesota Multiphasic Personality Inventory. *Journal of Consulting Psychology, 14,* 408–413.

Gough, H. G. (1956). The F minus K Dissimulation Index for the MMPI. In G. S. Welsh & W. G. Dahlstrom (Eds.), *Basic readings on the MMPI in psychology and medicine* (pp. 321–327). Minneapolis: University of Minnesota Press.

McKinley, J. C., & Hathaway, S. R. (1944). The Minnesota Multiphasic Personality Inventory: V. Hysteria, hypomania and psychopathic deviate. *Journal of Applied Psychology, 28,* 153–174.

---

[1]Not "ten of the eleven simulated records . . ." (Gough, 1950, p. 408). Gough, H. G., October 1984, Personal communication, IPAR, University of California, Berkeley, CA.

Research/Supplemental Scales for the MMPI

Females   F Minus K Dissimulation Index   (F - K)

		Age, yr				
	Total Sample	13	14	15	16	17
N	691	136	153	127	138	137
Median	-6	-5	-5	-6	-4	-7
Mean	-4.85	-3.97	-5.39	-4.80	-3.51	-6.50
SD	8.35	8.26	8.20	8.75	8.40	7.96
Min	-24	-23	-23	-24	-24	-20
Max	26	17	16	26	21	21

	Percentage of Sample with Raw Score < X					
X	Total Sample	13	14	15	16	17
-24	0.0	0.0	0.0	0.0	0.0	0.0
-23	0.3	0.0	0.0	0.8	0.7	0.0
-22	0.6	0.7	0.7	0.8	0.7	0.0
-21	0.6	0.7	0.7	0.8	0.7	0.0
-20	0.9	0.7	1.3	1.6	0.7	0.0
-19	2.0	1.5	3.3	2.4	1.4	1.5
-18	3.0	1.5	5.9	4.7	1.4	1.5
-17	4.5	2.2	7.2	5.5	1.4	5.8
-16	5.8	3.7	8.5	5.5	2.9	8.0
-15	7.7	5.1	9.8	6.3	5.1	11.7
-14	11.1	9.6	11.8	9.4	8.7	16.1
-13	15.1	15.4	15.7	11.8	11.6	20.4
-12	17.8	16.2	19.0	14.2	13.0	26.3
-11	22.4	18.4	25.5	21.3	17.4	29.2
-10	26.8	21.3	30.7	25.2	21.7	34.3
-9	32.0	27.2	36.6	31.5	23.9	40.1
-8	37.0	31.6	40.5	38.6	28.3	46.0
-7	41.4	36.0	43.8	42.5	34.8	49.6
-6	46.3	44.1	46.4	47.2	39.1	54.7
-5	50.5	47.8	49.0	51.2	43.5	61.3
-4	54.7	52.2	51.6	59.1	48.6	62.8
-3	59.9	55.9	55.6	63.0	54.3	71.5
-2	64.3	60.3	63.4	66.1	59.4	72.3
-1	68.9	62.5	69.9	70.1	66.7	75.2
0	71.3	65.4	74.5	72.4	68.1	75.9
1	75.0	70.6	78.4	76.4	70.3	78.8
2	78.6	75.0	79.7	81.1	75.4	81.8
3	81.6	77.9	82.4	83.5	77.5	86.9
4	83.8	80.9	85.0	85.0	80.4	87.6
5	86.3	82.4	88.2	87.4	82.6	90.5

Research/Supplemental Scales for the MMPI

Females   F Minus K Dissimulation Index   (F - K)
(Continued)

X	Total Sample	Percentage of Sample with Raw Score < X				
		13	14	15	16	17
6	88.3	84.6	90.8	89.0	84.8	92.0
7	90.3	88.2	92.2	89.8	86.2	94.9
8	91.9	90.4	94.1	89.8	88.4	96.4
9	92.8	92.6	94.8	91.3	88.4	96.4
10	94.1	93.4	95.4	93.7	90.6	97.1
11	95.1	94.9	96.1	95.3	92.0	97.1
12	95.9	96.3	96.1	95.3	94.9	97.1
13	96.7	97.1	97.4	95.3	96.4	97.1
14	97.8	97.8	98.7	96.9	97.8	97.8
15	98.0	97.8	98.7	96.9	97.8	98.5
16	98.4	97.8	99.3	97.6	97.8	99.3
17	99.0	99.3	100.0	97.6	98.6	99.3
18	99.4	100.0	100.0	98.4	99.3	99.3
19	99.4	100.0	100.0	98.4	99.3	99.3
20	99.4	100.0	100.0	98.4	99.3	99.3
21	99.4	100.0	100.0	98.4	99.3	99.3
22	99.7	100.0	100.0	98.4	100.0	100.0
23	99.7	100.0	100.0	98.4	100.0	100.0
24	99.7	100.0	100.0	98.4	100.0	100.0
25	99.7	100.0	100.0	98.4	100.0	100.0
26	99.9	100.0	100.0	99.2	100.0	100.0

Research/Supplemental Scales for the MMPI

Males   F Minus K Dissimulation Index   (F - K)

		Age, yr				
	Total Sample	13	14	15	16	17
N	624	112	147	130	122	113
Median	-5	-5	-3	-6	-4	-5
Mean	-4.19	-4.88	-2.44	-4.98	-3.75	-5.36
SD	8.70	8.68	9.00	8.76	8.55	8.16
Min	-25	-23	-24	-24	-22	-25
Max	24	17	22	17	18	24

Percentage of Sample with Raw Score < X

X	Total Sample	13	14	15	16	17
-25	0.0	0.0	0.0	0.0	0.0	0.0
-24	0.2	0.0	0.0	0.0	0.0	0.9
-23	0.5	0.0	0.7	0.8	0.0	0.9
-22	0.8	1.8	0.7	0.8	0.0	0.9
-21	1.3	1.8	1.4	0.8	0.8	1.8
-20	1.8	2.7	2.0	0.8	0.8	2.7
-19	3.0	4.5	3.4	3.8	0.8	2.7
-18	4.0	4.5	3.4	6.9	1.6	3.5
-17	5.8	7.1	4.8	8.5	3.3	5.3
-16	6.9	8.0	4.8	10.0	4.9	7.1
-15	8.5	13.4	5.4	10.8	6.6	7.1
-14	11.1	15.2	7.5	12.3	10.7	10.6
-13	12.8	17.0	8.8	15.4	12.3	11.5
-12	16.5	19.6	12.9	20.8	15.6	14.2
-11	21.8	22.3	16.3	27.7	21.3	22.1
-10	25.0	26.8	17.7	30.0	23.8	28.3
-9	29.6	34.8	23.1	31.5	27.0	33.6
-8	34.5	42.0	25.2	36.2	32.8	38.9
-7	38.5	42.0	30.6	40.0	38.5	43.4
-6	42.9	46.4	32.7	46.2	45.9	46.0
-5	47.0	49.1	38.1	53.1	46.7	49.6
-4	50.8	53.6	42.9	56.2	48.4	54.9
-3	54.2	55.4	46.9	56.9	51.6	61.9
-2	59.1	57.1	52.4	60.0	56.6	71.7
-1	63.0	60.7	58.5	62.3	61.5	73.5
0	66.0	64.3	61.2	67.7	63.1	75.2
1	70.2	67.9	64.6	72.3	68.0	79.6
2	74.0	71.4	66.7	78.5	73.0	82.3
3	77.7	77.7	70.7	83.1	73.8	85.0
4	82.1	83.0	76.9	86.9	78.7	85.8

X	Percentage of Sample with Raw Score < X					
	Total Sample	13	14	15	16	17
5	85.1	86.6	78.9	87.7	82.8	91.2
6	87.0	88.4	82.3	87.7	85.2	92.9
7	88.8	92.0	83.7	87.7	88.5	93.8
8	89.6	92.9	84.4	89.2	89.3	93.8
9	90.9	94.6	85.7	91.5	90.2	93.8
10	92.6	97.3	87.1	91.5	93.4	95.6
11	94.4	97.3	90.5	93.1	95.9	96.5
12	95.8	97.3	93.2	96.9	95.9	96.5
13	96.3	97.3	93.9	97.7	95.9	97.3
14	97.1	98.2	95.9	98.5	95.9	97.3
15	97.6	98.2	98.0	98.5	95.9	97.3
16	98.6	99.1	98.0	98.5	99.2	98.2
17	98.7	99.1	98.0	99.2	99.2	98.2
18	99.2	100.0	98.6	100.0	99.2	98.2
19	99.5	100.0	98.6	100.0	100.0	99.1
20	99.5	100.0	98.6	100.0	100.0	99.1
21	99.7	100.0	99.3	100.0	100.0	99.1
22	99.7	100.0	99.3	100.0	100.0	99.1
23	99.8	100.0	100.0	100.0	100.0	99.1
24	99.8	100.0	100.0	100.0	100.0	99.1

DISSIMULATION (ORIGINAL) (Ds)

During an investigation of prevailing beliefs about neuroticism, Gough (1954) identified 74 MMPI items that clearly differentiated persons who had been requested to take the MMPI in the role of a patient experiencing a psychoneurotic reaction from a sample of actual psychoneurotic patients. The patient sample consisted of 125 men and 51 women diagnosed as psychoneurotic. Responses from these patients were compared with those from 111 students in a psychology class and from 11 professional workers who were asked to emulate a patient experiencing a psychoneurotic reaction. Subsequently, cross validation of the Dissimulation Scale (Ds) was carried out with three new samples: 507 junior and senior high school students, 915 new clinical cases, and 343 dissemblers who were college students in psychology courses. Patients diagnosed as psychoneurotic achieved a mean score (15.9, SD = 7.9) nearly identical with that of the normal sample of junior and senior high school students (15.9, SD = 10.0). Thus, both the patients and the normal control samples obtained scores considerably below the mean of the subjects who were faking a psychoneurotic reaction (mean, 54.1; SD = 11.7). A cutting score of $\geq$ 35 was suggested for alerting clinicians to the possibility that the profile was being faked in the neurotic direction because 93% of the faked profiles had Ds scores of 35 or higher, but only 6% of the clinical cases and 2% of the student sample were in that range.

REFERENCE

Gough, H. G. (1954). Some common misconceptions about neuroticism. *Journal of Consulting Psychology, 18,* 287–292.

The following items score if answered true:

10.   There seems to be a lump in my throat much of the time.
14.[a]   I have diarrhea once a month or more.
16.   I am sure I get a raw deal from life.
19.   When I take a new job, I like to be tipped off on who should be gotten next to.
23.   I am troubled by attacks of nausea and vomiting.
24.   No one seems to understand me.
29.   I am bothered by acid stomach several times a week.
31.   I have nightmares every few nights.
35.   If people had not had it in for me I would have been much more successful.
42.   My family does not like the work I have chosen (or the work I intend to choose for my life work).
44.   Much of the time my head seems to hurt all over.
47.   Once a week or oftener I feel suddenly hot all over, without apparent cause.
50.   My soul sometimes leaves my body.
53.[a]   A minister can cure disease by praying and putting his hand on your head.
73.   I am an important person.
93.   I think most people would lie to get ahead.
97.   At times I have a strong urge to do something harmful or shocking.
104.   I don't seem to care what happens to me.
125.   I have a great deal of stomach trouble.
179.   I am worried about sex matters.
206.[a]   I am very religious (more than most people).
210.   Everything tastes the same.
211.   I can sleep during the day but not at night.

212. My people treat me more like a child than a grown-up.
216. There is very little love and companionship in my family as compared to other homes.
226. Some of my family have habits that bother and annoy me very much.
241. I dream frequently about things that are best kept to myself.
246. My neck spots with red often.
247. I have reason for feeling jealous of one or more members of my family.
297. I wish I were not bothered by thoughts about sex.
303. I am so touchy on some subjects that I can't talk about them.
320. Many of my dreams are about sex matters.
325. The things that some of my family have done have frightened me.
328. I find it hard to keep my mind on a task or job.
341. At times I hear so well it bothers me.
344. Often I cross the street in order not to meet someone I see.
352. I have been afraid of things or people that I knew could not hurt me.
360. Almost every day something happens to frighten me.
375.[a] When I am feeling very happy and active, someone who is blue or low will spoil it all.
388. I am afraid to be alone in the dark.
419. I played hooky from school quite often as a youngster.
422.[a] I have felt embarrassed over the type of work that one or more members of my family have done.
433.[a] I used to have imaginary companions.
438. There are certain people whom I dislike so much that I am inwardly pleased when they are catching it for something they have done.
443. I am apt to pass up something I want to do because others feel that I am not going about it in the right way.
453.[a] When I was a child I didn't care to be a member of a crowd or gang.
458. The man who had most to do with me when I was a child (such as my father, stepfather, etc.) was very strict with me.
459.[a] I have one or more bad habits which are so strong that it is no use in fighting against them.
471. In school my marks in deportment were quite regularly bad.
475. When I am cornered I tell that portion of the truth which is not likely to hurt me.
476.[a] I am a special agent of God.
480. I am often afraid of the dark.
481. I can remember "playing sick" to get out of something.
485. When a man is with a woman he is usually thinking about things related to her sex.
518. I have often felt guilty because I have pretended to feel more sorry about something than I really was.
519.[a] There is something wrong with my sex organs.
525. I am made nervous by certain animals.
535.[a] My mouth feels dry almost all the time.
541.[a] My skin seems to be unusually sensitive to touch.
543. Several times a week I feel as if something dreadful is about to happen.
545.[a] Sometimes I have the same dream over and over.
565.[a] I feel like jumping off when I am on a high place.

The following items score if answered false:

68. I hardly ever feel pain in the back of my neck.
83. Any man who is able and willing to work hard has a good chance of succeeding.
88. I usually feel that life is worthwhile.

96. I have very few quarrels with members of my family.
137. I believe that my home life is as pleasant as that of most people I know.
207. I enjoy many different kinds of play and recreation.
257. I usually expect to succeed in things I do.
306. I get all the sympathy I should.
405. I have no trouble swallowing.
466. Except by a doctor's orders I never take drugs or sleeping powders.
524.[a] I am not afraid of picking up a disease or germs from doorknobs.
528.[a] I blush no more often than others.

---

[a]Items that were deleted from the original MMPI item pool during construction of the MMPI-2.

Research/Supplemental Scales for the MMPI

Females   Dissimulation (Original)   (Ds)

		Age, yr				
	Total Sample	13	14	15	16	17
N	691	136	153	127	138	137
Median	19	19	18	19	20	17
Mean	19.49	20.10	19.18	19.76	21.12	17.36
SD	8.44	8.18	8.30	8.61	9.09	7.62
Min	3	5	5	5	6	3
Max	58	42	48	58	49	39

	Percentage of Sample with Raw Score < X					
X	Total Sample	13	14	15	16	17
3	0.0	0.0	0.0	0.0	0.0	0.0
4	0.3	0.0	0.0	0.0	0.0	1.5
5	0.6	0.0	0.0	0.0	0.0	2.9
6	1.4	1.5	1.3	0.8	0.0	3.6
7	3.2	3.7	2.0	1.6	1.4	7.3
8	5.2	5.9	4.6	3.9	2.9	8.8
9	6.7	7.4	5.9	5.5	5.1	9.5
10	9.7	9.6	9.2	8.7	5.8	15.3
11	12.9	11.0	11.8	11.0	10.1	20.4
12	17.8	14.0	17.0	16.5	15.2	26.3
13	22.3	15.4	24.8	20.5	18.8	31.4
14	25.9	19.9	28.1	24.4	21.7	35.0
15	30.4	24.3	33.3	29.9	26.1	38.0
16	36.0	33.1	38.6	34.6	29.7	43.8
17	40.1	37.5	43.1	38.6	34.8	46.0
18	45.0	41.9	45.8	44.1	42.0	51.1
19	49.6	45.6	51.6	49.6	43.5	57.7
20	53.4	51.5	55.6	52.8	44.9	62.0
21	58.5	53.7	60.8	57.5	52.9	67.2
22	63.4	59.6	64.7	63.0	58.7	70.8
23	68.5	63.2	68.0	70.9	64.5	75.9
24	72.9	70.6	75.2	72.4	68.1	78.1
25	75.1	72.1	76.5	75.6	69.6	81.8
26	78.6	75.0	80.4	81.1	71.0	85.4
27	82.1	80.9	84.3	83.5	72.5	89.1
28	84.4	82.4	86.3	84.3	76.8	92.0
29	86.5	84.6	89.5	84.3	79.0	94.9
30	88.4	87.5	89.5	88.2	81.9	94.9
31	89.4	89.0	90.8	89.0	82.6	95.6
32	90.3	90.4	92.2	89.8	83.3	95.6

X	Total Sample	Percentage of Sample with Raw Score < X				
		13	14	15	16	17
33	92.0	92.6	92.8	91.3	87.0	96.4
34	92.9	94.1	93.5	91.3	89.1	96.4
35	93.2	94.1	93.5	92.1	89.9	96.4
36	94.5	95.6	94.8	92.9	92.0	97.1
37	95.9	95.6	95.4	96.9	94.2	97.8
38	96.5	95.6	96.1	97.6	94.2	99.3
39	97.1	97.1	96.7	97.6	94.9	99.3
40	97.7	97.8	97.4	97.6	95.7	100.0
41	98.4	98.5	98.0	98.4	97.1	100.0
42	98.8	98.5	98.7	99.2	97.8	100.0
43	99.3	100.0	98.7	99.2	98.6	100.0
44	99.3	100.0	98.7	99.2	98.6	100.0
45	99.6	100.0	99.3	99.2	99.3	100.0
46	99.6	100.0	99.3	99.2	99.3	100.0
47	99.6	100.0	99.3	99.2	99.3	100.0
48	99.6	100.0	99.3	99.2	99.3	100.0
49	99.7	100.0	100.0	99.2	99.3	100.0
50	99.9	100.0	100.0	99.2	100.0	100.0
51	99.9	100.0	100.0	99.2	100.0	100.0
52	99.9	100.0	100.0	99.2	100.0	100.0
53	99.9	100.0	100.0	99.2	100.0	100.0
54	99.9	100.0	100.0	99.2	100.0	100.0
55	99.9	100.0	100.0	99.2	100.0	100.0
56	99.9	100.0	100.0	99.2	100.0	100.0
57	99.9	100.0	100.0	99.2	100.0	100.0
58	99.9	100.0	100.0	99.2	100.0	100.0

Research/Supplemental Scales for the MMPI

Males   Dissimulation (Original)   (Ds)

		Age, yr				
	Total Sample	13	14	15	16	17
N	624	112	147	130	122	113
Median	17	18	19	15	17	15
Mean	18.23	18.21	19.86	17.34	18.80	16.56
SD	8.27	8.27	9.39	7.36	8.19	7.42
Min	2	2	2	2	7	2
Max	45	39	45	34	41	41

	Percentage of Sample with Raw Score < X					
X	Total Sample	13	14	15	16	17
2	0.0	0.0	0.0	0.0	0.0	0.0
3	0.8	0.9	0.7	0.8	0.0	1.8
4	1.3	2.7	1.4	0.8	0.0	1.8
5	2.1	3.6	3.4	1.5	0.0	1.8
6	2.6	3.6	4.8	2.3	0.0	1.8
7	4.5	5.4	6.8	3.8	0.0	6.2
8	6.6	8.0	6.8	6.2	2.5	9.7
9	10.6	12.5	10.2	9.2	5.7	15.9
10	13.3	14.3	12.2	12.3	10.7	17.7
11	18.1	18.8	16.3	19.2	18.0	18.6
12	21.8	22.3	19.0	23.1	22.1	23.0
13	26.6	27.7	25.2	30.0	23.8	26.5
14	31.7	33.9	29.9	34.6	27.0	33.6
15	37.8	38.4	34.0	43.1	33.6	40.7
16	44.4	42.9	38.8	51.5	39.3	50.4
17	48.6	45.5	41.5	52.3	45.1	60.2
18	52.7	49.1	44.9	56.2	52.5	62.8
19	56.7	54.5	46.9	60.8	55.7	68.1
20	60.9	56.3	52.4	66.2	61.5	69.9
21	64.3	59.8	54.4	68.5	65.6	75.2
22	67.9	65.2	58.5	69.2	69.7	79.6
23	71.5	70.5	61.9	71.5	73.8	82.3
24	74.2	73.2	65.3	75.4	76.2	83.2
25	77.1	77.7	68.7	78.5	77.9	85.0
26	80.0	81.3	74.8	80.8	77.9	86.7
27	83.0	83.9	76.2	85.4	82.8	88.5
28	85.6	84.8	80.3	88.5	85.2	90.3
29	87.5	86.6	82.3	90.8	86.1	92.9
30	89.1	90.2	82.3	93.1	86.1	95.6
31	90.4	92.9	83.0	94.6	87.7	95.6

Research/Supplemental Scales for the MMPI

Males   Dissimulation (Original)   (Ds)
                                   (Continued)

X	Total Sample	Percentage of Sample with Raw Score < X 13	14	15	16	17
32	92.3	94.6	85.0	98.5	89.3	95.6
33	93.8	94.6	87.1	98.5	93.4	96.5
34	95.4	96.4	91.2	99.2	94.3	96.5
35	96.2	96.4	93.2	100.0	94.3	97.3
36	96.6	97.3	93.9	100.0	95.1	97.3
37	97.1	97.3	94.6	100.0	95.1	99.1
38	97.9	98.2	95.9	100.0	96.7	99.1
39	98.4	98.2	97.3	100.0	97.5	99.1
40	99.0	100.0	98.0	100.0	98.4	99.1
41	99.4	100.0	98.6	100.0	99.2	99.1
42	99.7	100.0	98.6	100.0	100.0	100.0
43	99.8	100.0	99.3	100.0	100.0	100.0
44	99.8	100.0	99.3	100.0	100.0	100.0
45	99.8	100.0	99.3	100.0	100.0	100.0

TEST-RETEST (Tr); TR INDEX (TRI)

It is widely believed by patients that the 16 duplicated items in the MMPI are routinely inspected by clinicians in order to determine response consistency, but this is not so. Although such an approach appears to have utility, these items had originally been "duplicated in the booklet and on the answer sheet to obtain a more economical method of scoring the answer sheets by the IBM 805 machine" (Hathaway & McKinley, 1967, p. 10).

Buechley and Ball (1952) noted that the items on scale F, viewed as being the most important of the three original validity scales, occurred only among the first 300 MMPI statements (that is, the front side of the standard IBM answer sheet). They thought that random marking such as that due to boredom might be more likely to occur during the remaining items. If true, then seven of the basic clinical scales could be affected because 30% of the items on scale K, 35% on scale 6 (Pa), 48% on scale 7 (Pt), 40% on scale 8 (Sc), and 54% on scale 0 (Si) occur after item 300. Only scales 2 (D), 3 (Hy), and 5 (Mf) would not be affected.

The Tr scale is made up of the 16 repeated items in the MMPI. The Tr score is the number of contradictory responses among these identical items. A point is earned if both items of the pair are not answered in the same direction. This score was developed to aid in detecting random response bias and in determining profile validity, especially when F was elevated.

Buechley and Ball (1952) used only 14 of the 16 pairs in developing the Tr scale for ease in hand scoring (that is, it required examination of only the front side of the answer sheet). They considered the answer to the original and the repeated item to represent a test-retest relationship and used Phi coefficients to measure the degree of agreement between the two responses.

The Tr scale was developed on a sample of 137 uncooperative and poorly motivated adolescent inmates of the Fred C. Neloes School for Boys in California. Buechley and Ball (1952) found a cutting score of 3 to be helpful in separating borderline-valid (raw F = 8–11) and invalid profiles (F ≥ 12), which they thought were due to a random response set, from those "whose responses may be validly and consistently bizarre" (p. 301).

Later, Greene (1979) noted that the TR index (TRI), calculated as the sum of the inconsistent responses to all 16 repeated items, is relatively independent of psychopathology and recommended a cutting score of 4 or greater as indicating a lack of response consistency.

REFERENCES

Buechley, R., & Ball, H. (1952). A new test of "validity" for the group MMPI. *Journal of Consulting Psychology, 16*, 299–301.

Greene, R. L. (1979). Response consistency on the MMPI: The TR Index. *Journal of Personality Assessment, 43*, 69–71.

Hathaway, S. R., & McKinley, J. C. (1967). *Minnesota Multiphasic Personality Inventory Manual* (rev. ed.). Minneapolis: University of Minnesota Press.

Item pairs:[a]

8–318. My daily life is full of things that keep me interested.
13–290. I work under a great deal of tension.
15–314. Once in a while I think of things too bad to talk about.
16–315. I am sure I got a raw deal from life.
20–310. My sex life is satisfactory.

21–308. At times I have very much wanted to leave home.
22–326. At times I have fits of laughing and crying that I cannot control.
23–288. I am troubled by attacks of nausea and vomiting.
24–333. No one seems to understand me.
32–328. I find it hard to keep my mind on a task or job.
33–323. I have had very peculiar and strange experiences.
35–331. If people had not had it in for me I would have been much more successful.
37–302. I have never been in trouble because of my sex behavior.
38–311. During one period when I was a youngster I engaged in petty thievery.
305–366. Even when I am with people I feel lonely much of the time.
317–362. I am more sensitive than most other people.

---

[a]One item from each of the 16 pairs was deleted from the original MMPI item pool during construction of the MMPI-2. Thus, there are no repeated items on the MMPI-2.

Research/Supplemental Scales for the MMPI

Females   Test-Retest   (Tr;TRI)

		Age, yr				
	Total Sample	13	14	15	16	17
N	691	136	153	127	138	137
Median	1	2	2	1	1	1
Mean	1.79	2.28	2.04	1.54	1.54	1.51
SD	1.72	1.87	1.77	1.55	1.55	1.69
Min	0	0	0	0	0	0
Max	11	8	11	7	7	8

Percentage of Sample with Raw Score < X

X	Total Sample	13	14	15	16	17
0	0.0	0.0	0.0	0.0	0.0	0.0
1	27.4	19.1	23.5	29.1	28.3	37.2
2	51.7	39.0	43.1	58.3	60.1	59.1
3	70.9	59.6	62.1	78.0	78.3	78.1
4	84.9	78.7	81.7	90.6	88.4	86.1
5	92.3	86.8	92.2	94.5	94.9	93.4
6	96.2	94.1	96.7	96.1	97.1	97.1
7	98.3	95.6	99.3	99.2	98.6	98.5
8	99.6	99.3	99.3	100.0	100.0	99.3
9	99.9	100.0	99.3	100.0	100.0	100.0
10	99.9	100.0	99.3	100.0	100.0	100.0
11	99.9	100.0	99.3	100.0	100.0	100.0

Research/Supplemental Scales for the MMPI

Males   Test-Retest   (Tr;TRI)

		Age, yr				
	Total Sample	13	14	15	16	17
N	624	112	147	130	122	113
Median	2	2	2	2	2	2
Mean	2.43	2.65	2.55	2.09	2.66	2.21
SD	2.19	2.14	2.22	2.04	2.31	2.17
Min	0	0	0	0	0	0
Max	12	12	11	9	10	9

Percentage of Sample with Raw Score < X

X	Total Sample	13	14	15	16	17
0	0.0	0.0	0.0	0.0	0.0	0.0
1	19.9	10.7	19.0	29.2	14.8	24.8
2	39.1	33.9	35.4	48.5	32.0	46.0
3	60.7	57.1	59.2	59.2	61.5	67.3
4	74.2	71.4	70.1	79.2	74.6	76.1
5	84.9	83.9	84.4	88.5	83.6	84.1
6	90.7	92.0	90.5	92.3	88.5	90.3
7	94.2	94.6	93.9	96.9	91.0	94.7
8	96.3	95.5	97.3	97.7	93.4	97.3
9	97.9	98.2	97.3	99.2	96.7	98.2
10	99.2	99.1	98.6	100.0	98.4	100.0
11	99.7	99.1	99.3	100.0	100.0	100.0
12	99.8	99.1	100.0	100.0	100.0	100.0

CARELESSNESS (Cs)

The Tr index (TRI)—the number of inconsistent responses to the 16 identical repeated items in the MMPI—may be a helpful adjunct to the other validity scales in detecting response bias (Buechley & Ball, 1952; Greene, 1979). However, Dahlstrom, Welsh, and Dahlstrom (1972, p. 141) believed that psychologically opposite items might be more sensitive than repeated identical items for detecting a patient's inability or unwillingness to complete the inventory in a meaningful or consistent manner (Haertzen & Hill, 1963). Subsequently, Greene (1978) developed a Carelessness scale (Cs) for the MMPI that was composed of 12 nonidentical pairs of items that were described as being psychologically opposite.

Three samples of 50 subjects (sex not specified) from a Veterans Administration hospital, a university psychology clinic, and college students enrolled in an introductory psychology course completed the MMPI. All possible nonredundant pairs of items that were answered in a consistent direction more than 90% of the time in each of the three subject groups were identified. After the pairs had been selected empirically, a three-judge panel was used to select the pairs that were psychological opposites.

Points are scored if the patient does not respond in a consistent fashion to the pairs of items. In the list below, pairs marked "S" earn 1 point toward the total score if both items receive the same response (that is, both items answered true or both answered false). Items marked "D" also earn 1 point toward the total score but only if the pair of items receives different responses (that is, one item marked true and the other false).

A cutting score of 4 or more was recommended for identifying invalid profiles.

REFERENCES

Buechley, R., & Ball, H. (1952). A new test of "validity" for the group MMPI. *Journal of Consulting Psychology, 16, 299–301.*

Dahlstrom, W. G., Welsh, G. S., & Dahlstrom, L. E. (1972). *An MMPI handbook, Volume I: Clinical interpretation.* Minneapolis: University of Minnesota Press.

Greene, R. L. (1978). An empirically derived MMPI carelessness scale. *Journal of Clinical Psychology, 34, 407–410.*

Greene, R. L. (1979). Response consistency on the MMPI: The TR Index. *Journal of Personality Assessment, 43, 69–71.*

Haertzen, C. A., & Hill, H. E. (1963). Assessing subjective effects of drugs: An index of carelessness and confusion for use with the Addiction Research Center Inventory (ARCI). *Journal of Clinical Psychology, 19, 407–412.*

Items:

S   10.   There seems to be a lump in my throat much of the time.
     405.   I have no trouble swallowing.

D   17.   My father was a good man.
     65.   I loved my father.

D   18.   I am very seldom troubled by constipation.
     63.[a]   I have no difficulty in starting or holding my bowel movement.

S   49.   It would be better if almost all laws were thrown away.
     113.   I believe in law enforcement.

S   76.   Most of the time I feel blue.
     107. I am happy most of the time.

S   88.   I usually feel that life is worthwhile.
     526. The future seems hopeless to me.

S   137.   I believe that my home life is as pleasant as that of most people I know.
     216. There is very little love and companionship in my family as compared to other homes.

D   177.   My mother was a good woman.
     220. I loved my mother.

S   178.   My memory seems to be all right.
     342. I forget right away what people say to me.

D   286.   I am never happier than when alone.
     312. I dislike having people about me.

S   329.   I almost never dream.
     425.[a] I dream frequently.

D   388.   I am afraid to be alone in the dark.
     480. I am often afraid of the dark.

---

[a]Items that were deleted from the original MMPI item pool during construction of the MMPI-2.

Research/Supplemental Scales for the MMPI

Females   Carelessness   (Cs)

		Age, yr				
	Total Sample	13	14	15	16	17
N	691	136	153	127	138	137
Median	1	1	1	1	1	1
Mean	1.47	1.71	1.57	1.54	1.51	1.01
SD	1.33	1.37	1.41	1.47	1.20	1.09
Min	0	0	0	0	0	0
Max	8	6	6	8	6	6

	Percentage of Sample with Raw Score < X					
X	Total Sample	13	14	15	16	17
0	0.0	0.0	0.0	0.0	0.0	0.0
1	25.9	18.4	23.5	28.3	21.7	38.0
2	57.7	52.9	56.2	54.3	52.9	72.3
3	82.1	74.3	80.4	78.7	83.3	93.4
4	92.5	88.2	90.2	92.1	94.2	97.8
5	96.7	97.1	94.8	96.1	97.8	97.8
6	98.6	98.5	98.0	97.6	99.3	99.3
7	99.9	100.0	100.0	99.2	100.0	100.0
8	99.9	100.0	100.0	99.2	100.0	100.0

Research/Supplemental Scales for the MMPI

Males   Carelessness   (Cs)

		Age, yr				
	Total Sample	13	14	15	16	17
N	624	112	147	130	122	113
Median	1	2	2	1	1	1
Mean	1.67	1.78	1.93	1.51	1.65	1.41
SD	1.47	1.52	1.49	1.43	1.45	1.43
Min	0	0	0	0	0	0
Max	7	7	6	6	7	6

Percentage of Sample with Raw Score < X

X	Total Sample	13	14	15	16	17
0	0.0	0.0	0.0	0.0	0.0	0.0
1	26.1	24.1	20.4	26.9	25.4	35.4
2	51.6	48.2	42.2	59.2	51.6	58.4
3	73.9	70.5	66.7	78.5	75.4	79.6
4	88.3	86.6	85.0	91.5	88.5	90.3
5	95.4	95.5	93.9	95.4	95.9	96.5
6	98.6	98.2	98.6	97.7	99.2	99.1
7	99.7	99.1	100.0	100.0	99.2	100.0

177

SUBTLE AND OBVIOUS KEYS (S AND O)

Much attention was given to the development of scales, such as L, F, and K, that could provide clinicians with information about the potential response bias of persons completing the MMPI. It was apparent that either conscious or unconscious bias could exert considerable influence on the MMPI profile, to present an excessively favorable or an excessively unfavorable self-description.

Because the items on each of the MMPI scales were selected empirically, there is remarkably diverse content. In addition, some of the items contain clear statements of unusual beliefs (such as item 151: "Someone has been trying to poison me"), whereas other items have no clear relationship to unusual patterns of thinking or to psychopathology (such as item 263: "I sweat very easily even on cool days").

Wiener (1948) believed that it was important to distinguish nondisabling personality factors present among the individual MMPI scales. It was further believed that the subtle MMPI items would be more useful than the overall validity scales, particularly with a relatively normally functioning population. Thus, Wiener thought that the items whose content was most obvious, in the sense of describing psychopathologic features, would be most helpful with seriously disturbed persons but that the subtle items of a scale would have greater usefulness in describing personality characteristics of normal groups who would be unlikely to endorse the frankly pathologic items.

Therefore, Wiener and Harmon (cited in Wiener, 1956) divided the items of the MMPI scales into two groups: those relatively clear as indicating emotional disturbance ("obvious" items), and those for which the relationship to emotional disturbance was relatively difficult to detect ("subtle" items). All of the F-scale items among the clinical scales were assigned to the obvious category. The pooled judgment of two raters, apparently using several criteria that were not described in the article, were used to sort the items into the subtle and obvious categories.

Examination of the items indicated that those in the obvious (O) category were most characteristic of an institutionalized population, and their frequency distribution carried a positive skew. The subtle (S) items were distributed in a relatively normal fashion. Among 139 normal men the mean percentage of endorsement ranged from 10% (6,Pa) to 23% (9,Ma) for the O items (mean, 17%) and from 32% (6,Pa) to 48% (2,D) for the S items (mean, 39%).

Originally it was planned to develop S and O keys for all of the clinical scales of the MMPI. However, it was not possible to do so for scales 1 (Hs), 7 (Pt), 8 (Sc), and 5 (Mf) because scales 1, 7, and 8 consisted almost entirely of obvious items, and the questionable validity of scale 5 was believed responsible for its negative results.

Subsequently, norms for the S and O keys were obtained from a sample of 100 cases from the original Minnesota male normative sample (Wiener, 1956) and, even though response patterns were different for each sex, apparently separate norms were never derived for women.

REFERENCES

Wiener, D. N. (1948). Subtle and obvious keys for the Minnesota Multiphasic Personality Inventory. *Journal of Consulting Psychology, 12*, 164–170.

Wiener, D. N. (1956). Subtle and obvious keys for the MMPI. In G. S. Welsh & W. G. Dahlstrom (Eds.), *Basic readings on the MMPI in psychology and medicine* (pp. 195–204). Minneapolis: University of Minnesota Press.

The items composing the S and O categories for scales 2 (D), 3 (Hy), 4 (Pd), 6 (Pa), and 9 (Ma) listed by direction of scoring follow:

Scale 2 (D): Depression—Obvious (D-O; 40 Items)

The following items score if answered *true*:

23. I am troubled by attacks of nausea and vomiting.
32. I find it hard to keep my mind on a task or job.
41. I have had periods of days, weeks, or months when I couldn't take care of things because I couldn't "get going."
43. My sleep is fitful and disturbed.
52. I prefer to pass by school friends, or people I know but have not seen for a long time, unless they speak to me first.
67. I wish I could be as happy as others seem to be.
86. I am certainly lacking in self-confidence.
104. I don't seem to care what happens to me.
138. Criticism or scolding hurts me terribly.
142. I certainly feel useless at times.
158. I cry easily.
159. I cannot understand what I read as well as I used to.
182. I am afraid of losing my mind.
189. I feel weak all over much of the time.
236. I brood a great deal.
259. I have difficulty in starting to do things.
290. I work under a great deal of tension.

The following items score if answered *false*:

2.   I have a good appetite.
8.   My daily life is full of things that keep me interested.
9.   I am about as able to work as I ever was.
18. I am very seldom troubled by constipation.
36. I seldom worry about my health.
46. My judgment is better than it ever was.
51. I am in just as good physical health as most of my friends.
57. I am a good mixer.
88. I usually feel that life is worthwhile.
95.[a] I go to church almost every week.
107. I am happy most of the time.
122. I seem to be about as capable and smart as most others around me.
131. I do not worry about catching diseases.
152. Most nights I go to sleep without thoughts or ideas bothering me.
153. During the past few years I have been well most of the time.
154. I have never had a fit or convulsion.
178. My memory seems to be all right.
207. I enjoy many different kinds of play and recreation.
242. I believe I am no more nervous than most others.
270. When I leave home I do not worry about whether the door is locked and the windows closed.
271. I do not blame a person for taking advantage of someone who lays himself open to it.
272. At times I am all full of energy.
285. Once in a while I laugh at a dirty joke.

Scale 2 (D): Depression—Subtle (D-S; 20 Items)

The following items score if answered *true:*

5.	I am easily awakened by noise.
130.	I have never vomited blood or coughed up blood.
193.	I do not have spells of hay fever or asthma.

The following items score if answered *false:*

30. At times I feel like swearing.
39. At times I feel like smashing things.
58.[a] Everything is turning out just like the prophets of the Bible said it would.
64. I sometimes keep on at a thing until others lose their patience with me.
80. I sometimes tease animals.
89. It takes a lot of argument to convince most people of the truth.
98.[a] I believe in the second coming of Christ.
145. At times I feel like picking a fist fight with someone.
155. I am neither gaining nor losing weight.
160. I have never felt better in my life than I do now.
191. Sometimes, when embarrassed, I break out in a sweat which annoys me greatly.
208. I like to flirt.
233. I have at times stood in the way of people who were trying to do something, not because it amounted to much but because of the principle of the thing.
241. I dream frequently about things that are best kept to myself.
248. Sometimes without any reason or even when things are going wrong I feel excitedly happy, "on top of the world."
263. I sweat very easily even on cool days.
296. I have periods in which I feel unusually cheerful without any special reason.

Scale 3 (Hy): Hysteria—Obvious (Hy-O; 32 Items)

The following items score if answered *true:*

10. There seems to be a lump in my throat much of the time.
23. I am troubled by attacks of nausea and vomiting.
32. I find it hard to keep my mind on a task or job.
43. My sleep is fitful and disturbed.
44. Much of the time my head seems to hurt all over.
47. Once a week or oftener I feel suddenly hot all over, without apparent cause.
76. Most of the time I feel blue.
114. Often I feel as if there were a tight band about my head.
179. I am worried about sex matters.
186. I frequently notice my hand shakes when I try to do something.
189. I feel weak all over much of the time.
238. I have periods of such great restlessness that I cannot sit long in a chair.

The following items score if answered *false:*

2. I have a good appetite.
3. I wake up fresh and rested most mornings.
7. My hands and feet are usually warm enough.
8. My daily life is full of things that keep me interested.

9.   I am about as able to work as I ever was.
51.   I am in just as good physical health as most of my friends.
55.   I am almost never bothered by pains over my heart or in my chest.
103.   I have little or no trouble with my muscles twitching or jumping.
107.   I am happy most of the time.
128.   The sight of blood neither frightens me nor makes me sick.
137.   I believe that my home life is as pleasant as that of most people I know.
153.   During the past few years I have been well most of the time.
163.   I do not tire quickly.
174.   I have never had a fainting spell.
175.   I seldom or never have dizzy spells.
188.   I can read a long while without tiring my eyes.
192.   I have had no difficulty in keeping my balance in walking.
230.   I hardly ever notice my heart pounding and I am seldom short of breath.
243.   I have few or no pains.
274.   My eyesight is as good as it has been for years.

Scale 3 (Hy): Hysteria—Subtle (Hy-S; 28 Items)

The following item scores if answered *true*:

253.   I can be friendly with people who do things which I consider wrong.

The following items score if answered *false*:

6.   I like to read newspaper articles on crime.
12.   I enjoy detective or mystery stories.
26.   I feel that it is certainly best to keep my mouth shut when I'm in trouble.
30.   At times I feel like swearing.
71.   I think a great many people exaggerate their misfortunes in order to gain the sympathy and help of others.
89.   It takes a lot of argument to convince most people of the truth.
93.   I think most people would lie to get ahead.
109.   Some people are so bossy that I feel like doing the opposite of what they request even though I know they are right.
124.   Most people will use somewhat unfair means to gain profit or an advantage rather than to lose it.
129.   Often I can't understand why I have been so cross and grouchy.
136.   I commonly wonder what hidden reason another person may have for doing something nice for me.
141.   My conduct is largely controlled by the customs of those about me.
147.   I have often lost out on things because I couldn't make up my mind soon enough.
160.   I have never felt better in my life than I do now.
162.   I resent having anyone take me in so cleverly that I have had to admit that it was one on me.
170.   What others think of me does not bother me.
172.   I frequently have to fight against showing that I am bashful.
180.   I find it hard to make talk when I meet new people.
190.   I have very few headaches.
201.   I wish I were not so shy.
213.   In walking I am very careful to step over sidewalk cracks.
234.   I get mad easily and then get over it soon.
265.   It is safer to trust nobody.
267.   When in a group of people I have trouble thinking of the right things to talk about.

279.   I drink an unusually large amount of water every day.
289.   I am always disgusted with the law when a criminal is freed through the arguments of a smart lawyer.
292.   I am likely not to speak to people until they speak to me.

Scale 4 (Pd): Psychopathic Deviate—Obvious (Pd-O; 28 Items)

The following items score if answered *true:*

16.   I am sure I get a raw deal from life.
24.   No one seems to understand me.
32.   I find it hard to keep my mind on a task or job.
33.   I have had very peculiar and strange experiences.
35.   If people had not had it in for me I would have been much more successful.
38.   During one period when I was a youngster I engaged in petty thievery.
42.   My family does not like the work I have chosen (or the work I intend to choose for my life work).
61.   I have not lived the right kind of life.
67.   I wish I could be as happy as others seem to be.
84.   These days I find it hard not to give up hope of amounting to something.
94.   I do many things which I regret afterwards (I regret things more or more often than others seem to).
106.   Much of the time I feel as if I have done something wrong or evil.
110.   Someone has it in for me.
118.   In school I was sometimes sent to the principal for cutting up.
215.   I have used alcohol excessively.
216.   There is very little love and companionship in my family as compared to other homes.
224.   My parents have often objected to the kind of people I went around with.
244.   My way of doing things is apt to be misunderstood by others.
245.   My parents and family find more fault with me than they should.
284.   I am sure I am being talked about.

The following items score if answered *false:*

8.   My daily life is full of things that keep me interested.
20.   My sex life is satisfactory.
37.   I have never been in trouble because of my sex behavior.
91.   I do not mind being made fun of.
107.   I am happy most of the time.
137.   I believe that my home life is as pleasant as that of most people I know.
287.   I have very few fears compared to my friends.
294.   I have never been in trouble with the law.

Scale 4 (Pd): Psychopathic Deviate—Subtle (Pd-S; 22 Items)

The following items score if answered *true:*

21.   At times I have very much wanted to leave home.
102.   My hardest battles are with myself.
127.   I know who is responsible for most of my troubles.
239.   I have been disappointed in love.

The following items score if answered *false:*

82.   I am easily downed in an argument.
96.   I have very few quarrels with members of my family.
134. At times my thoughts have raced ahead faster than I could speak them.
141. My conduct is largely controlled by the customs of those about me.
155. I am neither gaining nor losing weight.
170. What others think of me does not bother me.
171. It makes me uncomfortable to put on a stunt at a party even when others are doing the same sort of things.
173. I liked school.
180. I find it hard to make talk when I meet new people.
183. I am against giving money to beggars.
201. I wish I were not so shy.
231. I like to talk about sex.
235. I have been quite independent and free from family rule.
237. My relatives are nearly all in sympathy with me.
248. Sometimes without any reason or even when things are going wrong I feel excitedly happy, "on top of the world."
267. When in a group of people I have trouble thinking of the right things to talk about.
289. I am always disgusted with the law when a criminal is freed through the arguments of a smart lawyer.
296. I have periods in which I feel unusually cheerful without any special reason.

Scale 6 (Pa): Paranoia—Obvious (Pa-O; 23 Items)

The following items score if answered *true:*

16.   I am sure I get a raw deal from life.
24.   No one seems to understand me.
27.   Evil spirits possess me at times.
35.   If people had not had it in for me I would have been much more successful.
110. Someone has it in for me.
121. I believe I am being plotted against.
123. I believe I am being followed.
151. Someone has been trying to poison me.
158. I cry easily.
202. I believe I am a condemned person.
275. Someone has control over my mind.
284. I am sure I am being talked about.
291. At one or more times in my life I felt that someone was making me do things by hypnotizing me.
293. Someone has been trying to influence my mind.
305. Even when I am with people I feel lonely much of the time.
317. I am more sensitive than most other people.
326. At times I have fits of laughing and crying that I cannot control.
338. I have certainly had more than my share of things to worry about.
341. At times I hear so well it bothers me.
364. People say insulting and vulgar things about me.

The following items score if answered *false:*

281. I do not often notice my ears ringing or buzzing.

294. I have never been in trouble with the law.
347. I have no enemies who really wish to harm me.

Scale 6 (Pa): Paranoia—Subtle (Pa-S; 17 Items)

The following items score if answered *true*:

15. Once in a while I think of things too bad to talk about.
127. I know who is responsible for most of my troubles.
157. I feel that I have often been punished without cause.
299. I think that I feel more intensely than most people do.
365. I feel uneasy indoors.

The following items score if answered *false*:

93. I think most people would lie to get ahead.
107. I am happy most of the time.
109. Some people are so bossy that I feel like doing the opposite of what they request even though I know they are right.
111. I have never done anything dangerous for the thrill of it.
117. Most people are honest chiefly through fear of being caught.
124. Most people will use somewhat unfair means to gain profit or an advantage rather than to lose it.
268. Something exciting will almost always pull me out of it when I am feeling low.
313. The man who provides temptation by leaving valuable property unprotected is about as much to blame for its theft as the one who steals it.
316. I think nearly anyone would tell a lie to keep out of trouble.
319. Most people inwardly dislike putting themselves out to help other people.
327. My mother or father often made me obey even when I thought that it was unreasonable.
348. I tend to be on my guard with people who are somewhat more friendly than I had expected.

Scale 9 (Ma): Hypomania—Obvious (Ma-O; 23 Items)

The following items score if answered *true*:

13. I work under a great deal of tension.
22. At times I have fits of laughing and crying that I cannot control.
59. I have often had to take orders from someone who did not know as much as I did.
73. I am an important person.
97. At times I have a strong urge to do something harmful or shocking.
100. I have met problems so full of possibilities that I have been unable to make up my mind about them.
156. I have had periods in which I carried on activities without knowing later what I had been doing.
157. I feel that I have often been punished without cause.
167. It wouldn't make me nervous if any members of my family got into trouble with the law.
194. I have had attacks in which I could not control my movements or speech but in which I knew what was going on around me.
212. My people treat me more like a child than a grown-up.
226. Some of my family have habits that bother and annoy me very much.

238. I have periods of such great restlessness that I cannot sit long in a chair.
250. I don't blame anyone for trying to grab everything he can get in this world.
251. I have had blank spells in which my activities were interrupted and I did not know what was going on around me.
263. I sweat very easily even on cool days.
266. Once a week or oftener I become very excited.
277. At times I have been so entertained by the cleverness of a crook that I have hoped he would get by with it.
279. I drink an unusually large amount of water every day.
298. If several people find themselves in trouble, the best thing for them to do is to agree upon a story and stick to it.

The following items score if answered *false:*

111. I have never done anything dangerous for the thrill of it.
119. My speech is the same as always (not faster or slower, no slurring; no hoarseness).
120. My table manners are not quite as good at home as when I am out in company.

Scale 9 (Ma): Hypomania—Subtle (Ma-S; 23 Items)

The following items score if answered *true:*

11.   A person should try to understand his dreams and be guided by or take warning from them.
21.   At times I have very much wanted to leave home.
64.   I sometimes keep on at a thing until others lose their patience with me.
109. Some people are so bossy that I feel like doing the opposite of what they request even though I know they are right.
127. I know who is responsible for most of my troubles.
134. At times my thoughts have raced ahead faster than I could speak them.
143. When I was a child, I belonged to a crowd or gang that tried to stick together through thick and thin.
181. When I get bored I like to stir up some excitement.
222. It is not hard for me to ask help from my friends even though I cannot return the favor.
228. At times I feel that I can make up my mind with unusually great ease.
232. I have been inspired to a program of life based on duty which I have since carefully followed.
233. I have at times stood in the way of people who were trying to do something, not because it amounted to much but because of the principle of the thing.
240. I never worry about my looks.
268. Something exciting will almost always pull me out of it when I am feeling low.
271. I do not blame a person for taking advantage of someone who lays himself open to it.

The following items score if answered *false:*

101. I believe women ought to have as much sexual freedom as men.
105. Sometimes when I am not feeling well I am cross.
148. It makes me impatient to have people ask my advice or otherwise interrupt me when I am working on something important.
166. I am afraid when I look down from a high place.

171.   It makes me uncomfortable to put on a stunt at a party even when others are doing the same sort of things.

180.   I find it hard to make talk when I meet new people.

267.   When in a group of people I have trouble thinking of the right things to talk about.

289.   I am always disgusted with the law when a criminal is freed through the arguments of a smart lawyer.

------

[a]Items that were deleted from the original MMPI item pool during construction of the MMPI-2.

Research/Supplemental Scales for the MMPI

Females   Depression--Obvious   (D-O)

		Age, yr				
	Total Sample	13	14	15	16	17
N	691	136	153	127	138	137
Median	10	10	9	10	11	9
Mean	10.28	9.93	9.72	10.51	11.64	9.64
SD	5.03	4.42	4.71	5.53	5.73	4.45
Min	0	1	2	0	1	2
Max	30	23	27	29	30	22

	Percentage of Sample with Raw Score < X					
X	Total Sample	13	14	15	16	17
0	0.0	0.0	0.0	0.0	0.0	0.0
1	0.1	0.0	0.0	0.8	0.0	0.0
2	0.9	1.5	0.0	2.4	0.7	0.0
3	2.7	1.5	4.6	3.9	2.2	1.5
4	6.4	5.9	9.2	5.5	4.3	6.6
5	11.7	12.5	14.4	10.2	8.7	12.4
6	18.2	19.1	19.6	15.7	14.5	21.9
7	24.5	26.5	26.8	23.6	18.1	27.0
8	32.1	34.6	34.6	33.9	23.2	34.3
9	39.8	40.4	41.2	44.9	29.7	43.1
10	48.8	47.1	53.6	49.6	39.9	53.3
11	55.1	53.7	58.2	57.5	47.8	58.4
12	62.5	59.6	65.4	63.8	55.8	67.9
13	69.9	67.6	73.9	69.3	61.6	76.6
14	75.7	77.2	79.7	73.2	67.4	80.3
15	81.2	85.3	83.7	77.2	73.2	86.1
16	85.7	90.4	89.5	81.9	76.8	89.1
17	88.9	93.4	92.2	84.3	81.9	92.0
18	91.5	94.9	95.4	87.4	84.1	94.9
19	94.1	98.5	96.1	91.3	88.4	95.6
20	95.5	99.3	97.4	92.9	90.6	97.1
21	96.8	99.3	98.7	94.5	92.8	98.5
22	97.7	99.3	98.7	96.9	94.2	99.3
23	98.0	99.3	98.7	96.9	94.9	100.0
24	98.4	100.0	98.7	97.6	95.7	100.0
25	98.8	100.0	99.3	98.4	96.4	100.0
26	99.1	100.0	99.3	98.4	97.8	100.0
27	99.1	100.0	99.3	98.4	97.8	100.0
28	99.6	100.0	100.0	99.2	98.6	100.0
29	99.7	100.0	100.0	99.2	99.3	100.0

Females   Depression--Obvious   (D-O)
                        (Continued)

X	Total Sample	Percentage of Sample with Raw Score < X				
		13	14	15	16	17
30	99.9	100.0	100.0	100.0	99.3	100.0

Research/Supplemental Scales for the MMPI

Females · Depression--Subtle · (D-S)

		Age, yr				
	Total Sample	13	14	15	16	17
N	691	136	153	127	138	137
Median	9	10	9	9	9	9
Mean	9.20	9.45	9.26	8.69	9.36	9.20
SD	2.57	2.68	2.80	2.44	2.39	2.44
Min	3	3	3	3	4	4
Max	18	18	17	15	16	15

Percentage of Sample with Raw Score < X

X	Total Sample	13	14	15	16	17
3	0.0	0.0	0.0	0.0	0.0	0.0
4	0.9	1.5	0.7	2.4	0.0	0.0
5	2.7	1.5	2.6	3.9	2.2	3.6
6	8.2	8.1	9.8	10.2	6.5	6.6
7	14.2	13.2	14.4	17.3	12.3	13.9
8	25.3	25.7	26.1	31.5	20.3	23.4
9	39.9	36.0	43.1	44.9	35.5	40.1
10	55.9	47.1	58.2	66.1	51.4	56.9
11	69.6	66.9	68.0	77.2	69.6	67.2
12	81.8	79.4	78.4	87.4	82.6	81.8
13	90.3	86.0	88.9	94.5	91.3	91.2
14	94.9	95.6	91.5	96.9	94.9	96.4
15	97.8	97.1	95.4	99.2	98.6	99.3
16	99.0	98.5	97.4	100.0	99.3	100.0
17	99.7	99.3	99.3	100.0	100.0	100.0
18	99.9	99.3	100.0	100.0	100.0	100.0

Research/Supplemental Scales for the MMPI

Females   Hysteria--Obvious   (Hy-O)

| | | Age, yr | | | | |
	Total Sample	13	14	15	16	17
N	691	136	153	127	138	137
Median	7	7	6	7	8	6
Mean	7.78	7.57	7.14	8.19	8.65	7.43
SD	4.56	4.02	4.07	5.15	5.06	4.35
Min	1	1	1	1	1	1
Max	29	22	19	29	25	21

Percentage of Sample with Raw Score < X

X	Total Sample	13	14	15	16	17
1	0.0	0.0	0.0	0.0	0.0	0.0
2	2.5	1.5	0.7	3.1	2.2	5.1
3	8.2	9.6	7.2	10.2	5.8	8.8
4	16.5	14.7	19.6	18.1	13.8	16.1
5	26.9	27.2	32.0	27.6	22.5	24.8
6	36.3	34.6	44.4	33.1	31.9	36.5
7	45.4	41.9	52.3	41.7	39.9	50.4
8	54.7	51.5	61.4	51.2	49.3	59.1
9	64.8	65.4	68.6	64.6	57.2	67.9
10	70.9	73.5	72.5	68.5	63.0	76.6
11	76.4	78.7	78.4	74.0	71.0	79.6
12	80.8	81.6	85.0	78.0	73.2	85.4
13	84.9	87.5	90.2	80.3	78.3	87.6
14	87.7	91.9	91.5	84.3	81.2	89.1
15	90.3	93.4	93.5	85.8	87.0	91.2
16	93.2	96.3	94.8	90.6	90.6	93.4
17	94.6	97.8	95.4	92.9	92.0	94.9
18	96.4	98.5	98.7	94.5	93.5	96.4
19	97.4	99.3	99.3	95.3	95.7	97.1
20	98.0	99.3	100.0	96.1	95.7	98.5
21	98.6	99.3	100.0	98.4	96.4	98.5
22	99.0	99.3	100.0	98.4	97.1	100.0
23	99.7	100.0	100.0	99.2	99.3	100.0
24	99.7	100.0	100.0	99.2	99.3	100.0
25	99.7	100.0	100.0	99.2	99.3	100.0
26	99.9	100.0	100.0	99.2	100.0	100.0
27	99.9	100.0	100.0	99.2	100.0	100.0
28	99.9	100.0	100.0	99.2	100.0	100.0
29	99.9	100.0	100.0	99.2	100.0	100.0

Research/Supplemental Scales for the MMPI

Females Hysteria--Subtle (Hy-S)

		Age, yr				
	Total Sample	13	14	15	16	17
N	691	136	153	127	138	137
Median	13	13	13	13	13	14
Mean	13.47	13.05	13.82	13.13	13.07	14.20
SD	3.86	3.96	4.00	3.86	3.80	3.56
Min	2	3	5	3	2	4
Max	24	22	23	21	24	23

Percentage of Sample with Raw Score < X

X	Total Sample	13	14	15	16	17
2	0.0	0.0	0.0	0.0	0.0	0.0
3	0.1	0.0	0.0	0.0	0.7	0.0
4	0.4	0.7	0.0	0.8	0.7	0.0
5	0.7	1.5	0.0	0.8	0.7	0.7
6	1.6	2.2	0.7	1.6	2.2	1.5
7	2.5	4.4	1.3	1.6	2.9	2.2
8	5.2	6.6	3.3	6.3	6.5	3.6
9	10.1	14.0	7.8	14.2	10.9	4.4
10	16.1	19.1	15.0	18.9	18.8	8.8
11	22.3	25.0	22.2	23.6	26.1	14.6
12	30.4	35.3	29.4	33.9	32.6	21.2
13	41.4	50.0	38.6	44.9	43.5	30.7
14	51.5	52.2	50.3	55.9	55.8	43.8
15	61.4	63.2	60.8	66.1	64.5	52.6
16	70.9	74.3	68.0	74.8	73.9	64.2
17	79.2	80.9	75.8	81.1	83.3	75.2
18	84.8	87.5	83.7	82.7	87.7	82.5
19	89.4	89.7	87.6	89.0	93.5	87.6
20	92.9	93.4	90.2	93.7	95.7	92.0
21	95.9	95.6	92.8	96.9	97.8	97.1
22	97.8	99.3	94.1	100.0	97.8	98.5
23	98.8	100.0	96.7	100.0	98.6	99.3
24	99.9	100.0	100.0	100.0	99.3	100.0

Research/Supplemental Scales for the MMPI

Females   Psychopathic Deviate--Obvious   (Pd-O)

		Age, yr				
	Total Sample	13	14	15	16	17
N	691	136	153	127	138	137
Median	7	7	7	7	9	7
Mean	8.12	8.01	7.82	8.41	8.83	7.59
SD	4.63	4.25	4.70	4.87	4.98	4.28
Min	0	1	1	0	1	1
Max	24	23	24	22	20	20

Percentage of Sample with Raw Score < X

X	Total Sample	13	14	15	16	17
0	0.0	0.0	0.0	0.0	0.0	0.0
1	0.3	0.0	0.0	1.6	0.0	0.0
2	2.3	1.5	3.3	2.4	2.9	1.5
3	7.8	7.4	7.8	6.3	8.0	9.5
4	15.8	12.5	20.3	12.6	15.9	16.8
5	25.6	22.8	30.7	26.0	21.0	27.0
6	34.4	30.1	39.2	33.1	33.3	35.8
7	44.1	44.1	46.4	44.9	37.7	47.4
8	50.8	51.5	52.3	50.4	44.9	54.7
9	57.0	57.4	61.4	55.1	48.6	62.0
10	65.8	66.9	69.9	62.2	55.8	73.7
11	72.2	73.5	74.5	67.7	66.7	78.1
12	78.6	79.4	78.4	76.4	74.6	83.9
13	82.6	85.3	81.7	79.5	79.0	87.6
14	86.5	89.0	85.0	85.8	84.1	89.1
15	89.3	94.1	87.6	89.0	84.8	91.2
16	91.6	96.3	91.5	89.8	87.0	93.4
17	94.5	97.8	96.7	92.1	89.1	96.4
18	95.5	97.8	96.7	95.3	91.3	96.4
19	97.0	97.8	98.0	96.1	94.9	97.8
20	98.0	98.5	98.7	96.1	97.8	98.5
21	99.1	98.5	99.3	97.6	100.0	100.0
22	99.4	98.5	99.3	99.2	100.0	100.0
23	99.6	98.5	99.3	100.0	100.0	100.0
24	99.9	100.0	99.3	100.0	100.0	100.0

Research/Supplemental Scales for the MMPI

Females   Psychopathic Deviate--Subtle   (Pd-S)

	Total Sample	Age, yr				
		13	14	15	16	17
N	691	136	153	127	138	137
Median	11	10	11	11	11	11
Mean	10.75	10.31	10.74	10.73	11.01	10.95
SD	2.30	2.24	2.13	2.50	2.31	2.33
Min	2	4	6	2	4	5
Max	18	16	17	17	18	16

Percentage of Sample with Raw Score < X

X	Total Sample	13	14	15	16	17
2	0.0	0.0	0.0	0.0	0.0	0.0
3	0.1	0.0	0.0	0.8	0.0	0.0
4	0.1	0.0	0.0	0.8	0.0	0.0
5	0.7	0.7	0.0	2.4	0.7	0.0
6	1.0	1.5	0.0	2.4	0.7	0.7
7	2.9	3.7	2.6	4.7	2.2	1.5
8	7.8	11.0	7.2	7.1	5.1	8.8
9	17.2	22.1	13.1	18.1	15.2	18.2
10	28.8	34.6	26.8	31.5	25.4	26.3
11	44.9	52.2	47.1	43.3	38.4	43.1
12	60.9	71.3	63.4	57.5	57.2	54.7
13	78.4	83.8	83.7	76.4	76.1	71.5
14	88.9	91.9	88.2	88.2	89.1	86.9
15	95.7	97.1	96.7	96.9	93.5	94.2
16	98.1	99.3	98.0	97.6	96.4	99.3
17	99.6	100.0	99.3	99.2	99.3	100.0
18	99.9	100.0	100.0	100.0	99.3	100.0

Research/Supplemental Scales for the MMPI

Females   Paranoia--Obvious   (Pa-O)

	Total Sample	Age, yr				
		13	14	15	16	17
N	691	136	153	127	138	137
Median	4	5	4	4	5	4
Mean	4.90	4.94	5.01	5.10	5.28	4.15
SD	3.52	3.20	3.69	3.66	3.82	3.09
Min	0	0	0	0	0	0
Max	21	14	19	21	16	16

Percentage of Sample with Raw Score < X

X	Total Sample	13	14	15	16	17
0	0.0	0.0	0.0	0.0	0.0	0.0
1	5.6	3.7	5.9	5.5	3.6	9.5
2	13.0	11.8	14.4	9.4	12.3	16.8
3	27.9	27.9	28.8	25.2	28.3	29.2
4	40.7	39.0	40.5	37.0	39.1	47.4
5	54.6	50.0	54.2	52.0	50.0	66.4
6	65.1	60.3	63.4	64.6	62.3	75.2
7	72.9	69.9	69.3	73.2	69.6	83.2
8	81.3	80.1	79.1	81.1	78.3	88.3
9	86.3	87.5	85.6	85.0	82.6	90.5
10	88.7	89.7	88.2	88.2	84.1	93.4
11	91.0	94.1	89.5	90.6	86.2	94.9
12	94.2	96.3	92.8	94.5	91.3	96.4
13	95.5	97.8	94.8	96.1	92.0	97.1
14	96.7	97.8	96.1	96.1	94.9	98.5
15	98.8	100.0	98.7	97.6	98.6	99.3
16	99.0	100.0	99.3	97.6	98.6	99.3
17	99.7	100.0	99.3	99.2	100.0	100.0
18	99.7	100.0	99.3	99.2	100.0	100.0
19	99.7	100.0	99.3	99.2	100.0	100.0
20	99.9	100.0	100.0	99.2	100.0	100.0
21	99.9	100.0	100.0	99.2	100.0	100.0

Research/Supplemental Scales for the MMPI

Females   Paranoia--Subtle   (Pa-S)

	Total Sample	Age, yr				
		13	14	15	16	17
N	691	136	153	127	138	137
Median	6	6	6	6	6	7
Mean	6.25	5.52	6.07	6.24	6.51	6.91
SD	2.20	2.21	2.23	2.05	2.14	2.15
Min	1	1	1	2	3	2
Max	13	11	11	12	13	13

X	Percentage of Sample with Raw Score < X					
	Total Sample	13	14	15	16	17
1	0.0	0.0	0.0	0.0	0.0	0.0
2	0.6	1.5	1.3	0.0	0.0	0.0
3	2.7	5.9	5.9	0.8	0.0	0.7
4	9.7	18.4	10.5	7.1	8.7	3.6
5	22.9	39.0	24.2	20.5	15.9	14.6
6	39.9	50.0	41.8	42.5	35.5	29.9
7	56.6	69.1	60.8	57.5	53.6	41.6
8	71.5	81.6	75.2	71.7	68.8	59.9
9	83.5	89.7	83.7	87.4	79.7	77.4
10	92.2	94.9	92.8	92.9	91.3	89.1
11	96.8	97.8	96.7	96.9	97.1	95.6
12	99.1	100.0	100.0	99.2	98.6	97.8
13	99.7	100.0	100.0	100.0	99.3	99.3

Research/Supplemental Scales for the MMPI

Females   Hypomania--Obvious   (Ma-O)

		Age, yr				
	Total Sample	13	14	15	16	17
N	691	136	153	127	138	137
Median	9	9	9	10	10	8
Mean	9.31	9.24	9.14	9.77	9.83	8.63
SD	3.58	3.65	3.53	3.44	3.64	3.53
Min	2	2	2	3	2	2
Max	19	18	18	18	19	19

Percentage of Sample with Raw Score < X

X	Total Sample	13	14	15	16	17
2	0.0	0.0	0.0	0.0	0.0	0.0
3	1.3	2.2	2.0	0.0	0.7	1.5
4	4.1	3.7	3.9	2.4	3.6	6.6
5	9.6	8.1	8.5	7.9	8.0	15.3
6	17.1	14.7	19.0	11.8	15.2	24.1
7	24.6	27.2	28.1	18.9	18.8	29.2
8	32.3	37.5	34.6	25.2	26.1	37.2
9	41.8	45.6	41.8	35.4	35.5	50.4
10	51.7	55.9	52.9	46.5	44.2	58.4
11	63.8	64.0	64.1	61.4	59.4	70.1
12	71.6	70.6	71.9	69.3	68.8	77.4
13	79.6	77.9	83.0	77.2	75.4	83.9
14	87.0	84.6	88.2	85.0	83.3	93.4
15	92.3	91.9	93.5	92.1	89.9	94.2
16	95.8	96.3	96.7	94.5	93.5	97.8
17	97.7	97.1	98.0	96.9	97.1	99.3
18	98.8	99.3	99.3	98.4	97.8	99.3
19	99.7	100.0	100.0	100.0	99.3	99.3

196

Research/Supplemental Scales for the MMPI

Females   Hypomania--Subtle   (Ma-S)

	Total Sample	Age, yr				
		13	14	15	16	17
N	691	136	153	127	138	137
Median	11	11	11	11	11	11
Mean	11.08	10.84	11.40	11.40	10.84	10.88
SD	2.70	2.56	2.77	2.75	2.87	2.52
Min	3	4	5	5	3	5
Max	19	16	19	19	17	17

X	Percentage of Sample with Raw Score < X					
	Total Sample	13	14	15	16	17
3	0.0	0.0	0.0	0.0	0.0	0.0
4	0.1	0.0	0.0	0.0	0.7	0.0
5	0.4	1.5	0.0	0.0	0.7	0.0
6	1.9	2.2	1.3	1.6	3.6	0.7
7	4.3	2.9	3.9	4.7	7.2	2.9
8	9.6	8.8	7.8	8.7	13.8	8.8
9	18.7	19.9	16.3	13.4	23.2	20.4
10	27.6	29.4	24.2	21.3	31.9	31.4
11	42.4	44.9	39.2	40.2	43.5	44.5
12	54.6	60.3	51.0	50.4	55.1	56.2
13	69.6	72.8	66.7	66.9	69.6	72.3
14	81.2	86.0	74.5	77.2	81.2	87.6
15	89.6	92.6	85.0	88.2	89.9	92.7
16	94.5	94.9	93.5	92.9	96.4	94.9
17	98.7	100.0	98.0	96.9	99.3	99.3
18	99.6	100.0	99.3	98.4	100.0	100.0
19	99.7	100.0	99.3	99.2	100.0	100.0

Research/Supplemental Scales for the MMPI

Males   Depression--Obvious   (D-O)

		Age, yr				
	Total Sample	13	14	15	16	17
N	624	112	147	130	122	113
Median	8	8	9	8	9	7
Mean	9.12	9.13	9.54	8.85	9.65	8.30
SD	4.65	5.20	4.66	4.47	4.30	4.58
Min	0	2	0	1	1	1
Max	27	26	23	21	21	27

Percentage of Sample with Raw Score < X

X	Total Sample	13	14	15	16	17
0	0.0	0.0	0.0	0.0	0.0	0.0
1	0.2	0.0	0.7	0.0	0.0	0.0
2	1.0	0.0	1.4	1.5	0.8	0.9
3	3.8	1.8	4.8	4.6	2.5	5.3
4	9.0	9.8	10.2	9.2	5.7	9.7
5	15.7	21.4	12.2	16.2	9.8	20.4
6	24.4	34.8	19.7	24.6	17.2	27.4
7	32.5	39.3	27.9	33.8	23.8	39.8
8	42.5	48.2	36.1	44.6	35.2	50.4
9	51.0	50.9	46.3	53.8	43.4	61.9
10	59.3	58.0	52.4	63.8	54.9	69.0
11	65.1	60.7	63.3	69.2	61.5	70.8
12	71.6	68.8	68.7	71.5	68.9	81.4
13	77.2	75.0	74.8	76.9	74.6	85.8
14	81.6	76.8	78.2	82.3	82.0	89.4
15	86.7	84.8	85.7	86.9	85.2	91.2
16	89.6	88.4	87.8	90.8	87.7	93.8
17	93.4	94.6	92.5	93.8	92.6	93.8
18	94.9	95.5	94.6	96.2	94.3	93.8
19	96.8	95.5	95.9	97.7	98.4	96.5
20	97.6	96.4	97.3	98.5	98.4	97.3
21	97.9	96.4	98.0	98.5	98.4	98.2
22	98.9	97.3	98.6	100.0	100.0	98.2
23	99.0	97.3	99.3	100.0	100.0	98.2
24	99.5	98.2	100.0	100.0	100.0	99.1
25	99.5	98.2	100.0	100.0	100.0	99.1
26	99.5	98.2	100.0	100.0	100.0	99.1
27	99.8	100.0	100.0	100.0	100.0	99.1

Research/Supplemental Scales for the MMPI

Males   Depression--Subtle   (D-S)

| | | Age, yr | | | | |
	Total Sample	13	14	15	16	17
N	624	112	147	130	122	113
Median	9	9	9	9	8	9
Mean	8.86	9.14	8.84	8.98	8.59	8.74
SD	2.78	2.84	2.81	2.67	2.73	2.85
Min	2	3	2	4	4	2
Max	18	16	18	15	14	16

Percentage of Sample with Raw Score < X

X	Total Sample	13	14	15	16	17
2	0.0	0.0	0.0	0.0	0.0	0.0
3	0.3	0.0	0.7	0.0	0.0	0.9
4	1.4	1.8	2.0	0.0	0.0	3.5
5	5.4	4.5	6.8	3.8	5.7	6.2
6	10.6	8.0	10.2	10.0	13.9	10.6
7	21.2	17.0	22.4	17.7	25.4	23.0
8	34.0	28.6	34.7	31.5	39.3	35.4
9	47.9	45.5	45.6	47.7	54.9	46.0
10	58.7	57.1	56.5	57.7	59.8	62.8
11	70.2	69.6	69.4	70.0	71.3	70.8
12	83.3	81.3	83.7	83.1	82.8	85.8
13	90.4	88.4	92.5	89.2	91.0	90.3
14	94.9	91.1	96.6	94.6	96.7	94.7
15	97.4	94.6	98.0	96.9	100.0	97.3
16	99.0	98.2	98.6	100.0	100.0	98.2
17	99.8	100.0	99.3	100.0	100.0	100.0
18	99.8	100.0	99.3	100.0	100.0	100.0

Research/Supplemental Scales for the MMPI

Males   Hysteria--Obvious   (Hy-O)

		Age, yr				
	Total Sample	13	14	15	16	17
N	624	112	147	130	122	113
Median	6	5	6	6	6	6
Mean	6.55	6.17	6.97	6.19	7.10	6.21
SD	3.94	4.33	4.22	3.51	3.80	3.73
Min	0	0	0	1	1	0
Max	25	22	25	16	17	19

X	Percentage of Sample with Raw Score < X					
	Total Sample	13	14	15	16	17
0	0.0	0.0	0.0	0.0	0.0	0.0
1	0.6	1.8	0.7	0.0	0.0	0.9
2	4.3	7.1	4.1	6.2	2.5	1.8
3	13.9	21.4	12.9	15.4	8.2	12.4
4	25.6	31.3	24.5	27.7	19.7	25.7
5	36.1	43.8	33.3	37.7	29.5	37.2
6	44.2	52.7	40.1	43.1	41.0	46.0
7	56.1	59.8	50.3	60.0	51.6	60.2
8	66.0	69.6	59.2	69.2	59.8	74.3
9	72.8	79.5	68.0	73.1	63.1	82.3
10	79.5	82.1	73.5	81.5	74.6	87.6
11	83.8	83.9	81.6	85.4	80.3	88.5
12	88.5	87.5	87.8	92.3	83.6	91.2
13	92.1	89.3	91.8	95.4	91.0	92.9
14	93.6	91.1	94.6	96.2	92.6	92.9
15	95.8	94.6	95.9	98.5	95.1	94.7
16	97.1	95.5	95.9	99.2	98.4	96.5
17	98.1	97.3	97.3	100.0	99.2	96.5
18	99.0	98.2	98.6	100.0	100.0	98.2
19	99.4	99.1	98.6	100.0	100.0	99.1
20	99.5	99.1	98.6	100.0	100.0	100.0
21	99.5	99.1	98.6	100.0	100.0	100.0
22	99.5	99.1	98.6	100.0	100.0	100.0
23	99.8	100.0	99.3	100.0	100.0	100.0
24	99.8	100.0	99.3	100.0	100.0	100.0
25	99.8	100.0	99.3	100.0	100.0	100.0

Research/Supplemental Scales for the MMPI

Males   Hysteria--Subtle   (Hy-S)

		Age, yr				
	Total Sample	13	14	15	16	17
N	624	112	147	130	122	113
Median	12	12	11	13	12	13
Mean	12.47	12.29	11.78	12.68	12.38	13.42
SD	4.12	3.60	4.23	4.46	3.89	4.15
Min	3	3	4	4	5	5
Max	25	21	25	24	24	24

Percentage of Sample with Raw Score < X

X	Total Sample	13	14	15	16	17
3	0.0	0.0	0.0	0.0	0.0	0.0
4	0.2	0.9	0.0	0.0	0.0	0.0
5	1.1	0.9	2.0	2.3	0.0	0.0
6	2.7	0.9	3.4	5.4	2.5	0.9
7	6.7	2.7	10.2	8.5	6.6	4.4
8	12.2	8.0	17.7	13.1	9.8	10.6
9	18.3	11.6	24.5	20.8	18.0	14.2
10	23.7	22.3	32.0	23.1	22.1	16.8
11	34.0	34.8	42.9	30.8	33.6	25.7
12	43.1	46.4	50.3	42.3	42.6	31.9
13	51.6	54.5	57.8	50.0	54.9	38.9
14	59.6	64.3	63.3	56.2	62.3	51.3
15	70.2	77.7	73.5	66.9	70.5	61.9
16	79.2	83.0	83.7	76.2	82.8	69.0
17	83.7	87.5	87.8	80.0	85.2	77.0
18	87.8	89.3	91.8	84.6	88.5	84.1
19	91.5	92.9	94.6	89.2	91.0	89.4
20	95.0	95.5	96.6	93.1	95.9	93.8
21	96.8	98.2	96.6	95.4	98.4	95.6
22	97.9	100.0	97.3	96.9	99.2	96.5
23	98.4	100.0	98.0	98.5	99.2	96.5
24	99.0	100.0	98.6	98.5	99.2	99.1
25	99.8	100.0	99.3	100.0	100.0	100.0

Research/Supplemental Scales for the MMPI

Males   Psychopathic Deviate--Obvious   (Pd-O)

	Total Sample	Age, yr				
		13	14	15	16	17
N	624	112	147	130	122	113
Median	8	8	9	8	8	8
Mean	8.54	8.00	9.27	8.44	8.78	7.97
SD	4.56	4.33	4.93	4.77	4.33	4.20
Min	0	1	1	0	1	1
Max	24	20	24	23	19	19

X	Percentage of Sample with Raw Score < X					
	Total Sample	13	14	15	16	17
0	0.0	0.0	0.0	0.0	0.0	0.0
1	0.2	0.0	0.0	0.8	0.0	0.0
2	2.1	1.8	2.7	2.3	0.8	2.7
3	7.4	8.9	9.5	7.7	3.3	7.1
4	14.4	17.0	14.3	19.2	7.4	14.2
5	21.5	25.9	18.4	24.6	16.4	23.0
6	31.1	34.8	27.2	30.0	29.5	35.4
7	38.6	43.8	34.7	39.2	36.1	40.7
8	45.0	50.0	38.1	48.5	41.8	48.7
9	53.0	54.5	45.6	56.9	50.8	59.3
10	60.6	64.3	54.4	57.7	62.3	66.4
11	66.8	69.6	59.2	65.4	69.7	72.6
12	73.2	76.8	64.6	73.1	73.0	81.4
13	79.8	81.3	72.8	82.3	80.3	84.1
14	85.1	91.1	77.6	85.4	85.2	88.5
15	89.4	93.8	85.0	89.2	89.3	91.2
16	92.3	94.6	89.1	93.1	91.8	93.8
17	94.6	95.5	93.2	94.6	92.6	97.3
18	95.8	98.2	94.6	94.6	95.1	97.3
19	97.3	99.1	95.9	96.2	96.7	99.1
20	99.2	99.1	98.6	98.5	100.0	100.0
21	99.5	100.0	99.3	98.5	100.0	100.0
22	99.7	100.0	99.3	99.2	100.0	100.0
23	99.7	100.0	99.3	99.2	100.0	100.0
24	99.8	100.0	99.3	100.0	100.0	100.0

Research/Supplemental Scales for the MMPI

Males   Psychopathic Deviate--Subtle   (Pd-S)

	Total Sample	Age, yr				
		13	14	15	16	17
N	624	112	147	130	122	113
Median	10	10	11	10	11	10
Mean	10.52	10.37	10.66	10.49	10.70	10.34
SD	2.54	2.51	2.48	2.66	2.46	2.61
Min	3	3	6	4	3	5
Max	18	17	18	17	18	17

Percentage of Sample with Raw Score < X

X	Total Sample	13	14	15	16	17
3	0.0	0.0	0.0	0.0	0.0	0.0
4	0.3	0.9	0.0	0.0	0.8	0.0
5	0.8	0.9	0.0	1.5	1.6	0.0
6	1.8	2.7	0.0	2.3	1.6	2.7
7	4.3	4.5	2.0	5.4	3.3	7.1
8	10.7	9.8	8.2	13.8	8.2	14.2
9	21.5	23.2	20.4	20.8	18.9	24.8
10	36.4	38.4	37.4	36.9	30.3	38.9
11	50.5	56.3	49.0	53.1	43.4	51.3
12	67.0	67.9	66.7	66.9	63.9	69.9
13	78.0	77.7	78.9	76.2	79.5	77.9
14	87.7	89.3	85.7	85.4	88.5	90.3
15	93.6	94.6	91.2	93.1	95.1	94.7
16	97.0	98.2	96.6	96.2	97.5	96.5
17	98.7	99.1	98.6	99.2	98.4	98.2
18	99.7	100.0	99.3	100.0	99.2	100.0

Research/Supplemental Scales for the MMPI

Males   Paranoia--Obvious   (Pa-O)

		Age, yr				
	Total Sample	13	14	15	16	17
N	624	112	147	130	122	113
Median	4	4	4	4	4	4
Mean	4.67	4.86	4.93	4.64	4.68	4.19
SD	3.51	3.59	3.94	3.24	3.24	3.43
Min	0	0	0	0	0	0
Max	17	14	15	14	14	17

Percentage of Sample with Raw Score < X

X	Total Sample	13	14	15	16	17
0	0.0	0.0	0.0	0.0	0.0	0.0
1	8.0	6.3	12.2	7.7	4.9	8.0
2	19.1	17.0	23.8	15.4	14.8	23.9
3	33.0	29.5	33.3	29.2	32.8	40.7
4	45.0	47.3	42.9	45.4	42.6	47.8
5	56.4	58.0	50.3	56.9	56.6	61.9
6	65.4	64.3	60.5	67.7	63.1	72.6
7	72.1	68.8	70.7	70.8	72.1	78.8
8	78.7	75.9	76.9	78.5	81.1	81.4
9	84.3	81.3	81.6	83.8	86.1	89.4
10	88.5	85.7	85.7	88.5	90.2	92.9
11	92.8	91.1	88.4	95.4	93.4	96.5
12	95.2	93.8	90.5	98.5	97.5	96.5
13	97.0	96.4	94.6	99.2	97.5	97.3
14	98.4	99.1	97.3	99.2	99.2	97.3
15	99.0	100.0	98.0	100.0	100.0	97.3
16	99.8	100.0	100.0	100.0	100.0	99.1
17	99.8	100.0	100.0	100.0	100.0	99.1

Research/Supplemental Scales for the MMPI

Males   Paranoia--Subtle   (Pa-S)

		Age, yr			
	Total Sample	13	14	15	16	17
N	624	112	147	130	122	113
Median	6	6	6	7	7	7
Mean	6.47	5.95	6.19	6.58	6.75	6.95
SD	2.19	2.16	2.15	2.16	2.06	2.33
Min	1	2	1	2	2	2
Max	13	11	11	12	13	13

Percentage of Sample with Raw Score < X

X	Total Sample	13	14	15	16	17
1	0.0	0.0	0.0	0.0	0.0	0.0
2	0.3	0.0	1.4	0.0	0.0	0.0
3	2.7	5.4	3.4	3.1	0.8	0.9
4	7.5	12.5	9.5	7.7	2.5	5.3
5	19.2	26.8	23.1	16.2	14.8	15.0
6	34.5	43.8	37.4	31.5	29.5	30.1
7	51.6	61.6	55.1	50.0	46.7	44.2
8	69.6	76.8	76.2	66.2	65.6	61.9
9	82.4	86.6	85.7	83.1	82.0	73.5
10	90.2	94.6	92.5	87.7	90.2	85.8
11	96.3	97.3	96.6	96.9	96.7	93.8
12	98.9	100.0	100.0	99.2	98.4	96.5
13	99.4	100.0	100.0	100.0	98.4	98.2

Research/Supplemental Scales for the MMPI

Males   Hypomania--Obvious   (Ma-O)

| | | Age, yr | | | | |
	Total Sample	13	14	15	16	17
N	624	112	147	130	122	113
Median	9	9	10	9	10	9
Mean	9.59	9.27	9.99	9.14	10.16	9.30
SD	3.46	3.67	3.87	3.31	2.97	3.26
Min	1	1	1	2	3	3
Max	20	19	19	18	20	18

Percentage of Sample with Raw Score < X

X	Total Sample	13	14	15	16	17
1	0.0	0.0	0.0	0.0	0.0	0.0
2	0.3	0.9	0.7	0.0	0.0	0.0
3	1.0	1.8	2.0	0.8	0.0	0.0
4	2.9	4.5	4.1	3.1	0.8	1.8
5	6.7	9.8	7.5	6.9	3.3	6.2
6	12.0	16.1	13.6	12.3	4.1	14.2
7	20.8	24.1	22.4	25.4	9.0	23.0
8	27.9	33.0	27.2	33.8	16.4	29.2
9	39.3	43.8	35.4	45.4	31.1	41.6
10	51.4	55.4	47.6	56.2	43.4	55.8
11	61.9	64.3	56.5	66.2	57.4	66.4
12	69.9	74.1	63.3	75.4	66.4	71.7
13	78.0	76.8	70.1	83.8	78.7	82.3
14	85.3	85.7	76.2	87.7	89.3	89.4
15	91.8	92.0	86.4	93.8	95.1	92.9
16	95.5	96.4	91.8	96.9	95.9	97.3
17	98.1	97.3	98.0	99.2	96.7	99.1
18	98.7	98.2	98.6	99.2	98.4	99.1
19	99.5	99.1	99.3	100.0	99.2	100.0
20	99.8	100.0	100.0	100.0	99.2	100.0

Research/Supplemental Scales for the MMPI

Males   Hypomania--Subtle   (Ma-S)

		Age, yr				
	Total Sample	13	14	15	16	17
N	624	112	147	130	122	113
Median	11	11	11	11	11	11
Mean	11.20	11.00	11.16	11.05	11.37	11.44
SD	2.67	2.54	3.19	2.55	2.56	2.33
Min	4	4	4	4	6	6
Max	20	16	20	17	19	17

Percentage of Sample with Raw Score < X

X	Total Sample	13	14	15	16	17
4	0.0	0.0	0.0	0.0	0.0	0.0
5	0.5	0.9	0.7	0.8	0.0	0.0
6	1.9	1.8	5.4	1.5	0.0	0.0
7	4.5	3.6	8.2	6.2	0.8	2.7
8	9.1	8.9	14.3	9.2	6.6	5.3
9	16.3	17.0	22.4	16.9	14.8	8.8
10	25.0	28.6	27.9	23.8	23.0	21.2
11	38.6	42.9	40.8	36.9	36.9	35.4
12	53.0	52.7	52.4	55.4	54.1	50.4
13	67.9	71.4	64.6	71.5	69.7	62.8
14	81.1	83.0	76.9	85.4	79.5	81.4
15	89.9	92.0	87.1	91.5	87.7	92.0
16	95.0	97.3	91.2	96.2	95.1	96.5
17	97.9	100.0	95.2	99.2	96.7	99.1
18	99.5	100.0	98.6	100.0	99.2	100.0
19	99.7	100.0	99.3	100.0	99.2	100.0
20	99.8	100.0	99.3	100.0	100.0	100.0

APPENDIX A

Set 2: Subscales, Item Clusters, Content Scales

HARRIS AND LINGOES SUBSCALES

To help clinicians understand the reasons for the peaks and valleys of an MMPI profile, Harris and Lingoes (1955) constructed subscales based on item content (Lingoes, 1960). More specifically,

> the items scored in each scale were examined, and those which seemed similar in content, or to reflect a single attitude or trait were grouped into a subscale. In effect, the item intercorrelations were estimated, purely subjectively. The items were grouped on the basis of these estimates, and then given a name which was thought to be descriptive of the inferred attitude underlying the sorting of the items in the scored direction. (Harris & Lingoes, 1955, p. 1)

The names of the subscales were derived from the content of the items and from a review of profiles of scores for groups and individuals for whom other information was available. Preliminary norms were developed from six independent samples of 50 men and 50 women psychiatric patients from the Langley Porter Clinic; normal samples were not included. The authors suggested that users establish their own local norms. The names and brief descriptions of the subscales follow.

Scale 2 (D, Depression)

D1: *Subjective Depression*. Pessimism, poor morale, low self-esteem, lack of energy for coping, feelings of psychologic inertia, lack of joy in doing things.

D2: *Psychomotor Retardation*. Feelings of immobilization, lack of participation in social interactions.

D3: *Physical Malfunctioning*. Report of physical symptoms, preoccupation with self.

D4: *Mental Dullness*. Distrust of one's psychologic functioning, feelings of unresponsiveness.

D5: *Brooding*. Irritability, proneness toward rumination.

Scale 3 (Hy, Hysteria)

Hy1: *Denial of Social Anxiety.* Social extroversion.

Hy2: *Need for Affection and Reinforcement From Others.* Denial of critical or resentful attitude toward others, impunitiveness, strong views of optimism, and faith in others.

Hy3: *Lassitude-Malaise.* Feelings of needing attention and reassurance, efforts to keep up a good front, complaints about physical and mental dysfunction.

Hy4: *Somatic Complaints.* Endorsement of physical complaints suggestive of repression or conversion symptoms.

Hy5: *Inhibition of Aggression.* Disavowal of violence.

Scale 4 (Pd, Psychopathic Deviate)

Pd1: *Familial Discord.* Feelings of struggle against family control.

Pd2: *Authority Conflict.* Expressions of resentment of the demands, conventions, and standards of parents and society.

Pd3: *Social Imperturbability.* Denial of social anxiety, denial of dependency needs, blandness.

Pd4A: *Social Alienation.* Feelings of isolation, lack of gratification in social relationships, lack of feelings of belonging, externalization of blame for difficulties.

Pd4B: *Self-Alienation.* Feelings of despondency and lack of self-integration, exhibitionistically stated feelings of guilt.

Pd4: *Alienation.* Sum of Pd4A and Pd4B.

Scale 6 (Pa, Paranoia)

Pa1: *Ideas of External Influence.* Externalization of blame for problems, frustrations, and failures; projection, persecutory ideas.

Pa2: *Poignancy.* High-strung, prone to think of oneself as special and different from others, overly subjective, cherishes sensitive feelings, thin-skinned.

Pa3: *Moral Virtue.* Denial of distrust and hostility, excessive generosity or naivete about motives of others, righteousness about ethical matters.

Scale 7 (Pt, Psychasthenia)

Harris and Lingoes (1955) found that the items of scale 7 did not lend themselves to classification.

Scale 8 (Sc, Schizophrenia)

Sc1A: *Social Alienation.* Lack of rapport with others, withdrawal from meaningful relationships.

Sc1B: *Emotional Alienation.* Feelings of lack of rapport with oneself, apathy, flatness or distorted affect, experiencing oneself as strange.

Sc1: *Object Loss.* Sum of Sc1A and Sc1B.

Sc2A: *Lack of Ego Mastery, Cognitive.* Strange and puzzling ideas, admission of autonomous thought processes.

Sc2B: *Lack of Ego Mastery, Conative.* Feelings of psychologic weakness, abulia, inertia, massive inhibition, regression.

Sc2C: *Lack of Ego Mastery, Defect of Inhibition and Control.* Feelings of not being in control of one's impulses, feelings of being at the mercy of strange and alien impulses and emotions, dissociation of affect.

Sc2: *Lack of Ego Mastery, Intrapsychic Autonomy.* Sum of Sc2A, Sc2B, and Sc2C.

Sc3: Sensorimotor Dissociation. Feelings of depersonalization, feeling of change in self-perception.

Scale 9 (Ma, Hypomania)

Ma1: Amorality. Disarming frankness, denial of feelings of guilt, callousness about motives and means and ends in self and in others.

Ma2: Psychomotor Acceleration. Hyperactivity, lability, pressure for action.

Ma3: Imperturbability. Confidence in social situations, denial of sensitivity, independent from opinions of others.

Ma4: Ego Inflation. Feelings of self-importance extending to the point of unrealistic grandiosity.

REFERENCES

Harris, R. E., & Lingoes, J. C. (1955). *Subscales for the Minnesota Multiphasic Personality Inventory—An aid to profile interpretation.* Unpublished data (mimeographed). University of California, School of Medicine and the Langley-Porter Clinic, Department of Psychiatry, San Francisco, CA. (Available from J. C. Lingoes, PhD, Computing Center, University of Michigan, 1075 Beal Avenue, Ann Arbor, MI 48109–2112; Personal communication, September 1984.)

Lingoes, J. C. (1960). MMPI factors of the Harris and the Wiener subscales. *Journal of Consulting Psychology, 24,* 74–83.

The items of the Harris and Lingoes subscales, and their direction of scoring, are listed below.

Scale 2 (D, Depression)

D1: Subjective Depression (32 Items)

The following items score if answered *true:*

32.	I find it hard to keep my mind on a task or job.
41.	I have had periods of days, weeks, or months when I couldn't take care of things because I couldn't "get going."
43.	My sleep is fitful and disturbed.
52.	I prefer to pass by school friends, or people I know but have not seen for a long time, unless they speak to me first.
67.	I wish I could be as happy as others seem to be.
86.	I am certainly lacking in self-confidence.
104.	I don't seem to care what happens to me.
138.	Criticism or scolding hurts me terribly.
142.	I certainly feel useless at times.
158.	I cry easily.
159.	I cannot understand what I read as well as I used to.
182.	I am afraid of losing my mind.
189.	I feel weak all over much of the time.
236.	I brood a great deal.
259.	I have difficulty in starting to do things.

The following items score if answered *false*:

2.   I have a good appetite.
8.   My daily life is full of things that keep me interested.
46. My judgment is better than it ever was.
57. I am a good mixer.
88. I usually feel that life is worthwhile.
107. I am happy most of the time.
122. I seem to be about as capable and smart as most others around me.
131. I do not worry about catching diseases.
152. Most nights I go to sleep without thoughts or ideas bothering me.
160. I have never felt better in my life than I do now.
191. Sometimes, when embarrassed, I break out in a sweat which annoys me greatly.
207. I enjoy many different kinds of play and recreation.
208. I like to flirt.
242. I believe I am no more nervous than most others.
272. At times I am all full of energy.
285. Once in a while I laugh at a dirty joke.
296. I have periods in which I feel unusually cheerful without any special reason.

D2: *Psychomotor Retardation (15 Items)*

The following items score if answered *true*:

41. I have had periods of days, weeks, or months when I couldn't take care of things because I couldn't "get going."
52. I prefer to pass by school friends, or people I know but have not seen for a long time, unless they speak to me first.
182. I am afraid of losing my mind.
259. I have difficulty in starting to do things.

The following items score if answered *false*:

8.   My daily life is full of things that keep me interested.
30. At times I feel like swearing.
39. At times I feel like smashing things.
57. I am a good mixer.
64. I sometimes keep on at a thing until others lose their patience with me.
89. It takes a lot of argument to convince most people of the truth.
95.[a] I go to church almost every week.
145. At times I feel like picking a fist fight with someone.
207. I enjoy many different kinds of play and recreation.
208. I like to flirt.
233. I have at times stood in the way of people who were trying to do something, not because it amounted to much but because of the principle of the thing.

---

[a]Items that were deleted from the original MMPI item pool during construction of the MMPI-2.

D3: *Physical Malfunctioning (11 Items)*

The following items score if answered *true*:

130. I have never vomited blood or coughed up blood.
189. I feel weak all over much of the time.

193.   I do not have spells of hay fever or asthma.
288.   I am troubled by attacks of nausea and vomiting.

The following items score if answered *false:*

 2.   I have a good appetite.
 18.   I am very seldom troubled by constipation.
 51.   I am in just as good physical health as most of my friends.
153.   During the past few years I have been well most of the time.
154.   I have never had a fit or convulsion.
155.   I am neither gaining nor losing weight.
160.   I have never felt better in my life than I do now.

D4: Mental Dullness (15 Items)

The following items score if answered *true:*

 32.   I find it hard to keep my mind on a task or job.
 41.   I have had periods of days, weeks, or months when I couldn't take care of things because I couldn't "get going."
 86.   I am certainly lacking in self-confidence.
104.   I don't seem to care what happens to me.
159.   I cannot understand what I read as well as I used to.
182.   I am afraid of losing my mind.
259.   I have difficulty in starting to do things.
290.   I work under a great deal of tension.

The following items score if answered *false:*

 8.   My daily life is full of things that keep me interested.
 9.   I am about as able to work as I ever was.
 46.   My judgment is better than it ever was.
 88.   I usually feel that life is worthwhile.
122.   I seem to be about as capable and smart as most others around me.
178.   My memory seems to be all right.
207.   I enjoy many different kinds of play and recreation.

D5: Brooding (10 Items)

The following items score if answered *true:*

 41.   I have had periods of days, weeks, or months when I couldn't take care of things because I couldn't "get going."
 67.   I wish I could be as happy as others seem to be.
104.   I don't seem to care what happens to me.
138.   Criticism or scolding hurts me terribly.
142.   I certainly feel useless at times.
158.   I cry easily.
182.   I am afraid of losing my mind.
236.   I brood a great deal.

The following items score if answered *false:*

 88.   I usually feel that life is worthwhile.
107.   I am happy most of the time.

Scale 3 (Hy, Hysteria)

Hy1: Denial of Social Anxiety (6 Items)

The following items score if answered *true:*
(none)

The following items score if answered *false:*

  141.   My conduct is largely controlled by the customs of those about me.
  172.   I frequently have to fight against showing that I am bashful.
  180.   I find it hard to make talk when I meet new people.
  201.   I wish I were not so shy.
  267.   When in a group of people I have trouble thinking of the right things to talk about.
  292.   I am likely not to speak to people until they speak to me.

Hy2: Need for Affection and Reinforcement From Others (12 Items)

The following item scores if answered *true:*

  253.   I can be friendly with people who do things which I consider wrong.

The following items score if answered *false:*

  26.   I feel that it is certainly best to keep my mouth shut when I'm in trouble.
  71.   I think a great many people exaggerate their misfortunes in order to gain the sympathy and help of others.
  89.   It takes a lot of argument to convince most people of the truth.
  93.   I think most people would lie to get ahead.
  109.   Some people are so bossy that I feel like doing the opposite of what they request even though I know they are right.
  124.   Most people will use somewhat unfair means to gain profit or an advantage rather than to lose it.
  136.   I commonly wonder what hidden reason another person may have for doing something nice for me.
  162.   I resent having anyone take me in so cleverly that I have had to admit that it was one on me.
  234.   I get mad easily and then get over it soon.
  265.   It is safer to trust nobody.
  289.   I am always disgusted with the law when a criminal is freed through the arguments of a smart lawyer.

Hy3: Lassitude-Malaise (15 Items)

The following items score if answered *true:*

  32.   I find it hard to keep my mind on a task or job.
  43.   My sleep is fitful and disturbed.
  76.   Most of the time I feel blue.
  189.   I feel weak all over much of the time.
  238.   I have periods of such great restlessness that I cannot sit long in a chair.

The following items score if answered *false:*

2. I have a good appetite.
3. I wake up fresh and rested most mornings.
8. My daily life is full of things that keep me interested.
9. I am about as able to work as I ever was.
51. I am in just as good physical health as most of my friends.
107. I am happy most of the time.
137. I believe that my home life is as pleasant as that of most people I know.
153. During the past few years I have been well most of the time.
160. I have never felt better in my life than I do now.
163. I do not tire quickly.

Hy4: Somatic Complaints (17 Items)

The following items score if answered *true*:

10. There seems to be a lump in my throat much of the time.
23. I am troubled by attacks of nausea and vomiting.
44. Much of the time my head seems to hurt all over.
47. Once a week or oftener I feel suddenly hot all over, without apparent cause.
114. Often I feel as if there were a tight band about my head.
186. I frequently notice my hand shakes when I try to do something.

The following items score if answered *false*:

7. My hands and feet are usually warm enough.
55. I am almost never bothered by pains over the heart or in my chest.
103. I have little or no trouble with my muscles twitching or jumping.
174. I have never had a fainting spell.
175. I seldom or never have dizzy spells.
188. I can read a long while without tiring my eyes.
190. I have very few headaches.
192. I have had no difficulty in keeping my balance in walking.
230. I hardly ever notice my heart pounding and I am seldom short of breath.
243. I have few or no pains.
274. My eyesight is as good as it has been for years.

Hy5: Inhibition of Aggression (7 Items)

The following items score if answered *true*:
(none)

The following items score if answered *false*:

6. I like to read newspaper articles on crime.
12. I enjoy detective or mystery stories.
30. At times I feel like swearing.
128. The sight of blood neither frightens me nor makes me sick.
129. Often I can't understand why I have been so cross and grouchy.
147. I have often lost out on things because I couldn't make up my mind soon enough.
170. What others think of me does not bother me.

Scale 4 (Pd, Psychopathic Deviate)

In their original mimeographed paper, Harris and Lingoes (1955) stated that the items for the subscales they derived for scale 4 (Pd) were drawn from both the unrevised and the published version of the scale (Dahlstrom & Welsh, 1960). More specifically, Lingoes (1988) noted that "nine items on the Pd subscales were taken from the original Pd scale (PD_0), but were retained by us since they seemed to add to the interpretability and reliability of the subscales" (p. 4). As a result, some of the items on the original Harris and Lingoes subscales for scale 4 (Pd) are not found on scale 4 (Pd) as it appeared in its final form (Dahlstrom & Welsh, 1960). These items, as well as those that Harris and Lingoes included on their subscales for scale 4 (Pd) but that were not a part of scale 4 (for example, item 212 falls on scales 8 and 9 but not on scale 4), are identified by a "b" and were deleted from the Harris and Lingoes subscales for scale 4 (Pd) during construction of the MMPI-2.

REFERENCES

Dahlstrom, W. G., & Welsh, G. S. (1960). *An MMPI handbook: A guide to use in clinical practice and research* (p. 462). Minneapolis: University of Minnesota Press.

Harris, R. E. & Lingoes, J. C. (1955). *Subscales for the Minnesota Multiphasic Personality Inventory—An aid to profile interpretation.* Mimeographed unpublished data. University of California, School of Medicine and the Langley-Porter Clinic, Department of Psychiatry, San Francisco, CA. (Available from J. C. Lingoes, PhD, Computing Center, University of Michigan, 1075 Beal Avenue, Ann Arbor, MI 48109–2112.)

Lingoes, J. C. (1988, August). *MMPI subscales and profile interpretation: Harris and Lingoes revisited* (discussion). Paper presented at the 96th Annual Convention of the American Psychological Association, Atlanta, GA.

Pd1: Familial Discord (11 Items)

The following items score if answered *true*:

    21.   At times I have very much wanted to leave home.
    42.   My family does not like the work I have chosen (or the work I intend to choose for my life work).
    212.[b] My people treat me more like a child than a grown-up.
    216.   There is very little love and companionship in my family as compared to other homes.
    224.   My parents have often objected to the kind of people I went around with.
    245.   My parents and family find more fault with me than they should.

The following items score if answered *false*:

    96.   I have very few quarrels with members of my family.
    137.   I believe that my home life is as pleasant as that of most people I know.
    235.   I have been quite independent and free from family rule.
    237.   My relatives are nearly all in sympathy with me.
    527.[b] The members of my family and my close relatives get along quite well.

Pd2: Authority Conflict (11 Items)

The following items score if answered true:

38.   During one period when I was a youngster I engaged in petty thievery.
59.[b] I have often had to take orders from someone who did not know as much as I did.
118. In school I was sometimes sent to the principal for cutting up.
520.[b] I strongly defend my own opinions as a rule.

The following items score if answered *false:*

37.   I have never been in trouble because of my sex behavior.
82.   I am easily downed in an argument.
141. My conduct is largely controlled by the customs of those about me.
173. I liked school.
289. I am always disgusted with the law when a criminal is freed through the arguments of a smart lawyer.
294. I have never been in trouble with the law.
429.[a,b] I like to attend lectures on serious subjects.

Pd3: Social Imperturbability (12 Items)

The following items score if answered *true:*

64.[b] I sometimes keep on at a thing until others lose their patience with me.
479.[b] I do not mind meeting strangers.
520.[b] I strongly defend my own opinions as a rule.
521.[b] In a group of people I would not be embarrassed to be called upon to start a discussion or give an opinion about something I know well.

The following items score if answered *false:*

82.   I am easily downed in an argument.
141. My conduct is largely controlled by the customs of those about me.
171. It makes me uncomfortable to put on a stunt at a party even when others are doing the same sort of things.
180. I find it hard to make talk when I meet new people.
201. I wish I were not so shy.
267. When in a group of people I have trouble thinking of the right things to talk about.
304.[b] In school I found it very hard to talk before the class.
352.[b] I have been afraid of things or people that I knew could not hurt me.

Pd4A: Social Alienation (18 Items)

The following items score if answered *true:*

16.   I am sure I get a raw deal from life.
24.   No one seems to understand me.
35.   If people had not had it in for me I would have been much more successful.
64.[b] I sometimes keep on at a thing until others lose their patience with me.
67.   I wish I could be as happy as others seem to be.
94.   I do many things which I regret afterwards (I regret things more or more often than others seem to).
110. Someone has it in for me.
127. I know who is responsible for most of my troubles.
146.[b] I have the wanderlust and am never happy unless I am roaming or traveling about.
239. I have been disappointed in love.

244.   My way of doing things is apt to be misunderstood by others.
284.   I am sure I am being talked about.
305.[b] Even when I am with people I feel lonely much of the time.
368.[b] I have sometimes stayed away from another person because I feared doing or saying something that I might regret afterwards.
520.[b] I strongly defend my own opinions as a rule.

The following items score if answered *false:*

20.   My sex life is satisfactory.
141.   My conduct is largely controlled by the customs of those about me.
170.   What others think of me does not bother me.

Pd4B: Self-Alienation (15 Items)

The following items score if answered *true:*

32.   I find it hard to keep my mind on a task or job.
33.   I have had very peculiar and strange experiences.
61.   I have not lived the right kind of life.
67.   I wish I could be as happy as others seem to be.
76.[b]   Most of the time I feel blue.
84.   These days I find it hard not to give up hope of amounting to something.
94.   I do many things which I regret afterwards (I regret things more or more often than others seem to).
102.   My hardest battles are with myself.
106.   Much of the time I feel as if I have done something wrong or evil.
127.   I know who is responsible for most of my troubles.
146.[b] I have the wanderlust and am never happy unless I am roaming or traveling about.
215.   I have used alcohol excessively.
368.[b] I have sometimes stayed away from another person because I feared doing or saying something that I might regret afterwards.

The following items score if answered *false:*

8.   My daily life is full of things that keep me interested.
107.   I am happy most of the time.

---

[a]Items that were deleted from the original MMPI item pool during construction of the MMPI-2.
[b]Items (n = 19) included by Harris and Lingoes from the original scale 4 (at that time labeled PD$_0$) that were deleted from the Harris and Lingoes subscales for scale 4 (Pd) during construction of the MMPI-2.

Scale 6 (Pa, Paranoia)

Pa1: Ideas of External Influence (17 Items)

The following items score if answered *true:*

16.   I am sure I get a raw deal from life.
24.   No one seems to understand me.
35.   If people had not had it in for me I would have been much more successful.

110. Someone has it in for me.
121. I believe I am being plotted against.
123. I believe I am being followed.
127. I know who is responsible for most of my troubles.
151. Someone has been trying to poison me.
157. I feel that I have often been punished without cause.
202. I believe I am a condemned person.
275. Someone has control over my mind.
284. I am sure I am being talked about.
291. At one or more times in my life I felt that someone was making me do things by hypnotizing me.
293. Someone has been trying to influence my mind.
338. I have certainly had more than my share of things to worry about.
364. People say insulting and vulgar things about me.

The following item scores if answered *false:*

347. I have no enemies who really wish to harm me.

Pa2: Poignancy (9 Items)

The following items score if answered *true:*

24. No one seems to understand me.
158. I cry easily.
299. I think that I feel more intensely than most people do.
305. Even when I am with people I feel lonely much of the time.
317. I am more sensitive than most other people.
341. At times I hear so well it bothers me.
365. I feel uneasy indoors.

The following items score if answered *false:*

111. I have never done anything dangerous for the thrill of it.
268. Something exciting will almost always pull me out of it when I am feeling low.

Pa3: Moral Virtue (9 Items)

The following item scores if answered *true:*

314. Once in a while I think of things too bad to talk about.

The following items score if answered *false:*

93. I think most people would lie to get ahead.
109. Some people are so bossy that I feel like doing the opposite of what they request even though I know they are right.
117. Most people are honest chiefly through fear of being caught.
124. Most people will use somewhat unfair means to gain profit or an advantage rather than to lose it.
313. The man who provides temptation by leaving valuable property unprotected is about as much to blame for its theft as the one who steals it.
316. I think nearly anyone would tell a lie to keep out of trouble.

319.   Most people inwardly dislike putting themselves out to help other people.
348.   I tend to be on my guard with people who are somewhat more friendly than I had expected.

Scale 8 (Sc, Schizophrenia)

Sc1A: Social Alienation (21 Items)

The following items score if answered *true:*

16.   I am sure I get a raw deal from life.
21.   At times I have very much wanted to leave home.
24.   No one seems to understand me.
35.   If people had not had it in for me I would have been much more successful.
52.   I prefer to pass by school friends, or people I know but have not seen for a long time, unless they speak to me first.
121.   I believe I am being plotted against.
157.   I feel that I have often been punished without cause.
212.   My people treat me more like a child than a grown-up.
241.   I dream frequently about things that are best kept to myself.
282.   Once in a while I feel hate toward members of my family whom I usually love.
305.   Even when I am with people I feel lonely much of the time.
312.   I dislike having people about me.
324.   I have never been in love with anyone.
325.   The things that some of my family have done have frightened me.
352.   I have been afraid of things or people that I knew could not hurt me.
364.   People say insulting and vulgar things about me.

The following items score if answered *false:*

65.   I loved my father.
220.   I loved my mother.
276.   I enjoy children.
306.   I get all the sympathy I should.
309.   I seem to make friends about as quickly as others do.

Sc1B: Emotional Alienation (11 Items)

The following items score if answered *true:*

76.   Most of the time I feel blue.
104.   I don't seem to care what happens to me.
202.   I believe I am a condemned person.
301.   Life is a strain for me much of the time.
339.   Most of the time I wish I were dead.
355.   Sometimes I enjoy hurting persons I love.
360.   Almost every day something happens to frighten me.
363.   At times I have enjoyed being hurt by someone I loved.

The following items score if answered *false:*

8.   My daily life is full of things that keep me interested.
196.   I like to visit places where I have never been before.
322.   I worry over money and business.

Sc2A: Lack of Ego Mastery, Cognitive (10 Items)

The following items score if answered *true:*

32. I find it hard to keep my mind on a task or job.
33. I have had very peculiar and strange experiences.
159. I cannot understand what I read as well as I used to.
168. There is something wrong with my mind.
182. I am afraid of losing my mind.
335. I cannot keep my mind on one thing.
345. I often feel as if things were not real.
349. I have strange and peculiar thoughts.
356. I have more trouble concentrating than others seem to have.

The following item scores if answered *false:*

178. My memory seems to be all right.

Sc2B: Lack of Ego Mastery, Conative (14 Items)

The following items score if answered *true:*

32. I find it hard to keep my mind on a task or job.
40. Most any time I would rather sit and daydream than to do anything else.
41. I have had periods of days, weeks, or months when I couldn't take care of things because I couldn't "get going."
76. Most of the time I feel blue.
104. I don't seem to care what happens to me.
202. I believe I am a condemned person.
259. I have difficulty in starting to do things.
301. Life is a strain for me much of the time.
335. I cannot keep my mind on one thing.
339. Most of the time I wish I were dead.
356. I have more trouble concentrating than others seem to have.

The following items score if answered *false:*

8. My daily life is full of things that keep me interested.
196. I like to visit places where I have never been before.
322. I worry over money and business.

Sc2C: Lack of Ego Mastery, Defect of Inhibition and Control (11 Items)

The following items score if answered *true:*

22. At times I have fits of laughing and crying that I cannot control.
97. At times I have a strong urge to do something harmful or shocking.
156. I have had periods in which I carried on activities without knowing later what I had been doing.
194. I have had attacks in which I could not control my movements or speech but in which I knew what was going on around me.
238. I have periods of such great restlessness that I cannot sit long in a chair.
266. Once a week or oftener I become very excited.

291.   At one or more times in my life I felt that someone was making me do things by hypnotizing me.
303.   I am so touchy on some subjects that I can't talk about them.
352.   I have been afraid of things or people that I knew could not hurt me.
354.   I am afraid of using a knife or anything very sharp or pointed.
360.   Almost every day something happens to frighten me.

The following items score if answered *false:*
(none)

Sc3: Sensorimotor Dissociation (20 Items)

The following items score if answered *true:*

22.   At times I have fits of laughing and crying that I cannot control.
33.   I have had very peculiar and strange experiences.
47.   Once a week or oftener I feel suddenly hot all over, without apparent cause.
156.   I have had periods in which I carried on activities without knowing later what I had been doing.
194.   I have had attacks in which I could not control my movements or speech but in which I knew what was going on around me.
210.   Everything tastes the same.
251.   I have had blank spells in which my activities were interrupted and I did not know what was going on around me.
273.   I have numbness in one or more regions of my skin.
291.   At one or more times in my life I felt that someone was making me do things by hypnotizing me.
332.   Sometimes my voice leaves me or changes even though I have no cold.
334.   Peculiar odors come to me at times.
341.   At times I hear so well it bothers me.
345.   I often feel as if things were not real.
350.   I hear strange things when I am alone.

The following items score if answered *false:*

103.   I have little or no trouble with my muscles twitching or jumping.
119.   My speech is the same as always (not faster or slower, or slurring; no hoarseness).
187.   My hands have not become clumsy or awkward.
192.   I have had no difficulty in keeping my balance in walking.
281.   I do not often notice my ears ringing or buzzing.
330.   I have never been paralyzed or had any unusual weakness of any of my muscles.

Scale 9 (Ma, Hypomania)

Ma1: Amorality (6 Items)

The following items score if answered *true:*

143.   When I was a child, I belonged to a crowd or gang that tried to stick together through thick and thin.
250.   I don't blame anyone for trying to grab everything he can get in this world.
271.   I do not blame a person for taking advantage of someone who lays himself open to it.
277.   At times I have been so entertained by the cleverness of a crook that I have hoped he would get by with it.

298.   If several people find themselves in trouble, the best thing for them to do is to agree upon a story and stick to it.

The following item scores if answered *false:*

289.   I am always disgusted with the law when a criminal is freed through the arguments of a smart lawyer.

Ma2: Psychomotor Acceleration (11 Items)

The following items score if answered *true:*

13.   I work under a great deal of tension.
97.   At times I have a strong urge to do something harmful or shocking.
100.   I have met problems so full of possibilities that I have been unable to make up my mind about them.
134.   At times my thoughts have raced ahead faster than I could speak them.
181.   When I get bored I like to stir up some excitement.
228.   At times I feel that I can make up my mind with unusually great ease.
238.   I have periods of such great restlessness that I cannot sit long in a chair.
266.   Once a week or oftener I become very excited.
268.   Something exciting will almost always pull me out of it when I am feeling low.

The following items score if answered *false:*

111.   I have never done anything dangerous for the thrill of it.
119.   My speech is the same as always (not faster or slower, or slurring; no hoarseness).

Ma3: Imperturbability (8 Items)

The following items score if answered *true:*

167.   It wouldn't make me nervous if any members of my family got into trouble with the law.
222.   It is not hard for me to ask help from my friends even though I cannot return the favor.
240.   I never worry about my looks.

The following items score if answered *false:*

105.   Sometimes when I am not feeling well I am cross.
148.   It makes me impatient to have people ask my advice or otherwise interrupt me when I am working on something important.
171.   It makes me uncomfortable to put on a stunt at a party even when others are doing the same sort of things.
180.   I find it hard to make talk when I meet new people.
267.   When in a group of people I have trouble thinking of the right things to talk about.

Ma4: Ego Inflation (9 Items)

The following items score if answered *true:*

11.   A person should try to understand his dreams and be guided by or take warning from them.

59. I have often had to take orders from someone who did not know as much as I did.
64. I sometimes keep on at a thing until others lose their patience with me.
73. I am an important person.
109. Some people are so bossy that I feel like doing the opposite of what they request even though I know they are right.
157. I feel that I have often been punished without cause.
212. My people treat me more like a child than a grown-up.
232. I have been inspired to a program of life based on duty which I have since carefully followed.
233. I have at times stood in the way of people who were trying to do something, not because it amounted to much but because of the principle of the thing.

The following items score if answered *false:*
(none)

Research/Supplemental Scales for the MMPI

Females   Subjective Depression   (D1)

| | Total Sample | Age, yr | | | | |
		13	14	15	16	17
N	691	136	153	127	138	137
Median	8	8	8	8	9	7
Mean	8.65	8.56	8.28	8.76	9.93	7.79
SD	4.33	3.71	4.10	4.74	4.96	3.80
Min	1	1	1	1	1	1
Max	26	20	21	23	26	19

Percentage of Sample with Raw Score < X

X	Total Sample	13	14	15	16	17
1	0.0	0.0	0.0	0.0	0.0	0.0
2	1.9	2.2	3.3	2.4	0.7	0.7
3	5.2	3.7	5.9	4.7	4.3	7.3
4	10.9	9.6	13.7	10.2	6.5	13.9
5	18.1	15.4	19.6	19.7	13.0	22.6
6	25.3	22.1	26.8	31.5	16.7	29.9
7	33.1	30.1	35.9	37.0	23.2	39.4
8	44.0	39.7	46.4	47.2	35.5	51.1
9	52.7	50.7	52.3	55.1	43.5	62.0
10	59.9	61.0	60.8	59.1	52.9	65.7
11	69.3	67.6	73.2	68.5	61.6	75.2
12	76.0	77.2	79.7	70.9	67.4	83.9
13	82.2	84.6	84.3	78.7	73.2	89.8
14	86.8	91.2	88.9	82.7	79.0	92.0
15	91.5	95.6	94.8	87.4	84.1	94.9
16	93.3	97.1	94.8	90.6	87.0	97.1
17	95.9	98.5	98.0	94.5	90.6	97.8
18	96.7	99.3	98.0	94.5	92.8	98.5
19	97.5	99.3	98.0	96.9	94.2	99.3
20	97.8	99.3	98.0	96.9	94.9	100.0
21	98.6	100.0	99.3	97.6	95.7	100.0
22	99.1	100.0	100.0	99.2	96.4	100.0
23	99.4	100.0	100.0	99.2	97.8	100.0
24	99.7	100.0	100.0	100.0	98.6	100.0
25	99.7	100.0	100.0	100.0	98.6	100.0
26	99.9	100.0	100.0	100.0	99.3	100.0

Research/Supplemental Scales for the MMPI

Females   Psychomotor Retardation   (D2)

| | Total Sample | Age, yr | | | | |
		13	14	15	16	17
N	691	136	153	127	138	137
Median	5	5	5	5	5	5
Mean	4.81	4.79	4.73	4.74	4.86	4.92
SD	1.91	1.82	1.85	1.99	2.12	1.77
Min	0	0	0	0	0	1
Max	11	10	11	10	11	9

| X | Percentage of Sample with Raw Score < X | | | | | |
	Total Sample	13	14	15	16	17
0	0.0	0.0	0.0	0.0	0.0	0.0
1	0.6	0.7	0.7	0.8	0.7	0.0
2	3.0	1.5	3.3	4.7	2.9	2.9
3	11.1	10.3	9.8	14.2	12.3	9.5
4	24.2	25.7	24.8	24.4	26.8	19.0
5	44.9	42.6	47.7	48.0	46.4	39.4
6	66.6	66.9	68.0	65.4	68.1	64.2
7	82.9	84.6	83.0	81.9	80.4	84.7
8	91.0	92.6	92.8	91.3	86.2	92.0
9	96.2	97.1	98.0	96.1	93.5	96.4
10	99.3	99.3	99.3	99.2	98.6	100.0
11	99.6	100.0	99.3	100.0	98.6	100.0

Research/Supplemental Scales for the MMPI

Females   Physical Malfunctioning   (D3)

| | Total Sample | Age, yr | | | | |
		13	14	15	16	17
N	691	136	153	127	138	137
Median	3	3	3	3	3	3
Mean	3.20	3.32	3.21	3.08	3.38	2.99
SD	1.35	1.31	1.31	1.35	1.32	1.42
Min	0	0	0	0	1	0
Max	9	7	8	7	7	9

| X | Percentage of Sample with Raw Score < X | | | | | |
	Total Sample	13	14	15	16	17
0	0.0	0.0	0.0	0.0	0.0	0.0
1	0.9	0.7	0.7	1.6	0.0	1.5
2	6.5	5.1	5.9	7.1	2.9	11.7
3	33.7	29.4	30.7	39.4	29.7	40.1
4	62.8	58.1	64.1	66.1	58.0	67.9
5	83.6	81.6	84.3	84.3	80.4	87.6
6	94.9	94.1	96.1	94.5	93.5	96.4
7	98.4	99.3	98.0	99.2	97.8	97.8
8	99.7	100.0	99.3	100.0	100.0	99.3
9	99.9	100.0	100.0	100.0	100.0	99.3

Research/Supplemental Scales for the MMPI

Females   Mental Dullness   (D4)

		Age, yr				
	Total Sample	13	14	15	16	17
N	691	136	153	127	138	137
Median	3	3	2	3	3	2
Mean	3.10	3.12	2.84	3.39	3.67	2.55
SD	2.51	2.42	2.26	2.66	2.95	2.08
Min	0	0	0	0	0	0
Max	14	10	11	12	14	11

Percentage of Sample with Raw Score < X

X	Total Sample	13	14	15	16	17
0	0.0	0.0	0.0	0.0	0.0	0.0
1	14.2	14.7	18.3	12.6	10.1	14.6
2	28.9	28.7	30.7	28.3	23.2	33.6
3	48.8	44.9	51.6	45.7	42.8	58.4
4	62.7	63.2	62.1	58.3	57.2	72.3
5	74.4	73.5	76.5	68.5	68.1	84.7
6	85.1	84.6	90.8	78.0	79.0	92.0
7	90.2	89.7	93.5	85.0	86.2	95.6
8	93.5	93.4	95.4	92.9	88.4	97.1
9	96.8	97.1	98.7	96.1	93.5	98.5
10	97.5	98.5	99.3	96.9	94.2	98.5
11	98.6	100.0	99.3	99.2	94.9	99.3
12	99.4	100.0	100.0	99.2	97.8	100.0
13	99.7	100.0	100.0	100.0	98.6	100.0
14	99.9	100.0	100.0	100.0	99.3	100.0

```
                  Research/Supplemental Scales for the MMPI

Females                    Brooding      (D5)

                                            Age, yr

                 Total Sample    13      14      15      16      17

         N           691        136     153     127     138     137
         Median        3          3       3       3       4       3
         Mean        3.37       3.16    3.07    3.41    4.10    3.17
         SD          2.06       1.88    1.92    2.19    2.25    1.89
         Min           0          0       0       0       0       0
         Max          10          9       9       9      10       9


                   Percentage of Sample with Raw Score < X
         X       Total Sample    13      14      15      16      17

         0           0.0         0.0     0.0     0.0     0.0     0.0
         1           6.2         5.9     8.5     4.7     3.6     8.0
         2          20.0        23.5    22.9    19.7    12.3    21.2
         3          36.2        37.5    40.5    40.9    23.9    38.0
         4          54.6        55.9    60.8    55.9    44.2    55.5

         5          73.4        78.7    78.4    74.0    60.1    75.2
         6          86.4        89.7    89.5    84.3    74.6    93.4
         7          92.2        94.9    96.1    89.0    84.8    95.6
         8          95.5        98.5    97.4    93.7    90.6    97.1
         9          98.3        99.3    99.3    96.9    96.4    99.3

        10          99.9       100.0   100.0   100.0    99.3   100.0
```

Research/Supplemental Scales for the MMPI

Females   Denial Of Social Anxiety   (Hy1)

	Total Sample	Age, yr				
		13	14	15	16	17
N	691	136	153	127	138	137
Median	3	3	3	3	3	4
Mean	3.09	2.90	3.15	2.98	2.88	3.50
SD	1.78	1.70	1.70	1.89	1.82	1.75
Min	0	0	0	0	0	0
Max	6	6	6	6	6	6

X	Percentage of Sample with Raw Score < X					
	Total Sample	13	14	15	16	17
0	0.0	0.0	0.0	0.0	0.0	0.0
1	8.4	8.8	7.8	10.2	9.4	5.8
2	23.4	25.0	20.3	26.8	27.5	18.2
3	38.4	40.4	33.3	43.3	47.1	28.5
4	56.3	62.5	54.9	59.8	60.9	43.8
5	74.0	79.4	77.1	73.2	76.1	63.5
6	91.0	94.1	91.5	88.2	91.3	89.8

Research/Supplemental Scales for the MMPI

Females   Need For Affection and Reinforcement from Others   (Hy2)

| | Total Sample | Age, yr | | | | |
		13	14	15	16	17
N	691	136	153	127	138	137
Median	5	4	5	5	5	6
Mean	5.27	4.82	5.44	5.28	5.07	5.69
SD	2.35	2.31	2.36	2.33	2.34	2.34
Min	0	1	0	0	0	1
Max	12	11	12	11	11	11

| X | Percentage of Sample with Raw Score < X | | | | | |
	Total Sample	13	14	15	16	17
0	0.0	0.0	0.0	0.0	0.0	0.0
1	0.6	0.0	0.7	0.8	1.4	0.0
2	3.0	2.2	2.0	4.7	3.6	2.9
3	11.3	14.0	9.2	10.2	13.0	10.2
4	26.8	35.3	23.5	26.8	28.3	20.4
5	39.5	50.7	36.6	35.4	44.2	30.7
6	55.7	67.6	52.3	55.1	59.4	44.5
7	72.4	77.9	71.2	74.0	75.4	63.5
8	80.6	83.1	80.4	80.3	81.9	77.4
9	89.7	91.9	89.5	87.4	91.3	88.3
10	95.4	96.3	93.5	97.6	95.7	94.2
11	98.6	98.5	97.4	99.2	99.3	98.5
12	99.9	100.0	99.3	100.0	100.0	100.0

Research/Supplemental Scales for the MMPI

Females   Lassitude-Malaise   (Hy3)

		Age, yr				
	Total Sample	13	14	15	16	17
N	691	136	153	127	138	137
Median	3	3	2	3	3	3
Mean	3.39	3.38	3.03	3.63	3.75	3.23
SD	2.60	2.25	2.41	2.93	2.90	2.47
Min	0	0	0	0	0	0
Max	14	12	10	14	14	11

Percentage of Sample with Raw Score < X

X	Total Sample	13	14	15	16	17
0	0.0	0.0	0.0	0.0	0.0	0.0
1	10.0	6.6	11.1	15.7	6.5	10.2
2	25.8	21.3	29.4	29.1	21.7	27.0
3	44.4	40.4	52.9	40.2	44.2	43.1
4	59.6	55.1	66.7	54.3	56.5	64.2
5	71.3	72.8	75.2	64.6	68.1	75.2
6	80.8	83.1	83.7	77.2	73.9	85.4
7	88.0	94.1	88.9	82.7	85.5	88.3
8	91.6	95.6	93.5	86.6	89.1	92.7
9	94.8	97.1	96.7	92.9	92.0	94.9
10	97.1	98.5	98.7	96.9	94.2	97.1
11	98.6	98.5	100.0	99.2	95.7	99.3
12	99.4	99.3	100.0	99.2	98.6	100.0
13	99.7	100.0	100.0	99.2	99.3	100.0
14	99.7	100.0	100.0	99.2	99.3	100.0

Research/Supplemental Scales for the MMPI

Females   Somatic Complaints   (Hy4)

	Total Sample	Age, yr				
		13	14	15	16	17
N	691	136	153	127	138	137
Median	3	3	3	3	4	3
Mean	3.70	3.55	3.33	3.92	4.32	3.45
SD	2.95	2.78	2.67	3.22	3.25	2.77
Min	0	0	0	0	0	0
Max	16	12	13	16	15	12

X	Percentage of Sample with Raw Score < X					
	Total Sample	13	14	15	16	17
0	0.0	0.0	0.0	0.0	0.0	0.0
1	10.9	9.6	11.1	14.2	8.0	11.7
2	25.5	25.7	28.8	26.8	19.6	26.3
3	41.5	44.9	41.8	37.0	37.7	46.0
4	56.7	59.6	63.4	51.2	47.1	61.3
5	67.4	67.6	75.8	62.2	59.4	70.8
6	76.1	76.5	81.7	75.6	68.1	78.1
7	82.8	86.0	84.3	81.9	76.8	84.7
8	87.6	88.2	92.2	85.8	81.9	89.1
9	92.6	94.1	94.8	90.6	89.1	94.2
10	95.4	96.3	96.7	94.5	92.8	96.4
11	97.3	97.8	98.7	96.1	95.7	97.8
12	98.0	98.5	98.7	96.9	96.4	99.3
13	99.0	100.0	99.3	97.6	97.8	100.0
14	99.6	100.0	100.0	99.2	98.6	100.0
15	99.7	100.0	100.0	99.2	99.3	100.0
16	99.9	100.0	100.0	99.2	100.0	100.0

Research/Supplemental Scales for the MMPI

Females   Inhibition Of Aggression   (Hy5)

| | Total Sample | Age, yr | | | | |
		13	14	15	16	17
N	691	136	153	127	138	137
Median	3	3	3	3	3	3
Mean	2.99	3.23	3.14	2.81	2.82	2.90
SD	1.28	1.21	1.36	1.20	1.30	1.26
Min	0	0	0	0	0	0
Max	7	6	6	5	7	6

| | Percentage of Sample with Raw Score < X | | | | | |
X	Total Sample	13	14	15	16	17
0	0.0	0.0	0.0	0.0	0.0	0.0
1	1.7	0.7	0.7	2.4	2.9	2.2
2	12.0	6.6	12.4	12.6	13.0	15.3
3	36.6	27.9	33.3	42.5	43.5	36.5
4	65.4	59.6	60.1	69.3	72.5	66.4
5	87.8	85.3	83.7	92.1	88.4	90.5
6	98.0	97.1	95.4	100.0	98.6	99.3
7	99.9	100.0	100.0	100.0	99.3	100.0

Research/Supplemental Scales for the MMPI

Females   Familial Discord   (Pd1)

		Age, yr			
	Total Sample	13	14	15	16	17
N	691	136	153	127	138	137
Median	4	4	4	5	4	4
Mean	4.23	4.13	4.19	4.43	4.46	3.97
SD	2.28	2.12	2.23	2.44	2.32	2.30
Min	0	1	1	0	1	0
Max	10	10	9	10	10	10

Percentage of Sample with Raw Score < X

X	Total Sample	13	14	15	16	17
0	0.0	0.0	0.0	0.0	0.0	0.0
1	0.9	0.0	0.0	2.4	0.0	2.2
2	9.7	8.1	9.2	11.8	7.2	12.4
3	26.5	27.9	26.8	27.6	19.6	30.7
4	44.3	44.1	45.1	38.6	44.9	48.2
5	57.6	57.4	60.1	49.6	56.5	63.5
6	72.4	76.5	72.5	69.3	65.9	77.4
7	82.1	86.0	81.7	78.0	80.4	83.9
8	89.7	91.2	90.8	85.8	89.1	91.2
9	95.1	97.1	94.8	95.3	93.5	94.9
10	98.6	99.3	100.0	98.4	96.4	98.5

235

Research/Supplemental Scales for the MMPI

Females   Authority Conflict   (Pd2)

	Total Sample	Age, yr				
		13	14	15	16	17
N	691	136	153	127	138	137
Median	4	4	4	4	3	4
Mean	3.83	3.63	4.00	4.03	3.68	3.82
SD	1.58	1.38	1.55	1.42	1.70	1.79
Min	0	0	1	1	0	0
Max	9	8	9	8	8	9

Percentage of Sample with Raw Score < X

X	Total Sample	13	14	15	16	17
0	0.0	0.0	0.0	0.0	0.0	0.0
1	0.9	1.5	0.0	0.0	1.4	1.5
2	5.2	7.4	2.6	3.1	7.2	5.8
3	19.4	15.4	15.7	14.2	25.4	26.3
4	44.1	46.3	41.2	34.6	50.7	47.4
5	69.5	78.7	66.0	63.8	72.5	66.4
6	85.7	91.2	83.7	87.4	83.3	83.2
7	94.1	97.8	94.1	94.5	92.8	91.2
8	98.4	99.3	98.0	99.2	98.6	97.1
9	99.6	100.0	98.7	100.0	100.0	99.3

Research/Supplemental Scales for the MMPI

Females   Social Imperturbability   (Pd3)

		Age, yr				
	Total Sample	13	14	15	16	17
N	691	136	153	127	138	137
Median	7	6	7	7	6	7
Mean	6.52	6.13	6.66	6.57	6.20	7.03
SD	2.54	2.42	2.43	2.63	2.62	2.54
Min	0	1	1	0	1	1
Max	12	12	12	11	12	12

	Percentage of Sample with Raw Score < X					
X	Total Sample	13	14	15	16	17
0	0.0	0.0	0.0	0.0	0.0	0.0
1	0.3	0.0	0.0	1.6	0.0	0.0
2	1.6	2.2	0.7	1.6	2.9	0.7
3	5.2	7.4	5.2	5.5	5.8	2.2
4	13.3	17.6	11.8	10.2	18.1	8.8
5	24.5	27.2	19.6	25.2	30.4	20.4
6	36.6	36.8	32.0	38.6	44.2	32.1
7	48.8	52.9	47.1	49.6	52.9	41.6
8	62.1	69.1	61.4	61.4	65.9	52.6
9	74.5	83.8	75.2	72.4	74.6	66.4
10	87.7	94.1	87.6	83.5	89.9	83.2
11	93.9	96.3	94.1	92.9	95.7	90.5
12	99.3	99.3	99.3	100.0	99.3	98.5

Research/Supplemental Scales for the MMPI

Females   Social Alienation   (Pd4A)

		Age, yr				
	Total Sample	13	14	15	16	17
N	691	136	153	127	138	137
Median	7	7	7	7	7	6
Mean	7.18	6.99	7.19	7.47	7.66	6.60
SD	3.11	2.92	3.16	3.30	3.19	2.87
Min	1	1	1	1	1	1
Max	16	15	15	16	15	14

Percentage of Sample with Raw Score < X

X	Total Sample	13	14	15	16	17
1	0.0	0.0	0.0	0.0	0.0	0.0
2	1.0	1.5	0.7	0.8	0.7	1.5
3	3.8	5.9	3.9	1.6	0.7	6.6
4	10.7	13.2	11.1	6.3	5.8	16.8
5	21.4	20.6	21.6	21.3	18.8	24.8
6	34.3	35.3	33.3	33.9	28.3	40.9
7	44.9	44.1	42.5	44.9	42.8	50.4
8	57.2	55.9	60.8	54.3	54.3	59.9
9	67.4	66.2	70.6	63.8	63.8	72.3
10	78.6	80.9	77.8	77.2	72.5	84.7
11	84.9	89.0	85.0	84.3	76.8	89.8
12	89.9	94.1	88.2	87.4	84.1	95.6
13	93.9	97.1	92.2	89.8	92.0	98.5
14	96.4	98.5	94.8	93.7	96.4	98.5
15	98.3	99.3	98.7	96.1	97.1	100.0
16	99.6	100.0	100.0	97.6	100.0	100.0

Research/Supplemental Scales for the MMPI

Females   Self-Alienation   (Pd4B)

		Age, yr				
	Total Sample	13	14	15	16	17
N	691	136	153	127	138	137
Median	5	4	4	5	5	5
Mean	5.05	4.85	4.63	5.26	5.67	4.91
SD	2.89	2.85	2.64	3.08	3.22	2.54
Min	0	0	1	0	0	0
Max	15	15	14	14	14	12

	Percentage of Sample with Raw Score < X					
X	Total Sample	13	14	15	16	17
0	0.0	0.0	0.0	0.0	0.0	0.0
1	1.4	2.2	0.0	2.4	1.4	1.5
2	7.8	8.1	7.8	10.2	6.5	6.6
3	19.4	23.5	23.5	17.3	15.2	16.8
4	34.4	36.0	41.2	28.3	32.6	32.8
5	47.9	51.5	56.2	44.9	39.9	46.0
6	62.1	62.5	66.7	62.2	51.4	67.2
7	72.5	74.3	75.8	72.4	63.8	75.9
8	81.2	83.1	85.6	79.5	76.1	81.0
9	86.8	89.0	90.8	84.3	80.4	89.1
10	91.5	93.4	94.8	88.2	86.2	94.2
11	94.9	96.3	97.4	92.1	89.9	98.5
12	97.1	97.8	98.7	96.1	93.5	99.3
13	98.4	98.5	99.3	97.6	96.4	100.0
14	99.3	99.3	·99.3	98.4	99.3	100.0
15	99.9	99.3	100.0	100.0	100.0	100.0

Research/Supplemental Scales for the MMPI

Females   Alienation (Sum of Pd4A and Pd4B)   (Pd4)

		Age, yr				
	Total Sample	13	14	15	16	17
N	691	136	153	127	138	137
Median	12	12	11	12	13	11
Mean	12.23	11.84	11.82	12.73	13.33	11.51
SD	5.65	5.46	5.39	6.10	6.08	5.11
Min	1	1	2	1	2	2
Max	30	30	28	30	28	26

	Percentage of Sample with Raw Score < X					
X	Total Sample	13	14	15	16	17
1	0.0	0.0	0.0	0.0	0.0	0.0
2	0.3	0.7	0.0	0.8	0.0	0.0
3	1.0	0.7	0.7	0.8	0.7	2.2
4	2.0	2.2	1.3	1.6	1.4	3.6
5	5.8	8.8	5.9	3.9	2.9	7.3
6	10.0	11.8	10.5	10.2	5.1	12.4
7	15.9	17.6	15.0	17.3	11.6	18.2
8	22.9	25.0	24.2	21.3	20.3	23.4
9	29.5	31.6	30.7	26.0	28.3	30.7
10	36.0	38.2	35.9	33.1	34.1	38.7
11	43.1	42.6	48.4	40.2	38.4	45.3
12	49.5	49.3	55.6	47.2	42.0	52.6
13	55.9	55.9	59.5	53.5	50.0	59.9
14	61.6	62.5	66.0	56.7	55.1	67.2
15	68.2	69.9	71.2	67.7	60.1	71.5
16	74.0	75.7	77.8	74.0	65.2	76.6
17	79.2	80.9	82.4	77.2	71.7	83.2
18	82.2	84.6	84.3	81.9	73.9	86.1
19	85.4	89.7	85.6	83.5	79.7	88.3
20	88.1	92.6	88.2	85.0	81.2	93.4
21	90.9	94.1	92.2	86.6	84.8	96.4
22	92.9	95.6	94.8	90.6	87.0	96.4
23	94.6	96.3	95.4	91.3	91.3	98.5
24	96.2	97.1	97.4	94.5	93.5	98.5
25	97.3	97.8	98.7	95.3	94.9	99.3
26	97.7	97.8	98.7	96.1	96.4	99.3
27	98.4	99.3	98.7	96.1	97.8	100.0
28	99.1	99.3	99.3	97.6	99.3	100.0
29	99.4	99.3	100.0	97.6	100.0	100.0
30	99.7	99.3	100.0	99.2	100.0	100.0

Research/Supplemental Scales for the MMPI

Females   Ideas of External Influence   (Pa1)

		Age, yr				
	Total Sample	13	14	15	16	17
N	691	136	153	127	138	137
Median	3	3	3	3	3	2
Mean	3.50	3.66	3.79	3.64	3.60	2.77
SD	2.75	2.60	2.87	2.94	2.88	2.33
Min	0	0	0	0	0	0
Max	16	13	14	16	13	13

	Percentage of Sample with Raw Score < X					
X	Total Sample	13	14	15	16	17
0	0.0	0.0	0.0	0.0	0.0	0.0
1	6.5	7.4	3.3	6.3	5.8	10.2
2	27.2	23.5	26.8	26.0	26.1	33.6
3	45.6	39.7	43.8	40.2	47.8	56.2
4	57.9	52.9	54.2	54.3	57.2	70.8
5	71.8	64.7	64.7	75.6	72.5	82.5
6	80.6	79.4	75.8	81.9	78.3	88.3
7	86.1	84.6	83.0	86.6	83.3	93.4
8	90.4	91.9	87.6	89.8	87.7	95.6
9	92.9	94.1	90.8	92.1	90.6	97.1
10	96.2	97.8	94.8	95.3	94.9	98.5
11	97.8	99.3	98.0	95.3	97.8	98.5
12	98.4	99.3	99.3	96.1	98.6	98.5
13	99.3	99.3	99.3	99.2	99.3	99.3
14	99.7	100.0	99.3	99.2	100.0	100.0
15	99.9	100.0	100.0	99.2	100.0	100.0
16	99.9	100.0	100.0	99.2	100.0	100.0

241

Research/Supplemental Scales for the MMPI

Females   Poignancy   (Pa2)

		Age, yr				
	Total Sample	13	14	15	16	17
N	691	136	153	127	138	137
Median	3	2	2	3	3	3
Mean	2.88	2.49	2.61	3.02	3.33	3.00
SD	1.75	1.65	1.50	1.66	2.07	1.72
Min	0	0	0	0	0	0
Max	9	8	6	7	9	7

Percentage of Sample with Raw Score < X

X	Total Sample	13	14	15	16	17
0	0.0	0.0	0.0	0.0	0.0	0.0
1	6.5	8.8	7.2	4.7	6.5	5.1
2	24.3	33.8	23.5	20.5	20.3	23.4
3	45.0	54.4	50.3	39.4	37.7	42.3
4	65.7	70.6	75.2	62.2	60.1	59.1
5	81.9	88.2	86.3	81.9	71.7	81.0
6	92.3	96.3	96.7	92.9	84.1	91.2
7	96.8	99.3	100.0	96.9	89.9	97.8
8	99.4	99.3	100.0	100.0	97.8	100.0
9	99.9	100.0	100.0	100.0	99.3	100.0

Research/Supplemental Scales for the MMPI

Females   Moral Virtue   (Pa3)

| | | Age, yr | | | | |
	Total Sample	13	14	15	16	17
N	691	136	153	127	138	137
Median	4	3	4	3	4	4
Mean	3.70	3.32	3.63	3.57	3.68	4.27
SD	1.99	1.92	1.97	1.92	1.91	2.14
Min	0	0	0	0	0	0
Max	9	9	9	8	9	9

Percentage of Sample with Raw Score < X

X	Total Sample	13	14	15	16	17
0	0.0	0.0	0.0	0.0	0.0	0.0
1	1.9	0.7	2.6	1.6	1.4	2.9
2	13.9	19.1	15.0	12.6	10.9	11.7
3	32.0	38.2	33.3	35.4	31.2	21.9
4	49.6	60.3	49.0	52.8	50.0	36.5
5	66.6	75.7	66.7	69.3	68.1	53.3
6	81.3	85.3	81.0	83.5	84.8	72.3
7	90.3	91.2	92.8	91.3	91.3	84.7
8	95.5	97.8	96.7	96.1	95.7	91.2
9	99.1	99.3	99.3	100.0	98.6	98.5

Research/Supplemental Scales for the MMPI

Females   Social Alienation   (Sc1A)

		Age, yr				
	Total Sample	13	14	15	16	17
N	691	136	153	127	138	137
Median	5	6	5	6	6	5
Mean	5.67	5.88	5.78	6.04	5.93	4.74
SD	3.21	3.01	3.26	3.33	3.42	2.89
Min	0	1	0	0	0	0
Max	18	14	15	18	17	13

Percentage of Sample with Raw Score < X

X	Total Sample	13	14	15	16	17
0	0.0	0.0	0.0	0.0	0.0	0.0
1	1.9	0.0	1.3	1.6	0.7	5.8
2	7.7	6.6	9.2	4.7	5.8	11.7
3	15.8	14.0	13.7	15.0	14.5	21.9
4	27.5	22.1	26.8	22.0	27.5	38.7
5	40.8	36.8	40.5	36.2	41.3	48.9
6	53.0	50.0	50.3	48.8	50.0	65.7
7	63.7	61.8	62.7	58.3	59.4	75.9
8	75.5	72.8	75.8	71.7	73.2	83.9
9	80.6	77.2	78.4	78.0	81.2	88.3
10	86.4	83.8	85.6	87.4	83.3	92.0
11	91.8	91.9	90.8	91.3	89.1	95.6
12	94.8	97.8	93.5	92.9	92.0	97.8
13	97.0	98.5	96.1	95.3	95.7	99.3
14	98.6	99.3	98.0	97.6	97.8	100.0
15	99.0	100.0	99.3	97.6	97.8	100.0
16	99.6	100.0	100.0	99.2	98.6	100.0
17	99.7	100.0	100.0	99.2	99.3	100.0
18	99.9	100.0	100.0	99.2	100.0	100.0

Research/Supplemental Scales for the MMPI

Females   Emotional Alienation   (Sc1B)

		Age, yr				
	Total Sample	13	14	15	16	17
N	691	136	153	127	138	137
Median	1	1	1	1	1	1
Mean	1.77	1.91	1.69	1.92	1.86	1.48
SD	1.58	1.64	1.52	1.68	1.66	1.36
Min	0	0	0	0	0	0
Max	9	9	7	9	7	6

Percentage of Sample with Raw Score < X

X	Total Sample	13	14	15	16	17
0	0.0	0.0	0.0	0.0	0.0	0.0
1	14.6	10.3	15.7	11.0	13.0	22.6
2	57.2	52.9	57.5	53.5	58.0	63.5
3	77.6	76.5	80.4	75.6	75.4	79.6
4	88.6	86.0	90.8	85.8	87.7	92.0
5	92.5	91.9	92.8	92.1	89.1	96.4
6	95.4	95.6	96.1	94.5	92.8	97.8
7	98.3	97.8	97.4	97.6	98.6	100.0
8	99.4	98.5	100.0	98.4	100.0	100.0
9	99.7	99.3	100.0	99.2	100.0	100.0

Research/Supplemental Scales for the MMPI

Females   Object Loss (Sum of Sc1A and Sc1B)   (Sc1)

| | | Age, yr | | | | |
	Total Sample	13	14	15	16	17
N	691	136	153	127	138	137
Median	7	7	7	7	7	6
Mean	7.44	7.79	7.47	7.96	7.78	6.23
SD	4.29	4.08	4.37	4.50	4.54	3.74
Min	0	2	0	0	1	1
Max	24	20	22	24	23	18

Percentage of Sample with Raw Score < X

X	Total Sample	13	14	15	16	17
0	0.0	0.0	0.0	0.0	0.0	0.0
1	0.3	0.0	0.7	0.8	0.0	0.0
2	2.0	0.0	2.0	1.6	2.2	4.4
3	8.5	6.6	9.8	6.3	8.0	11.7
4	16.5	14.0	15.7	11.8	15.2	25.5
5	27.1	22.1	26.8	22.8	26.8	36.5
6	39.7	34.6	41.2	32.3	39.9	49.6
7	49.1	43.4	48.4	44.1	45.7	63.5
8	58.2	55.9	56.9	52.8	52.9	72.3
9	66.6	64.0	66.7	60.6	61.6	79.6
10	74.0	70.6	73.9	71.7	70.3	83.2
11	79.5	74.3	79.1	78.7	78.3	86.9
12	82.6	77.9	83.0	81.9	80.4	89.8
13	87.3	86.0	87.6	86.6	84.1	92.0
14	90.4	91.2	90.2	89.8	87.7	93.4
15	93.2	94.1	92.2	91.3	92.8	95.6
16	95.2	96.3	94.1	93.7	94.9	97.1
17	96.1	97.1	95.4	95.3	94.9	97.8
18	96.7	97.1	96.1	96.1	95.7	98.5
19	97.8	97.8	97.4	96.1	97.8	100.0
20	98.3	98.5	98.0	96.9	97.8	100.0
21	98.7	100.0	98.7	96.9	97.8	100.0
22	99.0	100.0	99.3	97.6	97.8	100.0
23	99.7	100.0	100.0	99.2	99.3	100.0
24	99.9	100.0	100.0	99.2	100.0	100.0

Research/Supplemental Scales for the MMPI

Females   Lack Of Ego Mastery, Cognitive   (Sc2A)

		Age, yr				
	Total Sample	13	14	15	16	17
N	691	136	153	127	138	137
Median	2	2	2	2	3	1
Mean	2.39	2.34	2.30	2.54	2.91	1.89
SD	2.29	2.27	2.00	2.38	2.64	2.03
Min	0	0	0	0	0	0
Max	10	9	8	9	10	10

	Percentage of Sample with Raw Score < X					
X	Total Sample	13	14	15	16	17
0	0.0	0.0	0.0	0.0	0.0	0.0
1	25.2	22.8	24.8	26.8	21.7	29.9
2	45.4	47.8	43.8	45.7	39.1	51.1
3	58.8	60.3	55.6	55.9	50.0	72.3
4	72.8	76.5	71.9	64.6	65.9	84.7
5	82.2	83.8	84.3	79.5	73.2	89.8
6	88.6	87.5	92.8	85.8	84.8	91.2
7	93.3	93.4	97.4	91.3	88.4	95.6
8	96.5	95.6	99.3	97.6	92.0	97.8
9	98.4	98.5	100.0	99.2	94.9	99.3
10	99.6	100.0	100.0	100.0	98.6	99.3

Research/Supplemental Scales for the MMPI

Females　　　　　Lack Of Ego Mastery, Conative　　(Sc2B)

		Age, yr				
	Total Sample	13	14	15	16	17
N	691	136	153	127	138	137
Median	3	3	3	3	3	3
Mean	3.68	3.86	3.54	3.98	4.00	3.06
SD	2.64	2.68	2.50	2.85	2.90	2.13
Min	0	0	0	0	0	0
Max	13	12	12	13	12	10

	Percentage of Sample with Raw Score < X					
X	Total Sample	13	14	15	16	17
0	0.0	0.0	0.0	0.0	0.0	0.0
1	3.6	0.7	6.5	3.1	2.9	4.4
2	24.3	20.6	26.8	22.0	21.0	30.7
3	40.5	39.7	41.2	39.4	38.4	43.8
4	55.0	55.1	50.3	54.3	53.6	62.0
5	69.3	66.2	68.0	63.0	68.1	81.0
6	77.4	74.3	81.0	70.9	72.5	87.6
7	84.5	83.1	86.3	79.5	79.7	93.4
8	90.2	88.2	94.8	86.6	84.8	95.6
9	94.1	94.1	96.7	92.1	89.1	97.8
10	95.9	95.6	97.4	96.1	92.8	97.8
11	98.3	97.8	98.0	97.6	97.8	100.0
12	99.1	98.5	99.3	98.4	99.3	100.0
13	99.9	100.0	100.0	99.2	100.0	100.0

Research/Supplemental Scales for the MMPI

Females   Lack Of Ego Mastery, Defect of Inhibition and Control   (Sc2C)

		Age, yr				
	Total Sample	13	14	15	16	17
N	691	136	153	127	138	137
Median	3	3	3	3	4	3
Mean	3.61	3.65	3.56	3.79	3.93	3.12
SD	2.09	2.10	2.09	2.00	2.19	1.98
Min	0	0	0	0	0	0
Max	11	9	9	9	11	8

	Percentage of Sample with Raw Score < X					
X	Total Sample	13	14	15	16	17
0	0.0	0.0	0.0	0.0	0.0	0.0
1	5.2	3.7	4.6	2.4	8.7	6.6
2	17.8	16.2	19.6	13.4	14.5	24.8
3	32.7	33.1	32.0	27.6	26.1	44.5
4	50.4	51.5	53.6	51.2	36.2	59.1
5	66.9	65.4	68.0	63.0	63.8	73.7
6	80.6	80.9	81.0	78.7	76.8	85.4
7	90.4	90.4	90.8	89.0	87.7	94.2
8	96.5	95.6	96.1	96.9	94.9	99.3
9	99.0	97.8	98.7	99.2	99.3	100.0
10	99.9	100.0	100.0	100.0	99.3	100.0
11	99.9	100.0	100.0	100.0	99.3	100.0

Research/Supplemental Scales for the MMPI

Females   Lack of Ego Mastery, Intrapsychic Autonomy (Sc2)

		Age, yr				
	Total Sample	13	14	15	16	17
N	691	136	153	127	138	137
Median	9	9	9	10	10	7
Mean	9.68	9.85	9.39	10.30	10.85	8.07
SD	6.17	6.27	5.70	6.40	6.90	5.23
Min	0	1	1	0	0	0
Max	29	28	27	29	29	23

	Percentage of Sample with Raw Score < X					
X	Total Sample	13	14	15	16	17
0	0.0	0.0	0.0	0.0	0.0	0.0
1	0.4	0.0	0.0	0.8	0.7	0.7
2	4.2	3.7	3.3	2.4	5.1	6.6
3	9.7	7.4	11.1	6.3	10.1	13.1
4	14.9	13.2	13.7	13.4	15.9	18.2
5	22.4	21.3	22.2	22.0	21.0	25.5
6	29.7	29.4	28.8	30.7	23.2	36.5
7	37.8	35.3	39.2	37.8	29.0	47.4
8	44.0	43.4	44.4	41.7	36.2	54.0
9	49.3	49.3	49.0	44.9	42.0	61.3
10	54.4	55.1	54.2	49.6	47.8	65.0
11	60.8	61.8	60.8	54.3	54.3	72.3
12	67.3	69.1	68.6	59.8	61.6	76.6
13	71.3	72.1	74.5	62.2	65.9	81.0
14	75.7	75.0	77.1	69.3	69.6	86.9
15	79.0	77.9	79.7	75.6	71.7	89.8
16	82.3	80.9	83.7	81.9	73.9	91.2
17	85.1	83.8	88.2	84.3	76.8	92.0
18	87.6	85.3	89.5	86.6	82.6	93.4
19	89.9	88.2	91.5	87.4	87.0	94.9
20	91.6	91.2	94.1	89.8	87.0	95.6
21	93.2	93.4	95.4	90.6	89.9	96.4
22	94.6	94.1	96.7	92.1	92.8	97.1
23	96.2	96.3	97.4	96.9	93.5	97.1
24	97.4	96.3	99.3	96.9	94.2	100.0
25	97.5	96.3	99.3	97.6	94.2	100.0
26	98.3	97.8	99.3	98.4	95.7	100.0
27	98.6	98.5	99.3	98.4	96.4	100.0
28	99.1	98.5	100.0	99.2	97.8	100.0
29	99.7	100.0	100.0	99.2	99.3	100.0

Research/Supplemental Scales for the MMPI

Females   Sensorimotor Dissociation   (Sc3)

	Total Sample	Age, yr				
		13	14	15	16	17
N	691	136	153	127	138	137
Median	3	3	3	3	4	3
Mean	4.11	4.13	4.20	4.22	4.70	3.28
SD	3.25	3.16	3.29	3.22	3.51	2.91
Min	0	0	0	0	0	0
Max	17	13	15	17	15	13

Percentage of Sample with Raw Score < X

X	Total Sample	13	14	15	16	17
0	0.0	0.0	0.0	0.0	0.0	0.0
1	10.7	8.8	10.5	8.7	10.9	14.6
2	24.2	21.3	22.9	19.7	20.3	36.5
3	36.9	36.8	36.6	33.1	29.7	48.2
4	52.1	51.5	51.6	54.3	42.8	60.6
5	61.8	61.8	60.1	61.4	54.3	71.5
6	71.3	72.1	68.6	72.4	63.8	80.3
7	79.0	81.6	77.8	77.2	72.5	86.1
8	84.1	84.6	83.7	81.9	79.0	91.2
9	87.8	86.8	87.6	85.0	86.2	93.4
10	92.0	91.9	90.8	92.1	90.6	94.9
11	95.1	94.9	94.8	96.9	92.0	97.1
12	97.1	96.3	97.4	99.2	94.2	98.5
13	98.7	99.3	98.7	99.2	97.1	99.3
14	99.4	100.0	99.3	99.2	98.6	100.0
15	99.4	100.0	99.3	99.2	98.6	100.0
16	99.9	100.0	100.0	99.2	100.0	100.0
17	99.9	100.0	100.0	99.2	100.0	100.0

Research/Supplemental Scales for the MMPI

Females   Amorality   (Ma1)

	Total Sample	Age, yr				
		13	14	15	16	17
N	691	136	153	127	138	137
Median	2	2	2	2	2	2
Mean	2.06	2.07	2.14	2.25	1.99	1.86
SD	1.30	1.25	1.28	1.41	1.34	1.22
Min	0	0	0	0	0	0
Max	6	6	6	6	5	5

X	Total Sample	Percentage of Sample with Raw Score < X				
		13	14	15	16	17
0	0.0	0.0	0.0	0.0	0.0	0.0
1	11.1	9.6	6.5	10.2	15.2	14.6
2	36.6	37.5	34.0	33.9	37.0	40.9
3	64.7	60.3	66.7	58.3	68.8	68.6
4	85.7	89.7	85.0	78.7	83.3	91.2
5	96.5	97.1	95.4	94.5	97.1	98.5
6	99.4	99.3	98.7	99.2	100.0	100.0

Research/Supplemental Scales for the MMPI

Females   Psychomotor Acceleration   (Ma2)

				Age, yr		
	Total Sample	13	14	15	16	17
N	691	136	153	127	138	137
Median	7	6	7	7	7	7
Mean	6.72	6.47	6.58	6.98	7.05	6.54
SD	1.95	2.03	2.00	1.77	2.01	1.87
Min	1	2	1	3	3	2
Max	11	11	10	10	11	11

	Percentage of Sample with Raw Score < X					
X	Total Sample	13	14	15	16	17
1	0.0	0.0	0.0	0.0	0.0	0.0
2	0.1	0.0	0.7	0.0	0.0	0.0
3	1.3	1.5	3.3	0.0	0.0	1.5
4	6.4	8.1	8.5	4.7	6.5	3.6
5	14.9	19.9	17.6	10.2	11.6	14.6
6	27.4	30.9	28.8	18.9	23.9	33.6
7	43.0	51.5	41.2	38.6	37.0	46.7
8	61.4	66.2	62.7	55.1	55.1	67.2
9	79.9	81.6	83.0	78.0	71.7	84.7
10	94.9	94.9	96.7	96.1	91.3	95.6
11	99.0	98.5	100.0	100.0	97.8	98.5

Research/Supplemental Scales for the MMPI

Females   Imperturbability   (Ma3)

		Age, yr				
	Total Sample	13	14	15	16	17
N	691	136	153	127	138	137
Median	3	2	3	3	3	3
Mean	2.82	2.54	2.90	2.80	2.86	2.97
SD	1.51	1.46	1.58	1.53	1.50	1.46
Min	0	0	0	0	0	0
Max	6	6	6	6	6	6

	Percentage of Sample with Raw Score < X					
X	Total Sample	13	14	15	16	17
0	0.0	0.0	0.0	0.0	0.0	0.0
1	5.8	9.6	4.6	4.7	6.5	3.6
2	21.3	22.8	20.9	25.2	20.3	17.5
3	43.3	50.7	43.8	44.1	39.1	38.7
4	65.8	74.3	64.1	63.8	64.5	62.8
5	85.4	90.4	82.4	85.0	86.2	83.2
6	96.7	97.8	94.1	97.6	97.1	97.1

Research/Supplemental Scales for the MMPI

Females   Ego Inflation   (Ma4)

| | | Age, yr | | | | |
	Total Sample	13	14	15	16	17
N	691	136	153	127	138	137
Median	5	5	5	5	5	4
Mean	4.58	4.86	4.76	4.72	4.44	4.09
SD	1.81	1.83	1.77	1.78	1.80	1.77
Min	0	0	1	1	0	0
Max	9	9	9	9	9	9

Percentage of Sample with Raw Score < X

X	Total Sample	13	14	15	16	17
0	0.0	0.0	0.0	0.0	0.0	0.0
1	0.4	0.7	0.0	0.0	0.7	0.7
2	3.8	2.9	3.9	3.9	3.6	4.4
3	12.9	8.1	10.5	10.2	16.7	19.0
4	29.7	25.7	23.5	27.6	32.6	39.4
5	49.1	44.9	44.4	44.9	49.3	62.0
6	68.3	59.6	65.4	65.4	69.6	81.8
7	84.4	80.9	82.4	81.1	87.7	89.8
8	95.1	92.6	94.1	96.1	96.4	96.4
9	98.8	98.5	99.3	99.2	99.3	97.8

Research/Supplemental Scales for the MMPI

Males   Subjective Depression   (D1)

		Age, yr				
	Total Sample	13	14	15	16	17
N	624	112	147	130	122	113
Median	7	7	7	7	8	6
Mean	7.78	7.85	8.23	7.38	8.39	6.89
SD	4.11	4.18	4.16	4.04	3.99	4.07
Min	1	1	1	1	1	1
Max	23	20	21	18	19	23

Percentage of Sample with Raw Score < X

X	Total Sample	13	14	15	16	17
1	0.0	0.0	0.0	0.0	0.0	0.0
2	2.1	3.6	0.7	4.6	0.8	0.9
3	6.7	6.3	3.4	10.0	3.3	11.5
4	13.5	15.2	8.8	16.2	7.4	21.2
5	24.5	22.3	20.4	28.5	19.7	32.7
6	35.1	34.8	29.9	37.7	28.7	46.0
7	43.8	42.0	40.8	46.2	36.1	54.9
8	54.0	50.9	51.7	55.4	50.0	62.8
9	61.5	58.9	58.5	66.2	54.9	69.9
10	68.6	70.5	65.3	70.8	62.3	75.2
11	76.6	76.8	74.8	77.7	71.3	83.2
12	80.4	79.5	77.6	82.3	77.0	86.7
13	84.5	85.7	81.6	87.7	79.5	88.5
14	89.3	91.1	87.1	91.5	85.2	92.0
15	93.9	92.9	92.5	95.4	92.6	96.5
16	95.8	94.6	95.2	96.2	95.9	97.3
17	96.6	95.5	95.9	96.9	97.5	97.3
18	98.1	98.2	96.6	98.5	99.2	98.2
19	98.9	98.2	98.0	100.0	99.2	99.1
20	99.2	98.2	98.6	100.0	100.0	99.1
21	99.7	100.0	99.3	100.0	100.0	99.1
22	99.8	100.0	100.0	100.0	100.0	99.1
23	99.8	100.0	100.0	100.0	100.0	99.1

Research/Supplemental Scales for the MMPI

Males   Psychomotor Retardation   (D2)

		Age, yr				
	Total Sample	13	14	15	16	17
N	624	112	147	130	122	113
Median	5	4	4	4	5	5
Mean	4.61	4.33	4.45	4.58	5.04	4.66
SD	1.91	1.90	1.94	1.75	2.03	1.91
Min	1	1	1	1	1	1
Max	10	9	9	10	10	10

	Percentage of Sample with Raw Score < X					
X	Total Sample	13	14	15	16	17
1	0.0	0.0	0.0	0.0	0.0	0.0
2	4.0	4.5	6.1	2.3	4.1	2.7
3	14.6	16.1	17.7	10.8	13.1	15.0
4	30.3	39.3	32.7	27.7	22.1	30.1
5	48.4	56.3	52.4	51.5	36.1	45.1
6	69.2	75.0	71.4	71.5	60.7	67.3
7	83.0	83.9	83.0	86.9	77.0	84.1
8	92.3	92.9	92.5	94.6	88.5	92.9
9	98.1	99.1	99.3	97.7	96.7	97.3
10	99.2	100.0	100.0	99.2	97.5	99.1

Research/Supplemental Scales for the MMPI

Males   Physical Malfunctioning   (D3)

	Total Sample	Age, yr				
		13	14	15	16	17
N	624	112	147	130	122	113
Median	3	3	3	3	3	2
Mean	3.09	3.39	3.29	3.20	2.85	2.68
SD	1.25	1.23	1.21	1.10	1.38	1.20
Min	0	1	0	1	0	1
Max	8	8	7	6	8	6

X	Percentage of Sample with Raw Score < X					
	Total Sample	13	14	15	16	17
0	0.0	0.0	0.0	0.0	0.0	0.0
1	0.6	0.0	1.4	0.0	1.6	0.0
2	7.9	3.6	4.8	6.9	12.3	12.4
3	33.2	22.3	23.8	25.4	45.1	52.2
4	65.1	56.3	60.5	58.5	73.0	78.8
5	89.3	87.5	86.4	90.8	90.2	92.0
6	95.7	92.9	95.2	98.5	95.1	96.5
7	99.4	99.1	99.3	100.0	98.4	100.0
8	99.7	99.1	100.0	100.0	99.2	100.0

Research/Supplemental Scales for the MMPI

Males   Mental Dullness   (D4)

	Total Sample	Age, yr				
		13	14	15	16	17
N	624	112	147	130	122	113
Median	2	2	3	2	3	2
Mean	2.88	2.78	3.14	2.79	3.24	2.37
SD	2.38	2.47	2.50	2.37	2.30	2.14
Min	0	0	0	0	0	0
Max	11	10	11	10	9	11

X	Percentage of Sample with Raw Score < X					
	Total Sample	13	14	15	16	17
0	0.0	0.0	0.0	0.0	0.0	0.0
1	16.3	22.3	15.6	13.8	13.1	17.7
2	33.7	36.6	30.6	36.9	25.4	39.8
3	51.8	53.6	46.9	55.4	41.8	62.8
4	65.9	64.3	63.3	68.5	59.0	75.2
5	77.2	75.9	71.4	79.2	73.8	87.6
6	84.0	87.5	77.6	85.4	79.5	92.0
7	91.7	92.9	89.8	91.5	88.5	96.5
8	95.4	95.5	94.6	94.6	95.9	96.5
9	97.4	95.5	98.0	96.9	99.2	97.3
10	98.7	98.2	98.6	98.5	100.0	98.2
11	99.7	100.0	99.3	100.0	100.0	99.1

Research/Supplemental Scales for the MMPI

Males   Brooding   (D5)

| | Total Sample | Age, yr | | | | |
		13	14	15	16	17
N	624	112	147	130	122	113
Median	2	2	2	2	2	2
Mean	2.52	2.47	2.83	2.28	2.74	2.19
SD	1.92	1.92	2.03	1.70	1.96	1.94
Min	0	0	0	0	0	0
Max	9	8	8	6	8	9

| X | Percentage of Sample with Raw Score < X | | | | | |
	Total Sample	13	14	15	16	17
0	0.0	0.0	0.0	0.0	0.0	0.0
1	16.0	14.3	13.6	20.8	10.7	21.2
2	34.6	38.4	28.6	35.4	29.5	43.4
3	55.6	57.1	51.0	56.9	52.5	61.9
4	71.0	71.4	64.6	72.3	70.5	77.9
5	84.1	83.9	78.9	89.2	81.1	88.5
6	91.2	91.1	85.0	97.7	89.3	93.8
7	96.6	97.3	95.9	100.0	93.4	96.5
8	99.2	99.1	99.3	100.0	99.2	98.2
9	99.8	100.0	100.0	100.0	100.0	99.1

Research/Supplemental Scales for the MMPI

Males   Denial Of Social Anxiety   (Hy1)

	Total Sample	Age, yr				
		13	14	15	16	17
N	624	112	147	130	122	113
Median	3	3	2	3	3	3
Mean	2.91	3.13	2.63	2.97	2.77	3.13
SD	1.83	1.79	1.78	1.86	1.79	1.89
Min	0	0	0	0	0	0
Max	6	6	6	6	6	6

X	Percentage of Sample with Raw Score < X					
	Total Sample	13	14	15	16	17
0	0.0	0.0	0.0	0.0	0.0	0.0
1	11.1	7.1	12.2	13.1	12.3	9.7
2	26.0	20.5	31.3	25.4	27.0	23.9
3	45.0	42.0	52.4	40.8	49.2	38.9
4	60.3	55.4	68.0	56.9	62.3	56.6
5	75.5	74.1	78.9	76.9	76.2	69.9
6	91.5	88.4	94.6	90.0	95.9	87.6

Research/Supplemental Scales for the MMPI

Males   Need For Affection and Reinforcement from Others   (Hy2)

| | | Age, yr | | | | |
	Total Sample	13	14	15	16	17
N	624	112	147	130	122	113
Median	5	5	4	4	5	5
Mean	4.87	4.67	4.46	4.97	4.89	5.45
SD	2.37	2.12	2.32	2.46	2.38	2.49
Min	0	0	0	0	1	0
Max	12	10	12	11	12	12

| | Percentage of Sample with Raw Score < X | | | | | |
X	Total Sample	13	14	15	16	17
0	0.0	0.0	0.0	0.0	0.0	0.0
1	1.1	0.9	2.0	1.5	0.0	0.9
2	4.6	4.5	6.1	4.6	5.7	1.8
3	14.6	12.5	21.1	12.3	16.4	8.8
4	31.6	33.9	35.4	30.8	31.1	25.7
5	48.7	48.2	55.1	51.5	48.4	38.1
6	65.1	66.1	72.8	65.4	63.1	55.8
7	77.7	87.5	83.7	71.5	74.6	70.8
8	85.7	91.1	89.8	83.8	84.4	78.8
9	91.2	92.9	94.6	89.2	91.8	86.7
10	95.0	95.5	95.9	94.6	96.7	92.0
11	98.2	100.0	98.0	97.7	99.2	96.5
12	99.5	100.0	99.3	100.0	99.2	99.1

Research/Supplemental Scales for the MMPI

Males   Lassitude-Malaise   (Hy3)

		Age, yr				
	Total Sample	13	14	15	16	17
N	624	112	147	130	122	113
Median	2	2	3	3	3	2
Mean	2.96	2.87	3.23	2.75	3.13	2.76
SD	2.35	2.47	2.51	2.14	2.20	2.40
Min	0	0	0	0	0	0
Max	14	11	13	8	10	14

	Percentage of Sample with Raw Score < X					
X	Total Sample	13	14	15	16	17
0	0.0	0.0	0.0	0.0	0.0	0.0
1	12.2	15.2	10.2	16.9	5.7	13.3
2	30.8	36.6	27.9	34.6	25.4	30.1
3	50.6	54.5	46.9	48.5	47.5	57.5
4	65.1	66.1	59.9	66.2	63.9	70.8
5	76.8	73.2	72.8	77.7	75.4	85.8
6	87.2	85.7	85.0	90.8	85.2	89.4
7	92.5	94.6	89.8	93.1	92.6	92.9
8	95.0	95.5	93.9	96.9	95.1	93.8
9	97.0	96.4	95.9	100.0	97.5	94.7
10	98.4	97.3	97.3	100.0	98.4	99.1
11	99.2	98.2	98.6	100.0	100.0	99.1
12	99.7	100.0	99.3	100.0	100.0	99.1
13	99.7	100.0	99.3	100.0	100.0	99.1
14	99.8	100.0	100.0	100.0	100.0	99.1

Research/Supplemental Scales for the MMPI

Males   Somatic Complaints   (Hy4)

	Total Sample	Age, yr				
		13	14	15	16	17
N	624	112	147	130	122	113
Median	3	2	3	2	3	2
Mean	3.05	2.90	3.28	2.78	3.41	2.81
SD	2.44	2.64	2.50	2.29	2.48	2.23
Min	0	0	0	0	0	0
Max	13	11	13	13	10	10

X	Percentage of Sample with Raw Score < X					
	Total Sample	13	14	15	16	17
0	0.0	0.0	0.0	0.0	0.0	0.0
1	12.3	16.1	12.2	13.1	7.4	13.3
2	31.3	35.7	25.9	33.1	28.7	34.5
3	49.5	57.1	40.8	54.6	43.4	54.0
4	62.5	68.8	55.1	68.5	59.0	62.8
5	76.6	76.8	78.9	80.0	68.0	78.8
6	84.8	83.9	85.0	88.5	77.9	88.5
7	90.9	89.3	91.2	93.8	86.1	93.8
8	94.2	91.1	93.9	96.9	92.6	96.5
9	96.5	94.6	95.9	97.7	96.7	97.3
10	98.4	98.2	97.3	98.5	99.2	99.1
11	99.2	98.2	98.6	99.2	100.0	100.0
12	99.5	100.0	98.6	99.2	100.0	100.0
13	99.5	100.0	98.6	99.2	100.0	100.0

Research/Supplemental Scales for the MMPI

Males   Inhibition Of Aggression   (Hy5)

		Age, yr				
	Total Sample	13	14	15	16	17
N	624	112	147	130	122	113
Median	3	2	2	3	3	3
Mean	2.68	2.52	2.65	2.75	2.75	2.73
SD	1.26	1.19	1.30	1.31	1.31	1.15
Min	0	0	0	0	0	0
Max	6	5	6	6	6	6

	Percentage of Sample with Raw Score < X					
X	Total Sample	13	14	15	16	17
0	0.0	0.0	0.0	0.0	0.0	0.0
1	3.2	2.7	2.7	3.8	4.1	2.7
2	17.6	21.4	18.4	20.0	16.4	11.5
3	46.0	50.9	51.7	38.5	44.3	44.2
4	73.4	77.7	72.1	71.5	72.1	74.3
5	92.5	95.5	91.8	91.5	89.3	94.7
6	99.2	100.0	98.6	99.2	99.2	99.1

Research/Supplemental Scales for the MMPI

Males   Familial Discord   (Pd1)

	Total Sample	13	14	15	16	17
				Age, yr.		
N	624	112	147	130	122	113
Median	3	3	4	4	4	3
Mean	3.74	3.45	4.16	3.73	3.75	3.49
SD	2.06	1.99	2.14	1.96	2.17	1.97
Min	0	1	0	0	0	0
Max	10	10	9	9	10	9

Percentage of Sample with Raw Score < X

X	Total Sample	13	14	15	16	17
0	0.0	0.0	0.0	0.0	0.0	0.0
1	1.9	0.0	1.4	1.5	3.3	3.5
2	13.3	18.8	6.1	13.1	16.4	14.2
3	32.4	40.2	25.2	32.3	33.6	32.7
4	51.0	56.3	46.3	46.9	50.0	57.5
5	66.2	67.9	63.9	63.8	63.1	73.5
6	79.2	83.9	70.1	83.1	77.0	84.1
7	88.8	92.9	81.0	91.5	89.3	91.2
8	95.0	97.3	91.2	95.4	95.9	96.5
9	98.6	99.1	98.6	99.2	97.5	98.2
10	99.7	99.1	100.0	100.0	99.2	100.0

266

Research/Supplemental Scales for the MMPI

Males   Authority Conflict   (Pd2)

		Age, yr				
	Total Sample	13	14	15	16	17
N	624	112	147	130	122	113
Median	5	4	5	5	5	5
Mean	4.87	4.35	4.83	4.91	5.00	5.27
SD	1.78	1.57	1.68	1.80	1.92	1.85
Min	0	1	0	1	1	1
Max	10	9	9	10	10	10

Percentage of Sample with Raw Score < X

X	Total Sample	13	14	15	16	17
0	0.0	0.0	0.0	0.0	0.0	0.0
1	0.2	0.0	0.7	0.0	0.0	0.0
2	2.1	2.7	2.7	2.3	1.6	0.9
3	8.8	11.6	6.1	6.9	11.5	8.8
4	20.7	28.6	22.4	18.5	20.5	13.3
5	43.9	56.3	43.5	45.4	41.0	33.6
6	65.9	78.6	63.9	67.7	62.3	57.5
7	82.7	91.1	83.7	82.3	79.5	77.0
8	92.3	97.3	94.6	92.3	88.5	88.5
9	97.1	99.1	99.3	96.2	95.9	94.7
10	99.0	100.0	100.0	97.7	99.2	98.2

Research/Supplemental Scales for the MMPI

Males Social Imperturbability (Pd3)

		Age, yr				
	Total Sample	13	14	15	16	17
N	624	112	147	130	122	113
Median	7	7	6	7	7	7
Mean	6.87	6.79	6.44	6.98	6.80	7.47
SD	2.36	2.47	2.38	2.34	2.41	2.08
Min	0	0	1	0	1	3
Max	12	12	12	12	12	12

	Percentage of Sample with Raw Score < X					
X	Total Sample	13	14	15	16	17
0	0.0	0.0	0.0	0.0	0.0	0.0
1	0.3	0.9	0.0	0.8	0.0	0.0
2	1.1	0.9	2.0	0.8	1.6	0.0
3	4.0	3.6	6.8	3.8	4.9	0.0
4	7.7	8.0	11.6	6.9	9.8	0.9
5	16.2	18.8	21.8	13.8	16.4	8.8
6	29.0	33.0	33.3	24.6	32.0	21.2
7	43.8	45.5	51.7	42.3	45.1	31.9
8	59.1	60.7	63.9	61.5	56.6	51.3
9	72.4	74.1	78.2	71.5	71.3	65.5
10	85.4	85.7	89.1	83.1	86.9	81.4
11	95.5	92.9	98.6	93.8	96.7	94.7
12	98.6	97.3	99.3	99.2	99.2	97.3

Research/Supplemental Scales for the MMPI

Males   Social Alienation   (Pd4A)

		Age, yr				
	Total Sample	13	14	15	16	17
N	624	112	147	130	122	113
Median	7	6	7	7	7	6
Mean	7.02	6.74	7.54	7.09	7.16	6.39
SD	3.18	3.22	3.37	3.25	2.95	2.94
Min	0	0	1	1	2	1
Max	16	14	15	15	15	16

Percentage of Sample with Raw Score < X

X	Total Sample	13	14	15	16	17
0	0.0	0.0	0.0	0.0	0.0	0.0
1	0.2	0.9	0.0	0.0	0.0	0.0
2	1.4	1.8	2.0	2.3	0.0	0.9
3	6.1	5.4	6.8	10.0	1.6	6.2
4	15.1	18.8	15.0	16.2	8.2	17.7
5	23.9	28.6	19.7	23.8	21.3	27.4
6	35.1	42.0	27.9	31.5	33.6	43.4
7	47.9	53.6	39.5	46.2	47.5	55.8
8	57.7	58.9	51.7	53.1	59.0	68.1
9	67.6	67.9	62.6	63.1	68.9	77.9
10	77.6	77.7	71.4	77.7	77.0	85.8
11	83.3	85.7	76.9	83.8	82.8	89.4
12	90.5	90.2	86.4	90.8	90.2	96.5
13	94.7	95.5	90.5	95.4	95.9	97.3
14	97.9	99.1	96.6	97.7	98.4	98.2
15	99.2	100.0	99.3	99.2	99.2	98.2
16	99.7	100.0	100.0	100.0	100.0	98.2

Research/Supplemental Scales for the MMPI

Males   Self-Alienation   (Pd4B)

		Age, yr				
	Total Sample	13	14	15	16	17
N	624	112	147	130	122	113
Median	5	4	5	4	5	4
Mean	4.90	4.55	5.24	4.63	5.28	4.69
SD	2.78	2.55	2.99	2.75	2.77	2.72
Min	0	0	0	0	0	0
Max	14	11	14	12	13	13

Percentage of Sample with Raw Score < X

X	Total Sample	13	14	15	16	17
0	0.0	0.0	0.0	0.0	0.0	0.0
1	2.6	0.9	2.7	3.8	1.6	3.5
2	9.8	8.9	10.2	12.3	7.4	9.7
3	21.5	25.9	20.4	25.4	16.4	19.5
4	34.3	42.0	31.3	36.2	27.0	36.3
5	48.1	51.8	42.9	51.5	43.4	52.2
6	63.1	66.1	56.5	68.5	57.4	69.0
7	72.4	75.9	66.7	74.6	68.0	78.8
8	82.9	87.5	78.9	84.6	78.7	85.8
9	88.9	92.0	86.4	90.0	86.9	90.3
10	93.1	96.4	89.1	94.6	93.4	92.9
11	95.8	97.3	94.6	96.9	95.1	95.6
12	98.2	100.0	97.3	98.5	97.5	98.2
13	99.5	100.0	99.3	100.0	99.2	99.1
14	99.8	100.0	99.3	100.0	100.0	100.0

Research/Supplemental Scales for the MMPI

Males   Alienation (Sum of Pd4A and Pd4B)   (Pd4)

		Age, yr				
	Total Sample	13	14	15	16	17
N	624	112	147	130	122	113
Median	12	11	13	12	11	10
Mean	11.92	11.29	12.78	11.72	12.44	11.08
SD	5.59	5.46	6.03	5.64	5.29	5.27
Min	1	1	2	2	4	2
Max	29	24	29	26	28	28

Percentage of Sample with Raw Score < X

X	Total Sample	13	14	15	16	17
1	0.0	0.0	0.0	0.0	0.0	0.0
2	0.2	0.9	0.0	0.0	0.0	0.0
3	2.1	1.8	2.7	3.1	0.0	2.7
4	5.0	2.7	6.8	8.5	0.0	6.2
5	8.2	8.9	9.5	11.5	2.5	8.0
6	13.0	17.0	12.9	17.7	4.9	12.4
7	17.8	23.2	15.0	20.8	13.1	17.7
8	24.2	30.4	21.8	25.4	19.7	24.8
9	31.6	36.6	27.2	32.3	28.7	34.5
10	38.3	46.4	31.3	37.7	34.4	44.2
11	43.4	49.1	38.1	40.0	40.2	52.2
12	49.8	54.5	41.5	44.6	51.6	60.2
13	56.3	57.1	49.0	56.9	56.6	63.7
14	62.3	62.5	55.8	63.8	62.3	69.0
15	69.4	69.6	66.0	70.8	64.8	77.0
16	73.6	76.8	68.0	73.1	71.3	80.5
17	79.2	82.1	72.8	80.0	77.0	85.8
18	82.1	86.6	74.8	82.3	81.1	87.6
19	86.1	88.4	80.3	86.2	84.4	92.9
20	89.3	90.2	85.0	89.2	88.5	94.7
21	91.8	92.0	88.4	93.8	90.2	95.6
22	94.4	95.5	91.2	96.2	94.3	95.6
23	96.0	99.1	92.5	96.9	95.9	96.5
24	97.6	99.1	96.6	98.5	97.5	96.5
25	98.7	100.0	97.3	99.2	99.2	98.2
26	99.2	100.0	99.3	99.2	99.2	98.2
27	99.4	100.0	99.3	100.0	99.2	98.2
28	99.5	100.0	99.3	100.0	99.2	99.1
29	99.8	100.0	99.3	100.0	100.0	100.0

Research/Supplemental Scales for the MMPI

Males   Ideas of External Influence   (Pa1)

| | Total Sample | Age, yr | | | | |
		13	14	15	16	17
N	624	112	147	130	122	113
Median	3	3	4	4	3	3
Mean	3.82	4.09	4.07	3.87	3.67	3.32
SD	2.70	2.66	3.03	2.65	2.40	2.61
Min	0	0	0	0	0	0
Max	12	10	12	12	11	12

| X | Percentage of Sample with Raw Score < X | | | | | |
	Total Sample	13	14	15	16	17
0	0.0	0.0	0.0	0.0	0.0	0.0
1	7.5	2.7	11.6	7.7	4.1	10.6
2	21.5	16.1	25.9	22.3	13.9	28.3
3	37.5	31.3	36.7	36.9	40.2	42.5
4	53.0	51.8	46.9	47.7	59.0	61.9
5	64.7	63.4	58.5	63.1	68.9	71.7
6	75.0	75.0	66.7	73.8	79.5	82.3
7	82.5	81.3	78.9	80.8	82.8	90.3
8	88.6	84.8	86.4	89.2	91.0	92.0
9	93.3	90.2	90.5	94.6	95.1	96.5
10	97.0	94.6	95.9	98.5	99.2	96.5
11	98.4	100.0	96.6	99.2	99.2	97.3
12	99.0	100.0	98.0	99.2	100.0	98.2

Research/Supplemental Scales for the MMPI

Males   Poignancy   (Pa2)

		Age, yr				
	Total Sample	13	14	15	16	17
N	624	112	147	130	122	113
Median	2	2	2	2	3	2
Mean	2.61	2.23	2.62	2.52	2.98	2.69
SD	1.83	1.66	2.00	1.71	1.93	1.72
Min	0	0	0	0	0	0
Max	8	6	8	8	8	8

	Percentage of Sample with Raw Score < X					
X	Total Sample	13	14	15	16	17
0	0.0	0.0	0.0	0.0	0.0	0.0
1	9.1	14.3	10.9	9.2	8.2	2.7
2	33.5	39.3	37.4	30.8	27.0	32.7
3	53.7	63.4	55.8	55.4	43.4	50.4
4	70.7	75.0	70.7	74.6	62.3	70.8
5	84.0	89.3	80.3	88.5	77.9	85.0
6	92.1	95.5	89.1	93.8	88.5	94.7
7	96.6	100.0	95.2	96.9	95.1	96.5
8	99.0	100.0	98.6	99.2	99.2	98.2

Research/Supplemental Scales for the MMPI

Males   Moral Virtue   (Pa3)

		Age, yr				
	Total Sample	13	14	15	16	17
N	624	112	147	130	122	113
Median	3	3	3	4	3	4
Mean	3.69	3.53	3.37	3.94	3.65	4.04
SD	1.99	1.95	1.87	2.09	1.95	2.07
Min	0	0	0	0	0	0
Max	9	9	8	9	9	9

	Percentage of Sample with Raw Score < X					
X	Total Sample	13	14	15	16	17
0	0.0	0.0	0.0	0.0	0.0	0.0
1	2.1	1.8	2.7	2.3	1.6	1.8
2	12.3	16.1	14.3	8.5	13.1	9.7
3	31.3	35.7	36.1	26.9	31.1	25.7
4	50.6	50.9	59.9	49.2	51.6	38.9
5	69.7	70.5	75.5	65.4	68.9	67.3
6	81.9	84.8	84.4	77.7	83.6	78.8
7	89.4	91.1	92.5	86.2	91.8	85.0
8	94.4	97.3	97.3	91.5	94.3	91.2
9	99.0	99.1	100.0	98.5	99.2	98.2

274

Research/Supplemental Scales for the MMPI

Males   Social Alienation   (Sc1A)

		Age, yr				
	Total Sample	13	14	15	16	17
N	624	112	147	130	122	113
Median	5	5	6	5	5	4
Mean	5.62	5.59	6.08	5.73	5.77	4.76
SD	3.41	3.32	3.61	3.27	3.48	3.22
Min	0	0	0	0	0	0
Max	17	14	15	15	17	15

Percentage of Sample with Raw Score < X

X	Total Sample	13	14	15	16	17
0	0.0	0.0	0.0	0.0	0.0	0.0
1	2.7	2.7	1.4	3.1	0.8	6.2
2	8.5	6.3	7.5	7.7	7.4	14.2
3	19.7	21.4	15.0	17.7	19.7	26.5
4	30.4	32.1	26.5	30.0	27.0	38.1
5	43.1	42.9	38.8	37.7	44.3	54.0
6	53.8	53.6	49.7	53.1	50.8	63.7
7	64.6	64.3	61.2	59.2	63.9	76.1
8	73.4	71.4	69.4	72.3	72.1	83.2
9	80.9	81.3	76.9	78.5	81.1	88.5
10	86.1	86.6	83.0	86.9	84.4	90.3
11	89.9	88.4	88.4	90.0	90.2	92.9
12	92.9	92.9	89.8	94.6	93.4	94.7
13	96.2	98.2	93.2	97.7	94.3	98.2
14	97.3	99.1	93.2	99.2	97.5	98.2
15	98.9	100.0	98.0	99.2	98.4	99.1
16	99.7	100.0	100.0	100.0	98.4	100.0
17	99.8	100.0	100.0	100.0	99.2	100.0

Research/Supplemental Scales for the MMPI

Males   Emotional Alienation   (Sc1B)

	Total Sample	Age, yr				
		13	14	15	16	17
N	624	112	147	130	122	113
Median	1	2	2	1	2	1
Mean	1.88	2.01	2.14	1.62	1.96	1.64
SD	1.48	1.35	1.60	1.30	1.50	1.55
Min	0	0	0	0	0	0
Max	8	7	8	7	7	8

X	Percentage of Sample with Raw Score < X					
	Total Sample	13	14	15	16	17
0	0.0	0.0	0.0	0.0	0.0	0.0
1	10.9	4.5	9.5	13.1	10.7	16.8
2	51.3	45.5	42.9	59.2	48.4	61.9
3	74.4	70.5	66.7	81.5	72.1	82.3
4	87.0	88.4	82.3	90.8	85.2	89.4
5	92.8	92.9	91.2	96.2	91.8	92.0
6	96.8	98.2	95.2	98.5	96.7	95.6
7	99.0	99.1	98.6	99.2	99.2	99.1
8	99.7	100.0	99.3	100.0	100.0	99.1

Research/Supplemental Scales for the MMPI

Males   Object Loss (Sum of Sc1A and Sc1B)   (Sc1)

		Age, yr				
	Total Sample	13	14	15	16	17
N	624	112	147	130	122	113
Median	7	7	7	7	7	6
Mean	7.50	7.60	8.22	7.35	7.73	6.40
SD	4.45	4.22	4.89	4.10	4.47	4.30
Min	0	0	0	0	1	1
Max	23	21	23	17	22	20

	Percentage of Sample with Raw Score < X					
X	Total Sample	13	14	15	16	17
0	0.0	0.0	0.0	0.0	0.0	0.0
1	0.5	0.9	0.7	0.8	0.0	0.0
2	4.0	2.7	2.7	5.4	0.8	8.8
3	8.3	4.5	6.1	7.7	7.4	16.8
4	18.6	19.6	16.3	18.5	17.2	22.1
5	29.0	30.4	22.4	30.0	27.0	37.2
6	38.3	35.7	34.0	38.5	38.5	46.0
7	49.5	48.2	42.9	47.7	46.7	64.6
8	58.7	55.4	54.4	56.9	56.6	71.7
9	65.7	61.6	61.9	63.8	63.1	79.6
10	72.6	66.1	68.0	74.6	72.1	83.2
11	77.6	75.9	72.8	77.7	77.0	85.8
12	81.6	82.1	78.2	80.8	80.3	87.6
13	84.8	85.7	81.0	85.4	83.6	89.4
14	88.0	88.4	84.4	90.8	86.1	91.2
15	91.2	93.8	87.8	91.5	89.3	94.7
16	94.4	96.4	91.2	96.9	92.6	95.6
17	95.8	97.3	91.8	98.5	96.7	95.6
18	96.6	98.2	92.5	100.0	97.5	95.6
19	97.9	99.1	95.2	100.0	98.4	97.3
20	98.2	99.1	96.6	100.0	98.4	97.3
21	99.0	99.1	98.0	100.0	98.4	100.0
22	99.7	100.0	99.3	100.0	99.2	100.0
23	99.8	100.0	99.3	100.0	100.0	100.0

Research/Supplemental Scales for the MMPI

Males   Lack Of Ego Mastery, Cognitive   (Sc2A)

| | Total Sample | Age, yr | | | | |
		13	14	15	16	17
N	624	112	147	130	122	113
Median	2	2	2	2	2	2
Mean	2.28	2.09	2.65	2.02	2.64	1.92
SD	2.06	1.96	2.19	1.99	2.10	1.91
Min	· 0	0	0	0	0	0
Max	9	8	8	8	8	9

| | Percentage of Sample with Raw Score < X | | | | | |
X	Total Sample	13	14	15	16	17
0	0.0	0.0	0.0	0.0	0.0	0.0
1	23.4	25.0	19.7	30.8	17.2	24.8
2	43.9	49.1	37.4	49.2	36.9	48.7
3	61.1	64.3	51.7	65.4	54.9	71.7
4	74.5	77.7	68.7	76.9	66.4	85.0
5	83.5	85.7	78.9	86.2	77.0	91.2
6	91.2	92.9	86.4	93.1	89.3	95.6
7	96.2	97.3	94.6	97.7	95.9	95.6
8	98.1	99.1	97.3	99.2	98.4	96.5
9	99.8	100.0	100.0	100.0	100.0	99.1

Research/Supplemental Scales for the MMPI

Males   Lack Of Ego Mastery, Conative   (Sc2B)

		Age, yr				
	Total Sample	13	14	15	16	17
N	624	112	147	130	122	113
Median	3	3	4	3	4	2
Mean	3.58	3.41	4.08	3.26	4.07	2.93
SD	2.49	2.32	2.63	2.34	2.56	2.35
Min	0	0	0	0	0	0
Max	11	10	11	10	11	11

	Percentage of Sample with Raw Score < X					
X	Total Sample	13	14	15	16	17
0	0.0	0.0	0.0	0.0	0.0	0.0
1	3.5	0.9	2.7	3.1	3.3	8.0
2	22.9	24.1	18.4	26.2	17.2	30.1
3	43.3	43.8	34.7	50.0	34.4	55.8
4	56.3	59.8	48.3	62.3	45.9	67.3
5	69.4	74.1	60.5	74.6	60.7	79.6
6	77.7	82.1	70.7	81.5	68.9	87.6
7	85.6	87.5	79.6	86.9	83.6	92.0
8	91.8	92.0	87.8	94.6	90.2	95.6
9	95.2	96.4	93.9	96.2	93.4	96.5
10	97.4	98.2	96.6	98.5	97.5	96.5
11	99.0	100.0	98.6	100.0	98.4	98.2

Research/Supplemental Scales for the MMPI

Males Lack Of Ego Mastery, Defect of Inhibition and Control (Sc2C)

		Age, yr				
	Total Sample	13	14	15	16	17
N	624	112	147	130	122	113
Median	3	3	3	3	3	2
Mean	3.01	3.04	3.27	2.72	3.28	2.71
SD	2.02	2.16	2.01	1.87	1.99	2.00
Min	0	0	0	0	0	0
Max	10	9	9	8	8	10

Percentage of Sample with Raw Score < X

X	Total Sample	13	14	15	16	17
0	0.0	0.0	0.0	0.0	0.0	0.0
1	10.3	14.3	8.2	13.1	6.6	9.7
2	25.6	24.1	21.8	30.0	22.1	31.0
3	42.3	41.1	38.1	46.9	35.2	51.3
4	63.6	67.9	55.1	67.7	58.2	71.7
5	77.6	77.7	72.1	80.8	75.4	83.2
6	88.3	84.8	87.8	92.3	84.4	92.0
7	94.6	91.1	93.9	98.5	91.8	97.3
8	97.6	96.4	97.3	98.5	98.4	97.3
9	99.2	99.1	99.3	100.0	100.0	97.3
10	99.7	100.0	100.0	100.0	100.0	98.2

Research/Supplemental Scales for the MMPI

Males   Lack of Ego Mastery, Intrapsychic Autonomy (Sc2)

		Age, yr				
	Total Sample	13	14	15	16	17
N	624	112	147	130	122	113
Median	8	8	9	6	10	6
Mean	8.88	8.54	10.00	8.00	9.98	7.56
SD	5.71	5.65	5.90	5.42	5.66	5.51
Min	0	0	1	0	2	0
Max	30	23	26	22	25	30

X	Percentage of Sample with Raw Score < X					
	Total Sample	13	14	15	16	17
0	0.0	0.0	0.0	0.0	0.0	0.0
1	0.8	0.9	0.0	1.5	0.0	1.8
2	4.0	5.4	2.0	6.2	0.0	7.1
3	10.9	11.6	11.6	12.3	6.6	12.4
4	19.2	22.3	17.0	21.5	14.8	21.2
5	28.2	32.1	21.1	33.8	23.0	32.7
6	34.5	36.6	24.5	40.0	30.3	43.4
7	42.8	44.6	34.0	50.8	32.8	54.0
8	48.9	49.1	40.8	56.2	37.7	62.8
9	53.5	55.4	44.9	60.0	41.8	68.1
10	59.9	65.2	51.0	66.9	45.9	73.5
11	64.6	68.8	54.4	72.3	54.9	75.2
12	69.4	72.3	59.2	76.9	63.1	77.9
13	74.5	74.1	67.3	79.2	70.5	83.2
14	78.2	78.6	72.1	81.5	73.0	87.6
15	82.1	83.9	74.1	86.2	78.7	89.4
16	84.8	84.8	79.6	86.9	82.0	92.0
17	87.7	87.5	85.7	87.7	83.6	94.7
18	90.5	89.3	89.8	91.5	87.7	94.7
19	93.1	92.0	92.5	93.8	91.8	95.6
20	95.4	95.5	93.9	96.9	94.3	96.5
21	96.5	98.2	95.2	98.5	94.3	96.5
22	97.8	99.1	96.6	99.2	97.5	96.5
23	98.4	99.1	96.6	100.0	99.2	97.3
24	98.9	100.0	97.3	100.0	99.2	98.2
25	99.4	100.0	99.3	100.0	99.2	98.2
26	99.5	100.0	99.3	100.0	100.0	98.2
27	99.7	100.0	100.0	100.0	100.0	98.2
28	99.8	100.0	100.0	100.0	100.0	99.1
29	99.8	100.0	100.0	100.0	100.0	99.1

Research/Supplemental Scales for the MMPI

Males Lack of Ego Mastery, Intrapsychic Autonomy (Sc2)
(Continued)

		Percentage of Sample with Raw Score < X				
X	Total Sample	13	14	15	16	17
30	99.8	100.0	100.0	100.0	100.0	99.1

Research/Supplemental Scales for the MMPI

Males   Sensorimotor Dissociation   (Sc3)

		Age, yr				
	Total Sample	13	14	15	16	17
N	624	112	147	130	122	113
Median	3	4	4	2	3	3
Mean	3.86	4.17	4.08	3.39	4.13	3.53
SD	3.03	3.14	3.15	2.87	2.99	2.96
Min	0	0	0	0	0	0
Max	15	15	14	14	12	15

	Percentage of Sample with Raw Score < X					
X	Total Sample	13	14	15	16	17
0	0.0	0.0	0.0	0.0	0.0	0.0
1	8.8	8.9	9.5	9.2	7.4	8.8
2	25.6	22.3	25.2	30.8	22.1	27.4
3	41.5	39.3	38.8	50.8	34.4	44.2
4	53.8	47.3	47.6	62.3	50.8	61.9
5	64.4	59.8	59.2	70.0	61.5	72.6
6	74.2	6ᴗ.⁀	72.8	77.7	71.3	80.5
7	80.4	75.0	81.6	84.6	76.2	84.1
8	86.5	83.9	84.4	90.8	84.4	89.4
9	90.7	91.1	89.8	93.1	88.5	91.2
10	93.9	94.6	91.2	96.9	93.4	93.8
11	97.1	97.3	95.2	98.5	97.5	97.3
12	98.4	98.2	98.0	98.5	99.2	98.2
13	99.0	98.2	99.3	98.5	100.0	99.1
14	99.4	99.1	99.3	99.2	100.0	99.1
15	99.7	99.1	100.0	100.0	100.0	99.1

Research/Supplemental Scales for the MMPI

Males   Amorality   (Mal)

		Age, yr				
	Total Sample	13	14	15	16	17
N	624	112	147	130	122	113
Median	2	2	3	2	3	3
Mean	2.49	2.16	2.65	2.36	2.67	2.57
SD	1.39	1.31	1.51	1.38	1.31	1.37
Min	0	0	0	0	0	0
Max	6	6	6	6	6	6

Percentage of Sample with Raw Score < X

X	Total Sample	13	14	15	16	17
0	0.0	0.0	0.0	0.0	0.0	0.0
1	6.4	9.8	7.5	4.6	3.3	7.1
2	25.5	32.1	25.2	30.0	17.2	23.0
3	52.4	61.6	48.3	58.5	47.5	46.9
4	77.2	85.7	68.7	82.3	76.2	75.2
5	91.7	96.4	87.8	91.5	91.8	92.0
6	97.8	98.2	98.0	96.9	96.7	99.1

Research/Supplemental Scales for the MMPI

Males   Psychomotor Acceleration   (Ma2)

		Age, yr				
	Total Sample	13	14	15	16	17
N	624	112	147	130	122	113
Median	7	7	7	6	7	7
Mean	6.61	6.46	6.69	6.38	6.80	6.70
SD	1.98	1.99	2.15	1.97	1.92	1.80
Min	1	2	1	2	2	2
Max	11	10	11	11	11	10

Percentage of Sample with Raw Score < X

X	Total Sample	13	14	15	16	17
1	0.0	0.0	0.0	0.0	0.0	0.0
2	0.5	0.0	2.0	0.0	0.0	0.0
3	2.4	3.6	3.4	2.3	1.6	0.9
4	7.2	8.0	9.5	8.5	4.1	5.3
5	15.1	17.9	15.0	16.2	13.1	13.3
6	28.4	30.4	27.9	35.4	23.8	23.9
7	44.7	47.3	42.2	50.8	41.8	41.6
8	65.7	67.0	62.6	68.5	65.6	65.5
9	82.2	86.6	76.2	85.4	79.5	85.0
10	93.9	93.8	93.2	96.2	91.8	94.7
11	99.2	100.0	99.3	98.5	98.4	100.0

Research/Supplemental Scales for the MMPI

Males   Imperturbability (Ma3)

		Age, yr				
	Total Sample	13	14	15	16	17
N	624	112	147	130	122	113
Median	3	3	3	3	3	4
Mean	3.18	3.10	2.84	3.19	3.34	3.49
SD	1.61	1.62	1.65	1.60	1.57	1.58
Min	0	0	0	0	0	0
Max	7	7	7	7	7	7

	Percentage of Sample with Raw Score < X					
X	Total Sample	13	14	15	16	17
0	0.0	0.0	0.0	0.0	0.0	0.0
1	4.3	5.4	6.8	4.6	2.5	1.8
2	16.0	17.0	22.4	13.8	13.9	11.5
3	35.1	34.8	44.9	36.2	28.7	28.3
4	57.1	59.8	64.6	56.2	54.1	48.7
5	80.1	84.8	85.0	79.2	77.0	73.5
6	92.1	91.1	93.9	92.3	91.8	91.2
7	97.6	97.3	98.0	98.5	97.5	96.5

Research/Supplemental Scales for the MMPI

Males   Ego Inflation   (Ma4)

	Total Sample	Age, yr				
		13	14	15	16	17
N	624	112	147	130	122	113
Median	5	5	5	5	5	4
Mean	4.64	4.73	4.84	4.66	4.60	4.32
SD	1.80	1.87	1.82	1.82	1.78	1.70
Min	0	1	0	1	1	0
Max	9	9	8	8	9	8

X	Percentage of Sample with Raw Score < X					
	Total Sample	13	14	15	16	17
0	0.0	0.0	0.0	0.0	0.0	0.0
1	0.5	0.0	1.4	0.0	0.0	0.9
2	5.0	2.7	5.4	6.2	4.9	5.3
3	13.0	10.7	11.6	13.8	11.5	17.7
4	26.4	29.5	21.1	26.2	28.7	28.3
5	45.4	47.3	37.4	45.4	45.9	53.1
6	67.3	67.9	65.3	62.3	69.7	72.6
7	83.7	78.6	79.6	83.1	86.1	92.0
8	95.0	91.1	94.6	96.9	94.3	98.2
9	99.7	99.1	100.0	100.0	99.2	100.0

SERKOWNEK SUBSCALES[1] FOR SCALES 5 (Mf) AND 0 (Si)

Scale 5 (Mf, Masculinity-Femininity)

The development of subscales for scale 5 (Mf) was initiated by Pepper and Strong (1958), who rationally divided the 60 items of this scale into five categories: ego sensitivity, sexual identification, altruism, endorsement of culturally feminine occupations, and denial of culturally masculine occupations. Subsequently, Graham, Schroeder, and Lilly (1971) factor analyzed scale 5 on a heterogeneous sample of 422 subjects, including psychiatric inpatients (29%), psychiatric outpatients (29%), and normal people (42%). Their ages ranged from 15 to 70 years (mean, 26 years), and their education ranged from 5 years to postgraduate training (mean, 14 years). Overall, 57% of the sample were women, 50% were single, 37% were married, and 13% were separated, divorced, or widowed. The "normal sample" included hospital employees, policemen, social workers, secretaries, students, and teachers.

Results of the analysis yielded seven factors: (I) *sensitivity-narcissism*, sensitivity to the reactions of others, proneness to worry or be easily hurt or upset; (II) *feminine interests*, endorsement of items clearly feminine in nature; (III) *masculine interests*, endorsement of items clearly masculine in nature; (IV) *demographic*, a relationship among three (education, age, marital status) of the five demographic variables included in the analysis; (V) *homosexual concern, passivity*, discomfort in discussing sexual matters, admitting homosexual impulses; (VI) social *extroversion*, enjoyment and comfort in loud, active social gatherings; and (VII) *exhibitionism*, enjoyment of activities having a dominant and conspicuous role. These findings were viewed as consistent with the clusters derived rationally by Pepper and Strong (1958). Graham et al. (1971) noted that masculine and feminine interests did not appear as opposite tendencies on a single continuum but that endorsements of items professing interests that are masculine or feminine in character are relatively independent of each other.

Later, Serkownek (1975; Schuerger, Foerstner, Serkownek, & Ritz, 1987) utilized the information from the study by Graham et al. (1971) to derive subscales that could be scored for clinical interpretation. Preliminary norms were established (K. Serkownek, personal communication, 1984) by using MMPI data from the 50,000 medical patients reported by Swenson, Pearson, and Osborne (1973). It was believed that such subscales could then be used as moderator variables to enhance the interpretation of scale 5 and to provide additional information as to the dynamics that might have led to an elevation on the scale. There is some overlap because an item was included on any subscale if its factor loading was 0.30 or larger. However, an exception was made for two subscales (Stereotypic Feminine Interest, Denial of Stereotypic Masculine Interest) on which no overlap was permitted. Factor IV (demographic) was omitted and the remaining factors from the Graham study were renamed and described as follows:

Mf1: Narcissism-Hypersensitivity. Worrisome, easily hurt, preoccupied with sexual matters, views self as awkward, concerned about personal appearance.

Mf2: Stereotypic Feminine Interests. Reports interest in occupations or pastimes that are considered traditionally or culturally feminine.

Mf3: Denial of Stereotypic Masculine Interests. Denies interest in occupations or pastimes traditionally considered culturally masculine (such as military service, hunting, sports).

Mf4: Heterosexual Discomfort, Passivity. Same-sex attraction, discomfort talking about sex, unaspiring.

---

[1]The scales as listed herein correct the errors printed in the composition of the Serkownek subscales as reported in Graham, J. R. (1977). *The MMPI: A practical guide.* New York: Oxford University Press; and Greene, R. L. (1980). *The MMPI: An interpretive manual.* New York: Grune & Stratton.

Mf5: Introspective, Critical. Serious, rational, dislikes loud parties, does not believe in afterlife.

Mf6: Socially Retiring. Timid, unassertive, dislikes dramatics.

Scale 0 (Si, Social Introversion-Extroversion)

Using the same sample described above, Graham et al. (1971) also factor analyzed scale 0 (Si). The analysis yielded seven interpretable factors measuring extent of social participation and reasons for social involvement (or lack of it) and suggested that scale 0 may also reflect the patient's degree of general psychologic adjustment: (I) *inferiority and discomfort*, unhappiness and discomfort because of perceived lack of interpersonal skills; (II) *affiliation*, enjoyment from being with other people; (III) *social excitement*, enjoyment associated with participation in active social groups; (IV) *demographic*, a relationship among four (age, education, pathology, marital status) of the five demographic variables analyzed; (V) *sensitivity*, shy, easily embarrassed, sensitive to reactions of others, unlikely to be assertive in stressful situations; (VI) *interpersonal trust*, feels that others are honest, sincere, and unselfish; (VII) *physical-somatic concern*, reports somatic symptoms, expresses concern about physical appearance.

Serkownek (1975; Schuerger et al., 1987) then utilized information from the factor analysis by Graham et al. (1971) to construct scales that could readily be scored to provide supplemental information for understanding the patient's score on scale 0. Preliminary norms (K. Serkownek, personal communication, 1984) for his tables were derived from the MMPI responses obtained from the large sample of medical patients described by Swenson et al. (1973). The names and brief descriptions of the subscales are as follows.

Si1: Inferiority, Personal Discomfort. Shy, easily embarrassed, socially awkward, vulnerable to criticism, lack of skill in interpersonal relations, excessively sensitive.

Si2: Discomfort With Others. Lacks confidence, tends to withdraw, fails to enjoy social contacts (particularly groups).

Si3: Staid, Personal Rigidity. Avoids social groups, dislikes excitement, avoids social risks and competition, primarily a follower and not a leader.

Si4: Hypersensitivity. Easily embarrassed, unlikely to be assertive in stressful situations, sensitive to reactions of others.

Si5: Distrust. Use of denial, disappointment in self and others, inferred use of regressive behavior to gain attention.

Si6: Physical-Somatic Concerns. Brooding, worrisome, inferred somatic changes when stressed, inferred stage fright.

REFERENCES

Graham, J. R., Schroeder, H. E., & Lilly, R. S. (1971). Factor analysis of items on the social introversion and masculinity-femininity scales of the MMPI. *Journal of Clinical Psychology, 27*, 367–370.

Pepper, L., & Strong, P. (1958). *Judgmental subscales for the Mf scale of the MMPI.* Unpublished materials. (Cited in Dahlstrom, W. G., & Welsh, G. S. [1960]. *An MMPI handbook: A guide to use in clinical practice and research.* Minneapolis: University of Minnesota Press.)

Schuerger, J. M., Foerstner, S. B., Serkownek, K., & Ritz, G. (1987). History and validities of the Serkownek subscales for MMPI scales 5 and 0. *Psychological Reports, 61,* 227–235.

Serkownek, K. (1975). *Subscales for scales 5 and 0 of the Minnesota Multiphasic Personality Inventory.* Unpublished preliminary version dated June 1975.

Swenson, W. M., Pearson, J. S., & Osborne, D. (1973). *An MMPI source book: Basic item, scale, and pattern data on 50,000 medical patients.* Minneapolis: University of Minnesota Press.

The items composing each of the Serkownek subscales for scales 5 (Mf) and 0 (Si), and their direction of scoring, are listed below.

Scale 5 (Mf, Masculinity-Femininity)

Mf1: Narcissism-Hypersensitivity (18 Items)

The following items score if answered *true*:

25.   I would like to be a singer.
89.   It takes a lot of argument to convince most people of the truth.
117.   Most people are honest chiefly through fear of being caught.
179.   I am worried about sex matters.
217.   I frequently find myself worrying about something.
226.   Some of my family have habits that bother and annoy me very much.
239.   I have been disappointed in love.
278.   I have often felt that strangers were looking at me critically.
282.   Once in a while I feel hate toward members of my family whom I usually love.
297.   I wish I were not bothered by thoughts about sex.
299.   I think that I feel more intensely than most people do.

The following items score if answered *false*:

79.   My feelings are not easily hurt.
133.   I have never indulged in any unusual sex practices.
187.   My hands have not become clumsy or awkward.
198.   I daydream very little.
214.   I have never had any breaking out on my skin that has worried me.
262.   It does not bother me that I am not better looking.
264.   I am entirely self-confident.

Mf2: Stereotypic Feminine Interests (14 Items)

The following items score if answered true:

4.   I think I would like the work of a librarian.
70.[a]   I used to like drop-the-handkerchief.
74.   I have often wished I were a girl. (Or if you are a girl) I have never been sorry that I am a girl.
77.   I enjoy reading love stories.
78.   I like poetry.
87.   I would like to be a florist.
92.   I would like to be a nurse.
132.   I like collecting flowers or growing house plants.
140.   I like to cook.
149.   I used to keep a diary.
204.   I would like to be a journalist.
261.   If I were an artist I would like to draw flowers.
295.[a]   I liked "Alice in Wonderland" by Lewis Carroll.

The following item scores if answered *false*:

300.   There never was a time in my life when I liked to play with dolls.

Mf3: Denial of Stereotypic Masculine Interests (8 Items)

The following items score if answered *true:*
(none)

The following items score if answered *false:*

  1.   I like mechanics magazines.
  81. I think I would like the kind of work a forest ranger does.
144. I would like to be a soldier.
176. I do not have a great fear of snakes.
219. I think I would like the work of a building contractor.
221. I like science.
223. I very much like hunting.
283. If I were a reporter I would very much like to report sporting news.

Mf4: Heterosexual Discomfort, Passivity (4 Items)

The following item scores if answered *true:*

  69.[a] I am very strongly attracted by members of my own sex.

The following items score if answered *false:*

  19. When I take a new job, I like to be tipped off on who should be gotten next to.
  80. I sometimes tease animals.
231. I like to talk about sex.

Mf5: Introspective, Critical (7 Items)

The following item scores if answered *true:*

204. I would like to be a journalist.

The following items score if answered *false:*

  92. I would like to be a nurse.
  99. I like to go to parties and other affairs where there is lots of loud fun.
115. I believe in a life hereafter.
249.[a] I believe there is a Devil and a Hell in afterlife.
254. I like to be with a crowd who play jokes on one another.
264. I am entirely self-confident.

Mf6: Socially Retiring (9 Items)

The following items score if answered *true:*
(none)

The following items score if answered *false:*

  89. It takes a lot of argument to convince most people of the truth.
  99. I like to go to parties and other affairs where there is lots of loud fun.
112. I frequently find it necessary to stand up for what I think is right.

116. I enjoy a race or game better when I bet on it.
117. Most people are honest chiefly through fear of being caught.
126. I like dramatics.
140. I like to cook.
203. If I were a reporter I would very much like to report news of the theater.
229. I should like to belong to several clubs or lodges.

ªItems that were deleted from the original MMPI item pool during construction of the MMPI-2.

Scale 0 (Si, Social Introversion-Extroversion)

Si1: Inferiority, Personal Discomfort (27 Items)

The following items score if answered *true*:

32. I find it hard to keep my mind on a task or job.
67. I wish I could be as happy as others seem to be.
82. I am easily downed in an argument.
138. Criticism or scolding hurts me terribly.
147. I have often lost out on things because I couldn't make up my mind soon enough.
171. It makes me uncomfortable to put on a stunt at a party even when others are doing the same sort of things.
172. I frequently have to fight against showing that I am bashful.
180. I find it hard to make talk when I meet new people.
201. I wish I were not so shy.
236. I brood a great deal.
267. When in a group of people I have trouble thinking of the right things to talk about.
278. I have often felt that strangers were looking at me critically.
292. I am likely not to speak to people until they speak to me.
304. In school I found it very hard to talk before the class.
321. I am easily embarrassed.
336. I easily become impatient with people.
359. Sometimes some unimportant thought will run through my mind and bother me for days.
377. At parties I am more likely to sit by myself or with just one other person than to join in with the crowd.
383. People often disappoint me.
411. It makes me feel like a failure when I hear of the success of someone I know well.
455. I am quite often not in on the gossip and talk of the group I belong to.
549. I shrink from facing a crisis or difficulty.
564. I am apt to pass up something I want to do when others feel that it isn't worth doing.

The following items score if answered *false*:

57. I am a good mixer.
309. I seem to make friends about as quickly as others do.
353. I have no dread of going into a room by myself where other people have already gathered and are talking.
371. I am not unusually self-conscious.

Si2: Discomfort With Others (14 Items)

The following items score if answered *true:*

357. I have several times given up doing a thing because I thought too little of my ability.
377. At parties I am more likely to sit by myself or with just one other person than to join in with the crowd.
427. I am embarrassed by dirty stories.
469. I have often found people jealous of my good ideas, just because they had not thought of them first.
473. Whenever possible I avoid being in a crowd.
487. I feel like giving up quickly when things go wrong.
505. I have had periods when I felt so full of pep that sleep did not seem necessary for days at a time.

The following items score if answered *false:*

449. I enjoy social gatherings just to be with people.
450. I enjoy the excitement of a crowd.
462.[a] I have had no difficulty starting or holding my urine.
479. I do not mind meeting strangers.
481. I can remember "playing sick" to get out of something.
521. In a group of people I would not be embarrassed to be called upon to start a discussion or give an opinion about something I know well.
547. I like parties and socials.

Si3: Staid, Personal Rigidity (16 Items)

The following items score if answered *true:*
(none)

The following items score if answered *false:*

33. I have had very peculiar and strange experiences.
91. I do not mind being made fun of.
99. I like to go to parties and other affairs where there is lots of loud fun.
143. When I was a child, I belonged to a crowd or gang that tried to stick together through thick and thin.
208. I like to flirt.
229. I should like to belong to several clubs or lodges.
231. I like to talk about sex.
254. I like to be with a crowd who play jokes on one another.
400. If given the chance I could do some things that would be of great benefit to the world.
415. If given the chance I would make a good leader of people.
440. I try to remember good stories to pass them on to other people.
446. I enjoy gambling for small stakes.
449. I enjoy social gatherings just to be with people.
450. I enjoy the excitement of a crowd.
469. I have often found people jealous of my good ideas, just because they had not thought of them first.

505. I have had periods when I felt so full of pep that sleep did not seem necessary for days at a time.

Si4: Hypersensitivity (10 Items)

The following items score if answered *true*:

25.   I would like to be a singer.
32.   I find it hard to keep my mind on a task or job.
126. I like dramatics.
138. Criticism or scolding hurts me terribly.
236. I brood a great deal.
278. I have often felt that strangers were looking at me critically.
391. I love to go to dances.
427. I am embarrassed by dirty stories.
487. I feel like giving up quickly when things go wrong.
549. I shrink from facing a crisis or difficulty.

The following items score if answered *false*:
(none)

Si5: Distrust (12 Items)

The following items score if answered *true*:

117. Most people are honest chiefly through fear of being caught.
124. Most people will use somewhat unfair means to gain profit or an advantage rather than to lose it.
147. I have often lost out on things because I couldn't make up my mind soon enough.
278. I have often felt that strangers were looking at me critically.
316. I think nearly anyone would tell a lie to keep out of trouble.
359. Sometimes some unimportant thought will run through my mind and bother me for days.
383. People often disappoint me.
398. I often think, "I wish I were a child again."
411. It makes me feel like a failure when I hear of the success of someone I know well.
436. People generally demand more respect for their own rights than they are willing to allow for others.
481. I can remember "playing sick" to get out of something.
482. While in trains, busses, etc., I often talk to strangers.

The following items score if answered *false*:
(none)

Si6: Physical-Somatic Concerns (10 Items)

The following items score if answered *true*:

33.   I have had very peculiar and strange experiences.
236. I brood a great deal.
332. Sometimes my voice leaves me or changes even though I have no cold.

The following items score if answered *false*:

119.   My speech is the same as always (not faster or slower, or slurring; no hoarseness).
193.   I do not have spells of hay fever or asthma.
262.   It does not bother me that I am not better looking.
281.   I do not often notice my ears ringing or buzzing.
309.   I seem to make friends about as quickly as others do.
449.   I enjoy social gatherings just to be with people.
451.   My worries seem to disappear when I get into a crowd of lively friends.

---

[a]Items that were deleted from the original MMPI item pool during construction of the MMPI-2.

Research/Supplemental Scales for the MMPI

Females   Narcissism-Hypersensitivity   (Mf1)

| | | Age, yr | | | | |
	Total Sample	13	14	15	16	17
N	691	136	153	127	138	137
Median	10	9	10	10	10	9
Mean	9.48	8.85	9.44	9.76	10.25	9.14
SD	3.11	3.15	3.02	2.89	3.16	3.16
Min	0	1	2	2	0	1
Max	17	16	17	15	17	17

Percentage of Sample with Raw Score < X

X	Total Sample	13	14	15	16	17
0	0.0	0.0	0.0	0.0	0.0	0.0
1	0.1	0.0	0.0	0.0	0.7	0.0
2	0.6	1.5	0.0	0.0	0.7	0.7
3	1.4	1.5	0.7	1.6	1.4	2.2
4	2.9	2.9	3.3	2.4	1.4	4.4
5	7.1	9.6	7.8	4.7	4.3	8.8
6	12.2	17.6	12.4	7.9	7.2	15.3
7	19.2	26.5	17.6	15.7	13.8	22.6
8	25.5	35.3	25.5	20.5	16.7	29.2
9	33.3	41.2	33.3	29.9	25.4	36.5
10	46.6	55.1	43.8	41.7	42.0	50.4
11	60.2	66.9	61.4	58.3	50.7	63.5
12	73.2	77.2	77.1	71.7	63.8	75.9
13	84.7	89.0	86.9	84.3	76.1	86.9
14	91.3	94.1	93.5	89.0	84.8	94.9
15	95.8	97.8	96.1	96.9	91.3	97.1
16	98.6	99.3	98.0	100.0	97.1	98.5
17	99.1	100.0	98.7	100.0	97.8	99.3

Research/Supplemental Scales for the MMPI

Females   Stereotypic Feminine Interests   (Mf2)

		Age, yr				
	Total Sample	13	14	15	16	17
N	691	136	153	127	138	137
Median	7	7	7	7	7	7
Mean	7.16	6.93	7.22	7.24	7.18	7.23
SD	2.25	2.28	2.24	2.25	2.30	2.18
Min	0	2	0	1	2	1
Max	14	14	13	13	13	12

	Percentage of Sample with Raw Score < X					
X	Total Sample	13	14	15	16	17
0	0.0	0.0	0.0	0.0	0.0	0.0
1	0.1	0.0	0.7	0.0	0.0	0.0
2	0.6	0.0	0.7	1.6	0.0	0.7
3	2.5	2.2	0.7	3.1	2.9	3.6
4	4.6	4.4	3.3	6.3	5.1	4.4
5	11.1	14.7	8.5	9.4	13.8	9.5
6	23.7	30.1	22.9	20.5	22.5	22.6
7	38.2	43.4	39.9	33.1	39.1	35.0
8	55.3	59.6	58.8	53.5	53.6	50.4
9	72.1	74.3	71.2	72.4	70.3	72.3
10	85.7	87.5	84.3	85.8	85.5	85.4
11	93.5	94.9	90.8	95.3	92.0	94.9
12	97.3	97.1	96.7	96.1	97.8	98.5
13	99.4	99.3	99.3	99.2	99.3	100.0
14	99.9	99.3	100.0	100.0	100.0	100.0

Research/Supplemental Scales for the MMPI

Females   Denial Of Stereotypic Masculine Interests   (Mf3)

	Total Sample	Age, yr				
		13	14	15	16	17
N	691	136	153	127	138	137
Median	6	7	6	6	6	6
Mean	6.23	6.49	6.05	6.13	6.31	6.21
SD	1.26	1.18	1.29	1.45	1.13	1.22
Min	1	2	2	2	3	1
Max	8	8	8	8	8	8

	Percentage of Sample with Raw Score < X					
X	Total Sample	13	14	15	16	17
1	0.0	0.0	0.0	0.0	0.0	0.0
2	0.1	0.0	0.0	0.0	0.0	0.7
3	1.2	0.7	2.0	2.4	0.0	0.7
4	2.7	1.5	3.9	3.9	1.4	2.9
5	9.1	5.1	11.8	15.0	7.2	6.6
6	23.9	17.6	27.5	29.9	20.3	24.1
7	54.6	47.8	60.8	52.8	53.6	56.9
8	84.9	78.7	89.5	82.7	86.2	86.9

Research/Supplemental Scales for the MMPI

Females   Heterosexual Discomfort, Passivity   (Mf4)

| | | Age, yr | | | | |
	Total Sample	13	14	15	16	17
N	691	136	153	127	138	137
Median	2	2	2	2	2	2
Mean	1.89	1.88	1.98	1.72	1.83	2.01
SD	0.93	0.94	0.94	0.93	0.89	0.95
Min	0	0	0	0	0	0
Max	4	4	3	3	4	3

| | Percentage of Sample with Raw Score < X | | | | | |
X	Total Sample	13	14	15	16	17
0	0.0	0.0	0.0	0.0	0.0	0.0
1	8.7	7.4	9.2	11.8	7.2	8.0
2	32.0	34.6	26.8	37.8	33.3	28.5
3	71.1	70.6	66.0	78.7	78.3	62.8
4	99.6	99.3	100.0	100.0	98.6	100.0

Research/Supplemental Scales for the MMPI

Females   Introspective, Critical   (Mf5)

		Age, yr				
	Total Sample	13	14	15	16	17
N	691	136	153	127	138	137
Median	3	3	3	3	3	3
Mean	2.98	2.89	2.87	2.83	3.03	3.26
SD	1.18	1.29	1.10	1.19	1.15	1.12
Min	0	0	0	0	1	1
Max	6	6	5	6	6	6

	Percentage of Sample with Raw Score < X					
X	Total Sample	13	14	15	16	17
0	0.0	0.0	0.0	0.0	0.0	0.0
1	0.6	1.5	0.7	0.8	0.0	0.0
2	10.4	16.2	7.8	13.4	9.4	5.8
3	35.0	36.0	41.8	39.4	32.6	24.8
4	67.9	70.6	71.2	72.4	65.9	59.1
5	89.9	89.0	91.5	92.1	90.6	86.1
6	98.7	97.8	100.0	98.4	98.6	98.5

Research/Supplemental Scales for the MMPI

Females   Socially Retiring   (Mf6)

		Age, yr				
	Total Sample	13	14	15	16	17
N	691	136	153	127	138	137
Median	4	4	4	4	4	4
Mean	4.04	4.01	3.84	3.80	4.21	4.37
SD	1.61	1.61	1.52	1.60	1.54	1.75
Min	0	0	1	1	0	0
Max	9	7	8	8	8	9

	Percentage of Sample with Raw Score < X					
X	Total Sample	13	14	15	16	17
0	0.0	0.0	0.0	0.0	0.0	0.0
1	0.7	0.7	0.0	0.0	0.7	2.2
2	5.2	8.1	3.9	7.1	2.2	5.1
3	17.2	17.6	20.9	21.3	13.8	12.4
4	37.8	33.8	45.1	45.7	34.1	29.9
5	62.1	61.8	66.7	68.5	57.2	56.2
6	80.8	83.8	84.3	85.0	79.0	71.5
7	92.8	92.6	96.1	93.7	92.8	88.3
8	99.1	100.0	99.3	99.2	99.3	97.8
9	99.9	100.0	100.0	100.0	100.0	99.3

Research/Supplemental Scales for the MMPI

Females   Inferiority, Personal Discomfort   (Si1)

		Age, yr				
	Total Sample	13	14	15	16	17
N	691	136	153	127	138	137
Median	11	12	12	11	12	10
Mean	11.48	11.70	11.12	11.85	12.65	10.15
SD	5.51	5.10	5.29	5.86	5.77	5.29
Min	0	2	1	0	0	0
Max	25	25	25	24	25	23

Percentage of Sample with Raw Score < X

X	Total Sample	13	14	15	16	17
0	0.0	0.0	0.0	0.0	0.0	0.0
1	0.4	0.0	0.0	0.8	0.7	0.7
2	2.0	0.0	0.7	2.4	2.2	5.1
3	3.9	2.2	3.3	4.7	2.9	6.6
4	6.9	4.4	6.5	7.1	3.6	13.1
5	11.6	8.8	13.1	11.0	6.5	18.2
6	15.5	13.2	17.6	13.4	8.7	24.1
7	21.6	18.4	24.2	18.1	18.1	28.5
8	27.4	22.8	31.4	27.6	22.5	32.1
9	31.3	28.7	34.6	30.7	26.1	35.8
10	38.1	35.3	39.2	37.8	33.3	44.5
11	44.6	43.4	45.1	44.1	38.4	51.8
12	50.8	49.3	49.0	52.0	44.2	59.9
13	58.8	55.9	60.8	56.7	51.4	68.6
14	63.1	59.6	66.0	64.6	52.9	72.3
15	68.5	66.9	71.2	66.1	59.4	78.1
16	75.5	76.5	77.8	72.4	68.1	82.5
17	80.5	83.8	81.0	76.4	75.4	85.4
18	84.5	87.5	86.9	78.7	79.0	89.8
19	89.7	91.2	92.2	85.0	84.1	95.6
20	92.3	93.4	95.4	88.2	87.0	97.1
21	93.9	95.6	96.7	90.6	88.4	97.8
22	95.7	97.1	98.0	92.9	91.3	98.5
23	97.5	97.8	98.7	96.1	95.7	99.3
24	98.6	99.3	99.3	97.6	96.4	100.0
25	99.4	99.3	99.3	100.0	98.6	100.0

Research/Supplemental Scales for the MMPI

Females   Discomfort With Others   (Si2)

| | Total Sample | Age, yr | | | | |
		13	14	15	16	17
N	691	136	153	127	138	137
Median	3	4	3	3	4	3
Mean	3.79	4.26	3.63	3.58	4.24	3.26
SD	2.27	2.14	2.31	2.37	2.22	2.17
Min	0	0	0	0	0	0
Max	11	11	10	10	11	10

| X | Percentage of Sample with Raw Score < X | | | | | |
	Total Sample	13	14	15	16	17
0	0.0	0.0	0.0	0.0	0.0	0.0
1	4.2	1.5	5.9	6.3	2.2	5.1
2	14.8	8.1	19.0	17.3	7.2	21.9
3	32.3	21.3	34.6	40.2	21.7	43.8
4	50.2	40.4	53.6	55.9	39.9	61.3
5	67.3	57.4	71.2	70.1	61.6	75.9
6	77.9	72.8	77.8	78.7	76.1	83.9
7	86.0	85.3	83.7	85.8	85.5	89.8
8	93.3	91.2	94.1	92.9	92.0	96.4
9	96.5	97.8	97.4	96.1	93.5	97.8
10	98.4	98.5	99.3	98.4	97.1	98.5
11	99.7	99.3	100.0	100.0	99.3	100.0

Research/Supplemental Scales for the MMPI

Females   Staid, Personal Rigidity   (Si3)

| | Total Sample | Age, yr | | | | |
		13	14	15	16	17
N	691	136	153	127	138	137
Median	7	8	8	7	8	7
Mean	7.52	7.63	7.58	7.13	7.64	7.57
SD	2.73	2.73	2.58	2.61	2.87	2.86
Min	0	1	1	0	1	1
Max	16	14	14	14	16	15

Percentage of Sample with Raw Score < X

X	Total Sample	13	14	15	16	17
0	0.0	0.0	0.0	0.0	0.0	0.0
1	0.1	0.0	0.0	0.8	0.0	0.0
2	0.9	0.7	0.7	1.6	0.7	0.7
3	1.9	1.5	1.3	2.4	1.4	2.9
4	5.9	4.4	4.6	8.7	5.1	7.3
5	12.4	12.5	9.8	14.2	13.8	12.4
6	25.6	25.7	24.2	24.4	27.5	26.3
7	37.8	37.5	36.6	39.4	37.7	38.0
8	51.5	50.0	48.4	60.6	48.6	51.1
9	64.7	62.5	62.1	74.0	61.6	64.2
10	76.4	72.8	79.1	81.1	74.6	74.5
11	85.7	81.6	88.9	89.8	84.1	83.9
12	91.6	91.2	92.2	93.7	92.0	89.1
13	96.2	97.1	96.7	96.9	94.9	95.6
14	98.0	99.3	97.4	99.2	96.4	97.8
15	99.6	100.0	100.0	100.0	98.6	99.3
16	99.9	100.0	100.0	100.0	99.3	100.0

Research/Supplemental Scales for the MMPI

Females   Hypersensitivity   (Si4)

		Age, yr				
	Total Sample	13	14	15	16	17
N	691	136	153	127	138	137
Median	4	4	4	5	5	4
Mean	4.56	4.48	4.44	4.72	5.09	4.10
SD	1.89	1.76	1.85	1.98	1.91	1.82
Min	0	1	1	0	1	0
Max	10	9	10	10	9	8

Percentage of Sample with Raw Score < X

X	Total Sample	13	14	15	16	17
0	0.0	0.0	0.0	0.0	0.0	0.0
1	0.3	0.0	0.0	0.8	0.0	0.7
2	4.1	3.7	4.6	2.4	2.2	7.3
3	13.9	12.5	13.7	13.4	9.4	20.4
4	31.3	30.9	34.6	29.1	23.2	38.0
5	50.5	52.2	52.9	48.8	37.0	61.3
6	69.8	71.3	71.9	68.5	59.4	77.4
7	82.8	88.2	86.3	77.2	73.9	87.6
8	93.1	94.9	93.5	89.8	89.9	97.1
9	98.6	98.5	99.3	98.4	96.4	100.0
10	99.7	100.0	99.3	99.2	100.0	100.0

Research/Supplemental Scales for the MMPI

Females   Distrust   (Si5)

		Age, yr				
	Total Sample	13	14	15	16	17
N	691	136	153	127	138	137
Median	7	6	7	7	7	6
Mean	6.53	6.63	6.47	6.48	6.99	6.10
SD	2.58	2.57	2.47	2.52	2.53	2.76
Min	0	0	0	0	1	0
Max	12	12	12	12	12	12

	Percentage of Sample with Raw Score < X					
X	Total Sample	13	14	15	16	17
0	0.0	0.0	0.0	0.0	0.0	0.0
1	0.9	1.5	0.7	0.8	0.0	1.5
2	3.5	3.7	3.9	0.8	2.2	6.6
3	7.4	5.1	6.5	7.1	6.5	11.7
4	13.3	8.1	13.1	15.0	13.0	17.5
5	21.3	19.9	20.3	22.8	15.9	27.7
6	34.0	35.3	34.6	36.2	23.2	40.9
7	47.9	52.9	47.7	44.1	39.1	55.5
8	61.6	60.3	62.7	64.6	55.1	65.7
9	74.8	71.3	75.8	77.2	71.0	78.8
10	88.1	85.3	90.8	89.0	84.1	91.2
11	95.1	94.1	97.4	96.1	92.0	95.6
12	98.7	99.3	99.3	98.4	99.3	97.1

Research/Supplemental Scales for the MMPI

Females   Physical-Somatic Concerns   (Si6)

| | Total Sample | Age, yr | | | | |
		13	14	15	16	17
N	691	136	153	127	138	137
Median	3	3	3	3	3	2
Mean	2.80	2.74	2.81	2.90	3.11	2.47
SD	1.64	1.44	1.60	1.60	1.94	1.56
Min	0	0	0	0	0	0
Max	8	6	7	7	8	8

| X | Percentage of Sample with Raw Score < X | | | | | |
	Total Sample	13	14	15	16	17
0	0.0	0.0	0.0	0.0	0.0	0.0
1	5.1	5.1	3.9	3.9	6.5	5.8
2	24.0	19.9	24.8	22.8	21.7	30.7
3	46.7	45.6	43.8	42.5	43.5	58.4
4	68.6	70.6	70.6	65.4	62.3	73.7
5	83.9	89.0	83.7	81.9	75.4	89.8
6	93.5	96.3	93.5	95.3	87.0	95.6
7	98.3	100.0	98.7	98.4	94.9	99.3
8	99.4	100.0	100.0	100.0	97.8	99.3

Research/Supplemental Scales for the MMPI

Males   Narcissism-Hypersensitivity   (Mf1)

	Total Sample	Age, yr				
		13	14	15	16	17
N	624	112	147	130	122	113
Median	8	7	8	8	8	8
Mean	7.88	7.18	8.15	7.75	8.37	7.87
SD	3.38	3.50	3.29	3.50	3.24	3.31
Min	0	0	1	0	0	1
Max	16	15	16	16	15	16

Percentage of Sample with Raw Score < X

X	Total Sample	13	14	15	16	17
0	0.0	0.0	0.0	0.0	0.0	0.0
1	0.8	2.7	0.0	0.8	0.8	0.0
2	1.9	2.7	2.0	1.5	0.8	2.7
3	4.6	9.8	4.1	3.8	2.5	3.5
4	9.8	17.0	8.2	12.3	4.1	8.0
5	16.8	24.1	13.6	16.9	12.3	18.6
6	26.3	31.3	23.1	29.2	22.1	26.5
7	36.9	43.8	34.0	40.0	32.0	35.4
8	46.5	55.4	44.2	48.5	41.0	44.2
9	57.4	64.3	53.7	62.3	51.6	55.8
10	68.4	74.1	61.9	72.3	62.3	73.5
11	76.9	83.9	72.8	78.5	72.1	78.8
12	83.5	88.4	82.3	81.5	82.0	84.1
13	90.2	92.0	91.8	88.5	87.7	91.2
14	94.9	95.5	95.2	93.8	94.3	95.6
15	97.3	97.3	98.6	96.2	97.5	96.5
16	99.4	100.0	99.3	98.5	100.0	99.1

Research/Supplemental Scales for the MMPI

Males   Stereotypic Feminine Interests   (Mf2)

	Total Sample	Age, yr				
		13	14	15	16	17
N	624	112	147	130	122	113
Median	2	3	2	2	2	2
Mean	2.52	2.57	2.35	2.64	2.60	2.47
SD	1.81	1.68	1.85	1.90	1.87	1.73
Min	0	0	0	0	0	0
Max	10	7	8	10	10	8

Percentage of Sample with Raw Score < X

X	Total Sample	13	14	15	16	17
0	0.0	0.0	0.0	0.0	0.0	0.0
1	10.1	9.8	12.9	7.7	8.2	11.5
2	33.2	32.1	38.8	31.5	32.8	29.2
3	56.6	49.1	60.5	56.9	54.1	61.1
4	74.7	72.3	79.6	71.5	75.4	73.5
5	85.7	85.7	86.4	84.6	85.2	86.7
6	92.8	94.6	93.2	90.8	91.0	94.7
7	96.8	99.1	95.9	96.2	95.9	97.3
8	98.9	100.0	98.0	98.5	99.2	99.1
9	99.7	100.0	100.0	99.2	99.2	100.0
10	99.7	100.0	100.0	99.2	99.2	100.0

Research/Supplemental Scales for the MMPI

Males   Denial Of Stereotypic Masculine Interests   (Mf3)

		Age, yr				
	Total Sample	13	14	15	16	17
N	624	112	147	130	122	113
Median	4	4	4	4	4	4
Mean	3.75	3.86	3.80	3.69	3.69	3.72
SD	1.65	1.60	1.48	1.56	1.83	1.82
Min	0	1	1	0	0	0
Max	8	8	7	7	8	7

	Percentage of Sample with Raw Score < X					
X	Total Sample	13	14	15	16	17
0	0.0	0.0	0.0	0.0	0.0	0.0
1	1.8	0.0	0.0	2.3	3.3	3.5
2	8.0	3.6	6.1	7.7	11.5	11.5
3	24.7	24.1	20.4	20.8	30.3	29.2
4	45.0	45.5	42.2	46.9	45.1	46.0
5	66.0	65.2	68.0	69.2	65.6	61.1
6	84.5	81.3	85.7	87.7	82.8	84.1
7	95.2	95.5	97.3	96.2	93.4	92.9
8	99.7	99.1	100.0	100.0	99.2	100.0

Research/Supplemental Scales for the MMPI

Males   Heterosexual Discomfort, Passivity   (Mf4)

		Age, yr				
	Total Sample	13	14	15	16	17
N	624	112	147	130	122	113
Median	2	2	2	1	1	2
Mean	1.55	1.65	1.56	1.48	1.48	1.58
SD	0.89	0.95	0.93	0.93	0.86	0.79
Min	0	0	0	0	0	0
Max	4	4	3	3	3	3

Percentage of Sample with Raw Score < X

X	Total Sample	13	14	15	16	17
0	0.0	0.0	0.0	0.0	0.0	0.0
1	11.9	8.9	15.0	14.6	12.3	7.1
2	48.6	48.2	44.2	52.3	51.6	46.9
3	84.9	79.5	84.4	84.6	87.7	88.5
4	99.7	98.2	100.0	100.0	100.0	100.0

Research/Supplemental Scales for the MMPI

Males   Introspective, Critical   (Mf5)

	Total Sample	Age, yr				
		13	14	15	16	17
N	624	112	147	130	122	113
Median	3	3	3	3	3	3
Mean	2.83	2.92	2.86	2.92	2.70	2.74
SD	1.19	1.17	1.25	1.29	1.08	1.15
Min	0	1	0	1	0	1
Max	7	6	6	6	6	7

X	Percentage of Sample with Raw Score < X					
	Total Sample	13	14	15	16	17
0	0.0	0.0	0.0	0.0	0.0	0.0
1	0.3	0.0	0.7	0.0	0.8	0.0
2	11.9	7.1	15.0	16.9	10.7	8.0
3	42.9	44.6	39.5	36.9	45.9	49.6
4	73.4	68.8	70.7	68.5	80.3	79.6
5	90.7	88.4	91.2	88.5	93.4	92.0
6	98.1	99.1	97.3	97.7	99.2	97.3
7	99.8	100.0	100.0	100.0	100.0	99.1

Research/Supplemental Scales for the MMPI

Males   Socially Retiring   (Mf6)

		Age, yr				
	Total Sample	13	14	15	16	17
N	624	112	147	130	122	113
Median	4	5	4	4	5	4
Mean	4.47	4.46	4.39	4.48	4.52	4.52
SD	1.61	1.50	1.69	1.64	1.55	1.64
Min	0	1	0	1	1	1
Max	9	8	9	8	9	8

	Percentage of Sample with Raw Score < X					
X	Total Sample	13	14	15	16	17
0	0.0	0.0	0.0	0.0	0.0	0.0
1	0.2	0.0	0.7	0.0	0.0	0.0
2	2.7	3.6	2.0	2.3	2.5	3.5
3	11.4	10.7	13.6	13.1	10.7	8.0
4	26.9	25.0	29.9	30.0	23.0	25.7
5	51.3	48.2	53.7	51.5	48.4	54.0
6	74.5	73.2	78.9	67.7	77.0	75.2
7	89.7	93.8	87.8	88.5	91.8	87.6
8	96.5	99.1	94.6	99.2	95.9	93.8
9	99.7	100.0	99.3	100.0	99.2	100.0

Research/Supplemental Scales for the MMPI

Males   Inferiority, Personal Discomfort   (Si1)

		Age, yr				
	Total Sample	13	14	15	16	17
N	624	112	147	130	122	113
Median	10	9	11	10	10	10
Mean	10.60	10.13	11.43	10.45	11.03	9.69
SD	5.58	5.41	5.78	5.53	5.56	5.49
Min	0	0	0	1	1	0
Max	25	24	25	25	25	23

	Percentage of Sample with Raw Score < X					
X	Total Sample	13	14	15	16	17
0	0.0	0.0	0.0	0.0	0.0	0.0
1	0.5	0.9	0.7	0.0	0.0	0.9
2	3.0	3.6	2.7	3.1	1.6	4.4
3	5.8	6.3	3.4	7.7	3.3	8.8
4	9.3	10.7	4.8	13.1	5.7	13.3
5	13.9	12.5	10.9	16.9	12.3	17.7
6	21.0	22.3	17.0	22.3	17.2	27.4
7	27.6	31.3	22.4	26.9	25.4	33.6
8	33.3	37.5	27.9	32.3	31.1	39.8
9	40.9	48.2	36.1	39.2	36.1	46.9
10	45.7	50.9	41.5	44.6	43.4	49.6
11	52.1	52.7	47.6	52.3	52.5	56.6
12	57.2	57.1	54.4	56.2	54.9	64.6
13	62.8	64.3	59.9	61.5	58.2	71.7
14	70.0	70.5	66.0	71.5	69.7	73.5
15	75.3	78.6	70.1	76.2	73.8	79.6
16	80.3	83.0	76.2	80.0	79.5	84.1
17	83.8	86.6	79.6	83.8	83.6	86.7
18	87.5	89.3	83.0	88.5	86.1	92.0
19	89.9	92.0	85.7	90.8	88.5	93.8
20	92.5	93.8	89.1	95.4	90.2	94.7
21	94.6	97.3	91.2	96.9	92.6	95.6
22	96.2	99.1	92.5	97.7	95.9	96.5
23	98.4	99.1	97.3	99.2	97.5	99.1
24	98.9	99.1	98.0	99.2	98.4	100.0
25	99.5	100.0	99.3	99.2	99.2	100.0

Research/Supplemental Scales for the MMPI

Males   Discomfort With Others   (Si2)

	Total Sample	Age, yr				
		13	14	15	16	17
N	624	112	147	130	122	113
Median	3	4	4	3	3	3
Mean	3.93	4.62	4.33	3.65	3.61	3.42
SD	2.60	2.63	2.62	2.56	2.42	2.58
Min	0	0	0	0	0	0
Max	12	12	10	10	11	10

	Percentage of Sample with Raw Score < X					
X	Total Sample	13	14	15	16	17
0	0.0	0.0	0.0	0.0	0.0	0.0
1	4.3	1.8	1.4	6.2	4.9	8.0
2	17.6	6.3	15.6	20.0	19.7	26.5
3	37.5	25.9	32.0	42.3	40.2	47.8
4	50.5	36.6	43.5	55.4	57.4	60.2
5	63.1	55.4	55.8	69.2	67.2	69.0
6	73.4	70.5	68.0	76.9	75.4	77.0
7	82.9	76.8	77.6	84.6	89.3	86.7
8	88.1	85.7	84.4	88.5	92.6	90.3
9	93.3	90.2	91.8	93.8	95.9	94.7
10	97.0	92.9	97.3	97.7	98.4	98.2
11	99.2	97.3	100.0	100.0	98.4	100.0
12	99.8	99.1	100.0	100.0	100.0	100.0

Research/Supplemental Scales for the MMPI

Males   Staid, Personal Rigidity   (Si3)

	Total Sample	Age, yr				
		13	14	15	16	17
N	624	112	147	130	122	113
Median	7	8	7	7	7	6
Mean	7.03	7.69	7.20	6.77	7.10	6.40
SD	2.84	2.77	3.19	2.74	2.65	2.62
Min	0	0	1	1	0	1
Max	16	15	16	14	14	14

X	Percentage of Sample with Raw Score < X					
	Total Sample	13	14	15	16	17
0	0.0	0.0	0.0	0.0	0.0	0.0
1	0.3	0.9	0.0	0.0	0.8	0.0
2	1.4	0.9	1.4	2.3	1.6	0.9
3	3.8	0.9	4.8	6.2	2.5	4.4
4	10.9	8.0	14.3	13.1	6.6	11.5
5	21.3	15.2	25.9	19.2	17.2	28.3
6	30.0	20.5	33.3	28.5	27.9	38.9
7	44.7	33.0	43.5	49.2	43.4	54.0
8	56.7	46.4	51.7	63.1	55.7	67.3
9	70.0	61.6	63.3	74.6	71.3	80.5
10	81.1	72.3	76.2	85.4	82.8	89.4
11	88.5	83.9	84.4	90.8	91.0	92.9
12	93.8	94.6	90.5	95.4	94.3	94.7
13	96.8	95.5	96.6	97.7	95.9	98.2
14	98.1	98.2	96.6	97.7	99.2	99.1
15	99.5	99.1	98.6	100.0	100.0	100.0
16	99.8	100.0	99.3	100.0	100.0	100.0

Research/Supplemental Scales for the MMPI

Males   Hypersensitivity   (Si4)

	Total Sample	Age, yr				
		13	14	15	16	17
N	624	112	147	130	122	113
Median	3	3	3	3	3	3
Mean	3.13	3.04	3.18	3.10	3.25	3.03
SD	1.93	2.01	1.88	1.86	1.99	1.95
Min	0	0	0	0	0	0
Max	10	8	8	10	9	9

X	Percentage of Sample with Raw Score < X					
	Total Sample	13	14	15	16	17
0	0.0	0.0	0.0	0.0	0.0	0.0
1	6.4	9.8	6.8	3.8	6.6	5.3
2	19.2	23.2	17.0	17.7	15.6	23.9
3	42.8	45.5	40.1	44.6	38.5	46.0
4	62.8	61.6	61.9	62.3	63.9	64.6
5	77.9	75.9	77.6	81.5	77.0	77.0
6	88.1	88.4	85.7	90.8	86.1	90.3
7	93.9	93.8	94.6	93.8	92.6	94.7
8	97.1	97.3	98.6	96.9	95.9	96.5
9	99.4	100.0	100.0	99.2	98.4	99.1
10	99.8	100.0	100.0	99.2	100.0	100.0

Research/Supplemental Scales for the MMPI

Males   Distrust   (Si5)

	Total Sample	13	14	15	16	17
				Age, yr		
N	624	112	147	130	122	113
Median	6	6	7	6	6	6
Mean	6.17	5.95	6.59	6.06	6.33	5.81
SD	2.65	2.57	2.75	2.69	2.69	2.45
Min	0	0	0	0	1	0
Max	12	11	11	11	12	11

X	Total Sample	13	14	15	16	17
	Percentage of Sample with Raw Score < X					
0	0.0	0.0	0.0	0.0	0.0	0.0
1	1.3	1.8	2.0	1.5	0.0	0.9
2	3.8	4.5	4.8	3.8	1.6	4.4
3	9.1	10.7	8.2	10.0	6.6	10.6
4	18.4	19.6	12.9	20.0	18.9	22.1
5	27.9	28.6	21.8	33.8	28.7	27.4
6	40.9	40.2	36.7	42.3	42.6	43.4
7	53.2	56.3	49.0	53.8	51.6	56.6
8	65.2	72.3	58.5	62.3	61.5	74.3
9	77.6	82.1	68.7	76.9	75.4	87.6
10	89.3	91.1	85.0	90.8	87.7	92.9
11	96.6	98.2	93.2	98.5	95.1	99.1
12	99.5	100.0	100.0	100.0	97.5	100.0

Research/Supplemental Scales for the MMPI

Males   Physical-Somatic Concerns   (Si6)

		Age, yr				
	Total Sample	13	14	15	16	17
N	624	112	147	130	122	113
Median	3	3	3	3	3	3
Mean	3.05	3.17	3.17	2.87	3.17	2.87
SD	1.83	1.89	1.90	1.62	1.84	1.86
Min	0	0	0	0	0	0
Max	9	9	9	7	8	8

	Percentage of Sample with Raw Score < X					
X	Total Sample	13	14	15	16	17
0	0.0	0.0	0.0	0.0	0.0	0.0
1	6.9	5.4	6.8	8.5	6.6	7.1
2	20.7	20.5	18.4	20.0	19.7	25.7
3	41.5	42.0	42.2	42.3	35.2	46.0
4	62.5	57.1	58.5	65.4	61.5	70.8
5	78.8	76.8	76.9	83.1	77.0	80.5
6	90.2	88.4	87.8	94.6	90.2	90.3
7	95.8	95.5	95.2	99.2	95.1	93.8
8	98.6	98.2	98.0	100.0	97.5	99.1
9	99.7	99.1	99.3	100.0	100.0	100.0

WIGGINS CONTENT SCALES

The items of the 10 basic clinical scales of the MMPI were primarily selected by empirical means. Response patterns obtained from criterion groups having known psychologic and behavioral characteristics were compared with those of normal people, medical patients, and persons with various psychiatric diagnoses. Thus, the scales of the MMPI contain diverse item content and, in addition, some items are included on more than one scale because of the empirical selection procedures that were used.

However, another view also may be considered. Wiggins (1966, 1969) contended that a patient completing the MMPI is likely to view the experience as an opportunity to communicate symptoms, feelings, and attitudes to the examiner. Thus, the individual can choose to endorse various types of item content and may do so in a characteristic pattern. While there may be conscious or unconscious bias in the respondent's communication through the MMPI items, Wiggins stressed that such relatively direct messages from the patient should not be overlooked because they might provide useful information to supplement interpretations made from the basic clinical scales.

With these views in mind, Wiggins began his work by considering each of the original Hathaway and McKinley MMPI content categories as a scale. These Hathaway content-category scales were then scored on the MMPIs of 500 college students to yield a single value for each scale for each student. Internal consistency was evaluated by correlations between the totals for odd and even items. Subsequently, factor analytic procedures were carried out on the intercorrelation matrix composed of the 26 Hathaway content-category scores separately by sex; this yielded six interpretable factors for both men and women.

Encouraged by the internal consistency and factor structure, Wiggins then revised the original 26 Hathaway content categories. Items were reassigned, some original categories were eliminated and others were created, and some original categories were collapsed; all procedures, with one minor exception (unspecified), were carried out on a completely intuitive basis. This yielded 15 dimensions. The final selection of items was based on statistical procedures, however. An item was retained only if its point-biserial correlation with its category exceeded 0.30 and the correlation with its scale also exceeded its correlation with the remaining 14 categories. As a result, two categories (sleeping habits, obsessive-compulsive) were abandoned.

These procedures resulted in

> 13 mutually exclusive scales which were considered to be internally consistent, moderately independent, and representative of the major substantive clusters of the MMPI. All of these scales were based on rational regroupings of the original content categories proposed by Hathaway and McKinley. Six of these scales were further refined by item-analytic procedures. (Wiggins, 1966, p. 12)

Later, further work established norms and relationships with other MMPI scales (Wiggins, 1984; Wiggins, Goldberg, & Appelbaum, 1971). An annotated description of the Wiggins content categories follows.

1: Social Maladjustment (SOC). Approximates the concept of introversion-extroversion with high scorers tending to be socially bashful, shy, embarrassed, reticent, self-conscious, and extremely reserved. Low scorers are gregarious, confident, assertive, and fun-loving and relate quickly and easily to others.

2: Depression (DEP). High scorers represent classic depression with feelings of guilt, regret, worry, unhappiness, loss of concentration and motivation, reduced self-esteem, anxiety and apprehension, oversensitivity, being misunderstood and unworthy, and deserving of punishment.

3: Feminine Interests (FEM). High scorers admit to liking feminine games, hobbies, and vocations with denial of liking masculine games, hobbies, and vocations. High scores also may be earned by expressing a like for a broad range of interests and those viewed as socially desirable (e.g., the fine arts).

4: Poor Morale (MOR). High scores indicate lack of self-confidence, feelings of failure and despair, and tendencies to give up hope. Oversensitive to feelings and reactions of others, feels misunderstood or useless, and is likely to be socially suggestible. While there is overlap among MOR, SOC, and DEP, MOR emphasizes a lack of self-confidence and hypersensitivity to the opinions of others, whereas feelings of guilt and apprehension are stronger on DEP and lack of social poise is stronger on SOC.

5: Religious Fundamentalism (REL). A high score indicates a view of the self as religious and churchgoing, with many fundamentalist beliefs and a view of his or her faith as the true one.

6: Authority Conflict (AUT). High scorers tend to view life as a jungle with others seen as unscrupulous, dishonest, hypocritical, and motivated only by personal profit. They are competitive, feel rules are for others, have little respect for experts, and are mistrustful in general.

7: Psychoticism (PSY). High scorers admit to hallucinations, strange experiences, loss of control, and classic paranoid delusions of grandeur and persecution, feelings of unreality, daydreaming, and the sense that things are wrong while feeling misunderstood.

8: Organic Symptoms (ORG). High scorers describe symptoms of headache, nausea, dizziness, loss of motility and coordination, poor concentration and memory, and difficulty in speaking and reading. They describe sensations of hearing, smell, and skin, as well as loss of consciousness, that may be indicative of organic involvement.

9: Family Problems (FAM). High scorers feel that their home life was unpleasant and characterized by a lack of love, with parents viewed as unnecessarily critical, nervous, quarrelsome, and quick-tempered.

10: Manifest Hostility (HOS). High scorers admit to sadistic impulses with tendencies to be cross, grouchy, competitive, argumentative, uncooperative, socially aggressive, and retaliatory in interpersonal relationships.

11: Phobias (PHO). High scorers admit to many fears of the classic phobic variety (e.g., heights; dark, closed spaces).

12: Hypomania (HYP). High scorers are characterized by feelings of excitement, well-being, restlessness, tension, enthusiasm, broad interests, seeking change, cheerfulness, great energy, and difficulty with temper control.

13: Poor Health (HEA). High scorers express concern about their health and admit to various gastrointestinal symptoms, primarily those related to upset stomach and difficulty in elimination.

REFERENCES

Wiggins, J. S. (1966). Substantive dimensions of self-report in the MMPI item pool. *Psychological Monographs, 80*(22, Whole no. 630), 1–42.

Wiggins, J. S. (1969). Content dimensions in the MMPI. In J. N. Butcher (Ed.), *MMPI: Research developments and clinical applications* (pp. 127–180). New York: McGraw-Hill Book Company.

Wiggins, J. S. (1984). *MMPI content scales: Basic data for scoring and interpretation.* Unpublished data. (Personal communication: Dr. Jerry S. Wiggins, Department of Psychology, University of British Columbia, Vancouver, Canada).

Wiggins, J. S., Goldberg, L. R., & Appelbaum, M. (1971). MMPI content scales: Interpretative norms and correlations with other scales. *Journal of Consulting and Clinical Psychology, 37,* 403–410.

The items of the Wiggins Content Scales, and their direction for scoring, are listed below.

SOC: Social Maladjustment (27 Items)

The following items score if answered *true:*

52. I prefer to pass by school friends, or people I know but have not seen for a long time, unless they speak to me first.
171. It makes me uncomfortable to put on a stunt at a party even when others are doing the same sort of things.
172. I frequently have to fight against showing that I am bashful.
180. I find it hard to make talk when I meet new people.
201. I wish I were not so shy.
267. When in a group of people I have trouble thinking of the right things to talk about.
292. I am likely not to speak to people until they speak to me.
304. In school I found it very hard to talk before the class.
377. At parties I am more likely to sit by myself or with just one other person than to join in with the crowd.
384. I feel unable to tell anyone all about myself.
453.ª When I was a child I didn't care to be a member of a crowd or gang.
455. I am quite often not in on the gossip and talk of the group I belong to.
509. I sometimes find it hard to stick up for my rights because I am so reserved.

The following items score if answered *false:*

57. I am a good mixer.
91. I would like to be a nurse.
99. I like to go to parties and other affairs where there is lots of loud fun.
309. I seem to make friends about as quickly as others do.
371. I am not unusually self-conscious.
391. I love to go to dances.
449. I enjoy social gatherings just to be with people.
450. I enjoy the excitement of a crowd.
479. I do not mind meeting strangers.
482. While in trains, busses, etc., I often talk to strangers.
502. I like to let people know where I stand on things.
520. I strongly defend my own opinions as a rule.
521. In a group of people I would not be embarrassed to be called upon to start a discussion or give an opinion about something I know well.
547. I like parties and socials.

DEP: Depression (33 Items)

The following items score if answered *true:*

41. I have had periods of days, weeks, or months when I couldn't take care of things because I couldn't "get going."
61. I have not lived the right kind of life.
67. I wish I could be as happy as others seem to be.
76. Most of the time I feel blue.
94. I do many things which I regret afterwards (I regret things more or more often than others seem to).

104.   I don't seem to care what happens to me.
106.   Much of the time I feel as if I have done something wrong or evil.
158.   I cry easily.
202.   I believe I am a condemned person.
209.   I believe my sins are unpardonable.
210.   Everything tastes the same.
217.   I frequently find myself worrying about something.
259.   I have difficulty in starting to do things.
305.   Even when I am with people I feel lonely much of the time.
337.   I feel anxiety about something or someone almost all the time.
338.   I have certainly had more than my share of things to worry about.
339.   Most of the time I wish I were dead.
374.   At periods my mind seems to work more slowly than usual.
390.   I have often felt badly over being misunderstood when trying to keep someone from making a mistake.
396.   Often, even though everything is going fine for me, I feel that I don't care about anything.
413.   I deserve severe punishment for my sins.
414.   I am apt to take disappointments so keenly that I can't put them out of my mind.
487.   I feel like giving up quickly when things go wrong.
517.   I cannot do anything well.
518.   I have often felt guilty because I have pretended to feel more sorry about something than I really was.
526.   The future seems hopeless to me.
543.   Several times a week I feel as if something dreadful is about to happen.

The following items score if answered *false:*

  8.   My daily life is full of things that keep me interested.
 79.   My feelings are not easily hurt.
 88.   I usually feel that life is worthwhile.
207.   I enjoy many different kinds of play and recreation.
379.   I very seldom have spells of the blues.
407.   I am usually calm and not easily upset.

FEM: Feminine interests (30 Items)

The following items score if answered *true:*

 70.[a] I used to like drop-the-handkerchief.
 74.   I have often wished I were a girl. (Or if you are a girl) I have never been sorry that I am a girl.
 77.   I enjoy reading love stories.
 78.   I like poetry.
 87.   I would like to be a florist.
 92.   I would like to be a nurse.
126.   I like dramatics.
132.   I like collecting flowers or growing house plants.
140.   I like to cook.
149.   I used to keep a diary.
203.   If I were a reporter I would very much like to report news of the theater.
261.   If I were an artist I would like to draw flowers.
295.[a] I liked "Alice in Wonderland" by Lewis Carroll.

463.   I used to like hopscotch.
538.[a] I think I would like the work of a dressmaker.
554.[a] If I were an artist I would like to draw children.
557.[a] I would like to be a private secretary.
562.   The one to whom I was most attached and whom I most admired as a child was a woman. (Mother, sister, aunt, or other woman.)

The following items score if answered *false*:

1.   I like mechanics magazines.
81.   I think I would like the kind of work a forest ranger does.
219.   I think I would like the work of a building contractor.
221.   I like science.
223.   I very much like hunting.
283.   If I were a reporter I would very much like to report sporting news.
300.   There never was a time in my life when I liked to play with dolls.
423.[a] I like or have liked fishing very much.
434.   I would like to be an auto racer.
537.[a] I would like to hunt lions in Africa.
552.   I like to read about science.
563.   I like adventure stories better than romantic stories.

MOR: *Poor Morale (23 Items)*

The following items score if answered *true*:

84.   These days I find it hard not to give up hope of amounting to something.
86.   I am certainly lacking in self-confidence.
138.   Criticism or scolding hurts me terribly.
142.   I certainly feel useless at times.
244.   My way of doing things is apt to be misunderstood by others.
321.   I am easily embarrassed.
357.   I have several times given up doing a thing because I thought too little of my ability.
361.   I am inclined to take things hard.
375.[a] When I am feeling very happy and active, someone who is blue or low will spoil it all.
382.   I wish I could get over worrying about things I have said that may have injured other people's feelings.
389.   My plans have frequently seemed so full of difficulties that I have had to give them up.
395.   The future is too uncertain for a person to make serious plans.
397.   I have sometimes felt that difficulties were piling up so high that I could not overcome them.
398.   I often think, "I wish I were a child again."
411.   It makes me feel like a failure when I hear of the success of someone I know well.
416.   It bothers me to have someone watch me at work even though I know I can do it well.
418.   At times I think I am no good at all.
431.   I worry quite a bit over possible misfortunes.
531.   People can pretty easily change me even though I thought that my mind was already made up on a subject.
549.   I shrink from facing a crisis or difficulty.
555.   I sometimes feel that I am about to go to pieces.

The following items score if answered *false:*

122.   I seem to be about as capable and smart as most others around me.
264.   I am entirely self-confident.

REL: *Religious Fundamentalism (12 Items)*

The following items score if answered *true:*

58.[a]   Everything is turning out just like the prophets of the Bible said it would.
95.[a]   I go to church almost every week.
98.[a]   I believe in the second coming of Christ.
115.   I believe in a life hereafter.
206.[a]   I am very religious (more than most people).
249.[a]   I believe there is a Devil and a Hell in afterlife.
258.[a]   I believe there is a God.
373.[a]   I feel sure that there is only one true religion.
483.   Christ performed miracles such as changing water into wine.
488.   I pray several times every week.
490.   I read in the Bible several times a week.

The following item scores if answered *false:*

491.   I have no patience with people who believe there is only one true religion.

AUT: *Authority Conflict (20 Items)*

The following items score if answered *true:*

59.   I have often had to take orders from someone who did not know as much as I did.
71.   I think a great many people exaggerate their misfortunes in order to gain the sympathy and help of others.
93.   I think most people would lie to get ahead.
116.   I enjoy a race or game better when I bet on it.
117.   Most people are honest chiefly through fear of being caught.
118.   In school I was sometimes sent to the principal for cutting up.
124.   Most people will use somewhat unfair means to gain profit or an advantage rather than to lose it.
250.   I don't blame anyone for trying to grab everything he can get in this world.
265.   It is safer to trust nobody.
277.   At times I have been so entertained by the cleverness of a crook that I have hoped he would get by with it.
280.   Most people make friends because friends are likely to be useful to them.
298.   If several people find themselves in trouble, the best thing for them to do is to agree upon a story and stick to it.
313.   The man who provides temptation by leaving valuable property unprotected is about as much to blame for its theft as the one who steals it.
316.   I think nearly anyone would tell a lie to keep out of trouble.
319.   Most people inwardly dislike putting themselves out to help other people.
406.   I have often met people who were supposed to be experts who were no better than I.
436.   People generally demand more respect for their own rights than they are willing to allow for others.

437.   It is all right to get around the law if you don't actually break it.
446.   I enjoy gambling for small stakes.

The following item scores if answered *false:*

294.   I have never been in trouble with the law.

PSY: Psychoticism (48 Items)

The following items score if answered *true:*

16.   I am sure I get a raw deal from life.
22.   At times I have fits of laughing and crying that I cannot control.
24.   No one seems to understand me.
27.   Evil spirits possess me at times.
33.   I have had very peculiar and strange experiences.
35.   If people had not had it in for me I would have been much more successful.
40.   Most any time I would rather sit and daydream than to do anything else.
48.   When I am with people, I am bothered by hearing very queer things.
50.   My soul sometimes leaves my body.
66.   I see things or animals or people around me that others do not see.
73.   I am an important person.
110.   Someone has it in for me.
121.   I believe I am being plotted against.
123.   I believe I am being followed.
127.   I know who is responsible for most of my troubles.
136.   I commonly wonder what hidden reason another person may have for doing something nice for me.
151.   Someone has been trying to poison me.
168.   There is something wrong with my mind.
184.   I commonly hear voices without knowing where they come from.
194.   I have had attacks in which I could not control my movements or speech but in which I knew what was going on around me.
197.   Someone has been trying to rob me.
200.   There are persons who are trying to steal my thoughts and ideas.
232.   I have been inspired to a program of life based on duty which I have since carefully followed.
275.   Someone has control over my mind.
278.   I have often felt that strangers were looking at me critically.
284.   I am sure I am being talked about.
291.   At one or more times in my life I felt that someone was making me do things by hypnotizing me.
293.   Someone has been trying to influence my mind.
299.   I think that I feel more intensely than most people do.
312.   I dislike having people about me.
317.   I am more sensitive than most other people.
334.   Peculiar odors come to me at times.
341.   At times I hear so well it bothers me.
345.   I often feel as if things were not real.
348.   I tend to be on my guard with people who are somewhat more friendly than I had expected.
349.   I have strange and peculiar thoughts.
350.   I hear strange things when I am alone.

364.   People say insulting and vulgar things about me.
400.   If given the chance I could do some things that would be of great benefit to the world.
420.   I have had some very unusual religious experiences.
433.[a] I used to have imaginary companions.
448.   I am bothered by people outside, on streetcars, in stores, etc., watching me.
476.[a] I am a special agent of God.
511.   I have a daydream life about which I do not tell other people.
551.   Sometimes I am sure that other people can tell what I am thinking.

The following items score if answered *false:*

198.   I daydream very little.
347.   I have no enemies who really wish to harm me.
464.   I have never seen a vision.

ORG: *Organic Symptoms (36 Items)*

The following items score if answered *true:*

23.   I am troubled by attacks of nausea and vomiting.
44.   Much of the time my head seems to hurt all over.
108.   There seems to be a fullness in my head or nose most of the time.
114.   Often I feel as if there were a tight band around my head.
156.   I have had periods in which I carried on activities without knowing later what I had been doing.
159.   I cannot understand what I read as well as I used to.
161.   The top of my head sometimes feels tender.
186.   I frequently notice my hand shakes when I try to do something.
189.   I feel weak all over much of the time.
251.   I have had blank spells in which my activities were interrupted and I did not know what was going on around me.
273.   I have numbness in one or more regions of my skin.
332.   Sometimes my voice leaves me or changes even though I have no cold.
335.   I cannot keep my mind on one thing.
541.[a] My skin seems to be unusually sensitive to touch.
560.   I am greatly bothered by forgetting where I put things.

The following items score if answered *false:*

46.   My judgment is better than it ever was.
68.   I hardly ever feel pain in the back of the neck.
103.   I have little or no trouble with my muscles twitching or jumping.
119.   My speech is the same as always (not faster or slower, or slurring; no hoarseness).
154.   I have never had a fit or convulsion.
174.   I have never had a fainting spell.
175.   I seldom or never have dizzy spells.
178.   My memory seems to be all right.
185.   My hearing is apparently as good as that of most people.
187.   My hands have not become clumsy or awkward.
188.   I can read a long while without tiring my eyes.
190.   I have very few headaches.
192.   I have had no difficulty in keeping my balance in walking.

243.   I have few or no pains.
274.   My eyesight is as good as it has been for years.
281.   I do not often notice my ears ringing or buzzing.
330.   I have never been paralyzed or had any unusual weakness of any of my muscles.
405.   I have no trouble swallowing.
496.[a]   I have never seen things doubled (that is, an object never looks like two objects to me without my being able to make it look like one object).
508.[a]   I believe my sense of smell is as good as other people's.
540.[a]   My face has never been paralyzed.

FAM: Family Problems (16 Items)

The following items score if answered *true*:

21.   At times I have very much wanted to leave home.
212.   My people treat me more like a child than a grown-up.
216.   There is very little love and companionship in my family as compared to other homes.
224.   My parents have often objected to the kind of people I went around with.
226.   Some of my family have habits that bother and annoy me very much.
239.   I have been disappointed in love.
245.   My parents and family find more fault with me than they should.
325.   The things that some of my family have done have frightened me.
327.   My mother or father often made me obey even when I thought that it was unreasonable.
421.   One or more members of my family is very nervous.
516.   Some of my family have quick tempers.

The following items score if answered *false*:

65.   I loved my father.
96.   I have very few quarrels with members of my family.
137.   I believe that my home life is as pleasant as that of most people I know.
220.   I loved my mother.
527.   The members of my family and my close relatives get along quite well.

HOS: Manifest Hostility (27 Items)

The following items score if answered *true*:

28.   When someone does me a wrong, I feel I should pay him back if I can, just for the principle of the thing.
39.   At times I feel like smashing things.
80.   I sometimes tease animals.
89.   It takes a lot of argument to convince most people of the truth.
109.   Some people are so bossy that I feel like doing the opposite of what they request, even though I know they are right.
129.   Often I can't understand why I have been so cross and grouchy.
139.   Sometimes I feel as if I must injure either myself or someone else.
145.   At times I feel like picking a fist fight with someone.
162.   I resent having anyone take me in so cleverly that I have had to admit that it was one on me.
218.   It does not bother me particularly to see animals suffer.

269. I can easily make other people afraid of me, and sometimes do for the fun of it.
282. Once in a while I feel hate toward members of my family whom I usually love.
336. I easily become impatient with people.
355. Sometimes I enjoy hurting persons I love.
363. At times I have enjoyed being hurt by someone I loved.
368. I have sometimes stayed away from another person because I feared doing or saying something that I might regret afterwards.
393. Horses that don't pull should be beaten or kicked.
410. I would certainly enjoy beating a crook at his own game.
417. I am often so annoyed when someone tries to get ahead of me in a line of people that I speak to him about it.
426. I have at times had to be rough with people who were rude or annoying.
438. There are certain people whom I dislike so much that I am inwardly pleased when they are catching it for something they have done.
447. I am often inclined to go out of my way to win a point with someone who opposed me.
452.[a] I like to poke fun at people.
468. I am often sorry because I am so cross and grouchy.
469. I have often found people jealous of my good ideas, just because they had not thought of them first.
495. I usually "lay my cards on the table" with people that I am trying to correct or improve.
536. It makes me angry to have people hurry me.

The following items score if answered *false*:
(none)

PHO: Phobias (27 Items)

The following items score if answered *true*:

166. I am afraid when I look down from a high place.
182. I am afraid of losing my mind.
351. I get anxious and upset when I have to make a short trip away from home.
352. I have been afraid of things or people that I knew could not hurt me.
360. Almost every day something happens to frighten me.
365. I feel uneasy indoors.
385. Lightning is one of my fears.
388. I am afraid to be alone in the dark.
392. A windstorm terrifies me.
473. Whenever possible I avoid being in a crowd.
480. I am often afraid of the dark.
492. I dread the thought of an earthquake.
494. I am afraid of finding myself in a closet or small closed place.
499. I must admit that I have at times been worried beyond reason over something that really did not matter.
525. I am made nervous by certain animals.
553. I am afraid of being alone in a wide-open place.

The following items score if answered *false*:

128. The sight of blood neither frightens me nor makes me sick.
131. I do not worry about catching diseases.
169. I am not afraid to handle money.

176.   I do not have a great fear of snakes.
287.   I have very few fears compared to my friends.
353.   I have no dread of going into a room by myself where other people have already gathered and are talking.
367.   I am not afraid of fire.
401.   I have no fear of water.
412.[a] I do not dread seeing a doctor about a sickness or injury.
522.   I have no fear of spiders.
539.   I am not afraid of mice.

HYP: Hypomania (25 Items)

The following items score if answered *true:*

13.   I work under a great deal of tension.
134.   At times my thoughts have raced ahead faster than I could speak them.
146.   I have the wanderlust and am never happy unless I am roaming or traveling about.
181.   When I get bored I like to stir up some excitement.
196.   I like to visit places where I have never been before.
228.   At times I feel that I can make up my mind with unusually great ease.
234.   I get mad easily and then get over it soon.
238.   I have periods of such great restlessness that I cannot sit long in a chair.
248.   Sometimes without any reason or even when things are going wrong, I feel excitedly happy, "on top of the world."
266.   Once a week or oftener I become very excited.
268.   Something exciting will almost always pull me out of it when I am feeling low.
272.   At times I am all full of energy.
296.   I have periods in which I feel unusually cheerful without any special reason.
340.   Sometimes I become so excited that I find it hard to get to sleep.
342.   I forget right away what people say to me.
372.[a] I tend to be interested in several different hobbies rather than to stick to one of them for a long time.
381.   I am often said to be hotheaded.
386.   I like to keep people guessing what I'm going to do next.
409.[a] At times I have worn myself out by undertaking too much.
439.   It makes me nervous to have to wait.
445.   I was fond of excitement when I was young (or in childhood).
465.   I have several times had a change of heart about my life work.
500.   I readily become one hundred per cent sold on a good idea.
505.   I have had periods when I felt so full of pep that sleep did not seem necessary for days at a time.
506.   I am a high-strung person.

The following items score if answered *false:*
(none)

HEA: Poor Health (28 Items)

The following items score if answered *true:*

10.   There seems to be a lump in my throat much of the time.
14.[a] I have diarrhea once a month or more.
29.   I am bothered by acid stomach several times a week.

34.   I have a cough most of the time.
72.   I am troubled by discomfort in the pit of my stomach every few days or oftener.
125. I have a great deal of stomach trouble.
279. I drink an unusually large amount of water every day.
424.[a] I feel hungry almost all the time.
519.[a] There is something wrong with my sex organs.
544. I feel tired a good deal of the time.

The following items score if answered *false:*

2.   I have a good appetite.
18.   I am very seldom troubled by constipation.
36.   I seldom worry about my health.
51.   I am in just as good physical health as most of my friends.
55.   I am almost never bothered by pains over the heart or in my chest.
63.[a]   I have had no difficulty in starting or holding my bowel movement.
130. I have never vomited blood or coughed up blood.
153. During the past few years I have been well most of the time.
155. I am neither gaining nor losing weight.
163. I do not tire quickly.
193. I do not have spells of hay fever or asthma.
214. I have never had any breaking out on my skin that has worried me.
230. I hardly ever notice my heart pounding and I am seldom short of breath.
462.[a] I have had no difficulty starting or holding my urine.
474.[a] I have to urinate no more often than others.
486.[a] I have never noticed any blood in my urine.
533.[a] I am not bothered by a great deal of belching of gas from my stomach.
542.[a] I have never had any black tarry-looking bowel movements.

---

[a]Items that were deleted from the original MMPI item pool during construction of the MMPI-2.

Research/Supplemental Scales for the MMPI

Females   Social Maladjustment   (SOC)

		Age, yr				
	Total Sample	13	14	15	16	17
N	691	136	153	127	138	137
Median	9	10	10	9	10	8
Mean	9.72	10.42	9.65	9.40	10.24	8.87
SD	5.06	4.50	4.92	5.10	5.48	5.19
Min	0	1	1	1	1	0
Max	27	25	27	24	27	23

	Percentage of Sample with Raw Score < X					
X	Total Sample	13	14	15	16	17
0	0.0	0.0	0.0	0.0	0.0	0.0
1	0.3	0.0	0.0	0.0	0.0	1.5
2	1.6	0.7	2.6	1.6	1.4	1.5
3	4.8	2.2	6.5	4.7	2.9	7.3
4	9.6	5.1	9.2	12.6	5.8	15.3
5	15.8	8.8	17.0	15.0	14.5	23.4
6	22.1	11.8	23.5	25.2	21.0	29.2
7	30.2	21.3	27.5	35.4	31.9	35.8
8	37.3	26.5	34.0	42.5	36.2	48.2
9	45.6	37.5	40.5	49.6	47.1	54.0
10	51.7	44.1	49.7	54.3	50.0	60.6
11	59.0	53.7	58.8	62.2	54.3	66.4
12	67.4	63.2	69.9	69.3	62.3	72.3
13	73.4	68.4	75.8	74.0	69.6	78.8
14	79.0	75.7	81.7	78.7	76.1	82.5
15	81.8	80.9	83.7	81.9	78.3	83.9
16	86.1	85.3	87.6	87.4	83.3	86.9
17	89.0	89.0	89.5	91.3	85.5	89.8
18	92.2	94.1	92.8	92.1	88.4	93.4
19	94.1	97.1	94.8	93.7	91.3	93.4
20	95.2	98.5	96.7	94.5	91.3	94.9
21	97.1	98.5	98.0	97.6	94.9	96.4
22	98.0	98.5	98.7	97.6	96.4	98.5
23	98.8	98.5	99.3	99.2	97.8	99.3
24	99.3	99.3	99.3	99.2	98.6	100.0
25	99.4	99.3	99.3	100.0	98.6	100.0
26	99.7	100.0	99.3	100.0	99.3	100.0
27	99.7	100.0	99.3	100.0	99.3	100.0

Research/Supplemental Scales for the MMPI

Females   Depression   (DEP)

	Total Sample	Age, yr				
		13	14	15	16	17
N	691	136	153	127	138	137
Median	10	9	9	10	11	9
Mean	10.26	9.67	9.87	10.46	11.75	9.57
SD	5.84	5.56	5.43	6.19	6.30	5.54
Min	0	0	0	0	0	0
Max	29	26	28	29	28	28

X	Percentage of Sample with Raw Score < X					
	Total Sample	13	14	15	16	17
0	0.0	0.0	0.0	0.0	0.0	0.0
1	1.6	3.7	1.3	0.8	0.7	1.5
2	2.7	3.7	2.6	2.4	1.4	3.6
3	4.8	5.9	3.9	5.5	2.9	5.8
4	11.3	14.0	9.8	13.4	8.0	11.7
5	17.4	22.1	15.7	18.1	11.6	19.7
6	24.0	26.5	25.5	24.4	15.9	27.7
7	29.7	32.4	30.1	31.5	22.5	32.1
8	35.6	39.7	35.3	37.0	27.5	38.7
9	42.5	46.3	43.8	40.9	36.2	45.3
10	49.5	52.9	51.6	48.8	40.6	53.3
11	57.0	58.8	59.5	56.7	48.6	61.3
12	63.0	65.4	66.7	61.4	52.2	68.6
13	68.3	68.4	71.9	65.4	60.1	75.2
14	73.2	71.3	77.1	73.2	65.9	78.1
15	78.7	77.9	83.0	78.0	70.3	83.9
16	82.1	83.8	86.3	79.5	73.9	86.1
17	85.4	89.7	88.2	81.1	78.3	89.1
18	88.3	92.6	92.2	84.3	79.7	92.0
19	90.7	93.4	93.5	89.0	83.3	94.2
20	91.8	94.9	93.5	90.6	84.8	94.9
21	93.5	96.3	94.1	92.9	88.4	95.6
22	95.1	97.8	96.1	93.7	92.0	95.6
23	96.1	98.5	96.7	96.1	93.5	95.6
24	97.3	98.5	98.0	96.9	95.7	97.1
25	98.1	99.3	98.7	96.9	97.1	98.5
26	98.7	99.3	99.3	98.4	97.1	99.3
27	99.0	100.0	99.3	98.4	97.8	99.3
28	99.3	100.0	99.3	99.2	98.6	99.3
29	99.9	100.0	100.0	99.2	100.0	100.0

Research/Supplemental Scales for the MMPI

Females   Feminine Interests   (FEM)

		Age, yr				
	Total Sample	13	14	15	16	17
N	691	136	153	127	138	137
Median	19	19	19	19	19	19
Mean	18.92	18.84	18.76	19.11	19.07	18.85
SD	3.37	3.49	3.39	3.29	3.29	3.40
Min	8	9	10	9	9	8
Max	29	28	29	27	27	25

Percentage of Sample with Raw Score < X

X	Total Sample	13	14	15	16	17
8	0.0	0.0	0.0	0.0	0.0	0.0
9	0.1	0.0	0.0	0.0	0.0	0.7
10	0.7	0.7	0.0	0.8	0.7	1.5
11	1.4	2.2	1.3	1.6	0.7	1.5
12	2.2	2.2	2.0	1.6	2.2	2.9
13	3.6	3.7	2.6	3.1	2.9	5.8
14	5.9	5.9	5.9	5.5	5.1	7.3
15	9.4	11.8	9.8	6.3	8.0	10.9
16	14.8	18.4	16.3	11.8	12.3	14.6
17	23.6	25.7	26.8	19.7	23.2	21.9
18	31.5	34.6	34.6	26.8	28.3	32.8
19	42.1	41.2	45.8	40.2	42.0	40.9
20	55.3	52.2	60.1	55.9	54.3	53.3
21	68.5	68.4	69.3	70.1	68.1	66.4
22	77.3	76.5	79.1	79.5	76.1	75.2
23	86.1	88.2	86.9	85.8	82.6	86.9
24	92.2	92.6	92.2	91.3	90.6	94.2
25	96.4	95.6	96.7	93.7	97.1	98.5
26	98.3	97.8	97.4	96.9	99.3	100.0
27	99.1	99.3	98.7	98.4	99.3	100.0
28	99.7	99.3	99.3	100.0	100.0	100.0
29	99.9	100.0	99.3	100.0	100.0	100.0

Research/Supplemental Scales for the MMPI

Females   Poor Morale   (MOR)

	Total Sample	13	14	15	16	17
N	691	136	153	127	138	137
Median	11	11	10	11	12	11
Mean	11.06	11.07	10.55	11.32	12.49	9.93
SD	5.03	4.89	4.93	5.22	4.92	4.91
Min	0	1	0	2	1	0
Max	22	22	21	22	22	21

Percentage of Sample with Raw Score < X

X	Total Sample	13	14	15	16	17
0	0.0	0.0	0.0	0.0	0.0	0.0
1	0.4	0.0	0.7	0.0	0.0	1.5
2	2.6	2.9	3.9	0.0	0.7	5.1
3	4.3	3.7	4.6	1.6	2.2	9.5
4	6.4	4.4	6.5	3.9	2.9	13.9
5	10.0	8.8	11.8	8.7	5.1	15.3
6	15.8	15.4	19.0	15.0	8.0	21.2
7	21.1	19.9	24.8	23.6	13.8	23.4
8	27.2	27.2	30.1	30.7	17.4	30.7
9	33.0	33.8	34.6	34.6	23.2	38.7
10	39.9	40.4	42.5	40.2	29.0	47.4
11	45.4	47.1	50.3	44.9	34.8	49.6
12	52.8	51.5	55.6	52.8	44.9	59.1
13	58.8	55.1	62.7	57.5	50.7	67.2
14	66.4	65.4	68.6	66.1	56.5	75.2
15	72.5	72.1	76.5	69.3	62.3	81.8
16	78.1	78.7	80.4	75.6	67.4	88.3
17	84.9	86.8	88.9	81.1	76.1	91.2
18	89.4	91.2	93.5	87.4	81.2	93.4
19	93.2	94.9	95.4	90.6	88.4	96.4
20	95.1	95.6	96.7	92.1	92.0	98.5
21	97.3	98.5	98.0	94.5	95.7	99.3
22	99.3	99.3	100.0	97.6	99.3	100.0

Research/Supplemental Scales for the MMPI

Females   Religious Fundamentalism   (REL)

		Age, yr				
	Total Sample	13	14	15	16	17
N	691	136	153	127	138	137
Median	7	7	7	7	7	7
Mean	7.03	6.93	7.42	6.90	6.78	7.04
SD	2.50	2.43	2.34	2.51	2.73	2.48
Min	0	0	1	1	1	1
Max	12	12	12	12	12	12

	Percentage of Sample with Raw Score < X					
X	Total Sample	13	14	15	16	17
0	0.0	0.0	0.0	0.0	0.0	0.0
1	0.1	0.7	0.0	0.0	0.0	0.0
2	1.7	2.2	2.0	1.6	1.4	1.5
3	4.8	4.4	3.3	5.5	5.8	5.1
4	9.7	8.8	4.6	11.0	14.5	10.2
5	15.8	14.7	9.2	18.1	22.5	15.3
6	25.5	25.0	17.6	26.8	33.3	25.5
7	38.9	39.7	33.3	39.4	44.9	38.0
8	57.3	61.8	52.9	56.7	60.1	55.5
9	72.4	73.5	69.3	77.2	72.5	70.1
10	82.8	84.6	80.4	85.8	79.7	83.9
11	91.2	93.4	88.9	91.3	89.1	93.4
12	97.3	97.8	96.7	96.9	97.8	97.1

336

Research/Supplemental Scales for the MMPI

Females   Authority Conflict   (AUT)

| | | Age, yr | | | | |
	Total Sample	13	14	15	16	17
N	691	136	153	127	138	137
Median	9	9	9	10	10	8
Mean	9.18	9.41	9.15	9.55	9.36	8.47
SD	3.72	3.55	3.66	3.59	3.88	3.83
Min	0	0	0	0	0	0
Max	19	17	18	19	19	16

Percentage of Sample with Raw Score < X

X	Total Sample	13	14	15	16	17
0	0.0	0.0	0.0	0.0	0.0	0.0
1	0.9	0.7	0.7	0.8	0.7	1.5
2	2.3	2.2	0.7	0.8	4.3	3.6
3	4.6	3.7	3.9	2.4	6.5	6.6
4	7.7	6.6	7.2	5.5	7.2	11.7
5	11.9	9.6	10.5	11.8	10.1	17.5
6	16.2	13.2	15.7	13.4	15.9	22.6
7	23.6	19.1	22.9	18.1	24.6	32.8
8	32.3	27.2	32.7	28.3	31.9	40.9
9	41.2	38.2	42.5	37.0	37.7	50.4
10	52.5	50.7	56.2	48.8	48.6	57.7
11	62.1	60.3	67.3	59.1	59.4	63.5
12	71.6	72.8	73.9	65.4	70.3	75.2
13	79.6	79.4	78.4	78.7	79.0	82.5
14	88.1	86.0	88.9	89.8	84.8	91.2
15	92.6	94.1	91.5	92.9	88.4	96.4
16	96.4	96.3	94.8	95.3	97.1	98.5
17	98.8	98.5	98.0	98.4	99.3	100.0
18	99.6	100.0	99.3	99.2	99.3	100.0
19	99.7	100.0	100.0	99.2	99.3	100.0

Research/Supplemental Scales for the MMPI

Females   Psychoticism   (PSY)

| | | Age, yr | | | | |
	Total Sample	13	14	15	16	17
N	691	136	153	127	138	137
Median	12	12	12	12	13	11
Mean	13.19	13.46	13.42	13.31	13.93	11.78
SD	6.73	6.91	6.87	6.44	7.29	5.91
Min	1	3	2	2	1	1
Max	37	33	36	37	36	35

Percentage of Sample with Raw Score < X

X	Total Sample	13	14	15	16	17
1	0.0	0.0	0.0	0.0	0.0	0.0
2	0.3	0.0	0.0	0.0	0.7	0.7
3	1.2	0.0	0.7	0.8	2.9	1.5
4	3.2	2.2	2.0	1.6	5.1	5.1
5	6.2	5.9	4.6	3.9	7.2	9.5
6	10.1	11.8	9.8	5.5	10.9	12.4
7	14.3	14.7	12.4	11.0	13.8	19.7
8	20.7	19.9	20.9	18.9	16.7	27.0
9	27.1	25.0	25.5	26.0	24.6	34.3
10	32.4	33.1	30.7	30.7	29.7	38.0
11	39.9	39.7	40.5	34.6	39.1	45.3
12	46.3	47.1	48.4	40.2	43.5	51.8
13	52.4	51.5	52.9	50.4	47.1	59.9
14	58.3	55.9	58.2	60.6	53.6	63.5
15	64.1	62.5	65.4	64.6	58.0	70.1
16	68.3	67.6	67.3	70.1	62.3	74.5
17	72.6	71.3	70.6	74.8	68.8	78.1
18	77.4	73.5	75.2	81.1	73.9	83.9
19	80.8	77.2	77.8	83.5	76.8	89.1
20	83.2	80.1	81.7	85.8	79.0	89.8
21	86.3	84.6	83.7	88.2	81.9	93.4
22	88.4	88.2	87.6	89.0	82.6	94.9
23	90.3	89.7	89.5	89.8	85.5	97.1
24	91.8	90.4	90.8	91.3	89.1	97.1
25	93.1	92.6	92.2	92.1	90.6	97.8
26	94.2	92.6	92.8	96.1	92.0	97.8
27	95.2	94.1	94.8	96.1	92.8	98.5
28	96.2	95.6	96.1	96.9	94.2	98.5
29	96.7	95.6	96.7	97.6	94.9	98.5
30	97.1	96.3	97.4	97.6	95.7	98.5

Females   Psychoticism   (PSY)
                      (Continued)

X	Total Sample	Percentage of Sample with Raw Score < X				
		13	14	15	16	17
31	97.8	97.8	98.0	97.6	97.1	98.5
32	98.6	98.5	98.0	97.6	99.3	99.3
33	98.7	98.5	98.0	98.4	99.3	99.3
34	99.1	100.0	98.7	98.4	99.3	99.3
35	99.4	100.0	99.3	99.2	99.3	99.3
36	99.6	100.0	99.3	99.2	99.3	100.0
37	99.9	100.0	100.0	99.2	100.0	100.0

Research/Supplemental Scales for the MMPI

Females   Organic Symptoms   (ORG)

		Age, yr				
	Total Sample	13	14	15	16	17
N	691	136	153	127	138	137
Median	6	6	5	6	6	5
Mean	6.75	7.00	6.31	6.94	7.75	5.83
SD	5.05	4.77	4.50	5.61	5.76	4.41
Min	0	0	0	0	0	0
Max	31	19	18	31	26	21

Percentage of Sample with Raw Score < X

X	Total Sample	13	14	15	16	17
0	0.0	0.0	0.0	0.0	0.0	0.0
1	3.3	2.2	2.6	4.7	2.9	4.4
2	10.3	12.5	9.8	14.2	6.5	8.8
3	21.6	18.4	23.5	26.0	15.2	24.8
4	30.2	24.3	33.3	32.3	26.8	34.3
5	39.8	36.0	44.4	34.6	35.5	47.4
6	49.9	47.1	52.9	48.0	42.0	59.1
7	58.9	55.1	62.1	56.7	52.9	67.2
8	64.4	61.0	65.4	63.8	59.4	72.3
9	69.8	64.7	70.6	70.9	64.5	78.1
10	74.5	72.8	73.9	75.6	67.4	83.2
11	78.6	78.7	79.7	77.2	71.7	85.4
12	82.9	83.8	85.6	81.1	76.8	86.9
13	87.0	84.6	90.2	85.8	81.9	92.0
14	89.1	85.3	90.8	87.4	87.7	94.2
15	91.0	88.2	92.8	89.8	89.1	94.9
16	93.3	92.6	94.8	92.9	90.6	95.6
17	94.9	95.6	97.4	93.7	91.3	96.4
18	95.9	97.8	98.7	93.7	92.8	96.4
19	97.0	99.3	100.0	93.7	94.2	97.1
20	98.0	100.0	100.0	95.3	94.9	99.3
21	98.4	100.0	100.0	97.6	94.9	99.3
22	99.0	100.0	100.0	98.4	96.4	100.0
23	99.1	100.0	100.0	99.2	96.4	100.0
24	99.3	100.0	100.0	99.2	97.1	100.0
25	99.4	100.0	100.0	99.2	97.8	100.0
26	99.6	100.0	100.0	99.2	98.6	100.0
27	99.9	100.0	100.0	99.2	100.0	100.0
28	99.9	100.0	100.0	99.2	100.0	100.0
29	99.9	100.0	100.0	99.2	100.0	100.0

Females   Organic Symptoms   (ORG)
                                      (Continued)

X	Total Sample	Percentage of Sample with Raw Score < X				
		13	14	15	16	17
30	99.9	100.0	100.0	99.2	100.0	100.0
31	99.9	100.0	100.0	99.2	100.0	100.0

Research/Supplemental Scales for the MMPI

Females   Family Problems   (FAM)

				Age, yr		
	Total Sample	13	14	15	16	17
N	691	136	153	127	138	137
Median	6	6	6	7	7	6
Mean	6.44	6.13	6.13	6.95	7.01	6.05
SD	3.18	3.04	3.24	3.17	3.18	3.18
Min	0	0	0	1	1	0
Max	15	14	14	15	15	14

	Percentage of Sample with Raw Score < X					
X	Total Sample	13	14	15	16	17
0	0.0	0.0	0.0	0.0	0.0	0.0
1	1.2	2.2	1.3	0.0	0.0	2.2
2	5.8	6.6	9.2	3.9	3.6	5.1
3	10.1	8.8	12.4	8.7	6.5	13.9
4	18.7	21.3	20.9	13.4	13.8	23.4
5	31.0	31.6	36.6	27.6	24.6	33.6
6	40.8	45.6	45.1	33.1	35.5	43.8
7	52.1	55.9	56.2	44.9	44.2	58.4
8	63.7	67.6	66.7	54.3	57.2	71.5
9	74.4	78.7	77.1	66.1	68.8	80.3
10	83.2	87.5	83.7	81.1	77.5	86.1
11	88.1	89.0	88.9	89.0	84.1	89.8
12	92.5	96.3	92.8	91.3	88.4	93.4
13	96.1	97.1	96.7	94.5	96.4	95.6
14	98.6	99.3	99.3	97.6	98.6	97.8
15	99.7	100.0	100.0	99.2	99.3	100.0

Research/Supplemental Scales for the MMPI

Females   Manifest Hostility   (HOS)

				Age, yr		
	Total Sample	13	14	15	16	17
N	691	136	153	127	138	137
Median	12	12	12	13	13	11
Mean	12.14	12.46	11.97	12.54	12.75	11.04
SD	4.47	4.54	4.56	4.47	4.30	4.31
Min	1	3	2	3	1	1
Max	24	23	23	24	21	23

Percentage of Sample with Raw Score < X

X	Total Sample	13	14	15	16	17
1	0.0	0.0	0.0	0.0	0.0	0.0
2	0.3	0.0	0.0	0.0	0.7	0.7
3	1.2	0.0	2.6	0.0	0.7	2.2
4	2.6	1.5	3.3	2.4	1.4	4.4
5	4.1	2.9	3.9	3.1	3.6	6.6
6	6.8	5.9	9.2	3.9	4.3	10.2
7	11.9	11.0	13.1	12.6	8.7	13.9
8	16.9	12.5	18.3	18.1	13.8	21.9
9	23.0	19.1	22.9	22.0	20.3	30.7
10	28.2	29.4	28.8	26.0	22.5	34.3
11	36.0	36.0	37.9	33.9	30.4	41.6
12	44.7	47.1	45.1	38.6	37.0	55.5
13	52.8	52.9	55.6	46.5	44.2	64.2
14	61.4	58.8	62.7	56.7	55.8	72.3
15	67.6	66.9	69.3	62.2	59.4	79.6
16	75.0	70.6	77.1	70.1	71.0	85.4
17	81.5	76.5	83.0	78.7	78.3	90.5
18	87.6	83.8	87.6	86.6	85.5	94.2
19	91.9	89.7	90.8	92.1	92.0	94.9
20	96.4	95.6	96.1	96.9	97.1	96.4
21	98.0	97.1	98.0	98.4	98.6	97.8
22	99.0	97.8	98.7	99.2	100.0	99.3
23	99.3	98.5	99.3	99.2	100.0	99.3
24	99.9	100.0	100.0	99.2	100.0	100.0

Research/Supplemental Scales for the MMPI

Females   Phobias   (PHO)

		Age, yr				
	Total Sample	13	14	15	16	17
N	691	136	153	127	138	137
Median	9	9	9	10	10	8
Mean	9.49	9.44	9.08	9.69	10.19	9.09
SD	4.52	4.47	4.83	4.23	4.56	4.38
Min	0	0	0	0	0	0
Max	24	21	24	20	21	21

Percentage of Sample with Raw Score < X

X	Total Sample	13	14	15	16	17
0	0.0	0.0	0.0	0.0	0.0	0.0
1	0.9	1.5	0.7	0.8	0.7	0.7
2	1.2	1.5	0.7	1.6	1.4	0.7
3	3.9	2.2	5.2	3.1	5.1	3.6
4	8.4	8.1	11.8	7.1	6.5	8.0
5	14.5	15.4	18.3	11.8	10.9	15.3
6	20.0	19.9	27.5	15.7	15.2	20.4
7	27.4	24.3	35.3	26.8	21.0	28.5
8	36.2	35.3	41.2	34.6	28.3	40.9
9	45.4	47.1	49.7	41.7	37.0	51.1
10	52.7	55.1	55.6	48.0	43.5	60.6
11	61.5	64.0	68.0	55.1	52.9	66.4
12	68.6	69.1	73.2	61.4	63.8	74.5
13	75.3	75.0	77.1	72.4	73.9	77.4
14	81.0	81.6	81.0	80.3	79.7	82.5
15	85.7	84.6	84.3	89.8	84.1	86.1
16	89.1	90.4	86.3	93.7	86.2	89.8
17	92.5	94.1	90.8	95.3	87.7	94.9
18	94.4	94.9	93.5	96.1	92.8	94.9
19	96.2	95.6	96.7	96.1	95.7	97.1
20	98.0	97.8	98.7	99.2	96.4	97.8
21	99.0	98.5	98.7	100.0	98.6	99.3
22	99.7	100.0	98.7	100.0	100.0	100.0
23	99.9	100.0	99.3	100.0	100.0	100.0
24	99.9	100.0	99.3	100.0	100.0	100.0

Research/Supplemental Scales for the MMPI

Females   Hypomania   (HYP)

		Age, yr				
	Total Sample	13	14	15	16	17
N	691	136	153	127	138	137
Median	15	14	15	16	16	15
Mean	15.10	14.83	14.69	15.64	15.29	15.12
SD	3.56	3.55	3.78	3.38	3.72	3.30
Min	2	8	2	7	5	7
Max	24	23	23	22	24	23

	Percentage of Sample with Raw Score < X					
X	Total Sample	13	14	15	16	17
2	0.0	0.0	0.0	0.0	0.0	0.0
3	0.1	0.0	0.7	0.0	0.0	0.0
4	0.1	0.0	0.7	0.0	0.0	0.0
5	0.1	0.0	0.7	0.0	0.0	0.0
6	0.3	0.0	0.7	0.0	0.7	0.0
7	0.4	0.0	1.3	0.0	0.7	0.0
8	1.6	0.0	4.6	0.8	1.4	0.7
9	3.5	2.2	5.9	3.1	4.3	1.5
10	6.5	7.4	9.2	7.9	5.8	2.2
11	11.1	11.0	15.0	7.9	10.9	10.2
12	16.4	16.9	19.6	14.2	16.7	13.9
13	23.9	26.5	26.1	18.9	23.9	23.4
14	33.1	39.7	34.6	26.0	33.3	31.4
15	42.3	50.7	45.8	31.5	39.9	42.3
16	52.4	60.3	56.9	39.4	48.6	55.5
17	63.2	66.2	67.3	55.9	58.0	67.9
18	73.7	75.7	74.5	69.3	72.5	75.9
19	81.9	83.1	84.3	77.2	81.9	82.5
20	89.3	88.2	91.5	89.0	87.7	89.8
21	94.4	94.1	96.1	96.9	91.3	93.4
22	97.3	96.3	97.4	98.4	96.4	97.8
23	98.8	98.5	98.7	100.0	97.8	99.3
24	99.9	100.0	100.0	100.0	99.3	100.0

Research/Supplemental Scales for the MMPI

Females   Poor Health   (HEA)

		Age, yr				
	Total Sample	13	14	15	16	17
N	691	136	153	127	138	137
Median	5	5	4	5	5	5
Mean	5.36	5.34	4.89	5.47	5.85	5.31
SD	3.36	2.90	3.17	3.77	3.78	3.12
Min	0	0	0	0	0	0
Max	22	14	15	22	16	15

Percentage of Sample with Raw Score < X

X	Total Sample	13	14	15	16	17
0	0.0	0.0	0.0	0.0	0.0	0.0
1	3.0	2.2	2.6	3.9	3.6	2.9
2	10.6	6.6	13.1	11.8	10.1	10.9
3	18.2	14.7	22.9	17.3	18.8	16.8
4	33.7	28.7	37.9	33.9	31.9	35.8
5	46.0	40.4	51.0	49.6	42.8	46.0
6	60.5	61.8	66.7	61.4	55.1	56.9
7	68.2	70.6	75.2	69.3	62.3	62.8
8	75.7	77.9	79.7	75.6	70.3	74.5
9	82.6	84.6	88.2	78.7	76.8	83.9
10	87.6	90.4	91.5	84.3	81.9	89.1
11	92.2	94.1	94.1	91.3	86.2	94.9
12	94.2	96.3	95.4	92.1	89.9	97.1
13	96.4	98.5	96.1	95.3	93.5	98.5
14	97.7	99.3	97.4	96.9	95.7	99.3
15	98.7	100.0	99.3	97.6	97.1	99.3
16	99.6	100.0	100.0	98.4	99.3	100.0
17	99.9	100.0	100.0	99.2	100.0	100.0
18	99.9	100.0	100.0	99.2	100.0	100.0
19	99.9	100.0	100.0	99.2	100.0	100.0
20	99.9	100.0	100.0	99.2	100.0	100.0
21	99.9	100.0	100.0	99.2	100.0	100.0
22	99.9	100.0	100.0	99.2	100.0	100.0

Research/Supplemental Scales for the MMPI

Males   Social Maladjustment   (SOC)

		Age, yr				
	Total Sample	13	14	15	16	17
N	624	112	147	130	122	113
Median	10	10	11	9	11	9
Mean	10.68	10.75	11.41	10.15	11.16	9.73
SD	5.13	4.92	5.27	5.28	4.73	5.27
Min	0	1	1	1	0	0
Max	26	26	24	25	25	22

Percentage of Sample with Raw Score < X

X	Total Sample	13	14	15	16	17
0	0.0	0.0	0.0	0.0	0.0	0.0
1	0.3	0.0	0.0	0.0	0.8	0.9
2	1.3	0.9	0.7	1.5	0.8	2.7
3	3.0	2.7	0.7	4.6	1.6	6.2
4	5.6	5.4	3.4	7.7	1.6	10.6
5	10.1	6.3	8.8	12.3	5.7	17.7
6	15.9	15.2	11.6	17.7	10.7	25.7
7	22.8	23.2	19.7	23.1	16.4	32.7
8	30.4	29.5	25.9	35.4	23.0	39.8
9	37.8	33.9	33.3	46.2	28.7	47.8
10	46.0	43.8	40.1	52.3	42.6	52.2
11	52.6	53.6	48.3	57.7	46.7	57.5
12	60.9	59.8	57.1	65.4	58.2	64.6
13	65.9	63.4	63.3	70.0	63.9	69.0
14	72.4	71.4	68.7	77.7	71.3	73.5
15	76.1	75.0	72.1	80.8	76.2	77.0
16	80.8	81.3	74.8	84.6	82.0	82.3
17	86.1	88.4	78.9	88.5	87.7	88.5
18	89.7	91.1	85.7	92.3	90.2	90.3
19	92.1	93.8	88.4	93.1	92.6	93.8
20	93.9	94.6	91.2	93.8	95.1	95.6
21	95.7	97.3	93.2	94.6	95.1	99.1
22	96.8	98.2	95.9	94.6	96.7	99.1
23	98.1	99.1	98.0	95.4	98.4	100.0
24	98.9	99.1	98.6	97.7	99.2	100.0
25	99.4	99.1	100.0	98.5	99.2	100.0
26	99.8	99.1	100.0	100.0	100.0	100.0

Research/Supplemental Scales for the MMPI

Males   Depression   (DEP)

				Age, yr		
	Total Sample	13	14	15	16	17
N	624	112	147	130	122	113
Median	8	7	8	7	8	7
Mean	8.91	8.59	9.76	8.30	9.48	8.19
SD	5.82	5.72	6.36	5.34	5.88	5.53
Min	0	0	0	0	0	0
Max	27	24	27	23	27	24

Percentage of Sample with Raw Score < X

X	Total Sample	13	14	15	16	17
0	0.0	0.0	0.0	0.0	0.0	0.0
1	2.6	1.8	3.4	3.8	1.6	1.8
2	7.2	8.0	8.2	8.5	3.3	8.0
3	11.5	12.5	10.9	14.6	5.7	14.2
4	17.5	21.4	15.0	19.2	12.3	20.4
5	26.0	33.0	23.1	27.7	21.3	25.7
6	33.7	39.3	29.9	36.2	27.9	36.3
7	40.7	45.5	35.4	42.3	36.9	45.1
8	48.6	51.8	42.9	52.3	42.6	54.9
9	55.4	57.1	50.3	56.9	53.3	61.1
10	60.7	59.8	53.7	62.3	60.7	69.0
11	65.4	62.5	59.9	67.7	64.8	73.5
12	69.2	65.2	63.9	70.8	70.5	77.0
13	73.1	67.9	68.7	77.7	73.8	77.9
14	76.8	75.0	72.8	79.2	77.0	80.5
15	81.4	82.1	77.6	83.1	80.3	85.0
16	85.3	87.5	81.0	89.2	82.8	86.7
17	88.8	91.1	83.7	93.1	86.1	91.2
18	92.1	92.9	88.4	96.2	90.2	93.8
19	93.8	96.4	90.5	96.2	91.8	94.7
20	94.6	97.3	91.8	97.7	91.8	94.7
21	95.2	97.3	93.2	97.7	93.4	94.7
22	96.2	98.2	93.2	98.5	94.3	97.3
23	97.1	98.2	95.2	99.2	95.1	98.2
24	98.6	99.1	96.6	100.0	98.4	99.1
25	99.2	100.0	98.0	100.0	98.4	100.0
26	99.5	100.0	98.6	100.0	99.2	100.0
27	99.5	100.0	98.6	100.0	99.2	100.0

Research/Supplemental Scales for the MMPI

Males   Feminine Interests   (FEM)

	Total Sample	Age, yr				
		13	14	15	16	17
N	624	112	147	130	122	113
Median	8	8	8	9	8	8
Mean	8.56	8.80	8.52	8.59	8.67	8.19
SD	3.04	3.10	2.76	3.11	3.22	3.07
Min	0	2	2	0	2	2
Max	19	16	17	17	19	16

Percentage of Sample with Raw Score < X

X	Total Sample	13	14	15	16	17
0	0.0	0.0	0.0	0.0	0.0	0.0
1	0.2	0.0	0.0	0.8	0.0	0.0
2	0.2	0.0	0.0	0.8	0.0	0.0
3	1.0	0.9	0.7	0.8	1.6	0.9
4	3.7	3.6	2.7	3.8	3.3	5.3
5	7.9	7.1	6.8	9.2	5.7	10.6
6	13.5	15.2	8.2	13.1	11.5	21.2
7	25.8	25.9	21.1	26.2	25.4	31.9
8	40.2	35.7	37.4	38.5	44.3	46.0
9	52.9	50.9	54.4	50.0	53.3	55.8
10	65.1	55.4	72.1	66.2	62.3	67.3
11	75.2	71.4	81.6	73.8	72.1	75.2
12	83.2	78.6	84.4	83.1	85.2	84.1
13	89.1	86.6	89.8	88.5	90.2	90.3
14	93.4	92.9	93.9	93.1	92.6	94.7
15	96.6	96.4	95.9	96.9	95.9	98.2
16	98.2	99.1	99.3	97.7	95.9	99.1
17	98.9	100.0	99.3	98.5	96.7	100.0
18	99.5	100.0	100.0	100.0	97.5	100.0
19	99.8	100.0	100.0	100.0	99.2	100.0

Research/Supplemental Scales for the MMPI

Males   Poor Morale   (MOR)

| | | Age, yr | | | | |
	Total Sample	13	14	15	16	17
N	624	112	147	130	122	113
Median	9	9	9	9	9	8
Mean	9.12	9.13	9.86	9.04	9.32	8.04
SD	5.19	5.13	5.50	5.22	4.93	4.95
Min	0	0	0	0	0	0
Max	22	20	22	19	22	21

| | Percentage of Sample with Raw Score < X | | | | | |
X	Total Sample	13	14	15	16	17
0	0.0	0.0	0.0	0.0	0.0	0.0
1	1.6	0.9	1.4	2.3	0.8	2.7
2	4.0	4.5	2.7	5.4	1.6	6.2
3	8.8	9.8	5.4	12.3	4.1	13.3
4	14.6	15.2	10.9	16.2	9.8	22.1
5	21.6	24.1	19.7	22.3	14.8	28.3
6	30.6	30.4	29.3	31.5	29.5	32.7
7	37.3	38.4	36.1	36.9	36.1	39.8
8	43.9	42.9	40.1	43.8	44.3	49.6
9	49.5	48.2	43.5	50.0	49.2	58.4
10	56.4	56.3	51.0	53.8	55.7	67.3
11	62.2	60.7	56.5	62.3	62.3	70.8
12	66.2	64.3	59.9	65.4	66.4	77.0
13	71.6	68.8	64.6	73.1	71.3	82.3
14	76.9	72.3	74.8	74.6	77.9	85.8
15	81.4	77.7	79.6	80.0	81.1	89.4
16	85.7	83.9	84.4	83.8	86.1	91.2
17	89.7	92.9	84.4	87.7	91.8	93.8
18	93.6	98.2	87.1	96.2	93.4	94.7
19	96.0	99.1	91.2	98.5	96.7	95.6
20	97.6	99.1	95.2	100.0	97.5	96.5
21	98.7	100.0	96.6	100.0	98.4	99.1
22	99.7	100.0	99.3	100.0	99.2	100.0

Research/Supplemental Scales for the MMPI

Males   Religious Fundamentalism   (REL)

		Age, yr				
	Total Sample	13	14	15	16	17
N	624	112	147	130	122	113
Median	7	8	7	7	7	7
Mean	7.05	7.57	7.08	7.06	7.04	6.50
SD	2.65	2.66	2.52	2.75	2.76	2.53
Min	0	0	1	0	0	1
Max	12	12	12	12	12	11

Percentage of Sample with Raw Score < X

X	Total Sample	13	14	15	16	17
0	0.0	0.0	0.0	0.0	0.0	0.0
1	1.1	0.9	0.0	2.3	2.5	0.0
2	3.7	1.8	3.4	3.8	4.9	4.4
3	6.6	3.6	6.1	6.9	8.2	8.0
4	10.3	7.1	9.5	12.3	10.7	11.5
5	17.0	14.3	15.0	17.7	17.2	21.2
6	26.0	24.1	23.1	23.8	25.4	34.5
7	39.4	33.9	40.1	39.2	37.7	46.0
8	52.2	42.9	51.0	52.3	52.5	62.8
9	67.9	58.9	68.0	66.9	67.2	78.8
10	81.1	73.2	83.7	79.2	79.5	89.4
11	90.9	83.9	93.9	91.5	91.0	92.9
12	98.6	98.2	98.0	97.7	99.2	100.0

Research/Supplemental Scales for the MMPI

Males   Authority Conflict (AUT)

		Age, yr				
	Total Sample	13	14	15	16	17
N	624	112	147	130	122	113
Median	11	11	11	11	12	12
Mean	10.97	10.41	11.17	10.56	11.53	11.13
SD	3.74	3.49	3.88	3.73	3.52	3.98
Min	0	1	0	2	2	0
Max	20	20	20	19	19	19

Percentage of Sample with Raw Score < X

X	Total Sample	13	14	15	16	17
0	0.0	0.0	0.0	0.0	0.0	0.0
1	0.3	0.0	0.7	0.0	0.0	0.9
2	0.5	0.9	0.7	0.0	0.0	0.9
3	1.8	1.8	2.0	1.5	0.8	2.7
4	3.5	3.6	4.1	3.1	1.6	5.3
5	6.3	7.1	6.8	5.4	4.9	7.1
6	8.5	8.9	8.2	9.2	6.6	9.7
7	12.2	10.7	11.6	14.6	9.0	15.0
8	18.3	18.8	17.7	23.8	13.1	17.7
9	24.0	25.0	22.4	30.0	18.9	23.9
10	33.2	34.8	32.0	40.0	27.9	31.0
11	42.6	50.0	40.1	47.7	36.1	39.8
12	52.7	64.3	50.3	58.5	43.4	47.8
13	61.5	75.0	59.2	66.2	52.5	55.8
14	74.5	83.9	71.4	75.4	71.3	71.7
15	83.7	91.1	81.0	85.4	82.0	79.6
16	89.4	92.9	87.8	90.0	89.3	87.6
17	94.7	96.4	93.2	95.4	94.3	94.7
18	96.8	96.4	95.9	98.5	95.9	97.3
19	98.7	98.2	98.6	99.2	99.2	98.2
20	99.7	99.1	99.3	100.0	100.0	100.0

Research/Supplemental Scales for the MMPI

Males   Psychoticism   (PSY)

		Age, yr				
	Total Sample	13	14	15	16	17
N	624	112	147	130	122	113
Median	12	11	13	12	12	10
Mean	12.60	12.67	13.26	12.15	13.15	11.60
SD	6.68	6.66	7.07	6.50	6.64	6.36
Min	1	2	1	2	2	1
Max	36	33	35	33	32	36

Percentage of Sample with Raw Score < X

X	Total Sample	13	14	15	16	17
1	0.0	0.0	0.0	0.0	0.0	0.0
2	0.6	0.0	2.0	0.0	0.0	0.9
3	2.2	0.9	4.8	1.5	1.6	1.8
4	5.4	5.4	7.5	4.6	3.3	6.2
5	8.5	8.9	10.2	10.8	4.9	7.1
6	13.6	12.5	13.6	17.7	11.5	12.4
7	19.2	17.0	19.0	23.1	15.6	21.2
8	25.0	23.2	23.1	30.8	20.5	27.4
9	31.4	32.1	27.2	36.2	24.6	38.1
10	37.5	37.5	32.0	42.3	32.8	44.2
11	42.8	42.9	36.7	44.6	41.0	50.4
12	48.9	51.8	44.2	47.7	46.7	55.8
13	54.3	57.1	49.0	53.1	53.3	61.1
14	60.3	60.7	54.4	59.2	61.5	67.3
15	65.4	63.4	59.2	66.9	65.6	73.5
16	70.2	69.6	63.3	71.5	69.7	78.8
17	75.2	72.3	70.7	76.2	73.8	84.1
18	78.0	76.8	73.5	80.0	75.4	85.8
19	82.1	78.6	81.0	83.1	79.5	88.5
20	84.8	83.0	83.7	84.6	82.8	90.3
21	86.5	86.6	85.0	86.9	82.8	92.0
22	88.9	90.2	87.1	90.8	85.2	92.0
23	90.5	91.1	87.8	94.6	86.1	93.8
24	92.8	94.6	91.2	96.2	88.5	93.8
25	94.6	96.4	91.2	96.2	94.3	95.6
26	95.4	96.4	93.2	96.2	95.1	96.5
27	96.3	96.4	94.6	97.7	96.7	96.5
28	97.4	97.3	97.3	97.7	98.4	96.5
29	97.9	97.3	98.0	98.5	98.4	97.3
30	98.4	97.3	98.6	99.2	98.4	98.2

Research/Supplemental Scales for the MMPI

Males   Psychoticism   (PSY)
                          (Continued)

| X | Total Sample | Percentage of Sample with Raw Score < X | | | | |
		13	14	15	16	17
31	98.4	97.3	98.6	99.2	98.4	98.2
32	98.9	99.1	98.6	99.2	99.2	98.2
33	99.4	99.1	99.3	99.2	100.0	99.1
34	99.7	100.0	99.3	100.0	100.0	99.1
35	99.7	100.0	99.3	100.0	100.0	99.1
36	99.8	100.0	100.0	100.0	100.0	99.1

Research/Supplemental Scales for the MMPI

Males   Organic Symptoms   (ORG)

		Age, yr				
	Total Sample	13	14	15	16	17
N	624	112	147	130	122	113
Median	6	5	7	5	6	5
Mean	6.48	6.68	6.99	5.87	7.09	5.67
SD	4.53	4.79	4.54	4.31	4.55	4.38
Min	0	0	0	0	0	0
Max	26	24	21	26	20	22

	Percentage of Sample with Raw Score < X					
X	Total Sample	13	14	15	16	17
0	0.0	0.0	0.0	0.0	0.0	0.0
1	3.5	4.5	4.1	1.5	2.5	5.3
2	10.6	9.8	10.2	10.8	9.0	13.3
3	20.2	18.8	17.7	23.8	16.4	24.8
4	29.3	30.4	23.8	32.3	24.6	37.2
5	39.9	42.0	32.0	43.1	35.2	49.6
6	49.4	52.7	40.8	53.8	43.4	58.4
7	56.9	56.3	49.0	66.2	50.8	63.7
8	64.7	59.8	59.9	73.1	58.2	73.5
9	71.2	66.1	67.3	80.0	64.8	77.9
10	78.0	74.1	74.8	84.6	73.0	84.1
11	82.4	78.6	79.6	90.0	77.0	86.7
12	86.7	85.7	86.4	90.0	80.3	91.2
13	89.6	88.4	89.1	91.5	85.2	93.8
14	91.3	89.3	90.5	93.1	89.3	94.7
15	93.8	94.6	93.2	94.6	91.8	94.7
16	95.2	95.5	93.9	96.2	95.1	95.6
17	96.5	96.4	95.2	96.9	97.5	96.5
18	97.3	97.3	96.6	97.7	98.4	96.5
19	98.6	97.3	98.6	99.2	99.2	98.2
20	98.9	98.2	98.6	99.2	99.2	99.1
21	99.4	99.1	99.3	99.2	100.0	99.1
22	99.5	99.1	100.0	99.2	100.0	99.1
23	99.7	99.1	100.0	99.2	100.0	100.0
24	99.7	99.1	100.0	99.2	100.0	100.0
25	99.8	100.0	100.0	99.2	100.0	100.0
26	99.8	100.0	100.0	99.2	100.0	100.0

Research/Supplemental Scales for the MMPI

Males   Family Problems   (FAM)

		Age, yr				
	Total Sample	13	14	15	16	17
N	624	112	147	130	122	113
Median	5	5	6	6	5	5
Mean	5.61	4.97	6.03	5.65	5.84	5.39
SD	2.98	3.03	3.33	2.80	2.89	2.67
Min	0	0	0	0	1	1
Max	14	12	14	12	14	13

	Percentage of Sample with Raw Score < X					
X	Total Sample	13	14	15	16	17
0	0.0	0.0	0.0	0.0	0.0	0.0
1	2.2	6.3	4.1	0.8	0.0	0.0
2	6.6	13.4	7.5	5.4	3.3	3.5
3	16.3	25.0	16.3	15.4	11.5	14.2
4	27.4	36.6	23.1	26.9	25.4	26.5
5	40.9	45.5	38.8	39.2	37.7	44.2
6	51.6	56.3	47.6	48.5	52.5	54.9
7	62.2	67.0	55.8	60.8	61.5	68.1
8	71.3	80.4	64.6	69.2	68.0	77.0
9	81.9	87.5	76.9	83.1	77.0	86.7
10	89.4	91.1	83.7	91.5	89.3	92.9
11	93.8	95.5	87.8	95.4	95.1	96.5
12	97.3	98.2	93.9	99.2	97.5	98.2
13	98.9	100.0	98.0	100.0	98.4	98.2
14	99.7	100.0	99.3	100.0	99.2	100.0

Research/Supplemental Scales for the MMPI

Males   Manifest Hostility   (HOS)

		Age, yr				
	Total Sample	13	14	15	16	17
N	624	112	147	130	122	113
Median	13	13	14	13	13	13
Mean	13.23	13.54	13.90	12.84	13.05	12.70
SD	4.85	5.06	4.95	4.84	4.46	4.87
Min	0	0	0	2	4	1
Max	25	24	23	24	23	25

	Percentage of Sample with Raw Score < X					
X	Total Sample	13	14	15	16	17
0	0.0	0.0	0.0	0.0	0.0	0.0
1	0.3	0.9	0.7	0.0	0.0	0.0
2	0.5	0.9	0.7	0.0	0.0	0.9
3	1.4	2.7	2.7	0.8	0.0	0.9
4	2.6	5.4	2.7	1.5	0.0	3.5
5	5.0	7.1	4.8	6.2	0.8	6.2
6	7.1	7.1	6.1	7.7	5.7	8.8
7	10.3	8.9	8.2	13.8	8.2	12.4
8	14.3	12.5	10.9	17.7	15.6	15.0
9	17.9	15.2	15.0	20.0	19.7	20.4
10	21.8	17.0	17.0	25.4	24.6	25.7
11	26.8	21.4	23.1	30.0	27.9	31.9
12	32.9	29.5	27.2	36.9	31.1	40.7
13	42.1	42.0	36.1	44.6	42.6	46.9
14	50.6	50.9	44.9	53.1	53.3	52.2
15	58.7	58.0	54.4	60.0	62.3	59.3
16	66.5	65.2	60.5	66.2	70.5	71.7
17	73.2	71.4	67.3	73.8	76.2	78.8
18	80.3	78.6	74.8	83.8	82.0	83.2
19	86.1	79.5	82.3	90.8	90.2	87.6
20	91.5	87.5	89.1	93.8	93.4	93.8
21	93.3	91.1	89.8	96.9	94.3	94.7
22	96.6	96.4	93.9	97.7	97.5	98.2
23	98.1	97.3	97.3	97.7	99.2	99.1
24	99.2	99.1	100.0	97.7	100.0	99.1
25	99.8	100.0	100.0	100.0	100.0	99.1

Research/Supplemental Scales for the MMPI

Males   Phobias   (PHO)

	Total Sample	Age, yr				
		13	14	15	16	17
N	624	112	147	130	122	113
Median	6	6	6	5	6	5
Mean	6.37	6.95	6.47	6.25	6.48	5.68
SD	4.02	4.43	3.70	4.17	4.03	3.77
Min	0	0	0	0	0	0
Max	19	19	15	17	18	18

	Percentage of Sample with Raw Score < X					
X	Total Sample	13	14	15	16	17
0	0.0	0.0	0.0	0.0	0.0	0.0
1	1.6	2.7	0.7	1.5	1.6	1.8
2	7.5	5.4	6.8	8.5	8.2	8.8
3	17.6	15.2	15.6	19.2	19.7	18.6
4	28.2	25.0	25.2	27.7	27.9	36.3
5	39.4	31.3	36.7	43.1	37.7	48.7
6	49.7	42.9	45.6	56.2	44.3	60.2
7	56.4	53.6	52.4	60.0	54.1	62.8
8	66.0	63.4	63.3	70.0	63.9	69.9
9	73.2	71.4	72.1	73.1	72.1	77.9
10	77.4	74.1	76.2	76.2	77.9	83.2
11	83.0	81.3	83.7	80.8	81.1	88.5
12	87.3	85.7	87.8	86.9	85.2	91.2
13	90.7	88.4	90.5	90.0	91.0	93.8
14	94.1	89.3	97.3	93.1	94.3	95.6
15	95.8	91.1	99.3	93.8	96.7	97.3
16	97.8	93.8	100.0	96.9	98.4	99.1
17	98.6	95.5	100.0	98.5	99.2	99.1
18	99.2	97.3	100.0	100.0	99.2	99.1
19	99.7	98.2	100.0	100.0	100.0	100.0

Research/Supplemental Scales for the MMPI

Males   Hypomania   (HYP)

		Age, yr				
	Total Sample	13	14	15	16	17
N	624	112	147	130	122	113
Median	15	14	15	14	15	15
Mean	14.38	14.04	14.43	14.28	14.61	14.54
SD	3.81	3.76	3.91	3.72	3.97	3.69
Min	0	2	2	5	4	0
Max	23	21	22	23	23	23

Percentage of Sample with Raw Score < X

X	Total Sample	13	14	15	16	17
0	0.0	0.0	0.0	0.0	0.0	0.0
1	0.2	0.0	0.0	0.0	0.0	0.9
2	0.2	0.0	0.0	0.0	0.0	0.9
3	0.5	0.9	0.7	0.0	0.0	0.9
4	0.6	0.9	1.4	0.0	0.0	0.9
5	1.0	0.9	1.4	0.0	1.6	0.9
6	1.9	2.7	2.0	0.8	3.3	0.9
7	3.2	3.6	2.7	4.6	4.1	0.9
8	4.8	5.4	4.8	5.4	4.9	3.5
9	7.1	8.0	6.8	6.9	8.2	5.3
10	10.9	13.4	10.2	12.3	9.0	9.7
11	15.5	17.9	17.0	15.4	13.1	14.2
12	20.2	20.5	21.8	20.8	19.7	17.7
13	27.7	30.4	29.3	28.5	27.0	23.0
14	37.3	42.0	38.8	36.9	36.9	31.9
15	49.7	51.8	47.6	51.5	48.4	49.6
16	59.5	60.7	58.5	60.8	55.7	61.9
17	70.2	72.3	68.0	71.5	67.2	72.6
18	79.0	83.0	74.1	82.3	75.4	81.4
19	85.9	88.4	85.0	86.9	83.6	85.8
20	92.0	93.8	91.8	92.3	90.2	92.0
21	96.3	99.1	95.9	96.9	95.1	94.7
22	98.6	100.0	99.3	98.5	97.5	97.3
23	99.4	100.0	100.0	99.2	98.4	99.1

Research/Supplemental Scales for the MMPI

Males   Poor Health   (HEA)

	Total Sample	Age, yr				
		13	14	15	16	17
N	624	112	147	130	122	113
Median	4	4	5	4	6	4
Mean	4.96	4.93	5.10	4.70	5.44	4.60
SD	2.94	3.29	2.65	2.87	2.69	3.21
Min	0	0	0	0	0	0
Max	18	18	15	15	11	18

Percentage of Sample with Raw Score < X

X	Total Sample	13	14	15	16	17
0	0.0	0.0	0.0	0.0	0.0	0.0
1	3.2	5.4	0.7	3.8	3.3	3.5
2	8.5	10.7	4.1	9.2	5.7	14.2
3	21.6	21.4	17.0	26.9	16.4	27.4
4	34.9	38.4	29.9	39.2	23.8	45.1
5	50.2	56.3	47.6	52.3	39.3	56.6
6	61.1	64.3	60.5	63.8	50.0	67.3
7	72.6	71.4	70.1	76.9	68.0	77.0
8	80.4	78.6	81.0	83.1	76.2	83.2
9	87.8	86.6	91.2	88.5	82.0	90.3
10	93.3	92.9	95.9	92.3	92.6	92.0
11	96.5	95.5	97.3	96.9	98.4	93.8
12	98.1	95.5	98.6	99.2	100.0	96.5
13	98.6	96.4	98.6	99.2	100.0	98.2
14	98.9	98.2	98.6	99.2	100.0	98.2
15	99.0	98.2	98.6	99.2	100.0	99.1
16	99.7	99.1	100.0	100.0	100.0	99.1
17	99.7	99.1	100.0	100.0	100.0	99.1
18	99.7	99.1	100.0	100.0	100.0	99.1

TSC ITEM-CLUSTER SCALES

Early factor and cluster analyses of the MMPI were limited to examination of the basic clinical scales or of the items composing single scales, with each scale considered separately. Cluster or factor studies using the entire MMPI item pool could not be carried out because the computer hardware and software were limited.

However, a system of cluster and factor analytic programs (Tryon, 1966, 1967; Tryon & Bailey, 1966) was the first to allow examination of the MMPI factor structure at the item level, an important research step because prior studies were believed by these authors to have been flawed by the amount of item overlap among the clinical scales.

The program used in developing the TSC scales (standing for Tryon, Stein, and Chu, the principal investigators in the project) estimated the internal structure of the MMPI by making use of random samples of 120 items from the MMPI item pool. Thus, all of the MMPI items were not included simultaneously but rather by samples of 120 items each. The communality of each item was calculated and the items were then ordered by magnitude. The 120 items having the largest communalities were then processed into clusters. The remaining items, after exclusion of those with "trivial generality," were related to the existing clusters. The process of final item selection used both statistical and rational procedures. The items included in each cluster depended on the magnitude of the oblique factor coefficient for that cluster, the existence of low coefficients for other clusters, and also some attention to the apparent content meaning of the cluster. The clusters of items that remained were homogeneous both statistically and rationally. More specifically, 317 items were eliminated because of low communality and 57 more were dropped because of ambiguity in relation to the content of the items within the cluster.

Thus, the 550 different MMPI items were reduced to seven scales containing 192 items believed to reproduce the generality of the total item pool.

The analysis was carried out on a sample of 70 male schizophrenic outpatients and 150 neurotic outpatients (anxiety reaction) at a Veterans Administration hospital. In addition, 90 military officers were included as a normal or contrast group. The two groups were matched for age and education.

The results (Stein, 1968) yielded three relatively independent clusters of items:

Cluster I: I. Social introversion vs. interpersonal poise and outgoingness.
Cluster II: B. Body symptoms vs. lack of physical complaints.
Cluster III: S. Suspicion and mistrust vs. absence of suspicion.

Four additional dependent clusters also were constructed but they were well correlated with the other clusters:

Cluster IV: D. Depression and apathy vs. positive and optimistic outlook.
Cluster V: R. Resentment and aggression vs. lack of resentment and aggression.
Cluster VI: A. Autism and disruptive thought vs. absence of such disturbance.
Cluster VII: T. Tension, worry, and fears vs. absence of such complaints.

REFERENCES

Stein, K. B. (1968). The TSC scales: The outcome of a cluster analysis of the 550 MMPI items. In P. McReynolds (Ed.), *Advances in psychological assessment* (Vol. 1, pp. 80–104). Palo Alto, CA: Science and Behavior Books.

Tryon, R. C. (1966). Unrestricted cluster and factor analysis, with applications to the MMPI and Holzinger-Harman problems. *Multivariate Behavioral Research, 1,* 229–244.

Tryon, R. C. (1967). Person-clusters on intellectual abilities and on MMPI attributes. *Multivariate Behavioral Research, 2,* 5–34.

Tryon, R. C., & Bailey, D. E. (1966). The BC TRY computer system of cluster and factor analysis. *Multivariate Behavioral Research, 1,* 95–111.

The items of the TSC scales, and their direction of scoring, are listed below.

I: *Social Introversion (26 Items)*

The following items score if answered *true:*

52. I prefer to pass by school friends, or people I know but have not seen for a long time, unless they speak to me first.
86. I am certainly lacking in self-confidence.
138. Criticism or scolding hurts me terribly.
171. It makes me uncomfortable to put on a stunt at a party even when others are doing the same sort of things.
172. I frequently have to fight against showing that I am bashful.
180. I find it hard to make talk when I meet new people.
201. I wish I were not so shy.
267. When in a group of people I have trouble thinking of the right things to talk about.
292. I am likely not to speak to people until they speak to me.
304. In school I found it very hard to talk before the class.
317. I am more sensitive than most other people.
321. I am easily embarrassed.
371. I am not unusually self-conscious.
377. At parties I am more likely to sit by myself or with just one other person than to join in with the crowd.
509. I sometimes find it hard to stick up for my rights because I am so reserved.

The following items score if answered *false:*

57. I am a good mixer.
79. My feelings are not easily hurt.
264. I am entirely self-confident.
309. I seem to make friends about as quickly as others do.
353. I have no dread of going into a room by myself where other people have already gathered and are talking.
415. If given the chance I would make a good leader of people.
449. I enjoy social gatherings just to be with people.
479. I do not mind meeting strangers.
482. While in trains, busses, etc., I often talk to strangers.
521. In a group of people I would not be embarrassed to be called upon to start a discussion or give an opinion about something I know well.
547. I like parties and socials.

B: *Body Symptoms (33 Items)*

The following items score if answered *true:*

10. There seems to be a lump in my throat much of the time.
14.[a] I have diarrhea once a month or more.
23. I am troubled by attacks of nausea and vomiting.
29. I am bothered by acid stomach several times a week.
44. Much of the time my head seems to hurt all over.
47. Once a week or oftener I feel suddenly hot all over, without apparent cause.
62. Parts of my body often have feelings like burning, tingling, crawling, or like "going to sleep."

72. I am troubled by discomfort in the pit of my stomach every few days or oftener.
108. There seems to be a fullness in my head or nose most of the time.
114. Often I feel as if there were a tight band about my head.
125. I have a great deal of stomach trouble.
161. The top of my head sometimes feels tender.
189. I feel weak all over much of the time.
191. Sometimes, when embarrassed, I break out in a sweat which annoys me greatly.
263. I sweat very easily even on cool days.
544. I feel tired a good deal of the time.

The following items score if answered *false:*

2. I have a good appetite.
3. I wake up fresh and rested most mornings.
18. I am very seldom troubled by constipation.
36. I seldom worry about my health.
51. I am in just as good physical health as most of my friends.
55. I am almost never bothered by pains over the heart or in my chest.
68. I hardly ever feel pain in the back of the neck.
103. I have little or no trouble with my muscles twitching or jumping.
153. During the past few years I have been well most of the time.
160. I have never felt better in my life than I do now.
163. I do not tire quickly.
175. I seldom or never have dizzy spells.
190. I have very few headaches.
192. I have had no difficulty in keeping my balance in walking.
230. I hardly ever notice my heart pounding and I am seldom short of breath.
243. I have few or no pains.
330. I have never been paralyzed or had any unusual weakness of any of my muscles.

S: Suspicion (25 Items)

The following items score if answered *true:*

71. I think a great many people exaggerate their misfortunes in order to gain the sympathy and help of others.
89. It takes a lot of argument to convince most people of the truth.
112. I frequently find it necessary to stand up for what I think is right.
136. I commonly wonder what hidden reason another person may have for doing something nice for me.
244. My way of doing things is apt to be misunderstood by others.
265. It is safer to trust nobody.
278. I have often felt that strangers were looking at me critically.
280. Most people make friends because friends are likely to be useful to them.
284. I am sure I am being talked about.
316. I think nearly anyone would tell a lie to keep out of trouble.
319. Most people inwardly dislike putting themselves out to help other people.
348. I tend to be on my guard with people who are somewhat more friendly than I had expected.
368. I have sometimes stayed away from another person because I feared doing or saying something that I might regret afterwards.
383. People often disappoint me.

390. I have often felt badly over being misunderstood when trying to keep someone from making a mistake.
404. People have often misunderstood my intentions when I was trying to put them right and be helpful.
406. I have often met people who were supposed to be experts who were no better than I.
426. I have at times had to be rough with people who were rude or annoying.
436. People generally demand more respect for their own rights than they are willing to allow for others.
438. There are certain people whom I dislike so much that I am inwardly pleased when they are catching it for something they have done.
447. I am often inclined to go out of my way to win a point with someone who has opposed me.
455. I am quite often not in on the gossip and talk of the group I belong to.
469. I have often found people jealous of my good ideas, just because they had not thought of them first.
507. I have frequently worked under people who seem to have things arranged so that they get credit for good work but are able to pass off mistakes onto those under them.
558. A large number of people are guilty of bad sexual conduct.

The following items score if answered *false*:
(none)

D: Depression (28 Items)

The following items score if answered true:

41.   I have had periods of days, weeks, or months when I couldn't take care of things because I couldn't "get going."
61.   I have not lived the right kind of life.
67.   I wish I could be as happy as others seem to be.
76.   Most of the time I feel blue.
84.   These days I find it hard not to give up hope of amounting to something.
104. I don't seem to care what happens to me.
142. I certainly feel useless at times.
168. There is something wrong with my mind.
236. I brood a great deal.
259. I have difficulty in starting to do things.
301. Life is a strain for me much of the time.
339. Most of the time I wish I were dead.
357. I have several times given up doing a thing because I thought too little of my ability.
361. I am inclined to take things hard.
384. I feel unable to tell anyone all about myself.
396. Often, even though everything is going fine for me, I feel that I don't care about anything.
397. I have sometimes felt that difficulties were piling up so high that I could not overcome them.
411. It makes me feel like a failure when I hear of the success of someone I know well.
414. I am apt to take disappointments so keenly that I can't put them out of my mind.
418. At times I think I am no good at all.
487. I feel like giving up quickly when things go wrong.

526.   The future seems hopeless to me.
549.   I shrink from facing a crisis or difficulty.

The following items score if answered *false:*

8.   My daily life is full of things that keep me interested.
46.   My judgment is better than it ever was.
88.   I usually feel that life is worthwhile.
107.   I am happy most of the time.
379.   I very seldom have spells of the blues.

R: Resentment (20 Items)

The following items score if answered *true:*

28.   When someone does me a wrong, I feel I should pay him back if I can just for the principle of the thing.
39.   At times I feel like smashing things.
94.   I do many things which I regret afterwards (I regret things more or more often than others seem to).
97.   At times I have a strong urge to do something harmful or shocking.
106.   Much of the time I feel as if I have done something wrong or evil.
129.   Often I can't understand why I have been so cross and grouchy.
139.   Sometimes I feel as if I must injure either myself or someone else.
145.   At times I feel like picking a fist fight with someone.
147.   I have often lost out on things because I couldn't make up my mind soon enough.
148.   It makes me impatient to have people ask my advice or otherwise interrupt me when I am working on something important.
162.   I resent having anyone take me in so cleverly that I have had to admit that it was one on me.
234.   I get mad easily and then get over it soon.
336.   I easily become impatient with people.
375.[a]   When I am feeling very happy and active, someone who is blue or low will spoil it all.
381.   I am often said to be hotheaded.
382.   I wish I could get over worrying about things I have said that may have injured other people's feelings.
416.   It bothers me to have someone watch me at work even though I know I can do it well.
443.   I am apt to pass up something I want to do because others feel that I am not going about it in the right way.
468.   I am often sorry because I am so cross and grouchy.
536.   It makes me angry to have people hurry me.

The following items score if answered *false:*
(none)

A: Autism (23 Items)

The following items score if answered *true:*

15.   Once in a while I think of things too bad to talk about.
31.   I have nightmares every few nights.

33.   I have had very peculiar and strange experiences.
40.   Most any time I would rather sit and daydream than to do anything else.
100. I have met problems so full of possibilities that I have been unable to make up my mind about them.
134. At times my thoughts have raced ahead faster than I could speak them.
241. I dream frequently about things that are best kept to myself.
297. I wish I were not bothered by thoughts about sex.
342. I forget right away what people say to me.
345. I often feel as if things were not real.
349. I have strange and peculiar thoughts.
356. I have more trouble concentrating than others seem to have.
358. Bad words, often terrible words, come into my mind and I cannot get rid of them.
359. Sometimes some unimportant thought will run through my mind and bother me for days.
374. At periods my mind seems to work more slowly than usual.
389. My plans have frequently seemed so full of difficulties that I have had to give them up.
425.[a] I dream frequently.
459.[a] I have one or more bad habits which are so strong that it is no use in fighting against them.
511. I have a daydream life about which I do not tell other people.
545.[a] Sometimes I have the same dream over and over.
559. I have often been frightened in the middle of the night.
560. I am greatly bothered by forgetting where I put things.

The following item scores if answered *false*:

329. I almost never dream.

T: Tension (36 Items)

The following items score if answered true:

13.   I work under a great deal of tension.
22.   At times I have fits of laughing and crying that I cannot control.
32.   I find it hard to keep my mind on a task or job.
43.   My sleep is fitful and disturbed.
102. My hardest battles are with myself.
158. I cry easily.
166. I am afraid when I look down from a high place.
182. I am afraid of losing my mind.
186. I frequently notice my hand shakes when I try to do something.
217. I frequently find myself worrying about something.
238. I have periods of such great restlessness that I cannot sit long in a chair.
303. I am so touchy on some subjects that I can't talk about them.
322. I worry over money and business.
335. I cannot keep my mind on one thing.
337. I feel anxiety about something or someone almost all the time.
338. I have certainly had more than my share of things to worry about.
340. Sometimes I become so excited that I find it hard to get to sleep.
351. I get anxious and upset when I have to make a short trip away from home.
360. Almost every day something happens to frighten me.
365. I feel uneasy indoors.

388. I am afraid to be alone in the dark.
431. I worry quite a bit over possible misfortune.
439. It makes me nervous to have to wait.
442.[a] I have had periods in which I lost sleep over worry.
448. I am bothered by people outside, on streetcars, in stores, etc., watching me.
473. Whenever possible I avoid being in a crowd.
492. I dread the thought of an earthquake.
494. I am afraid of finding myself in a closet or small closed place.
499. I must admit that I have at times been worried beyond reason over something that really did not matter.
506. I am a high-strung person.
543. Several times a week I feel as if something dreadful is about to happen.
555. I sometimes feel that I am about to go to pieces.

The following items score if answered *false*:

131. I do not worry about catching diseases.
152. Most nights I go to sleep without thoughts or ideas bothering me.
242. I believe I am no more nervous than most others.
407. I am usually calm and not easily upset.

---

[a]Items that were deleted from the original MMPI item pool during construction of the MMPI-2.

Research/Supplemental Scales for the MMPI

Females   Cluster I (Social Introversion)   (I)

	Total Sample	Age, yr				
		13	14	15	16	17
N	691	136	153	127	138	137
Median	11	11	11	11	12	10
Mean	11.05	11.26	10.83	11.26	11.64	10.28
SD	5.11	4.80	4.92	5.11	5.50	5.16
Min	1	1	1	1	1	1
Max	25	25	24	23	25	25

	Percentage of Sample with Raw Score < X					
X	Total Sample	13	14	15	16	17
1	0.0	0.0	0.0	0.0	0.0	0.0
2	1.0	0.7	1.3	0.8	1.4	0.7
3	3.0	2.2	3.9	4.7	2.9	1.5
4	5.1	2.9	5.9	6.3	4.3	5.8
5	10.0	8.1	11.1	8.7	8.7	13.1
6	15.3	11.8	14.4	13.4	15.9	21.2
7	20.1	15.4	18.3	18.1	20.3	28.5
8	27.1	22.1	26.1	24.4	28.3	34.3
9	34.3	31.6	35.3	30.7	34.1	39.4
10	42.3	39.7	43.8	38.6	39.9	48.9
11	48.2	45.6	46.4	48.0	44.2	56.9
12	55.4	55.1	57.5	54.3	47.1	62.8
13	62.5	62.5	63.4	60.6	55.8	70.1
14	68.0	67.6	71.2	66.9	60.9	73.0
15	75.0	74.3	79.1	74.0	68.1	78.8
16	80.5	80.9	83.0	78.0	76.1	83.9
17	84.8	85.3	86.3	84.3	80.4	87.6
18	88.3	88.2	89.5	89.0	85.5	89.1
19	91.8	94.1	93.5	91.3	87.7	92.0
20	92.9	94.9	94.1	92.1	89.9	93.4
21	94.9	95.6	96.1	95.3	92.8	94.9
22	97.4	98.5	98.0	96.1	96.4	97.8
23	98.6	98.5	99.3	98.4	97.1	99.3
24	99.4	99.3	99.3	100.0	99.3	99.3
25	99.6	99.3	100.0	100.0	99.3	99.3

Research/Supplemental Scales for the MMPI

Females   Cluster II (Body Symptoms)   (B)

		Age, yr				
	Total Sample	13	14	15	16	17
N	691	136	153	127	138	137
Median	6	6	5	6	7	6
Mean	6.67	6.28	5.92	6.84	7.78	6.62
SD	4.77	3.82	4.34	5.26	5.69	4.40
Min	0	0	0	0	0	0
Max	30	17	20	30	27	21

Percentage of Sample with Raw Score < X

X	Total Sample	13	14	15	16	17
0	0.0	0.0	0.0	0.0	0.0	0.0
1	2.9	2.2	3.3	3.9	3.6	1.5
2	10.1	8.1	10.5	13.4	12.3	6.6
3	19.5	15.4	22.9	21.3	18.8	19.0
4	29.1	26.5	35.3	28.3	25.4	29.2
5	38.4	37.5	44.4	38.6	33.3	37.2
6	47.9	50.0	54.2	47.2	42.0	45.3
7	56.9	59.6	67.3	59.1	44.2	53.3
8	64.3	64.7	73.2	63.8	52.9	65.7
9	71.6	73.5	77.8	70.9	62.3	73.0
10	76.6	79.4	81.7	76.4	67.4	77.4
11	81.2	84.6	84.3	78.0	76.1	82.5
12	83.9	86.8	88.2	79.5	78.3	86.1
13	88.6	91.9	90.8	86.6	84.1	89.1
14	91.3	97.1	91.5	89.0	86.2	92.7
15	93.1	97.8	94.1	90.6	87.0	95.6
16	94.6	98.5	95.4	93.7	89.1	96.4
17	95.7	98.5	96.7	95.3	90.6	97.1
18	96.7	100.0	98.0	96.1	92.0	97.1
19	97.3	100.0	98.7	96.1	94.2	97.1
20	97.8	100.0	99.3	96.9	95.7	97.1
21	98.8	100.0	100.0	98.4	96.4	99.3
22	99.3	100.0	100.0	99.2	97.1	100.0
23	99.4	100.0	100.0	99.2	97.8	100.0
24	99.6	100.0	100.0	99.2	98.6	100.0
25	99.6	100.0	100.0	99.2	98.6	100.0
26	99.7	100.0	100.0	99.2	99.3	100.0
27	99.7	100.0	100.0	99.2	99.3	100.0
28	99.9	100.0	100.0	99.2	100.0	100.0
29	99.9	100.0	100.0	99.2	100.0	100.0

Research/Supplemental Scales for the MMPI

Females   Cluster II (Body Symptoms)   (B)
                                (Continued)

| X | Total Sample | Percentage of Sample with Raw Score < X | | | | |
		13	14	15	16	17
30	99.9	100.0	100.0	99.2	100.0	100.0

Research/Supplemental Scales for the MMPI

Females   Cluster III (Suspicion and Mistrust)   (S)

	Total Sample	Age, yr				
		13	14	15	16	17
N	691	136	153	127	138	137
Median	14	14	14	14	15	13
Mean	13.72	14.44	13.71	13.93	13.99	12.56
SD	5.26	5.06	5.28	5.07	5.21	5.55
Min	1	2	2	3	2	1
Max	25	24	25	25	24	24

	Percentage of Sample with Raw Score < X					
X	Total Sample	13	14	15	16	17
1	0.0	0.0	0.0	0.0	0.0	0.0
2	0.4	0.0	0.0	0.0	0.0	2.2
3	1.2	0.7	1.3	0.0	0.7	2.9
4	2.6	2.9	2.6	1.6	0.7	5.1
5	4.3	2.9	3.9	3.1	2.9	8.8
6	6.8	4.4	5.9	4.7	7.2	11.7
7	10.9	6.6	10.5	8.7	11.6	16.8
8	14.3	8.8	15.7	12.6	13.0	21.2
9	18.7	12.5	17.6	18.9	15.9	28.5
10	22.4	15.4	20.9	24.4	18.8	32.8
11	27.9	22.1	28.1	27.6	26.1	35.8
12	33.6	30.9	34.6	30.7	32.6	38.7
13	39.2	33.8	43.1	36.2	38.4	43.8
14	47.0	41.9	46.4	42.5	47.1	56.9
15	53.5	51.5	53.6	50.4	49.3	62.8
16	60.5	57.4	62.7	56.7	59.4	65.7
17	68.7	65.4	69.3	66.9	67.4	74.5
18	74.8	70.6	75.2	77.2	73.2	78.1
19	79.6	72.8	79.1	81.1	80.4	84.7
20	84.5	83.8	83.7	84.3	83.3	87.6
21	89.3	88.2	88.9	92.1	86.2	91.2
22	93.2	91.2	92.2	93.7	92.8	96.4
23	96.2	94.1	95.4	96.9	96.4	98.5
24	98.1	97.8	98.7	97.6	97.1	99.3
25	99.7	100.0	99.3	99.2	100.0	100.0

Research/Supplemental Scales for the MMPI

Females   Cluster IV (Depression and Apathy)   (D)

| | Total Sample | Age, yr | | | | |
		13	14	15	16	17
N	691	136	153	127	138	137
Median	8	9	7	9	10	8
Mean	9.04	8.77	8.31	9.18	10.92	8.09
SD	5.72	5.33	5.21	6.19	6.12	5.38
Min	0	0	0	0	0	0
Max	28	25	25	26	28	24

Percentage of Sample with Raw Score < X

X	Total Sample	13	14	15	16	17
0	0.0	0.0	0.0	0.0	0.0	0.0
1	2.7	2.9	3.3	3.1	1.4	2.9
2	6.9	8.1	7.2	8.7	1.4	9.5
3	11.7	11.0	12.4	14.2	5.1	16.1
4	18.8	19.1	17.6	21.3	10.1	26.3
5	24.3	22.1	26.8	26.8	13.8	32.1
6	30.7	31.6	34.0	32.3	19.6	35.8
7	37.5	37.5	42.5	38.6	27.5	40.9
8	44.4	43.4	50.3	44.9	33.3	49.6
9	50.9	49.3	56.9	49.6	42.0	56.2
10	57.2	55.9	62.1	55.9	48.6	62.8
11	63.4	66.2	66.0	62.2	52.9	69.3
12	69.3	73.5	73.2	68.5	55.8	75.2
13	74.8	76.5	81.0	74.8	63.0	78.1
14	79.3	82.4	83.7	77.2	69.6	83.2
15	83.1	86.0	88.9	81.9	72.5	85.4
16	86.8	89.0	91.5	84.3	76.1	92.7
17	89.6	91.9	92.8	86.6	81.9	94.2
18	90.3	92.6	93.5	86.6	83.3	94.9
19	93.1	95.6	95.4	89.8	87.7	96.4
20	95.1	96.3	96.7	93.7	92.0	96.4
21	95.7	97.1	97.4	94.5	92.8	96.4
22	97.0	97.8	98.7	96.1	93.5	98.5
23	97.4	98.5	98.7	96.9	94.2	98.5
24	98.3	99.3	99.3	97.6	95.7	99.3
25	98.8	99.3	99.3	97.6	97.8	100.0
26	99.4	100.0	100.0	98.4	98.6	100.0
27	99.7	100.0	100.0	100.0	98.6	100.0
28	99.9	100.0	100.0	100.0	99.3	100.0

Research/Supplemental Scales for the MMPI

Females   Cluster V (Resentment and Aggression)   (R)

		Age, yr				
	Total Sample	13	14	15	16	17
N	691	136	153	127	138	137
Median	10	11	10	10	10	9
Mean	9.76	10.06	9.44	9.87	10.45	9.05
SD	4.12	4.08	4.16	4.36	3.90	4.01
Min	0	0	1	0	0	1
Max	20	18	18	20	20	18

Percentage of Sample with Raw Score < X

X	Total Sample	13	14	15	16	17
0	0.0	0.0	0.0	0.0	0.0	0.0
1	0.4	0.7	0.0	0.8	0.7	0.0
2	1.4	0.7	2.6	1.6	0.7	1.5
3	4.3	1.5	7.2	3.9	1.4	7.3
4	8.1	7.4	9.2	9.4	2.9	11.7
5	11.6	12.5	12.4	12.6	5.1	15.3
6	16.4	18.4	17.6	15.7	9.4	20.4
7	22.9	22.8	28.1	20.5	15.2	27.0
8	30.2	28.7	33.3	31.5	23.9	33.6
9	38.2	31.6	41.8	41.7	33.3	42.3
10	46.2	39.7	49.0	46.5	41.3	54.0
11	55.4	48.5	56.9	55.1	52.9	63.5
12	64.4	56.6	64.7	64.6	63.0	73.0
13	73.2	72.8	73.2	72.4	69.6	78.1
14	81.2	81.6	83.0	78.7	78.3	83.9
15	86.7	87.5	89.5	83.5	82.6	89.8
16	91.0	91.2	92.8	88.2	87.0	95.6
17	95.1	94.1	96.1	93.7	92.8	98.5
18	97.8	97.8	98.7	96.1	97.1	99.3
19	99.3	100.0	100.0	97.6	98.6	100.0
20	99.7	100.0	100.0	99.2	99.3	100.0

Research/Supplemental Scales for the MMPI

Females   Cluster VI (Autism and Disruptive Thought)   (A)

| | Total Sample | Age, yr | | | | |
		13	14	15	16	17
N	691	136	153	127	138	137
Median	11	11	10	11	12	10
Mean	10.98	10.96	10.69	11.09	12.07	10.13
SD	4.75	4.89	4.59	4.90	4.78	4.48
Min	1	1	1	1	2	1
Max	22	22	22	22	21	21

| X | Percentage of Sample with Raw Score < X | | | | | |
	Total Sample	13	14	15	16	17
1	0.0	0.0	0.0	0.0	0.0	0.0
2	0.7	0.7	0.7	0.8	0.0	1.5
3	2.6	2.9	2.0	2.4	1.4	4.4
4	4.8	2.9	3.9	6.3	4.3	6.6
5	7.8	7.4	7.8	8.7	5.8	9.5
6	13.9	12.5	14.4	16.5	9.4	16.8
7	19.7	19.9	22.2	18.9	13.0	24.1
8	26.6	29.4	26.1	24.4	19.6	33.6
9	33.1	38.2	34.0	31.5	24.6	37.2
10	40.1	42.6	41.2	42.5	31.2	43.1
11	47.5	48.5	50.3	48.0	37.7	52.6
12	55.3	58.8	59.5	52.0	44.2	61.3
13	63.2	64.0	68.0	60.6	54.3	68.6
14	69.2	66.9	73.2	67.7	61.6	75.9
15	75.0	73.5	78.4	71.7	68.8	81.8
16	81.0	80.1	81.0	79.5	74.6	89.8
17	86.3	85.3	86.3	86.6	80.4	92.7
18	89.0	87.5	90.2	89.0	83.3	94.9
19	92.5	91.2	94.8	92.1	87.7	96.4
20	95.7	94.1	98.0	95.3	93.5	97.1
21	98.6	98.5	99.3	97.6	97.8	99.3
22	99.6	99.3	99.3	99.2	100.0	100.0

Research/Supplemental Scales for the MMPI

Females   Cluster VII (Tension, Worry, and Fears)   (T)

			Age, yr			
	Total Sample	13	14	15	16	17
N	691	136	153	127	138	137
Median	14	12	13	14	15	13
Mean	13.97	13.28	13.44	14.44	15.51	13.27
SD	6.48	6.13	6.48	6.42	6.96	6.13
Min	1	1	1	2	1	2
Max	32	31	29	32	31	30

Percentage of Sample with Raw Score < X

X	Total Sample	13	14	15	16	17
1	0.0	0.0	0.0	0.0	0.0	0.0
2	0.9	0.7	2.0	0.0	1.4	0.0
3	2.3	2.2	3.3	1.6	3.6	0.7
4	3.9	5.1	3.9	3.9	3.6	2.9
5	5.8	5.1	6.5	5.5	5.1	6.6
6	9.6	8.8	11.8	6.3	8.0	12.4
7	13.3	11.0	16.3	9.4	10.1	19.0
8	16.8	16.9	20.3	12.6	11.6	21.9
9	22.0	24.3	24.8	18.9	16.7	24.8
10	27.9	33.1	29.4	24.4	21.7	30.7
11	33.0	39.0	34.0	30.7	24.6	36.5
12	39.2	44.1	39.2	39.4	31.9	41.6
13	44.6	50.7	47.7	44.1	33.3	46.7
14	49.6	54.4	53.6	48.0	39.1	52.6
15	55.3	58.8	60.1	52.8	47.1	56.9
16	59.6	63.2	62.7	57.5	52.9	61.3
17	64.7	68.4	68.0	63.8	58.7	64.2
18	68.7	71.3	72.5	64.6	62.3	72.3
19	74.5	78.7	79.1	70.9	65.9	77.4
20	77.7	83.1	82.4	73.2	68.1	81.0
21	83.1	86.8	85.6	80.3	72.5	89.8
22	87.0	90.4	86.9	87.4	78.3	92.0
23	90.4	91.9	92.8	90.6	81.9	94.9
24	92.5	95.6	93.5	91.3	85.5	96.4
25	93.8	95.6	93.5	92.9	89.1	97.8
26	95.2	97.1	94.8	95.3	91.3	97.8
27	96.7	98.5	95.4	96.1	94.9	98.5
28	97.8	99.3	97.4	97.6	96.4	98.5
29	98.4	99.3	98.7	99.2	96.4	98.5
30	99.1	99.3	100.0	99.2	97.8	99.3

Research/Supplemental Scales for the MMPI

Females Cluster VII (Tension, Worry, and Fears) (T)
(Continued)

		Percentage of Sample with Raw Score < X				
X	Total Sample	13	14	15	16	17
31	99.4	99.3	100.0	99.2	98.6	100.0
32	99.9	100.0	100.0	99.2	100.0	100.0

Research/Supplemental Scales for the MMPI

Males   Cluster I (Social Introversion)   (I)

		Age, yr				
	Total Sample	13	14	15	16	17
N	624	112	147	130	122	113
Median	9	10	9	9	9	9
Mean	10.13	10.08	10.64	9.73	10.61	9.49
SD	5.13	4.88	5.39	5.30	5.07	4.88
Min	0	2	1	0	1	2
Max	25	23	24	23	25	22

Percentage of Sample with Raw Score < X

X	Total Sample	13	14	15	16	17
0	0.0	0.0	0.0	0.0	0.0	0.0
1	0.2	0.0	0.0	0.8	0.0	0.0
2	1.1	0.0	2.0	2.3	0.8	0.0
3	3.5	4.5	2.0	6.2	2.5	2.7
4	9.1	11.6	5.4	11.5	4.9	13.3
5	12.8	14.3	7.5	15.4	9.8	18.6
6	19.9	22.3	14.3	23.1	15.6	25.7
7	27.2	25.9	25.9	31.5	21.3	31.9
8	34.8	34.8	34.7	36.2	28.7	39.8
9	42.5	40.2	40.8	45.4	39.3	46.9
10	51.0	47.3	51.7	52.3	50.8	52.2
11	58.5	52.7	59.9	62.3	55.7	61.1
12	64.4	61.6	63.9	66.9	64.8	64.6
13	69.4	67.0	68.0	73.1	66.4	72.6
14	73.9	72.3	72.1	77.7	71.3	76.1
15	76.8	74.1	74.1	80.0	73.8	82.3
16	83.5	83.9	78.9	86.2	82.0	87.6
17	88.1	92.9	82.3	90.8	86.1	90.3
18	90.5	95.5	85.0	91.5	88.5	93.8
19	92.5	96.4	87.1	92.3	91.0	97.3
20	94.6	97.3	91.2	93.1	94.3	98.2
21	96.5	99.1	94.6	94.6	96.7	98.2
22	97.8	99.1	96.6	96.9	98.4	98.2
23	98.6	99.1	98.6	96.9	98.4	100.0
24	99.7	100.0	99.3	100.0	99.2	100.0
25	99.8	100.0	100.0	100.0	99.2	100.0

Research/Supplemental Scales for the MMPI

Males　　　　　Cluster II (Body Symptoms)　　(B)

		Age, yr				
	Total Sample	13	14	15	16	17
N	624	112	147	130	122	113
Median	5	4	6	5	6	5
Mean	5.93	5.81	6.40	5.43	6.43	5.49
SD	4.19	4.73	4.38	3.78	3.77	4.17
Min	0	0	0	0	0	0
Max	23	20	23	19	16	21

Percentage of Sample with Raw Score < X

X	Total Sample	13	14	15	16	17
0	0.0	0.0	0.0	0.0	0.0	0.0
1	4.0	6.3	3.4	3.8	0.8	6.2
2	10.7	14.3	9.5	13.8	4.1	12.4
3	21.6	25.0	18.4	23.8	14.8	27.4
4	34.1	42.9	25.9	36.2	29.5	38.9
5	43.9	52.7	38.1	46.2	37.7	46.9
6	53.5	58.9	49.0	56.9	45.1	59.3
7	60.9	63.4	56.5	65.4	54.9	65.5
8	69.7	67.9	67.3	76.9	64.8	71.7
9	77.4	77.7	76.2	80.0	71.3	82.3
10	82.9	83.0	81.0	86.2	78.7	85.8
11	87.2	83.9	84.4	92.3	85.2	90.3
12	90.2	85.7	88.4	93.1	90.2	93.8
13	91.8	89.3	90.5	95.4	90.2	93.8
14	93.4	90.2	93.2	96.2	93.4	93.8
15	96.2	94.6	95.2	96.9	98.4	95.6
16	96.3	94.6	95.9	96.9	98.4	95.6
17	97.9	96.4	97.3	98.5	100.0	97.3
18	98.2	96.4	98.0	99.2	100.0	97.3
19	98.7	97.3	98.0	99.2	100.0	99.1
20	99.0	98.2	98.0	100.0	100.0	99.1
21	99.4	100.0	98.0	100.0	100.0	99.1
22	99.7	100.0	98.6	100.0	100.0	100.0
23	99.8	100.0	99.3	100.0	100.0	100.0

Research/Supplemental Scales for the MMPI

Males   Cluster III (Suspicion and Mistrust)   (S)

		Age, yr				
	Total Sample	13	14	15	16	17
N	624	112	147	130	122	113
Median	15	15	16	15	15	14
Mean	14.25	14.10	14.78	14.19	14.19	13.84
SD	5.29	5.03	5.45	5.45	5.17	5.34
Min	0	1	0	0	2	0
Max	25	24	25	24	24	25

Percentage of Sample with Raw Score < X

X	Total Sample	13	14	15	16	17
0	0.0	0.0	0.0	0.0	0.0	0.0
1	0.6	0.0	0.7	0.8	0.0	1.8
2	1.1	0.9	2.0	0.8	0.0	1.8
3	1.8	0.9	2.7	1.5	0.8	2.7
4	3.0	1.8	4.1	1.5	2.5	5.3
5	4.5	2.7	4.1	5.4	4.1	6.2
6	6.3	4..	6.1	6.2	6.6	8.0
7	7.9	6.3	7.5	8.5	6.6	10.6
8	11.7	12.5	10.9	12.3	9.8	13.3
9	16.5	17.0	17.0	16.9	14.8	16.8
10	20.5	22.3	19.0	22.3	20.5	18.6
11	24.2	26.8	20.4	26.9	25.4	22.1
12	29.6	28.6	26.5	32.3	32.0	29.2
13	35.7	36.6	31.3	39.2	34.4	38.1
14	42.6	45.5	36.7	45.4	42.6	44.2
15	47.9	48.2	43.5	48.5	48.4	52.2
16	54.8	55.4	47.6	53.1	59.0	61.1
17	61.4	63.4	54.4	60.0	67.2	63.7
18	70.0	68.8	63.3	70.8	74.6	74.3
19	78.4	77.7	75.5	78.5	79.5	81.4
20	83.0	86.6	78.9	81.5	83.6	85.8
21	87.8	92.9	87.1	84.6	85.2	90.3
22	91.7	94.6	91.2	88.5	91.0	93.8
23	95.7	97.3	94.6	96.2	94.3	96.5
24	98.7	99.1	98.0	99.2	98.4	99.1
25	99.7	100.0	99.3	100.0	100.0	99.1

Research/Supplemental Scales for the MMPI

Males   Cluster IV (Depression and Apathy)   (D)

	Total Sample	Age, yr				
		13	14	15	16	17
N	624	112	147	130	122	113
Median	7	7	7	6	7	6
Mean	8.08	7.75	8.83	7.68	8.73	7.16
SD	5.56	5.27	6.03	5.24	5.76	5.25
Min	0	0	0	0	0	0
Max	26	21	26	21	22	24

Percentage of Sample with Raw Score < X

X	Total Sample	13	14	15	16	17
0	0.0	0.0	0.0	0.0	0.0	0.0
1	2.9	1.8	2.7	4.6	1.6	3.5
2	9.8	11.6	7.5	12.3	6.6	11.5
3	16.5	21.4	13.6	16.9	10.7	21.2
4	23.2	26.8	19.0	21.5	23.0	27.4
5	32.5	34.8	29.3	34.6	27.9	37.2
6	40.2	42.0	34.7	42.3	37.7	46.0
7	46.6	44.6	43.5	50.8	41.0	54.0
8	54.5	56.3	50.3	56.2	51.6	59.3
9	60.1	59.8	59.2	61.5	54.9	65.5
10	64.3	63.4	62.6	63.8	60.7	71.7
11	68.1	66.1	63.9	70.0	64.8	77.0
12	72.4	71.4	68.0	73.1	69.7	81.4
13	76.3	75.9	72.8	76.2	74.6	83.2
14	80.3	82.1	76.2	81.5	77.0	85.8
15	85.6	88.4	80.3	88.5	82.0	90.3
16	88.9	92.0	85.0	92.3	85.2	91.2
17	91.3	93.8	87.8	94.6	87.7	93.8
18	93.9	96.4	89.8	96.9	91.0	96.5
19	95.0	98.2	91.2	97.7	92.6	96.5
20	96.2	99.1	93.2	97.7	94.3	97.3
21	97.0	99.1	94.6	98.5	95.9	97.3
22	98.2	100.0	96.6	100.0	96.7	98.2
23	99.2	100.0	97.3	100.0	100.0	99.1
24	99.7	100.0	99.3	100.0	100.0	99.1
25	99.8	100.0	99.3	100.0	100.0	100.0
26	99.8	100.0	99.3	100.0	100.0	100.0

Research/Supplemental Scales for the MMPI

Males   Cluster V (Resentment and Aggression)   (R)

	Total Sample	Age, yr				
		13	14	15	16	17
N	624	112	147	130	122	113
Median	10	11	11	10	10	9
Mean	9.79	10.05	10.71	9.54	9.80	8.62
SD	4.50	4.46	4.36	4.61	4.17	4.71
Min	0	0	0	0	1	0
Max	20	18	20	20	19	20

Percentage of Sample with Raw Score < X

X	Total Sample	13	14	15	16	17
0	0.0	0.0	0.0	0.0	0.0	0.0
1	1.3	1.8	1.4	1.5	0.0	1.8
2	2.9	4.5	3.4	2.3	0.8	3.5
3	6.6	7.1	4.1	5.4	4.1	13.3
4	10.1	10.7	6.8	11.5	6.6	15.9
5	13.0	11.6	8.8	15.4	8.2	22.1
6	19.6	17.0	11.6	22.3	19.7	29.2
7	25.5	24.1	15.6	29.2	26.2	34.5
8	32.2	29.5	21.8	38.5	31.1	42.5
9	38.6	34.8	28.6	43.8	38.5	49.6
10	45.5	39.3	36.7	49.2	46.7	57.5
11	53.7	46.4	46.9	54.6	53.3	69.0
12	62.8	59.8	57.8	60.8	64.8	72.6
13	70.5	68.8	63.9	70.0	73.8	77.9
14	78.0	74.1	74.1	80.0	81.1	81.4
15	84.6	82.1	85.0	85.4	83.6	86.7
16	88.8	90.2	86.4	87.7	89.3	91.2
17	92.9	95.5	87.8	93.1	95.1	94.7
18	96.0	97.3	91.8	96.9	97.5	97.3
19	98.7	100.0	97.3	99.2	99.2	98.2
20	99.5	100.0	99.3	99.2	100.0	99.1

Research/Supplemental Scales for the MMPI

Males Cluster VI (Autism and Disruptive Thought) (A)

		Age, yr				
	Total Sample	13	14	15	16	17
N	624	112	147	130	122	113
Median	10	10	10	10	11	9
Mean	10.09	9.72	10.48	9.81	10.75	9.57
SD	4.50	4.65	4.85	4.23	4.23	4.42
Min	0	0	1	0	1	1
Max	22	22	20	22	20	22

Percentage of Sample with Raw Score < X

X	Total Sample	13	14	15	16	17
0	0.0	0.0	0.0	0.0	0.0	0.0
1	0.3	0.9	0.0	0.8	0.0	0.0
2	2.2	2.7	3.4	2.3	0.8	1.8
3	4.3	4.5	6.1	4.6	3.3	2.7
4	6.6	6.3	8.8	6.9	4.1	6.2
5	11.9	12.5	14.3	11.5	7.4	13.3
6	15.9	23.2	15.0	13.8	10.7	17.7
7	23.6	32.1	21.1	22.3	16.4	27.4
8	31.4	36.6	27.9	33.1	23.8	37.2
9	38.0	43.8	34.7	38.5	29.5	45.1
10	45.7	50.0	42.2	47.7	37.7	52.2
11	55.3	53.6	55.1	56.9	48.4	62.8
12	62.0	61.6	58.5	63.8	59.0	68.1
13	68.6	67.9	64.6	71.5	67.2	72.6
14	75.3	75.0	70.7	79.2	72.1	80.5
15	81.4	82.1	76.9	85.4	79.5	84.1
16	86.7	89.3	80.3	90.8	86.1	88.5
17	91.2	94.6	86.4	95.4	88.5	92.0
18	95.0	96.4	92.5	97.7	93.4	95.6
19	97.6	97.3	95.9	99.2	97.5	98.2
20	98.9	99.1	98.0	99.2	99.2	99.1
21	99.5	99.1	100.0	99.2	100.0	99.1
22	99.5	99.1	100.0	99.2	100.0	99.1

Research/Supplemental Scales for the MMPI

Males   Cluster VII (Tension, Worry, and Fears)   (T)

	Total Sample	Age, yr				
		13	14	15	16	17
N	624	112	147	130	122	113
Median	10	10	11	11	11	10
Mean	11.17	10.86	11.87	10.75	11.67	10.53
SD	6.32	6.20	6.40	6.15	6.35	6.44
Min	0	0	0	0	0	0
Max	30	30	26	26	28	28

X	Percentage of Sample with Raw Score < X					
	Total Sample	13	14	15	16	17
0	0.0	0.0	0.0	0.0	0.0	0.0
1	1.8	0.9	2.7	0.8	1.6	2.7
2	3.5	1.8	3.4	6.2	2.5	3.5
3	7.4	5.4	7.5	9.2	5.7	8.8
4	11.1	9.8	10.2	12.3	9.0	14.2
5	16.0	16.1	14.3	19.2	13.1	17.7
6	20.7	21.4	17.0	23.8	16.4	25.7
7	25.5	27.7	20.4	26.9	21.3	32.7
8	31.6	33.9	27.9	32.3	28.7	36.3
9	37.7	42.9	32.0	41.5	32.0	41.6
10	43.1	50.0	36.1	46.2	38.5	46.9
11	50.6	58.0	46.9	50.0	45.9	54.0
12	55.6	58.9	51.7	53.1	52.5	63.7
13	60.4	60.7	57.1	60.0	58.2	67.3
14	65.4	66.1	59.9	66.2	64.8	71.7
15	71.6	70.5	66.0	75.4	73.8	73.5
16	75.0	75.0	70.1	76.2	78.7	76.1
17	79.2	78.6	75.5	83.8	79.5	78.8
18	83.0	85.7	78.9	85.4	83.6	82.3
19	86.1	87.5	82.3	88.5	86.1	86.7
20	89.1	91.1	87.1	89.2	86.9	92.0
21	91.5	92.9	89.1	93.1	88.5	94.7
22	92.9	92.9	91.8	95.4	90.2	94.7
23	95.4	96.4	95.2	96.9	92.6	95.6
24	95.7	96.4	95.2	96.9	94.3	95.6
25	97.3	98.2	96.6	98.5	95.9	97.3
26	97.9	99.1	98.0	98.5	96.7	97.3
27	98.9	99.1	100.0	100.0	97.5	97.3
28	99.2	99.1	100.0	100.0	98.4	98.2
29	99.8	99.1	100.0	100.0	100.0	100.0

Research/Supplemental Scales for the MMPI

Males   Cluster VII (Tension, Worry, and Fears)   (T)
(Continued)

X	Total Sample	Percentage of Sample with Raw Score < X				
		13	14	15	16	17
30	99.8	99.1	100.0	100.0	100.0	100.0

APPENDIX A

Set 3: State/Trait Personality Characteristics

WELSH FACTOR DIMENSIONS—SCALES A AND R

After some initial work to develop a scale for general maladjustment or general malaise (GM), Welsh (1956) identified four general dimensions of the MMPI. This was done by cluster-analytic studies on 287 male psychiatric patients in a Veterans Administration hospital. However, Welsh was able to construct only two independent scales with items of sufficient purity to represent the cluster dimensions. Items were selected by using a variant of the internal consistency method. Welsh used groups of subjects scoring at opposite extremes on the GM scale and from the nonoverlapping items of scale 2 (D) (that is, 2') to carry out an item analysis of the 550 MMPI items. The items showing the greatest separation on GM were retained as scale A and those from 2', as scale R.

Welsh's first factor, A, generally is believed to be a dimension of anxiety or general maladjustment (39 items). Later, Welsh (1965) described A as being "related to anxiety or general emotional upset as reflected by dysphoria, tension, inefficiency, and symptomatic complaints" (p. 43).

The items on scale A fell into five clusters: (a) a set related to a decrease in thinking efficiency because of mental slowness and decreased concentration accompanied by obsessive thoughts and feelings of doubt or indecision; (b) items referring to negative emotional tone, dysphoria, anxiety, and worry; (c) items describing feelings of pessimism and loss of energy; (d) items indicating feelings of interpersonal oversensitivity; and (e) items suggesting "malignant mentation" or schizoid mentation. It is interesting that all of the items on scale A are scored when the opposite of the direction given by the majority of the members in the original Minnesota sample of normal people are marked.

Welsh's second factor, R, typically is thought of as representing proneness for repression, or perhaps conscious inhibition and control over expressions of psychopathology (40 items) accompanied by "denial with rationalization and lack of effective insight . . . ." (Welsh, 1965, p. 43).

Five clusters of items were also described for R: (a) a set expressing physical symptoms and concern about general health; (b) items denying feelings of anger, resentment, or loss of control; (c) items describing a lack of social enjoyment; (d) items reporting feelings of social inadequacy; and (e) items referring to personal and vocational interests with some suggesting denial of intellectual and mechanical or manual activities as well as denying feelings of hostility or those of a sexual nature.

The mean (± SD) score for men in the original Minnesota normal sample was 12.2 ± 8.0 for factor A and 15.6 ± 4.8 for factor R; women in the original Minnesota normal sample earned a mean score of 14.8 ± 8.5 for factor A and 17.7 ± 4.3 for factor R.

REFERENCES

Welsh, G. S. (1956). Factor dimensions A and R. In G. S. Welsh & W. G. Dahlstrom (Eds.), *Basic readings on the MMPI in psychology and medicine* (pp. 264–281). Minneapolis: University of Minnesota Press.

Welsh, G. S. (1965). MMPI profiles and factor scales A and R. *Journal of Clinical Psychology, 21,* 43–47.

The 39 items for factor A and the 40 items for R, and their direction of scoring, are listed below.

First Factor: A

These items score if answered *true:*

32. I find it hard to keep my mind on a task or job.
41. I have had periods of days, weeks, or months when I couldn't take care of things because I couldn't "get going."
67. I wish I could be as happy as others seem to be.
76. Most of the time I feel blue.
94. I do many things which I regret afterwards (I regret things more or more often than others seem to).
138. Criticism or scolding hurts me terribly.
147. I have often lost out on things because I couldn't make up my mind soon enough.
236. I brood a great deal.
259. I have difficulty in starting to do things.
267. When in a group of people I have trouble thinking of the right things to talk about.
278. I have often felt that strangers were looking at me critically.
301. Life is a strain for me much of the time.
305. Even when I am with people I feel lonely much of the time.
331. If people had not had it in for me I would have been much more successful.
337. I feel anxiety about something or someone almost all of the time.
343. I usually have to stop and think before I act even in trifling matters.
344. Often I cross the street in order not to meet someone I see.
345. I often feel as if things were not real.
356. I have more trouble concentrating than others seem to have.
359. Sometimes some unimportant thought will run through my mind and bother me for days.
374. At periods my mind seems to work more slowly than usual.
382. I wish I could get over worrying about things I have said that may have injured other people's feelings.
383. People often disappoint me.
384. I feel unable to tell anyone all about myself.
389. My plans have frequently seemed so full of difficulties that I have had to give them up.

396. Often, even though everything is going fine for me, I feel that I don't care about anything.
397. I have sometimes felt that difficulties were piling up so high that I could not overcome them.
411. It makes me feel like a failure when I hear of the success of someone I know well.
414. I am apt to take disappointments so keenly that I can't put them out of my mind.
418. At times I think I am no good at all.
431. I worry quite a bit over possible misfortune.
443. I am apt to pass up something I want to do because others feel that I am not going about it in the right way.
465. I have several times had a change of heart about my life work.
499. I must admit that I have at times been worried beyond reason over something that really did not matter.
511. I have a daydream life about which I do not tell other people.
518. I have often felt guilty because I have pretended to feel more sorry about something than I really was.
544. I feel tired a good deal of the time.
555. I sometimes feel that I am about to go to pieces.

This item scores if answered *false:*

379. I very seldom have spells of the blues.

Second Factor: R

These items score if answered *true:*
(none)

These items score if answered *false:*

1. I like mechanics magazines.
6. I like to read newspaper articles on crime.
9. I am about as able to work as I ever was.
12. I enjoy detective or mystery stories.
39. At times I feel like smashing things.
51. I am in just as good physical health as most of my friends.
81. I think I would like the kind of work a forest ranger does.
112. I frequently find it necessary to stand up for what I think is right.
126. I like dramatics.
131. I do not worry about catching diseases.
140. I like to cook.
145. At times I feel like picking a fist fight with someone.
154. I have never had a fit or convulsion.
156. I have had periods in which I carried on activities without knowing later what I had been doing.
191. Sometimes, when embarrassed, I break out in a sweat which annoys me greatly.
208. I like to flirt.
219. I think I would like the work of a building contractor.
221. I like science.
271. I do not blame a person for taking advantage of someone who lays himself open to it.
272. At times I am all full of energy.
281. I do not often notice my ears ringing or buzzing.

282. Once in a while I feel hate toward members of my family whom I usually love.
327. My mother or father often made me obey even when I thought that it was unreasonable.
406. I have often met people who were supposed to be experts who were no better than I.
415. If given the chance I would make a good leader of people.
429.ᵃ I like to attend lectures on serious subjects.
440. I try to remember good stories to pass them on to other people.
445. I was fond of excitement when I was young (or in childhood).
447. I am often inclined to go out of my way to win a point with someone who has opposed me.
449. I enjoy social gatherings just to be with people.
450. I enjoy the excitement of a crowd.
451. My worries seem to disappear when I get into a crowd of lively friends.
462.ᵃ I have had no difficulty starting or holding my urine.
468. I am often sorry because I am so cross and grouchy.
472. I am fascinated by fire.
502. I like to let people know where I stand on things.
516. Some of my family have quick tempers.
529. I would like to wear expensive clothes.
550. I like repairing a door latch.
556.ᵃ I am very careful about my manner of dress.

ᵃItems that were deleted from the original MMPI item pool during construction of the MMPI-2.

Females   Welsh Factor Dimension--Scale A   (A)

	Total Sample	Age, yr				
		13	14	15	16	17
N	691	136	153	127	138	137
Median	17	16	16	16	19	16
Mean	17.19	16.93	16.38	17.46	19.40	15.87
SD	8.70	8.59	8.13	9.32	9.00	8.22
Min	0	0	0	2	0	0
Max	39	37	34	37	39	33

X	Percentage of Sample with Raw Score < X					
	Total Sample	13	14	15	16	17
0	0.0	0.0	0.0	0.0	0.0	0.0
1	0.9	0.7	1.3	0.0	0.7	1.5
2	1.2	0.7	1.3	0.0	0.7	2.9
3	2.9	1.5	3.3	2.4	2.9	4.4
4	4.5	5.1	3.3	4.7	3.6	5.8
5	7.1	6.6	5.9	7.9	5.1	10.2
6	9.7	8.8	10.5	8.7	7.2	13.1
7	12.6	13.2	14.4	11.8	8.0	15.3
8	14.6	14.7	17.0	15.0	9.4	16.8
9	18.1	19.1	19.6	19.7	10.9	21.2
10	21.4	23.5	22.2	23.6	13.0	24.8
11	26.3	27.9	26.1	26.0	19.6	32.1
12	28.5	30.9	28.1	29.1	21.0	33.6
13	33.1	33.1	35.9	34.6	25.4	36.5
14	36.6	36.8	40.5	37.8	28.3	39.4
15	40.4	41.2	41.8	42.5	33.3	43.1
16	45.4	46.3	47.1	48.8	35.5	49.6
17	49.2	51.5	50.3	52.8	39.1	52.6
18	53.1	55.1	56.9	54.3	44.2	54.7
19	56.7	58.8	59.5	57.5	50.0	57.7
20	59.6	61.0	61.4	60.6	50.7	64.2
21	64.7	64.0	67.3	64.6	55.8	71.5
22	67.6	68.4	71.2	66.1	58.7	73.0
23	71.1	72.8	74.5	70.9	60.1	76.6
24	74.5	73.5	80.4	72.4	65.9	79.6
25	78.4	77.2	85.0	73.2	69.6	86.1
26	81.0	82.4	86.9	76.4	69.6	89.1
27	83.6	83.8	88.9	81.9	73.2	89.8
28	85.7	87.5	89.5	84.3	76.8	89.8
29	88.1	91.2	92.2	85.0	80.4	91.2

Research/Supplemental Scales for the MMPI

Females Welsh Factor Dimension--Scale A (A)
(Continued)

X	Percentage of Sample with Raw Score < X					
	Total Sample	13	14	15	16	17
30	90.4	93.4	93.5	86.6	84.8	93.4
31	92.3	93.4	94.8	89.0	87.7	96.4
32	93.3	94.1	94.8	89.8	89.9	97.8
33	95.2	94.9	97.4	92.9	91.3	99.3
34	97.1	97.1	99.3	93.7	94.9	100.0
35	98.1	98.5	100.0	94.5	97.1	100.0
36	98.8	99.3	100.0	96.9	97.8	100.0
37	99.3	99.3	100.0	97.6	99.3	100.0
38	99.9	100.0	100.0	100.0	99.3	100.0
39	99.9	100.0	100.0	100.0	99.3	100.0

Females   Welsh Factor Dimension--Scale R   (R)

		Age, yr				
	Total Sample	13	14	15	16	17
N	691	136	153	127	138	137
Median	15	15	16	14	15	16
Mean	15.17	15.25	15.54	14.76	15.02	15.22
SD	3.55	3.38	3.65	3.82	3.41	3.46
Min	4	7	4	5	8	5
Max	28	24	25	28	24	24

	Percentage of Sample with Raw Score < X					
X	Total Sample	13	14	15	16	17
4	0.0	0.0	0.0	0.0	0.0	0.0
5	0.1	0.0	0.7	0.0	0.0	0.0
6	0.4	0.0	0.7	0.8	0.0	0.7
7	0.4	0.0	0.7	0.8	0.0	0.7
8	0.9	0.7	1.3	0.8	0.0	1.5
9	2.0	1.5	2.6	3.1	0.7	2.2
10	4.6	2.9	3.3	6.3	4.3	6.6
11	9.1	8.1	9.2	10.2	8.0	10.2
12	15.1	14.7	12.4	20.5	15.2	13.1
13	23.0	21.3	19.6	27.6	25.4	21.9
14	32.6	30.1	28.1	40.2	36.2	29.2
15	44.4	42.6	41.2	50.4	47.8	40.9
16	53.8	53.7	49.0	59.1	58.7	49.6
17	64.3	62.5	56.9	69.3	68.1	65.7
18	76.0	78.7	73.2	81.9	72.5	74.5
19	83.8	84.6	82.4	89.0	81.9	81.8
20	88.9	89.0	86.9	89.8	90.6	88.3
21	92.5	91.9	90.2	92.1	94.2	94.2
22	95.9	95.6	94.1	94.5	97.1	98.5
23	97.7	97.8	96.7	96.1	98.6	99.3
24	98.6	99.3	98.7	96.9	98.6	99.3
25	99.3	100.0	98.7	97.6	100.0	100.0
26	99.9	100.0	100.0	99.2	100.0	100.0
27	99.9	100.0	100.0	99.2	100.0	100.0
28	99.9	100.0	100.0	99.2	100.0	100.0

Research/Supplemental Scales for the MMPI

Males   Welsh Factor Dimension--Scale A   (A)

		Age, yr				
	Total Sample	13	14	15	16	17
N	624	112	147	130	122	113
Median	14	13	14	15	14	13
Mean	14.95	14.05	15.97	14.76	15.87	13.72
SD	8.79	8.65	9.12	8.66	8.85	8.46
Min	0	0	0	1	1	1
Max	38	35	36	35	35	38

Percentage of Sample with Raw Score < X

X	Total Sample	13	14	15	16	17
0	0.0	0.0	0.0	0.0	0.0	0.0
1	0.5	1.8	0.7	0.0	0.0	0.0
2	3.2	4.5	4.1	3.8	2.5	0.9
3	5.6	6.3	5.4	6.9	5.7	3.5
4	9.6	12.5	8.8	10.0	7.4	9.7
5	12.3	15.2	10.2	13.1	9.8	14.2
6	15.1	18.8	10.9	16.9	12.3	17.7
7	19.2	20.5	17.0	20.8	15.6	23.0
8	23.9	27.7	19.0	24.6	19.7	30.1
9	28.4	34.8	23.1	30.8	22.1	32.7
10	32.1	38.4	28.6	33.1	24.6	37.2
11	35.9	41.1	31.3	40.0	29.5	38.9
12	41.3	48.2	36.7	42.3	36.1	45.1
13	44.9	50.0	42.2	44.6	41.0	47.8
14	49.2	53.6	46.3	48.5	45.1	54.0
15	52.7	55.4	50.3	50.0	51.6	57.5
16	56.3	57.1	51.7	55.4	54.9	63.7
17	59.5	60.7	55.1	57.7	57.4	68.1
18	62.5	62.5	57.1	61.5	61.5	71.7
19	65.1	64.3	61.9	63.1	63.1	74.3
20	67.8	66.1	66.0	66.2	66.4	75.2
21	69.7	69.6	67.3	68.5	67.2	77.0
22	74.7	74.1	72.1	71.5	73.8	83.2
23	76.3	75.9	73.5	73.8	74.6	85.0
24	79.3	80.4	74.8	79.2	77.0	86.7
25	83.2	87.5	78.2	84.6	78.7	88.5
26	86.7	93.8	81.6	87.7	81.1	91.2
27	88.3	94.6	83.7	89.2	83.6	92.0
28	91.5	96.4	87.8	94.6	86.9	92.9
29	93.3	97.3	90.5	96.9	88.5	93.8

Males   Welsh Factor Dimension--Scale A   (A)
(Continued)

X	Total Sample	Percentage of Sample with Raw Score < X				
		13	14	15	16	17
30	94.4	97.3	91.8	96.9	91.0	95.6
31	95.2	97.3	92.5	96.9	94.3	95.6
32	96.0	97.3	93.9	97.7	95.9	95.6
33	96.8	97.3	95.9	98.5	96.7	95.6
34	97.9	98.2	96.6	99.2	98.4	97.3
35	98.4	98.2	98.0	99.2	99.2	97.3
36	99.4	100.0	98.6	100.0	100.0	98.2
37	99.7	100.0	100.0	100.0	100.0	98.2
38	99.8	100.0	100.0	100.0	100.0	99.1

Research/Supplemental Scales for the MMPI

Males   Welsh Factor Dimension--Scale R   (R)

		Age, yr				
	Total Sample	13	14	15	16	17
N	624	112	147	130	122	113
Median	14	15	14	14	15	14
Mean	14.54	15.23	14.51	14.09	14.87	14.06
SD	4.48	4.10	4.60	4.10	5.10	4.36
Min	3	3	5	3	5	4
Max	30	28	29	25	30	25

	Percentage of Sample with Raw Score < X					
X	Total Sample	13	14	15	16	17
3	0.0	0.0	0.0	0.0	0.0	0.0
4	0.3	0.9	0.0	0.8	0.0	0.0
5	0.6	0.9	0.0	0.8	0.0	1.8
6	1.4	0.9	0.7	0.8	2.5	2.7
7	3.4	2.7	2.0	2.3	4.9	5.3
8	5.1	2.7	4.1	3.8	9.0	6.2
9	8.0	3.6	9.5	6.2	11.5	8.8
10	11.1	5.4	10.9	12.3	13.9	12.4
11	17.9	9.8	21.1	21.5	18.0	17.7
12	25.6	17.0	28.6	27.7	28.7	24.8
13	33.8	22.3	36.1	36.9	35.2	37.2
14	42.9	29.5	46.9	45.4	41.8	49.6
15	53.2	46.4	52.4	57.7	50.0	59.3
16	61.2	58.0	61.2	65.4	56.6	64.6
17	67.1	62.5	68.7	70.8	59.8	73.5
18	75.2	75.0	74.1	78.5	69.7	78.8
19	81.1	83.9	78.9	83.8	74.6	85.0
20	86.4	86.6	85.7	90.8	80.3	88.5
21	90.1	90.2	89.8	94.6	83.6	92.0
22	92.6	92.9	91.8	96.2	89.3	92.9
23	95.4	94.6	95.2	96.2	94.3	96.5
24	97.9	97.3	98.0	99.2	96.7	98.2
25	98.2	97.3	98.0	99.2	98.4	98.2
26	99.0	98.2	98.6	100.0	98.4	100.0
27	99.2	99.1	98.6	100.0	98.4	100.0
28	99.4	99.1	98.6	100.0	99.2	100.0
29	99.7	100.0	99.3	100.0	99.2	100.0
30	99.8	100.0	100.0	100.0	99.2	100.0

394

COLLEGE MALADJUSTMENT (MT;Mt)

Because of the difficulty in differentiating MMPI profiles obtained from college students viewed as psychologically adjusted from those of students identified as maladjusted, Kleinmuntz (1960) attempted to develop a scale that would reliably predict proneness toward maladjustment in college.

The MMPIs from 40 students (both men and women, not distinguished in report) were randomly selected from students coming to a university mental hygiene clinic for a routine, but required, mental health screening interview. Only profiles from students whose health questionnaires contained no indication of prior psychiatric treatment were included in this group of "adjusted" students. The "maladjusted" group consisted of 40 students (both men and women, not distinguished in report) who had been involved in psychotherapy for three or more interviews at the same university mental hygiene clinic.

When the responses of the adjusted and maladjusted groups were compared, 43 items were found that discriminated between the groups at a statistically significant level ($p \leq$ 0.01). These items were combined into a scale of college maladjustment (MT;Mt). The mean ($\pm$ SD) raw scores on the MT scale were 23.2 $\pm$ 9.4 for the maladjusted group and 6.8 $\pm$ 5.2 for the criterion group of well-adjusted students.

Subsequently, 50 new profiles (all from women students) were compared with profiles from a new group of 21 maladjusted students (both men and women, not distinguished in report). The mean raw scores were 7.3 $\pm$ 4.9 for the cross-validation group of adjusted students and 28.3 $\pm$ 9.4 for the maladjusted students.

With a cutting score of $\geq$ 15, 96% of the well-adjusted students and 95% of the maladjusted sample would be accurately identified. In the cross-validation groups, 93% of the well-adjusted students and 96% of the members of the maladjusted sample were correctly identified.

Test-retest reliabilities ranging from 0.88 to 0.93 were reported. Because of the differences in MT scores among certain types of college groups, adjustment of cutting scores was recommended.

Six clusters of items were apparent: (a) items suggesting feelings of ineffectualness or worthlessness; (b) items suggesting decreased initiative and a lack of interest in life; (c) items suggesting difficulty in coping with college; (d) items suggesting proneness to worry or nervousness; (e) items suggesting preoccupation with gastrointestinal functions; and (f) items suggesting difficulty with concentration. Overall, high scorers were viewed as ineffectual, pessimistic, procrastinating, anxious, worried persons who tended to somatize and to find life being generally stressful.

Subsequently, Kleinmuntz (1961) developed T-score tables (apparently a linear trans-formation) based on MMPIs from 140 women and 68 men who were college sophomores. The scores for both sexes were similar so a single normative table was constructed. The mean raw score on MT for a new sample of 45 students referred for "emotional counseling" was 20.8 $\pm$ 6.9. A new group of 81 students referred for vocational or academic counseling earned a significantly ($p \leq$ 0.01) lower mean raw score, 12.2 $\pm$ 6.1.

With the cutting score of $\geq$ 15 developed from the derivation study, 84% of the students in the group referred for emotional counseling and 72% of the students referred for vocational or academic counseling would be identified as maladjusted and adjusted, respectively.

REFERENCES

Kleinmuntz, B. (1960). Identification of maladjusted college students. *Journal of Coun-seling Psychology, 7,* 209–211.

Kleinmuntz, B. (1961). The college maladjustment scale (MT): Norms and predictive validity. *Educational and Psychological Measurement, 21*, 1029–1033.

The 43 items of the MT scale, and their direction of scoring, are listed below.

These items score if answered *true:*

   13.   I work under a great deal of tension.
   29.   I am bothered by acid stomach several times a week.
   32.   I find it hard to keep my mind on a task or job.
   41.   I have had periods of days, weeks, or months when I couldn't take care of things because I couldn't "get going."
   84.   These days I find it hard not to give up hope of amounting to something.
   86.   I am certainly lacking in self-confidence.
   93.   I think most people would lie to get ahead.
   94.   I do many things which I regret afterwards (I regret things more or more often than others seem to).
  124.   Most people will use somewhat unfair means to gain profit or an advantage rather than to lose it.
  142.   I certainly feel useless at times.
  236.   I brood a great deal.
  238.   I have periods of such great restlessness that I cannot sit long in a chair.
  259.   I have difficulty in starting to do things.
  298.   If several people find themselves in trouble, the best thing for them to do is to agree upon a story and stick to it.
  301.   Life is a strain for me much of the time.
  314.   Once in a while I think of things too bad to talk about.
  335.   I cannot keep my mind on one thing.
  336.   I easily become impatient with people.
  356.   I have more trouble concentrating than others seem to have.
  361.   I am inclined to take things hard.
  397.   I have sometimes felt that difficulties were piling up so high that I could not overcome them.
  414.   I am apt to take disappointments so keenly that I can't put them out of my mind.
  418.   At times I think I am no good at all.
  442.[a]   I have had periods in which I lost sleep over worry.
  455.   I am quite often not in on the gossip and talk of the group I belong to.
  516.   Some of my family have quick tempers.
  544.   I feel tired a good deal of the time.
  555.   I sometimes feel that I am about to go to pieces.
  560.   I am greatly bothered by forgetting where I put things.

These items score if answered *false:*

    2.   I have a good appetite.
    3.   I wake up fresh and rested most mornings.
    8.   My daily life is full of things that keep me interested.
    9.   I am about as able to work as I ever was.
   18.   I am very seldom troubled by constipation.
   46.   My judgment is better than it ever was.
   63.[a]   I have had no difficulty in starting or holding my bowel movement.
  107.   I am happy most of the time.
  143.   When I was a child, I belonged to a crowd or gang that tried to stick together through thick and thin.

152.   Most nights I go to sleep without thoughts or ideas bothering me.
160.   I have never felt better in my life than I do now.
163.   I do not tire quickly.
242.   I believe I am no more nervous than most others.
407.   I am usually calm and not easily upset.

---

[a]Items that were deleted from the original MMPI item pool during construction of the MMPI-2.

Research/Supplemental Scales for the MMPI

Females   College Maladjustment   (MT;Mt)

		Age, yr				
	Total Sample	13	14	15	16	17
N	691	136	153	127	138	137
Median	17	17	15	17	19	16
Mean	17.01	16.88	16.01	17.44	19.04	15.80
SD	7.83	7.42	7.46	8.64	7.89	7.44
Min	0	1	2	0	2	2
Max	40	33	34	40	37	33

Percentage of Sample with Raw Score < X

X	Total Sample	13	14	15	16	17
0	0.0	0.0	0.0	0.0	0.0	0.0
1	0.1	0.0	0.0	0.8	0.0	0.0
2	0.3	0.7	0.0	0.8	0.0	0.0
3	1.2	0.7	2.0	1.6	0.7	0.7
4	2.5	1.5	2.6	3.1	1.4	3.6
5	4.5	5.1	3.3	4.7	1.4	8.0
6	7.1	8.1	7.8	7.9	2.2	9.5
7	9.3	8.8	9.8	9.4	3.6	14.6
8	12.6	11.0	14.4	14.2	5.8	17.5
9	15.6	14.0	17.0	18.1	9.4	19.7
10	19.7	18.4	24.2	23.6	11.6	20.4
11	22.7	22.8	26.8	26.0	13.0	24.8
12	26.5	26.5	29.4	29.1	16.7	30.7
13	30.7	30.9	35.9	29.9	23.9	32.1
14	35.6	34.6	39.9	37.0	26.8	39.4
15	40.7	39.7	47.1	40.2	32.6	43.1
16	44.7	44.1	52.3	43.3	34.1	48.9
17	48.9	49.3	53.6	45.7	42.0	53.3
18	52.7	51.5	56.2	50.4	46.4	58.4
19	58.0	56.6	62.7	55.9	50.0	64.2
20	64.0	61.8	68.0	61.4	58.7	69.3
21	66.9	64.7	71.9	63.0	60.1	73.7
22	71.3	69.9	75.2	67.7	64.5	78.8
23	74.8	75.7	79.1	70.9	65.9	81.8
24	77.4	79.4	81.0	73.2	68.8	83.9
25	79.9	82.4	83.7	74.0	73.2	85.4
26	83.9	87.5	87.6	78.7	76.8	88.3
27	87.1	89.0	89.5	85.8	79.7	91.2
28	89.6	92.6	91.5	88.2	84.1	91.2
29	91.5	95.6	93.5	89.8	84.8	93.4

Females   College Maladjustment   (MT;Mt)
                              (Continued)

X	Total Sample	Percentage of Sample with Raw Score < X				
		13	14	15	16	17
30	93.6	96.3	96.7	90.6	87.7	96.4
31	95.2	96.3	98.0	91.3	91.3	98.5
32	96.4	97.8	99.3	92.9	92.0	99.3
33	97.8	98.5	99.3	96.1	95.7	99.3
34	98.7	100.0	99.3	96.9	97.1	100.0
35	99.1	100.0	100.0	98.4	97.1	100.0
36	99.3	100.0	100.0	98.4	97.8	100.0
37	99.7	100.0	100.0	99.2	99.3	100.0
38	99.9	100.0	100.0	99.2	100.0	100.0
39	99.9	100.0	100.0	99.2	100.0	100.0
40	99.9	100.0	100.0	99.2	100.0	100.0

Research/Supplemental Scales for the MMPI

Males   College Maladjustment   (MT;Mt)

	Total Sample	Age, yr				
		13	14	15	16	17
N	624	112	147	130	122	113
Median	15	15	16	14	16	14
Mean	15.76	14.95	16.56	15.43	16.96	14.58
SD	7.40	7.64	7.56	7.47	7.03	7.04
Min	1	2	1	3	3	1
Max	34	32	34	31	33	33

	Percentage of Sample with Raw Score < X					
X	Total Sample	13	14	15	16	17
1	0.0	0.0	0.0	0.0	0.0	0.0
2	0.3	0.0	0.7	0.0	0.0	0.9
3	1.4	1.8	2.7	0.0	0.0	2.7
4	3.0	4.5	3.4	3.1	1.6	2.7
5	5.1	6.3	5.4	6.9	1.6	5.3
6	7.1	7.1	7.5	8.5	2.5	9.7
7	9.3	9.8	10.2	10.8	4.1	11.5
8	13.8	17.9	12.2	16.9	8.2	14.2
9	17.8	22.3	13.6	20.8	13.9	19.5
10	22.9	30.4	17.0	25.4	17.2	26.5
11	28.4	37.5	21.8	30.8	20.5	33.6
12	33.0	43.8	27.2	33.8	22.1	40.7
13	37.0	46.4	30.6	38.5	27.9	44.2
14	41.8	47.3	35.4	46.9	32.8	48.7
15	46.3	48.2	43.5	51.5	38.5	50.4
16	52.1	56.3	48.3	53.8	46.7	56.6
17	56.9	60.7	52.4	56.9	53.3	62.8
18	61.2	63.4	57.8	60.8	58.2	67.3
19	64.7	67.9	60.5	64.6	61.5	70.8
20	68.6	70.5	65.3	68.5	65.6	74.3
21	72.4	74.1	69.4	72.3	67.2	80.5
22	76.1	77.7	72.8	76.2	72.1	83.2
23	79.5	82.1	76.9	77.7	76.2	85.8
24	83.3	83.0	81.0	83.1	81.1	89.4
25	86.1	87.5	83.0	85.4	84.4	91.2
26	88.5	91.1	85.7	90.0	85.2	91.2
27	90.4	92.0	87.8	91.5	87.7	93.8
28	92.8	92.0	93.9	92.3	90.2	95.6
29	94.2	93.8	94.6	94.6	92.6	95.6
30	95.7	95.5	94.6	96.2	95.9	96.5

Research/Supplemental Scales for the MMPI

Males   College Maladjustment   (MT;Mt)
(Continued)

X	Total Sample	Percentage of Sample with Raw Score < X				
		13	14	15	16	17
31	97.0	95.5	95.2	99.2	96.7	98.2
32	98.6	99.1	95.9	100.0	99.2	99.1
33	99.2	100.0	98.0	100.0	99.2	99.1
34	99.8	100.0	99.3	100.0	100.0	100.0

MANIFEST ANXIETY (MAS;At)

The Manifest Anxiety scale (MAS) was originally constructed by Taylor (1951, 1953) for use in experimental studies on the role of drive or motivation, as formulated by Hull (1943), in performance on experimental tasks (such as eyelid conditioning). To select subjects, the MAS, a self-report questionnaire describing overt manifestations of anxiety, was used rather than introduction of stress by experimental manipulation (such as electric shock or stress-producing instructions).

To develop the MAS, approximately 200 items from the MMPI were submitted to five clinician-judges who were asked to identify the items reflecting manifest anxiety according to a description of "chronic anxiety reactions." This procedure yielded 65 items on which there was at least 80% agreement among the judges. In its original form, then called the Iowa Manifest Anxiety scale (At), the MAS consisted of these 65 statements supplemented by 135 buffer items that had been unanimously classified by the judges as nonindicative of anxiety, forming a scale of 200 items.

Subsequently, the scale was modified to include only the 50 of the original 65 items that showed a high correlation with the total anxiety scores earned by the original normative group. This group was described as 352 students in an introductory psychology course who earned scores ranging from 1 to 36.

Further normative data were obtained by administering the MAS (however, entitled "Biographical Inventory" for the study) to 1,971 students taking an introductory psychology course at Iowa State University. The mean score for this group was 14.6 (80th percentile, 21; 20th percentile, 7). Women obtained slightly higher scores than men, but the difference was not statistically significant. Scores ranged from 1 to 46 and the distribution was markedly skewed to the right, with the 50th percentile falling at a point slightly above raw score 13. No other descriptive statistics were provided.

Subsequently, the Biographical Inventory was administered to several neurotic and psychotic persons who were undergoing psychiatric treatment (as inpatients and outpatients). Scores ranged from 4 to 49; the median, approximately 34, was equivalent to the 98.8 percentile in the normal sample.

REFERENCES

Hull, C. L. (1943). *Principles of behavior: An introduction to behavior theory.* New York: D. Appleton-Century Company.

Taylor, J. A. (1951). The relationship of anxiety to the conditioned eyelid response. *Journal of Experimental Psychology, 41,* 81–92.

Taylor, J. A. (1953). A personality scale of manifest anxiety. *Journal of Abnormal and Social Psychology, 48,* 285–290.

The 50 items of the MAS;At scale, and their direction of scoring, are listed below.

These items score if answered *true:*

13. I work under a great deal of tension.
14.[a] I have diarrhea once a month or more.
23. I am troubled by attacks of nausea and vomiting.
31. I have nightmares every few nights.
32. I find it hard to keep my mind on a task or job.
43. My sleep is fitful and disturbed.

67.   I wish I could be as happy as others seem to be.
86.   I am certainly lacking in self-confidence.
125.   I have a great deal of stomach trouble.
142.   I certainly feel useless at times.
158.   I cry easily.
186.   I frequently notice my hand shakes when I try to do something.
191.   Sometimes, when embarrassed, I break out in a sweat which annoys me greatly.
217.   I frequently find myself worrying about something.
238.   I have periods of such great restlessness that I cannot sit long in a chair.
241.   I dream frequently about things that are best kept to myself.
263.   I sweat very easily even on cool days.
301.   Life is a strain for me much of the time.
317.   I am more sensitive than most other people.
321.   I am easily embarrassed.
322.   I worry over money and business.
335.   I cannot keep my mind on one thing.
337.   I feel anxiety about something or someone almost all the time.
340.   Sometimes I become so excited that I find it hard to get to sleep.
352.   I have been afraid of things or people that I knew could not hurt me.
361.   I am inclined to take things hard.
397.   I have sometimes felt that difficulties were piling up so high that I could not overcome them.
418.   At times I think I am no good at all.
424.[a]   I feel hungry almost all the time.
431.   I worry quite a bit over possible misfortune.
439.   It makes me nervous to have to wait.
442.[a]   I have had periods in which I lost sleep over worry.
499.   I must admit that I have at times been worried beyond reason over something that really did not matter.
506.   I am a high-strung person.
530.[a]   I am often afraid that I am going to blush.
549.   I shrink from facing a crisis or difficulty.
555.   I sometimes feel that I am about to go to pieces.

These items score if answered *false*:

7.   My hands and feet are usually warm enough.
18.   I am very seldom troubled by constipation.
107.   I am happy most of the time.
163.   I do not tire quickly.
190.   I have very few headaches.
230.   I hardly ever notice my heart pounding and I am seldom short of breath.
242.   I believe I am no more nervous than most others.
264.   I am entirely self-confident.
287.   I have very few fears compared to my friends.
371.   I am not unusually self-conscious.
407.   I am usually calm and not easily upset.
523.[a]   I practically never blush.
528.[a]   I blush no more often than others.

---

[a]Items that were deleted from the original MMPI item pool during construction of the MMPI-2.

Research/Supplemental Scales for the MMPI

Females   Manifest Anxiety   (MAS;At)

	Total Sample	Age, yr				
		13	14	15	16	17
N	691	136	153	127	138	137
Median	20	19	19	20	22	20
Mean	20.05	19.15	18.92	20.98	21.88	19.49
SD	8.60	8.11	8.47	8.88	8.77	8.49
Min	1	3	1	4	3	3
Max	45	37	43	45	42	40

Percentage of Sample with Raw Score < X

X	Total Sample	13	14	15	16	17
1	0.0	0.0	0.0	0.0	0.0	0.0
2	0.3	0.0	1.3	0.0	0.0	0.0
3	0.3	0.0	1.3	0.0	0.0	0.0
4	0.9	1.5	1.3	0.0	0.7	0.7
5	2.9	2.2	3.3	1.6	2.2	5.1
6	4.3	2.9	5.2	3.9	2.9	6.6
7	6.1	5.1	5.9	3.9	5.1	10.2
8	8.1	6.6	9.8	6.3	6.5	10.9
9	10.6	11.0	11.1	10.2	8.0	12.4
10	12.2	14.0	13.7	10.2	8.7	13.9
11	14.3	15.4	16.3	12.6	10.1	16.8
12	17.2	19.1	21.6	15.7	11.6	17.5
13	19.7	21.3	26.1	17.3	13.8	19.0
14	23.9	25.7	29.4	19.7	18.1	25.5
15	28.1	33.1	34.0	22.8	20.3	29.2
16	31.8	36.8	36.6	26.8	23.9	34.3
17	36.5	41.2	40.5	34.6	26.1	39.4
18	40.5	47.8	43.8	37.8	31.2	41.6
19	44.4	48.5	47.7	44.1	37.7	43.8
20	48.9	52.2	54.2	46.5	41.3	49.6
21	53.1	56.6	56.9	51.2	46.4	54.0
22	56.2	60.3	60.1	54.3	50.0	55.5
23	60.9	63.2	64.7	59.8	55.1	61.3
24	64.5	66.2	71.2	63.0	55.8	65.7
25	67.9	72.1	75.2	63.8	58.7	68.6
26	71.9	75.0	78.4	66.1	65.9	73.0
27	75.1	77.9	81.0	69.3	69.6	76.6
28	79.3	84.6	83.7	73.2	72.5	81.8
29	83.1	89.0	86.9	78.0	76.1	84.7
30	86.0	90.4	88.9	81.9	78.3	89.8

Females   Manifest Anxiety   (MAS;At)
                        (Continued)

X	Total Sample	Percentage of Sample with Raw Score < X				
		13	14	15	16	17
31	88.0	91.2	90.8	85.0	81.2	91.2
32	90.6	91.9	93.5	87.4	87.0	92.7
33	91.8	93.4	94.1	90.6	87.7	92.7
34	93.5	94.9	94.8	92.9	89.1	95.6
35	95.2	97.1	95.4	94.5	92.0	97.1
36	96.7	98.5	97.4	95.3	93.5	98.5
37	96.8	98.5	97.4	95.3	94.2	98.5
38	97.8	100.0	98.0	96.1	96.4	98.5
39	98.4	100.0	99.3	96.1	97.1	99.3
40	99.0	100.0	99.3	97.6	98.6	99.3
41	99.6	100.0	99.3	99.2	99.3	100.0
42	99.6	100.0	99.3	99.2	99.3	100.0
43	99.7	100.0	99.3	99.2	100.0	100.0
44	99.9	100.0	100.0	99.2	100.0	100.0
45	99.9	100.0	100.0	99.2	100.0	100.0

Research/Supplemental Scales for the MMPI

Males   Manifest Anxiety   (MAS;At)

| | Total Sample | Age, yr | | | | |
		13	14	15	16	17
N	624	112	147	130	122	113
Median	15	14	16	15	17	15
Mean	16.07	15.07	16.79	15.70	17.08	15.43
SD	8.31	8.46	8.55	8.04	8.17	8.26
Min	0	0	1	0	2	2
Max	38	38	37	34	36	35

| | Percentage of Sample with Raw Score < X | | | | | |
X	Total Sample	13	14	15	16	17
0	0.0	0.0	0.0	0.0	0.0	0.0
1	0.3	0.9	0.0	0.8	0.0	0.0
2	0.6	0.9	0.7	1.5	0.0	0.0
3	2.7	2.7	2.7	3.1	1.6	3.5
4	5.0	5.4	4.8	5.4	3.3	6.2
5	6.4	8.0	5.4	6.2	5.7	7.1
6	8.5	12.5	7.5	8.5	6.6	8.0
7	11.7	17.0	8.8	11.5	9.0	13.3
8	16.5	20.5	12.9	17.7	11.5	21.2
9	20.2	25.9	15.6	22.3	14.8	23.9
10	25.6	33.0	23.1	25.4	18.9	29.2
11	29.5	35.7	26.5	32.3	20.5	33.6
12	34.5	39.3	31.3	37.7	27.9	37.2
13	38.5	43.8	36.1	40.0	33.6	39.8
14	42.9	47.3	39.5	45.4	38.5	45.1
15	47.4	52.7	44.2	49.2	43.4	48.7
16	51.4	56.3	49.7	53.1	46.7	52.2
17	54.8	60.7	53.1	54.6	48.4	58.4
18	58.3	62.5	58.5	56.9	53.3	61.1
19	62.2	67.0	62.6	60.0	56.6	65.5
20	67.5	70.5	66.0	66.9	63.1	71.7
21	70.5	72.3	68.7	70.8	68.0	73.5
22	74.4	76.8	70.7	73.8	73.0	78.8
23	76.4	79.5	72.8	77.7	73.8	79.6
24	78.4	80.4	74.8	78.5	77.0	82.3
25	82.2	86.6	78.9	80.0	81.1	85.8
26	84.1	87.5	80.3	84.6	82.8	86.7
27	87.3	88.4	85.7	86.9	87.7	88.5
28	90.2	90.2	87.8	93.8	91.0	88.5
29	91.8	92.9	89.1	94.6	91.8	91.2

Males   Manifest Anxiety   (MAS;At)
                                    (Continued)

X	Total Sample	Percentage of Sample with Raw Score < X				
		13	14	15	16	17
30	93.3	93.8	91.8	96.9	91.8	92.0
31	94.6	95.5	94.6	97.7	91.8	92.9
32	95.2	96.4	94.6	97.7	91.8	95.6
33	96.6	97.3	95.2	99.2	93.4	98.2
34	97.4	98.2	95.2	99.2	96.7	98.2
35	98.2	98.2	95.9	100.0	98.4	99.1
36	98.7	98.2	97.3	100.0	98.4	100.0
37	99.5	99.1	98.6	100.0	100.0	100.0
38	99.8	99.1	100.0	100.0	100.0	100.0

OVERCONTROLLED HOSTILITY (O-H)

Although Megargee's work (1964) in prisoner typology is well known, many clinicians are unaware of his early research with assaultive and homicidal adolescents regarding the construct of "undercontrol" and "overcontrol." In his dissertation Megargee (1964) studied 76 male adolescents whose average age was 14 to 15 years and who had been incarcerated because of their physical aggressiveness. As contrast samples, 20 boys described as being unmanageable by their parents, but without assaultive crimes, and 26 nonviolent delinquents who had committed offenses against property were studied. It was believed that assaultive delinquents could be divided into two groups: those habitually or chronically aggressive and those chronically overcontrolled. The first group was capable of violence under extreme conditions but had a propensity to engage in chronic but relatively mild forms of aggression. However, the second group was believed to be so inhibited or overcontrolled that the instigation for aggressiveness needed to reach murderous levels before any direct expression of these feelings could occur. This research and the associated views were subsequently summarized (Megargee, 1966) and later led to the development of the Overcontrolled Hostility scale (O-H) for the MMPI (Megargee, Cook, & Mendelsohn, 1967; Megargee & Mendelsohn, 1962).

Because of a need to evaluate the likelihood of aggressive behavior in adjudicated males being considered for probationary status, Megargee and Mendelsohn (1962) reviewed 10 MMPI supplemental scales and 2 special indices believed to have potential for such a task. The scales selected for evaluation purported to measure traits such as hostility, impulsivity, and self-control. Specifically, the scales included Ap (Adjustment to Prison), Hc (Hostility Control), Ho (Hostility), Hv (Overt Hostility), Hy-5 (Inhibition of Aggression), Im (Impulsivity), Jh (Judged Manifest Hostility), Eo (Ego Overcontrol), Nu (Neurotic Undercontrol), and Bc (Bimodal Control). The two MMPI indices were AHI (Active Hostility Index) and FTI (Frustration Tolerance Index).

To cross-validate these scales and to evaluate their practical usefulness, 14 extremely assaultive men, ages 20 to 51 years (mean, 30 years), who had been convicted of such crimes as voluntary manslaughter, second-degree murder, and assault with a deadly weapon were used. A second group of 25 moderately assaultive men, ages 18 to 68 years (mean, 36 years), had been convicted of "battery," defined in the State of California Penal Code as the "unlawful use of force or violence on the person of another." A third group of 25 men, ages 19 to 62 years (mean, 41 years), had been convicted of a nonassaultive crime such as theft or homosexual activity. The fourth group consisted of normal men who were participating in a longitudinal follow-up project (Oakland Adolescent Growth Study); their ages ranged from 36 to 39 years (mean, 37 years; number of subjects not specified).

The results of this evaluation were dismaying because none of the measures discriminated among the groups in the correct direction. Indeed, it was found that assaultive subjects scored higher than the nonviolent criminals on a scale called "Inhibition of Aggression."

Subsequently, primarily because of the frequency with which the scales functioned in the opposite direction from that anticipated, as noted in the example above, the entire study was replicated with new samples (Megargee et al., 1967, p. 519). The results of this cross-validation were essentially the same—none of the measures discriminated among the groups and many of the scales tended to assess the assaultive criminals as being more controlled than their nonassaultive counterparts. It was believed that the heterogeneous nature of the criterion group of assaultive subjects contributed to the notable lack of success of these aggression and hostility scales.

Therefore, prior to initiating a study to develop a new scale for hostility/assaultiveness, Megargee et al. (1967) reexamined the important differences between the chronically overcontrolled-aggressive and the undercontrolled-aggressive types of personality.

The chronically overcontrolled-aggressive person is characterized by strong inhibitions against the expression of virtually any form of aggression. Thus, socially accepted outlets for anger may not be available to this type of person who therefore could experience extreme frustration. Without an appropriate outlet for aggression, these feelings may accumulate to the point such that defense mechanisms are insufficient and an aggressive act then takes place. Because of the considerable instigation necessary to overcome the defenses, the aggressive act is likely to be of extreme intensity. Therefore, Megargee et al. (1967) believed that the chronically overcontrolled-aggressive offender would be likely to commit a more violent crime than the undercontrolled-aggressive offender.

Because persons with the undercontrolled-aggressive type of personality have not appropriately learned the typical middle-class inhibitions or proscriptions against expression of aggression, they are more likely to express such feelings when provoked. Because scale 4 (Pd) was thought to be a satisfactory measure for detecting persons who are undercontrolled, Megargee et al. (1967) attempted to produce a scale that would detect the overcontrolled-aggressive person who represents a greater diagnostic problem for those working with offenders (that is, before an offense, it is important to distinguish between the well-controlled but relatively passive individual who is potentially assaultive and the individual who is not; after an offense it is equally important to discriminate overcontrolled-aggressive offenders from undercontrolled-aggressive offenders because different rehabilitation and management techniques are indicated).

By using two assaultive groups, a nonassaultive convicted group and 46 normal subjects (apparently the samples used in the prior study) as a basis for item analyses, six provisional assaultiveness scales were developed. One of these, a 55-item scale, was able to detect all of the 14 members of the extremely assaultive group and all of the 25 moderately assaultive criminals using a cutting score of ≥ 22. Only 4 of the 25 nonviolent criminals were misclassified.

Subsequently, this scale, at that time labeled As-3r, was cross-validated against three new samples of offenders. These included 14 extremely assaultive, 28 moderately assaultive, and 44 nonviolent criminals. The initial evaluation found excessive overlap in the scores earned by members of the three new criminal samples. The authors then eliminated items that were not discriminating between the assaultive and the nonassaultive groups. This resulted in a 31-item scale of overcontrolled-hostility (O-H). Cutting scores of ≥ 18 or ≥ 21 were suggested, depending on the base rates for assaultiveness in the population being studied; conversely, scores below 12 were suggested as an indication that the person was not likely to be an overcontrolled-aggressive individual with assaultive potential.

For comparison, it should be noted that the offenders described as extremely assaultive obtained a mean ($\pm$ SD) O-H score of 18 $\pm$ 4 and the nonviolent criminals obtained a mean score of 13 $\pm$ 4; two study samples of undergraduate psychology students earned mean scores of 12 $\pm$ 3, and a comparable sample of women undergraduate students earned a mean score of 14 $\pm$ 3.

The authors suggested that the O-H scale assessed two personality constructs, impulse control and hostile alienation, with a high O-H score indicating a conflict between strong aggressive impulses and strong inhibition against their expression. They also recognized that their quest for a scale of general assaultiveness had not been realized.

Later, a factor analysis carried out on O-H scale scores from 200 male prisoners found five major factors (Walters & Greene, 1983): (a) absence of symptoms such as anxiety and depression, (b) defensiveness and denial, (c) chronic hostility and anger, (d) persistent dreaming, and (e) compliance and unassertiveness. Their analysis suggests that high scorers on the O-H scale would tend to carry significant and chronic hostility or resentment while tending to behave in a defensive, unassertive, and compliant manner.

REFERENCES

Megargee, E. I. (1964). *Undercontrol and overcontrol in assaultive and homicidal adolescents.* Berkeley: University of California (University Microfilms, Inc., no. 64–9923, Ann Arbor, MI).

Megargee, E. I. (1966). Undercontrolled and overcontrolled personality types in extreme antisocial aggression. *Psychological Monographs: General and Applied*, 80 no. 3; whole no. 611.

Megargee, E. I., Cook, P. E., & Mendelsohn, G. A. (1967). Development and validation of an MMPI scale of assaultiveness in overcontrolled individuals. *Journal of Abnormal Psychology*, 72, 519–528.

Megargee, E. I., & Mendelsohn, G. A. (1962). A cross-validation of twelve MMPI indices of hostility and control. *Journal of Abnormal and Social Psychology*, 65, 431–438.

Walters, G. D., & Greene, R. L. (1983). Factor structure of the overcontrolled-hostility scale of the MMPI. *Journal of Clinical Psychology*, 39, 560–562.

The 31 items of the O-H scale, and their direction of scoring, are listed below.

These items score if answered *true*:

78.	I like poetry.
91.	I do not mind being made fun of.
229.	I should like to belong to several clubs or lodges.
319.	Most people inwardly dislike putting themselves out to help other people.
338.	I have certainly had more than my share of things to worry about.
373.[a]	I feel sure that there is only one true religion.
394.	I frequently ask people for advice.
425.[a]	I dream frequently.
488.[a]	I pray several times every week.
559.	I have often been frightened in the middle of the night.

These items score if answered *false*:

1.	I like mechanics magazines.
30.	At times I feel like swearing.
81.	I think I would like the kind of work a forest ranger does.
90.	Once in a while I put off until tomorrow what I ought to do today.
102.	My hardest battles are with myself.
109.	Some people are so bossy that I feel like doing the opposite of what they request even though I know they are right.
129.	Often I can't understand why I have been so cross and grouchy.
130.	I have never vomited blood or coughed up blood.
141.	My conduct is largely controlled by the customs of those about me.
165.	I like to know some important people because it makes me feel important.
181.	When I get bored I like to stir up some excitement.
183.	I am against giving money to beggars.
290.	I work under a great deal of tension.
329.	I almost never dream.
382.	I wish I could get over worrying about things I have said that may have injured other people's feelings.
396.	Often, even though everything is going fine for me, I feel that I don't care about anything.
439.	It makes me nervous to have to wait.
446.	I enjoy gambling for small stakes.
475.	When I am cornered I tell that portion of the truth which is not likely to hurt me.
501.	I usually work things out for myself rather than get someone to show me how.
534.	Several times I have been the last to give up trying to do a thing.

---

[a]Items that were deleted from the original MMPI item pool during construction of the MMPI-2.

Research/Supplemental Scales for the MMPI

Females   Overcontrolled Hostility   (O-H)

		Age, yr				
	Total Sample	13	14	15	16	17
N	691	136	153	127	138	137
Median	14	14	14	14	13	14
Mean	13.67	13.66	13.99	13.62	13.36	13.69
SD	2.60	2.33	2.57	2.59	2.64	2.82
Min	6	6	8	8	6	6
Max	22	20	22	21	21	22

	Percentage of Sample with Raw Score < X					
X	Total Sample	13	14	15	16	17
6	0.0	0.0	0.0	0.0	0.0	0.0
7	0.4	0.7	0.0	0.0	0.7	0.7
8	0.7	1.5	0.0	0.0	1.4	0.7
9	2.0	1.5	2.0	0.8	3.6	2.2
10	5.4	5.1	4.6	5.5	6.5	5.1
11	10.4	7.4	7.8	14.2	10.9	12.4
12	18.8	14.7	15.0	19.7	22.5	22.6
13	33.1	31.6	26.8	33.9	39.9	34.3
14	47.0	43.4	42.5	48.8	52.2	48.9
15	63.2	64.7	58.8	60.6	68.8	63.5
16	77.7	78.7	74.5	78.7	81.2	75.9
17	87.6	90.4	86.9	87.4	89.1	83.9
18	93.1	96.3	92.2	94.5	92.8	89.8
19	96.8	98.5	94.8	97.6	97.1	96.4
20	98.3	99.3	98.0	97.6	98.6	97.8
21	98.7	100.0	98.0	98.4	99.3	97.8
22	99.7	100.0	99.3	100.0	100.0	99.3

Research/Supplemental Scales for the MMPI

Males　　　　　　　Overcontrolled Hostility　　(O-H)

	Total Sample	Age, yr				
		13	14	15	16	17
N	624	112	147	130	122	113
Median	12	14	12	12	13	12
Mean	12.41	12.94	12.12	12.32	12.59	12.19
SD	2.93	3.07	3.00	2.76	2.70	3.09
Min	5	6	6	5	5	5
Max	22	22	19	19	20	20

Percentage of Sample with Raw Score < X

X	Total Sample	13	14	15	16	17
5	0.0	0.0	0.0	0.0	0.0	0.0
6	0.8	0.0	0.0	0.8	1.6	1.8
7	1.9	1.8	2.0	1.5	1.6	2.7
8	4.5	4.5	5.4	5.4	2.5	4.4
9	9.0	7.1	10.2	8.5	6.6	12.4
10	15.5	10.7	20.4	15.4	10.7	19.5
11	27.2	24.1	33.3	23.8	20.5	33.6
12	39.7	36.6	42.9	40.0	34.4	44.2
13	51.1	43.8	54.4	53.1	47.5	55.8
14	62.8	50.0	71.4	63.1	66.4	60.2
15	76.1	69.6	78.9	77.7	77.0	76.1
16	84.9	82.1	85.7	87.7	84.4	84.1
17	91.2	88.4	89.8	95.4	91.8	90.3
18	96.5	94.6	94.6	97.7	97.5	98.2
19	98.4	96.4	98.6	98.5	99.2	99.1
20	99.4	98.2	100.0	100.0	99.2	99.1
21	99.8	99.1	100.0	100.0	100.0	100.0
22	99.8	99.1	100.0	100.0	100.0	100.0

CONTROL IN PSYCHOLOGICAL ADJUSTMENT (Cn)

Some persons have psychological resilience, ego strength, stability, and general personal intactness, allowing them to cope successfully with life stresses that may incapacitate others to a point requiring hospitalization. To assess these factors, Cuadra (1956) studied two groups of psychiatric patients who differed in the severity of their psychiatric illness but had comparable MMPI profiles.

The criterion group of abnormally functioning adolescent and young adult patients, all of whom had required hospitalization, was composed of 15 men and 15 women ages 19 to 26. All had completed at least one semester of college and had applied voluntarily for psychiatric treatment. MMPIs were obtained within 21 days after hospitalization; profiles from those with more than 40 unanswered items were excluded. Members of the contrast group, psychiatric patients functioning relatively normally, were selected from outpatient psychiatric clinics; none of these patients had been hospitalized for treatment. More than 4,000 MMPI profiles were reviewed in order to find profiles whose configuration satisfactorily matched those of the criterion group. Scores on scales L, F, and K were not included in the matching process.

Item analysis found 12 items statistically significant with $p < 0.01$ level and 27 with $p < 0.05$ level. However, because the response frequency was low for some of the items and others discriminated successfully only for persons of one sex, seven items were excluded. Additional items selected from those nearly reaching statistically significant levels were included to bring the scale to a total of 50 items.

Scores for the contrast group of relatively normally functioning psychiatric outpatients ranged from 27 to 45 (mean [± SD] raw score, 34.8 ± 4.6); scores for the abnormally functioning group (hospitalized psychiatric patients) ranged from 9 to 33 (mean, 22.4 ± 5.5).

It was concluded that persons having virtually identical MMPI profiles may have answered a significantly different subset of items. Persons not requiring hospitalization but having profiles comparable to those of hospitalized psychiatric patients were successfully differentiated by their endorsement of items positively related to psychological insight and by an absence of rigidity of thinking and behavior.

REFERENCE

Cuadra, C. A. (1956). A scale for control in psychological adjustment (Cn). In G. S. Welsh & W. G. Dahlstrom (Eds.), *Basic readings on the MMPI in psychology and medicine* (pp. 235–254). Minneapolis: University of Minnesota Press.

The 50 items of the Cn scale, and their direction of scoring, are listed below.

These items score if answered *true:*

   6.   I like to read newspaper articles on crime.
  20.   My sex life is satisfactory.
  30.   At times I feel like swearing.
  56.   As a youngster I was suspended from school one or more times for cutting up.
  67.   I wish I could be as happy as others seem to be.
 105.   Sometimes when I am not feeling well I am cross.
 116.   I enjoy a race or game better when I bet on it.
 134.   At times my thoughts have raced ahead faster than I could speak them.
 145.   At times I feel like picking a fist fight with someone.

162. I resent having anyone take me in so cleverly that I have had to admit that it was one on me.
169. I am not afraid to handle money.
181. When I get bored I like to stir up some excitement.
225. I gossip a little at times.
236. I brood a great deal.
238. I have periods of such great restlessness that I cannot sit long in a chair.
285. Once in a while I laugh at a dirty joke.
296. I have periods in which I feel unusually cheerful without any special reason.
319. Most people inwardly dislike putting themselves out to help other people.
337. I feel anxiety about something or someone almost all the time.
382. I wish I could get over worrying about things I have said that may have injured other people's feelings.
411. It makes me feel like a failure when I hear of the success of someone I know well.
418. At times I think I am no good at all.
436. People generally demand more respect for their own rights than they are willing to allow for others.
446. I enjoy gambling for small stakes.
447. I am often inclined to go out of my way to win a point with someone who has opposed me.
460.[a] I have used alcohol moderately (or not at all).
529. I would like to wear expensive clothes.
555. I sometimes feel that I am about to go to pieces.

These items score if answered *false*:

58.[a] Everything is turning out just like the prophets of the Bible said it would.
80. I sometimes tease animals.
92. I would like to be a nurse.
96. I have very few quarrels with members of my family.
111. I have never done anything dangerous for the thrill of it.
167. It wouldn't make me nervous if any members of my family got into trouble with the law.
174. I have never had a fainting spell.
220. I loved my mother.
242. I believe I am no more nervous than most others.
249.[a] I believe there is a Devil and a Hell in afterlife.
250. I don't blame anyone for trying to grab everything he can get in this world.
291. At one or more times in my life I felt that someone was making me do things by hypnotizing me.
313. The man who provides temptation by leaving valuable property unprotected is about as much to blame for its theft as the one who steals it.
360. Almost every day something happens to frighten me.
378.[a] I do not like to see women smoke.
439. It makes me nervous to have to wait.
444.[a] I do not try to correct people who express an ignorant belief.
483.[a] Christ performed miracles such as changing water into wine.
488.[a] I pray several times every week.
489.[a] I feel sympathetic towards people who tend to hang on to their griefs and troubles.
527. The members of my family and my close relatives get along quite well.
548.[a] I never attend a sexy show if I can avoid it.

[a]Items that were deleted from the original MMPI item pool during construction of the MMPI-2.

Research/Supplemental Scales for the MMPI

Females   Control in Psychological Adjustment   (Cn)

| | Total Sample | Age, yr | | | | |
		13	14	15	16	17
N	691	136	153	127	138	137
Median	27	27	27	28	28	28
Mean	27.45	26.74	26.83	27.93	28.15	27.70
SD	4.44	4.58	4.28	4.61	4.26	4.34
Min	13	16	13	14	16	16
Max	42	40	37	42	39	39

| | Percentage of Sample with Raw Score < X | | | | | |
X	Total Sample	13	14	15	16	17
13	0.0	0.0	0.0	0.0	0.0	0.0
14	0.1	0.0	0.7	0.0	0.0	0.0
15	0.3	0.0	0.7	0.8	0.0	0.0
16	0.4	0.0	1.3	0.8	0.0	0.0
17	1.2	0.7	2.0	0.8	1.4	0.7
18	1.6	1.5	2.0	1.6	1.4	1.5
19	2.3	2.9	2.6	1.6	2.2	2.2
20	4.1	5.9	4.6	4.7	2.2	2.9
21	5.9	8.8	5.9	6.3	3.6	5.1
22	8.8	13.2	7.8	8.7	6.5	8.0
23	12.6	19.9	13.1	11.8	7.2	10.9
24	16.9	24.3	21.6	15.0	10.1	13.1
25	25.2	31.6	32.0	21.3	17.4	22.6
26	31.7	39.7	37.9	24.4	26.1	29.2
27	41.5	47.1	47.1	36.2	36.2	40.1
28	51.2	57.4	56.2	47.2	46.4	48.2
29	59.9	64.7	64.1	57.5	55.1	57.7
30	68.0	72.8	70.6	63.8	65.2	67.2
31	76.4	80.1	79.7	73.2	71.0	77.4
32	81.2	84.6	86.3	78.0	73.9	82.5
33	86.3	89.0	91.5	81.9	81.2	86.9
34	92.0	93.4	95.4	89.8	90.6	90.5
35	94.5	95.6	96.7	93.7	94.2	92.0
36	96.5	95.6	98.0	95.3	97.1	96.4
37	98.1	99.3	99.3	96.9	97.8	97.1
38	99.1	99.3	100.0	99.2	98.6	98.5
39	99.4	99.3	100.0	99.2	99.3	99.3
40	99.7	99.3	100.0	99.2	100.0	100.0
41	99.9	100.0	100.0	99.2	100.0	100.0
42	99.9	100.0	100.0	99.2	100.0	100.0

Research/Supplemental Scales for the MMPI

Males   Control in Psychological Adjustment   (Cn)

| | Total Sample | Age, yr | | | | |
		13	14	15	16	17
N	624	112	147	130	122	113
Median	27	26	27	27	27	28
Mean	26.82	25.92	26.69	26.95	27.24	27.28
SD	4.50	4.60	4.97	4.22	4.44	4.08
Min	14	14	15	15	14	17
Max	39	36	38	38	39	38

| X | Percentage of Sample with Raw Score < X | | | | | |
	Total Sample	13	14	15	16	17
14	0.0	0.0	0.0	0.0	0.0	0.0
15	0.5	1.8	0.0	0.0	0.8	0.0
16	1.3	3.6	1.4	0.8	0.8	0.0
17	1.8	4.5	2.7	0.8	0.8	0.0
18	1.9	4.5	2.7	0.8	0.8	0.9
19	3.4	5.4	6.8	1.5	1.6	0.9
20	4.8	8.0	7.5	3.1	3.3	1.8
21	8.7	12.5	11.6	6.9	7.4	4.4
22	12.3	17.0	14.3	10.8	11.5	8.0
23	17.1	22.3	21.8	13.1	13.9	14.2
24	22.4	25.9	26.5	19.2	19.7	20.4
25	29.8	33.9	34.0	27.7	27.0	25.7
26	39.1	42.9	42.9	38.5	36.9	33.6
27	46.2	53.6	48.3	46.2	44.3	38.1
28	54.5	63.4	52.4	57.7	52.5	46.9
29	63.6	72.3	61.2	65.4	58.2	61.9
30	72.0	78.6	70.7	71.5	68.0	71.7
31	78.2	82.1	74.8	79.2	74.6	81.4
32	84.5	89.3	83.0	84.6	79.5	86.7
33	89.9	93.8	87.1	90.0	86.9	92.9
34	94.6	95.5	92.5	96.2	95.1	93.8
35	96.5	98.2	93.9	97.7	96.7	96.5
36	97.8	99.1	96.6	97.7	98.4	97.3
37	98.7	100.0	99.3	97.7	99.2	97.3
38	98.9	100.0	99.3	98.5	99.2	97.3
39	99.8	100.0	100.0	100.0	99.2	100.0

EGO STRENGTH (Es)

The 68 items of the Ego Strength (Es) scale were selected for inclusion because of their correlation with response to psychotherapy in a sample of young adult and adult neurotic patients (Barron, 1953a, b). MMPI responses were obtained from 33 neurotic patients who were subsequently treated for 6 months in a psychiatric clinic. The sample was divided into 17 patients who were judged by two independent raters to have shown clear improvement and 16 patients who were judged to have shown no improvement. The sample consisted of 12 men and 21 women ranging in age from 20 to 45 years. About two-thirds were employed. Two had graduated from college and 28 were high-school graduates; 3 had not completed high school. The mean IQ score (Wechsler-Bellevue Intelligence Scale) was 117. Socioeconomic status was described as lower middle class.

Each had spontaneously sought treatment because of various symptoms; each was seen for 6 months of outpatient psychotherapy by inexperienced psychiatry residents. Patients in the group showing improvement reported improved feelings of well-being in contrast to symptoms of anxiety and depression prior to treatment; they also reported alleviation of symptoms such as headache, frigidity and impotence, and skin disorders and that they had better personal relationships with close family members.

The mean score on the Es scale of the patients showing improvement was 52.7, and the mean score of the group showing no improvement was 29.1 (standard deviations were not reported). From the code-type perspective, clinicians might find it instructive to learn that the mean profile for the unimproved group was characterized by an 8–2–7 code, and all three of these scales had a T score of more than 70, and the mean profile of the group that showed improvement had only one scale—2(D)—with a T score higher than 70.

Barron (1953a) did not present norms for the Es scale, stating that it had "not yet been put in a T-score form which would be comparable to the profile scores of other MMPI scales. This is principally because no representative sample of normal records has been available to the writer" (Barron, 1953a, p. 331).

Later, mean (± SD) raw scores of 44.3 ± 6.2 for men and 40.2 ± 6.2 for women were reported for the Es scale, based on the "improved" subsample of original Minnesota normal subjects (Hathaway & Briggs, 1957).

Still later, factor analysis of the Es scale yielded five factors (Stein & Chu, 1967): (a) emotional well-being, (b) cognitive well-being, (c) physical well-being, (d) areligious views, and (e) heterosexual interest. Normative data for these clusters will not be presented here for space reasons, but they are available upon request.

Barron (1953a) thought that scale Es measured "latent ego strength" (p. 329) and a "capacity for personal integration" (p. 329) and in general believed that the scale provided an "estimate of adaptability and personal resourcefulness" and "effective personal functioning" (p. 327).

REFERENCES

Barron, F. (1953a). An ego-strength scale which predicts response to psychotherapy. *Journal of Consulting Psychology, 17,* 327–333.

Barron, F. (1953b). Some test correlates of response to psychotherapy. *Journal of Consulting Psychology, 17,* 235–241.

Hathaway, S. R., & Briggs, P. F. (1957). Some normative data on the new MMPI scales. *Journal of Clinical Psychology, 13,* 364–368.

Stein, K. B., & Chu, C. L. (1967). Dimensionality of Barron's ego-strength scale. *Journal of Consulting Psychology, 31,* 153–161.

The 68 items composing the Es scale, and their direction of scoring, are listed below.

The following items score if answered *true:*

2. I have a good appetite.
36. I seldom worry about my health.
51. I am in just as good physical health as most of my friends.
95.[a] I go to church almost every week.
109. Some people are so bossy that I feel like doing the opposite of what they request, even though I know they are right.
153. During the past few years I have been well most of the time.
174. I have never had a fainting spell.
181. When I get bored I like to stir up some excitement.
187. My hands have not become clumsy or awkward.
192. I have had no difficulty in keeping my balance in walking.
208. I like to flirt.
221. I like science.
231. I like to talk about sex.
234. I get mad easily and then get over it soon.
253. I can be friendly with people who do things which I consider wrong.
270. When I leave home I do not worry about whether the door is locked and the windows closed.
355. Sometimes I enjoy hurting persons I love.
367. I am not afraid of fire.
380.[a] When someone says silly or ignorant things about something I know about, I try to set him right.
410. I would certainly enjoy beating a crook at his own game.
421. One or more members of my family is very nervous.
430.[a] I am attracted by members of the opposite sex.
458. The man who had most to do with me when I was a child (such as my father, stepfather, etc.) was very strict with me.
513.[a] I think Lincoln was greater than Washington.
515.[a] In my home we have always had the ordinary necessities (such as enough food, clothing, etc.).

The following items score if answered *false:*

14.[a] I have diarrhea once a month or more.
22. At times I have fits of laughing and crying that I cannot control.
32. I find it hard to keep my mind on a task or job.
33. I have had very peculiar and strange experiences.
34. I have a cough most of the time.
43. My sleep is fitful and disturbed.
48. When I am with people, I am bothered by hearing very queer things.
58.[a] Everything is turning out just like the prophets of the Bible said it would.
62. Parts of my body often have feelings like burning, tingling, crawling, or like "going to sleep."
82. I am easily downed in an argument.
94. I do many things which I regret afterwards (I regret things more or more often than others seem to).
100. I have met problems so full of possibilities that I have been unable to make up my mind about them.
132. I like collecting flowers or growing house plants.

140. I like to cook.
189. I feel weak all over much of the time.
209. I believe my sins are unpardonable.
217. I frequently find myself worrying about something.
236. I brood a great deal.
241. I dream frequently about things that are best kept to myself.
244. My way of doing things is apt to be misunderstood by others.
251. I have had blank spells in which my activities were interrupted and I did not know what was going on around me.
261. If I were an artist I would like to draw flowers.
341. At times I hear so well it bothers me.
344. Often I cross the street in order not to meet someone I see.
349. I have strange and peculiar thoughts.
359. Sometimes some unimportant thought will run through my mind and bother me for days.
378.[a] I do not like to see women smoke.
384. I feel unable to tell anyone all about myself.
389. My plans have frequently seemed so full of difficulties that I have had to give them up.
420.[a] I have had some very unusual religious experiences.
483.[a] Christ performed miracles such as changing water into wine.
488.[a] I pray several times every week.
489.[a] I feel sympathetic towards people who tend to hang on to their griefs and troubles.
494. I am afraid of finding myself in a closet or small closed space.
510. Dirt frightens or disgusts me.
525. I am made nervous by certain animals.
541.[a] My skin seems to be unusually sensitive to touch.
544. I feel tired a good deal of the time.
548.[a] I never attend a sexy show if I can avoid it.
554.[a] If I were an artist I would like to draw children.
555. I sometimes feel that I am about to go to pieces.
559. I have often been frightened in the middle of the night.
561.[a] I very much like horseback riding.

---

[a]Items that were deleted from the original MMPI item pool during construction of the MMPI-2.

Research/Supplemental Scales for the MMPI

Females   Ego Strength   (Es)

| | Total Sample | Age, yr | | | | |
		13	14	15	16	17
N	691	136	153	127	138	137
Median	42	42	43	43	42	43
Mean	42.08	40.96	42.56	42.38	40.98	43.47
SD	6.35	6.30	6.16	6.62	6.76	5.62
Min	21	23	21	23	21	32
Max	59	57	57	59	53	57

| X | Percentage of Sample with Raw Score < X | | | | | |
	Total Sample	13	14	15	16	17
21	0.0	0.0	0.0	0.0	0.0	0.0
22	0.3	0.0	0.7	0.0	0.7	0.0
23	0.4	0.0	0.7	0.0	1.4	0.0
24	0.7	0.7	0.7	0.8	1.4	0.0
25	0.9	0.7	0.7	0.8	2.2	0.0
26	0.9	0.7	0.7	0.8	2.2	0.0
27	1.7	1.5	1.3	2.4	3.6	0.0
28	1.9	2.2	1.3	2.4	3.6	0.0
29	2.3	3.7	1.3	3.1	3.6	0.0
30	2.9	4.4	1.3	3.9	5.1	0.0
31	3.6	5.9	2.0	3.9	6.5	0.0
32	5.2	6.6	3.9	5.5	10.1	0.0
33	6.5	8.8	4.6	6.3	12.3	0.7
34	8.5	12.5	6.5	7.9	13.0	2.9
35	12.4	16.2	11.1	11.0	16.7	7.3
36	16.2	19.1	15.0	16.5	21.7	8.8
37	20.1	24.3	18.3	20.5	26.8	10.9
38	24.0	27.9	22.2	24.4	29.7	16.1
39	28.7	36.0	25.5	27.6	32.6	21.9
40	32.4	39.0	29.4	31.5	35.5	27.0
41	37.6	42.6	34.0	38.6	42.8	30.7
42	42.7	49.3	37.9	40.9	48.6	37.2
43	50.5	57.4	45.1	48.8	55.1	46.7
44	56.0	64.0	54.2	51.2	58.7	51.8
45	62.7	71.3	60.8	57.5	67.4	56.2
46	68.2	77.9	66.0	63.8	71.7	61.3
47	73.7	81.6	71.9	70.9	79.7	64.2
48	79.6	83.1	79.1	79.5	82.6	73.7
49	83.9	86.8	83.0	83.5	87.7	78.8
50	89.3	93.4	88.9	87.4	90.6	86.1

Research/Supplemental Scales for the MMPI

Females   Ego Strength   (Es)
                              (Continued)

		Percentage of Sample with Raw Score < X				
X	Total Sample	13	14	15	16	17
51	92.8	96.3	92.2	90.6	94.2	90.5
52	94.8	97.1	95.4	92.1	95.7	93.4
53	97.0	97.8	96.1	96.1	98.6	96.4
54	97.8	98.5	96.7	97.6	100.0	96.4
55	˙98.4	98.5	98.0	98.4	100.0	97.1
56	98.7	98.5	98.7	98.4	100.0	97.8
57	99.4	99.3	99.3	99.2	100.0	99.3
58	99.9	100.0	100.0	99.2	100.0	100.0
59	99.9	100.0	100.0	99.2	100.0	100.0

Research/Supplemental Scales for the MMPI

Males   Ego Strength   (Es)

	Total Sample	Age, yr				
		13	14	15	16	17
N	624	112	147	130	122	113
Median	46	46	44	47	45	48
Mean	45.22	44.48	43.69	46.12	45.13	47.03
SD	5.89	6.25	6.05	5.54	5.27	5.77
Min	23	23	28	34	33	32
Max	58	57	56	58	57	57

Percentage of Sample with Raw Score < X

X	Total Sample	13	14	15	16	17
23	0.0	0.0	0.0	0.0	0.0	0.0
24	0.2	0.9	0.0	0.0	0.0	0.0
25	0.2	0.9	0.0	0.0	0.0	0.0
26	0.2	0.9	0.0	0.0	0.0	0.0
27	0.2	0.9	0.0	0.0	0.0	0.0
28	0.2	0.9	0.0	0.0	0.0	0.0
29	0.3	0.9	0.7	0.0	0.0	0.0
30	0.5	0.9	1.4	0.0	0.0	0.0
31	0.6	0.9	2.0	0.0	0.0	0.0
32	0.6	0.9	2.0	0.0	0.0	0.0
33	1.4	3.6	2.7	0.0	0.0	0.9
34	3.2	6.3	5.4	0.0	0.8	3.5
35	5.0	8.9	8.2	1.5	2.5	3.5
36	6.4	9.8	10.2	2.3	4.1	5.3
37	8.5	10.7	13.6	3.8	6.6	7.1
38	11.2	13.4	15.6	6.9	10.7	8.8
39	15.5	18.8	21.8	10.0	14.8	11.5
40	18.6	22.3	27.2	11.5	18.0	12.4
41	22.6	28.6	31.3	17.7	19.7	14.2
42	26.4	31.3	35.4	23.8	22.1	17.7
43	30.0	34.8	39.5	26.9	27.9	18.6
44	34.9	40.2	43.5	31.5	34.4	23.0
45	41.0	43.8	51.0	40.0	39.3	28.3
46	47.6	47.3	57.1	46.2	51.6	32.7
47	54.5	54.5	68.0	48.5	59.0	38.9
48	61.5	60.7	72.8	56.9	68.9	45.1
49	68.4	68.8	77.6	65.4	74.6	53.1
50	75.5	79.5	82.3	71.5	78.7	63.7
51	80.8	84.8	86.4	79.2	82.0	69.9
52	85.9	90.2	89.8	83.8	88.5	76.1

Research/Supplemental Scales for the MMPI

Males   Ego Strength   (Es)
                            (Continued)

| X | Percentage of Sample with Raw Score < X | | | | | |
	Total Sample	13	14	15	16	17
53	89.6	92.9	93.9	86.2	91.0	83.2
54	93.6	95.5	95.9	90.0	95.9	90.3
55	96.3	99.1	97.3	93.1	98.4	93.8
56	97.3	99.1	98.6	93.8	98.4	96.5
57	99.0	99.1	100.0	97.7	99.2	99.1
58	99.8	100.0	100.0	99.2	100.0	100.0

EGO-RESILIENCY (ER) AND EGO-CONTROL (EC)

In Block's monumental work (1965) in rebutting critics of the MMPI who believed that the patient's response set (for example, general acquiescence; responding to the social desirability level of the items) made the primary contribution to variance in MMPI scores, five useful scales were developed and reported.

After extensive factor analytic studies, Block (1965) characterized the first factor of the MMPI (Alpha) as reflecting ego-resiliency (ER). High scores on the Alpha scales (ER) indicate characteristics of resourcefulness, adaptability, and engagement with the world. Thus, such persons react to new situations in resourceful, tenacious, and elastic ways.

Persons scoring low on the ER scales appear to have little in the way of adaptive margins and tend to respond to stress in a rigid or chaotic manner. They are likely to be more disturbed and more brittle persons, relatively vulnerable to life stress.

The first of the two ER scales that Block (1965) developed to measure Alpha, Ego-Resiliency (Obvious) (ER-O), consisted of 108 MMPI items evenly balanced for the numbers of true and false items "to prevent the intrusion of an acquiescence interpretation" (p. 139); all were significantly related ($p \leq 0.01$) to the Alpha factor.

Because it was thought that ER-O items were relatively clear (that is, "obvious") with regard to intent, deliberate deception or unacknowledged defensiveness could exert a significant bias. Therefore, 40 additional items—20 scored true and 20 scored false—were selected according to the criteria noted above, but composed of relatively subtle content, to form the scale Ego-Resiliency (Subtle) (ER-S).

Persons scoring high on the ER-S and ER-O scales were described as having no undue persistent introspection about self, body, or others, being neither cynical nor overly credulous about others, and as having direction, stability, and an ability to function with relative autonomy. Low scorers on ER-S and ER-O were viewed as fitful, touchy, and ruminative.

The second factor of the MMPI (Beta) described the proneness of an individual to contain or suppress impulses. Thus, a series of Ego-Control (EC) scales measuring the Beta factor were developed. The fifth of these trial scales (EC-5) was composed of 32 items evenly divided between true and false responses. It was viewed as the most preferable of the EC scales because it was balanced for true and false items and also because of its higher reliability.

High scorers on EC were viewed as being overcontrolled, constrained, and distant with minimal expression of personal emotions. They were also described as highly organized and categoric in thinking style, prone to adhere rigidly to previous understandings, able to work on uninteresting tasks for long periods, overconforming, indecisive, and having narrow and relatively unchanging interests; gratification was described as likely to be delayed, even when pleasure was indicated.

Low scorers on EC were viewed as undercontrolled and were described as unduly spontaneous with enthusiasm neither checked nor sustained and as likely to make decisions rapidly and with noticeable emotional fluctuations; social customs and mores are likely to be disregarded or viewed with disdain; proneness for immediate gratification and nonconventional behavior was also suggested.

Because of sex differences, separate scales for men (EC-5M) and women (EC-5F) were developed as a supplement to EC-5. It appears that EC and EC-F,-M were intended to be used in concert.

The samples on which the scales were derived consisted of (a) 100 Air Force officers (Captains), (b) 95 normal men participating in a study of family factors in childhood diseases, (c) 46 normal men participating in a longitudinal study of development at Berkeley, (d) 110 women participating in a study of family factors in childhood diseases, (e) 49 normal women participating in a longitudinal study of growth and development at Berkeley, (f) 254 U.S. Marines who had various psychologic disturbances, (g) 79 women seen at various clinics in a university medical center, (h) 76 college women, of whom half were diagnosed as prehypertensive because of labile blood pressure and the other half were matched normal controls, and (i) 87 female clinic patients, about half of whom were hypertensive and the remainder controls who were comparable to those in the preceding sample (h).

REFERENCE

Block, J. (1965). *The challenge of response sets: Unconfounding meaning, acquiescence, and social desirability in the MMPI.* New York: Appleton-Century- Crofts.

The items composing the ER-O, ER-S, EC-5, EC-5F, and EC-5M scales, and their direction of scoring, are listed below.

Ego-Resiliency (Obvious) (ER-O) (108 Items)

These items score if answered *true:*

3. I wake up fresh and rested most mornings.
7. My hands and feet are usually warm enough.
8. My daily life is full of things that keep me interested.
9. I am about as able to work as I ever was.
18. I am very seldom troubled by constipation.
55. I am almost never bothered by pains over the heart or in my chest.
57. I am a good mixer.
63.[a] I have had no difficulty in starting or holding my bowel movement.
78. I like poetry.
79. My feelings are not easily hurt.
103. I have little or no trouble with my muscles twitching or jumping.
107. I am happy most of the time.
122. I seem to be about as capable and smart as most others around me.
130. I have never vomited blood or coughed up blood.
137. I believe that my home life is as pleasant as that of most people I know.
152. Most nights I go to sleep without thoughts or ideas bothering me.
153. During the past few years I have been well most of the time.
155. I am neither gaining nor losing weight.
160. I have never felt better in my life than I do now.
163. I do not tire quickly.
169. I am not afraid to handle money.
173. I liked school.
176. I do not have a great fear of snakes.
187. My hands have not become clumsy or awkward.
190. I have very few headaches.
207. I enjoy many different kinds of play and recreation.
214. I have never had any breaking out on my skin that has worried me.
230. I hardly ever notice my heart pounding and I am seldom short of breath.
243. I have few or no pains.
257. I usually expect to succeed in things I do.
262. It does not bother me that I am not better looking.
264. I am entirely self-confident.
274. My eyesight is as good as it has been for years.
281. I do not often notice my ears ringing or buzzing.

302.   I have never been in trouble because of my sex behavior.
309.   I seem to make friends about as quickly as others do.
318.   My daily life is full of things that keep me interested.
353.   I have no dread of going into a room by myself where other people have already gathered and are talking.
367.   I am not afraid of fire.
371.   I am not unusually self-conscious.
379.   I very seldom have spells of the blues.
399.   I am not easily angered.
401.   I have no fear of water.
407.   I am usually calm and not easily upset.
412.   I do not dread seeing a doctor about a sickness or injury.
429.[a]   I like to attend lectures on serious subjects.
462.[a]   I have had no difficulty starting or holding my urine.
464.   I have never seen a vision.
479.   I do not mind meeting strangers.
521.   In a group of people I would not be embarrassed to be called upon to start a discussion or give an opinion about something I know well.
527.   The members of my family and my close relatives get along quite well.
533.[a]   I am not bothered by a great deal of belching of gas from my stomach.
542.[a]   I have never had any black tarry-looking bowel movements.
547.   I like parties and socials.

These items score if answered *false:*

13.   I work under a great deal of tension.
15.   Once in a while I think of things too bad to talk about.
21.   At times I have very much wanted to leave home.
26.   I feel that it is certainly best to keep my mouth shut when I'm in trouble.
27.   Evil spirits possess me at times.
29.   I am bothered by acid stomach several times a week.
31.   I have nightmares every few nights.
32.   I find it hard to keep my mind on a task or job.
34.   I have a cough most of the time.
39.   At times I feel like smashing things.
40.   Most any time I would rather sit and daydream than to do anything else.
41.   I have had periods of days, weeks, or months when I couldn't take care of things because I couldn't "get going."
43.   My sleep is fitful and disturbed.
44.   Much of the time my head seems to hurt all over.
47.   Once a week or oftener I feel suddenly hot all over, without apparent cause.
52.   I prefer to pass by school friends, or people I know but have not seen for a long time, unless they speak to me first.
61.   I have not lived the right kind of life.
62.   Parts of my body often have feelings like burning, tingling, crawling, or like "going to sleep."
72.   I am troubled by discomfort in the pit of my stomach every few days or oftener.
76.   Most of the time I feel blue.
84.   These days I find it hard not to give up hope of amounting to something.
86.   I am certainly lacking in self-confidence.
93.   I think most people would lie to get ahead.
94.   I do many things which I regret afterwards (I regret things more or more often than others seem to).

97. At times I have a strong urge to do something harmful or shocking.
108. There seems to be a fullness in my head or nose most of the time.
109. Some people are so bossy that I feel like doing the opposite of what they request even though I know they are right.
114. Often I feel as if there were a tight band about my head.
117. Most people are honest chiefly through fear of being caught.
124. Most people will use somewhat unfair means to gain profit or an advantage rather than to lose it.
125. I have a great deal of stomach trouble.
129. Often I can't understand why I have been so cross and grouchy.
135. If I could get into a movie without paying and be sure I was not seen I would probably do it.
138. Criticism or scolding hurts me terribly.
139. Sometimes I feel as if I must injure either myself or someone else.
142. I certainly feel useless at times.
147. I have often lost out on things because I couldn't make up my mind soon enough.
148. It makes me impatient to have people ask my advice or otherwise interrupt me when I am working on something important.
156. I have had periods in which I carried on activities without knowing later what I had been doing.
157. I feel that I have often been punished without cause.
158. I cry easily.
161. The top of my head sometimes feels tender.
162. I resent having anyone take me in so cleverly that I have had to admit that it was one on me.
166. I am afraid when I look down from a high place.
182. I am afraid of losing my mind.
186. I frequently notice my hand shakes when I try to do something.
189. I feel weak all over much of the time.
215. I have used alcohol excessively.
216. There is very little love and companionship in my family as compared to other homes.
217. I frequently find myself worrying about something.
224. My parents have often objected to the kind of people I went around with.
226. Some of my family have habits that bother and annoy me very much.
234. I get mad easily and then get over it soon.
236. I brood a great deal.

---

[a]Items that were deleted from the original MMPI item pool during construction of the MMPI-2.

Ego-Resiliency (Subtle) (ER-S) (40 Items)

These items score if answered *true*:

36. I seldom worry about my health.
68. I hardly ever feel pain in the back of the neck.
73. I am an important person.
74. I have often wished I were a girl. (Or if you are a girl) I have never been sorry that I am a girl.
91. I do not mind being made fun of.
119. My speech is the same as always (not faster or slower, or slurring; no hoarseness).
131. I do not worry about catching diseases.

167. It wouldn't make me nervous if any members of my family got into trouble with the law.
198. I daydream very little.
222. It is not hard for me to ask help from my friends even though I cannot return the favor.
235. I have been quite independent and free from family rule.
242. I believe I am no more nervous than most others.
270. When I leave home I do not worry about whether the door is locked and the windows closed.
306. I get all the sympathy I should.
329. I almost never dream.
369.[a] Religion gives me no worry.
478.[a] I have never been made especially nervous over trouble that any members of my family have gotten into.
523.[a] I practically never blush.
528.[a] I blush no more often than others.
532. I can stand as much pain as others can.

These items score if answered *false*:

5. I am easily awakened by noise.
71. I think a great many people exaggerate their misfortunes in order to gain the sympathy and help of others.
89. It takes a lot of argument to convince most people of the truth.
102. My hardest battles are with myself.
112. I frequently find it necessary to stand up for what I think is right.
134. At times my thoughts have raced ahead faster than I could speak them.
201. I wish I were not so shy.
279. I drink an unusually large amount of water every day.
323. I have had very peculiar and strange experiences.
327. My mother or father often made me obey even when I thought that it was unreasonable.
382. I wish I could get over worrying about things I have said that may have injured other people's feelings.
390. I have often felt badly over being misunderstood when trying to keep someone from making a mistake.
394. I frequently ask people for advice.
402. I often must sleep over a matter before I decide what to do.
425.[a] I dream frequently.
458. The man who had most to do with me when I was a child (such as my father, stepfather, etc.) was very strict with me.
465. I have several times had a change of heart about my life work.
468. I am often sorry because I am so cross and grouchy.
489.[a] I feel sympathetic towards people who tend to hang on to their griefs and troubles.
505. I have had periods when I felt so full of pep that sleep did not seem necessary for days at a time.

Ego-Control—Scale 5 (EC-5) (32 Items)

These items score if answered *true*:

37. I have never been in trouble because of my sex behavior.
74. I have often wished I were a girl. (Or if you are a girl) I have never been sorry that I am a girl.

95.[a] I go to church almost every week.

96.   I have very few quarrels with members of my family.

111.   I have never done anything dangerous for the thrill of it.

132.   I like collecting flowers or growing house plants.

133.   I have never indulged in any unusual sex practices.

294.   I have never been in trouble with the law.

329.   I almost never dream.

373.[a] I feel sure that there is only one true religion.

377.   At parties I am more likely to sit by myself or with just one other person than to join in with the crowd.

453.   When I was a child I didn't care to be a member of a crowd or gang.

466.   Except by a doctor's orders I never take drugs or sleeping powders.

490.[a] I read in the Bible several times a week.

503.[a] It is unusual for me to express strong approval or disapproval of the actions of others.

548.[a] I never attend a sexy show if I can avoid it.

These items score if answered *false:*

38.   During one period when I was a youngster I engaged in petty thievery.

45.   I do not always tell the truth.

56.   As a youngster I was suspended from school one or more times for cutting up.

118.   In school I was sometimes sent to the principal for cutting up.

195.   I do not like everyone I know.

208.   I like to flirt.

215.   I have used alcohol excessively.

372.[a] I tend to be interested in several different hobbies rather than to stick to one of them for a long time.

415.   If given the chance I would make a good leader of people.

430.[a] I am attracted by members of the opposite sex.

434.   I would like to be an auto racer.

446.   I enjoy gambling for small stakes.

447.   I am often inclined to go out of my way to win a point with someone who has opposed me.

482.   While in trains, busses, etc., I often talk to strangers.

491.[a] I have no patience with people who believe there is only one true religion.

537.[a] I would like to hunt lions in Africa.

Ego-Control—Female (EC-5F) (34 Items)

These items score if answered *true:*

55.   I am almost never bothered by pains over the heart or in my chest.

68.   I hardly ever feel pain in the back of the neck.

82.   I am easily downed in an argument.

111.   I have never done anything dangerous for the thrill of it.

117.   Most people are honest chiefly through fear of being caught.

124.   Most people will use somewhat unfair means to gain profit or an advantage rather than to lose it.

141.   My conduct is largely controlled by the customs of those about me.

171.   It makes me uncomfortable to put on a stunt at a party even when others are doing the same sort of things.

180.   I find it hard to make talk when I meet new people.

201.   I wish I were not so shy.

260.   I was a slow learner in school.
267.   When in a group of people I have trouble thinking of the right things to talk about.
292.   I am likely not to speak to people until they speak to me.
304.   In school I found it very hard to talk before the class.
316.   I think nearly anyone would tell a lie to keep out of trouble.
321.   I am easily embarrassed.
377.   At parties I am more likely to sit by myself or with just one other person than to join in with the crowd.
530.[a]   I am often afraid that I am going to blush.

These items score if answered *false:*

21.   At times I have very much wanted to leave home.
57.   I am a good mixer.
126.   I like dramatics.
204.   I would like to be a journalist.
208.   I like to flirt.
226.   Some of my family have habits that bother and annoy me very much.
309.   I seem to make friends about as quickly as others do.
409.[a]   At times I have worn myself out by undertaking too much.
428.[a]   I like to read newspaper editorials.
429.[a]   I like to attend lectures on serious subjects.
432.   I have strong political opinions.
479.   I do not mind meeting strangers.
482.   While in trains, busses, etc., I often talk to strangers.
521.   In a group of people I would not be embarrassed to be called upon to start a discussion or give an opinion about something I know well.
523.[a]   I practically never blush.
529.   I would like to wear expensive clothes.

———————————

[a]Items that were deleted from the original MMPI item pool during construction of the MMPI-2.

Ego-Control—Male (EC-5M) (70 Items)

These items score if answered *true:*

58.   Everything is turning out just like the prophets of the Bible said it would.
82.   I am easily downed in an argument.
111.   I have never done anything dangerous for the thrill of it.
115.   I believe in a life hereafter.
133.   I have never indulged in any unusual sex practices.
171.   It makes me uncomfortable to put on a stunt at a party even when others are doing the same sort of things.
172.   I frequently have to fight against showing that I am bashful.
180.   I find it hard to make talk when I meet new people.
201.   I wish I were not so shy.
249.[a]   I believe there is a Devil and a Hell in afterlife.
267.   When in a group of people I have trouble thinking of the right things to talk about.
292.   I am likely not to speak to people until they speak to me.
304.   In school I found it very hard to talk before the class.
321.   I am easily embarrassed.
329.   I almost never dream.

377.   At parties I am more likely to sit by myself or with just one other person than to join in with the crowd.
378.ᵃ   I do not like to see women smoke.
385.   Lightning is one of my fears.
453.ᵃ   When I was a child I didn't care to be a member of a crowd or gang.
503.ᵃ   It is unusual for me to express strong approval or disapproval of the actions of others.
509.   I sometimes find it hard to stick up for my rights because I am so reserved.
548.ᵃ   I never attend a sexy show if I can avoid it.

These items score if answered *false:*

19.   When I take a new job, I like to be tipped off on who should be gotten next to.
21.   At times I have very much wanted to leave home.
38.   During one period when I was a youngster I engaged in petty thievery.
39.   At times I feel like smashing things.
45.   I do not always tell the truth.
56.   As a youngster I was suspended from school one or more times for cutting up.
57.   I am a good mixer.
78.   I like poetry.
99.   I like to go to parties and other affairs where there is lots of loud fun.
118.   In school I was sometimes sent to the principal for cutting up.
126.   I like dramatics.
142.   I certainly feel useless at times.
145.   At times I feel like picking a fist fight with someone.
149.   I used to keep a diary.
181.   When I get bored I like to stir up some excitement.
204.   I would like to be a journalist.
208.   I like to flirt.
229.   I should like to belong to several clubs or lodges.
231.   I like to talk about sex.
233.   I have at times stood in the way of people who were trying to do something, not because it amounted to much but because of the principle of the thing.
234.   I get mad easily and then get over it soon.
238.   I have periods of such great restlessness that I cannot sit long in a chair.
254.   I like to be with a crowd who play jokes on one another.
277.   At times I have been so entertained by the cleverness of a crook that I have hoped he would get by with it.
282.   Once in a while I feel hate toward members of my family whom I usually love.
322.   I worry over money and business.
400.   If given the chance I could do some things that would be of great benefit to the world.
417.   I am often so annoyed when someone tries to get ahead of me in a line of people that I speak to him about it.
425.ᵃ   I dream frequently.
426.   I have at times had to be rough with people who were rude or annoying.
430.   I am attracted by members of the opposite sex.
432.   I have strong political opinions.
438.   There are certain people whom I dislike so much that I am inwardly pleased when they are catching it for something they have done.
441.ᵃ   I like tall women.
446.   I enjoy gambling for small stakes.

447.   I am often inclined to go out of my way to win a point with someone who has opposed me.
449.   I enjoy social gatherings just to be with people.
450.   I enjoy the excitement of a crowd.
451.   My worries seem to disappear when I get into a crowd of lively friends.
452.   I like to poke fun at people.
463.   I used to like hopscotch.
465.   I have several times had a change of heart about my life work.
471.   In school my marks in deportment were quite regularly bad.
482.   While in trains, busses, etc., I often talk to strangers.
520.   I strongly defend my own opinions as a rule.
521.   In a group of people I would not be embarrassed to be called upon to start a discussion or give an opinion about something I know well.
529.   I would like to wear expensive clothes.
547.   I like parties and socials.

---

[a]Items that were deleted from the original MMPI item pool during construction of the MMPI-2.

Research/Supplemental Scales for the MMPI

Females   Ego-Resiliency (Obvious)   (ER-O)

| | | | | Age, yr | | |
	Total Sample	13	14	15	16	17
N	691	136	153	127	138	137
Median	72	72	74	73	67	73
Mean	71.07	71.10	73.03	69.84	67.57	73.53
SD	14.47	13.43	13.64	16.41	15.09	13.14
Min	18	38	33	18	30	38
Max	106	101	106	104	105	99

Percentage of Sample with Raw Score < X

X	Total Sample	13	14	15	16	17
18	0.0	0.0	0.0	0.0	0.0	0.0
19	0.1	0.0	0.0	0.8	0.0	0.0
20	0.1	0.0	0.0	0.8	0.0	0.0
21	0.1	0.0	0.0	0.8	0.0	0.0
22	0.1	0.0	0.0	0.8	0.0	0.0
23	0.1	0.0	0.0	0.8	0.0	0.0
24	0.1	0.0	0.0	0.8	0.0	0.0
25	0.1	0.0	0.0	0.8	0.0	0.0
26	0.1	0.0	0.0	0.8	0.0	0.0
27	0.1	0.0	0.0	0.8	0.0	0.0
28	0.1	0.0	0.0	0.8	0.0	0.0
29	0.1	0.0	0.0	0.8	0.0	0.0
30	0.1	0.0	0.0	0.8	0.0	0.0
31	0.3	0.0	0.0	0.8	0.7	0.0
32	0.3	0.0	0.0	0.8	0.7	0.0
33	0.6	0.0	0.0	0.8	2.2	0.0
34	0.9	0.0	0.7	0.8	2.9	0.0
35	1.0	0.0	0.7	1.6	2.9	0.0
36	1.0	0.0	0.7	1.6	2.9	0.0
37	1.0	0.0	0.7	1.6	2.9	0.0
38	1.6	0.0	0.7	3.1	4.3	0.0
39	2.3	0.7	0.7	3.9	5.8	0.7
40	2.7	1.5	1.3	4.7	5.8	0.7
41	3.5	1.5	1.3	6.3	6.5	2.2
42	4.2	1.5	2.0	7.1	8.0	2.9
43	4.3	1.5	2.0	7.9	8.0	2.9
44	4.5	1.5	2.0	8.7	8.0	2.9
45	4.9	2.2	2.0	9.4	8.7	2.9
46	5.5	2.9	2.6	10.2	8.7	3.6
47	5.5	2.9	2.6	10.2	8.7	3.6

Research/Supplemental Scales for the MMPI

Females   Ego-Resiliency (Obvious)   (ER-O)
(Continued)

| X | Percentage of Sample with Raw Score < X | | | | | |
	Total Sample	13	14	15	16	17
48	5.6	2.9	2.6	10.2	9.4	3.6
49	6.5	2.9	2.6	11.0	13.0	3.6
50	6.9	3.7	3.3	11.8	13.0	3.6
51	7.5	5.1	3.3	11.8	13.8	4.4
52	8.8	5.1	5.2	13.4	14.5	6.6
53	10.3	6.6	7.8	15.7	14.5	7.3
54	12.0	7.4	11.8	18.1	15.9	7.3
55	14.2	13.2	13.7	18.9	16.7	8.8
56	14.8	13.2	14.4	18.9	18.1	9.5
57	16.9	16.9	15.7	20.5	21.0	10.9
58	17.9	18.4	15.7	22.0	22.5	11.7
59	19.4	21.3	16.3	24.4	23.2	12.4
60	20.8	23.5	17.0	26.8	24.6	13.1
61	22.3	25.0	17.0	29.1	28.3	13.1
62	23.9	25.0	19.6	30.7	29.7	15.3
63	25.3	27.2	20.9	31.5	31.9	16.1
64	27.6	29.4	22.9	33.1	35.5	18.2
65	30.0	31.6	23.5	34.6	39.1	21.9
66	33.4	33.8	28.1	37.0	44.2	24.8
67	36.6	39.0	30.7	39.4	47.1	27.7
68	38.9	40.4	32.7	40.9	50.7	30.7
69	41.1	41.9	34.6	43.3	53.6	32.8
70	43.7	44.9	37.9	44.9	56.5	35.0
71	45.6	47.1	40.5	44.9	57.2	38.7
72	48.0	50.0	42.5	46.5	58.7	43.1
73	50.9	53.7	43.8	48.8	62.3	46.7
74	54.6	56.6	49.0	53.5	63.8	50.4
75	57.2	59.6	52.3	55.1	65.9	53.3
76	59.2	61.8	54.9	55.9	67.4	56.2
77	62.1	65.4	56.2	59.8	71.0	58.4
78	65.0	69.1	58.8	64.6	72.5	60.6
79	68.2	71.3	63.4	66.9	73.9	65.7
80	70.9	72.8	66.7	69.3	78.3	67.9
81	73.5	76.5	69.9	71.7	79.7	70.1
82	75.1	77.9	71.2	74.0	80.4	72.3
83	77.0	78.7	74.5	75.6	81.9	74.5
84	79.5	79.4	77.8	79.5	83.3	77.4
85	81.9	80.9	80.4	82.7	87.0	78.8
86	82.8	82.4	81.7	82.7	87.7	79.6
87	85.5	85.3	85.0	85.8	90.6	81.0

Females   Ego-Resiliency (Obvious)   (ER-O)
(Continued)

X	Percentage of Sample with Raw Score < X					
	Total Sample	13	14	15	16	17
88	87.7	87.5	86.9	87.4	92.0	84.7
89	89.0	89.0	88.2	89.8	93.5	84.7
90	90.7	91.2	89.5	90.6	94.9	87.6
91	91.8	91.9	89.5	91.3	95.7	90.5
92	92.9	93.4	90.8	92.1	96.4	92.0
93	94.4	94.1	92.8	94.5	97.8	92.7
94	95.2	95.6	93.5	95.3	97.8	94.2
95	95.8	96.3	94.1	95.3	97.8	95.6
96	96.5	96.3	95.4	96.9	98.6	95.6
97	97.7	97.1	98.0	97.6	98.6	97.1
98	98.1	98.5	98.0	97.6	98.6	97.8
99	98.6	98.5	98.7	97.6	99.3	98.5
100	99.1	98.5	99.3	98.4	99.3	100.0
101	99.4	99.3	99.3	99.2	99.3	100.0
102	99.6	100.0	99.3	99.2	99.3	100.0
103	99.6	100.0	99.3	99.2	99.3	100.0
104	99.6	100.0	99.3	99.2	99.3	100.0
105	99.7	100.0	99.3	100.0	99.3	100.0
106	99.9	100.0	99.3	100.0	100.0	100.0

Research/Supplemental Scales for the MMPI

Females   Ego-Resiliency (Subtle)   (ER-S)

		Age, yr				
	Total Sample	13	14	15	16	17
N	691	136	153	127	138	137
Median	20	20	20	19	18	19
Mean	19.48	19.93	19.97	19.09	18.65	19.68
SD	4.87	4.64	4.87	4.94	5.10	4.74
Min	5	10	8	5	8	9
Max	35	31	35	29	31	31

Percentage of Sample with Raw Score < X

X	Total Sample	13	14	15	16	17
5	0.0	0.0	0.0	0.0	0.0	0.0
6	0.1	0.0	0.0	0.8	0.0	0.0
7	0.4	0.0	0.0	2.4	0.0	0.0
8	0.4	0.0	0.0	2.4	0.0	0.0
9	0.9	0.0	0.7	2.4	1.4	0.0
10	1.7	0.0	1.3	4.7	2.2	0.7
11	2.9	1.5	2.6	5.5	4.3	0.7
12	5.1	3.7	5.2	6.3	8.0	2.2
13	7.5	5.9	7.2	10.2	10.1	4.4
14	12.0	9.6	11.8	13.4	17.4	8.0
15	15.6	14.0	13.1	18.9	20.3	12.4
16	21.7	19.1	17.0	22.0	29.7	21.2
17	27.8	25.0	24.2	27.6	35.5	27.0
18	34.6	30.1	30.7	31.5	44.9	35.8
19	42.5	36.8	39.2	39.4	53.6	43.8
20	49.9	43.4	44.4	52.0	56.5	54.0
21	58.6	55.9	53.6	58.3	63.8	62.0
22	65.1	63.2	59.5	66.1	70.3	67.2
23	72.1	70.6	66.7	74.8	77.5	71.5
24	78.6	76.5	73.9	83.5	82.6	77.4
25	84.7	82.4	82.4	89.0	88.4	81.8
26	89.0	87.5	89.5	91.3	89.1	87.6
27	92.3	91.9	92.2	94.5	92.8	90.5
28	94.6	96.3	95.4	96.1	93.5	92.0
29	97.1	97.1	98.0	98.4	96.4	95.6
30	98.3	97.8	98.0	100.0	97.8	97.8
31	99.0	99.3	98.7	100.0	98.6	98.5
32	99.9	100.0	99.3	100.0	100.0	100.0
33	99.9	100.0	99.3	100.0	100.0	100.0
34	99.9	100.0	99.3	100.0	100.0	100.0

Research/Supplemental Scales for the MMPI

Females   Ego-Resiliency (Subtle)   (ER-S)
                              (Continued)

| X | Total Sample | Percentage of Sample with Raw Score < X | | | | |
		13	14	15	16	17
35	99.9	100.0	99.3	100.0	100.0	100.0

Research/Supplemental Scales for the MMPI

Females   Ego-Control--Scale 5   (EC-5)

		Age, yr				
	Total Sample	13	14	15	16	17
N	691	136	153	127	138	137
Median	17	18	18	16	17	17
Mean	17.30	18.21	17.81	16.94	16.93	16.55
SD	3.61	3.42	3.33	3.58	3.73	3.77
Min	5	7	8	8	7	5
Max	29	26	28	29	27	25

Percentage of Sample with Raw Score < X

X	Total Sample	13	14	15	16	17
5	0.0	0.0	0.0	0.0	0.0	0.0
6	0.1	0.0	0.0	0.0	0.0	0.7
7	0.1	0.0	0.0	0.0	0.0	0.7
8	0.4	0.7	0.0	0.0	0.7	0.7
9	1.3	1.5	0.7	0.8	1.4	2.2
10	2.3	1.5	0.7	0.8	2.2	6.6
11	3.5	1.5	1.3	3.1	5.1	6.6
12	5.6	1.5	3.9	6.3	7.2	9.5
13	8.1	2.2	5.9	8.7	11.6	12.4
14	14.5	8.1	9.8	15.0	20.3	19.7
15	21.3	13.2	16.3	25.2	25.4	27.0
16	30.5	22.1	24.8	36.2	33.3	37.2
17	41.0	32.4	34.0	51.2	40.6	48.2
18	50.7	44.1	41.8	57.5	54.3	56.9
19	63.2	52.2	58.2	66.9	68.8	70.8
20	71.5	61.0	66.7	77.2	76.8	76.6
21	80.0	71.3	79.7	82.7	83.3	83.2
22	88.9	83.8	87.6	88.2	90.6	94.2
23	93.5	89.7	94.8	93.7	94.2	94.9
24	97.0	95.6	97.4	97.6	96.4	97.8
25	98.0	97.1	98.0	98.4	97.1	99.3
26	99.1	99.3	98.7	99.2	98.6	100.0
27	99.6	100.0	99.3	99.2	99.3	100.0
28	99.7	100.0	99.3	99.2	100.0	100.0
29	99.9	100.0	100.0	99.2	100.0	100.0

Research/Supplemental Scales for the MMPI

Females   Ego-Control--Male   (EC-5M)

		Age, yr				
	Total Sample	13	14	15	16	17
N	0	0	0	0	0	0
Median						
Mean						
SD						
Min						
Max						

		Percentage of Sample with Raw Score < X				
X	Total Sample	13	14	15	16	17

Research/Supplemental Scales for the MMPI

Females   Ego-Control--Female   (EC-5F)

| | Total Sample | Age, yr | | | | |
		13	14	15	16	17
N	691	136	153	127	138	137
Median	16	18	16	16	16	15
Mean	16.33	17.75	16.61	16.10	16.36	14.80
SD	4.76	4.00	4.91	4.85	4.59	4.97
Min	3	7	5	3	6	4
Max	29	26	29	28	28	27

Percentage of Sample with Raw Score < X

X	Total Sample	13	14	15	16	17
3	0.0	0.0	0.0	0.0	0.0	0.0
4	0.1	0.0	0.0	0.8	0.0	0.0
5	0.3	0.0	0.0	0.8	0.0	0.7
6	1.0	0.0	0.7	2.4	0.0	2.2
7	1.6	0.0	1.3	2.4	0.7	3.6
8	3.0	0.7	3.9	4.7	0.7	5.1
9	5.2	0.7	6.5	6.3	2.2	10.2
10	8.7	1.5	9.8	10.2	5.8	16.1
11	11.6	4.4	10.5	11.8	9.4	21.9
12	15.9	7.4	13.1	17.3	13.0	29.2
13	21.9	10.3	20.9	22.8	21.0	34.3
14	28.5	13.2	26.1	31.5	29.0	43.1
15	35.9	21.3	33.3	37.0	39.1	48.9
16	42.5	29.4	39.2	42.5	47.1	54.7
17	51.4	39.7	50.3	50.4	54.3	62.0
18	59.2	47.8	56.2	58.3	63.0	70.8
19	66.1	55.9	64.1	66.9	68.1	75.9
20	72.8	63.2	71.9	73.2	74.6	81.0
21	80.5	74.3	79.7	83.5	79.7	85.4
22	85.4	81.6	84.3	89.0	83.3	89.1
23	89.7	85.3	89.5	91.3	89.9	92.7
24	93.9	92.6	92.8	94.5	92.8	97.1
25	96.5	97.1	95.4	96.9	95.7	97.8
26	97.5	98.5	96.1	97.6	97.1	98.5
27	98.4	100.0	96.7	98.4	97.8	99.3
28	99.3	100.0	98.0	99.2	99.3	100.0
29	99.7	100.0	98.7	100.0	100.0	100.0

Research/Supplemental Scales for the MMPI

Males   Ego-Resiliency (Obvious)   (ER-O)

		Age, yr				
	Total Sample	13	14	15	16	17
N	624	112	147	130	122	113
Median	76	76	74	78	75	78
Mean	74.42	74.22	72.12	75.58	73.10	77.68
SD	13.42	14.27	13.53	13.51	12.54	12.65
Min	34	37	34	44	45	47
Max	103	101	102	102	98	103

Percentage of Sample with Raw Score < X

X	Total Sample	13	14	15	16	17
34	0.0	0.0	0.0	0.0	0.0	0.0
35	0.2	0.0	0.7	0.0	0.0	0.0
36	0.3	0.0	1.4	0.0	0.0	0.0
37	0.3	0.0	1.4	0.0	0.0	0.0
38	0.5	0.9	1.4	0.0	0.0	0.0
39	0.5	0.9	1.4	0.0	0.0	0.0
40	0.5	0.9	1.4	0.0	0.0	0.0
41	0.6	1.8	1.4	0.0	0.0	0.0
42	0.6	1.8	1.4	0.0	0.0	0.0
43	0.6	1.8	1.4	0.0	0.0	0.0
44	0.8	2.7	1.4	0.0	0.0	0.0
45	1.3	2.7	2.7	0.8	0.0	0.0
46	1.8	3.6	3.4	0.8	0.8	0.0
47	2.2	4.5	4.1	1.5	0.8	0.0
48	2.7	4.5	4.8	2.3	0.8	0.9
49	2.7	4.5	4.8	2.3	0.8	0.9
50	3.4	4.5	5.4	2.3	2.5	1.8
51	3.8	4.5	5.4	3.8	3.3	1.8
52	4.5	4.5	6.1	5.4	3.3	2.7
53	5.1	4.5	6.8	6.2	4.9	2.7
54	6.4	5.4	8.8	6.9	6.6	3.5
55	8.8	5.4	10.9	9.2	10.7	7.1
56	9.8	5.4	12.2	10.0	13.1	7.1
57	10.6	6.3	12.9	10.8	14.8	7.1
58	12.0	9.8	15.0	12.3	14.8	7.1
59	13.3	13.4	17.0	12.3	14.8	8.0
60	14.3	15.2	18.4	12.3	15.6	8.8
61	17.5	20.5	23.1	14.6	18.0	9.7
62	19.6	22.3	24.5	16.9	20.5	12.4
63	21.5	25.0	25.2	19.2	23.8	13.3

Males   Ego-Resiliency (Obvious)   (ER-O)
                        (Continued)

X	Percentage of Sample with Raw Score < X					
	Total Sample	13	14	15	16	17
64	23.1	25.0	27.2	20.8	26.2	15.0
65	24.8	27.7	29.3	22.3	28.7	15.0
66	26.6	30.4	29.9	25.4	29.5	16.8
67	28.4	32.1	32.7	26.9	31.1	17.7
68	30.8	36.6	34.7	29.2	32.8	19.5
69	33.0	41.1	36.7	30.8	33.6	22.1
70	35.4	42.0	38.8	32.3	38.5	24.8
71	38.6	43.8	42.2	35.4	43.4	27.4
72	40.5	44.6	44.9	36.9	45.1	30.1
73	42.0	46.4	46.3	40.0	45.1	31.0
74	45.0	49.1	49.7	41.5	47.5	36.3
75	47.1	49.1	52.4	44.6	50.0	38.1
76	49.5	50.0	54.4	47.7	53.3	40.7
77	51.9	51.8	55.8	49.2	57.4	44.2
78	54.3	54.5	58.5	50.0	60.7	46.9
79	58.3	57.1	67.3	52.3	61.5	51.3
80	61.9	60.7	70.7	55.4	64.8	55.8
81	63.8	62.5	72.1	59.2	66.4	56.6
82	67.0	64.3	78.2	60.0	69.7	60.2
83	69.6	67.0	78.9	64.6	72.1	62.8
84	70.8	67.9	80.3	64.6	74.6	64.6
85	74.0	68.8	83.0	70.8	77.0	68.1
86	77.7	73.2	85.0	74.6	82.0	71.7
87	79.8	74.1	87.1	76.9	83.6	75.2
88	83.0	78.6	89.1	80.8	86.1	78.8
89	85.7	80.4	91.8	83.1	90.2	81.4
90	87.7	83.9	92.5	85.4	92.6	82.3
91	89.7	89.3	93.2	86.9	94.3	84.1
92	91.2	92.0	93.2	88.5	95.1	86.7
93	92.5	92.0	93.9	90.8	96.7	88.5
94	93.6	92.0	95.9	92.3	97.5	89.4
95	94.2	93.8	95.9	93.1	97.5	90.3
96	95.0	94.6	96.6	93.8	97.5	92.0
97	95.7	95.5	96.6	93.8	99.2	92.9
98	96.3	96.4	96.6	96.2	99.2	92.9
99	97.6	97.3	96.6	98.5	100.0	95.6
100	98.2	97.3	98.0	99.2	100.0	96.5
101	98.6	98.2	98.6	99.2	100.0	96.5
102	99.4	100.0	99.3	99.2	100.0	98.2
103	99.8	100.0	100.0	100.0	100.0	99.1

Research/Supplemental Scales for the MMPI

Males   Ego-Resiliency (Subtle)   (ER-S)

	Total Sample	Age, yr				
		13	14	15	16	17
N	624	112	147	130	122	113
Median	20	21	20	20	20	21
Mean	20.49	20.52	20.20	20.58	20.23	21.00
SD	4.85	5.38	5.18	4.58	4.53	4.50
Min	7	7	8	11	8	11
Max	34	32	34	34	32	33

Percentage of Sample with Raw Score < X

X	Total Sample	13	14	15	16	17
7	0.0	0.0	0.0	0.0	0.0	0.0
8	0.2	0.9	0.0	0.0	0.0	0.0
9	0.8	1.8	0.7	0.0	1.6	0.0
10	0.8	1.8	0.7	0.0	1.6	0.0
11	1.3	2.7	1.4	0.0	2.5	0.0
12	2.4	2.7	4.8	0.8	2.5	0.9
13	4.6	5.4	8.2	2.3	4.1	2.7
14	7.4	8.0	10.2	5.4	6.6	6.2
15	10.7	11.6	13.6	7.7	9.8	10.6
16	15.4	18.8	18.4	13.8	13.9	11.5
17	20.8	25.0	22.4	18.5	19.7	18.6
18	27.1	32.1	29.3	26.2	24.6	23.0
19	34.8	41.1	37.4	36.2	31.1	27.4
20	42.9	45.5	48.3	42.3	42.6	34.5
21	50.5	50.0	55.1	50.8	54.1	40.7
22	59.1	54.5	61.9	59.2	63.9	54.9
23	67.6	62.5	68.0	71.5	71.3	63.7
24	74.7	70.5	75.5	76.9	77.9	71.7
25	80.1	76.8	78.9	80.0	86.1	78.8
26	83.7	82.1	81.6	82.3	89.3	83.2
27	88.1	84.8	87.8	89.2	91.0	87.6
28	92.0	89.3	91.8	93.1	92.6	92.9
29	94.7	92.0	95.2	94.6	95.1	96.5
30	96.3	92.9	96.6	96.2	97.5	98.2
31	97.6	97.3	96.6	97.7	98.4	98.2
32	98.4	98.2	97.3	98.5	99.2	99.1
33	99.4	100.0	98.6	99.2	100.0	99.1
34	99.7	100.0	99.3	99.2	100.0	100.0

Research/Supplemental Scales for the MMPI

Males   Ego-Control--Scale 5   (EC-5)

		Age, yr				
	Total Sample	13	14	15	16	17
N	624	112	147	130	122	113
Median	15	17	15	15	14	13
Mean	14.82	16.48	15.24	14.72	14.40	13.16
SD	3.91	3.34	3.86	3.85	3.82	3.93
Min	4	8	4	5	7	4
Max	25	25	24	24	24	23

Percentage of Sample with Raw Score < X

X	Total Sample	13	14	15	16	17
4	0.0	0.0	0.0	0.0	0.0	0.0
5	0.3	0.0	0.7	0.0	0.0	0.9
6	0.6	0.0	0.7	0.8	0.0	1.8
7	1.6	0.0	1.4	2.3	0.0	4.4
8	3.2	0.0	3.4	3.8	0.8	8.0
9	5.9	0.9	4.8	6.2	6.6	11.5
10	8.7	2.7	7.5	8.5	9.8	15.0
11	13.6	3.6	9.5	13.1	17.2	25.7
12	20.0	6.3	15.6	17.7	24.6	37.2
13	29.2	13.4	25.2	27.7	33.6	46.9
14	37.7	19.6	34.0	35.4	43.4	56.6
15	47.1	26.8	42.2	49.2	55.7	61.9
16	55.0	36.6	50.3	57.7	60.7	69.9
17	65.7	50.0	61.9	69.2	68.0	79.6
18	73.6	58.0	70.1	76.2	77.9	85.8
19	81.1	71.4	74.8	86.2	83.6	90.3
20	89.1	85.7	87.8	90.8	86.9	94.7
21	93.8	89.3	92.5	93.8	96.7	96.5
22	96.2	94.6	95.9	94.6	97.5	98.2
23	97.8	97.3	98.0	96.2	98.4	99.1
24	98.7	97.3	99.3	98.5	98.4	100.0
25	99.7	98.2	100.0	100.0	100.0	100.0

Research/Supplemental Scales for the MMPI

Males   Ego-Control--Male   (EC-5M)

		Age, yr				
	Total Sample	13	14	15	16	17
N	624	112	147	130	122	113
Median	32	33	32	31	32	30
Mean	31.75	33.24	32.35	31.29	31.66	30.14
SD	7.73	7.08	8.39	8.12	7.32	7.17
Min	11	13	15	11	13	13
Max	56	53	53	56	52	52

Percentage of Sample with Raw Score < X

X	Total Sample	13	14	15	16	17
11	0.0	0.0	0.0	0.0	0.0	0.0
12	0.2	0.0	0.0	0.8	0.0	0.0
13	0.2	0.0	0.0	0.8	0.0	0.0
14	0.8	0.9	0.0	1.5	0.8	0.9
15	0.8	0.9	0.0	1.5	0.8	0.9
16	1.3	0.9	0.7	1.5	0.8	2.7
17	1.9	1.8	1.4	3.1	0.8	2.7
18	2.4	1.8	2.0	3.1	0.8	4.4
19	3.2	1.8	3.4	3.1	2.5	5.3
20	5.0	2.7	5.4	5.4	4.1	7.1
21	6.9	3.6	8.8	6.9	5.7	8.8
22	8.8	3.6	12.2	7.7	9.0	10.6
23	11.7	3.6	15.0	12.3	14.8	11.5
24	14.6	6.3	18.4	15.4	16.4	15.0
25	17.1	10.7	19.0	16.9	18.9	19.5
26	20.8	13.4	21.8	24.6	20.5	23.0
27	24.8	16.1	25.9	28.5	22.1	31.0
28	28.7	19.6	29.3	30.8	27.9	35.4
29	35.9	26.8	36.7	40.8	32.8	41.6
30	39.7	32.1	38.1	46.9	34.4	46.9
31	44.6	36.6	42.9	47.7	41.0	54.9
32	49.7	41.1	44.2	53.8	48.4	61.9
33	55.6	45.5	50.3	56.9	57.4	69.0
34	61.2	50.9	53.7	63.8	66.4	72.6
35	66.3	56.3	61.2	70.8	68.0	76.1
36	69.4	61.6	64.6	75.4	69.7	76.1
37	73.6	67.9	68.7	76.9	73.0	82.3
38	77.9	74.1	72.1	82.3	77.0	85.0
39	80.4	79.5	72.8	83.8	81.1	86.7
40	84.1	81.3	76.9	86.9	86.9	90.3

Males   Ego-Control--Male   (EC-5M)
                        (Continued)

X	Total Sample	Percentage of Sample with Raw Score < X				
		13	14	15	16	17
41	87.2	84.8	83.7	87.7	89.3	91.2
42	88.9	86.6	86.4	89.2	91.0	92.0
43	91.8	90.2	89.8	90.8	93.4	95.6
44	93.4	93.8	93.2	90.8	94.3	95.6
45	94.7	94.6	93.9	92.3	95.9	97.3
46	95.2	94.6	95.2	93.1	95.9	97.3
47	96.6	97.3	95.2	94.6	97.5	99.1
48	97.3	98.2	95.2	96.2	98.4	99.1
49	97.8	98.2	95.9	96.9	99.2	99.1
50	98.1	99.1	96.6	96.9	99.2	99.1
51	98.2	99.1	97.3	96.9	99.2	99.1
52	98.7	99.1	98.0	98.5	99.2	99.1
53	99.5	99.1	99.3	99.2	100.0	100.0
54	99.8	100.0	100.0	99.2	100.0	100.0
55	99.8	100.0	100.0	99.2	100.0	100.0
56	99.8	100.0	100.0	99.2	100.0	100.0

Research/Supplemental Scales for the MMPI

Males   Ego-Control--Female (EC-5F)

	Total Sample	Age, yr				
		13	14	15	16	17
N	0	0	0	0	0	0
Median						
Mean						
SD						
Min						
Max						

Percentage of Sample with Raw Score < X

X	Total Sample	13	14	15	16	17

STATUS (St)

After reviewing the literature documenting the significant impact of socioeconomic status on personality and behavior, Gough (1946, 1948) constructed an MMPI scale that correlated with measures of status. However, this Status scale (St) contained no items or references specific to socioeconomic status and thus constituted an indirect measure.

The original sample was composed of 223 high school seniors (90 boys, 133 girls) from a Minnesota community of about 25,000 people. Item analyses of the MMPI responses were carried out on two groups of students representing the opposite ends of an index of socioeconomic status. Each sample contained 38 students (20 girls, 18 boys). The 34 items differentiating the two groups at a statistically significant level ($p \leq 0.02$) were assembled as an MMPI Status (St) scale.

The mean ($\pm$ SD) score for the total sample of 223 students was 17.4 ± 4.8; separately it was 17.5 ± 5.1 for the girls and 17.4 ± 4.4 for the boys. The correlation (r) between the index of socioeconomic status and scores on the St scale was 0.68. The St scale subsequently was cross-validated against a new high school class of 263 students (123 girls, 140 boys); for the correlation with a different index of socioeconomic status, $r = 0.50$. Later, a linear T-score conversion table was developed. A T score of 50 fell between raw scores 17 and 18. A T score of 70 fell between raw scores 26 and 27 (high scores are associated with high status), and a T score of 30 fell between raw scores 8 and 9 (low scores were associated with low status).

Examination of item content indicated that high scores reflected literary-aesthetic attitudes, social poise, security, and confidence in self and others, denial of fears and anxieties, having broad-minded, emancipated, and frank attitudes toward moral, religious, and sexual matters, and positive, dogmatic, and relatively self-righteous opinions.

REFERENCES

Gough, H. (1946). The relationship of socio-economic status to personality inventory and achievement test scores. *Journal of Educational Psychology, 37,* 527–540.

Gough, H. (1948). A new dimension in status: I. Development of a personality scale. *American Sociologic Review, 13,* 401–409.

The 34 items of the St scale, and their direction of scoring, are listed below.

These items score if answered *true:*

78.   I like poetry.
118.   In school I was sometimes sent to the principal for cutting up.
126.   I like dramatics.
149.   I used to keep a diary.
199.   Children should be taught all the main facts of sex.
204.   I would like to be a journalist.
229.   I should like to belong to several clubs or lodges.
237.   My relatives are nearly all in sympathy with me.
289.   I am always disgusted with the law when a criminal is freed through the arguments of a smart lawyer.
430.[a]   I am attracted by members of the opposite sex.
441.[a]   I like tall women.
452.[a]   I like to poke fun at people.
491.[a]   I have no patience with people who believe there is only one true religion.

513.[a] I think Lincoln was greater than Washington.

521. In a group of people I would not be embarrassed to be called upon to start a discussion or give an opinion about something I know well.

These items score if answered *false:*

136. I commonly wonder what hidden reason another person may have for doing something nice for me.

138. Criticism or scolding hurts me terribly.

180. I find it hard to make talk when I meet new people.

213. In walking I am very careful to step over sidewalk cracks.

249.[a] I believe there is a Devil and a Hell in afterlife.

267. When in a group of people I have trouble thinking of the right things to talk about.

280. Most people make friends because friends are likely to be useful to them.

297. I wish I were not bothered by thoughts about sex.

304. In school I found it very hard to talk before the class.

314. Once in a while I think of things too bad to talk about.

324. I have never been in love with anyone.

352. I have been afraid of things or people that I knew could not hurt me.

365. I feel uneasy indoors.

378.[a] I do not like to see women smoke.

388. I am afraid to be alone in the dark.

427. I am embarrassed by dirty stories.

448. I am bothered by people outside, on streetcars, in stores, etc., watching me.

480. I am often afraid of the dark.

488.[a] I pray several times every week.

---

[a]Items that were deleted from the original MMPI item pool during construction of the MMPI-2.

Research/Supplemental Scales for the MMPI

Females   Status   (St)

	Total Sample	Age, yr				
		13	14	15	16	17
N	691	136	153	127	138	137
Median	18	17	18	19	18	20
Mean	18.34	16.98	17.98	18.90	18.28	19.64
SD	3.92	3.93	4.00	4.03	3.42	3.70
Min	7	7	8	7	8	11
Max	29	27	27	29	27	28

X	Percentage of Sample with Raw Score < X					
	Total Sample	13	14	15	16	17
7	0.0	0.0	0.0	0.0	0.0	0.0
8	0.3	0.7	0.0	0.8	0.0	0.0
9	1.3	3.7	0.7	1.6	0.7	0.0
10	1.7	4.4	2.0	1.6	0.7	0.0
11	2.5	6.6	2.6	2.4	0.7	0.0
12	3.9	7.4	5.9	2.4	2.9	0.7
13	6.7	12.5	9.2	4.7	4.3	2.2
14	10.7	17.6	13.1	8.7	8.7	5.1
15	16.9	26.5	22.2	13.4	13.8	8.0
16	24.5	34.6	28.8	23.6	20.3	14.6
17	32.6	44.9	37.3	28.3	31.2	20.4
18	40.7	52.2	43.1	37.8	39.9	29.9
19	50.2	64.0	51.0	44.9	52.2	38.7
20	59.3	71.3	63.4	51.2	62.3	47.4
21	69.8	78.7	74.5	62.2	73.2	59.1
22	77.3	89.7	77.8	68.5	81.2	68.6
23	85.8	94.9	86.3	82.7	88.4	76.6
24	91.8	97.1	92.2	89.0	94.9	85.4
25	94.9	97.8	94.1	93.7	98.6	90.5
26	97.4	98.5	98.7	96.9	98.6	94.2
27	98.1	99.3	99.3	97.6	99.3	94.9
28	99.7	100.0	100.0	99.2	100.0	99.3
29	99.9	100.0	100.0	99.2	100.0	100.0

Research/Supplemental Scales for the MMPI

Males   Status   (St)

	Total Sample	Age, yr				
		13	14	15	16	17
N	624	112	147	130	122	113
Median	18	18	18	18	18	19
Mean	17.97	17.21	17.19	18.07	18.16	19.40
SD	3.64	3.75	2.93	3.89	3.73	3.53
Min	7	7	9	9	9	11
Max	28	26	23	28	28	28

X	Percentage of Sample with Raw Score < X					
	Total Sample	13	14	15	16	17
7	0.0	0.0	0.0	0.0	0.0	0.0
8	0.2	0.9	0.0	0.0	0.0	0.0
9	0.3	1.8	0.0	0.0	0.0	0.0
10	1.6	3.6	1.4	1.5	1.6	0.0
11	2.1	4.5	2.0	2.3	1.6	0.0
12	3.7	7.1	3.4	3.8	3.3	0.9
13	6.4	12.5	6.1	6.2	4.9	2.7
14	10.7	17.0	10.2	10.8	12.3	3.5
15	17.0	22.3	20.4	16.2	17.2	8.0
16	25.2	32.1	27.9	28.5	23.0	13.3
17	34.1	40.2	36.7	40.0	33.6	18.6
18	45.0	48.2	48.3	46.9	47.5	32.7
19	55.1	58.0	65.3	55.4	53.3	40.7
20	65.4	68.8	80.3	61.5	59.8	53.1
21	76.3	82.1	87.8	73.1	72.1	63.7
22	83.5	90.2	93.2	80.0	79.5	72.6
23	89.9	93.8	98.0	86.2	88.5	81.4
24	93.9	97.3	100.0	90.8	93.4	86.7
25	96.5	99.1	100.0	94.6	96.7	91.2
26	98.2	99.1	100.0	97.7	98.4	95.6
27	98.9	100.0	100.0	98.5	98.4	97.3
28	99.4	100.0	100.0	99.2	99.2	98.2

SOCIAL RESPONSIBILITY (Re)

Gough, McClosky, and Meehl (1952) were able to develop an MMPI scale to measure social responsibility (Re) by selecting items that differentiated between groups of people nominated by peers as having various degrees of personal responsibility.

The sample consisted of approximately 676 students, including members of one fraternity and one sorority at the University of Minnesota, social science classes at a Minneapolis high school, the senior class at the St. Cloud (Minnesota) Technical High School, and the 9th-grade class at St. Cloud Central Junior High School.

Nominations, according to a definition provided by the researchers, were obtained from teachers or principals for the St. Cloud samples; peer nominations were obtained for the Minneapolis high school and the college samples.

"Responsible people" were defined as those who were willing to accept the consequences of their own behavior, were dependable and trustworthy, and had a sense of obligation to their group. Although not necessarily leaders, responsible persons were described as having a sense of commitment and personal integrity. Persons identified as being low in responsibility were not to be viewed as irresponsible but as being deficient or lacking in the qualities of the responsible person.

Four criterion samples were developed based on the degree of peer-perceived characteristics of responsibility. In the college sample, 16 students were placed in the "most-responsible" category and 16 were in the "least-responsible" category; 55 high school students and 40 9th-grade students were placed in each of these categories.

Item analysis revealed 32 MMPI items that differentiated the two groups at a statistically significant level (unspecified) as well as 24 from a pool of items specifically prepared for the project. The correlation coefficient (r) for the association of the 32-item social-responsibility scale (Re) with the criterion ratings was 0.47 in the college sample and 0.53 in the high school sample. The mean (± SD) score for the total group was 18.5 ± 4.5. Mean scores among the groups described as being most responsible were relatively consistent, ranging from 22 ± 3.5 in the 9th-grade sample to 24 ± 3.5 in the college sample. Mean scores in the groups described as least responsible ranged from 14 ± 4.3 in the high school sample to 18 ± 2.9 in the college sample.

REFERENCE

Gough, H. G., McClosky, H., & Meehl, P. E. (1952). A personality scale for social responsibility. *Journal of Abnormal and Social Psychology, 47,* 73–80.

The 32 items of the Re scale, and their direction of scoring, are listed below.

These items score if answered *true:*

58.[a]   Everything is turning out just like the prophets of the Bible said it would.
111.   I have never done anything dangerous for the thrill of it.
173.   I liked school.
221.   I like science.
294.   I have never been in trouble with the law.
412.[a]   I do not dread seeing a doctor about a sickness or injury.
501.   I usually work things out for myself rather than get someone to show me how.
552.   I like to read about science.

These items score if answered *false*:

6. I like to read newspaper articles on crime.
28. When someone does me a wrong, I feel I should pay him back if I can just for the principle of the thing.
30. At times I feel like swearing.
33. I have had very peculiar and strange experiences.
56. As a youngster I was suspended from school one or more times for cutting up.
116. I enjoy a race or game better when I bet on it.
118. In school I was sometimes sent to the principal for cutting up.
157. I feel that I have often been punished without cause.
175. I seldom or never have dizzy spells.
181. When I get bored I like to stir up some excitement.
223. I very much like hunting.
224. My parents have often objected to the kind of people I went around with.
260. I was a slow learner in school.
304. In school I found it very hard to talk before the class.
419. I played hooky from school quite often as a youngster.
434. I would like to be an auto racer.
437. It is all right to get around the law if you don't actually break it.
468. I am often sorry because I am so cross and grouchy.
469. I have often found people jealous of my good ideas, just because they had not thought of them first.
471. In school my marks in deportment were quite regularly bad.
472. I am fascinated by fire.
529. I would like to wear expensive clothes.
553. I am afraid of being alone in a wide-open place.
558. A large number of people are guilty of bad sexual conduct.

---

[a]Items that were deleted from the original MMPI item pool during construction of the MMPI-2.

Research/Supplemental Scales for the MMPI

Females — Social Responsibility (Re)

				Age, yr		
	Total Sample	13	14	15	16	17
N	691	136	153	127	138	137
Median	19	19	20	19	18	19
Mean	18.90	18.99	19.07	18.64	18.30	19.48
SD	3.71	3.50	3.79	3.88	3.87	3.45
Min	8	9	9	8	8	11
Max	29	27	28	29	28	27

Percentage of Sample with Raw Score < X

X	Total Sample	13	14	15	16	17
8	0.0	0.0	0.0	0.0	0.0	0.0
9	0.4	0.0	0.0	1.6	0.7	0.0
10	1.2	0.7	0.7	2.4	2.2	0.0
11	1.4	0.7	0.7	3.1	2.9	0.0
12	2.5	1.5	1.3	3.9	4.3	1.5
13	4.2	3.7	3.9	5.5	4.3	3.6
14	7.8	6.6	7.8	8.7	10.1	5.8
15	12.6	11.8	12.4	13.4	17.4	8.0
16	18.5	15.4	21.6	19.7	24.6	10.9
17	26.5	22.8	28.8	27.6	32.6	20.4
18	34.3	33.1	32.7	37.8	42.0	26.3
19	44.1	45.6	41.8	45.7	52.9	35.0
20	54.3	53.7	49.7	56.7	60.9	51.1
21	64.5	64.7	61.4	66.9	68.1	62.0
22	75.0	73.5	73.9	79.5	76.8	71.5
23	83.8	83.8	81.7	85.8	87.0	81.0
24	89.9	91.2	89.5	90.6	91.3	86.9
25	94.1	96.3	93.5	93.7	94.2	92.7
26	97.0	96.3	96.1	96.9	98.6	97.1
27	98.4	99.3	97.4	98.4	99.3	97.8
28	99.4	100.0	98.7	99.2	99.3	100.0
29	99.9	100.0	100.0	99.2	100.0	100.0

Research/Supplemental Scales for the MMPI

Males　　　　　　　Social Responsibility　　　(Re)

		Age, yr				
	Total Sample	13	14	15	16	17
N	624	112	147	130	122	113
Median	18	19	17	18	18	18
Mean	17.76	18.57	17.35	18.14	17.32	17.52
SD	4.32	4.05	4.81	4.20	4.12	4.18
Min	5	8	5	8	5	7
Max	29	27	29	28	26	26

	Percentage of Sample with Raw Score < X					
X	Total Sample	13	14	15	16	17
5	0.0	0.0	0.0	0.0	0.0	0.0
6	0.3	0.0	0.7	0.0	0.8	0.0
7	0.6	0.0	2.0	0.0	0.8	0.0
8	0.8	0.0	2.0	0.0	0.8	0.9
9	1.9	0.9	2.7	0.8	2.5	2.7
10	2.9	0.9	4.8	1.5	4.1	2.7
11	5.3	0.9	8.8	3.8	8.2	3.5
12	8.5	4.5	10.2	6.9	9.8	10.6
13	11.9	8.0	15.0	8.5	13.9	13.3
14	17.6	12.5	24.5	13.8	15.6	20.4
15	23.4	16.1	30.6	21.5	21.3	25.7
16	30.6	23.2	36.7	27.7	32.0	31.9
17	37.2	30.4	42.2	34.6	41.0	36.3
18	45.8	40.2	51.0	44.6	46.7	45.1
19	54.8	49.1	56.5	53.8	56.6	57.5
20	63.0	56.3	64.6	63.1	68.0	61.9
21	72.4	66.1	75.5	69.2	77.9	72.6
22	78.8	75.0	78.2	73.8	84.4	83.2
23	85.6	83.0	81.6	83.1	91.0	90.3
24	91.3	91.1	89.1	88.5	95.9	92.9
25	95.4	92.9	93.2	95.4	98.4	97.3
26	97.4	94.6	97.3	97.7	98.4	99.1
27	99.0	97.3	99.3	98.5	100.0	100.0
28	99.7	100.0	99.3	99.2	100.0	100.0
29	99.8	100.0	99.3	100.0	100.0	100.0

DOMINANCE (Do)

Gough, McClosky, and Meehl (1951) used peer nominations to develop criterion groups of dominant and nondominant individuals. Subsequently, they developed a new MMPI scale for dominance (Do) that was correlated with these peer-report measures.

Subjects in the study included one fraternity and one sorority at the University of Minnesota (''approximately'' 100 college students) and 124 students from social science classes in a Minneapolis high school.

Each subject participating in the study was asked to nominate peers whom they considered to be most and least dominant according to a definition that they were given. High school students were asked to list the five most dominant and the five least dominant persons in their classrooms. College students were asked to list the 10 most and the 10 least dominant members of the sorority or fraternity to which they belonged.

The dominant person was described as able to influence others, not readily intimidated or defeated, and carrying feelings of self-confidence and was typically described by others as forceful, masterful, strong, confident, and authoritative.

Persons low in dominance were defined as submissive in appearance and feeling weaker in interpersonal contacts, finding it difficult to be self-assertive or to stand up for their rights and opinions, and more easily influenced or intimidated by others.

A pilot study of MMPI responses from 16 more dominant (8 men and 8 women) and 16 less dominant college students (8 men and 8 women) yielded 100 items that appeared to have potential for discriminating persons of high dominance from those of low dominance. These items, supplemented by an additional item pool constructed specifically for this study, were then administered to the total group of high school and college students. Item analyses were carried for the 25 most and 25 least dominant college (13 women and 12 men in each group) and high school students (12 girls and 13 boys in each group).

Analysis found 28 MMPI items that maintained their differentiating power in both samples. The mean score was 18.1 (SD = 3.8) for the college students and 15.5 (SD = 3.9) for the high school students. The correlation between scores on the Do scale and the peer nominations among the college students was 0.52; among the high school students it was 0.60.

Subjective review of item content suggested three main components. The largest number of items was related to poise, self-assurance and general self-confidence, resoluteness, and vigorous optimism; a second component suggested resourcefulness, efficiency, and perseverance; and the third was a factor of deep-seated seriousness and duty.

REFERENCE

Gough, H. G., McClosky, H., & Meehl, P. E. (1951). A personality scale for dominance. *Journal of Abnormal and Social Psychology, 46,* 360–366.

The 28 items of the Do scale, and their direction of scoring, are listed below.

These items score if answered *true*:

64. I sometimes keep on at a thing until others lose their patience with me.
229. I should like to belong to several clubs or lodges.
255. Sometimes at elections I vote for men about whom I know very little.
270. When I leave home I do not worry about whether the door is locked and the windows closed.
368. I have sometimes stayed away from another person because I feared doing or saying something that I might regret afterwards.

432.   I have strong political opinions.
523.[a] I practically never blush.

These items score if answered *false*:

32.   I find it hard to keep my mind on a task or job.
61.   I have not lived the right kind of life.
82.   I am easily downed in an argument.
86.   I am certainly lacking in self-confidence.
94.   I do many things which I regret afterwards (I regret things more or more often than others seem to).
186.   I frequently notice my hand shakes when I try to do something.
223.   I very much like hunting.
224.   My parents have often objected to the kind of people I went around with.
240.   I never worry about my looks.
249.   I believe there is a Devil and a Hell in afterlife.
250.   I don't blame anyone for trying to grab everything he can get in this world.
267.   When in a group of people I have trouble thinking of the right things to talk about.
268.   Something exciting will almost always pull me out of it when I am feeling low.
304.   In school I found it very hard to talk before the class.
343.   I usually have to stop and think before I act even in trifling matters.
356.   I have more trouble concentrating than others seem to have.
395.   The future is too uncertain for a person to make serious plans.
419.   I played hooky from school quite often as a youngster.
483.[a] Christ performed miracles such as changing water into wine.
558.   A large number of people are guilty of bad sexual conduct.
562.   The one to whom I was most attached and whom I most admired as a child was a woman. (Mother, sister, aunt, or other woman.)

---

[a]Items that were deleted from the original MMPI item pool during construction of the MMPI-2.

Research/Supplemental Scales for the MMPI

Females   Dominance   (Do)

	Total Sample	Age, yr				
		13	14	15	16	17
N	691	136	153	127	138	137
Median	15	15	15	15	15	16
Mean	15.14	14.87	15.02	15.11	14.96	15.75
SD	3.21	2.82	3.05	3.67	3.35	3.10
Min	5	7	5	5	6	7
Max	23	22	21	23	22	23

X	Percentage of Sample with Raw Score < X					
	Total Sample	13	14	15	16	17
5	0.0	0.0	0.0	0.0	0.0	0.0
6	0.3	0.0	0.7	0.8	0.0	0.0
7	0.4	0.0	0.7	0.8	0.7	0.0
8	1.2	0.7	0.7	0.8	2.2	1.5
9	2.3	1.5	1.3	3.9	3.6	1.5
10	4.2	2.9	4.6	7.1	5.1	1.5
11	7.4	5.9	6.5	11.0	9.4	4.4
12	13.3	11.8	12.4	20.5	16.7	5.8
13	20.5	18.4	22.2	26.0	23.9	12.4
14	30.8	31.6	31.4	34.6	31.9	24.8
15	41.8	46.3	43.1	40.2	42.0	37.2
16	53.4	58.1	51.6	51.2	57.2	48.9
17	65.4	71.3	68.0	60.6	65.2	61.3
18	74.4	82.4	76.5	68.5	74.6	69.3
19	84.4	89.7	85.6	82.7	85.5	78.1
20	91.3	94.1	94.8	89.0	90.6	87.6
21	96.8	99.3	98.0	96.1	96.4	94.2
22	98.6	99.3	100.0	96.9	99.3	97.1
23	99.6	100.0	100.0	98.4	100.0	99.3

Research/Supplemental Scales for the MMPI

Males   Dominance   (Do)

	Total Sample	Age, yr				
		13	14	15	16	17
N	624	112	147	130	122	113
Median	15	16	15	15	16	16
Mean	15.29	15.51	14.40	15.56	15.24	15.99
SD	3.14	2.83	3.30	2.96	3.19	3.15
Min	4	8	4	7	7	7
Max	22	22	21	21	22	22

Percentage of Sample with Raw Score < X

X	Total Sample	13	14	15	16	17
4	0.0	0.0	0.0	0.0	0.0	0.0
5	0.2	0.0	0.7	0.0	0.0	0.0
6	0.2	0.0	0.7	0.0	0.0	0.0
7	0.2	0.0	0.7	0.0	0.0	0.0
8	0.8	0.0	0.7	0.8	1.6	0.9
9	2.2	0.9	3.4	0.8	3.3	2.7
10	3.8	3.6	5.4	1.5	5.7	2.7
11	6.9	5.4	14.3	3.1	6.6	3.5
12	12.3	8.9	21.8	10.0	11.5	7.1
13	18.9	12.5	29.3	16.9	20.5	12.4
14	27.7	24.1	37.4	25.4	27.9	21.2
15	38.5	34.8	48.3	36.2	37.7	32.7
16	51.1	46.4	62.6	50.8	49.2	43.4
17	63.1	60.7	72.8	59.2	63.9	56.6
18	74.0	75.9	82.3	70.0	77.0	62.8
19	84.8	85.7	89.8	82.3	86.1	78.8
20	91.3	94.6	93.2	90.8	91.0	86.7
21	95.8	96.4	96.6	96.2	95.9	93.8
22	98.7	99.1	100.0	100.0	98.4	95.6

DEPENDENCY (Dy)

An effort to develop an MMPI scale empirically for measuring the personality construct of dependence was unsuccessful because experienced clinicians were unable to rate dependence reliably from case summaries. Therefore, Navran, as part of doctoral dissertation requirements (Navran, 1951, 1954), derived the scale through rational means. The items were not listed in his brief report (1954) but were presented later by Hathaway and Briggs (1957).

Sixteen judges selected MMPI items thought to be related to dependence. Subsequently, tetrachoric correlation coefficients were calculated for pairs of judges. Factor analysis of the resulting matrix yielded one main factor consisting of eight judges who collectively agreed on 157 items. Internal consistency and discriminability were evaluated on a sample of 50 neuropsychiatric patients and cross-validated on a comparable sample of 50 patients. This procedure was repeated with the same samples but in reversed order. The 57 items that survived this approach were then presented as a dependency scale.

Reliability was reported to be 0.91 for the 100 patients in the derivation sample. Scale Dy was also reported as correlating with scales 7 (Pt) ($r = 0.72$) and 2 (D) ($r = 0.60$). Other descriptive statistics were reported in the dissertation (Navran, 1951).

REFERENCES

Hathaway, S. R., & Briggs, P. F. (1957). Some normative data on new MMPI scales. *Journal of Clinical Psychology, 13,* 364–368.

Navran, L. (1951). *A rationally derived Minnesota Multiphasic Personality Inventory Scale to measure dependence.* Unpublished Doctoral Dissertation, Stanford University, Stanford, CA.

Navran, L. (1954). A rationally derived MMPI scale to measure dependence. *Journal of Consulting Psychology, 18,* 192.

The 57 items of the Dy scale, and their direction of scoring, are listed below.

These items score if answered true:

19. When I take a new job, I like to be tipped off on who should be gotten next to.
21. At times I have very much wanted to leave home.
24. No one seems to understand me.
41. I have had periods of days, weeks, or months when I couldn't take care of things because I couldn't "get going."
63.[a] I have had no difficulty in starting or holding my bowel movement.
67. I wish I could be as happy as others seem to be.
70.[a] I used to like drop-the-handkerchief.
82. I am easily downed in an argument.
86. I am certainly lacking in self-confidence.
98.[a] I believe in the second coming of Christ.
100. I have met problems so full of possibilities that I have been unable to make up my mind about them.
138. Criticism or scolding hurts me terribly.
141. My conduct is largely controlled by the customs of those about me.
158. I cry easily.
165. I like to know some important people because it makes me feel important.

180. I find it hard to make talk when I meet new people.
189. I feel weak all over much of the time.
201. I wish I were not so shy.
212. My people treat me more like a child than a grown-up.
236. I brood a great deal.
239. I have been disappointed in love.
259. I have difficulty in starting to do things.
267. When in a group of people I have trouble thinking of the right things to talk about.
304. In school I found it very hard to talk before the class.
305. Even when I am with people I feel lonely much of the time.
321. I am easily embarrassed.
337. I feel anxiety about something or someone almost all the time.
338. I have certainly had more than my share of things to worry about.
343. I usually have to stop and think before I act even in trifling matters.
357. I have several times given up doing a thing because I thought too little of my ability.
361. I am inclined to take things hard.
362. I am more sensitive than most other people.
375.[a] When I am feeling very happy and active, someone who is blue or low will spoil it all.
382. I wish I could get over worrying about things I have said that may have injured other people's feelings.
383. People often disappoint me.
390. I have often felt badly over being misunderstood when trying to keep someone from making a mistake.
394. I frequently ask people for advice.
397. I have sometimes felt that difficulties were piling up so high that I could not overcome them.
398. I often think, "I wish I were a child again."
408.[a] I am apt to hide my feelings in some things to the point that people may hurt me without their knowing about it.
443. I am apt to pass up something I want to do because others feel that I am not going about it in the right way.
487. I feel like giving up quickly when things go wrong.
488.[a] I pray several times every week.
489.[a] I feel sympathetic towards people who tend to hang on to their griefs and troubles.
509. I sometimes find it hard to stick up for my rights because I am so reserved.
531. People can pretty easily change me even though I thought that my mind was already made up on a subject.
549. I shrink from facing a crisis or difficulty.
554.[a] If I were an artist I would like to draw children.
564. I am apt to pass up something I want to do when others feel that it isn't worth doing.

These items score if answered *false:*

9. I am about as able to work as I ever was.
79. My feelings are not easily hurt.
107. I am happy most of the time.
163. I do not tire quickly.
170. What others think of me does not bother me.
193. I do not have spells of hay fever or asthma.

264.   I am entirely self-confident.
369.[a] Religion gives me no worry.

---

[a]Items that were deleted from the original MMPI item pool during construction of the MMPI-2.

Research/Supplemental Scales for the MMPI

Females   Dependency   (Dy)

		Age, yr				
	Total Sample	13	14	15	16	17
N	691	136	153	127	138	137
Median	27	27	26	27	29	26
Mean	26.69	26.35	25.73	27.18	29.20	25.13
SD	8.88	8.78	8.65	9.47	8.61	8.49
Min	4	8	5	10	8	4
Max	51	49	46	47	51	45

Percentage of Sample with Raw Score < X

X	Total Sample	13	14	15	16	17
4	0.0	0.0	0.0	0.0	0.0	0.0
5	0.1	0.0	0.0	0.0	0.0	0.7
6	0.3	0.0	0.7	0.0	0.0	0.7
7	0.3	0.0	0.7	0.0	0.0	0.7
8	0.9	0.0	2.6	0.0	0.0	1.5
9	1.3	0.7	2.6	0.0	0.7	2.2
10	2.0	2.2	3.3	0.0	1.4	2.9
11	2.5	2.2	3.9	0.8	1.4	3.6
12	3.5	3.7	4.6	1.6	2.2	5.1
13	4.8	5.9	5.9	3.1	2.2	6.6
14	6.1	7.4	7.2	4.7	2.2	8.8
15	9.0	8.8	10.5	8.7	3.6	13.1
16	11.4	11.0	12.4	14.2	3.6	16.1
17	13.9	13.2	15.7	17.3	5.8	17.5
18	16.8	17.6	19.0	19.7	7.2	20.4
19	20.4	24.3	22.2	23.6	8.7	23.4
20	23.6	27.9	25.5	26.0	12.3	26.3
21	26.2	29.4	28.1	29.9	15.2	28.5
22	28.9	31.6	32.0	30.7	18.8	31.4
23	34.9	37.5	37.9	33.9	26.1	38.7
24	37.3	39.0	39.2	38.6	28.3	41.6
25	40.5	41.2	44.4	40.2	30.4	46.0
26	44.6	41.9	49.7	44.9	36.2	49.6
27	47.3	45.6	52.9	47.2	37.0	53.3
28	53.3	52.9	55.6	54.3	42.0	61.3
29	57.9	58.1	58.2	57.5	47.8	67.9
30	63.0	64.7	63.4	59.8	54.3	72.3
31	66.1	66.9	68.6	62.2	58.0	74.5
32	70.0	71.3	75.2	64.6	60.9	77.4
33	72.9	75.7	77.1	68.5	63.8	78.8

Research/Supplemental Scales for the MMPI

Females   Dependency   (Dy)
                                (Continued)

X	Total Sample	Percentage of Sample with Raw Score < X				
		13	14	15	16	17
34	77.6	79.4	80.4	71.7	73.9	81.8
35	80.9	81.6	85.0	77.2	76.8	83.2
36	83.8	85.3	88.2	80.3	77.5	86.9
37	86.1	85.3	90.8	84.3	79.7	89.8
38	88.0	87.5	92.2	85.0	81.2	93.4
39	88.9	89.7	93.5	85.0	81.9	93.4
40	90.9	90.4	94.8	87.4	86.2	94.9
41	92.9	94.9	94.8	88.2	88.4	97.8
42	94.4	96.3	95.4	89.0	92.0	98.5
43	95.8	98.5	96.7	92.1	92.8	98.5
44	96.8	98.5	98.0	94.5	94.2	98.5
45	98.1	99.3	99.3	96.9	95.7	99.3
46	99.0	99.3	99.3	99.2	97.1	100.0
47	99.3	99.3	100.0	99.2	97.8	100.0
48	99.4	99.3	100.0	100.0	97.8	100.0
49	99.6	99.3	100.0	100.0	98.6	100.0
50	99.9	100.0	100.0	100.0	99.3	100.0
51	99.9	100.0	100.0	100.0	99.3	100.0

Research/Supplemental Scales for the MMPI

Males   Dependency   (Dy)

		Age, yr				
	Total Sample	13	14	15	16	17
N	624	112	147	130	122	113
Median	22	21	23	22	22	20
Mean	22.51	22.02	23.61	22.28	23.24	21.03
SD	9.29	9.26	9.77	9.10	9.37	8.69
Min	3	6	5	4	3	5
Max	49	44	49	40	47	44

Percentage of Sample with Raw Score < X

X	Total Sample	13	14	15	16	17
3	0.0	0.0	0.0	0.0	0.0	0.0
4	0.2	0.0	0.0	0.0	0.8	0.0
5	0.3	0.0	0.0	0.8	0.8	0.0
6	1.1	0.0	1.4	1.5	1.6	0.9
7	2.1	0.9	2.7	3.1	1.6	1.8
8	3.2	2.7	3.4	4.6	2.5	2.7
9	4.3	3.6	3.4	6.2	3.3	5.3
10	5.9	5.4	6.1	6.2	4.1	8.0
11	8.0	8.0	8.2	9.2	4.9	9.7
12	10.9	12.5	10.2	13.1	5.7	13.3
13	15.4	19.6	13.6	19.2	7.4	17.7
14	18.1	22.3	16.3	20.8	11.5	20.4
15	22.1	27.7	19.7	23.1	16.4	24.8
16	25.6	34.8	21.8	26.2	20.5	26.5
17	29.8	38.4	24.5	29.2	26.2	32.7
18	34.1	40.2	27.2	33.8	34.4	37.2
19	37.8	41.1	32.0	37.7	38.5	41.6
20	40.2	41.1	34.7	40.8	41.0	45.1
21	45.2	44.6	40.8	43.1	47.5	51.3
22	49.5	50.9	46.3	46.2	49.2	56.6
23	53.7	53.6	49.7	51.5	52.5	62.8
24	57.9	58.9	53.1	54.6	57.4	67.3
25	61.5	62.5	56.5	60.8	60.7	69.0
26	65.1	64.3	61.2	62.3	64.8	74.3
27	67.5	65.2	62.6	66.2	66.4	78.8
28	70.0	66.1	66.0	70.8	68.0	80.5
29	74.5	69.6	74.1	73.8	73.0	82.3
30	77.2	75.0	77.6	76.9	74.6	82.3
31	79.0	76.8	78.2	76.9	77.9	85.8
32	80.9	79.5	78.9	80.8	79.5	86.7

Males   Dependency   (Dy)
                          (Continued)

X	Total Sample	Percentage of Sample with Raw Score < X				
		13	14	15	16	17
33	83.0	83.0	80.3	84.6	79.5	88.5
34	85.1	87.5	82.3	86.9	80.3	89.4
35	87.2	91.1	83.7	87.7	84.4	90.3
36	89.4	93.8	85.7	89.2	87.7	92.0
37	91.8	94.6	88.4	93.1	91.0	92.9
38	93.9	96.4	91.2	95.4	92.6	94.7
39	94.4	96.4	91.2	96.9	93.4	94.7
40	95.5	97.3	91.8	98.5	94.3	96.5
41	96.2	97.3	92.5	100.0	94.3	97.3
42	97.0	98.2	93.9	100.0	95.1	98.2
43	98.1	98.2	96.6	100.0	97.5	98.2
44	98.6	99.1	97.3	100.0	97.5	99.1
45	99.2	100.0	98.0	100.0	98.4	100.0
46	99.4	100.0	98.6	100.0	98.4	100.0
47	99.7	100.0	99.3	100.0	99.2	100.0
48	99.8	100.0	99.3	100.0	100.0	100.0
49	99.8	100.0	99.3	100.0	100.0	100.0

PREJUDICE (Pr)

As part of a series of studies on social intolerance, Gough (1951a, b) administered the Levinson-Sanford Anti-Semitism Scale (Levinson & Sanford, 1944) to a class of 271 high school seniors in a Midwest community of about 25,000 population. The 40 students scoring highest (22 boys and 18 girls) and the 40 boys and girls scoring lowest on the scale (18 girls and 22 boys) were compared in regard to their MMPI responses.

The mean profile of the high-scoring group suggested that these students were given to impulsive and poorly controlled social behavior. They were also described as injudicious, disgruntled, having a complaining manner, lacking poise, socially timid, and harassed by fears and doubts about their own self-worth, capability, and integrity. They tended to come from homes of lower socioeconomic status, had lower levels of academic achievement and intellectual ability, and were characterized by an expectation of downward social mobility.

Subsequently, by item analysis, 47 MMPI items that separated ($p \leq 0.05$) the high-scoring students from the low-scoring students were identified. Cross-validation was carried out with a new sample of 263 12th-grade students who also completed the Levinson-Sanford Anti-Semitism Scale and the MMPI. Two new 38-person criterion subsamples, evenly divided by sex, were selected in the same manner as the original criterion group. Item analysis of the original 47 items found 32 that retained their differentiating power in the cross-validation sample and were subsequently called the Prejudice (Pr) scale.

From the item content it appears that persons scoring high on the Pr scale (mean raw scores were not reported) were characterized by attitudes of anti-intellectuality, pessimism or lack of hope and confidence in the future, cynicism, distrust, doubt, and suspicion and a bitter or hostile outlook toward others, leading to a tendency to debunk or discredit the ability and achievements of peers. Gough (1951a, b) believed that their feelings of discontent, of resentfulness of the manner in which they are perceived by others, and of isolation, lack of poise, and self-assurance and their rigid or dogmatic style of thinking could reach a degree such that distortion and impairment of efficient social interaction and response might be expected.

Later, T-score conversion tables were developed on the basis of the responses of 550 girls and 528 boys in high schools in several different communities. The table apparently was a linear transformation of raw scores; a T score of 50 represented a raw score between 13 and 14, a T score of 70 fell between raw scores 24 and 25, and a T score of 30 came from a raw score of 2.

REFERENCES

Gough, H. G. (1951a). Studies of social intolerance: I. Some psychological and sociological correlates of anti-semitism. *Journal of Social Psychology, 33,* 237–246.

Gough, H. G. (1951b). Studies of social intolerance: II. A personality scale for anti-semitism. *Journal of Social Psychology, 33,* 247–255.

Levinson, D. J., & Sanford, R. N. (1944). A scale for the measurement of anti-semitism. *Journal of Psychology, 17,* 339–370.

The 32 items of the Pr scale, and their direction of scoring, are listed below.

These items score if answered *true*:

47. Once a week or oftener I feel suddenly hot all over, without apparent cause.
84. These days I find it hard not to give up hope of amounting to something.

93. I think most people would lie to get ahead.
106. Much of the time I feel as if I have done something wrong or evil.
117. Most people are honest chiefly through fear of being caught.
124. Most people will use somewhat unfair means to gain profit or an advantage rather than to lose it.
136. I commonly wonder what hidden reason another person may have for doing something nice for me.
139. Sometimes I feel as if I must injure either myself or someone else.
157. I feel that I have often been punished without cause.
171. It makes me uncomfortable to put on a stunt at a party even when others are doing the same sort of things.
186. I frequently notice my hand shakes when I try to do something.
250. I don't blame anyone for trying to grab everything he can get in this world.
280. Most people make friends because friends are likely to be useful to them.
304. In school I found it very hard to talk before the class.
307. I refuse to play some games because I am not good at them.
313. The man who provides temptation by leaving valuable property unprotected is about as much to blame for its theft as the one who steals it.
319. Most people inwardly dislike putting themselves out to help other people.
323. I have had very peculiar and strange experiences.
338. I have certainly had more than my share of things to worry about.
349. I have strange and peculiar thoughts.
373.[a] I feel sure that there is only one true religion.
395. The future is too uncertain for a person to make serious plans.
406. I have often met people who were supposed to be experts who were no better than I.
411. It makes me feel like a failure when I hear of the success of someone I know well.
435.[a] Usually I would prefer to work with women.
437. It is all right to get around the law if you don't actually break it.
469. I have often found people jealous of my good ideas, just because they had not thought of them first.
485. When a man is with a woman he is usually thinking about things related to her sex.
543. Several times a week I feel as if something dreadful is about to happen.

These items score if answered *false:*

78. I like poetry.
176. I do not have a great fear of snakes.
221. I like science.

---

[a]Items that were deleted from the original MMPI item pool during construction of the MMPI-2.

```
                  Research/Supplemental Scales for the MMPI

    Females                    Prejudice    (Pr)

                                           Age, yr

                    Total Sample    13      14      15      16      17

    N                   691        136     153     127     138     137
    Median              14          15      14      14      14      12
    Mean               13.76      14.92   13.64   13.83   14.32   12.12
    SD                  5.88       5.80    5.79    6.09    5.82    5.62
    Min                  0           0       1       2       2       1
    Max                 30          30      28      27      27      25


                  Percentage of Sample with Raw Score < X
        X      Total Sample    13      14      15      16      17

        0         0.0          0.0     0.0     0.0     0.0     0.0
        1         0.1          0.7     0.0     0.0     0.0     0.0
        2         0.7          0.7     0.7     0.0     0.0     2.2
        3         1.9          0.7     1.3     2.4     1.4     3.6
        4         3.6          1.5     2.0     4.7     3.6     6.6

        5         5.4          2.2     4.6     7.9     4.3     8.0
        6         8.0          3.7     6.5    11.0     6.5    12.4
        7        11.9          7.4     9.2    14.2     9.4    19.7
        8        15.6         11.0    17.6    15.0    10.1    24.1
        9        21.3         18.4    21.6    22.0    16.7    27.7

       10        26.0         19.9    27.5    28.3    21.0    33.6
       11        31.4         25.7    32.0    32.3    27.5    39.4
       12        36.9         30.1    37.3    35.4    34.1    47.4
       13        43.6         34.6    44.4    41.7    42.0    54.7
       14        47.9         37.5    49.7    48.0    45.7    58.4

       15        54.8         45.6    58.8    55.1    50.7    63.5
       16        60.2         52.2    64.1    58.3    56.5    69.3
       17        66.4         58.8    68.0    60.6    65.9    78.1
       18        71.8         66.9    73.2    66.1    70.3    81.8
       19        77.3         71.3    78.4    75.6    75.4    85.4

       20        81.9         77.2    83.0    79.5    79.7    89.8
       21        87.3         82.4    88.9    86.6    84.1    94.2
       22        90.3         87.5    89.5    90.6    89.9    94.2
       23        92.5         91.2    92.2    92.1    89.9    97.1
       24        94.6         93.4    93.5    95.3    93.5    97.8

       25        96.5         94.9    96.1    97.6    95.7    98.5
       26        98.0         97.1    98.0    97.6    97.1   100.0
       27        98.6         97.8    98.7    99.2    97.1   100.0
       28        99.7         99.3    99.3   100.0   100.0   100.0
       29        99.9         99.3   100.0   100.0   100.0   100.0
```

Females   Prejudice   (Pr)
                          (Continued)

X	Total Sample	Percentage of Sample with Raw Score < X				
		13	14	15	16	17
30	99.9	99.3	100.0	100.0	100.0	100.0

Research/Supplemental Scales for the MMPI

Males   Prejudice   (Pr)

				Age, yr		
	Total Sample	13	14	15	16	17
N	624	112	147	130	122	113
Median	14	14	15	14	15	13
Mean	14.13	14.18	14.97	13.82	14.38	13.06
SD	5.54	5.07	5.72	5.82	5.65	5.17
Min	0	2	1	1	0	0
Max	28	24	27	26	27	28

Percentage of Sample with Raw Score < X

X	Total Sample	13	14	15	16	17
0	0.0	0.0	0.0	0.0	0.0	0.0
1	0.3	0.0	0.0	0.0	0.8	0.9
2	0.8	0.0	0.7	0.8	0.8	1.8
3	1.8	2.7	0.7	2.3	0.8	2.7
4	2.6	2.7	2.0	3.8	1.6	2.7
5	3.7	3.6	2.7	6.2	2.5	3.5
6	5.8	5.4	6.8	7.7	2.5	6.2
7	9.0	7.1	10.2	11.5	5.7	9.7
8	12.0	8.9	13.6	14.6	9.0	13.3
9	17.1	11.6	14.3	20.8	20.5	18.6
10	22.4	18.8	18.4	26.2	23.8	25.7
11	26.9	24.1	21.8	32.3	27.9	29.2
12	33.3	31.3	29.3	36.2	32.0	38.9
13	38.8	37.5	32.7	40.8	37.7	46.9
14	44.2	44.6	36.1	46.9	42.6	53.1
15	52.7	50.9	44.9	54.6	50.0	65.5
16	59.8	59.8	52.4	60.0	58.2	70.8
17	64.1	60.7	57.1	63.8	66.4	74.3
18	71.6	72.3	66.0	69.2	73.8	78.8
19	77.2	80.4	68.7	75.4	78.7	85.8
20	82.2	83.9	76.2	80.8	82.8	89.4
21	86.9	88.4	83.7	85.4	86.1	92.0
22	90.2	93.8	86.4	90.8	87.7	93.8
23	93.1	95.5	91.2	94.6	88.5	96.5
24	95.4	98.2	94.6	96.2	90.2	98.2
25	97.8	100.0	97.3	98.5	95.1	98.2
26	98.6	100.0	97.3	98.5	98.4	99.1
27	99.2	100.0	98.6	100.0	98.4	99.1
28	99.8	100.0	100.0	100.0	100.0	99.1

CONVERSION LOW-BACK PAIN (Lb)

As part of his doctoral research, Hanvik (1949) investigated the effectiveness with which the MMPI could differentiate between patients with psychosomatic or functional low-back pain without physical findings and patients with comparable low-back pain but for whom there was evidence of organic disease. Hanvik studied 60 male patients who had been admitted to a Veterans Administration hospital with back pain as the primary reason for admission. Of this sample, 28 required operation for a protruded intervertebral disc; the evidence for organic problems in 2 patients was based on history, report of pain, and "radiographs." The other 30 patients had essentially negative general physical and neurologic examinations. The two groups were similar in age (middle 30s), intellectual ability, marital status, socioeconomic level, and duration of low-back pain symptoms (3 to 3.5 years).

Comparison of the response patterns from the members of each group yielded 25 items that differentiated the two samples ($p \leq 0.05$ on 8 items; $p \leq 0.025$ on 17 items). The mean ($\pm$ SD) score on the Low-Back Pain (Lb) scale was 6.6 ± 2.5 for the group with organic disease and 13.9 ± 2.2 for the group who had low-back pain without signs of organicity ($p \leq 0.001$). Using a raw cutting score of ≥ 11 misclassified four cases: two from the functional back pain group were misclassified as having organic disease, and two from the organic dysfunction group were misplaced in the group with functional back pain.

Subsequently, cross-validation was carried out on a comparable sample of 40 different patients, 20 with surgical evidence of a herniated disc and 20 with a similar complaint of low-back pain but with essentially negative physical and neurologic examinations. Lb scores for the cross-validation group were similar to those in the criterion cases, 9.3 ± 2.6 and 13.1 ± 2.3 for the organic disease group and the functional back pain group, respectively ($p \leq 0.001$). The histogram (Hanvik, 1949, p. 63) indicates that six members of the group with functional back pain and four members of the group with organic dysfunction would be misclassified using the cutting score from the original derivation study (≥ 11).

Later, Hanvik (1951) reported on the mean profiles of these two groups, noting the clear-cut conversion V in the profile configuration of the group with functional low-back pain. Overall, scores on scales 1 (Hs), 2 (D), and 3 (Hy) were significantly increased (T = 73, 63, and 69, respectively), yielding this configuration. The T scores for scales 1 (Hs), 2 (D), and 3 (Hy) for the group with organic dysfunction yielded a nearly straight line (T = 58, 58, and 57, respectively). In addition, the mean scores for scales 4 (Pd), 7 (Pt), and 8 (Sc) were significantly higher ($p \leq 0.001$) in the group with functional low-back pain.

REFERENCES

Hanvik, L. J. (1949). *Some psychological dimensions of low back pain.* Unpublished Doctoral Dissertation, University of Minnesota, Minneapolis.

Hanvik, L. J. (1951). MMPI profiles in patients with low-back pain. *Journal of Consulting Psychology, 15,* 350–353.

The 25 items of the Lb scale, and their direction of scoring, follow.

These items score if answered *true:*

  67.   I wish I could be as happy as others seem to be.
111.   I have never done anything dangerous for the thrill of it.
127.   I know who is responsible for most of my troubles.

238. I have periods of such great restlessness that I cannot sit long in a chair.
346. I have a habit of counting things that are not important such as bulbs on electric signs, and so forth.

These items score if answered *false*:

3. I wake up fresh and rested most mornings.
45. I do not always tell the truth.
98.[a] I believe in the second coming of Christ.
109. Some people are so bossy that I feel like doing the opposite of what they request even though I know they are right.
148. It makes me impatient to have people ask my advice or otherwise interrupt me when I am working on something important.
153. During the past few years I have been well most of the time.
180. I find it hard to make talk when I meet new people.
190. I have very few headaches.
230. I hardly ever notice my heart pounding and I am seldom short of breath.
267. When in a group of people I have trouble thinking of the right things to talk about.
321. I am easily embarrassed.
327. My mother or father often made me obey even when I thought that it was unreasonable.
378.[a] I do not like to see women smoke.
394. I frequently ask people for advice.
429.[a] I like to attend lectures on serious subjects.
483.[a] Christ performed miracles such as changing water into wine.
502. I like to let people know where I stand on things.
504. I do not try to cover up my poor opinion or pity of a person so that he won't know how I feel.
516. Some of my family have quick tempers.
536. It makes me angry to have people hurry me.

---

[a]Items that were deleted from the original MMPI item pool during construction of the MMPI-2.

Research/Supplemental Scales for the MMPI

Females   Conversion Low-Back Pain   (Lb)

	Total Sample	Age, yr				
		13	14	15	16	17
N	691	136	153	127	138	137
Median	9	8	9	9	9	9
Mean	9.00	8.62	8.85	8.98	9.29	9.29
SD	2.36	2.18	2.33	2.63	2.27	2.36
Min	2	2	3	2	4	4
Max	17	15	15	17	16	15

X	Percentage of Sample with Raw Score < X					
	Total Sample	13	14	15	16	17
2	0.0	0.0	0.0	0.0	0.0	0.0
3	0.3	0.7	0.0	0.8	0.0	0.0
4	0.6	1.5	0.7	0.8	0.0	0.0
5	1.9	2.2	2.6	1.6	0.7	2.2
6	5.5	4.4	5.2	7.1	4.3	6.6
7	13.9	14.0	15.0	18.1	12.3	10.2
8	27.4	33.1	31.4	29.1	21.7	21.2
9	44.0	52.2	45.1	46.5	37.7	38.7
10	59.3	67.6	60.8	61.4	54.3	52.6
11	74.1	77.9	79.7	74.0	68.1	70.1
12	85.5	88.2	86.3	83.5	83.3	86.1
13	92.9	97.8	92.8	89.0	93.5	91.2
14	96.2	99.3	96.1	95.3	96.4	94.2
15	98.7	99.3	99.3	97.6	99.3	97.8
16	99.6	100.0	100.0	98.4	99.3	100.0
17	99.9	100.0	100.0	99.2	100.0	100.0

Research/Supplemental Scales for the MMPI

Males   Conversion Low-Back Pain   (Lb)

		Age, yr				
	Total Sample	13	14	15	16	17
N	624	112	147	130	122	113
Median	9	9	9	9	9	9
Mean	9.02	9.04	8.79	8.70	9.38	9.27
SD	2.43	2.17	2.34	2.30	2.54	2.73
Min	1	4	2	4	1	4
Max	18	16	15	14	18	18

Percentage of Sample with Raw Score < X

X	Total Sample	13	14	15	16	17
1	0.0	0.0	0.0	0.0	0.0	0.0
2	0.2	0.0	0.0	0.0	0.8	0.0
3	0.3	0.0	0.7	0.0	0.8	0.0
4	0.3	0.0	0.7	0.0	0.8	0.0
5	2.1	0.9	2.0	2.3	0.8	4.4
6	6.4	1.8	6.8	11.5	3.3	8.0
7	13.5	9	15.6	19.2	8.2	14.2
8	27.7	23.2	30.6	32.3	23.8	27.4
9	42.0	47.3	44.2	43.1	35.2	39.8
10	61.9	64.3	66.7	61.5	59.8	55.8
11	72.9	73.2	78.2	74.6	69.7	67.3
12	85.3	88.4	86.4	90.0	80.3	80.5
13	92.9	94.6	93.2	96.2	91.8	88.5
14	96.3	96.4	96.6	99.2	95.1	93.8
15	98.4	97.3	99.3	100.0	97.5	97.3
16	99.0	99.1	100.0	100.0	97.5	98.2
17	99.5	100.0	100.0	100.0	98.4	99.1
18	99.5	100.0	100.0	100.0	98.4	99.1

FUNCTIONAL DORSAL PAIN (DOR)

The Functional Dorsal Pain (DOR) scale was developed in France (Pichot et al., 1972) in a manner similar to that used by Hanvik (1949) but with 77 female and 7 male patients. Seventy percent of the subjects were typists or business machine operators. As a group they complained of "moderate back pains" and were diagnosed as falling in the category of benign, essential, or functional back pain. Spinal "radiographs" were either normal or showed only minimal changes described as being the sort that might be observed in subjects of the same age without any pain. A control group was composed of the 314 subjects used as the standardization group for the French version of the MMPI. Cross-validation was carried out with 22 new cases selected on the same basis as those used in the original sample.

Sixty-three items discriminated between the normal and patient samples (p ≤ 0.001). Mean scores for females were somewhat higher than for males, so separate T-score conversion tables were developed for each sex. Apparently, a linear transformation was used to establish a mean of 50 and a standard deviation of 10 with conversion tables provided in the article. For males, a raw score of 20 to 21 points fell at the middle of the average range and earned T-score values of 49 to 51. A raw score of 24 for women yielded a T score of 50.

No cutting scores were reported, although the authors used a T score of 70 (raw score 33 for men or 38 for women) in their examination of hit rates.

The correlation between the DOR and Lb scales was -0.17 among the reference group of normals and -0.22 among patients with functional back pain (p ≤ 0.05).

A number of profile subtypes were found. The first three were characterized by a conversion V pattern. A fourth group was typified primarily by higher scores on scales 2 (D) and 7 (Pt); a fifth group had elevations on scales 6 (Pa), 7 (Pt), 8 (Sc), and 9 (Ma); there also was a group of "normal profiles" in which no score exceeded 70 (29% of the group fell in this category). Five valid but nonnormal profiles were not classifiable.

Discriminatory power varied with profile subtype, with the best hit rate (about 70%) for the DOR scale occurring among the neurotic profiles. The Lb scale did well at discriminating among those with elevations on scales 6 (Pa), 7 (Pt), 8 (Sc), and 9 (Ma)—about 80%.

In summarizing their data the authors stated, "thus by using simultaneously two special scales, the Lb scale of Hanvik (1949) and DOR scale, we have shown that it is possible to recognize as pathologic 80% of the profiles of patients, with a proportion of 'false positives' of less than 5% in the 'normal' population" (Pichot et al., 1972, p. 168).

REFERENCES

Hanvik, L. J. (1949). *Some psychological dimensions of low back pain.* Unpublished Doctoral Dissertation, University of Minnesota, Minneapolis.

Pichot, P., Perse, J., Lebeaux, M., Dureau, J., Perez, C., and Ryckewaert, A. (1972). The personality of patients with functional back pains: The value of the Minnesota Multiphasic Personality Inventory (MMPI). (Translated by Robert E. Asnis, PhD, P.O. Box 255, Nottingham, PA 19362.) *Revue de Psychologie Applique, 22,* 145–172.

The 63 items of the DOR scale, and their direction of scoring, follow.

These items score if answered true:

10.   There seems to be a lump in my throat much of the time.
12.   I enjoy detective or mystery stories.

62. Parts of my body often have feelings like burning, tingling, crawling, or like "going to sleep."
74. I have often wished I were a girl. (Or if you are a girl) I have never been sorry that I am a girl.
114. Often I feel as if there were a tight band about my head.
158. I cry easily.
161. The top of my head sometimes feels tender.
186. I frequently notice my hand shakes when I try to do something.
189. I feel weak all over much of the time.
191. Sometimes, when embarrassed, I break out in a sweat which annoys me greatly.
194. I have had attacks in which I could not control my movements or speech but in which I knew what was going on around me.
199. Children should be taught all the main facts of sex.
238. I have periods of such great restlessness that I cannot sit long in a chair.
292. I am likely not to speak to people until they speak to me.
304. In school I found it very hard to talk before the class.
357. I have several times given up doing a thing because I thought too little of my ability.
361. I am inclined to take things hard.
403.[a] It is great to be living in these times when so much is going on.
493.[a] I prefer work which requires close attention, to work which allows me to be careless.
506. I am a high-strung person.
535.[a] My mouth feels dry almost all the time.
544. I feel tired a good deal of the time.
555. I sometimes feel that I am about to go to pieces.
556.[a] I am very careful about my manner of dress.

These items score if answered *false*:

3. I wake up fresh and rested most mornings.
7. My hands and feet are usually warm enough.
19. When I take a new job, I like to be tipped off on who should be gotten next to.
36. I seldom worry about my health.
46. My judgment is better than it ever was.
51. I am in just as good physical health as most of my friends.
58.[a] Everything is turning out just like the prophets of the Bible said it would.
68. I hardly ever feel pain in the back of the neck.
95.[a] I go to church almost every week.
107. I am happy most of the time.
117. Most people are honest chiefly through fear of being caught.
120. My table manners are not quite as good at home as when I am out in company.
124. Most people will use somewhat unfair means to gain profit or an advantage rather than to lose it.
153. During the past few years I have been well most of the time.
154. I have never had a fit or convulsion.
160. I have never felt better in my life than I do now.
163. I do not tire quickly.
175. I seldom or never have dizzy spells.
190. I have very few headaches.
192. I have had no difficulty in keeping my balance in walking.
206.[a] I am very religious (more than most people).
219. I think I would like the work of a building contractor.

233. I have at times stood in the way of people who were trying to do something, not because it amounted to much but because of the principle of the thing.
242. I believe I am no more nervous than most others.
243. I have few or no pains.
244. My way of doing things is apt to be misunderstood by others.
249.[a] I believe there is a Devil and a Hell in afterlife.
255. Sometimes at elections I vote for men about whom I know very little.
281. I do not often notice my ears ringing or buzzing.
300. There never was a time in my life when I liked to play with dolls.
330. I have never been paralyzed or had any unusual weakness of any of my muscles.
373.[a] I feel sure that there is only one true religion.
379. I very seldom have spells of the blues.
413. I deserve severe punishment for my sins.
482. While in trains, busses, etc., I often talk to strangers.
488.[a] I pray several times every week.
523.[a] I practically never blush.
528.[a] I blush no more often than others.
540.[a] My face has never been paralyzed.

---

[a]Items that were deleted from the original MMPI item pool during construction of the MMPI-2.

Research/Supplemental Scales for the MMPI

Females   Functional Dorsal Pain   (DOR)

		Age, yr				
	Total Sample	13	14	15	16	17
N	691	136	153	127	138	137
Median	26	25	24	26	27	26
Mean	25.98	25.59	24.77	26.43	26.73	26.53
SD	5.51	4.80	5.57	6.22	5.95	4.73
Min	11	14	11	16	15	15
Max	45	39	39	45	42	41

Percentage of Sample with Raw Score < X

X	Total Sample	13	14	15	16	17
11	0.0	0.0	0.0	0.0	0.0	0.0
12	0.1	0.0	0.7	0.0	0.0	0.0
13	0.1	0.0	0.7	0.0	0.0	0.0
14	0.3	0.0	1.3	0.0	0.0	0.0
15	0.4	0.7	1.3	0.0	0.0	0.0
16	1.3	2.2	2.0	0.0	1.4	0.7
17	2.9	2.9	3.9	3.9	2.9	0.7
18	5.8	4.4	6.5	8.7	6.5	2.9
19	8.2	5.9	10.5	10.2	9.4	5.1
20	11.0	8.1	17.0	12.6	10.1	6.6
21	16.5	14.7	24.2	17.3	15.2	10.2
22	21.1	17.6	30.7	22.8	19.6	13.9
23	27.1	27.2	34.6	29.9	23.2	19.7
24	34.4	35.3	44.4	34.6	31.9	24.8
25	41.2	41.9	52.9	40.2	38.4	31.4
26	48.9	50.7	61.4	45.7	43.5	41.6
27	56.7	60.3	66.7	53.5	50.0	51.8
28	63.2	66.2	72.5	62.2	55.1	59.1
29	69.8	72.1	76.5	66.9	63.0	69.3
30	75.8	78.7	83.7	70.9	70.3	74.5
31	80.5	85.3	85.6	74.0	76.8	80.3
32	83.8	90.4	86.3	76.4	80.4	84.7
33	87.1	92.6	87.6	79.5	84.8	90.5
34	90.6	94.1	91.5	87.4	86.2	93.4
35	92.2	96.3	92.8	89.8	87.0	94.9
36	94.8	97.1	94.8	92.9	91.3	97.8
37	96.1	98.5	96.7	94.5	92.8	97.8
38	97.1	98.5	97.4	96.1	94.9	98.5
39	98.0	99.3	98.7	96.9	96.4	98.5
40	98.8	100.0	100.0	97.6	97.8	98.5

Females   Functional Dorsal Pain   (DOR)
                           (Continued)

X	Total Sample	Percentage of Sample with Raw Score < X				
		13	14	15	16	17
41	99.3	100.0	100.0	98.4	98.6	99.3
42	99.6	100.0	100.0	98.4	99.3	100.0
43	99.7	100.0	100.0	98.4	100.0	100.0
44	99.7	100.0	100.0	98.4	100.0	100.0
45	99.9	100.0	100.0	99.2	100.0	100.0

Males　　　　　　Functional Dorsal Pain　　(DOR)

	Total Sample	Age, yr				
		13	14	15	16	17
N	624	112	147	130	122	113
Median	22	21	22	21	22	22
Mean	22.17	22.04	22.35	21.58	22.63	22.22
SD	5.35	5.86	5.45	5.11	5.14	5.19
Min	10	12	11	11	10	12
Max	44	44	41	36	38	39

	Percentage of Sample with Raw Score < X					
X	Total Sample	13	14	15	16	17
10	0.0	0.0	0.0	0.0	0.0	0.0
11	0.2	0.0	0.0	0.0	0.8	0.0
12	0.5	0.0	0.7	0.8	0.8	0.0
13	1.4	0.9	0.7	3.1	1.6	0.9
14	3.0	2.7	2.7	4.6	3.3	1.8
15	4.8	7.1	4.1	6.2	4.1	2.7
16	7.1	10.7	6.1	8.5	6.6	3.5
17	12.8	18.8	11.6	14.6	9.8	9.7
18	19.6	23.2	21.1	21.5	15.6	15.9
19	27.9	33.9	28.6	30.0	21.3	25.7
20	35.3	40.2	36.1	40.8	27.9	31.0
21	41.3	44.6	38.8	47.7	35.2	40.7
22	48.1	50.9	44.9	54.6	41.8	48.7
23	56.3	57.1	50.3	60.8	51.6	62.8
24	63.1	62.5	60.5	64.6	60.7	68.1
25	69.2	67.9	68.7	68.5	66.4	75.2
26	76.0	74.1	74.1	77.7	74.6	79.6
27	81.7	78.6	83.0	83.8	79.5	83.2
28	85.7	82.1	87.8	87.7	84.4	85.8
29	88.1	85.7	90.5	90.0	86.1	87.6
30	90.4	89.3	90.5	90.8	89.3	92.0
31	92.1	91.1	92.5	93.8	91.0	92.0
32	94.2	93.8	93.9	97.7	93.4	92.0
33	95.8	95.5	95.2	98.5	96.7	92.9
34	97.0	97.3	96.6	98.5	97.5	94.7
35	97.8	97.3	97.3	98.5	99.2	96.5
36	98.4	98.2	97.3	99.2	99.2	98.2
37	98.7	98.2	98.0	100.0	99.2	98.2
38	99.0	99.1	98.0	100.0	99.2	99.1
39	99.2	99.1	98.0	100.0	100.0	99.1

Research/Supplemental Scales for the MMPI

Males   Functional Dorsal Pain   (DOR)
(Continued)

X	Total Sample	Percentage of Sample with Raw Score < X				
		13	14	15	16	17
40	99.5	99.1	98.6	100.0	100.0	100.0
41	99.7	99.1	99.3	100.0	100.0	100.0
42	99.8	99.1	100.0	100.0	100.0	100.0
43	99.8	99.1	100.0	100.0	100.0	100.0
44	99.8	99.1	100.0	100.0	100.0	100.0

CAUDALITY (Ca)

Preliminary work (Andersen & Hanvik, 1950) had found that the MMPI response patterns of medical patients with focal lesions in the frontal lobes could be differentiated from those of patients with parietal lesions. Later, Williams (1951, 1952) carried out a cross-validation study that led to the development of a Caudality (Ca) scale. It had more generality than the original work, which had culminated in a parietofrontal scale (Friedman, 1950).

Williams' study sample was composed of 48 patients with frontal lobe damage, 48 patients with parietal lobe damage, and 20 patients with temporal lobe damage; 56 of these cases had been included in the Friedman (1950) study. The three subgroups were evenly divided with regard to the presence of dominant or nondominant hemispheric damage. All of the patients were men ranging in age from 17 to 64 years (mean ± SD, 36.4 ± 11.5 years). Focal cerebral damage was verified primarily by surgical procedures and radiographs. The author recognized the possibility of contrecoup or other unrecognized damage that might have contaminated the samples.

Two procedures were used in the development of the Ca scale. First, the response patterns of half of the 48 patients with frontal lobe damage and half of the 48 patients with parietal damage were carefully examined by item analysis. Items that separated the two groups at a statistically significant level ($p \leq 0.10$) were selected for further study. Cross-validation was carried out with the 48 remaining patients, half of whom had frontal damage and half with parietal damage. A scale of 20 items was constructed of the cross-validated items, which successfully differentiated the two groups ($p \leq 0.05$).

For the second approach, both subgroups were combined into one large sample and a second scale of 33 items was constructed by including those that discriminated between the patients with frontal damage and those with parietal damage at a more stringent level of statistical significance ($p \leq 0.02$).

Subsequently, the nonoverlapping items of the two scales developed by these two approaches were combined into a single Ca scale of 37 items (Williams, 1951, p. 59), with a low score suggesting frontal-lobe damage and a high score being indicative of non-frontal-lobe damage. A cutting score at the median (raw score ≥ 11) misclassified 12 of the patients with parietal damage and 10 of the patients with frontal lobe damage (22% error). The mean score for the patients with non-frontal-lobe damage fell between raw scores of 16 and 17; T-score equivalents based on the sample of patients having frontal lobe damage yield a T score of 70. Lower Ca scores were earned by patients with frontal-lobe damage (mean raw score, 8.2 ± 4.2).

In discussing his results, Williams (1952) indicated that patients with parietal damage endorse items suggesting anxiety, depression, guilt, introversion, feelings of inadequacy, worry about the future, and somatic concern. Those with frontal lobe damage tend to exhibit schizoid tendencies, and their MMPI responses are characterized by denial of anxiety or worry, attitudes of acceptance, affability, and self-confidence, and a relatively low level of aspiration. Williams thought that feelings reported by patients with parietal and temporal lobe damage were secondary to the frustration and stress imposed by the disability, whereas the patients with frontal lobe damage failed to react with anxiety to their disability.

Although Williams (1951, p. 59; 1952, p. 295) refers to a 37-item scale, both tables presented by Williams (1951, pp. 61–62; 1952, pp. 295–296) list only 36 items, as does a slightly later reference to his work (Hathaway & Briggs, 1957, p. 367), apparently because items 8 and 318 (card F-39) are duplicates in the booklet form of the MMPI.

REFERENCES

Andersen, A. L., & Hanvik, L. J. (1950). The psychometric localization of brain lesions: The differential effect of frontal and parietal lesions on MMPI profiles. *Journal of Clinical Psychology, 6,* 177–180.

Friedman, S. (1950). *Psychometric effects of frontal and parietal lobe brain damage.* Unpublished doctoral thesis, University of Minnesota, Minneapolis.

Hathaway, S. R., & Briggs, P. F. (1957). Some normative data on the new MMPI scales. *Journal of Clinical Psychology, 13,* 364–368.

Williams, H. L. (1951). *Differential effects of focal brain damage on the Minnesota Multiphasic Personality Inventory.* Unpublished doctoral dissertation, University of Minnesota, Minneapolis.

Williams, H. L. (1952). The development of a caudality scale for the MMPI. *Journal of Clinical Psychology, 8,* 293–297.

The 36 items of the Ca scale, and their direction of scoring, follow.

These items score if answered *true:*

28. When someone does me a wrong, I feel I should pay him back if I can just for the principle of the thing.
39. At times I feel like smashing things.
76. Most of the time I feel blue.
94. I do many things which I regret afterwards (I regret things more or more often than others seem to).
142. I certainly feel useless at times.
147. I have often lost out on things because I couldn't make up my mind soon enough.
159. I cannot understand what I read as well as I used to.
180. I find it hard to make talk when I meet new people.
182. I am afraid of losing my mind.
189. I feel weak all over much of the time.
236. I brood a great deal.
239. I have been disappointed in love.
273. I have numbness in one or more regions of my skin.
313. The man who provides temptation by leaving valuable property unprotected is about as much to blame for its theft as the one who steals it.
338. I have certainly had more than my share of things to worry about.
343. I usually have to stop and think before I act even in trifling matters.
361. I am inclined to take things hard.
389. My plans have frequently seemed so full of difficulties that I have had to give them up.
499. I must admit that I have at times been worried beyond reason over something that really did not matter.
512.[a] I dislike to take a bath.
544. I feel tired a good deal of the time.
549. I shrink from facing a crisis or difficulty.
551. Sometimes I am sure that other people can tell what I am thinking.
560. I am greatly bothered by forgetting where I put things.

These items score if answered *false:*

8. My daily life is full of things that keep me interested.
46. My judgment is better than it ever was.
57. I am a good mixer.
69.[a] I am very strongly attracted by members of my own sex.
163. I do not tire quickly.
188. I can read a long while without tiring my eyes.
242. I believe I am no more nervous than most others.

407.   I am usually calm and not easily upset.
412.[a] I do not dread seeing a doctor about a sickness or injury.
450.   I enjoy the excitement of a crowd.
513.[a] I think Lincoln was greater than Washington.
523.[a] I practically never blush.

---

[a]Items that were deleted from the original MMPI item pool during construction of the MMPI-2.

Research/Supplemental Scales for the MMPI

Females   Caudality   (Ca)

| | | Age, yr | | | | |
	Total Sample	13	14	15	16	17
N	691	136	153	127	138	137
Median	14	14	13	15	15	13
Mean	14.07	14.24	13.33	14.59	15.33	12.99
SD	5.65	5.61	5.35	5.99	5.78	5.32
Min	1	2	2	3	1	3
Max	29	28	27	28	29	27

Percentage of Sample with Raw Score < X

X	Total Sample	13	14	15	16	17
1	0.0	0.0	0.0	0.0	0.0	0.0
2	0.1	0.0	0.0	0.0	0.7	0.0
3	0.7	0.7	2.0	0.0	0.7	0.0
4	2.0	2.2	3.3	0.8	1.4	2.2
5	3.3	3.7	3.9	1.6	1.4	5.8
6	6.1	8.1	7.2	4.7	2.2	8.0
7	8.8	10.3	11.8	7.9	2.2	11.7
8	12.2	13.2	14.4	12.6	4.3	16.1
9	17.2	17.6	19.6	17.3	8.7	22.6
10	22.6	21.3	22.9	24.4	16.7	27.7
11	28.4	23.5	30.1	29.1	23.9	35.0
12	34.6	29.4	35.9	35.4	29.0	43.1
13	41.7	36.0	44.4	41.7	36.2	49.6
14	48.0	46.3	50.3	45.7	42.0	55.5
15	53.3	50.7	59.5	48.8	47.8	58.4
16	61.4	59.6	68.6	56.7	53.6	67.2
17	67.4	64.7	75.2	62.2	62.3	71.5
18	72.9	74.3	77.8	67.7	65.9	78.1
19	78.0	79.4	85.0	71.7	71.7	81.0
20	82.8	80.1	88.2	78.0	77.5	89.1
21	86.1	86.0	90.2	82.7	79.7	91.2
22	89.1	89.0	91.5	86.6	84.1	94.2
23	92.3	93.4	94.1	89.8	87.0	97.1
24	94.1	95.6	95.4	92.1	89.1	97.8
25	95.9	96.3	98.0	92.9	92.8	99.3
26	97.1	97.8	98.0	96.1	94.2	99.3
27	97.7	97.8	99.3	96.1	95.7	99.3
28	99.0	99.3	100.0	98.4	97.1	100.0
29	99.7	100.0	100.0	100.0	98.6	100.0

486

Research/Supplemental Scales for the MMPI

Males   Caudality   (Ca)

	Total Sample	Age, yr				
		13	14	15	16	17
N	624	112	147	130	122	113
Median	13	13	14	12	13	12
Mean	13.13	12.95	13.83	12.68	13.80	12.18
SD	5.63	5.66	5.74	5.58	5.52	5.55
Min	1	1	3	1	2	3
Max	30	30	27	24	29	25

Percentage of Sample with Raw Score < X

X	Total Sample	13	14	15	16	17
1	0.0	0.0	0.0	0.0	0.0	0.0
2	0.3	0.9	0.0	0.8	0.0	0.0
3	0.8	1.8	0.0	1.5	0.8	0.0
4	2.6	2.7	2.0	3.1	3.3	1.8
5	4.8	7.1	3.4	6.9	4.1	2.7
6	7.7	8.0	6.8	8.5	5.7	9.7
7	12.3	9.8	11.6	15.4	7.4	17.7
8	17.0	19.6	13.6	20.0	9.0	23.9
9	23.9	25.0	18.4	26.9	17.2	33.6
10	30.6	33.0	26.5	33.1	22.1	39.8
11	35.3	37.5	30.6	39.2	28.7	41.6
12	41.5	42.9	36.1	45.4	39.3	45.1
13	48.4	48.2	44.2	50.8	46.7	53.1
14	54.6	53.6	49.7	56.2	51.6	63.7
15	60.7	59.8	56.5	63.1	57.4	68.1
16	66.2	65.2	62.6	66.2	61.5	77.0
17	71.6	73.2	68.0	70.8	68.9	78.8
18	76.3	76.8	70.7	78.5	74.6	82.3
19	82.4	83.0	78.2	83.8	81.1	86.7
20	85.3	86.6	83.7	84.6	82.8	89.4
21	88.6	90.2	88.4	89.2	84.4	91.2
22	92.1	93.8	90.5	93.8	91.8	91.2
23	94.2	95.5	93.2	96.2	93.4	92.9
24	95.5	96.4	93.9	98.5	95.1	93.8
25	97.8	99.1	95.2	100.0	96.7	98.2
26	98.6	99.1	95.9	100.0	98.4	100.0
27	99.0	99.1	97.3	100.0	99.2	100.0
28	99.7	99.1	100.0	100.0	99.2	100.0
29	99.7	99.1	100.0	100.0	99.2	100.0
30	99.8	99.1	100.0	100.0	100.0	100.0

ALCOHOLISM—MacANDREW (MAC)

Early efforts to develop alcoholism-proneness scales for the MMPI were described as unsuccessful because they focused on response patterns of alcoholic patients contrasted with responses of normal persons (MacAndrew, 1981). Therefore, MacAndrew (1965) developed his alcoholism scale (MAC) by contrasting the responses from 300 men who voluntarily applied to a state-supported alcoholism outpatient treatment program in the Los Angeles area with responses from 300 men being evaluated for outpatient treatment in a state-supported psychiatric clinic (actually located in the same facility as the alcoholism program). The alcoholic patients ranged in age from 21 to 70 years (mean ± SD, 41.8 ± 9.2 years) and the nonalcoholic psychiatric patients, from 21 to 67 years (mean ± SD, 34.7 ± 10.6 years). Subsequently, each of the samples was subdivided into a standardization group of 200 and a cross-validation sample of 100.

Comparison of response patterns from the two groups, after cross-validation, yielded 51 items that discriminated between the two groups (p ≤ 0.01). The two items of greatest statistical significance were number 215 ("I have used alcohol excessively") and number 460 ("I have used alcohol moderately [or not at all]"), and they were subsequently omitted from the 51 items in order to avoid questions related directly to alcohol use. It was found that using a raw score ≥ 24 resulted in correct classification of 82% of the standardization and cross-validation samples. Approximately 9% were mislabeled false-negatives and 10% as false-positives. The scores did not appear to be related to age.

MacAndrew (1981) described high scorers on the MAC scale as appearing to be self-confident and social people who are relatively bold and uninhibited, showing rebellious urges, and being resentful of authority with character dimensions of reward-seeking and punishment-avoidance.

MacAndrew (1967) also reported that the following 13 factors were present in the diverse content of the scale:

I:	Interpersonal adroitness
II:	Good ability to concentrate
III:	Lack of sexual preoccupation
IV:	History of school difficulty
V:	Freedom from parental control
VI:	Female identification
VII:	Lived the wrong kind of life
VIII:	Orientation to religion and guilt
IX:	Self-responsibility for own troubles
X:	Deterioration of functioning
XI:	Report of blackout experiences
XII:	Bodily complaints
XIII:	Miscellaneous (unnamed)

REFERENCES

MacAndrew, C. (1965). The differentiation of male alcoholic outpatients from nonalcoholic psychiatric outpatients by means of the MMPI. *Quarterly Journal of Studies on Alcohol, 26,* 238–246.

MacAndrew, C. (1967). Self-reports of male alcoholics: A dimensional analysis of certain differences from nonalcoholic male psychiatric outpatients. *Quarterly Journal of Studies on Alcohol, 28,* 43–51.

MacAndrew, C. (1981). What the MAC scale tells us about men alcoholics: An interpretive review. *Journal of Studies on Alcohol, 42,* 604–625.

The 49 items of the MAC scale, and their direction of scoring, follow.

The following items score if answered *true*:

  6.   I like to read newspaper articles on crime.
  27.   Evil spirits possess me at times.
  34.   I have a cough most of the time.
  50.   My soul sometimes leaves my body.
  56.   As a youngster I was suspended from school one or more times for cutting up.
  57.   I am a good mixer.
  58.ᵃ Everything is turning out just like the prophets of the Bible said it would.
  61.   I have not lived the right kind of life.
  81.   I think I would like the kind of work a forest ranger does.
  94.   I do many things which I regret afterwards (I regret things more or more often than others seem to).
 116. I enjoy a race or game better when I bet on it.
 118. In school I was sometimes sent to the principal for cutting up.
 127. I know who is responsible for most of my troubles.
 128. The sight of blood neither frightens me nor makes me sick.
 140. I like to cook.
 156. I have had periods in which I carried on activities without knowing later what I had been doing.
 186. I frequently notice my hand shakes when I try to do something.
 224. My parents have often objected to the kind of people I went around with.
 235. I have been quite independent and free from family rule.
 243. I have few or no pains.
 251. I have had blank spells in which my activities were interrupted and I did not know what was going on around me.
 263. I sweat very easily even on cool days.
 283. If I were a reporter I would very much like to report sporting news.
 309. I seem to make friends about as quickly as others do.
 413. I deserve severe punishment for my sins.
 419. I played hooky from school quite often as a youngster.
 426. I have at times had to be rough with people who were rude or annoying.
 445. I was fond of excitement when I was young (or in childhood).
 446. I enjoy gambling for small stakes.
 477. If I were in trouble with several friends who were equally to blame, I would rather take the whole blame than to give them away.
 482. While in trains, busses, etc., I often talk to strangers.
 483.ᵃ Christ performed miracles such as changing water into wine.
 488.ᵃ I pray several times every week.
 500. I readily become one hundred per cent sold on a good idea.
 507. I have frequently worked under people who seem to have things arranged so that they get credit for good work but are able to pass off mistakes onto those under them.
 529. I would like to wear expensive clothes.
 562. The one to whom I was most attached and whom I most admired as a child was a woman. (Mother, sister, aunt, or other woman.)

The following items score if answered *false*:

  86.   I am certainly lacking in self-confidence.
 120. My table manners are not quite as good at home as when I am out in company.

130.   I have never vomited blood or coughed up blood.
149.   I used to keep a diary.
173.   I liked school.
179.   I am worried about sex matters.
278.   I have often felt that strangers were looking at me critically.
294.   I have never been in trouble with the law.
320.   Many of my dreams are about sex matters.
335.   I cannot keep my mind on one thing.
356.   I have more trouble concentrating than others seem to have.
378.[a]   I do not like to see women smoke.

---

[a]Items that were deleted from the original MMPI item pool during construction of the MMPI-2.

Research/Supplemental Scales for the MMPI

Females   Alcoholism--MacAndrew   (MAC)

| | Total Sample | Age, yr | | | | |
		13	14	15	16	17
N	691	136	153	127	138	137
Median	20	20	21	20	20	20
Mean	20.37	20.15	20.44	20.24	20.39	20.61
SD	3.70	3.63	3.57	3.70	3.63	4.00
Min	11	11	12	12	12	11
Max	33	33	32	31	29	33

Percentage of Sample with Raw Score < X

X	Total Sample	13	14	15	16	17
11	0.0	0.0	0.0	0.0	0.0	0.0
12	0.4	0.7	0.0	0.0	0.0	1.5
13	1.6	2.2	0.7	1.6	0.7	2.9
14	2.9	3.7	2.0	3.1	0.7	5.1
15	5.1	6.6	3.3	6.3	2.9	6.6
16	8.7	9.6	8.5	10.2	8.0	7.3
17	13.7	15.4	14.4	14.2	13.0	11.7
18	21.3	19.9	22.2	22.8	22.5	19.0
19	31.0	33.1	32.7	30.7	32.6	25.5
20	41.7	44.9	40.5	38.6	45.7	38.7
21	52.4	52.2	49.0	54.3	54.3	52.6
22	63.7	62.5	58.8	67.7	67.4	62.8
23	73.4	75.0	70.6	79.5	71.0	71.5
24	81.3	86.0	79.7	81.9	78.3	81.0
25	87.7	89.7	88.9	87.4	84.8	87.6
26	92.2	93.4	94.8	90.6	91.3	90.5
27	94.4	95.6	96.1	93.7	93.5	92.7
28	96.8	98.5	98.0	96.9	96.4	94.2
29	98.0	99.3	98.7	98.4	97.8	95.6
30	98.7	99.3	98.7	98.4	100.0	97.1
31	99.1	99.3	98.7	99.2	100.0	98.5
32	99.4	99.3	99.3	100.0	100.0	98.5
33	99.6	99.3	100.0	100.0	100.0	98.5

Research/Supplemental Scales for the MMPI

Males   Alcoholism--MacAndrew   (MAC)

	Total Sample	Age, yr				
		13	14	15	16	17
N	624	112	147	130	122	113
Median	22	22	22	21	23	22
Mean	22.18	22.29	22.20	21.32	22.49	22.69
SD	4.07	3.68	4.24	3.67	4.08	4.55
Min	10	13	12	13	10	14
Max	35	31	35	32	32	35

Percentage of Sample with Raw Score < X

X	Total Sample	13	14	15	16	17
10	0.0	0.0	0.0	0.0	0.0	0.0
11	0.2	0.0	0.0	0.0	0.8	0.0
12	0.3	0.0	0.0	0.0	1.6	0.0
13	0.6	0.0	0.7	0.0	2.5	0.0
14	1.8	0.9	4.1	0.8	2.5	0.0
15	3.0	2.7	5.4	2.3	2.5	1.8
16	4.8	2.7	6.8	6.9	2.5	4.4
17	8.0	5.4	8.2	10.8	6.6	8.8
18	12.0	8.9	11.6	14.6	9.0	15.9
19	17.5	14.3	17.0	20.8	15.6	19.5
20	25.5	25.0	25.2	30.0	21.3	25.7
21	34.5	30.4	34.7	42.3	31.1	32.7
22	43.9	40.2	42.9	53.8	39.3	42.5
23	54.3	54.5	53.1	63.1	49.2	51.3
24	63.0	65.2	61.2	72.3	58.2	57.5
25	72.1	71.4	71.4	82.3	68.9	65.5
26	80.1	79.5	79.6	86.2	81.1	73.5
27	85.4	86.6	84.4	92.3	85.2	77.9
28	89.9	92.0	90.5	95.4	90.2	80.5
29	93.4	93.8	93.2	96.9	93.4	89.4
30	96.3	98.2	95.2	98.5	95.1	94.7
31	97.8	99.1	98.0	99.2	96.7	95.6
32	98.7	100.0	99.3	99.2	97.5	97.3
33	99.5	100.0	99.3	100.0	100.0	98.2
34	99.7	100.0	99.3	100.0	100.0	99.1
35	99.7	100.0	99.3	100.0	100.0	99.1

SUBSTANCE ABUSE PROCLIVITY—MacANDREW (SAP)

MacAndrew (1986) constructed the Substance Abuse Proclivity (SAP) scale in an effort to develop "a psychometric instrument for the early detection of problem-engendering alcohol and drug use in young men . . . ." (p. 161). The criterion samples used in the normative work included "substance misusers" and "alcohol offenders," with members of both samples undergoing treatment for either alcohol or drug misuse at the time the MMPI data were obtained. MMPI responses from these two samples were contrasted with those from young males described as "putatively normal," "nonpsychiatric medical outpatients," and, finally, "nonsubstance-misusing psychiatric outpatients" (p. 161).

Six samples were used: first, 91 men ranging in age from 16 to 21 years who were court referrals to an alcoholism treatment program; second, 100 young men ranging from 16 to 22 years of age who were receiving inpatient treatment for either alcohol or drug misuse; and third, a sample of 70 young men ages 16 to 21 years who were psychiatric outpatients with no indication of substance use. The fourth sample of 550 young men ages 16 to 19 years was composed of medical outpatients whose MMPIs had been obtained at the Mayo Clinic during 1960 to 1965. The fifth sample was 113 college students ages 17 to 22 years who were enrolled in an introductory psychology course at the University of California. The sixth and final sample included 3,278 college freshmen at the University of Minnesota (their ages were not reported).

Thirty-six MMPI items were selected for inclusion on the new scale by a three-stage analysis of response frequencies among the criterion and contrast groups.

Six items containing relatively direct information about alcohol or substance use or its consequences and viewed as "circular in content" (MacAndrew, 1986, pp. 162, 163) were excluded: item 215, I have used alcohol excessively (T); item 460, I have used alcohol moderately (or not at all) (F); item 466, except by a doctor's order, I never take drugs or sleeping powders (F); item 496, I have never seen things doubled, that is, an object never looks like two objects without my being able to make it look like one object (T); item 156, I have had periods in which I carried on activities without knowing later what I had been doing (T); and item 251, I have had blank spells in which my activities were interrupted and I did not know what was going on around me (T).

When the SAP scale was applied to the standardization samples, detection rates ranged from 81% to 89% using a score of 16 or greater to indicate substance abuse proclivity.

Subsequently, six additional samples were obtained for cross-validation. The first was composed of 103 young male alcoholics or drug misusers ranging in age from 13 to 19 years who were being treated at a residential chemical dependency program. The second group contained 309 California college students ranging in age from 17 to 21 years. A third group of 152 young male college students attending the University of Minnesota in the late 1930s and a fourth sample of 96 young men attending the University of Minnesota in the early 1960s also were included; no information regarding age was provided. The fifth and sixth samples were comprised of 95 college students in Oregon and 225 freshmen men at a college in Maine; no information regarding their age range was provided.

The SAP scale identified 86% to 90% of the substance abusers among the 412 subjects who could be used for this purpose.

It should be noted that mean scores for the alcohol offenders (20.0; SD = 4.3) and the substance misusers (20.1; SD = 4.3) in the standardization criterion samples and for the combination group of alcohol and other substance abusers in the cross-validation group (21.6; SD = 4.3) are virtually identical. Mean values among the nonabusing samples were also comparable. Mean values for the two groups of college students, the medical outpatients, and the psychiatric outpatients ranged from 10 to 21 (standard deviation range, 3.7 to 4.0), consistent with the two contemporary samples of college students used in the cross-validation sample (range of means, 10 to 11), although the Minnesota college students from 1930 and 1960 earned slightly lower scores (8.3 and 9.8, respectively).

Subsequently, the SAP scale was applied with equally positive results to comparable male samples that were somewhat older, ranging from 22 to 26 years old (MacAndrew, 1987).

REFERENCES

MacAndrew, C. (1986). Toward the psychometric detection of substance misuse in young men: The SAP scale. *Journal of Studies on Alcohol, 47*, 161–166.

MacAndrew, C. (1987). An examination of the applicability of the substance abuse proclivity scale to young adult males. *Psychology of Addictive Behaviors, 1* (3), 140–145.

The 36 items of the SAP scale, and their direction of scoring, are listed below.

The following items score if answered *true:*

20.   My sex life is satisfactory.
56.[b]   As a youngster I was suspended from school one or more times for cutting up.
57.[b]   I am a good mixer.
61.[a,b] I have not lived the right kind of life.
98.[a]   I believe in the second coming of Christ.
99.   I like to go to parties and other affairs where there is lots of loud fun.
118.[a,b] In school I was sometimes sent to the principal for cutting up.
127.[a,b] I know who is responsible for most of my troubles.
143.   When I was a child, I belonged to a crowd or gang that tried to stick together through thick and thin.
157.   I feel that I have often been punished without cause.
202.   I believe I am a condemned person.
208.   I like to flirt.
219.   I think I would like the work of a building contractor.
224.[a,b] My parents have often objected to the kind of people I went around with.
250.   I don't blame anyone for trying to grab everything he can get in this world.
331.   If people had not had it in for me I would have been much more successful.
338.   I have certainly had more than my share of things to worry about.
347.   I have no enemies who really wish to harm me.
365.   I feel uneasy indoors.
419.[a,b] I played hooky from school quite often as a youngster.
423.[a]   I like or have liked fishing very much.
469.   I have often found people jealous of my good ideas, just because they had not thought of them first.
471.   In school my marks in deportment were quite regularly bad.
484.[a]   I have one or more faults which are so big that it seems better to accept them and try to control them rather than to try to get rid of them.
494.   I am afraid of finding myself in a closet or small closed place.
507.[a,b] I have frequently worked under people who seem to have things arranged so that they get credit for good work but are able to pass off mistakes onto those under them.
543.   Several times a week I feel as if something dreadful is about to happen.

The following items are scored if answered *false:*

137.   I believe that my home life is as pleasant as that of most people I know.
173.[a,b] I liked school.

179.[a,b] I am worried about sex matters.

294.[a,b] I have never been in trouble with the law.

376.[a] Policemen are usually honest.

377. At parties I am more likely to sit by myself or with just one other person than to join in with the crowd.

378.[a,b] I do not like to see women smoke.

464. I have never seen a vision.

532. I can stand as much pain as others can.

---

[a]Items that were deleted from the original MMPI item pool during construction of the MMPI-2.

[b]Items that are also on the MAC scale (MacAndrew, C. [1965]. The differentiation of male alcoholic outpatients from nonalcoholic psychiatric outpatients by means of the MMPI. *Quarterly Journal of Studies on Alcohol, 26,* 238–246).

Research/Supplemental Scales for the MMPI

Females   Substance Abuse Proclivity--MacAndrew   (SAP)

| | Total Sample | Age, yr | | | | |
		13	14	15	16	17
N	691	136	153	127	138	137
Median	13	13	13	13	13	13
Mean	13.37	13.14	13.25	13.54	13.64	13.31
SD	4.10	4.20	3.89	3.95	4.26	4.23
Min	5	5	6	5	5	5
Max	28	28	23	25	25	25

Percentage of Sample with Raw Score < X

X	Total Sample	13	14	15	16	17
5	0.0	0.0	0.0	0.0	0.0	0.0
6	1.2	2.2	0.0	0.8	0.7	2.2
7	3.2	4.4	1.3	2.4	5.1	2.9
8	6.2	8.1	3.9	4.7	8.0	6.6
9	10.7	11.8	9.2	9.4	12.3	10.9
10	16.9	19.9	18.3	13.4	15.2	17.5
11	25.6	25.0	26.8	24.4	22.5	29.2
12	35.3	36.8	39.9	30.7	31.2	37.2
13	46.6	48.5	47.7	46.5	44.2	46.0
14	55.0	55.9	58.8	52.8	52.2	54.7
15	63.0	64.7	62.7	61.4	61.6	64.2
16	70.8	73.5	70.6	68.5	68.1	73.0
17	77.6	80.1	77.1	77.2	75.4	78.1
18	83.2	86.8	83.0	84.3	78.3	83.9
19	88.1	90.4	89.5	89.0	84.1	87.6
20	91.9	93.4	92.8	92.9	89.1	91.2
21	94.8	96.3	94.8	94.5	94.2	94.2
22	97.3	97.1	98.7	97.6	96.4	96.4
23	98.1	97.8	99.3	98.4	98.6	96.4
24	98.8	98.5	100.0	98.4	99.3	97.8
25	99.3	98.5	100.0	99.2	99.3	99.3
26	99.7	98.5	100.0	100.0	100.0	100.0
27	99.7	98.5	100.0	100.0	100.0	100.0
28	99.9	99.3	100.0	100.0	100.0	100.0

Research/Supplemental Scales for the MMPI

Males   Substance Abuse Proclivity--MacAndrew   (SAP)

	Total Sample	Age, yr				
		13	14	15	16	17
N	624	112	147	130	122	113
Median	14	14	14	13	14	13
Mean	13.99	13.58	14.44	13.58	14.14	14.13
SD	4.27	3.51	4.48	3.95	4.82	4.38
Min	4	7	4	4	4	6
Max	28	21	27	23	28	26

Percentage of Sample with Raw Score < X

X	Total Sample	13	14	15	16	17
4	0.0	0.0	0.0	0.0	0.0	0.0
5	0.5	0.0	0.7	0.8	0.8	0.0
6	1.1	0.0	1.4	2.3	1.6	0.0
7	2.6	0.0	2.7	2.3	4.9	2.7
8	4.6	3.6	6.1	2.3	5.7	5.3
9	8.0	4.5	8.8	10.0	9.0	7.1
10	13.6	13.4	11.6	16.9	15.6	10.6
11	23.4	25.0	20.4	24.6	26.2	21.2
12	31.6	33.0	27.9	31.5	33.6	32.7
13	40.2	39.3	35.4	42.3	41.0	44.2
14	49.0	49.1	46.9	52.3	46.7	50.4
15	57.1	59.8	53.1	60.0	56.6	56.6
16	63.6	69.6	59.2	68.5	60.7	61.1
17	71.2	75.9	65.3	73.8	70.5	71.7
18	77.7	83.0	72.8	79.2	77.9	77.0
19	84.8	92.0	78.9	87.7 [c]	85.2	81.4
20	90.1	95.5	87.8	93.8	86.1	87.6
21	93.8	98.2	91.8	96.9	90.2	92.0
22	95.5	100.0	94.6	98.5	91.8	92.9
23	96.8	100.0	95.9	98.5	93.4	96.5
24	98.2	100.0	98.0	100.0	95.1	98.2
25	98.7	100.0	98.6	100.0	96.7	98.2
26	99.4	100.0	99.3	100.0	98.4	99.1
27	99.7	100.0	99.3	100.0	99.2	100.0
28	99.8	100.0	100.0	100.0	99.2	100.0

CRITICAL ITEMS: LACHAR-WROBEL CRITICAL ITEM SET (CI)

In addition to the basic clinical and supplemental scales, most clinicians believe that there are some single items of the MMPI that, if endorsed in the atypical direction, require further investigation because of their implication for serious life stress or psychopathology. This approach to the use of MMPI items has been questioned by other clinicians and researchers who object to the face-validity approach to using single MMPI items as though they were an entire scale, particularly without empirical support and knowledge of associated behavioral correlates.

Therefore, Lachar and Wrobel (1979) undertook a comprehensive investigation to determine whether the hunches of clinicians who used the items in this way were valid. They used 400 psychiatric patients divided into eight cells based on combinations of sex, race (white, black), and inpatient-outpatient status. Furthermore, another 197 black men, 281 black women, 192 white men, and 286 white women, all psychiatric patients, were used for additional analyses. Finally, data from the "improved" original Minnesota normal sample (Hathaway & Briggs, 1957) and 321 normal black men and 561 normal black women were used for comparative purposes.

Nominations for a potential pool of critical items (CI) were obtained from 14 clinical psychologists. Items were included if endorsed by at least 6 of the 14 clinicians, using the following definition of a critical item:

> certain questions of the MMPI considered to be face-valid indicators of psychopathology when endorsed in a certain way. They serve not only to separate empirically patients from normals, but indicate responses that the clinician would find useful to further investigate. (Lachar & Wrobel, 1979, p. 278)

This approach and the addition of items found on other lists of critical items yielded a total potential pool of 177 critical items.

The source of criterion data was the medical records of 130 psychiatric patients. Information from the psychiatric evaluations was reviewed to identify important topics that reflected the patient's motivation to seek mental health assistance as well as content that guided further inquiry by the interviewer. This approach yielded 14 criterion categories believed to reflect the problems that motivate people to seek psychological treatment and also to be indicative of the diagnostic concerns of clinicians. These criteria and their base rates among the 400 patients constituting the MMPI study sample are as follows:

Depression and suicidal ideation, 58%
Anxiety and worry, 34%
Sleep disturbance, 30%
Somatic concern, 24%
Deviant beliefs, 23%
Deviant thinking and experience, 22%
Family trouble, 22%
Drug or alcohol abuse, 20%
Problematic anger, 19%
Deviant behavior, 17%
Antisocial attitude, 12%
Sexual concern, 11%
Sexual deviation, 8%
Neurologic screening, 7%

In a careful process of analyzing MMPI item-to-criterion relationships, 111 items in 11 MMPI item content categories were obtained. Of these, 80% separated normal persons from the psychiatric patients for men and women and for blacks and whites in a statistically significant way. The authors noted that some of the old familiar critical items, such as item 27, "Evil spirits possess me at times," were not empirically supported; they also found that 91% of the validated critical items would be classified as "obvious" by the Wiener (1948) classification system for subtle and obvious items.

The 11 MMPI critical item content categories were the following:

Anxiety and tension
Depression and worry
Sleep disturbance
Deviant beliefs
Deviant thinking and experience
Substance abuse
Antisocial attitude
Family conflict
Problematic anger
Sexual concern and deviation
Somatic symptoms

In summary, Lachar and Wrobel (1979) noted that some individual MMPI items can be used as face-valid descriptions of psychological concerns of patients and are accurate representations of the patient's history and current behavior.

REFERENCES

Hathaway, S. R., & Briggs, P. F. (1957). Some normative data on the new MMPI scales. *Journal of Clinical Psychology, 13*, 364–368.

Lachar, D., & Wrobel, T. A. (1979). Validating clinician's hunches: Construction of a new MMPI critical item set. *Journal of Consulting and Clinical Psychology, 47*, 277–284.

Wiener, D. N. (1948). Subtle and obvious keys for the Minnesota Multiphasic Personality Inventory. *Journal of Consulting Psychology, 12*, 164–170.

The following list gives the MMPI items in each of the 11 CI content categories identified by Lachar and Wrobel, separated by direction of scoring. The percentages of women and men responding "true" to each item among members of the census-matched contemporary adult normal sample are shown before each item (women first). For comparison, the second set of values are the percentages of our adolescent normal sample responding "true" to each listed item, with the females listed first. However, the normative tables that follow are based on the *cumulative number of items endorsed* in the scorable direction for each of the 11 Lachar and Wrobel MMPI content categories.

I. Anxiety and Tension (11 items)

Adults		Adoles.			
F	M	F	M		Item

The following items score if answered *true*:

25%	35%	28%	27%	13.	I work under a great deal of tension.
4	5	13	17	16.	I am sure I get a raw deal from life.
11	13	26	20	186.	I frequently notice my hand shakes when I try to do something.
20	34	54	50	238.	I have periods of such great restlessness that I cannot sit long in a chair.
11	9	29	27	335.	I cannot keep my mind on one thing.
17	11	30	28	337.	I feel anxiety about something or someone almost all the time.
13	10	32	26	352.	I have been afraid of things or people that I knew could not hurt me.
6	5	17	17	543.	Several times a week I feel as if something dreadful is about to happen.

The following items score if answered *false*:

81	86	76	79	242.	I believe I am no more nervous than most others.
53	57	37	47	287.	I have very few fears compared to my friends.
75	79	61	69	407.	I am usually calm and not easily upset.

II. Depression and Worry (16 items)

The following items score if answered *true*:

7	5	13	12	76.	Most of the time I feel blue.
36	23	37	26	86.	I am certainly lacking in self-confidence.
2	4	20	24	139.	Sometimes I feel as if I must injure either myself or someone else.
44	42	64	56	142.	I certainly feel useless at times.
3	4	6	5	168.	There is something wrong with my mind.
12	11	19	25	301.	Life is a strain for me much of the time.
2	1	11	8	339.	Most of the time I wish I were dead.
37	33	61	49	397.	I have sometimes felt that difficulties were piling up so high that I could not overcome them.
30	22	59	43	418.	At times I think I am no good at all.
32	28	38	31	431.	I worry quite a bit over possible misfortune.
4	4	8	9	526.	The future seems hopeless to me.

The following items score if answered *false*:

95	98	94	97	2.	I have a good appetite.
73	74	49	45	3.	I wake up fresh and rested most mornings.
83	83	93	92	9.	I am about as able to work as I ever was.

96%	98%	91%	91%	88.	I usually feel that life is worthwhile.
89	89	92	93	178.	My memory seems to be all right.

III. Sleep Disturbance (6 items)

The following items score if answered *true:*

62	41	34	32	5.	I am easily awakened by noise.
7	7	17	11	31.	I have nightmares every few nights.
12	9	13	12	43.	My sleep is fitful and disturbed.
30	26	52	41	359.	Sometimes some unimportant thought will run through my mind and bother me for days.
17	6	37	24	559.	I have often been frightened in the middle of the night.

The following item scores if answered *false:*

73	78	47	56	152.	Most nights I go to sleep without thoughts or ideas bothering me.

IV. Deviant Beliefs (15 items)

The following items score if answered *true:*

4	5	18	26	110.	Someone has it in for me.
1	1	7	10	121.	I believe I am being plotted against.
0	1	4	5	123.	I believe I am being followed.
0	0	0	4	151.	Someone has been trying to poison me.
1	1	1	4	197.	Someone has been trying to rob me.
2	4	10	13	200.	There are persons who are trying to steal my thoughts and ideas.
2	4	1	4	275.	Someone has control over my mind.
27	34	48	46	284.	I am sure I am being talked about.
0	1	5	4	291.	At one or more times in my life I felt that someone was making me do things by hypnotizing me.
2	5	7	8	293.	Someone has been trying to influence my mind.
2	3	9	13	331.	If people had not had it in for me I would have been much more successful.
4	8	27	29	364.	People say insulting and vulgar things about me.
36	38	62	52	551.	Sometimes I am sure that other people can tell what I am thinking.

The following items score if answered *false:*

90	85	74	67	119.	My speech is the same as always (not faster or slower, or slurring; no hoarseness).
93	91	84	75	347.	I have no enemies who really wish to harm me.

V. Deviant Thinking and Experience (11 items)

The following items score if answered *true*:

9%	20%	39%	44%	33.	I have had very peculiar and strange experiences.
3	4	17	19	48.	When I am with people, I am bothered by hearing very queer things.
7	15	16	17	66.	I see things or animals or people around me that others do not see.
76	76	87	80	134.	At times my thoughts have raced ahead faster than I could speak them.
1	2	11	10	184.	I commonly hear voices without knowing where they come from.
12	15	20	24	334.	Peculiar odors come to me at times.
8	8	21	25	341.	At times I hear so well it bothers me.
6	15	34	36	349.	I have strange and peculiar thoughts.
15	8	35	27	350.	I hear strange things when I am alone.
6	9	6	9	420.[a]	I have had some very unusual religious experiences.

The following item scores if answered *false*:

87	84	73	72	464.	I have never seen a vision.

VI. Substance Abuse (4 items)

The following items score if answered *true*:

6	10	22	24	156.	I have had periods in which I carried on activities without knowing later what I had been doing.
17	35	14	14	215.	I have used alcohol excessively.

The following items score if answered *false*:

93	86	87	81	460.[a]	I have used alcohol moderately (or not at all).
87	85	81	81	466.	Except by a doctor's orders I never take drugs or sleeping powders.

VII. Antisocial Attitude (9 items)

The following items score if answered *true*:

12	31	33	51	28.	When someone does me a wrong, I feel I should pay him back if I can just for the principle of the thing.
21	40	30	41	38.	During one period when I was a youngster I engaged in petty thievery.
3	15	2	8	56.	As a youngster I was suspended from school one or more times for cutting up.

5%	33%	10%	28%	118.	In school I was sometimes sent to the principal for cutting up.
2	4	6	11	205.	At times it has been impossible for me to keep from stealing or shoplifting something.
42	36	56	59	250.	I don't blame anyone for trying to grab everything he can get in this world.
2	8	17	33	269.	I can easily make other people afraid of me, and sometimes do for the fun of it.
25	34	41	48	280.	Most people make friends because friends are likely to be useful to them.

The following item scores if answered *false*:

87	64	87	67	294.	I have never been in trouble with the law.

VIII. Family Conflict (4 items)

The following items score if answered *true*:

31	25	59	49	21.	At times I have very much wanted to leave home.
7	8	35	35	245.	My parents and family find more fault with me than they should.

The following items score if answered *false*:

84	81	39	46	96.	I have very few quarrels with members of my family.
91	90	75	81	137.	I believe that my home life is as pleasant as that of most people I know.

IX. Problematic Anger (4 items)

The following items score if answered *true*:

8	14	48	48	97.	At times I have a strong urge to do something harmful or shocking.
6	15	36	60	145.	At times I feel like picking a fist fight with someone.
43	45	57	59	234.	I get mad easily and then get over it soon.
13	22	28	32	381.	I am often said to be hotheaded.

The following items score if answered *false*:
(none)

X. Sexual Concern and Deviation[b] (8 items)

The following items score if answered *true*:

5	5	4	4	69.[a]	I am very strongly attracted by members of my own sex.

12%	18%	34%	23%	179.	I am worried about sex matters.
17	17	40	34	297.	I wish I were not bothered by thoughts about sex.
5	5	3	3	519.[a]	There is something wrong with my sex organs.

The following items score if answered *false:*

80	78	71	63	20.	My sex life is satisfactory.
83	84	89	84	37.	I have never been in trouble because of my sex behavior.
87	74	89	84	133.	I have never indulged in any unusual sex practices.

XI. Somatic Symptoms (23 items)

The following items score if answered *true:*

2	1	3	1	23.	I am troubled by attacks of nausea and vomiting.
17	20	7	6	29.	I am bothered by acid stomach several times a week.
6	4	11	5	44.	Much of the time my head seems to hurt all over.
16	6	14	11	47.	Once a week or oftener I feel suddenly hot all over, without apparent cause.
32	26	12	17	62.	Parts of my body often have feelings like burning, tingling, crawling, or like "going to sleep."
9	10	12	11	72.	I am troubled by discomfort in the pit of my stomach every few days or oftener.
7	4	11	10	114.	Often I feel as if there were a tight band about my head.
8	9	7	5	125.	I have a great deal of stomach trouble.
4	3	6	6	189.	I feel weak all over much of the time.
3	3	8	5	194.	I have had attacks in which I could not control my movements or speech but in which I knew what was going on around me.
6	6	15	16	251.	I have had blank spells in which my activities were interrupted and I did not know what was going on around me.
9	5	6	6	273.	I have numbness in one or more regions of my skin.
35	26	42	32	544.	I feel tired a good deal of the time.

The following items score if answered *false:*

67	56	50	53	36.	I seldom worry about my health.
79	81	73	72	55.	I am almost never bothered by pains over the heart or in my chest.
75	75	77	73	68.	I hardly ever feel pain in the back of the neck.
95	93	80	75	154.	I have never had a fit or convulsion.

54%	73%	75%	78%	174.	I have never had a fainting spell.
83	88	74	80	175.	I seldom or never have dizzy spells.
77	83	68	81	190.	I have very few headaches.
81	82	80	79	243.	I have few or no pains.
84	78	72	68	281.	I do not often notice my ears ringing or buzzing.
88	84	85	83	330.	I have never been paralyzed or had any unusual weakness of any of my muscles.

---

[a]Items that were deleted from the original MMPI item pool during construction of the MMPI-2.

[b]Item 74. "I have often wished I were a girl. (Or if you are a girl) I have never been sorry that I am a girl" was added to the CI list for males only. (77, 24) (70, 7) (See "X. Sexual Concern and Deviation," p. 503.)

Research/Supplemental Scales for the MMPI

Females   Lachar-Wrobel CI Set I: Anxiety and Tension

	Total Sample	Age, yr				
		13	14	15	16	17
N	691	136	153	127	138	137
Median	3	3	3	3	4	3
Mean	3.52	3.40	3.37	3.74	3.99	3.15
SD	2.31	2.20	2.42	2.36	2.39	2.06
Min	0	0	0	0	0	0
Max	11	9	10	11	11	9

X	Percentage of Sample with Raw Score < X					
	Total Sample	13	14	15	16	17
0	0.0	0.0	0.0	0.0	0.0	0.0
1	5.8	4.4	5.9	4.7	4.3	9.5
2	21.9	25.0	27.5	18.1	13.8	24.1
3	38.8	40.4	44.4	34.6	32.6	40.9
4	54.4	55.9	58.8	50.4	45.7	60.6
5	67.7	69.1	66.7	67.7	60.9	74.5
6	80.5	81.6	83.7	77.2	74.6	84.7
7	89.3	90.4	89.5	87.4	86.2	92.7
8	94.4	95.6	93.5	92.9	91.3	98.5
9	96.4	97.8	94.8	95.3	94.9	99.3
10	98.8	100.0	98.0	98.4	97.8	100.0
11	99.7	100.0	100.0	99.2	99.3	100.0

Females   Lachar-Wrobel CI Set II: Depression And Worry

| | Total Sample | Age, yr | | | | |
		13	14	15	16	17
N	691	136	153	127	138	137
Median	4	4	3	4	4	3
Mean	4.12	3.88	3.82	4.26	5.01	3.68
SD	3.02	2.79	2.81	3.25	3.37	2.71
Min	0	0	0	0	0	0
Max	16	13	14	15	16	15

| | Percentage of Sample with Raw Score < X | | | | | |
X	Total Sample	13	14	15	16	17
0	0.0	0.0	0.0	0.0	0.0	0.0
1	7.8	8.8	8.5	9.4	3.6	8.8
2	21.4	24.3	24.2	22.0	13.0	23.4
3	33.6	36.0	37.9	37.0	22.5	34.3
4	46.7	46.3	51.0	46.5	37.0	52.6
5	61.4	64.0	65.4	56.7	51.4	68.6
6	72.5	72.8	75.2	69.3	65.2	79.6
7	81.9	86.0	81.7	81.1	73.2	87.6
8	87.4	89.7	88.2	84.3	81.2	93.4
9	91.8	94.1	94.8	88.2	86.2	94.9
10	94.4	96.3	96.7	92.1	89.1	97.1
11	95.4	96.3	98.0	93.7	91.3	97.1
12	97.0	98.5	98.0	96.1	94.2	97.8
13	98.4	99.3	99.3	99.2	95.7	98.5
14	99.0	100.0	99.3	99.2	97.1	99.3
15	99.4	100.0	100.0	99.2	98.6	99.3
16	99.9	100.0	100.0	100.0	99.3	100.0

Research/Supplemental Scales for the MMPI

Females   Lachar-Wrobel CI Set III: Sleep Disturbance

| | Total Sample | Age, yr | | | | |
		13	14	15	16	17
N	691	136	153	127	138	137
Median	2	2	2	2	2	2
Mean	2.04	2.07	1.93	1.95	2.26	1.99
SD	1.44	1.51	1.38	1.47	1.43	1.44
Min	0	0	0	0	0	0
Max	6	6	6	6	5	5

| X | Percentage of Sample with Raw Score < X | | | | | |
	Total Sample	13	14	15	16	17
0	0.0	0.0	0.0	0.0	0.0	0.0
1	15.2	16.2	13.1	17.3	12.3	17.5
2	40.2	39.7	44.4	44.9	30.4	41.6
3	65.3	64.0	70.6	66.9	60.9	63.5
4	81.8	82.4	85.6	80.3	77.5	82.5
5	94.4	93.4	94.1	96.1	92.8	95.6
6	99.3	97.8	99.3	99.2	100.0	100.0

Research/Supplemental Scales for the MMPI

Females   Lachar-Wrobel CI Set IV: Deviant Beliefs

| | Total Sample | Age, yr | | | | |
		13	14	15	16	17
N	691	136	153	127	138	137
Median	2	2	2	2	2	2
Mean	2.40	2.61	2.61	2.48	2.40	1.91
SD	2.15	2.17	2.27	2.23	2.18	1.80
Min	0	0	0	0	0	0
Max	12	9	12	12	11	10

| X | Percentage of Sample with Raw Score < X | | | | | |
	Total Sample	13	14	15	16	17
0	0.0	0.0	0.0	0.0	0.0	0.0
1	17.1	18.4	15.7	15.0	15.9	20.4
2	40.7	36.0	38.6	38.6	42.0	48.2
3	61.8	53.7	56.2	63.8	63.0	73.0
4	76.7	69.9	73.2	75.6	77.5	87.6
5	85.8	83.8	82.4	85.0	85.5	92.7
6	90.3	88.2	89.5	89.8	89.9	94.2
7	93.6	93.4	90.8	93.7	93.5	97.1
8	96.4	97.8	96.1	94.5	95.7	97.8
9	98.6	97.8	98.7	98.4	98.6	99.3
10	99.4	100.0	99.3	99.2	99.3	99.3
11	99.6	100.0	99.3	99.2	99.3	100.0
12	99.7	100.0	99.3	99.2	100.0	100.0

Research/Supplemental Scales for the MMPI

Females   Lachar-Wrobel CI Set V: Deviant Thinking/Experience

	Total Sample	Age, yr				
		13	14	15	16	17
N	691	136	153	127	138	137
Median	3	3	2	3	3	2
Mean	3.11	3.29	3.05	3.24	3.23	2.77
SD	2.17	2.31	2.20	2.04	2.27	1.96
Min	0	0	0	0	0	0
Max	11	11	10	10	10	8

	Percentage of Sample with Raw Score < X					
X	Total Sample	13	14	15	16	17
0	0.0	0.0	0.0	0.0	0.0	0.0
1	5.1	5.9	5.2	3.1	5.1	5.8
2	28.2	25.7	31.4	23.6	28.3	31.4
3	47.8	46.3	51.6	40.9	44.9	54.0
4	63.1	60.3	63.4	59.8	62.3	69.3
5	74.8	71.3	72.5	74.8	72.5	83.2
6	85.1	81.6	85.0	88.2	82.6	88.3
7	91.2	88.2	90.8	92.1	89.9	94.9
8	95.8	95.6	96.7	96.1	94.2	96.4
9	98.6	97.8	98.7	98.4	97.8	100.0
10	99.4	99.3	99.3	99.2	99.3	100.0
11	99.9	99.3	100.0	100.0	100.0	100.0

Research/Supplemental Scales for the MMPI

Females   Lachar-Wrobel CI Set VI: Substance Abuse

	Total Sample	Age, yr				
		13	14	15	16	17
N	691	136	153	127	138	137
Median	1	1	1	1	1	1
Mean	1.12	1.00	1.08	1.04	1.28	1.23
SD	0.82	0.66	0.78	0.84	0.93	0.86
Min	0	0	0	0	0	0
Max	4	3	4	4	4	3

X	Percentage of Sample with Raw Score < X					
	Total Sample	13	14	15	16	17
0	0.0	0.0	0.0	0.0	0.0	0.0
1	20.7	20.6	21.6	25.2	16.7	19.7
2	73.5	80.1	75.2	77.2	69.6	65.7
3	94.2	99.3	96.1	95.3	88.4	92.0
4	99.1	100.0	99.3	98.4	97.8	100.0

Research/Supplemental Scales for the MMPI

Females   Lachar-Wrobel CI Set VII: Antisocial Attitude

	Total Sample	Age, yr				
		13	14	15	16	17
N	691	136	153	127	138	137
Median	2	2	2	2	2	1
Mean	2.08	2.10	2.13	2.17	2.14	1.84
SD	1.57	1.48	1.58	1.58	1.65	1.57
Min	0	0	0	0	0	0
Max	8	7	6	7	7	8

	Percentage of Sample with Raw Score < X					
X	Total Sample	13	14	15	16	17
0	0.0	0.0	0.0	0.0	0.0	0.0
1	15.2	13.2	16.3	14.2	13.0	19.0
2	41.4	38.2	38.6	36.2	43.5	50.4
3	66.1	64.7	63.4	66.1	66.7	70.1
4	82.1	82.4	81.0	79.5	79.0	88.3
5	92.0	94.9	90.2	92.1	89.9	93.4
6	96.7	97.1	97.4	96.9	94.9	97.1
7	99.1	99.3	100.0	98.4	99.3	98.5
8	99.9	100.0	100.0	100.0	100.0	99.3

Research/Supplemental Scales for the MMPI

Females   Lachar-Wrobel CI Set VIII: Family Conflict

		Age, yr				
	Total Sample	13	14	15	16	17
N	691	136	153	127	138	137
Median	2	1	1	2	2	1
Mean	1.79	1.68	1.68	1.96	1.98	1.66
SD	1.33	1.30	1.33	1.40	1.34	1.25
Min	0	0	0	0	0	0
Max	4	4	4	4	4	4

	Percentage of Sample with Raw Score < X					
X	Total Sample	13	14	15	16	17
0	0.0	0.0	0.0	0.0	0.0	0.0
1	19.7	21.3	22.9	18.1	15.9	19.7
2	47.5	51.5	51.0	42.5	41.3	50.4
3	68.3	69.9	69.9	63.8	62.3	75.2
4	85.8	89.0	88.2	79.5	82.6	89.1

Research/Supplemental Scales for the MMPI

Females   Lachar-Wrobel CI Set IX: Problematic Anger

| | | Age, yr | | | | |
	Total Sample	13	14	15	16	17
N	691	136	153	127	138	137
Median	2	2	2	2	2	1
Mean	1.68	1.72	1.55	1.73	1.84	1.60
SD	1.19	1.21	1.19	1.14	1.21	1.20
Min	0	0	0	0	0	0
Max	4	4	4	4	4	4

| | Percentage of Sample with Raw Score < X | | | | | |
X	Total Sample	13	14	15	16	17
0	0.0	0.0	0.0	0.0	0.0	0.0
1	19.1	21.3	22.9	14.2	15.2	21.2
2	46.0	41.9	49.7	47.2	39.9	51.1
3	73.8	70.6	79.7	70.9	72.5	74.5
4	92.6	94.1	92.8	94.5	88.4	93.4

Research/Supplemental Scales for the MMPI

Females   Lachar-Wrobel CI Set X: Sexual Concern/Deviation

	Total Sample	Age, yr				
		13	14	15	16	17
N	691	136	153	127	138	137
Median	1	1	1	1	1	1
Mean	1.25	1.23	1.35	1.13	1.36	1.16
SD	1.11	1.02	1.15	0.98	1.17	1.18
Min	0	0	0	0	0	0
Max	6	4	5	4	5	6

X	Percentage of Sample with Raw Score < X					
	Total Sample	13	14	15	16	17
0	0.0	0.0	0.0	0.0	0.0	0.0
1	28.9	28.7	24.8	32.3	24.6	35.0
2	62.8	61.0	60.8	63.8	62.3	66.4
3	87.8	89.0	86.9	92.1	83.3	88.3
4	97.1	98.5	95.4	99.2	95.7	97.1
5	98.6	100.0	97.4	100.0	97.8	97.8
6	99.9	100.0	100.0	100.0	100.0	99.3

Research/Supplemental Scales for the MMPI

Females   Lachar-Wrobel CI Set XI: Somatic Symptoms

		Age, yr				
	Total Sample	13	14	15	16	17
N	691	136	153	127	138	137
Median	4	4	3	4	4	4
Mean	4.45	4.28	4.03	4.61	5.22	4.16
SD	3.60	3.02	3.40	3.71	4.41	3.26
Min	0	0	0	0	0	0
Max	20	13	16	20	20	18

	Percentage of Sample with Raw Score < X					
X	Total Sample	13	14	15	16	17
0	0.0	0.0	0.0	0.0	0.0	0.0
1	7.7	6.6	8.5	7.9	8.7	6.6
2	21.7	22.1	25.5	17.3	22.5	20.4
3	35.6	33.8	39.9	34.6	31.2	38.0
4	48.2	46.3	54.9	45.7	44.2	48.9
5	60.6	59.6	64.7	60.6	53.6	64.2
6	68.5	64.0	74.5	69.3	62.3	71.5
7	76.4	77.9	81.7	74.8	68.1	78.8
8	81.9	82.4	85.6	81.1	72.5	87.6
9	87.3	91.2	87.6	85.0	80.4	92.0
10	90.7	93.4	90.8	89.8	86.2	93.4
11	93.5	97.8	94.1	91.3	89.1	94.9
12	94.8	98.5	96.1	93.7	90.6	94.9
13	96.1	98.5	97.4	96.1	91.3	97.1
14	97.1	100.0	97.4	96.9	92.8	98.5
15	98.1	100.0	98.7	98.4	94.2	99.3
16	98.7	100.0	99.3	99.2	95.7	99.3
17	99.4	100.0	100.0	99.2	98.6	99.3
18	99.4	100.0	100.0	99.2	98.6	99.3
19	99.6	100.0	100.0	99.2	98.6	100.0
20	99.7	100.0	100.0	99.2	99.3	100.0

Research/Supplemental Scales for the MMPI

Males   Lachar-Wrobel CI Set I: Anxiety and Tension

		Age, yr				
	Total Sample	13	14	15	16	17
N	624	112	147	130	122	113
Median	3	3	3	3	3	2
Mean	3.12	3.17	3.45	2.94	3.29	2.69
SD	2.22	2.22	2.32	2.00	2.40	2.08
Min	0	0	0	0	0	0
Max	10	10	10	9	10	9

	Percentage of Sample with Raw Score < X					
X	Total Sample	13	14	15	16	17
0	0.0	0.0	0.0	0.0	0.0	0.0
1	8.0	5.4	4.1	8.5	10.7	12.4
2	27.2	25.9	25.9	26.2	24.6	34.5
3	47.0	46.4	42.2	48.5	44.3	54.9
4	62.2	63.4	54.4	65.4	59.8	69.9
5	75.8	76.8	70.1	79.2	73.0	81.4
6	83.7	82.1	81.0	86.9	82.0	86.7
7	91.0	92.0	87.1	94.6	89.3	92.9
8	95.5	94.6	93.9	97.7	92.6	99.1
9	97.8	97.3	97.3	99.2	95.9	99.1
10	99.5	99.1	99.3	100.0	99.2	100.0

Research/Supplemental Scales for the MMPI

Males   Lachar-Wrobel CI Set II: Depression And Worry

		Age, yr				
	Total Sample	13	14	15	16	17
N	624	112	147	130	122	113
Median	3	3	3	3	4	3
Mean	3.67	3.31	4.15	3.45	3.89	3.43
SD	2.86	2.81	3.14	2.76	2.67	2.80
Min	0	0	0	0	0	0
Max	14	13	14	11	12	14

	Percentage of Sample with Raw Score < X					
X	Total Sample	13	14	15	16	17
0	0.0	0.0	0.0	0.0	0.0	0.0
1	11.2	17.0	9.5	14.6	7.4	8.0
2	27.2	33.9	23.1	32.3	18.9	29.2
3	39.7	45.5	33.3	43.1	35.2	43.4
4	54.3	58.9	50.3	55.4	50.0	58.4
5	66.3	66.1	61.2	68.5	63.9	73.5
6	76.8	79.5	72.1	75.4	77.0	81.4
7	83.8	86.6	77.6	83.8	83.6	89.4
8	88.8	92.0	85.0	88.5	87.7	92.0
9	93.4	96.4	88.4	96.2	92.6	94.7
10	96.2	97.3	93.2	98.5	96.7	95.6
11	97.3	98.2	95.9	98.5	98.4	95.6
12	98.4	98.2	97.3	100.0	99.2	97.3
13	99.4	99.1	98.6	100.0	100.0	99.1
14	99.7	100.0	99.3	100.0	100.0	99.1

Research/Supplemental Scales for the MMPI

Males   Lachar-Wrobel CI Set III: Sleep Disturbance

	Total Sample	Age, yr				
		13	14	15	16	17
N	624	112	147	130	122	113
Median	1	1	2	1	1	1
Mean	1.63	1.57	1.78	1.52	1.61	1.61
SD	1.29	1.26	1.43	1.19	1.17	1.37
Min	0	0	0	0	0	0
Max	6	6	6	6	5	5

X	Total Sample	Percentage of Sample with Raw Score < X				
		13	14	15	16	17
0	0.0	0.0	0.0	0.0	0.0	0.0
1	21.2	22.3	20.4	22.3	17.2	23.9
2	50.6	50.9	46.9	50.8	50.8	54.9
3	77.6	79.5	73.5	81.5	79.5	74.3
4	91.3	92.9	87.8	95.4	91.8	89.4
5	97.3	98.2	94.6	98.5	99.2	96.5
6	99.4	99.1	98.6	99.2	100.0	100.0

Research/Supplemental Scales for the MMPI

Males   Lachar-Wrobel CI Set IV: Deviant Beliefs

		Age, yr				
	Total Sample	13	14	15	16	17
N	624	112	147	130	122	113
Median	2	2	2	2	2	2
Mean	2.72	2.83	2.89	2.70	2.67	2.44
SD	2.28	2.35	2.46	2.29	2.03	2.21
Min	0	0	0	0	0	0
Max	13	10	10	13	9	10

	Percentage of Sample with Raw Score < X					
X	Total Sample	13	14	15	16	17
0	0.0	0.0	0.0	0.0	0.0	0.0
1	13.5	13.4	15.0	16.9	5.7	15.9
2	37.7	37.5	37.4	37.7	35.2	40.7
3	54.8	50.9	53.1	51.5	57.4	61.9
4	69.9	67.9	66.7	65.4	73.8	77.0
5	80.9	81.3	75.5	81.5	83.6	84.1
6	88.3	85.7	85.0	90.8	89.3	91.2
7	91.5	89.3	87.8	94.6	92.6	93.8
8	95.5	92.9	94.6	97.7	96.7	95.6
9	97.9	99.1	97.3	97.7	98.4	97.3
10	98.9	99.1	98.6	98.5	100.0	98.2
11	99.8	100.0	100.0	99.2	100.0	100.0
12	99.8	100.0	100.0	99.2	100.0	100.0
13	99.8	100.0	100.0	99.2	100.0	100.0

Research/Supplemental Scales for the MMPI

Males   Lachar-Wrobel CI Set V: Deviant Thinking/Experience

| | Total Sample | Age, yr | | | | |
		13	14	15	16	17
N	624	112	147	130	122	113
Median	3	3	3	3	3	3
Mean	3.18	3.28	3.29	2.88	3.46	2.98
SD	2.19	2.25	2.21	2.16	2.24	2.05
Min	0	0	0	0	0	0
Max	10	9	9	10	8	10

Percentage of Sample with Raw Score < X

X	Total Sample	13	14	15	16	17
0	0.0	0.0	0.0	0.0	0.0	0.0
1	7.7	11.6	7.5	9.2	4.9	5.3
2	24.5	21.4	23.8	33.1	21.3	22.1
3	44.7	42.9	42.2	49.2	40.2	49.6
4	60.9	58.0	57.1	65.4	54.9	69.9
5	76.6	73.2	75.5	80.8	73.0	80.5
6	84.9	81.3	83.0	89.2	82.0	89.4
7	90.5	91.1	89.8	92.3	86.9	92.9
8	94.4	93.8	94.6	96.2	91.0	96.5
9	98.4	99.1	98.0	97.7	100.0	97.3
10	99.5	100.0	100.0	99.2	100.0	98.2

Research/Supplemental Scales for the MMPI

Males   Lachar-Wrobel CI Set VI: Substance Abuse

| | Total Sample | Age, yr | | | | |
		13	14	15	16	17
N	624	112	147	130	122	113
Median	1	1	1	1	1	1
Mean	0.91	0.87	1.00	0.88	0.81	0.98
SD	0.86	0.77	0.81	0.88	0.88	0.98
Min	0	0	0	0	0	0
Max	4	3	3	4	4	4

| X | Percentage of Sample with Raw Score < X | | | | | |
	Total Sample	13	14	15	16	17
0	0.0	0.0	0.0	0.0	0.0	0.0
1	35.7	34.8	27.9	38.5	41.8	37.2
2	79.0	80.4	76.9	79.2	83.6	75.2
3	94.9	98.2	95.2	96.2	94.3	90.3
4	99.4	100.0	100.0	98.5	99.2	99.1

Males   Lachar-Wrobel CI Set VII: Antisocial Attitude

	Total Sample	Age, yr				
		13	14	15	16	17
N	624	112	147	130	122	113
Median	3	2	3	3	3	3
Mean	3.09	2.56	3.32	2.92	3.35	3.26
SD	1.94	1.70	2.05	1.96	1.98	1.84
Min	0	0	0	0	0	0
Max	9	8	9	9	8	8

Percentage of Sample with Raw Score < X

X	Total Sample	13	14	15	16	17
0	0.0	0.0	0.0	0.0	0.0	0.0
1	7.5	9.8	6.1	9.2	4.9	8.0
2	22.9	29.5	21.8	26.2	21.3	15.9
3	41.2	51.8	36.7	46.2	35.2	37.2
4	62.2	75.0	57.8	66.9	56.6	55.8
5	76.1	85.7	72.8	78.5	72.1	72.6
6	88.0	9 <->	85.0	87.7	83.6	90.3
7	95.4	98.2	92.5	96.9	93.4	96.5
8	97.6	99.1	95.9	97.7	97.5	98.2
9	99.7	100.0	99.3	99.2	100.0	100.0

Research/Supplemental Scales for the MMPI

Males   Lachar-Wrobel CI Set VIII: Family Conflict

| | | Age, yr | | | | |
	Total Sample	13	14	15	16	17
N	624	112	147	130	122	113
Median	1	1	2	2	2	1
Mean	1.55	1.43	1.80	1.48	1.58	1.41
SD	1.23	1.33	1.29	1.17	1.17	1.12
Min	0	0	0	0	0	0
Max	4	4	4	4	4	4

| | Percentage of Sample with Raw Score < X | | | | | |
X	Total Sample	13	14	15	16	17
0	0.0	0.0	0.0	0.0	0.0	0.0
1	24.4	33.0	18.4	26.9	20.5	24.8
2	51.1	57.1	44.9	49.2	49.2	57.5
3	76.6	76.8	69.4	79.2	79.5	79.6
4	92.5	90.2	87.1	96.2	92.6	97.3

Research/Supplemental Scales for the MMPI

Males   Lachar-Wrobel CI Set IX: Problematic Anger

		Age, yr				
	Total Sample	13	14	15	16	17
N	624	112	147	130	122	113
Median	2	2	2	2	2	2
Mean	1.99	1.96	2.23	1.94	2.01	1.73
SD	1.25	1.23	1.23	1.22	1.23	1.31
Min	0	0	0	0	0	0
Max	4	4	4	4	4	4

	Percentage of Sample with Raw Score < X					
X	Total Sample	13	14	15	16	17
0	0.0	0.0	0.0	0.0	0.0	0.0
1	16.0	13.4	13.6	16.2	13.9	23.9
2	35.4	38.4	25.2	36.2	35.2	45.1
3	61.2	63.4	52.4	63.1	61.5	68.1
4	88.6	88.4	85.7	90.8	88.5	90.3

Research/Supplemental Scales for the MMPI

Males   Lachar-Wrobel CI Set X: Sexual Concern/Deviation

	Total Sample	Age, yr				
		13	14	15	16	17
N	624	112	147	130	122	113
Median	1	1	1	1	1	1
Mean	1.33	1.17	1.37	1.29	1.49	1.32
SD	1.18	1.16	1.21	1.14	1.10	1.26
Min	0	0	0	0	0	0
Max	6	6	5	5	5	5

X	Percentage of Sample with Raw Score < X					
	Total Sample	13	14	15	16	17
0	0.0	0.0	0.0	0.0	0.0	0.0
1	26.9	33.0	29.3	26.2	16.4	30.1
2	62.8	67.9	57.8	66.2	58.2	65.5
3	83.3	88.4	81.6	83.8	82.0	81.4
4	95.0	95.5	94.6	96.2	95.9	92.9
5	98.7	99.1	99.3	98.5	98.4	98.2
6	99.8	99.1	100.0	100.0	100.0	100.0

Research/Supplemental Scales for the MMPI

Males   Lachar-Wrobel CI Set XI: Somatic Symptoms

		Age, yr				
	Total Sample	13	14	15	16	17
N	624	112	147	130	122	113
Median	3	3	4	3	4	3
Mean	4.03	4.04	4.46	3.61	4.38	3.54
SD	3.20	3.27	3.41	2.99	3.18	3.02
Min	0	0	0	0	0	0
Max	16	13	15	16	13	12

	Percentage of Sample with Raw Score < X					
X	Total Sample	13	14	15	16	17
0	0.0	0.0	0.0	0.0	0.0	0.0
1	8.8	7.1	9.5	10.8	7.4	8.8
2	24.8	26.8	18.4	28.5	20.5	31.9
3	39.7	41.1	33.3	43.1	34.4	48.7
4	51.9	56.3	46.9	54.6	45.1	58.4
5	62.0	62.5	58.5	66.9	55.7	67.3
6	72.1	68.8	68.7	79.2	66.4	77.9
7	81.6	79.5	76.2	86.2	79.5	87.6
8	85.9	83.9	80.3	90.8	86.1	89.4
9	90.1	89.3	88.4	93.8	88.5	90.3
10	92.6	91.1	91.8	96.2	90.2	93.8
11	94.6	94.6	92.5	96.9	93.4	95.6
12	96.5	96.4	96.6	96.9	95.9	96.5
13	98.4	98.2	96.6	98.5	99.2	100.0
14	99.0	100.0	97.3	98.5	100.0	100.0
15	99.5	100.0	98.6	99.2	100.0	100.0
16	99.8	100.0	100.0	99.2	100.0	100.0

Research/Supplemental Scales for the MMPI

Females   Lachar-Wrobel   Sum of CI Sets I through XI

| | Total Sample | Age, yr | | | | |
		13	14	15	16	17
N	691	136	153	127	138	137
Median	4	4	3	4	4	4
Mean	4.45	4.28	4.03	4.61	5.22	4.16
SD	3.60	3.02	3.40	3.71	4.41	3.26
Min	0	0	0	0	0	0
Max	20	13	16	20	20	18

| | Percentage of Sample with Raw Score < X | | | | | |
X	Total Sample	13	14	15	16	17
0	100.0	100.0	100.0	100.0	100.0	100.0
1	100.1	100.0	100.0	100.0	100.7	100.0
2	100.3	100.0	100.0	100.0	101.4	100.0
3	100.4	100.0	100.0	100.0	102.2	100.0
4	100.6	100.0	100.0	100.0	102.9	100.0
5	100.7	100.0	100.0	100.0	103.6	100.0
6	100.9	100.0	100.0	100.0	104.3	100.0
7	101.0	100.0	100.0	100.0	105.1	100.0
8	101.2	100.0	100.0	100.0	105.8	100.0
9	101.3	100.0	100.0	100.0	106.5	100.0
10	101.4	100.0	100.0	100.0	107.2	100.0
11	101.6	100.0	100.0	100.0	108.0	100.0
12	101.7	100.0	100.0	100.0	108.7	100.0
13	101.9	100.0	100.0	100.0	109.4	100.0
14	102.0	100.0	100.0	100.0	110.1	100.0
15	102.2	100.0	100.0	100.0	110.9	100.0
16	102.3	100.0	100.0	100.0	111.6	100.0
17	102.5	100.0	100.0	100.0	112.3	100.0
18	102.6	100.0	100.0	100.0	113.0	100.0
19	102.7	100.0	100.0	100.0	113.8	100.0
20	102.9	100.0	100.0	100.0	114.5	100.0

Research/Supplemental Scales for the MMPI

Males   Lachar-Wrobel   Sum of CI Sets I through XI

		Age, yr				
	Total Sample	13	14	15	16	17
N	624	112	147	130	122	113
Median	3	3	4	3	4	3
Mean	4.03	4.04	4.46	3.61	4.38	3.54
SD	3.20	3.27	3.41	2.99	3.18	3.02
Min	0	0	0	0	0	0
Max	16	13	15	16	13	12

	Percentage of Sample with Raw Score < X					
X	Total Sample	13	14	15	16	17
0	100.0	100.0	100.0	100.0	100.0	100.0
1	100.2	100.0	100.0	100.8	100.0	100.0
2	100.3	100.0	100.0	101.5	100.0	100.0
3	100.5	100.0	100.0	102.3	100.0	100.0
4	100.6	100.0	100.0	103.1	100.0	100.0
5	100.8	100.0	100.0	103.8	100.0	100.0
6	101.0	100.0	100.0	104.6	100.0	100.0
7	101.1	100.0	100.0	105.4	100.0	100.0
8	101.3	100.0	100.0	106.2	100.0	100.0
9	101.4	100.0	100.0	106.9	100.0	100.0
10	101.6	100.0	100.0	107.7	100.0	100.0
11	101.8	100.0	100.0	108.5	100.0	100.0
12	101.9	100.0	100.0	109.2	100.0	100.0
13	102.1	100.0	100.0	110.0	100.0	100.0
14	102.2	100.0	100.0	110.8	100.0	100.0
15	102.4	100.0	100.0	111.5	100.0	100.0
16	102.6	100.0	100.0	112.3	100.0	100.0

APPENDIX B

Mean T Scores for 13 Basic MMPI Scales Among Contemporary Normal Adolescents and Adults in Eight Age Groups, Using Original Hathaway Norms and K-Corrected Values

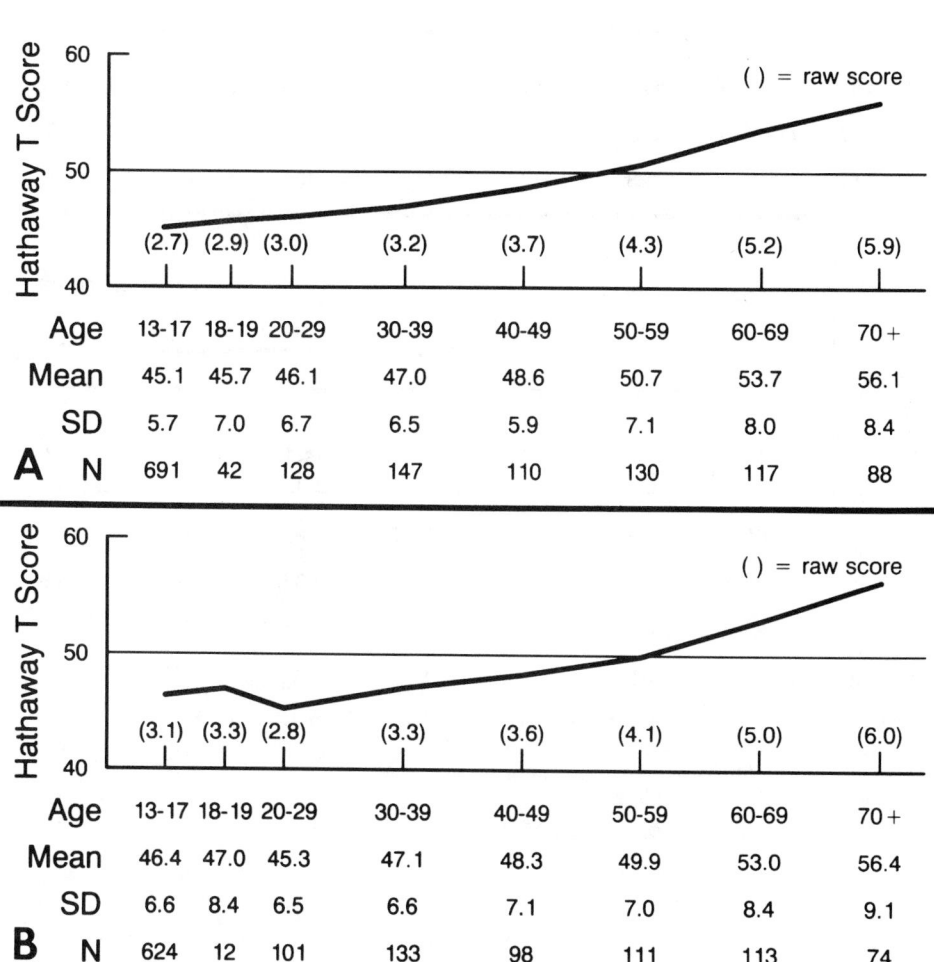

Figure 1. Mean scores for scale L. A, Females. B, Males. (From Colligan, R. C., Osborne, D., Swenson, W. M., & Offord, K. P. [1983]. *The MMPI: A contemporary normative study.* New York: Praeger Publishers. By permission of Mayo Foundation.)

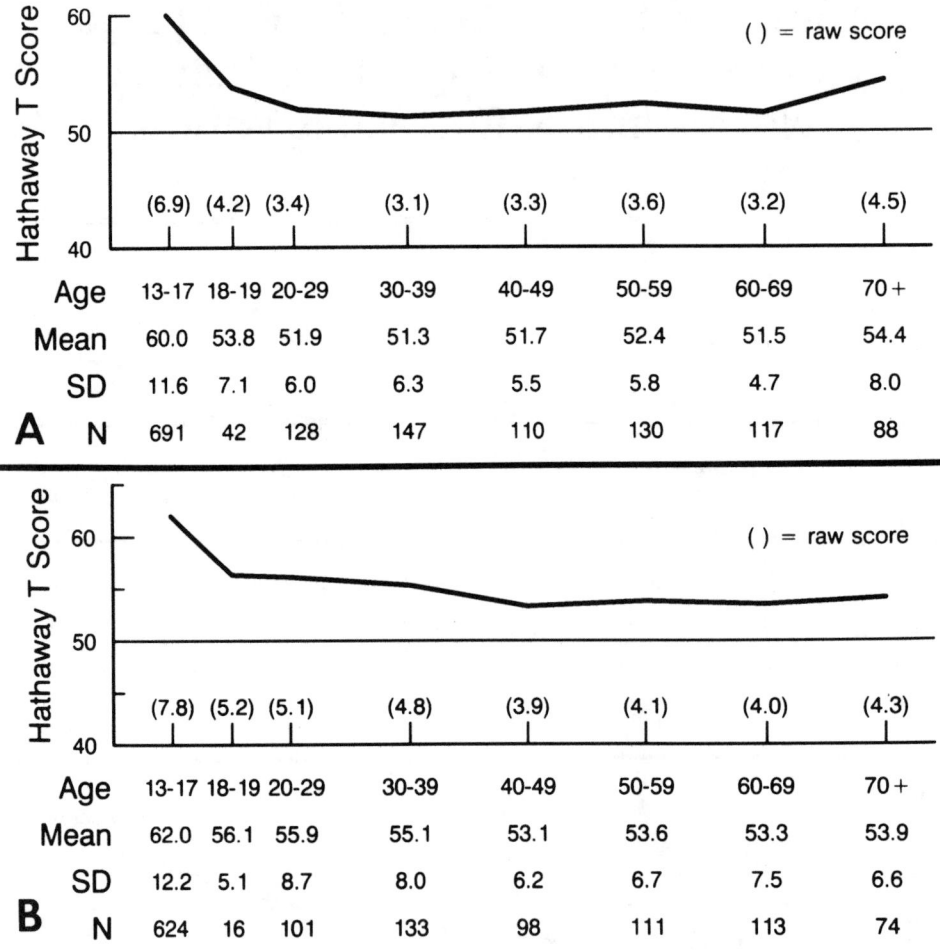

Figure 2. Mean scores for scale F. A, Females. B, Males. (From Colligan, R. C., Osborne, D., Swenson, W. M., & Offord, K. P. [1983]. *The MMPI: A contemporary normative study.* New York: Praeger Publishers. By permission of Mayo Foundation.)

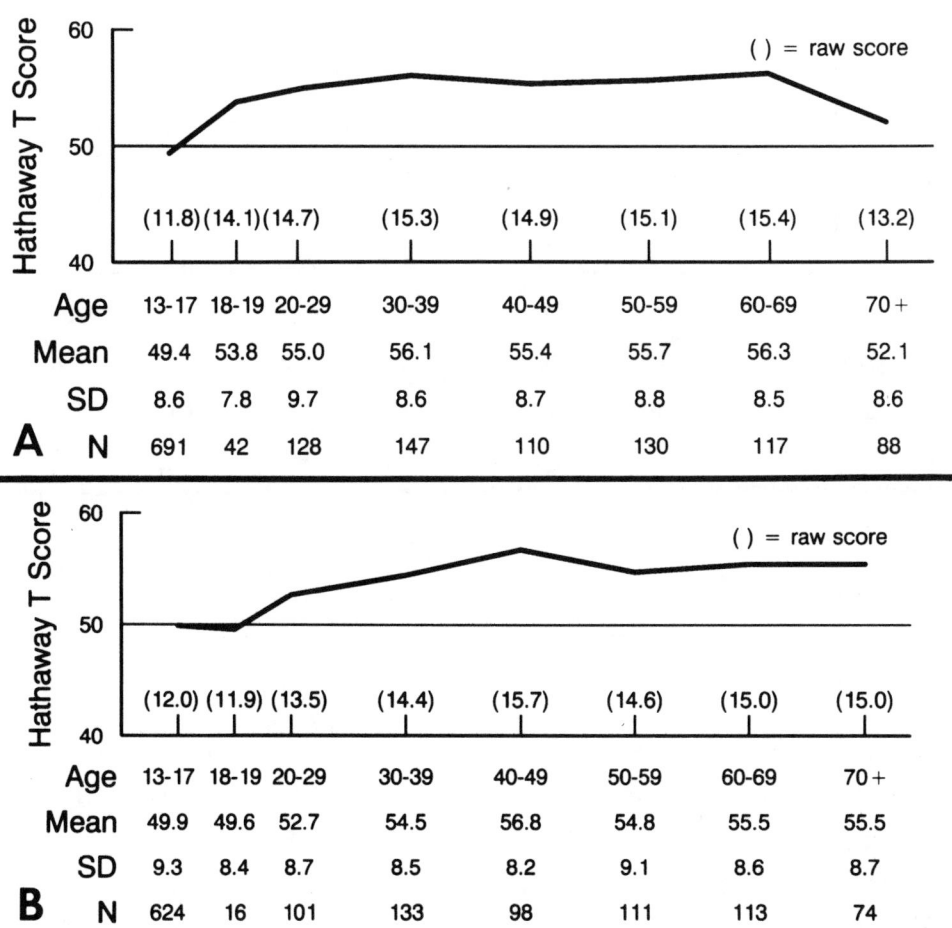

	( ) = raw score						
	(11.8) (14.1) (14.7)	(15.3)	(14.9)	(15.1)	(15.4)	(13.2)	
Age	13-17 18-19 20-29	30-39	40-49	50-59	60-69	70 +	
Mean	49.4 53.8 55.0	56.1	55.4	55.7	56.3	52.1	
SD	8.6 7.8 9.7	8.6	8.7	8.8	8.5	8.6	
A N	691 42 128	147	110	130	117	88	

	( ) = raw score						
	(12.0) (11.9) (13.5)	(14.4)	(15.7)	(14.6)	(15.0)	(15.0)	
Age	13-17 18-19 20-29	30-39	40-49	50-59	60-69	70 +	
Mean	49.9 49.6 52.7	54.5	56.8	54.8	55.5	55.5	
SD	9.3 8.4 8.7	8.5	8.2	9.1	8.6	8.7	
B N	624 16 101	133	98	111	113	74	

Figure 3.   Mean scores for scale K. A, Females. B, Males. (From Colligan, R. C., Osborne, D., Swenson, W. M., & Offord, K. P. [1983]. *The MMPI: A contemporary normative study*. New York: Praeger Publishers. By permission of Mayo Foundation.)

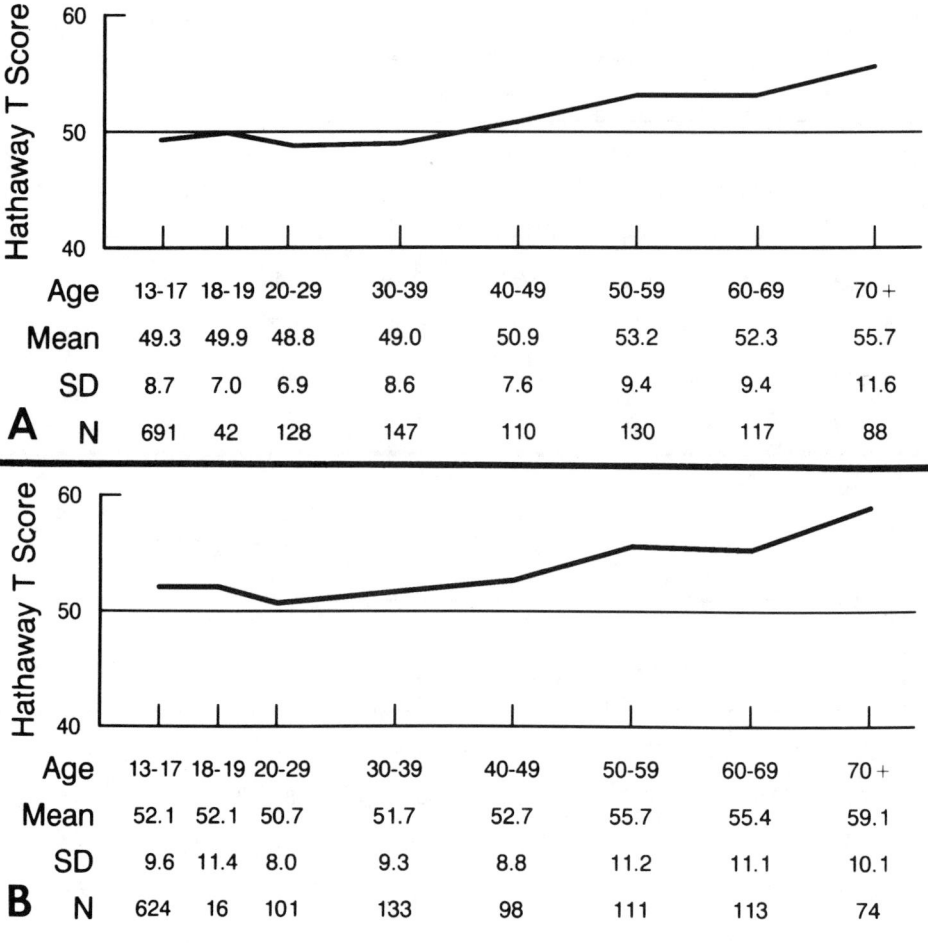

Figure 4.   Mean scores for scale 1 (Hs). A, Females. B, Males. (From Colligan, R. C., Osborne, D., Swenson, W. M., & Offord, K. P. [1983]. *The MMPI: A contemporary normative study.* New York: Praeger Publishers. By permission of Mayo Foundation.)

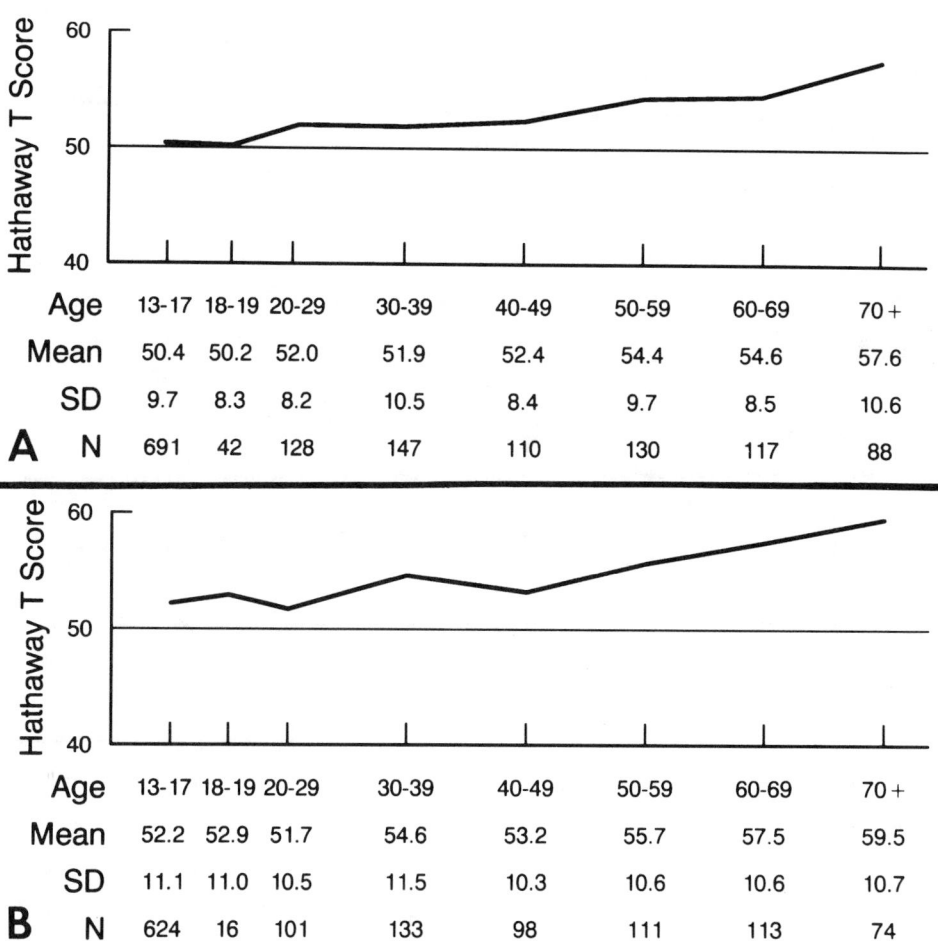

Age	13-17	18-19	20-29	30-39	40-49	50-59	60-69	70+
Mean	50.4	50.2	52.0	51.9	52.4	54.4	54.6	57.6
SD	9.7	8.3	8.2	10.5	8.4	9.7	8.5	10.6
A N	691	42	128	147	110	130	117	88

Age	13-17	18-19	20-29	30-39	40-49	50-59	60-69	70+
Mean	52.2	52.9	51.7	54.6	53.2	55.7	57.5	59.5
SD	11.1	11.0	10.5	11.5	10.3	10.6	10.6	10.7
B N	624	16	101	133	98	111	113	74

Figure 5.   Mean scores for scale 2 (D). A, Females. B, Males. (From Colligan, R. C., Osborne, D., Swenson, W. M., & Offord, K. P. [1983]. *The MMPI: A contemporary normative study.* New York: Praeger Publishers. By permission of Mayo Foundation.)

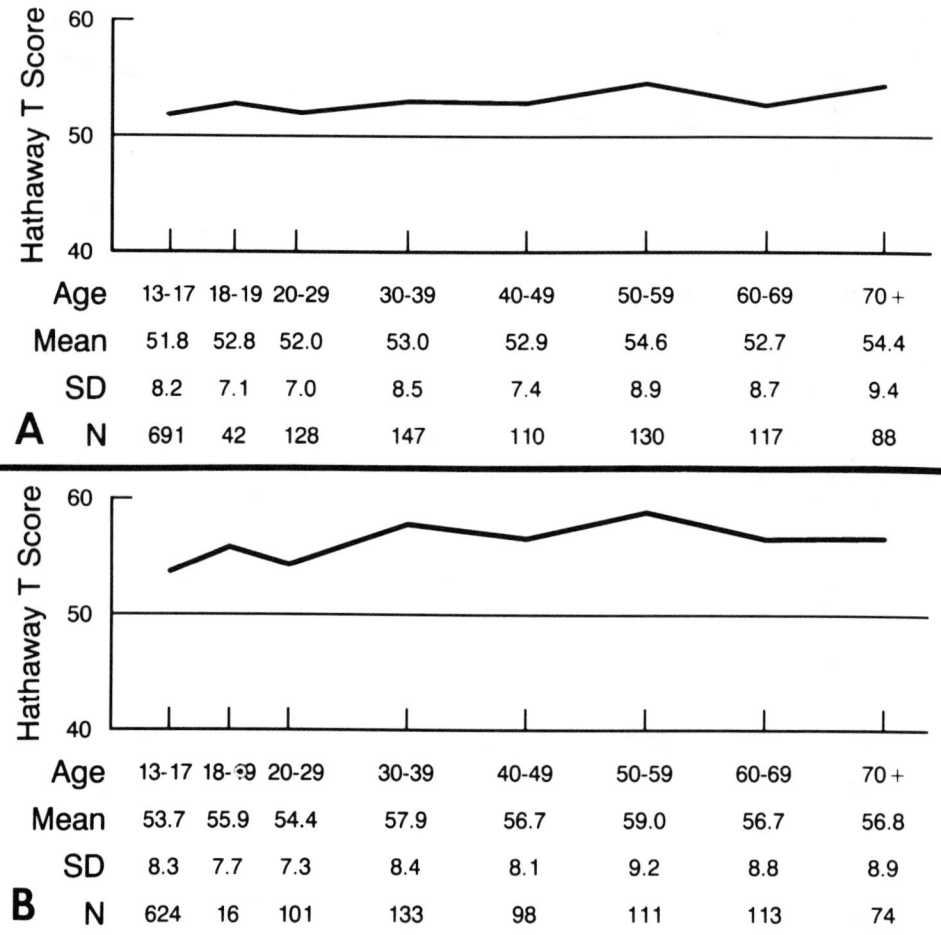

Age	13-17	18-19	20-29	30-39	40-49	50-59	60-69	70+
Mean	51.8	52.8	52.0	53.0	52.9	54.6	52.7	54.4
SD	8.2	7.1	7.0	8.5	7.4	8.9	8.7	9.4
A N	691	42	128	147	110	130	117	88

Age	13-17	18-19	20-29	30-39	40-49	50-59	60-69	70+
Mean	53.7	55.9	54.4	57.9	56.7	59.0	56.7	56.8
SD	8.3	7.7	7.3	8.4	8.1	9.2	8.8	8.9
B N	624	16	101	133	98	111	113	74

Figure 6. Mean scores for scale 3 (Hy). A, Females. B, Males. (From Colligan, R. C., Osborne, D., Swenson, W. M., & Offord, K. P. [1983]. *The MMPI: A contemporary normative study.* New York: Praeger Publishers. By permission of Mayo Foundation.)

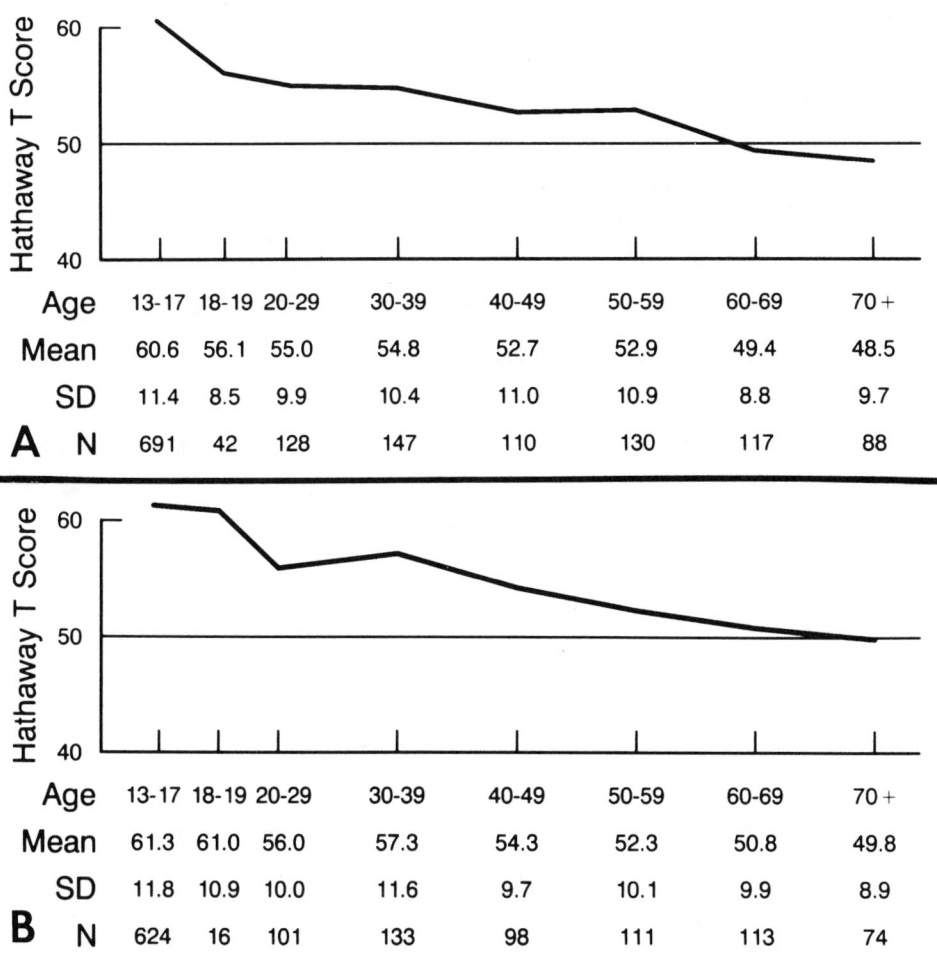

Age	13-17	18-19	20-29	30-39	40-49	50-59	60-69	70+
Mean	60.6	56.1	55.0	54.8	52.7	52.9	49.4	48.5
SD	11.4	8.5	9.9	10.4	11.0	10.9	8.8	9.7
A N	691	42	128	147	110	130	117	88

Age	13-17	18-19	20-29	30-39	40-49	50-59	60-69	70+
Mean	61.3	61.0	56.0	57.3	54.3	52.3	50.8	49.8
SD	11.8	10.9	10.0	11.6	9.7	10.1	9.9	8.9
B N	624	16	101	133	98	111	113	74

Figure 7.   Mean scores for scale 4 (Pd). A, Females. B, Males. (From Colligan, R. C., Osborne, D., Swenson, W. M., & Offord, K. P. [1983]. *The MMPI: A contemporary normative study.* New York: Praeger Publishers. By permission of Mayo Foundation.)

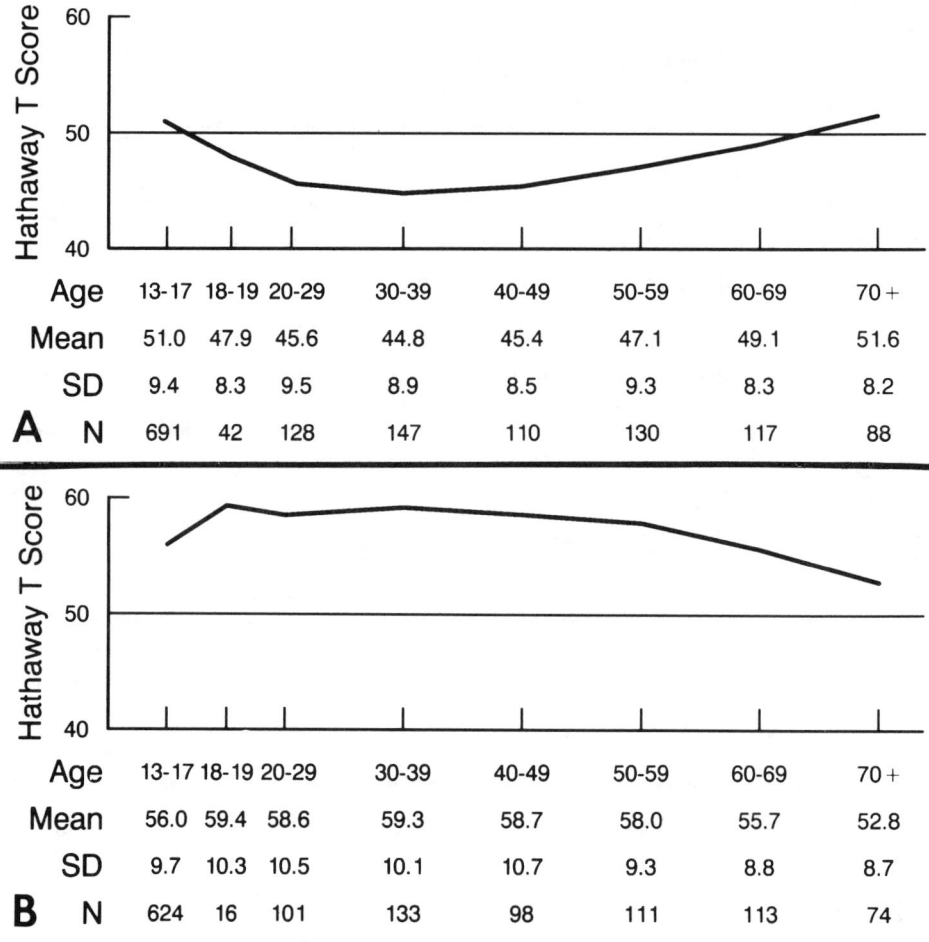

Figure 8. Mean scores for scale 5 (Mf). A, Females. B, Males. (From Colligan, R. C., Osborne, D., Swenson, W. M., & Offord, K. P. [1983]. *The MMPI: A contemporary normative study*. New York: Praeger Publishers. By permission of Mayo Foundation.)

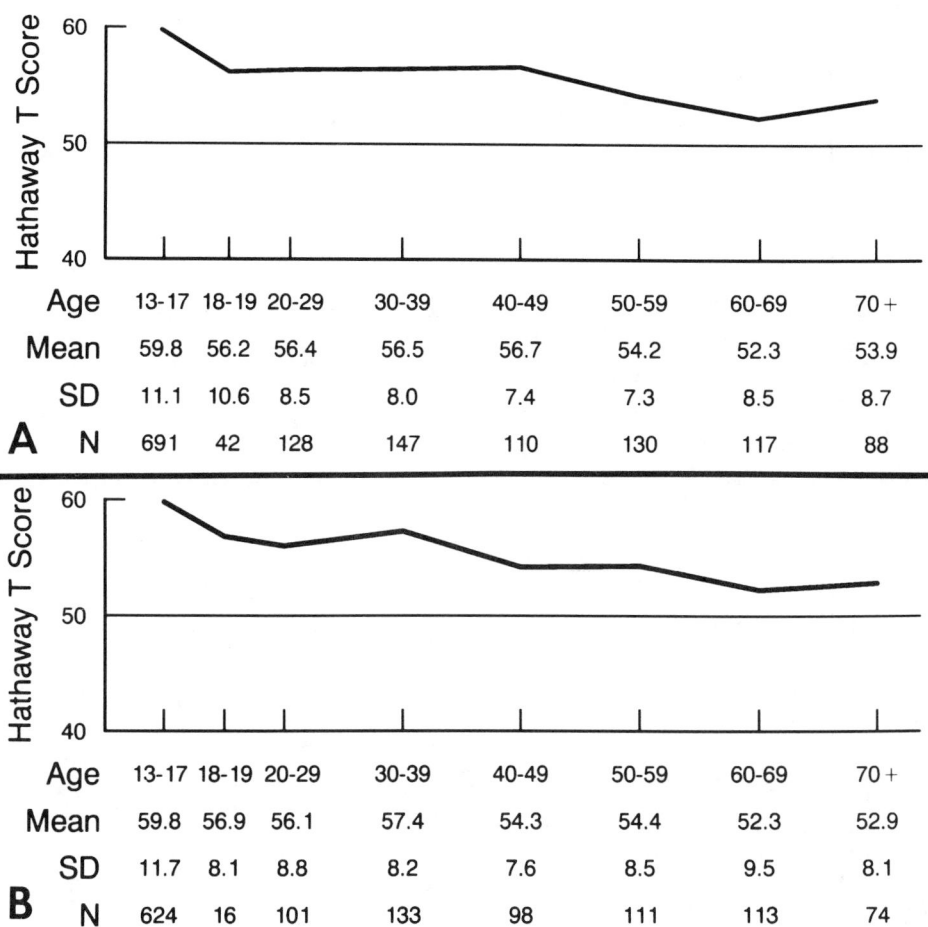

Figure 9. Mean scores for scale 6 (Pa). A, Females. B, Males. (From Colligan, R. C., Osborne, D., Swenson, W. M., & Offord, K. P. [1983]. *The MMPI: A contemporary normative study.* New York: Praeger Publishers. By permission of Mayo Foundation.)

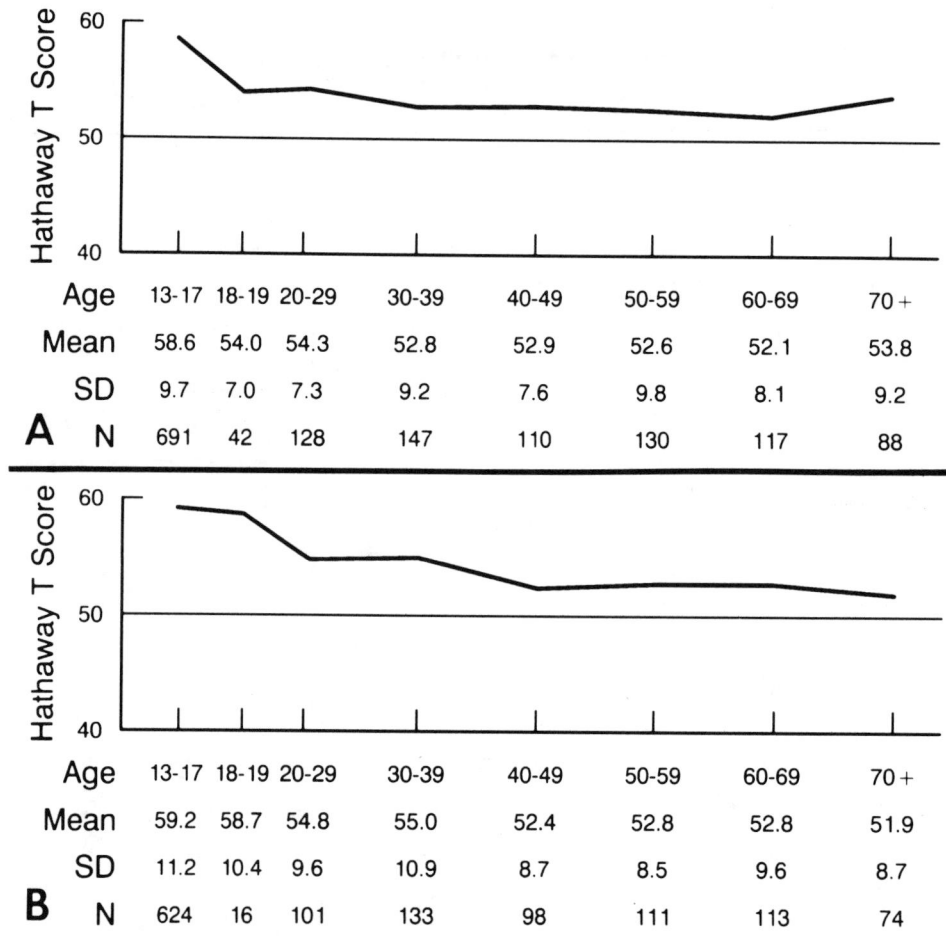

Age	13-17	18-19	20-29	30-39	40-49	50-59	60-69	70+
Mean	58.6	54.0	54.3	52.8	52.9	52.6	52.1	53.8
SD	9.7	7.0	7.3	9.2	7.6	9.8	8.1	9.2
A N	691	42	128	147	110	130	117	88

Age	13-17	18-19	20-29	30-39	40-49	50-59	60-69	70+
Mean	59.2	58.7	54.8	55.0	52.4	52.8	52.8	51.9
SD	11.2	10.4	9.6	10.9	8.7	8.5	9.6	8.7
B N	624	16	101	133	98	111	113	74

Figure 10.   Mean scores for scale 7 (Pt). A, Females. B, Males. (From Colligan, R. C., Osborne, D., Swenson, W. M., & Offord, K. P. [1983]. *The MMPI: A contemporary normative study.* New York: Praeger Publishers. By permission of Mayo Foundation.)

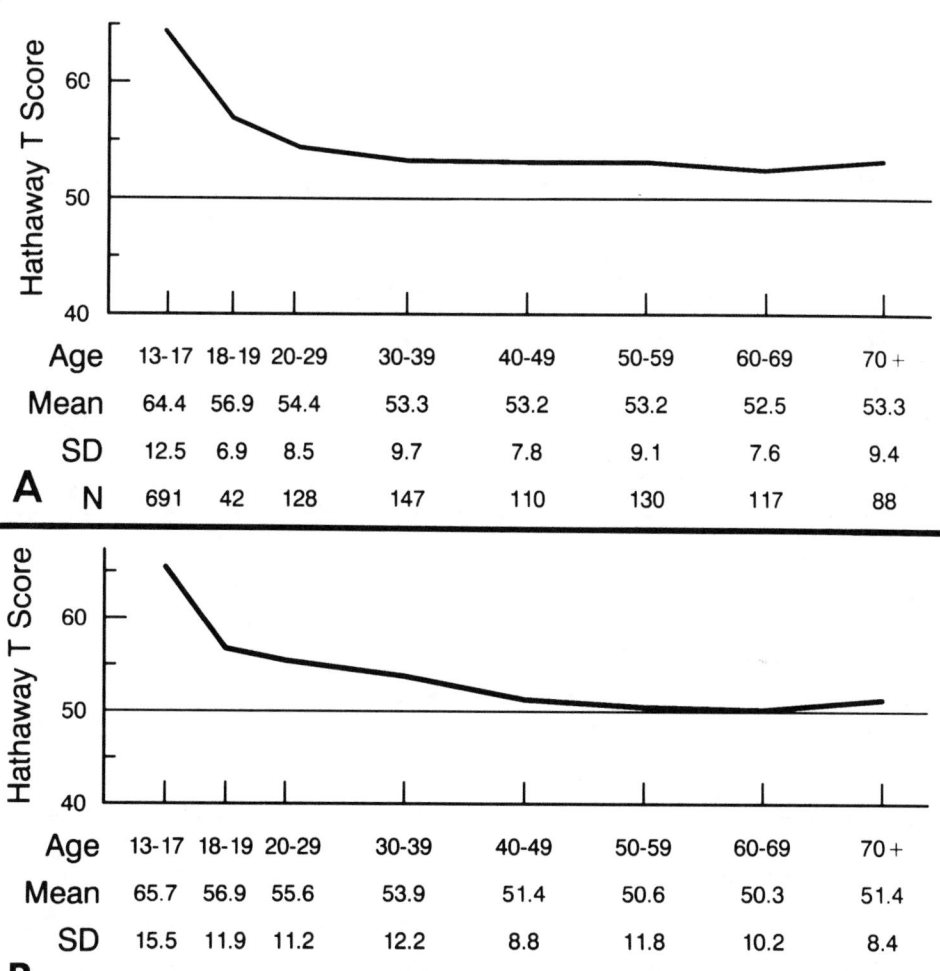

Figure 11. Mean scores for scale 8 (Sc). A, Females. B, Males. (From Colligan, R. C., Osborne, D., Swenson, W. M., & Offord, K. P. [1983]. *The MMPI: A contemporary normative study.* New York: Praeger Publishers. By permission of Mayo Foundation.)

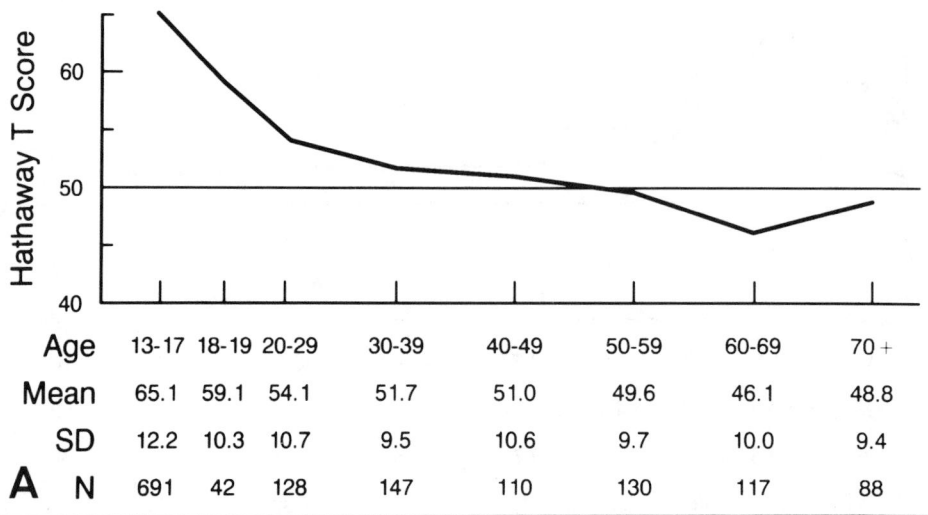

Age	13-17	18-19	20-29	30-39	40-49	50-59	60-69	70+
Mean	65.1	59.1	54.1	51.7	51.0	49.6	46.1	48.8
SD	12.2	10.3	10.7	9.5	10.6	9.7	10.0	9.4
A N	691	42	128	147	110	130	117	88

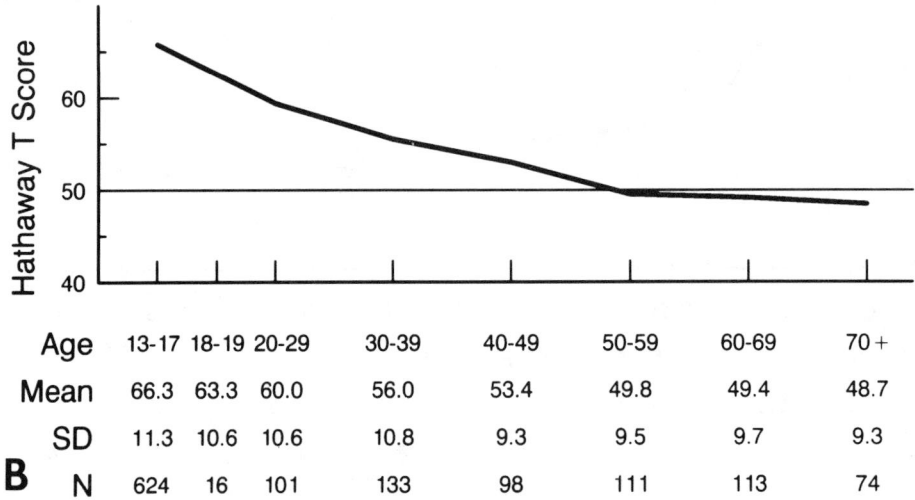

Age	13-17	18-19	20-29	30-39	40-49	50-59	60-69	70+
Mean	66.3	63.3	60.0	56.0	53.4	49.8	49.4	48.7
SD	11.3	10.6	10.6	10.8	9.3	9.5	9.7	9.3
B N	624	16	101	133	98	111	113	74

Figure 12. Mean scores for scale 9 (Ma). A, Females. B, Males. (From Colligan, R. C., Osborne, D., Swenson, W. M., & Offord, K. P. [1983]. *The MMPI: A contemporary normative study.* New York: Praeger Publishers. By permission of Mayo Foundation.)

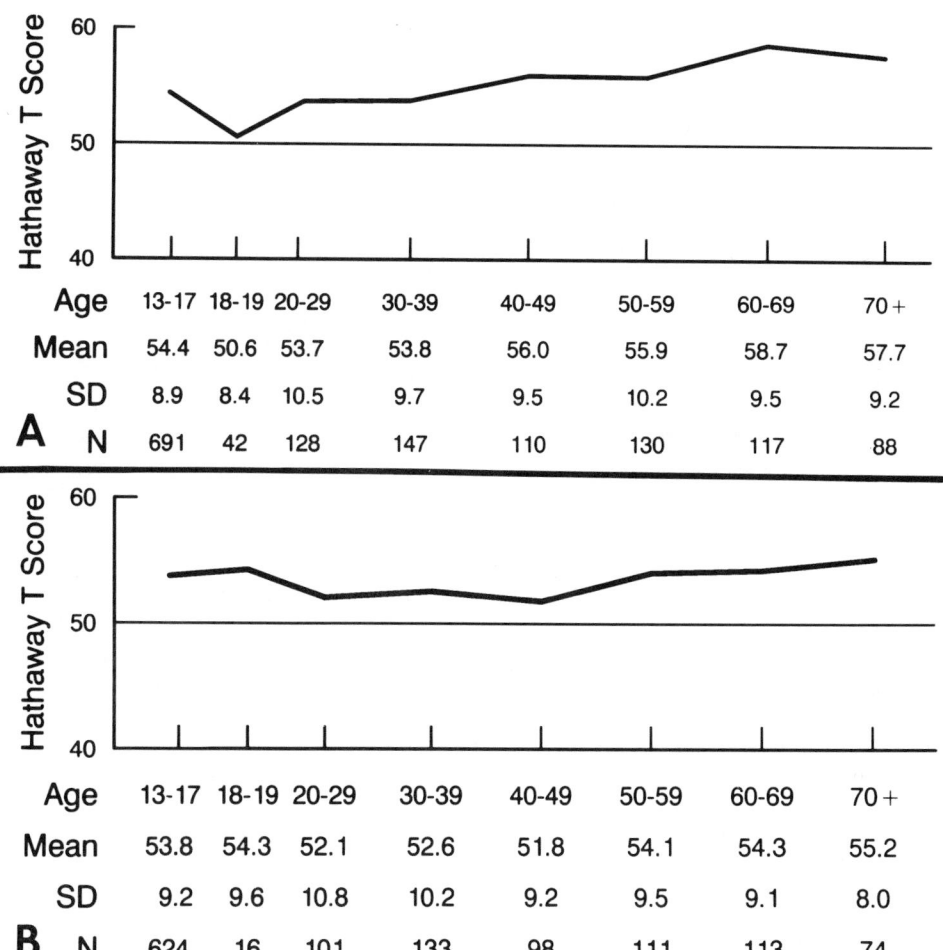

Figure 13.   Mean scores for scale 0 (Si). A, Females. B, Males. (From Colligan, R. C., Osborne, D., Swenson, W. M., & Offord, K. P. [1983]. *The MMPI: A contemporary normative study.* New York: Praeger Publishers. By permission of Mayo Foundation.)

APPENDIX C

Mean and Mean + 2 SD MMPI Profiles for Contemporary Normal Adolescents, Using Original Hathaway Adult Norms and K-Corrected Scores

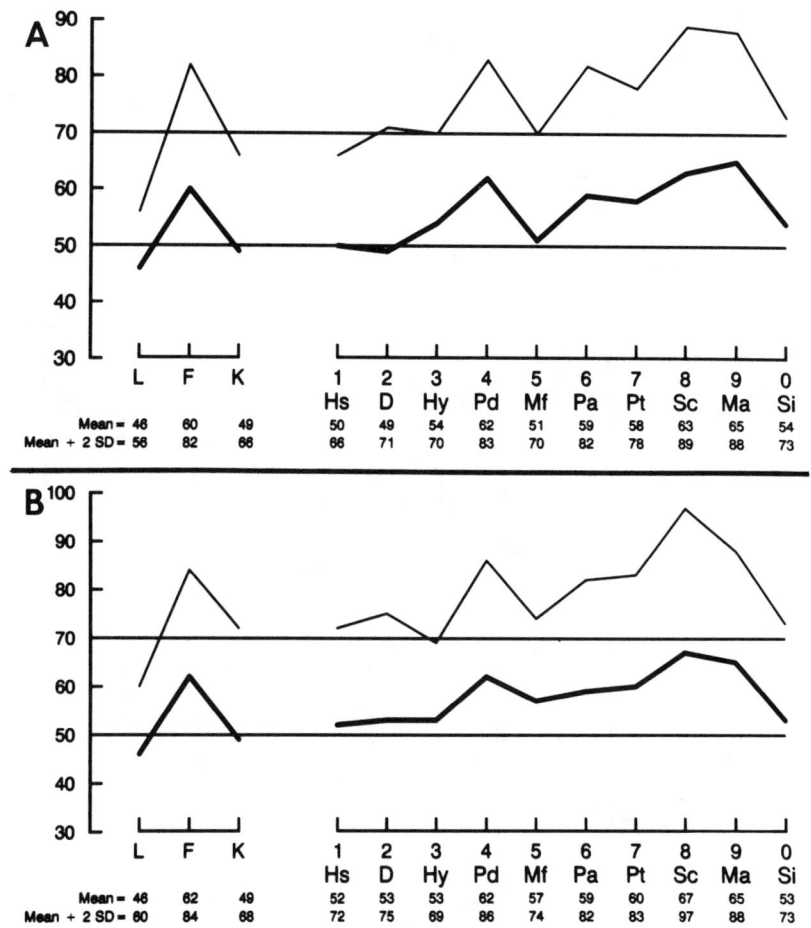

Figure 1.   Scores for adolescents ages 13 to 17 years. *A*, Female adolescents (n = 691). *B*, Male adolescents (n = 624).

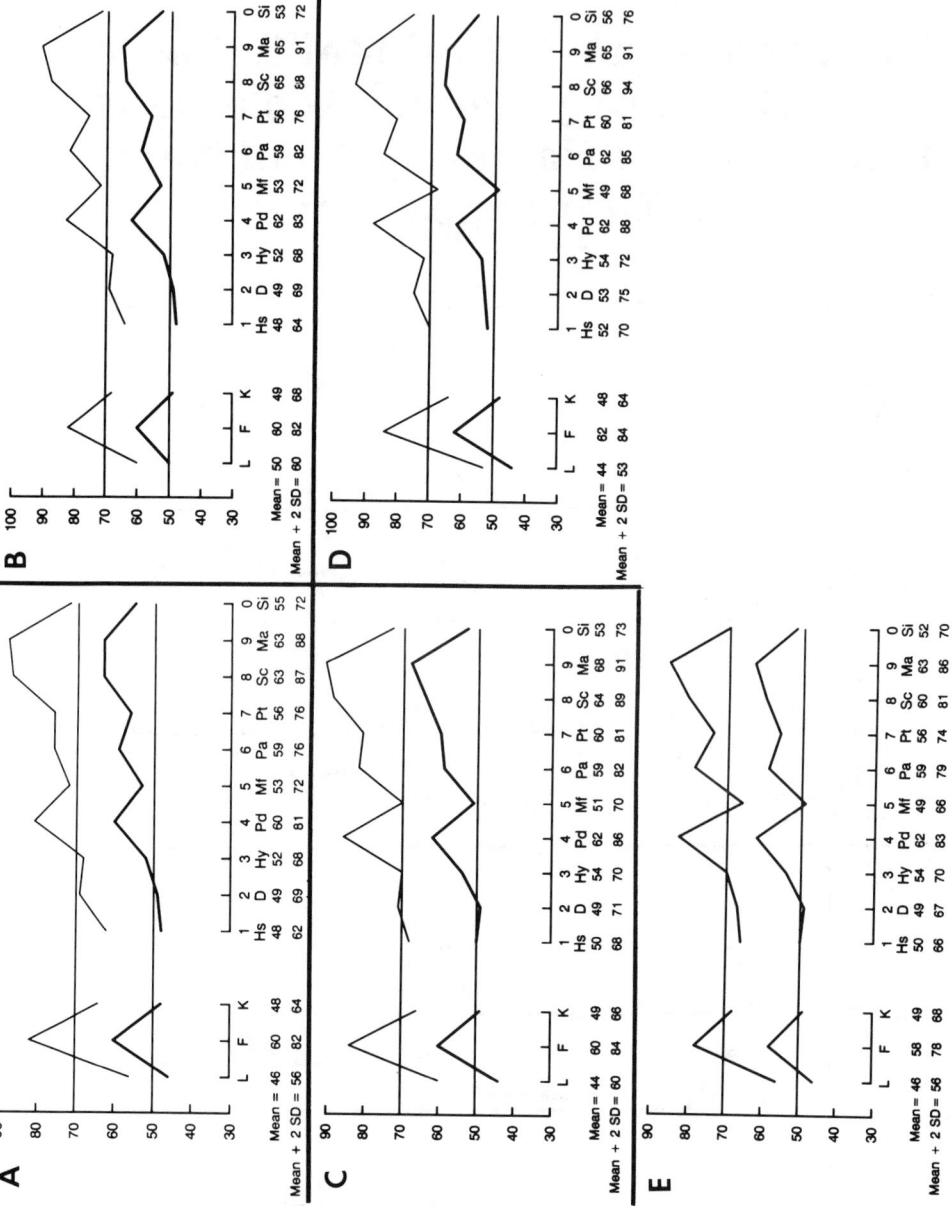

Figure 2.   Scores for female adolescents. A, Age 13 years. B, Age 14 years (n = 153). C, Age 15 years (n = 127). D, Age 16 years (n = 138). E, Age 17 years (n = 137).

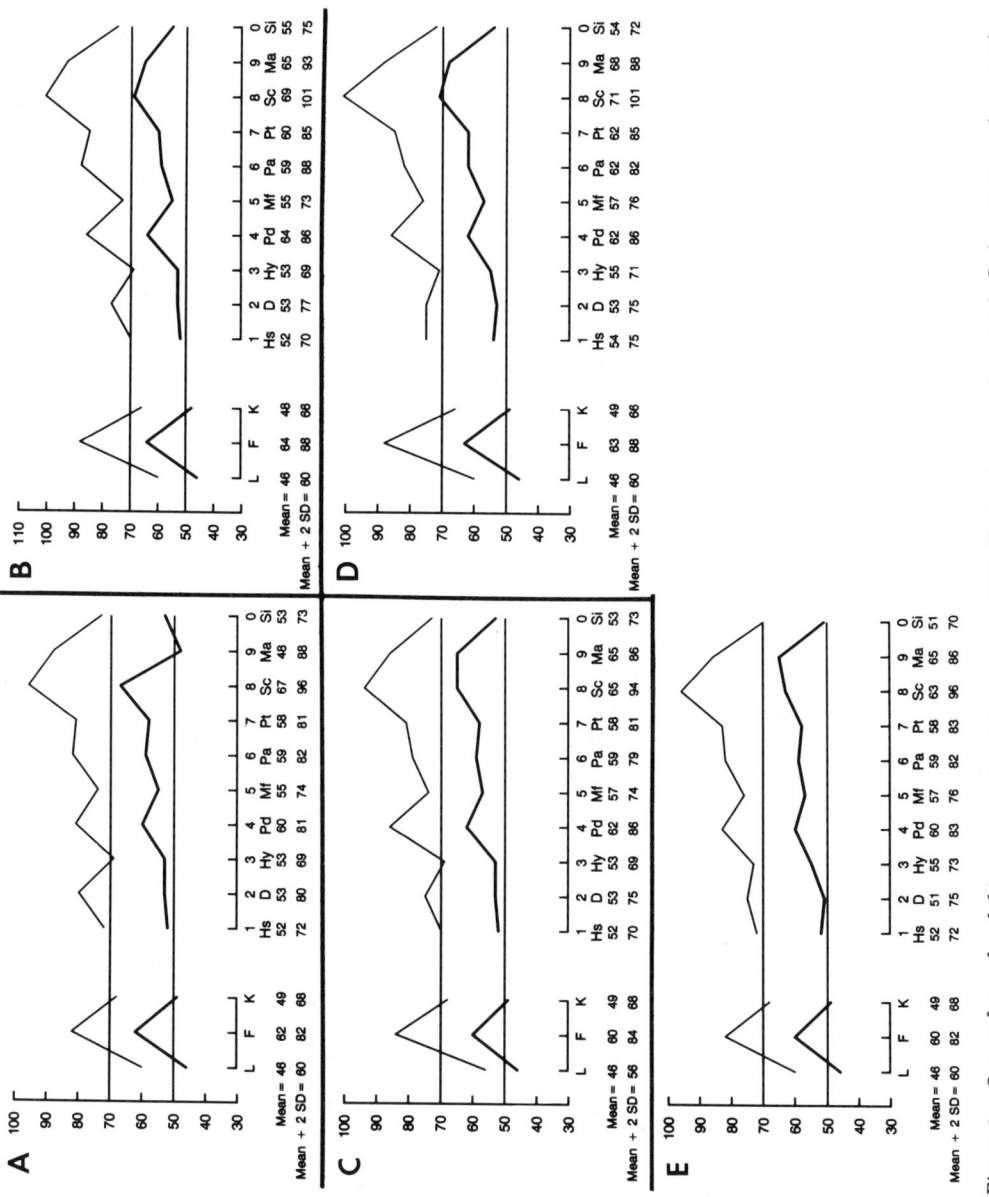

Figure 3. Scores for male adolescents. *A*, Age 13 years (n = 112). *B*, Age 14 years (n = 147). *C*, Age 15 years (n = 130). *D*, Age 16 years (n = 122). *E*, Age 17 years (n = 113).

APPENDIX D

Mean and Mean + 2 SD MMPI Profiles for Contemporary Normal Adolescents, Using Contemporary Adult Norms and K-Corrected Scores

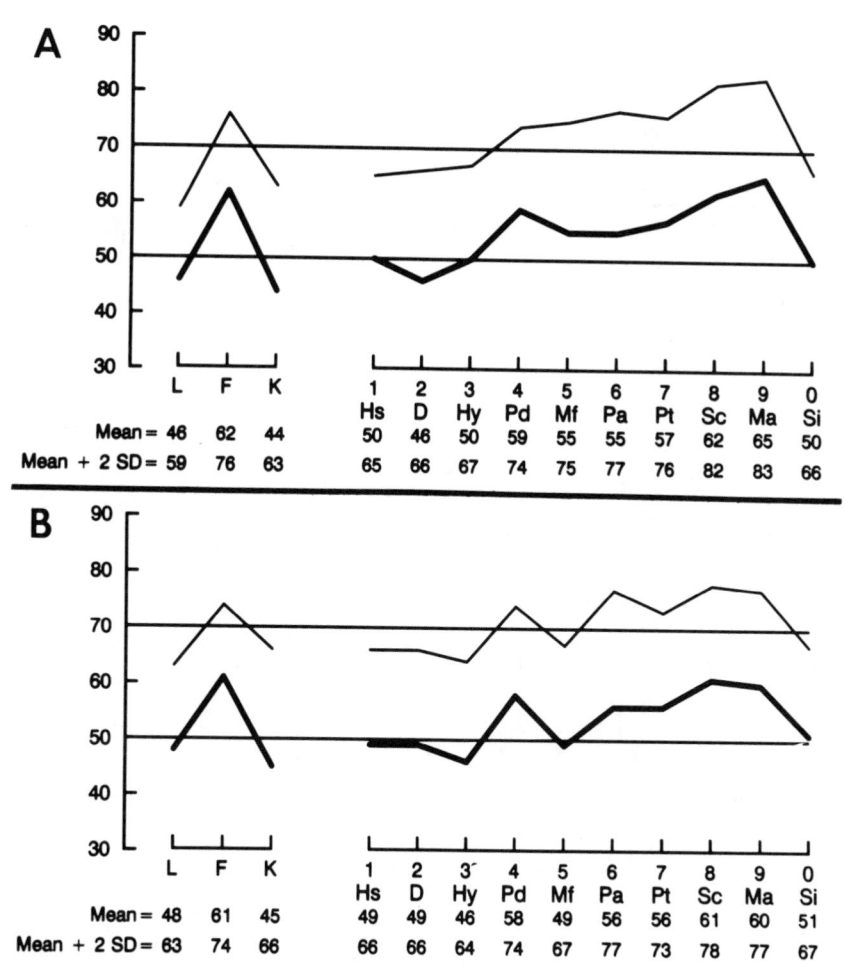

Figure 1.   Scores for adolescents ages 13 to 17 years. *A*, Female adolescents (n = 691). *B*, Male adolescents (n = 624).

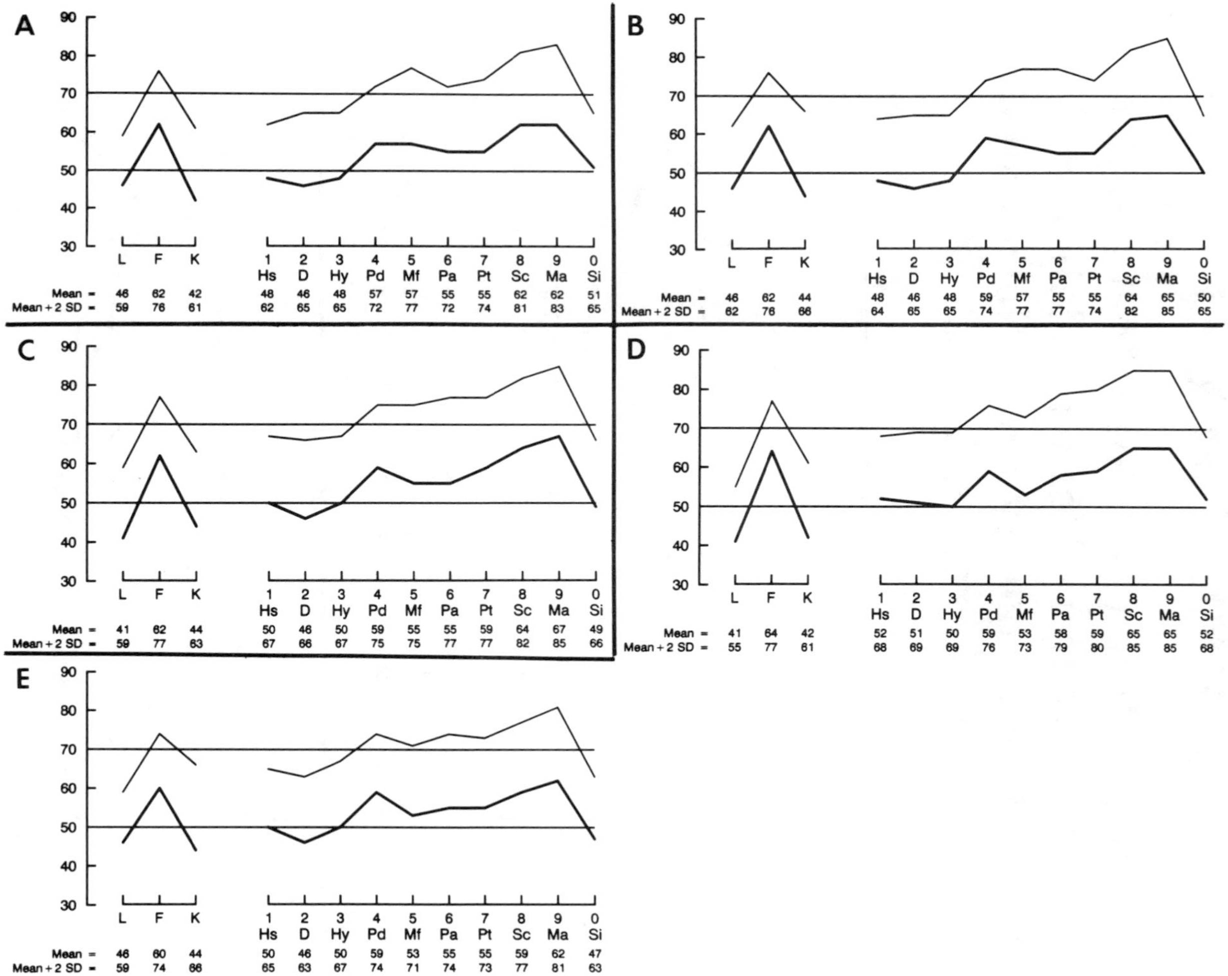

Figure 2. Scores for female adolescents. A, Age 13 years (n = 136). B, Age 14 years (n = 153). C. Age 15 years (n = 127).

550

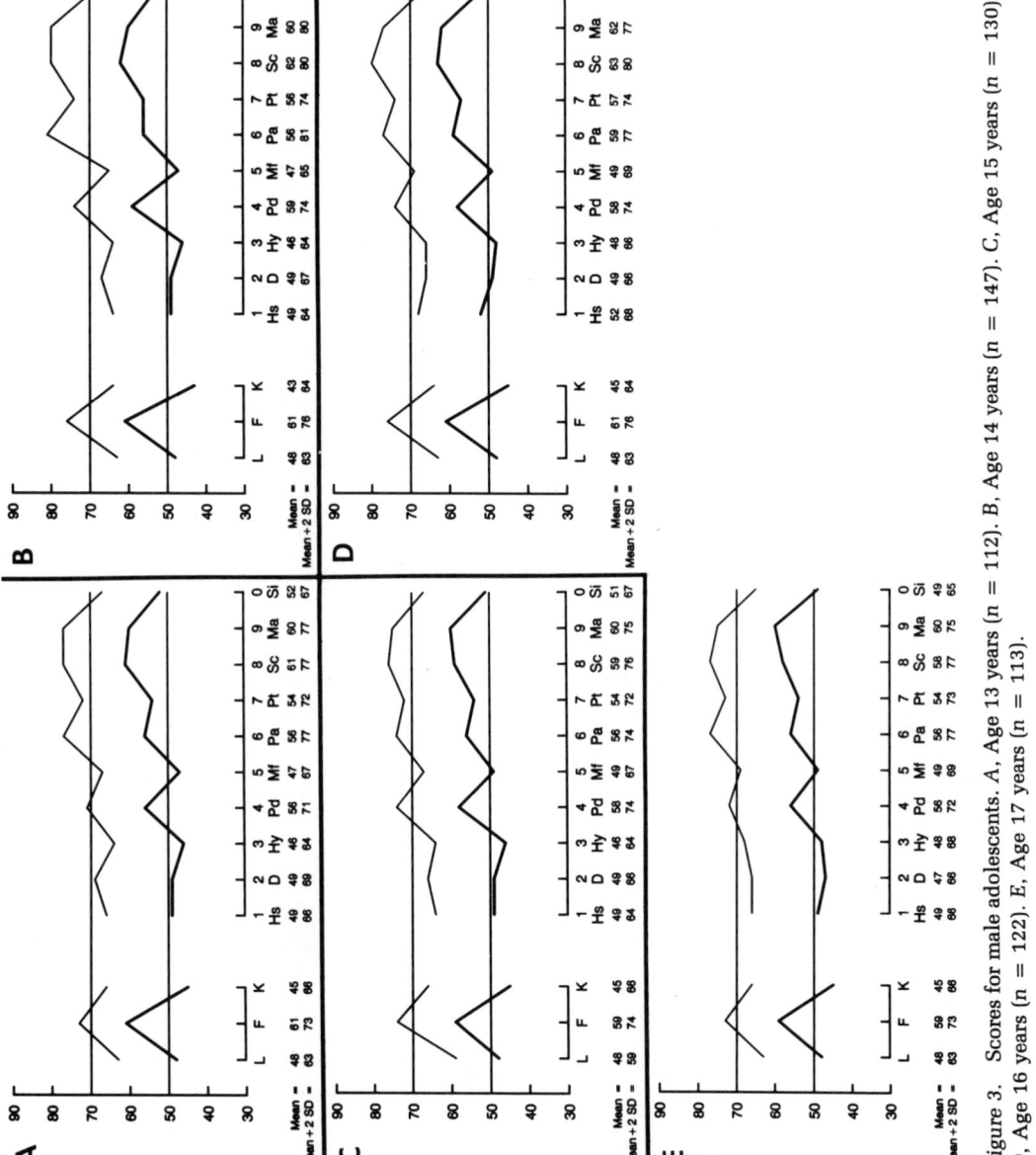

Figure 3. Scores for male adolescents. A, Age 13 years (n = 112). B, Age 14 years (n = 147). C, Age 15 years (n = 130). D, Age 16 years (n = 122). E, Age 17 years (n = 113).

551

APPENDIX E

Mean and Mean + 2 SD MMPI Profiles for Contemporary Normal Adolescents, Using Marks and Briggs Norms* and Scores Without K Correction

*Marks, P. A., Seeman, W., & Haller, D. L. (1974). *The Actuarial Use of the MMPI With Adolescents and Adults.* Baltimore: Williams & Wilkins (pp. 155–162).

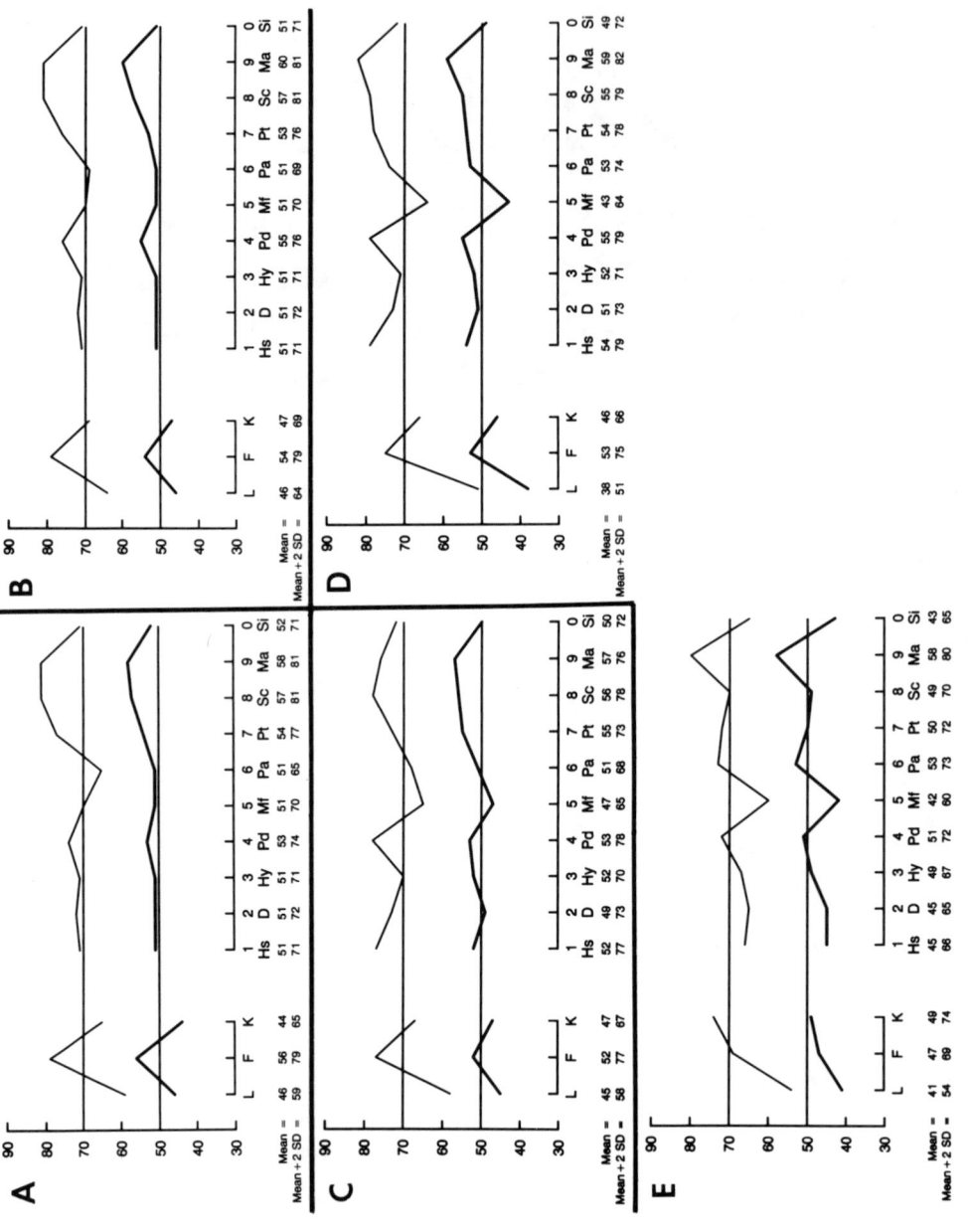

Figure 1. Scores for female adolescents. A, Age 13 years (n = 136). B, Age 14 years (n = 153). C, Age 15 years (n = 127).
D, Age 16 years (n = 138). E, Age 17 years (n = 137).

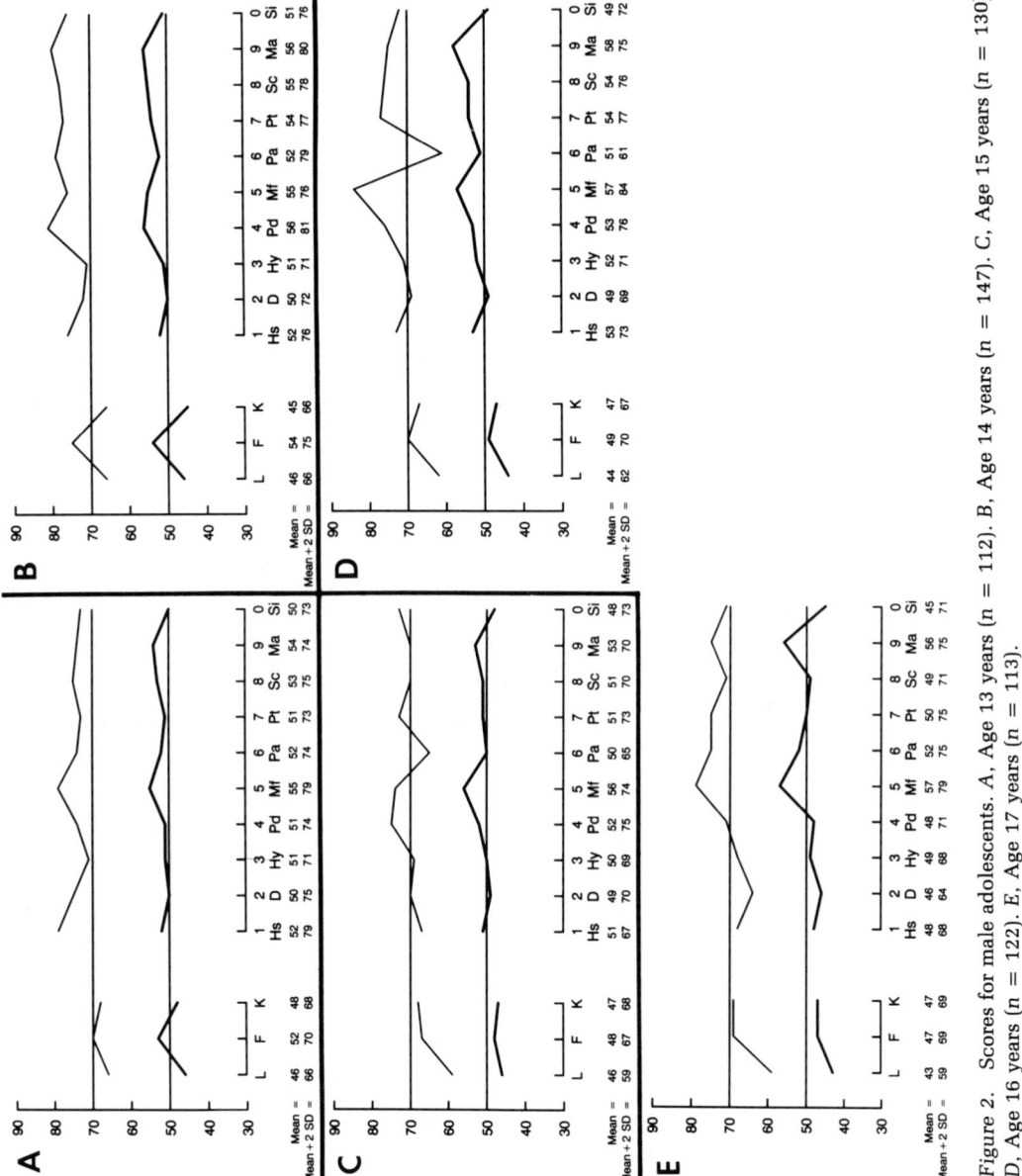

Figure 2. Scores for male adolescents. A, Age 13 years (n = 112). B, Age 14 years (n = 147). C, Age 15 years (n = 130). D, Age 16 years (n = 122). E, Age 17 years (n = 113).

APPENDIX F

Product-Moment Correlations Between Normalized T Scores With and Without K Correction and Age on Basic MMPI Validity and Clinical Scales for Contemporary Normal Adolescents

Pearson Product-Moment Correlations and Two-Tailed P Values Between Age and Normalized
T Scores With and Without K Correction on Basic MMPI Validity and Clinical Scales

Females, N=691

	Age	T L	T F	T K	T 1	T 2	T 3	T 4	T 5
Age	1.000	-0.084	-0.090	0.017	0.032	0.028	0.081	0.044	-0.152
		0.026	0.018	NS	NS	NS	0.034	NS	<0.001
T L	-0.084	1.000	-0.143	0.339	-0.168	-0.013	0.061	-0.172	0.012
	0.026		<0.001	<0.001	<0.001	NS	NS	<0.001	NS
T F	-0.090	-0.143	1.000	-0.547	0.590	0.440	0.268	0.677	0.128
	0.018	<0.001		<0.001	<0.001	<0.001	<0.001	<0.001	0.001
T K	0.017	0.339	-0.547	1.000	-0.466	-0.310	0.107	-0.442	-0.076
	NS	<0.001	<0.001		<0.001	<0.001	0.005	<0.001	0.046
T 1	0.032	-0.168	0.590	-0.466	1.000	0.502	0.567	0.548	0.029
	NS	<0.001	<0.001	<0.001		<0.001	<0.001	<0.001	NS
T 2	0.028	-0.013	0.440	-0.310	0.502	1.000	0.359	0.498	-0.101
	NS	NS	<0.001	<0.001	<0.001		<0.001	<0.001	0.008
T 3	0.081	0.061	0.268	0.107	0.567	0.359	1.000	0.373	-0.097
	0.034	NS	<0.001	0.005	<0.001	<0.001		<0.001	0.011
T 4	0.044	-0.172	0.677	-0.442	0.548	0.498	0.373	1.000	0.028
	NS	<0.001	<0.001	<0.001	<0.001	<0.001	<0.001		NS
T 5	-0.152	0.012	0.128	-0.076	0.029	-0.101	-0.097	0.028	1.000
	<0.001	NS	0.001	0.046	NS	0.008	0.011	NS	
T 6	0.069	-0.126	0.545	-0.355	0.503	0.438	0.362	0.597	-0.023
	NS	0.001	<0.001	<0.001	<0.001	<0.001	<0.001	<0.001	NS
T 7	0.033	-0.341	0.677	-0.749	0.653	0.565	0.190	0.649	0.020
	NS	<0.001	<0.001	<0.001	<0.001	<0.001	<0.001	<0.001	NS
T 8	-0.064	-0.288	0.769	-0.705	0.679	0.501	0.248	0.724	0.113
	NS	<0.001	<0.001	<0.001	<0.001	<0.001	<0.001	<0.001	0.003
T 9	-0.027	-0.215	0.522	-0.416	0.423	0.003	0.149	0.494	0.161
	NS	<0.001	<0.001	<0.001	<0.001	NS	<0.001	<0.001	<0.001
T 0	-0.073	-0.079	0.395	-0.532	0.339	0.579	-0.102	0.271	-0.008
	NS	0.038	<0.001	<0.001	<0.001	<0.001	0.007	<0.001	NS
T 1 +0.5K	0.052	0.044	0.325	0.092	0.800	0.394	0.739	0.341	-0.005
	NS	NS	<0.001	0.016	<0.001	<0.001	<0.001	<0.001	NS
T 4 +0.4K	0.059	-0.052	0.543	-0.108	0.426	0.442	0.471	0.929	0.009
	NS	NS	<0.001	0.004	<0.001	<0.001	<0.001	<0.001	NS
T 7 +1.0K	0.056	-0.202	0.545	-0.276	0.565	0.586	0.391	0.592	-0.019
	NS	<0.001	<0.001	<0.001	<0.001	<0.001	<0.001	<0.001	NS
T 8 +1.0K	-0.073	-0.151	0.682	-0.307	0.604	0.478	0.421	0.692	0.113
	NS	<0.001	<0.001	<0.001	<0.001	<0.001	<0.001	<0.001	0.003
T 9 +0.2K	-0.029	-0.162	0.453	-0.252	0.361	-0.056	0.181	0.442	0.156
	NS	<0.001	<0.001	<0.001	<0.001	NS	<0.001	<0.001	<0.001

Pearson Product-Moment Correlations and Two-Tailed P Values Between Age and Normalized
T Scores With and Without K Correction on Basic MMPI Validity and Clinical Scales

Females, N=691

	T 6	T 7	T 8	T 9	T 0	T 1 +0.5K	T 4 +0.4K	T 7 +1.0K	T 8 +1.0K	T 9 +0.2K
Age	0.069 NS	0.033 NS	-0.064 NS	-0.027 NS	-0.073 NS	0.052 NS	0.059 NS	0.056 NS	-0.073 NS	-0.029 NS
T L	-0.126 0.001	-0.341 <0.001	-0.288 <0.001	-0.215 <0.001	-0.079 0.038	0.044 NS	-0.052 NS	-0.202 <0.001	-0.151 <0.001	-0.162 <0.001
T F	0.545 <0.001	0.677 <0.001	0.769 <0.001	0.522 <0.001	0.395 <0.001	0.325 <0.001	0.543 <0.001	0.545 <0.001	0.682 <0.001	0.453 <0.001
T K	-0.355 <0.001	-0.749 <0.001	-0.705 <0.001	-0.416 <0.001	-0.532 <0.001	0.092 0.016	-0.108 0.004	-0.276 <0.001	-0.307 <0.001	-0.252 <0.001
T 1	0.503 <0.001	0.653 <0.001	0.679 <0.001	0.423 <0.001	0.339 <0.001	0.800 <0.001	0.426 <0.001	0.565 <0.001	0.604 <0.001	0.361 <0.001
T 2	0.438 <0.001	0.565 <0.001	0.501 <0.001	0.003 NS	0.579 <0.001	0.394 <0.001	0.442 <0.001	0.586 <0.001	0.478 <0.001	-0.056 NS
T 3	0.362 <0.001	0.190 <0.001	0.248 <0.001	0.149 <0.001	-0.102 0.007	0.739 <0.001	0.471 <0.001	0.391 <0.001	0.421 <0.001	0.181 <0.001
T 4	0.597 <0.001	0.649 <0.001	0.724 <0.001	0.494 <0.001	0.271 <0.001	0.341 <0.001	0.929 <0.001	0.592 <0.001	0.692 <0.001	0.442 <0.001
T 5	-0.023 NS	0.020 NS	0.113 0.003	0.161 <0.001	-0.008 NS	-0.005 NS	0.009 NS	-0.019 NS	0.113 0.003	0.156 <0.001
T 6	1.000	0.580 <0.001	0.645 <0.001	0.372 <0.001	0.254 <0.001	0.360 <0.001	0.556 <0.001	0.590 <0.001	0.663 <0.001	0.332 <0.001
T 7	0.580 <0.001	1.000	0.874 <0.001	0.488 <0.001	0.577 <0.001	0.252 <0.001	0.432 <0.001	0.823 <0.001	0.674 <0.001	0.375 <0.001
T 8	0.645 <0.001	0.874 <0.001	1.000	0.619 <0.001	0.483 <0.001	0.324 <0.001	0.539 <0.001	0.696 <0.001	0.877 <0.001	0.522 <0.001
T 9	0.372 <0.001	0.488 <0.001	0.619 <0.001	1.000	-0.066 NS	0.209 <0.001	0.388 <0.001	0.366 <0.001	0.556 <0.001	0.983 <0.001
T 0	0.254 <0.001	0.577 <0.001	0.483 <0.001	-0.066 NS	1.000	0.052 NS	0.095 0.012	0.397 <0.001	0.297 <0.001	-0.172 <0.001
T 1 +0.5K	0.360 <0.001	0.252 <0.001	0.324 <0.001	0.209 <0.001	0.052 NS	1.000	0.427 <0.001	0.475 <0.001	0.515 <0.001	0.242 <0.001
T 4 +0.4K	0.556 <0.001	0.432 <0.001	0.539 <0.001	0.388 <0.001	0.095 0.012	0.427 <0.001	1.000	0.567 <0.001	0.670 <0.001	0.394 <0.001
T 7 +1.0K	0.590 <0.001	0.823 <0.001	0.696 <0.001	0.366 <0.001	0.397 <0.001	0.475 <0.001	0.567 <0.001	1.000	0.771 <0.001	0.340 <0.001
T 8 +1.0K	0.663 <0.001	0.674 <0.001	0.877 <0.001	0.556 <0.001	0.297 <0.001	0.515 <0.001	0.670 <0.001	0.771 <0.001	1.000	0.535 <0.001
T 9 +0.2K	0.332 <0.001	0.375 <0.001	0.522 <0.001	0.983 <0.001	-0.172 <0.001	0.242 <0.001	0.394 <0.001	0.340 <0.001	0.535 <0.001	1.000

Pearson Product-Moment Correlations and Two-Tailed P Values Between Age and Normalized T Scores With and Without K Correction on Basic MMPI Validity and Clinical Scales

Males, N=624

	Age	T L	T F	T K	T 1	T 2	T 3	T 4	T 5
Age	1.000	-0.029 NS	-0.045 NS	0.033 NS	-0.031 NS	-0.081 0.042	0.081 0.044	-0.020 NS	0.070 NS
T L	-0.029 NS	1.000	-0.154 <0.001	0.382 <0.001	-0.229 <0.001	0.028 NS	0.066 NS	-0.223 <0.001	-0.132 0.001
T F	-0.045 NS	-0.154 <0.001	1.000	-0.509 <0.001	0.582 <0.001	0.433 <0.001	0.118 0.003	0.595 <0.001	0.075 NS
T K	0.033 NS	0.382 <0.001	-0.509 <0.001	1.000	-0.421 <0.001	-0.174 <0.001	0.262 <0.001	-0.331 <0.001	-0.171 <0.001
T 1	-0.031 NS	-0.229 <0.001	0.582 <0.001	-0.421 <0.001	1.000	0.459 <0.001	0.457 <0.001	0.463 <0.001	0.215 <0.001
T 2	-0.081 0.042	0.028 NS	0.433 <0.001	-0.174 <0.001	0.459 <0.001	1.000	0.311 <0.001	0.438 <0.001	0.238 <0.001
T 3	0.081 0.044	0.066 NS	0.118 0.003	0.262 <0.001	0.457 <0.001	0.311 <0.001	1.000	0.285 <0.001	0.239 <0.001
T 4	-0.020 NS	-0.223 <0.001	0.595 <0.001	-0.331 <0.001	0.463 <0.001	0.438 <0.001	0.285 <0.001	1.000	0.159 <0.001
T 5	0.070 NS	-0.132 0.001	0.075 NS	-0.171 <0.001	0.215 <0.001	0.238 <0.001	0.239 <0.001	0.159 <0.001	1.000
T 6	0.035 NS	-0.188 <0.001	0.525 <0.001	-0.325 <0.001	0.483 <0.001	0.355 <0.001	0.300 <0.001	0.529 <0.001	0.272 <0.001
T 7	-0.001 NS	-0.387 <0.001	0.680 <0.001	-0.758 <0.001	0.636 <0.001	0.460 <0.001	0.048 NS	0.550 <0.001	0.297 <0.001
T 8	-0.044 NS	-0.333 <0.001	0.791 <0.001	-0.684 <0.001	0.679 <0.001	0.452 <0.001	0.115 0.004	0.617 <0.001	0.252 <0.001
T 9	0.034 NS	-0.299 <0.001	0.522 <0.001	-0.453 <0.001	0.363 <0.001	-0.050 NS	0.009 NS	0.458 <0.001	0.050 NS
T 0	-0.142 <0.001	-0.113 0.005	0.443 <0.001	-0.509 <0.001	0.392 <0.001	0.537 <0.001	-0.116 0.004	0.228 <0.001	0.153 <0.001
T 1 +0.5K	-0.023 NS	0.030 NS	0.247 <0.001	0.261 <0.001	0.734 <0.001	0.378 <0.001	0.697 <0.001	0.252 <0.001	0.109 0.006
T 4 +0.4K	-0.019 NS	-0.083 0.038	0.423 <0.001	0.040 NS	0.318 <0.001	0.400 <0.001	0.410 <0.001	0.926 <0.001	0.103 0.010
T 7 +1.0K	0.014 NS	-0.206 <0.001	0.531 <0.001	-0.201 <0.001	0.543 <0.001	0.569 <0.001	0.360 <0.001	0.535 <0.001	0.299 <0.001
T 8 +1.0K	-0.053 NS	-0.165 <0.001	0.690 <0.001	-0.230 <0.001	0.604 <0.001	0.502 <0.001	0.359 <0.001	0.603 <0.001	0.227 <0.001
T 9 +0.2K	0.052 NS	-0.246 <0.001	0.449 <0.001	-0.277 <0.001	0.303 <0.001	-0.092 0.021	0.072 NS	0.421 <0.001	0.020 NS

Pearson Product-Moment Correlations and Two-Tailed P Values Between Age and Normalized T Scores With and Without K Correction on Basic MMPI Validity and Clinical Scales

Males, N=624

	T 6	T 7	T 8	T 9	T 0	T 1 +0.5K	T 4 +0.4K	T 7 +1.0K	T 8 +1.0K	T 9 +0.2K
Age	0.035 NS	-0.001 NS	-0.044 NS	0.034 NS	-0.142 <0.001	-0.023 NS	-0.019 NS	0.014 NS	-0.053 NS	0.052 NS
T L	-0.188 <0.001	-0.387 <0.001	-0.333 <0.001	-0.299 <0.001	-0.113 0.005	0.030 NS	-0.083 0.038	-0.206 <0.001	-0.165 <0.001	-0.246 <0.001
T F	0.525 <0.001	0.680 <0.001	0.791 <0.001	0.522 <0.001	0.443 <0.001	0.247 <0.001	0.423 <0.001	0.531 <0.001	0.690 <0.001	0.449 <0.001
T K	-0.325 <0.001	-0.758 <0.001	-0.684 <0.001	-0.453 <0.001	-0.509 <0.001	0.261 <0.001	0.040 NS	-0.201 <0.001	-0.230 <0.001	-0.277 <0.001
T 1	0.483 <0.001	0.636 <0.001	0.679 <0.001	0.363 <0.001	0.392 <0.001	0.734 <0.001	0.318 <0.001	0.543 <0.001	0.604 <0.001	0.303 <0.001
T 2	0.355 <0.001	0.460 <0.001	0.452 <0.001	-0.050 NS	0.537 <0.001	0.378 <0.001	0.400 <0.001	0.569 <0.001	0.502 <0.001	-0.092 0.021
T 3	0.300 <0.001	0.048 NS	0.115 0.004	0.009 NS	-0.116 0.004	0.697 <0.001	0.410 <0.001	0.360 <0.001	0.359 <0.001	0.072 NS
T 4	0.529 <0.001	0.550 <0.001	0.617 <0.001	0.458 <0.001	0.228 <0.001	0.252 <0.001	0.926 <0.001	0.535 <0.001	0.603 <0.001	0.421 <0.001
T 5	0.272 <0.001	0.297 <0.001	0.252 <0.001	0.050 NS	0.153 <0.001	0.109 0.006	0.103 0.010	0.299 <0.001	0.227 <0.001	0.020 NS
T 6	1.000	0.573 <0.001	0.625 <0.001	0.383 <0.001	0.226 <0.001	0.308 <0.001	0.441 <0.001	0.603 <0.001	0.644 <0.001	0.348 <0.001
T 7	0.573 <0.001	1.000	0.877 <0.001	0.509 <0.001	0.592 <0.001	0.121 0.002	0.277 <0.001	0.751 <0.001	0.628 <0.001	0.386 <0.001
T 8	0.625 <0.001	0.877 <0.001	1.000	0.582 <0.001	0.544 <0.001	0.233 <0.001	0.378 <0.001	0.661 <0.001	0.845 <0.001	0.480 <0.001
T 9	0.383 <0.001	0.509 <0.001	0.582 <0.001	1.000	-0.043 NS	0.057 NS	0.298 <0.001	0.308 <0.001	0.442 <0.001	0.978 <0.001
T 0	0.226 <0.001	0.592 <0.001	0.544 <0.001	-0.043 NS	1.000	0.050 NS	0.041 NS	0.418 <0.001	0.375 <0.001	-0.158 <0.001
T 1 +0.5K	0.308 <0.001	0.121 0.002	0.233 <0.001	0.057 NS	0.050 NS	1.000	0.368 <0.001	0.455 <0.001	0.506 <0.001	0.117 0.003
T 4 +0.4K	0.441 <0.001	0.277 <0.001	0.378 <0.001	0.298 <0.001	0.041 NS	0.368 <0.001	1.000	0.492 <0.001	0.551 <0.001	0.328 <0.001
T 7 +1.0K	0.603 <0.001	0.751 <0.001	0.661 <0.001	0.308 <0.001	0.418 <0.001	0.455 <0.001	0.492 <0.001	1.000	0.780 <0.001	0.290 <0.001
T 8 +1.0K	0.644 <0.001	0.628 <0.001	0.845 <0.001	0.442 <0.001	0.375 <0.001	0.506 <0.001	0.551 <0.001	0.780 <0.001	1.000	0.428 <0.001
T 9 +0.2K	0.348 <0.001	0.386 <0.001	0.480 <0.001	0.978 <0.001	-0.158 <0.001	0.117 0.003	0.328 <0.001	0.290 <0.001	0.428 <0.001	1.000

561

APPENDIX G

Product-Moment Correlations Between Raw Scores With and Without K Correction and Age on Basic MMPI Validity and Clinical Scales for Contemporary Normal Adolescents

Pearson Product-Moment Correlations and Two-Tailed P Values Between Age and Raw Scores
With and Without K Correction on Basic MMPI Validity and Clinical Scales

Females, N=691

	Age	Raw L	Raw F	Raw K	Raw 1	Raw 2	Raw 3	Raw 4	Raw 5
Age	1.000	-0.088	-0.072	0.015	0.050	0.034	0.083	0.046	0.152
		0.021	NS	NS	NS	NS	0.030	NS	<0.001
Raw L	-0.088	1.000	-0.130	0.390	-0.134	0.014	0.078	-0.182	-0.019
	0.021		0.001	<0.001	<0.001	NS	0.041	<0.001	NS
Raw F	-0.072	-0.130	1.000	-0.512	0.640	0.493	0.340	0.707	-0.157
	NS	0.001		<0.001	<0.001	<0.001	<0.001	<0.001	<0.001
Raw K	0.015	0.390	-0.512	1.000	-0.454	-0.317	0.096	-0.446	0.075
	NS	<0.001	<0.001		<0.001	<0.001	0.012	<0.001	0.050
Raw 1	0.050	-0.134	0.640	-0.454	1.000	0.554	0.624	0.555	-0.049
	NS	<0.001	<0.001	<0.001		<0.001	<0.001	<0.001	NS
Raw 2	0.034	0.014	0.493	-0.317	0.554	1.000	0.392	0.534	0.082
	NS	NS	<0.001	<0.001	<0.001		<0.001	<0.001	0.030
Raw 3	0.083	0.078	0.340	0.096	0.624	0.392	1.000	0.393	0.085
	0.030	0.041	<0.001	0.012	<0.001	<0.001		<0.001	0.025
Raw 4	0.046	-0.182	0.707	-0.446	0.555	0.534	0.393	1.000	-0.039
	NS	<0.001	<0.001	<0.001	<0.001	<0.001	<0.001		NS
Raw 5	0.152	-0.019	-0.157	0.075	-0.049	0.082	0.085	-0.039	1.000
	<0.001	NS	<0.001	0.050	NS	0.030	0.025	NS	
Raw 6	0.065	-0.141	0.652	-0.348	0.541	0.477	0.380	0.642	0.013
	NS	<0.001	<0.001	<0.001	<0.001	<0.001	<0.001	<0.001	NS
Raw 7	0.029	-0.338	0.701	-0.742	0.661	0.606	0.231	0.674	-0.036
	NS	<0.001	<0.001	<0.001	<0.001	<0.001	<0.001	<0.001	NS
Raw 8	-0.058	-0.273	0.821	-0.682	0.703	0.554	0.300	0.748	-0.126
	NS	<0.001	<0.001	<0.001	<0.001	<0.001	<0.001	<0.001	0.001
Raw 9	-0.028	-0.236	0.526	-0.419	0.419	0.026	0.161	0.504	-0.158
	NS	<0.001	<0.001	<0.001	<0.001	NS	<0.001	<0.001	<0.001
Raw 0	-0.066	-0.067	0.390	-0.527	0.352	0.590	-0.081	0.276	0.011
	NS	NS	<0.001	<0.001	<0.001	<0.001	0.034	<0.001	NS
Raw 1 +0.5K	0.063	0.058	0.439	0.032	0.875	0.449	0.750	0.380	-0.014
	NS	NS	<0.001	NS	<0.001	<0.001	<0.001	<0.001	NS
Raw 4 +0.4K	0.060	-0.055	0.588	-0.117	0.444	0.475	0.473	0.940	-0.014
	NS	NS	<0.001	0.002	<0.001	<0.001	<0.001	<0.001	NS
Raw 7 +1.0K	0.053	-0.183	0.607	-0.290	0.594	0.621	0.403	0.620	0.006
	NS	<0.001	<0.001	<0.001	<0.001	<0.001	<0.001	<0.001	NS
Raw 8 +1.0K	-0.066	-0.135	0.776	-0.323	0.656	0.539	0.441	0.719	-0.121
	NS	<0.001	<0.001	<0.001	<0.001	<0.001	<0.001	<0.001	0.001
Raw 9 +0.2K	-0.028	-0.179	0.463	-0.257	0.359	-0.035	0.188	0.450	-0.152
	NS	<0.001	<0.001	<0.001	<0.001	NS	<0.001	<0.001	<0.001

Pearson Product-Moment Correlations and Two-Tailed P Values Between Age and Raw Scores With and Without K Correction on Basic MMPI Validity and Clinical Scales

Females, N=691

	Raw 6	Raw 7	Raw 8	Raw 9	Raw 0	Raw 1 +0.5K	Raw 4 +0.4K	Raw 7 +1.0K	Raw 8 +1.0K	Raw 9 +0.2K
Age	0.065 NS	0.029 NS	-0.058 NS	-0.028 NS	-0.066 NS	0.063 NS	0.060 NS	0.053 NS	-0.066 NS	-0.028 NS
Raw L	-0.141 <0.001	-0.338 <0.001	-0.273 <0.001	-0.236 <0.001	-0.067 NS	0.058 NS	-0.055 NS	-0.183 <0.001	-0.135 <0.001	-0.179 <0.001
Raw F	0.652 <0.001	0.701 <0.001	0.821 <0.001	0.526 <0.001	0.390 <0.001	0.439 <0.001	0.588 <0.001	0.607 <0.001	0.776 <0.001	0.463 <0.001
Raw K	-0.348 <0.001	-0.742 <0.001	-0.682 <0.001	-0.419 <0.001	-0.527 <0.001	0.032 NS	-0.117 0.002	-0.290 <0.001	-0.323 <0.001	-0.257 <0.001
Raw 1	0.541 <0.001	0.661 <0.001	0.703 <0.001	0.419 <0.001	0.352 <0.001	0.875 <0.001	0.444 <0.001	0.594 <0.001	0.656 <0.001	0.359 <0.001
Raw 2	0.477 <0.001	0.606 <0.001	0.554 <0.001	0.026 NS	0.590 <0.001	0.449 <0.001	0.475 <0.001	0.621 <0.001	0.539 <0.001	-0.035 NS
Raw 3	0.380 <0.001	0.231 <0.001	0.300 <0.001	0.161 <0.001	-0.081 0.034	0.750 <0.001	0.473 <0.001	0.403 <0.001	0.441 <0.001	0.188 <0.001
Raw 4	0.642 <0.001	0.674 <0.001	0.748 <0.001	0.504 <0.001	0.276 <0.001	0.380 <0.001	0.940 <0.001	0.620 <0.001	0.719 <0.001	0.450 <0.001
Raw 5	0.013 NS	-0.036 NS	-0.126 0.001	-0.158 <0.001	0.011 NS	-0.014 NS	-0.014 NS	0.006 NS	-0.121 0.001	-0.152 <0.001
Raw 6	1.000	0.616 <0.001	0.692 <0.001	0.387 <0.001	0.280 <0.001	0.417 <0.001	0.581 <0.001	0.611 <0.001	0.701 <0.001	0.343 <0.001
Raw 7	0.616 <0.001	1.000	0.882 <0.001	0.491 <0.001	0.580 <0.001	0.340 <0.001	0.470 <0.001	0.857 <0.001	0.726 <0.001	0.382 <0.001
Raw 8	0.692 <0.001	0.882 <0.001	1.000	0.612 <0.001	0.486 <0.001	0.420 <0.001	0.573 <0.001	0.734 <0.001	0.913 <0.001	0.520 <0.001
Raw 9	0.387 <0.001	0.491 <0.001	0.612 <0.001	1.000	-0.064 NS	0.243 <0.001	0.398 <0.001	0.379 <0.001	0.557 <0.001	0.983 <0.001
Raw 0	0.280 <0.001	0.580 <0.001	0.486 <0.001	-0.064 NS	1.000	0.110 0.004	0.107 0.005	0.423 <0.001	0.334 <0.001	-0.168 <0.001
Raw 1 +0.5K	0.417 <0.001	0.340 <0.001	0.420 <0.001	0.243 <0.001	0.110 0.004	1.000	0.433 <0.001	0.510 <0.001	0.561 <0.001	0.263 <0.001
Raw 4 +0.4K	0.581 <0.001	0.470 <0.001	0.573 <0.001	0.398 <0.001	0.107 0.005	0.433 <0.001	1.000	0.581 <0.001	0.676 <0.001	0.400 <0.001
Raw 7 +1.0K	0.611 <0.001	0.857 <0.001	0.734 <0.001	0.379 <0.001	0.423 <0.001	0.510 <0.001	0.581 <0.001	1.000	0.788 <0.001	0.348 <0.001
Raw 8 +1.0K	0.701 <0.001	0.726 <0.001	0.913 <0.001	0.557 <0.001	0.334 <0.001	0.561 <0.001	0.676 <0.001	0.788 <0.001	1.000	0.528 <0.001
Raw 9 +0.2K	0.343 <0.001	0.382 <0.001	0.520 <0.001	0.983 <0.001	-0.168 <0.001	0.263 <0.001	0.400 <0.001	0.348 <0.001	0.528 <0.001	1.000

Pearson Product-Moment Correlations and Two-Tailed P Values Between Age and Raw Scores With and Without K Correction on Basic MMPI Validity and Clinical Scales

Males, N=624

	Age	Raw L	Raw F	Raw K	Raw 1	Raw 2	Raw 3	Raw 4	Raw 5
Age	1.000	-0.034 NS	-0.043 NS	0.028 NS	-0.031 NS	-0.078 NS	0.085 0.034	-0.021 NS	0.069 NS
Raw L	-0.034 NS	1.000	-0.137 0.001	0.391 <0.001	-0.190 <0.001	0.044 NS	0.091 0.023	-0.234 <0.001	-0.131 0.001
Raw F	-0.043 NS	-0.137 0.001	1.000	-0.464 <0.001	0.583 <0.001	0.466 <0.001	0.173 <0.001	0.595 <0.001	0.069 NS
Raw K	0.028 NS	0.391 <0.001	-0.464 <0.001	1.000	-0.414 <0.001	-0.181 <0.001	0.268 <0.001	-0.324 <0.001	-0.170 <0.001
Raw 1	-0.031 NS	-0.190 <0.001	0.583 <0.001	-0.414 <0.001	1.000	0.495 <0.001	0.497 <0.001	0.447 <0.001	0.208 <0.001
Raw 2	-0.078 NS	0.044 NS	0.466 <0.001	-0.181 <0.001	0.495 <0.001	1.000	0.336 <0.001	0.443 <0.001	0.247 <0.001
Raw 3	0.085 0.034	0.091 0.023	0.173 <0.001	0.268 <0.001	0.497 <0.001	0.336 <0.001	1.000	0.296 <0.001	0.241 <0.001
Raw 4	-0.021 NS	-0.234 <0.001	0.595 <0.001	-0.324 <0.001	0.447 <0.001	0.443 <0.001	0.296 <0.001	1.000	0.159 <0.001
Raw 5	0.069 NS	-0.131 0.001	0.069 NS	-0.170 <0.001	0.208 <0.001	0.247 <0.001	0.241 <0.001	0.159 <0.001	1.000
Raw 6	0.027 NS	-0.168 <0.001	0.619 <0.001	-0.325 <0.001	0.510 <0.001	0.395 <0.001	0.305 <0.001	0.543 <0.001	0.271 <0.001
Raw 7	-0.004 NS	-0.370 <0.001	0.675 <0.001	-0.745 <0.001	0.634 <0.001	0.511 <0.001	0.092 0.021	0.564 <0.001	0.309 <0.001
Raw 8	-0.050 NS	-0.314 <0.001	0.805 <0.001	-0.660 <0.001	0.690 <0.001	0.495 <0.001	0.158 <0.001	0.624 <0.001	0.246 <0.001
Raw 9	0.034 NS	-0.313 <0.001	0.502 <0.001	-0.466 <0.001	0.355 <0.001	-0.040 NS	0.008 NS	0.456 <0.001	0.050 NS
Raw 0	-0.135 0.001	-0.095 0.017	0.406 <0.001	-0.499 <0.001	0.387 <0.001	0.561 <0.001	-0.099 0.013	0.233 <0.001	0.165 <0.001
Raw 1 +0.5K	-0.015 NS	0.051 NS	0.325 <0.001	0.208 <0.001	0.802 <0.001	0.416 <0.001	0.708 <0.001	0.273 <0.001	0.114 0.004
Raw 4 +0.4K	-0.016 NS	-0.093 0.020	0.444 <0.001	0.050 NS	0.310 <0.001	0.399 <0.001	0.416 <0.001	0.927 <0.001	0.102 0.011
Raw 7 +1.0K	0.019 NS	-0.197 <0.001	0.580 <0.001	-0.208 <0.001	0.564 <0.001	0.589 <0.001	0.372 <0.001	0.541 <0.001	0.302 <0.001
Raw 8 +1.0K	-0.047 NS	-0.169 <0.001	0.758 <0.001	-0.247 <0.001	0.639 <0.001	0.529 <0.001	0.366 <0.001	0.609 <0.001	0.215 <0.001
Raw 9 +0.2K	0.043 NS	-0.254 <0.001	0.444 <0.001	-0.290 <0.001	0.297 <0.001	-0.080 0.047	0.071 NS	0.423 <0.001	0.020 NS

Pearson Product-Moment Correlations and Two-Tailed P Values Between Age and Raw Scores
With and Without K Correction on Basic MMPI Validity and Clinical Scales

Males, N=624

	Raw 6	Raw 7	Raw 8	Raw 9	Raw 0	Raw 1 +0.5K	Raw 4 +0.4K	Raw 7 +1.0K	Raw 8 +1.0K	Raw 9 +0.2K
e	0.027 NS	-0.004 NS	-0.050 NS	0.034 NS	-0.135 0.001	-0.015 NS	-0.016 NS	0.019 NS	-0.047 NS	0.043 NS
w L	-0.168 <0.001	-0.370 <0.001	-0.314 <0.001	-0.313 <0.001	-0.095 0.017	0.051 NS	-0.093 0.020	-0.197 <0.001	-0.169 <0.001	-0.254 <0.001
w F	0.619 <0.001	0.675 <0.001	0.805 <0.001	0.502 <0.001	0.406 <0.001	0.325 <0.001	0.444 <0.001	0.580 <0.001	0.758 <0.001	0.444 <0.001
w K	-0.325 <0.001	-0.745 <0.001	-0.660 <0.001	-0.466 <0.001	-0.499 <0.001	0.208 <0.001	0.050 NS	-0.208 <0.001	-0.247 <0.001	-0.290 <0.001
w 1	0.510 <0.001	0.634 <0.001	0.690 <0.001	0.355 <0.001	0.387 <0.001	0.802 <0.001	0.310 <0.001	0.564 <0.001	0.639 <0.001	0.297 <0.001
w 2	0.395 <0.001	0.511 <0.001	0.495 <0.001	-0.040 NS	0.561 <0.001	0.416 <0.001	0.399 <0.001	0.589 <0.001	0.529 <0.001	-0.080 0.047
w 3	0.305 <0.001	0.092 0.021	0.158 <0.001	0.008 NS	-0.099 0.013	0.708 <0.001	0.416 <0.001	0.372 <0.001	0.366 <0.001	0.071 NS
w 4	0.543 <0.001	0.564 <0.001	0.624 <0.001	0.456 <0.001	0.233 <0.001	0.273 <0.001	0.927 <0.001	0.541 <0.001	0.609 <0.001	0.423 <0.001
w 5	0.271 <0.001	0.309 <0.001	0.246 <0.001	0.050 NS	0.165 <0.001	0.114 0.004	0.102 0.011	0.302 <0.001	0.215 <0.001	0.020 NS
w 6	1.000	0.621 <0.001	0.676 <0.001	0.385 <0.001	0.259 <0.001	0.338 <0.001	0.445 <0.001	0.623 <0.001	0.676 <0.001	0.346 <0.001
w 7	0.621 <0.001	1.000	0.882 <0.001	0.495 <0.001	0.604 <0.001	0.195 <0.001	0.302 <0.001	0.807 <0.001	0.687 <0.001	0.377 <0.001
w 8	0.676 <0.001	0.882 <0.001	1.000	0.565 <0.001	0.538 <0.001	0.312 <0.001	0.399 <0.001	0.709 <0.001	0.891 <0.001	0.472 <0.001
w 9	0.385 <0.001	0.495 <0.001	0.565 <0.001	1.000	-0.054 NS	0.076 NS	0.297 <0.001	0.314 <0.001	0.447 <0.001	0.980 <0.001
w 0	0.259 <0.001	0.604 <0.001	0.538 <0.001	-0.054 NS	1.000	0.090 0.024	0.051 NS	0.445 <0.001	0.393 <0.001	-0.164 <0.001
w 1 .5K	0.338 <0.001	0.195 <0.001	0.312 <0.001	0.076 NS	0.090 0.024	1.000	0.370 <0.001	0.471 <0.001	0.529 <0.001	0.128 0.001
w 4 .4K	0.445 <0.001	0.302 <0.001	0.399 <0.001	0.297 <0.001	0.051 NS	0.370 <0.001	1.000	0.488 <0.001	0.545 <0.001	0.332 <0.001
w 7 .0K	0.623 <0.001	0.807 <0.001	0.709 <0.001	0.314 <0.001	0.445 <0.001	0.471 <0.001	0.488 <0.001	1.000	0.789 <0.001	0.296 <0.001
w 8 .0K	0.676 <0.001	0.687 <0.001	0.891 <0.001	0.447 <0.001	0.393 <0.001	0.529 <0.001	0.545 <0.001	0.789 <0.001	1.000	0.433 <0.001
w 9 .2K	0.346 <0.001	0.377 <0.001	0.472 <0.001	0.980 <0.001	-0.164 <0.001	0.128 0.001	0.332 <0.001	0.296 <0.001	0.433 <0.001	1.000

APPENDIX H

Percentage of Sample Responding True on Each MMPI Item From the Contemporary Normal Sample of Adolescents, by Age and Sex, and From a Random Sample of 100 Boys and 100 Girls in the Hathaway and Monachesi Minnesota Statewide Sample of Ninth-Grade Students

Percentage of Sample Responding True on Each MMPI Item

MMPI Item Number	Females, Age in Years							Males, Age in Years							MMPI Item Number
	13 (N=136)	14 (N=153)	15 (N=127)	16 (N=138)	17 (N=137)	Total (N=691)	H and M (N=100)	13 (N=112)	14 (N=147)	15 (N=130)	16 (N=122)	17 (N=113)	Total (N=624)	H and M (N=100)	
1	1.5	5.2	3.1	6.5	5.1	4.3	11.0	49.1	46.9	54.6	52.5	57.5	51.9	83.0	
2	96.3	92.2	93.7	90.6	96.4	93.8	99.0	93.8	98.0	95.4	98.4	98.2	96.8	94.0	
3	50.0	54.9	51.2	47.1	41.6	49.1	81.0	54.5	40.1	50.8	41.8	38.1	44.9	69.0	
4	20.6	19.6	15.7	15.9	12.4	16.9	47.0	8.9	4.8	7.7	4.9	7.1	6.6	4.0	
5	35.3	28.1	30.7	37.7	39.4	34.2	25.0	31.3	36.7	30.0	30.3	31.0	32.1	31.0	
6	36.8	41.8	50.4	57.2	51.1	47.3	64.0	36.6	42.2	42.3	45.9	49.6	43.3	65.0	
7	75.7	66.0	66.9	61.6	63.5	66.7	84.0	84.8	84.4	80.8	77.9	88.5	83.2	91.0	
8	73.5	79.7	72.4	78.3	75.2	76.0	85.0	75.9	75.5	74.6	71.3	81.4	75.6	89.0	
9	92.6	90.8	92.1	90.6	97.1	92.6	89.0	85.7	93.2	92.3	93.4	94.7	92.0	87.0	
10	4.4	3.9	7.1	5.8	2.9	4.8	2.0	10.7	12.2	3.8	4.1	6.2	7.5	5.0	1
11	50.7	49.0	52.8	29.7	36.5	43.7	16.0	43.8	44.9	43.8	45.1	34.5	42.6	13.0	1
12	58.8	54.2	67.7	61.6	61.3	60.5	78.0	78.6	72.8	69.2	64.8	69.0	70.8	79.0	1
13	23.5	24.8	32.3	33.3	24.8	27.6	9.0	25.0	30.6	23.8	27.9	26.5	26.9	10.0	1
14	4.4	4.6	4.7	10.1	8.0	6.4	4.0	8.0	9.5	6.2	6.6	6.2	7.4	6.0	1
15	62.5	62.7	69.3	76.1	66.4	67.3	45.0	63.4	64.6	66.2	64.8	63.7	64.6	62.0	1
16	13.2	17.6	11.0	13.8	8.8	13.0	7.0	15.2	24.5	18.5	14.8	8.8	16.8	4.0	1
17	91.9	87.6	89.0	88.4	90.5	89.4	94.0	93.8	92.5	92.3	91.0	89.4	91.8	90.0	1
18	84.6	83.0	81.9	82.6	85.4	83.5	75.0	76.8	81.6	80.8	82.0	90.3	82.2	78.0	1
19	34.6	26.8	33.1	33.3	23.4	30.1	38.0	32.1	36.7	38.5	39.3	29.2	35.4	37.0	1
20	70.6	64.7	69.3	71.0	77.4	70.5	93.0	64.3	61.2	63.8	58.2	69.9	63.3	90.0	2
21	53.7	52.9	64.6	62.3	62.8	59.0	40.0	40.2	55.8	43.1	52.5	50.4	48.7	37.0	2
22	52.9	56.2	61.4	58.7	46.0	55.0	24.0	28.6	30.6	19.2	23.8	20.4	24.7	13.0	2
23	2.9	2.0	3.1	4.3	4.4	3.3	2.0	0.9	1.4	1.5	0.8	2.7	1.4	5.0	2
24	29.4	26.1	26.8	32.6	24.8	27.9	13.0	25.0	23.1	27.7	27.9	21.2	25.0	8.0	2
25	41.2	47.1	43.3	40.6	40.9	42.7	44.0	25.0	25.2	27.7	35.2	31.0	28.7	24.0	2
26	61.8	56.2	49.6	57.2	45.3	54.1	40.0	58.0	53.7	48.5	52.5	52.2	52.9	56.0	2
27	13.2	15.0	11.0	10.1	5.8	11.1	21.0	14.3	11.6	10.0	15.6	6.2	11.5	26.0	2
28	41.2	36.6	33.9	31.9	19.7	32.7	28.0	32.7	61.9	49.2	53.3	37.2	51.4	36.0	2
29	3.7	5.9	6.3	12.3	5.8	6.8	6.0	5.4	6.1	5.4	8.2	4.4	5.9	2.0	2
30	92.6	92.8	94.5	96.4	95.6	94.4	73.0	92.0	90.5	96.2	96.7	92.9	93.6	76.0	3
31	22.1	16.3	14.2	15.2	14.6	16.5	11.0	14.3	12.2	8.5	9.0	11.5	11.1	8.0	3
32	33.8	35.9	38.6	39.1	21.9	33.9	24.0	21.4	35.4	28.5	29.5	20.4	27.6	20.0	3
33	35.3	34.0	42.5	42.8	40.1	38.8	37.0	42.0	42.9	37.7	47.5	49.6	43.8	36.0	3
34	8.8	8.5	4.7	11.6	7.3	8.2	13.0	2.7	6.8	6.2	5.7	7.1	5.8	3.0	3
35	13.2	14.4	10.2	10.9	3.6	10.6	6.0	19.6	16.3	13.8	12.3	12.4	14.9	8.0	3
36	47.8	52.9	48.0	51.4	47.4	49.6	57.0	53.6	55.1	53.1	47.5	54.0	52.7	61.0	3
37	90.4	90.8	88.2	90.6	86.1	89.3	88.0	86.6	83.7	86.2	78.7	84.1	83.8	87.0	3
38	19.9	29.4	37.0	31.9	32.1	30.0	11.0	19.6	39.5	41.5	50.0	51.3	40.5	29.0	3
39	75.7	60.8	76.4	81.9	65.7	71.8	45.0	78.6	78.2	68.5	80.3	73.5	75.8	48.0	3
40	49.3	43.1	41.7	51.4	33.6	43.8	32.0	38.4	46.3	32.3	40.2	30.1	37.8	21.0	4
41	43.4	41.8	46.5	55.1	43.1	45.9	22.0	30.4	37.4	36.2	50.0	33.6	37.7	25.0	4
42	7.4	3.9	4.7	5.1	6.6	5.5	4.0	1.8	8.8	6.9	6.6	3.5	5.8	5.0	4
43	13.2	11.8	15.0	13.0	10.2	12.6	7.0	10.7	16.3	6.2	8.2	15.9	11.5	7.0	4
44	14.0	5.2	11.0	17.4	6.6	10.7	7.0	4.5	8.8	2.3	5.7	5.3	5.4	2.0	
45	91.9	87.6	88.2	89.1	82.5	87.8	68.0	84.8	86.4	86.9	82.0	84.1	84.9	75.0	
46	69.1	79.1	80.3	74.6	78.8	76.4	72.0	67.9	81.6	78.5	79.5	88.5	79.3	85.0	
47	14.0	13.7	10.2	19.6	12.4	14.0	11.0	12.5	15.0	10.0	13.9	4.4	11.4	9.0	
48	20.6	17.0	16.5	20.3	8.8	16.6	6.0	26.8	23.1	14.6	16.4	11.5	18.6	0.0	
49	5.9	6.5	10.2	6.5	2.9	6.4	1.0	9.8	15.0	7.7	14.8	9.7	11.5	8.0	
50	8.1	5.2	2.4	6.5	5.8	5.6	12.0	8.0	6.8	3.8	9.0	6.2	6.7	8.0	
51	88.2	94.1	83.5	89.1	83.9	88.0	90.0	82.1	89.1	90.0	88.5	91.2	88.3	85.0	
52	20.6	24.8	21.3	17.4	18.2	20.5	14.0	28.6	30.6	27.7	36.1	28.3	30.3	12.0	

Percentage of Sample Responding True on Each MMPI Item

MMPI Item Number	Females, Age in Years							Males, Age in Years							MMPI Item Number
	13 (N=136)	14 (N=153)	15 (N=127)	16 (N=138)	17 (N=137)	Total (N=691)	H and M (N=100)	13 (N=112)	14 (N=147)	15 (N=130)	16 (N=122)	17 (N=113)	Total (N=624)	H and M (N=100)	
53	5.9	2.6	4.7	3.6	2.2	3.8	14.0	11.6	8.8	5.4	9.8	8.0	8.7	12.0	53
54	91.2	91.5	92.1	93.5	98.5	93.3	95.0	87.5	86.4	88.5	90.2	93.8	89.1	89.0	54
55	76.5	73.2	70.1	68.8	76.6	73.1	74.0	68.8	68.7	73.8	73.8	74.3	71.8	79.0	55
56	2.2	2.6	3.1	0.7	2.2	2.2	2.0	0.9	7.5	5.4	12.3	12.4	7.7	8.0	56
57	71.3	76.5	80.3	76.1	79.6	76.7	74.0	73.2	68.7	66.2	70.5	67.3	69.1	76.0	57
58	27.9	30.7	27.6	27.5	38.0	30.4	51.0	32.1	38.8	33.1	36.9	30.1	34.5	50.0	58
59	61.0	60.8	57.5	57.2	54.7	58.3	46.0	59.8	64.6	66.2	68.9	76.1	67.0	55.0	59
60	94.9	96.7	95.3	96.4	95.6	95.8	96.0	95.5	93.9	96.9	94.3	92.0	94.6	96.0	60
61	13.2	12.4	11.8	15.2	9.5	12.4	5.0	17.9	23.1	12.3	16.4	15.0	17.1	17.0	61
62	44.9	41.8	44.9	52.2	41.6	45.0	36.0	42.0	43.5	37.7	37.7	31.0	38.6	20.0	62
63	87.5	88.2	88.2	89.9	89.1	88.6	82.0	84.8	86.4	90.0	89.3	91.2	88.3	88.0	63
64	55.9	62.7	59.8	56.5	55.5	58.2	38.0	59.8	57.8	50.0	53.3	53.1	54.8	41.0	64
65	95.6	94.1	92.1	88.4	93.4	92.8	95.0	95.5	92.5	92.3	93.4	89.4	92.6	95.0	65
66	15.4	15.7	19.7	15.2	13.9	15.9	11.0	17.0	17.0	17.7	19.7	15.0	17.3	14.0	66
67	53.7	49.7	50.4	63.8	51.1	53.7	55.0	48.2	53.1	43.8	50.0	39.8	47.3	49.0	67
68	83.8	78.4	78.7	69.6	74.5	77.0	82.0	74.1	68.0	73.8	68.9	79.6	72.6	84.0	68
69	5.1	3.9	0.8	5.1	5.8	4.2	34.0	2.7	3.4	4.6	5.7	2.7	3.8	50.0	69
70	22.8	24.2	29.9	30.4	31.4	27.6	77.0	14.3	17.7	16.9	13.1	12.4	15.1	38.0	70
71	82.4	79.1	87.4	79.0	80.3	81.5	72.0	83.0	83.0	85.4	85.2	80.5	83.5	82.0	71
72	6.6	9.2	14.2	15.9	13.1	11.7	8.0	10.7	12.9	10.0	11.5	8.8	10.9	4.0	72
73	76.5	75.8	75.6	73.9	83.9	77.1	10.0	83.0	75.5	80.8	77.0	83.2	79.6	18.0	73
74	77.9	70.6	68.5	65.2	65.7	69.6	70.0	7.1	8.2	7.7	8.2	3.5	7.1	7.0	74
75	99.3	100.0	98.4	98.6	100.0	99.3	99.0	100.0	98.0	100.0	99.2	99.1	99.2	96.0	75
76	14.0	7.2	17.3	15.2	11.7	12.9	4.0	11.6	13.6	10.0	13.9	12.4	12.3	4.0	76
77	72.1	85.0	85.0	81.2	81.8	81.0	87.0	13.4	12.2	10.8	9.8	14.2	12.0	17.0	77
78	44.1	62.1	66.1	74.6	64.2	62.2	44.0	29.5	21.1	30.0	26.2	26.5	26.4	17.0	78
79	30.1	26.1	20.5	23.2	20.4	24.2	38.0	47.3	45.6	54.6	45.9	48.7	48.4	74.0	79
80	45.6	39.9	48.8	44.9	35.8	42.8	45.0	50.9	56.5	56.2	57.4	59.3	56.1	55.0	80
81	21.3	26.1	23.6	27.5	33.6	26.5	29.0	42.0	44.2	50.8	51.6	61.1	49.7	76.0	81
82	34.6	27.5	36.2	37.0	27.7	32.4	17.0	27.7	29.3	22.3	18.9	16.8	23.2	16.0	82
83	98.5	97.4	96.9	97.8	99.3	98.0	99.0	96.4	96.6	99.2	99.2	99.1	98.1	99.0	83
84	59.6	49.7	53.5	57.2	43.8	52.7	44.0	59.8	53.1	52.3	50.0	44.2	51.9	48.0	84
85	5.9	8.5	7.9	8.0	6.6	7.4	5.0	13.4	12.2	7.7	14.8	1.8	10.1	1.0	85
86	32.4	32.0	43.3	45.7	31.4	36.8	25.0	22.3	25.2	30.0	26.2	24.8	25.8	23.0	86
87	25.0	24.2	24.4	23.2	22.6	23.9	42.0	2.7	4.1	2.3	4.1	3.5	3.4	16.0	87
88	89.7	91.5	92.1	84.8	96.4	90.9	96.0	94.6	84.4	89.2	93.4	92.9	90.5	96.0	88
89	56.6	48.4	52.0	47.8	44.5	49.8	47.0	65.2	65.3	59.2	56.6	59.3	61.2	63.0	89
90	98.5	93.5	97.6	97.8	95.6	96.5	96.0	95.5	90.5	97.7	95.1	92.0	94.1	93.0	90
91	14.7	19.6	19.7	16.7	17.5	17.7	29.0	22.3	25.2	32.3	36.1	31.9	29.5	48.0	91
92	29.4	26.8	25.2	29.7	21.2	26.5	55.0	0.0	3.4	3.1	3.3	0.9	2.2	1.0	92
93	66.2	56.9	69.3	66.7	57.7	63.1	28.0	67.0	72.8	66.9	71.3	64.6	68.8	43.0	93
94	52.9	37.9	41.7	47.8	39.4	43.8	49.0	42.9	55.1	45.4	43.4	35.4	45.0	39.0	94
95	71.3	74.5	68.5	54.3	58.4	65.6	90.0	73.2	57.8	64.6	56.6	42.5	59.0	75.0	95
96	41.2	43.8	37.0	29.7	44.5	39.4	57.0	50.0	38.8	44.6	46.7	51.3	45.8	70.0	96
97	44.1	43.1	55.1	59.4	36.5	47.5	34.0	48.2	53.7	40.8	56.6	41.6	48.4	34.0	97
98	74.3	81.0	75.6	68.1	75.9	75.1	75.0	79.5	73.5	80.0	73.8	77.0	76.6	72.0	98
99	80.1	84.3	89.0	81.9	78.1	82.6	67.0	67.9	73.5	82.3	79.5	82.3	77.1	75.0	99
100	74.3	70.6	71.7	78.3	67.2	72.4	74.0	71.4	72.1	62.3	66.4	60.2	66.7	61.0	100
101	90.4	90.2	92.1	91.3	89.8	90.7	47.0	87.5	85.7	90.0	91.8	90.3	88.9	74.0	101
102	36.8	45.1	60.6	68.8	62.8	54.6	49.0	33.9	53.1	45.4	60.7	51.3	49.2	39.0	102
103	85.3	79.1	80.3	76.1	85.4	81.2	81.0	87.5	87.8	90.8	79.5	84.1	86.1	85.0	103
104	5.9	7.8	10.2	13.0	5.8	8.5	5.0	8.0	15.0	6.9	14.8	10.6	11.2	9.0	104

MMPI Item Number	Females, Age in Years							Males, Age in Years							MMPI Item Number
	13 (N=136)	14 (N=153)	15 (N=127)	16 (N=138)	17 (N=137)	Total (N=691)	H and M (N=100)	13 (N=112)	14 (N=147)	15 (N=130)	16 (N=122)	17 (N=113)	Total (N=624)	H and M (N=100)	
105	81.6	81.0	85.8	83.3	89.1	84.1	92.0	72.3	69.4	72.3	68.9	66.4	69.9	82.0	105
106	24.3	17.0	16.5	22.5	15.3	19.1	21.0	23.2	21.8	17.7	23.0	15.9	20.4	20.0	106
107	91.2	92.8	89.8	86.2	88.3	89.7	98.0	87.5	86.4	89.2	87.7	91.2	88.3	93.0	107
108	13.2	11.1	11.0	15.9	8.8	12.0	8.0	12.5	17.7	13.8	22.1	15.0	16.3	8.0	108
109	82.4	84.3	84.3	81.2	75.2	81.5	63.0	78.6	76.9	72.3	71.3	63.7	72.8	62.0	109
110	18.4	19.0	24.4	16.7	13.1	18.2	17.0	29.5	30.6	32.3	19.7	15.9	26.0	22.0	110
111	60.3	52.3	38.6	38.4	38.7	45.9	60.0	44.6	32.0	33.1	17.2	14.2	28.4	47.0	111
112	81.6	85.0	80.3	68.1	70.8	77.3	77.0	79.5	81.0	81.5	81.1	81.4	80.9	83.0	112
113	93.4	94.1	95.3	97.8	97.8	95.7	95.0	96.4	89.8	93.8	88.5	95.6	92.6	94.0	113
114	11.8	8.5	11.8	15.2	6.6	10.7	8.0	10.7	13.6	5.4	9.8	9.7	9.9	8.0	114
115	69.9	72.5	76.4	70.3	78.1	73.4	89.0	75.9	76.9	76.9	78.7	80.5	77.7	84.0	115
116	16.9	18.3	15.0	12.3	15.3	15.6	16.0	27.7	34.0	27.7	31.1	31.9	30.6	29.0	116
117	54.4	58.8	52.0	58.7	50.4	55.0	35.0	51.8	58.5	52.3	54.1	49.6	53.5	40.0	117
118	6.6	7.8	8.7	10.1	15.3	9.7	8.0	19.6	26.5	25.4	30.3	36.3	27.6	32.0	118
119	72.8	73.9	75.6	67.4	78.1	73.5	72.0	57.1	69.4	71.5	66.4	70.8	67.3	62.0	119
120	75.0	73.2	77.2	80.4	71.5	75.4	85.0	64.3	72.1	78.5	70.5	77.9	72.8	91.0	120
121	6.6	7.8	9.4	6.5	4.4	6.9	7.0	15.2	13.6	10.0	7.4	3.5	10.1	1.0	121
122	91.2	90.2	87.4	87.7	90.5	89.4	83.0	91.1	86.4	90.0	91.0	96.5	90.7	81.0	122
123	3.7	4.6	3.1	6.5	1.5	3.9	2.0	8.0	6.8	3.1	3.3	3.5	5.0	5.0	123
124	74.3	62.1	69.3	73.2	54.0	66.4	49.0	75.0	81.6	69.2	76.2	72.6	75.2	64.0	124
125	2.2	5.2	9.4	12.3	3.6	6.5	6.0	6.3	5.4	1.5	6.6	6.2	5.1	2.0	125
126	55.9	59.5	70.1	61.6	56.2	60.5	73.0	32.1	26.5	31.5	32.8	31.9	30.8	36.0	126
127	52.9	68.0	69.3	64.5	62.0	63.4	43.0	59.8	54.4	53.1	61.5	61.9	57.9	43.0	127
128	63.2	61.4	63.8	63.8	60.6	62.5	70.0	82.1	78.9	76.9	77.9	80.5	79.2	76.0	128
129	50.0	60.8	60.6	71.7	63.5	61.4	69.0	50.0	53.7	45.4	44.3	45.1	47.9	63.0	129
130	86.0	83.0	81.1	86.2	80.3	83.4	80.0	83.9	89.1	90.0	73.0	84.1	84.3	84.0	130
131	59.6	61.4	62.2	46.4	56.9	57.3	57.0	64.3	68.7	62.3	63.1	68.1	65.4	63.0	131
132	43.4	49.0	48.8	47.8	52.6	48.3	64.0	15.2	13.6	15.4	16.4	4.4	13.1	24.0	132
133	90.4	90.8	89.0	87.7	85.4	88.7	90.0	83.9	85.0	86.9	86.1	77.9	84.1	82.0	133
134	81.6	85.0	89.0	89.1	88.3	86.5	73.0	74.1	76.9	81.5	81.1	86.7	80.0	76.0	134
135	33.8	38.6	57.5	58.7	50.4	47.5	29.0	47.3	57.8	61.5	63.9	69.0	59.9	41.0	135
136	60.3	54.2	48.8	62.3	50.4	55.3	61.0	54.5	60.5	56.2	53.3	46.0	54.5	60.0	136
137	77.9	76.5	66.9	73.2	79.6	75.0	89.0	79.5	79.6	83.1	79.5	85.8	81.4	89.0	137
138	55.9	48.4	55.1	59.4	56.9	55.0	53.0	41.1	36.1	30.8	39.3	32.7	35.9	25.0	138
139	23.5	19.0	21.3	23.2	12.4	19.8	27.0	23.2	30.6	23.1	25.4	16.8	24.2	17.0	139
140	87.5	86.9	81.1	80.4	73.0	81.9	88.0	77.7	66.7	65.4	65.6	64.6	67.8	62.0	140
141	71.3	67.3	70.9	73.9	64.2	69.5	64.0	60.7	68.7	64.6	73.0	65.5	66.7	64.0	141
142	62.5	58.2	66.1	75.4	59.1	64.1	57.0	57.1	63.3	50.8	56.6	50.4	55.9	64.0	142
143	36.8	31.4	37.8	35.5	40.9	36.3	37.0	22.3	32.7	26.9	35.2	33.6	30.3	27.0	143
144	5.1	3.3	11.8	2.9	2.9	5.1	17.0	32.1	38.8	30.8	35.2	31.0	33.8	53.0	144
145	39.7	34.6	34.6	39.9	30.7	35.9	22.0	62.5	64.6	56.2	57.4	56.6	59.6	53.0	145
146	14.7	13.7	14.2	13.0	9.5	13.0	14.0	10.7	27.2	14.6	26.2	23.9	20.8	29.0	146
147	47.8	43.1	50.4	50.0	47.4	47.6	40.0	54.5	54.4	49.2	50.0	40.7	50.0	50.0	147
148	60.3	56.2	51.2	49.3	50.4	53.5	48.0	59.8	60.5	56.9	50.8	47.8	55.4	53.0	148
149	69.9	66.0	79.5	68.1	74.5	71.3	47.0	11.6	7.5	13.1	13.9	15.0	12.0	3.0	149
150	91.2	88.2	92.1	93.5	89.8	90.9	89.0	91.1	91.8	97.7	88.5	92.9	92.5	89.0	150
151	0.0	0.0	0.8	0.0	0.0	0.1	1.0	0.9	2.0	1.5	1.6	0.9	1.4	4.0	151
152	53.7	47.1	49.6	42.8	43.1	47.2	68.0	62.5	59.2	50.8	49.2	59.3	56.1	74.0	152
153	87.5	91.5	86.6	87.0	90.5	88.7	92.0	90.2	96.6	92.3	92.6	93.8	93.3	89.0	153
154	72.8	74.5	78.7	87.7	86.9	80.0	89.0	62.5	72.1	77.7	80.3	81.4	74.8	83.0	154
155	47.1	52.3	61.4	45.7	55.5	52.2	54.0	42.0	39.5	37.7	52.5	68.1	47.3	26.0	155
156	27.2	17.0	22.0	27.5	19.0	22.4	7.0	24.1	29.9	23.1	20.5	18.6	23.6	16.0	156

Percentage of Sample Responding True on Each MMPI Item

MMPI Item Number	Females, Age in Years							Males, Age in Years							MMPI Item Number
	13 (N=136)	14 (N=153)	15 (N=127)	16 (N=138)	17 (N=137)	Total (N=691)	H and M (N=100)	13 (N=112)	14 (N=147)	15 (N=130)	16 (N=122)	17 (N=113)	Total (N=624)	H and M (N=100)	
157	48.5	42.5	43.3	45.7	33.6	42.7	30.0	46.4	54.4	49.2	43.4	37.2	46.6	42.0	157
158	46.3	54.2	60.6	62.3	57.7	56.2	39.0	18.8	17.7	10.8	10.7	8.0	13.3	10.0	158
159	16.9	13.7	15.0	15.9	8.8	14.0	13.0	14.3	19.0	12.3	20.5	15.0	16.3	12.0	159
160	57.4	59.5	62.2	54.3	61.3	58.9	69.0	62.5	60.5	70.8	64.8	74.3	66.3	64.0	160
161	10.3	5.2	8.7	8.7	8.8	8.2	7.0	10.7	10.9	6.2	3.3	3.5	7.1	8.0	161
162	38.2	36.6	37.8	38.4	41.6	38.5	33.0	45.5	46.3	42.3	44.3	43.4	44.4	33.0	162
163	60.3	69.3	63.0	60.1	61.3	63.0	70.0	83.0	77.6	77.7	79.5	79.6	79.3	79.0	163
164	62.5	62.1	55.1	64.5	67.9	62.5	80.0	64.3	70.1	69.2	65.6	67.3	67.5	76.0	164
165	75.7	79.1	70.9	70.3	70.1	73.4	65.0	68.8	70.1	66.2	71.3	64.6	68.3	48.0	165
166	39.7	41.2	51.2	43.5	47.4	44.4	52.0	38.4	32.0	30.0	24.6	27.4	30.4	35.0	166
167	19.1	22.9	13.4	20.3	19.0	19.1	19.0	24.1	27.2	26.9	32.8	31.9	28.5	29.0	167
168	2.9	3.9	7.9	10.9	4.4	5.9	2.0	3.6	6.8	3.1	7.4	3.5	5.0	5.0	168
169	90.4	94.1	92.1	89.9	89.1	91.2	88.0	88.4	91.8	88.5	90.2	90.3	89.9	96.0	169
170	26.5	28.1	24.4	15.2	28.5	24.6	21.0	48.2	39.5	40.8	42.6	45.1	42.9	53.0	170
171	62.5	63.4	59.8	63.0	61.3	62.1	49.0	50.9	59.9	50.8	46.7	47.8	51.6	38.0	171
172	37.5	34.0	37.0	44.2	32.1	36.9	52.0	27.7	37.4	31.5	39.3	33.6	34.1	34.0	172
173	72.8	82.4	74.0	79.7	80.3	78.0	80.0	67.0	56.5	65.4	63.9	66.4	63.5	65.0	173
174	77.9	74.5	76.4	77.5	70.1	75.3	69.0	80.4	76.2	80.0	77.9	73.5	77.6	83.0	174
175	77.9	79.1	75.6	65.2	73.0	74.2	78.0	80.4	76.9	84.6	73.8	85.8	80.1	86.0	175
176	38.2	46.4	43.3	39.9	40.9	41.8	47.0	67.0	71.4	66.9	73.0	69.9	69.7	78.0	176
177	94.1	94.8	91.3	90.6	96.4	93.5	98.0	93.8	92.5	88.5	86.9	89.4	90.2	93.0	177
178	91.2	95.4	93.7	86.2	92.7	91.9	94.0	92.0	90.5	94.6	93.4	94.7	92.9	92.0	178
179	33.8	34.6	27.6	42.0	29.2	33.6	12.0	17.0	27.9	23.1	22.1	23.9	23.1	11.0	179
180	65.4	54.2	55.1	52.2	43.1	54.0	54.0	56.3	64.6	57.7	53.3	46.9	56.3	53.0	180
181	78.7	86.9	83.5	81.2	86.1	83.4	83.0	83.0	78.2	80.0	73.8	77.9	78.5	73.0	181
182	14.0	13.7	14.2	23.9	13.9	15.9	5.0	13.4	14.3	10.8	15.6	9.7	12.8	5.0	182
183	42.6	34.0	33.1	35.5	35.0	36.0	25.0	43.8	42.9	40.8	43.4	51.3	44.2	38.0	183
184	16.2	10.5	11.0	11.6	6.6	11.1	5.0	7.1	10.2	10.0	17.2	4.4	9.9	5.0	184
185	89.7	94.1	89.8	86.2	90.5	90.2	95.0	92.9	90.5	94.6	89.3	91.2	91.7	94.0	185
186	26.5	22.9	30.7	27.5	21.2	25.6	29.0	21.4	21.8	18.5	20.5	15.0	19.6	29.0	186
187	88.2	84.3	82.7	84.1	89.8	85.8	88.0	83.0	90.5	87.7	87.7	92.0	88.3	88.0	187
188	62.5	66.0	58.3	65.2	59.9	62.5	64.0	62.5	55.8	57.7	45.9	58.4	55.9	61.0	188
189	1.5	3.9	10.2	9.4	7.3	6.4	8.0	3.6	9.5	3.1	6.6	8.8	6.4	8.0	189
190	67.6	72.5	69.3	60.1	71.5	68.3	78.0	83.9	78.9	81.5	83.6	78.8	81.3	88.0	190
191	35.3	31.4	33.9	30.4	45.3	35.2	33.0	30.4	35.4	40.8	35.2	41.6	36.7	39.0	191
192	96.3	92.8	89.0	90.6	95.6	92.9	92.0	96.4	93.9	95.4	93.4	92.9	94.4	93.0	192
193	82.4	82.4	78.0	81.9	74.5	79.9	84.0	78.6	70.7	76.9	68.0	75.2	73.7	92.0	193
194	8.1	9.2	9.4	10.1	2.2	7.8	9.0	3.6	5.4	4.6	5.7	2.7	4.5	8.0	194
195	88.2	88.9	89.8	87.7	89.8	88.9	77.0	93.8	88.4	93.1	86.9	86.7	89.7	68.0	195
196	97.1	98.7	96.9	99.3	95.6	97.5	98.0	95.5	91.2	96.9	95.9	94.7	94.7	100	196
197	2.2	0.0	0.0	0.0	1.5	0.7	1.0	4.5	2.0	3.1	5.7	6.2	4.2	2.0	197
198	46.3	41.8	29.9	28.3	25.5	34.6	37.0	62.5	48.3	47.7	36.9	45.1	47.9	66.0	198
199	72.1	84.3	78.7	81.9	82.5	80.0	80.0	76.8	74.8	80.8	76.2	76.1	76.9	64.0	199
200	14.0	11.8	8.7	8.0	8.0	10.1	5.0	11.6	16.3	10.8	13.1	10.6	12.7	7.0	200
201	43.4	51.6	56.7	56.5	45.3	50.7	54.0	52.7	58.5	49.2	56.6	51.3	53.8	52.0	201
202	10.3	8.5	5.5	5.8	4.4	6.9	4.0	15.2	15.6	9.2	9.0	8.8	11.7	11.0	202
203	33.1	27.5	28.3	28.3	30.7	29.5	47.0	14.3	14.3	17.7	10.7	12.4	13.9	20.0	203
204	16.9	19.6	18.9	23.2	29.2	21.6	33.0	8.0	10.2	16.9	12.3	16.8	12.8	17.0	204
205	7.4	5.9	5.5	4.3	5.8	5.8	1.0	9.8	12.2	12.3	13.9	5.3	10.9	10.0	205
206	23.5	27.5	15.0	26.8	19.0	22.6	23.0	33.9	21.1	27.7	27.9	18.6	25.6	14.0	206
207	87.5	93.5	89.8	92.0	93.4	91.3	96.0	83.9	90.5	92.3	87.7	96.5	90.2	91.0	207
208	55.1	70.6	78.0	73.9	78.1	71.1	55.0	49.1	60.5	65.4	56.6	67.3	59.9	48.0	208

Percentage of Sample Responding True on Each MMPI Item

	Females, Age in Years							Males, Age in Years							
MMPI Item Number	13 (N=136)	14 (N=153)	15 (N=127)	16 (N=138)	17 (N=137)	Total (N=691)	H and M (N=100)	13 (N=112)	14 (N=147)	15 (N=130)	16 (N=122)	17 (N=113)	Total (N=624)	H and M (N=100)	MMPI Item Number
209	7.4	8.5	4.7	4.3	5.1	6.1	8.0	8.0	10.2	10.0	6.6	6.2	8.3	10.0	209
210	1.5	0.7	2.4	2.2	1.5	1.6	3.0	1.8	0.7	2.3	4.9	3.5	2.6	3.0	210
211	4.4	2.6	4.7	5.8	6.6	4.8	2.0	1.8	2.0	3.8	4.1	5.3	3.4	2.0	211
212	41.2	35.9	33.9	31.9	17.5	32.1	21.0	30.4	31.3	27.7	23.0	15.9	26.0	23.0	212
213	8.8	9.8	7.9	4.3	5.8	7.4	12.0	14.3	8.8	6.9	9.0	3.5	8.5	11.0	213
214	46.3	48.4	48.0	37.7	46.7	45.4	49.0	61.6	55.1	56.9	50.8	54.0	55.6	62.0	214
215	3.7	8.5	11.0	18.1	30.7	14.3	5.0	2.7	10.2	11.5	15.6	30.1	13.8	4.0	215
216	10.3	15.0	17.3	18.8	14.6	15.2	7.0	8.0	13.6	12.3	10.7	10.6	11.2	10.0	216
217	58.1	63.4	67.7	66.7	62.0	63.5	60.0	40.2	54.4	50.0	52.5	54.0	50.5	45.0	217
218	2.9	3.9	0.8	3.6	1.5	2.6	4.0	8.0	11.6	8.5	14.8	6.2	9.9	11.0	218
219	4.4	4.6	3.1	6.5	8.8	5.5	7.0	22.3	25.2	36.9	40.2	34.5	31.7	57.0	219
220	94.1	96.1	96.1	91.3	95.6	94.6	97.0	96.4	96.6	90.8	95.1	95.6	94.9	95.0	220
221	41.2	45.8	41.7	40.6	46.7	43.3	51.0	71.4	62.6	66.2	59.0	63.7	64.4	67.0	221
222	59.6	64.1	65.4	58.0	53.3	60.1	41.0	62.5	61.2	75.4	59.8	61.9	64.3	51.0	222
223	4.4	13.1	11.8	4.3	5.8	8.0	38.0	53.6	62.6	53.8	54.1	48.7	55.0	89.0	223
224	31.6	39.2	35.4	35.5	27.0	33.9	26.0	28.6	36.1	30.0	34.4	35.4	33.0	30.0	224
225	89.7	94.1	94.5	95.7	94.9	93.8	98.0	68.8	67.3	75.4	76.2	76.1	72.6	63.0	225
226	69.1	66.0	78.7	75.4	75.2	72.6	54.0	57.1	65.3	63.8	63.9	63.7	63.0	44.0	226
227	15.4	18.3	11.8	12.3	17.5	15.2	13.0	13.4	17.7	16.2	18.0	12.4	15.7	15.0	227
228	72.8	73.2	73.2	66.7	71.5	71.5	73.0	74.1	78.9	75.4	68.0	82.3	75.8	74.0	228
229	29.4	40.5	44.9	37.0	37.2	37.8	68.0	25.9	28.6	29.2	31.1	29.2	28.8	50.0	229
230	66.2	69.3	65.4	66.7	68.6	67.3	64.0	72.3	70.1	73.1	68.9	63.7	69.7	70.0	230
231	25.0	30.7	38.6	36.2	40.9	34.2	25.0	39.3	39.5	50.8	52.5	54.0	47.0	29.0	231
232	23.5	24.2	19.7	21.0	14.6	20.7	19.0	23.2	22.4	20.0	23.0	23.0	22.3	28.0	232
233	46.3	41.2	44.9	47.1	37.2	43.3	22.0	48.2	55.8	56.2	54.9	45.1	52.4	35.0	233
234	64.7	54.2	56.7	52.9	57.7	57.2	60.0	59.8	68.0	63.1	55.7	46.0	59.1	49.0	234
235	37.5	33.3	40.2	38.4	35.0	36.8	30.0	36.6	36.7	42.3	48.4	43.4	41.3	39.0	235
236	17.6	17.6	20.5	29.0	14.6	19.8	16.0	15.2	20.4	19.2	19.7	19.5	18.9	4.0	236
237	24.3	22.9	16.5	21.0	17.5	20.5	22.0	29.5	27.2	23.1	27.0	23.0	26.0	18.0	237
238	56.6	50.3	53.5	59.4	50.4	54.0	40.0	46.4	49.0	50.0	55.7	49.6	50.2	52.0	238
239	48.5	57.5	60.6	68.8	55.5	58.2	30.0	35.7	46.9	40.8	56.6	46.0	45.4	16.0	239
240	2.2	3.3	0.8	3.6	2.9	2.6	7.0	14.3	6.1	9.2	10.7	9.7	9.8	19.0	240
241	69.1	66.0	72.4	63.0	63.5	66.7	48.0	58.0	64.6	64.6	71.3	54.9	63.0	52.0	241
242	80.1	74.5	69.3	72.5	82.5	75.8	76.0	78.6	81.0	78.5	78.7	78.8	79.2	86.0	242
243	81.6	84.3	80.3	73.2	81.8	80.3	88.0	75.9	80.3	76.9	76.2	85.0	78.8	83.0	243
244	47.1	39.9	50.4	52.2	40.1	45.7	38.0	47.3	58.5	53.1	50.0	41.6	50.6	45.0	244
245	36.0	36.6	36.2	39.9	27.7	35.3	14.0	33.9	45.6	34.6	32.8	27.4	35.4	17.0	245
246	3.7	9.2	2.4	5.1	6.6	5.5	1.0	4.5	4.1	2.3	4.9	0.9	3.4	4.0	246
247	36.0	38.6	37.0	33.3	19.7	33.0	13.0	23.2	32.0	20.8	24.6	16.8	23.9	10.0	247
248	56.6	64.1	64.6	63.0	61.3	61.9	60.0	44.6	51.7	49.2	52.5	55.8	50.8	53.0	248
249	70.6	80.4	74.0	71.0	72.3	73.8	72.0	73.2	70.1	68.5	79.5	68.1	71.8	72.0	249
250	56.6	56.9	59.8	56.5	51.1	56.2	34.0	50.0	66.7	56.9	59.8	56.6	58.5	38.0	250
251	16.2	14.4	19.7	15.2	11.7	15.3	10.0	17.0	19.7	12.3	16.4	13.3	15.9	7.0	251
252	8.8	10.5	11.8	15.9	6.6	10.7	4.0	8.9	19.0	10.8	13.9	8.0	12.5	11.0	252
253	68.4	75.8	81.9	81.9	83.2	78.1	66.0	54.5	65.3	64.6	68.9	79.6	66.5	61.0	253
254	38.2	34.6	44.1	33.3	24.1	34.7	51.0	44.6	46.9	49.2	55.7	61.1	51.3	58.0	254
255	33.1	26.1	32.3	44.2	29.2	32.9	23.0	28.6	29.9	22.3	27.0	28.3	27.2	18.0	255
256	30.9	21.6	18.1	22.5	11.7	21.0	14.0	28.6	25.2	20.0	20.5	15.9	22.1	16.0	256
257	82.4	80.4	82.7	72.5	83.9	80.3	79.0	91.1	77.6	90.0	89.3	91.2	87.3	78.0	257
258	96.3	98.7	96.9	97.8	97.1	97.4	97.0	97.3	91.8	92.3	93.4	89.4	92.8	96.0	258
259	36.8	36.6	47.2	39.9	35.8	39.1	22.0	36.6	44.9	43.1	50.8	36.3	42.6	26.0	259
260	11.0	15.7	9.4	18.1	11.7	13.3	21.0	16.1	20.4	20.0	28.7	21.2	21.3	35.0	260

MMPI Item Number	Females, Age in Years 13 (N=136)	14 (N=153)	15 (N=127)	16 (N=138)	17 (N=137)	Total (N=691)	H and M (N=100)	Males, Age in Years 13 (N=112)	14 (N=147)	15 (N=130)	16 (N=122)	17 (N=113)	Total (N=624)	H and M (N=100)	MMPI Item Number
261	40.4	45.8	41.7	38.4	44.5	42.3	45.0	16.1	10.9	9.2	12.3	8.8	11.4	19.0	261
262	37.5	30.7	29.1	28.3	43.8	33.9	42.0	46.4	44.9	49.2	53.3	55.8	49.7	69.0	262
263	24.3	30.1	26.0	26.1	27.0	26.8	17.0	28.6	23.8	28.5	32.8	23.0	27.2	21.0	263
264	33.8	29.4	18.1	21.7	26.3	26.0	20.0	48.2	46.3	40.8	42.6	40.7	43.8	34.0	264
265	13.2	12.4	17.3	21.7	13.1	15.5	12.0	15.2	24.5	25.4	28.7	19.5	22.9	20.0	265
266	64.0	66.7	70.9	63.8	65.0	66.0	45.0	52.7	57.1	54.6	60.7	53.1	55.8	28.0	266
267	53.7	43.1	44.1	44.9	33.6	43.8	40.0	42.9	52.4	51.5	47.5	39.8	47.3	33.0	267
268	86.8	86.3	85.0	82.6	82.5	84.7	75.0	75.9	75.5	76.2	74.6	77.9	76.0	78.0	268
269	19.9	16.3	18.9	20.3	11.7	17.4	14.0	30.4	39.5	28.5	30.3	37.2	33.3	19.0	269
270	48.5	41.2	57.5	48.6	43.8	47.6	33.0	42.0	44.2	52.3	50.0	61.1	49.7	59.0	270
271	35.3	30.7	29.9	21.7	24.1	28.4	41.0	34.8	42.9	30.0	36.9	36.3	36.4	49.0	271
272	97.8	96.1	96.1	97.8	97.8	97.1	96.0	94.6	94.6	94.6	96.7	92.9	94.7	96.0	272
273	5.9	5.2	4.7	6.5	6.6	5.8	4.0	4.5	5.4	3.8	9.0	8.0	6.1	7.0	273
274	47.8	57.5	46.5	47.8	57.7	51.7	60.0	69.6	63.9	62.3	56.6	65.5	63.5	72.0	274
275	2.2	0.7	1.6	1.4	0.7	1.3	5.0	1.8	2.7	3.8	3.3	6.2	3.5	6.0	275
276	100.0	93.5	90.6	92.0	96.4	94.5	95.0	87.5	84.4	81.5	78.7	77.0	81.9	88.0	276
277	14.0	20.3	26.8	26.8	19.0	21.3	15.0	38.4	45.6	41.5	53.3	59.3	47.4	26.0	277
278	55.9	58.2	63.0	68.8	55.5	60.2	57.0	40.2	50.3	45.4	49.2	46.9	46.6	33.0	278
279	18.4	11.8	15.0	12.3	11.7	13.7	12.0	19.6	24.5	15.4	23.0	13.3	19.4	21.0	279
280	51.5	46.4	40.2	38.4	29.9	41.4	32.0	51.8	49.7	42.3	48.4	46.9	47.8	42.0	280
281	64.0	70.6	70.1	72.5	83.9	72.2	78.0	66.1	68.0	66.9	62.3	75.2	67.6	84.0	281
282	76.5	83.7	81.1	84.1	66.4	78.4	60.0	67.0	75.5	71.5	71.3	59.3	69.4	46.0	282
283	33.8	42.5	41.7	38.4	34.3	38.2	49.0	73.2	61.9	64.6	59.0	57.5	63.1	79.0	283
284	47.8	54.9	50.4	47.8	40.1	48.3	28.0	45.5	49.7	47.7	47.5	39.8	46.3	25.0	284
285	90.4	91.5	99.2	94.2	97.8	94.5	77.0	92.0	94.6	97.7	95.9	96.5	95.4	94.0	285
286	13.2	7.2	8.7	8.0	8.0	9.0	9.0	13.4	15.6	5.4	14.8	15.9	13.0	12.0	286
287	37.5	45.1	33.1	34.8	34.3	37.2	32.0	42.9	42.9	43.8	50.8	53.1	46.5	56.0	287
288	2.2	3.9	1.6	2.9	2.2	2.6	0.0	2.7	4.1	1.5	0.8	1.8	2.2	2.0	288
289	72.1	64.7	71.7	81.9	86.1	75.1	59.0	70.5	70.1	70.8	76.2	77.9	72.9	61.0	289
290	29.4	27.5	33.9	33.3	21.2	28.9	14.0	25.9	34.0	29.2	28.7	33.6	30.4	17.0	290
291	5.9	7.2	2.4	3.6	2.9	4.5	3.0	3.6	2.0	2.3	5.7	7.1	4.0	5.0	291
292	33.8	30.7	34.6	35.5	28.5	32.6	30.0	39.3	51.7	40.8	50.0	43.4	45.4	28.0	292
293	6.6	5.2	7.9	10.1	6.6	7.2	3.0	8.9	6.1	5.4	8.2	11.5	7.9	8.0	293
294	94.1	88.2	90.6	79.7	82.5	87.0	91.0	77.7	69.4	69.2	60.7	54.9	66.5	66.0	294
295	55.1	58.2	55.1	56.5	56.9	56.4	65.0	19.6	23.8	26.9	25.4	28.3	24.8	27.0	295
296	81.6	84.3	88.2	80.4	89.1	84.7	82.0	61.6	68.7	69.2	64.8	67.3	66.5	71.0	296
297	42.6	47.1	33.9	40.6	34.3	39.9	36.0	33.0	34.7	32.3	36.1	31.9	33.7	45.0	297
298	38.2	41.8	44.1	40.6	38.0	40.5	28.0	42.0	47.6	52.3	59.0	48.7	50.0	53.0	298
299	30.1	34.6	38.6	49.3	40.9	38.6	23.0	26.8	36.1	40.8	45.1	42.5	38.3	26.0	299
300	10.3	15.0	16.5	15.9	7.3	13.0	13.0	65.2	68.7	60.8	54.9	58.4	61.9	66.0	300
301	16.9	17.0	22.8	23.2	17.5	19.4	7.0	16.1	31.3	19.2	32.8	22.1	24.7	6.0	301
302	94.1	90.8	92.9	89.9	85.4	90.6	91.0	88.4	88.4	84.6	84.4	85.8	86.4	91.0	302
303	51.5	49.0	52.0	50.0	43.1	49.1	28.0	40.2	41.5	33.1	36.1	33.6	37.0	25.0	303
304	41.2	35.9	40.9	43.5	41.6	40.5	65.0	30.4	35.4	36.2	38.5	38.9	35.9	48.0	304
305	18.4	13.7	23.6	29.7	18.2	20.5	14.0	15.2	23.8	17.7	23.0	17.7	19.7	11.0	305
306	69.1	75.8	70.1	75.4	85.4	75.3	91.0	75.0	75.5	72.3	80.3	85.0	77.4	90.0	306
307	33.8	38.6	37.0	51.4	48.2	41.8	26.0	29.5	34.7	38.5	37.7	29.2	34.1	29.0	307
308	58.8	56.9	62.2	66.7	63.5	61.5	45.0	42.9	59.9	47.7	54.1	53.1	51.9	40.0	308
309	83.1	78.4	79.5	80.4	84.7	81.2	80.0	81.3	79.6	81.5	71.3	80.5	78.8	86.0	309
310	75.7	68.0	70.9	76.1	82.5	74.5	97.0	70.5	63.9	69.2	67.2	69.0	67.8	88.0	310
311	19.9	28.8	36.2	29.0	29.2	28.5	9.0	20.5	37.4	42.3	45.1	49.6	39.1	27.0	311
312	6.6	10.5	4.7	6.5	3.6	6.5	6.0	15.2	10.2	8.5	10.7	8.0	10.4	7.0	312

Percentage of Sample Responding True on Each MMPI Item

MMPI Item Number	Females, Age in Years							Males, Age in Years							MMPI Item Number
	13 (N=136)	14 (N=153)	15 (N=127)	16 (N=138)	17 (N=137)	Total (N=691)	H and M (N=100)	13 (N=112)	14 (N=147)	15 (N=130)	16 (N=122)	17 (N=113)	Total (N=624)	H and M (N=100)	
313	59.6	60.1	59.1	48.6	41.6	53.8	74.0	67.9	51.0	49.2	54.1	43.4	52.9	72.0	313
314	64.0	61.4	63.0	68.1	59.9	63.2	47.0	67.9	64.6	65.4	68.9	66.4	66.5	61.0	314
315	19.1	16.3	11.0	15.2	5.8	13.6	4.0	20.5	22.4	15.4	15.6	14.2	17.8	4.0	315
316	77.2	69.3	66.1	73.9	62.0	69.8	42.0	67.9	74.8	60.8	68.0	65.5	67.6	52.0	316
317	41.2	47.1	51.2	50.7	57.7	49.5	23.0	31.3	32.7	37.7	42.6	42.5	37.2	15.0	317
318	79.4	80.4	69.3	76.1	75.2	76.3	88.0	81.3	77.6	77.7	70.5	78.8	77.1	82.0	318
319	46.3	44.4	47.2	33.3	33.6	41.0	39.0	56.3	46.9	41.5	54.1	47.8	49.0	51.0	319
320	24.3	21.6	28.3	21.0	25.5	24.0	12.0	33.9	42.9	46.2	41.0	38.9	40.9	25.0	320
321	64.7	62.7	66.9	68.1	57.7	64.0	60.0	39.3	40.8	44.6	43.4	43.4	42.3	28.0	321
322	23.5	32.7	32.3	42.0	46.7	35.5	16.0	21.4	37.4	42.3	44.3	46.9	38.6	15.0	322
323	33.8	32.7	36.2	36.2	34.3	34.6	31.0	34.8	33.3	40.0	42.6	46.0	39.1	30.0	323
324	27.9	30.1	22.8	23.9	15.3	24.2	29.0	30.4	27.2	33.1	23.8	21.2	27.2	31.0	324
325	41.9	34.6	50.4	39.9	40.9	41.2	20.0	26.8	32.0	30.0	30.3	30.1	30.0	19.0	325
326	47.8	44.4	55.9	55.1	43.1	49.1	22.0	23.2	22.4	18.5	17.2	23.0	20.8	14.0	326
327	81.6	75.8	81.1	81.2	73.0	78.4	73.0	75.9	77.6	81.5	68.9	70.8	75.2	73.0	327
328	30.1	30.1	37.8	32.6	21.2	30.2	21.0	27.7	33.3	29.2	28.7	17.7	27.7	24.0	328
329	16.2	13.1	15.7	14.5	16.1	15.1	31.0	27.7	22.4	20.0	17.2	24.8	22.3	52.0	329
330	88.2	86.9	78.7	84.8	84.7	84.8	87.0	82.1	82.3	85.4	82.0	82.3	82.9	84.0	330
331	12.5	13.1	10.2	7.2	2.9	9.3	2.0	13.4	15.0	13.1	11.5	8.8	12.5	6.0	331
332	30.9	35.9	27.6	36.2	24.1	31.1	20.0	38.4	43.5	37.7	34.4	38.1	38.6	26.0	332
333	25.0	28.1	25.2	29.0	17.5	25.0	9.0	22.3	22.4	22.3	27.0	21.2	23.1	8.0	333
334	22.1	24.2	18.1	23.2	13.9	20.4	27.0	25.0	25.2	19.2	29.5	23.0	24.4	30.0	334
335	34.6	26.8	31.5	32.6	19.7	28.9	25.0	26.8	30.6	26.9	32.0	17.7	27.1	22.0	335
336	48.5	51.6	55.9	53.6	46.0	51.1	37.0	45.5	50.3	43.8	50.8	46.9	47.6	37.0	336
337	26.5	29.4	33.9	34.1	27.0	30.1	23.0	23.2	27.9	24.6	31.1	31.0	27.6	21.0	337
338	46.3	54.2	52.0	60.1	46.7	52.0	20.0	55.4	49.7	50.8	50.8	49.6	51.1	22.0	338
339	8.1	15.0	8.7	13.0	7.3	10.6	3.0	6.3	9.5	3.8	10.7	8.8	7.9	4.0	339
340	83.8	76.5	83.5	77.5	86.9	81.5	74.0	78.6	64.6	72.3	71.3	62.8	69.7	59.0	340
341	21.3	19.0	19.7	24.6	18.2	20.5	8.0	26.8	26.5	22.3	24.6	23.0	24.7	7.0	341
342	13.2	13.1	21.3	21.7	9.5	15.6	7.0	12.5	13.6	16.2	20.5	14.2	15.4	19.0	342
343	35.3	34.0	36.2	34.8	30.7	34.2	43.0	21.4	29.3	27.7	21.3	27.4	25.6	37.0	343
344	43.4	28.8	24.4	27.5	20.4	28.9	29.0	32.1	40.1	23.1	27.9	23.0	29.6	28.0	344
345	28.7	37.9	27.6	42.0	20.4	31.5	32.0	27.7	27.9	23.1	27.0	23.0	25.8	16.0	345
346	31.6	28.8	26.8	33.3	19.7	28.1	29.0	27.7	29.9	29.2	33.6	26.5	29.5	15.0	346
347	79.4	81.0	78.0	85.5	93.4	83.5	91.0	76.8	74.1	73.8	72.1	78.8	75.0	86.0	347
348	58.1	53.6	49.6	54.3	51.1	53.4	49.0	43.8	52.4	50.0	48.4	50.4	49.2	49.0	348
349	31.6	33.3	39.4	37.7	30.7	34.4	20.0	28.6	44.9	30.8	41.8	32.7	36.2	17.0	349
350	41.9	35.9	34.6	34.8	29.2	35.3	29.0	37.5	29.3	22.3	26.2	19.5	26.9	10.0	350
351	12.5	12.4	8.7	10.1	5.1	9.8	11.0	8.9	8.8	10.0	9.8	9.7	9.5	8.0	351
352	26.5	30.1	35.4	37.7	30.7	32.0	36.0	30.4	31.3	19.2	29.5	15.9	25.5	21.0	352
353	56.6	48.4	47.2	44.9	58.4	51.1	54.0	62.5	66.7	63.8	60.7	68.1	64.4	56.0	353
354	17.6	11.1	7.1	5.1	5.1	9.3	6.0	9.8	5.4	5.4	4.9	7.1	6.4	3.0	354
355	13.2	12.4	15.7	21.7	9.5	14.5	15.0	19.6	13.6	11.5	11.5	10.6	13.3	10.0	355
356	27.9	26.8	30.7	32.6	22.6	28.1	25.0	24.1	34.7	23.8	36.1	15.9	27.4	21.0	356
357	45.6	40.5	47.2	61.6	46.7	48.2	31.0	42.9	40.8	33.1	33.6	32.7	36.7	33.0	357
358	44.9	34.0	37.8	37.7	26.3	36.0	28.0	42.9	34.7	36.9	35.2	35.4	36.9	41.0	358
359	50.0	51.0	51.2	59.4	46.7	51.7	48.0	41.1	43.5	40.8	39.3	38.9	40.9	36.0	359
360	12.5	7.8	8.7	9.4	5.8	8.8	5.0	12.5	10.9	6.9	8.2	8.0	9.3	2.0	360
361	35.3	33.3	41.7	52.9	42.3	41.0	30.0	24.1	26.5	24.6	30.3	30.1	27.1	16.0	361
362	40.4	45.8	52.8	52.9	55.5	49.3	25.0	33.0	32.0	41.5	44.3	44.2	38.8	15.0	362
363	5.1	6.5	6.3	5.1	3.6	5.4	11.0	5.4	10.9	7.7	8.2	6.2	7.9	17.0	363
364	41.9	29.4	24.4	21.0	17.5	26.9	16.0	35.7	30.6	32.3	25.4	22.1	29.3	15.0	364

Percentage of Sample Responding True on Each MMPI Item

MMPI Item Number	Females, Age in Years							Males, Age in Years							MMPI Item Number
	13 (N=136)	14 (N=153)	15 (N=127)	16 (N=138)	17 (N=137)	Total (N=691)	H and M (N=100)	13 (N=112)	14 (N=147)	15 (N=130)	16 (N=122)	17 (N=113)	Total (N=624)	H and M (N=100)	
365	10.3	6.5	5.5	6.5	5.8	6.9	11.0	3.6	12.9	6.9	17.2	8.8	10.1	38.0	365
366	16.9	13.1	19.7	26.8	15.3	18.2	8.0	12.5	20.4	13.8	19.7	12.4	16.0	9.0	366
367	47.8	59.5	59.1	58.7	55.5	56.2	55.0	74.1	82.3	77.7	77.0	77.0	77.9	76.0	367
368	55.1	56.9	62.2	63.8	56.9	58.9	38.0	46.4	45.6	55.4	51.6	41.6	48.2	28.0	368
369	78.7	83.0	77.2	85.5	72.3	79.5	61.0	76.8	75.5	73.8	74.6	75.2	75.2	74.0	369
370	80.9	85.0	80.3	79.7	73.0	79.9	82.0	73.2	78.2	75.4	77.0	64.6	74.0	73.0	370
371	56.6	53.6	49.6	49.3	54.7	52.8	66.0	66.1	57.8	52.3	49.2	67.3	58.2	62.0	371
372	74.3	82.4	82.7	74.6	78.1	78.4	72.0	73.2	78.2	82.3	77.0	74.3	77.2	63.0	372
373	31.6	40.5	30.7	33.3	35.8	34.6	62.0	46.4	44.2	46.9	44.3	38.1	44.1	71.0	373
374	46.3	59.5	64.6	72.5	63.5	61.2	59.0	49.1	52.4	56.9	65.6	64.6	57.5	52.0	374
375	41.2	39.2	30.7	33.3	29.9	35.0	37.0	36.6	27.9	28.5	32.0	24.8	29.8	27.0	375
376	88.2	88.2	89.0	86.2	81.8	86.7	97.0	89.3	88.4	87.7	82.0	83.2	86.2	93.0	376
377	19.9	24.2	26.0	27.5	18.2	23.2	19.0	26.8	32.0	29.2	32.0	31.0	30.3	29.0	377
378	68.4	68.0	60.6	59.4	51.1	61.6	68.0	73.2	68.7	73.8	70.5	68.1	70.8	71.0	378
379	70.6	64.1	55.1	50.7	59.9	60.2	70.0	76.8	71.4	73.1	61.5	75.2	71.5	77.0	379
380	67.6	69.9	66.9	64.5	70.1	67.9	81.0	70.5	69.4	60.8	62.3	70.8	66.7	76.0	380
381	23.5	22.9	26.8	31.9	35.0	27.9	32.0	25.9	36.7	33.8	31.1	28.3	31.6	33.0	381
382	75.0	76.5	71.7	77.5	59.9	72.2	64.0	65.2	63.3	67.7	58.2	54.9	62.0	50.0	382
383	45.6	41.8	44.9	45.7	45.3	44.6	47.0	45.5	42.9	46.9	43.4	39.8	43.8	42.0	383
384	49.3	42.5	40.9	50.0	40.1	44.6	43.0	54.5	58.5	63.1	59.8	60.2	59.3	37.0	384
385	19.1	26.1	26.8	18.1	23.4	22.7	29.0	13.4	9.5	10.8	9.8	8.0	10.3	15.0	385
386	41.9	39.2	50.4	44.2	37.2	42.4	31.0	43.8	43.5	46.9	54.9	56.6	48.9	36.0	386
387	16.9	14.4	15.0	18.1	10.2	14.9	20.0	19.6	22.4	20.0	19.7	21.2	20.7	23.0	387
388	30.1	31.4	20.5	31.9	21.9	27.4	26.0	19.6	16.3	16.9	9.8	5.3	13.8	14.0	388
389	38.2	35.9	35.4	42.8	33.6	37.2	27.0	42.0	40.8	47.7	33.6	29.2	38.9	38.0	389
390	57.4	66.0	66.9	71.7	61.3	64.7	54.0	59.8	59.2	58.5	56.6	61.9	59.1	45.0	390
391	83.1	88.9	81.9	82.6	81.0	83.6	77.0	53.6	46.3	60.8	57.4	62.8	55.8	48.0	391
392	19.1	23.5	23.6	21.7	21.2	21.9	33.0	17.0	8.2	9.2	5.7	13.3	10.4	11.0	392
393	0.7	0.7	2.4	0.7	1.5	1.2	1.0	4.5	2.7	2.3	4.9	3.5	3.5	6.0	393
394	63.2	68.0	66.9	71.0	61.3	66.1	65.0	53.6	53.1	52.3	59.0	61.9	55.8	60.0	394
395	41.9	40.5	47.2	42.0	35.0	41.2	48.0	53.6	57.1	36.9	36.9	38.1	44.9	48.0	395
396	38.2	45.8	44.1	52.2	38.7	43.8	37.0	33.9	41.5	37.7	47.5	35.4	39.4	33.0	396
397	54.4	56.9	56.7	72.5	62.0	60.5	36.0	39.3	51.7	50.0	55.7	46.9	49.0	24.0	397
398	44.9	42.5	30.7	39.1	30.7	37.8	20.0	33.0	41.5	34.6	35.2	24.8	34.3	24.0	398
399	46.3	50.3	51.2	44.2	40.1	46.5	51.0	49.1	47.6	49.2	57.4	63.7	53.0	57.0	399
400	58.1	62.7	55.1	58.0	58.4	58.6	36.0	67.9	70.7	71.5	64.8	72.6	69.6	49.0	400
401	81.6	83.0	79.5	73.2	77.4	79.0	77.0	77.7	77.6	75.4	76.2	84.1	78.0	79.0	401
402	41.2	31.4	37.8	38.4	42.3	38.1	46.0	31.3	27.2	28.5	32.0	32.7	30.1	27.0	402
403	89.0	86.9	83.5	82.6	81.0	84.7	92.0	78.6	74.8	82.3	84.4	84.1	80.6	85.0	403
404	63.2	60.8	70.1	64.5	56.2	62.8	58.0	59.8	72.1	65.4	57.4	63.7	64.1	49.0	404
405	91.2	88.9	91.3	94.2	95.6	92.2	91.0	92.0	91.2	92.3	89.3	93.8	91.7	96.0	405
406	54.4	45.1	48.0	46.4	45.3	47.8	36.0	59.8	63.3	63.8	59.0	60.2	61.4	43.0	406
407	66.9	60.1	60.6	56.5	62.0	61.2	75.0	66.1	66.0	72.3	64.8	74.3	68.6	82.0	407
408	75.7	72.5	71.7	81.2	82.5	76.7	68.0	57.1	70.1	59.2	57.4	66.4	62.3	52.0	408
409	56.6	56.2	64.6	70.3	74.5	64.3	46.0	58.0	54.4	55.4	63.9	48.7	56.1	45.0	409
410	37.5	51.6	47.2	51.4	51.1	47.9	39.0	64.3	63.3	64.6	67.2	70.8	65.9	57.0	410
411	45.6	35.9	33.1	42.8	27.0	36.9	22.0	26.8	35.4	30.0	33.6	19.5	29.5	27.0	411
412	61.8	64.1	51.2	47.1	62.0	57.5	63.0	73.2	77.6	73.1	65.6	73.5	72.8	77.0	412
413	17.6	20.9	14.2	17.4	14.6	17.1	47.0	15.2	25.9	19.2	20.5	16.8	19.9	49.0	413
414	36.8	39.2	41.7	47.8	37.2	40.5	33.0	40.2	40.1	37.7	32.8	35.4	37.3	26.0	414
415	61.0	55.6	54.3	47.1	55.5	54.7	30.0	64.3	61.9	73.8	56.6	72.6	65.7	44.0	415
416	68.4	72.5	79.5	76.1	73.0	73.8	67.0	68.8	71.4	61.5	76.2	58.4	67.5	48.0	416

Percentage of Sample Responding True on Each MMPI Item

MMPI Item Number	Females, Age in Years 13 (N=136)	14 (N=153)	15 (N=127)	16 (N=138)	17 (N=137)	Total (N=691)	H and M (N=100)	Males, Age in Years 13 (N=112)	14 (N=147)	15 (N=130)	16 (N=122)	17 (N=113)	Total (N=624)	H and M (N=100)	MMPI Item Number
417	41.2	33.3	35.4	24.6	27.7	32.4	31.0	47.3	42.9	44.6	39.3	35.4	42.0	47.0	4
418	55.1	58.8	60.6	69.6	49.6	58.8	50.0	45.5	45.6	41.5	44.3	35.4	42.6	39.0	4
419	6.6	8.5	5.5	9.4	10.9	8.2	6.0	8.0	10.9	3.8	10.7	14.2	9.5	14.0	4
420	11.0	5.9	5.5	3.6	2.9	5.8	12.0	9.8	10.9	8.5	6.6	9.7	9.1	12.0	4
421	14.0	22.9	36.2	29.7	27.0	25.8	29.0	16.1	27.2	26.2	34.4	27.4	26.4	29.0	4
422	14.0	13.7	16.5	13.8	8.0	13.2	9.0	15.2	21.8	7.7	18.0	5.3	13.9	13.0	4
423	56.6	54.9	49.6	52.2	56.9	54.1	67.0	79.5	83.0	78.5	75.4	75.2	78.5	79.0	4
424	35.3	35.3	25.2	33.3	23.4	30.7	31.0	33.0	38.1	36.2	42.6	41.6	38.3	40.0	4
425	71.3	73.9	74.0	76.8	78.1	74.8	66.0	58.0	59.2	71.5	72.1	65.5	65.2	41.0	4
426	65.4	52.9	62.2	57.2	47.4	56.9	38.0	67.0	71.4	66.2	63.9	72.6	68.3	47.0	4
427	33.1	24.2	26.0	29.7	24.8	27.5	69.0	17.0	12.2	13.1	10.7	13.3	13.1	21.0	4
428	20.6	30.1	33.1	29.0	32.8	29.1	49.0	20.5	25.9	21.5	19.7	32.7	24.0	44.0	4
429	29.4	22.2	25.2	30.4	38.7	29.1	31.0	16.1	16.3	22.3	23.8	23.0	20.2	28.0	4
430	89.7	92.8	96.9	94.9	97.1	94.2	74.0	83.9	87.1	89.2	94.3	93.8	89.6	65.0	4
431	33.8	35.9	38.6	44.9	34.3	37.5	32.0	24.1	33.3	33.8	31.1	32.7	31.3	26.0	4
432	19.9	22.2	23.6	18.1	21.9	21.1	13.0	32.1	27.2	29.2	29.5	38.9	31.1	31.0	4
433	22.1	18.3	25.2	21.7	15.3	20.4	21.0	17.0	13.6	22.3	19.7	11.5	16.8	18.0	4
434	8.1	12.4	14.2	16.7	14.6	13.2	11.0	33.0	38.1	43.8	53.3	52.2	43.9	50.0	4
435	49.3	42.5	39.4	37.7	22.6	38.4	54.0	32.1	36.7	46.9	46.7	29.2	38.6	15.0	4
436	77.9	83.0	80.3	85.5	78.1	81.0	72.0	75.0	77.6	80.0	80.3	75.2	77.7	74.0	4
437	47.8	49.0	61.4	55.1	51.1	52.7	51.0	59.8	58.5	60.8	66.4	67.3	62.3	52.0	4
438	80.9	81.0	76.4	85.5	71.5	79.2	50.0	79.5	82.3	73.8	77.0	82.3	79.0	51.0	4
439	37.5	37.3	46.5	50.7	47.4	43.7	46.0	31.3	40.8	36.9	38.5	45.1	38.6	28.0	4
440	84.6	86.9	86.6	85.5	86.1	86.0	78.0	88.4	81.6	82.3	78.7	86.7	83.3	85.0	4
441	33.8	29.4	31.5	37.7	30.7	32.6	44.0	32.1	39.5	45.4	41.8	50.4	41.8	16.0	4
442	55.1	58.8	64.6	66.7	65.7	62.1	32.0	42.0	51.7	46.9	50.0	49.6	48.2	24.0	4
443	44.1	45.1	44.1	51.4	40.1	45.0	44.0	36.6	43.5	40.8	32.8	34.5	38.0	39.0	4
444	44.1	41.8	45.7	45.7	35.0	42.4	43.0	40.2	48.3	39.2	43.4	41.6	42.8	32.0	4
445	94.1	88.2	93.7	92.0	94.2	92.3	93.0	87.5	86.4	86.9	88.5	92.0	88.1	88.0	4
446	37.5	31.4	36.2	31.9	40.9	35.5	11.0	51.8	61.2	58.5	68.0	69.0	61.7	34.0	4
447	55.9	54.2	58.3	52.2	55.5	55.1	45.0	64.3	55.8	61.5	55.7	58.4	59.0	51.0	4
448	50.7	40.5	40.9	49.3	38.0	43.8	37.0	35.7	40.8	33.8	24.6	21.2	31.7	24.0	4
449	76.5	83.0	81.9	81.9	85.4	81.8	82.0	62.5	66.7	78.5	74.6	77.9	72.0	60.0	4
450	85.3	82.4	87.4	86.2	84.7	85.1	94.0	63.4	68.0	78.5	73.0	76.1	71.8	79.0	4
451	86.8	81.7	83.5	80.4	77.4	81.9	86.0	81.3	83.7	80.8	82.8	79.6	81.7	88.0	4
452	32.4	33.3	42.5	40.6	32.8	36.2	15.0	58.9	54.4	46.9	56.6	56.6	54.5	21.0	4
453	52.2	51.0	36.2	44.9	40.9	45.3	20.0	51.8	55.8	43.1	59.0	48.7	51.8	40.0	4
454	21.3	27.5	22.8	24.6	20.4	23.4	24.0	43.8	46.3	40.0	44.3	41.6	43.3	50.0	4
455	41.9	35.3	33.1	33.3	33.6	35.5	38.0	48.2	51.0	47.7	54.1	57.5	51.6	52.0	4
456	8.8	9.2	11.8	8.7	9.5	9.6	15.0	20.5	23.8	16.2	21.3	16.8	19.9	24.0	4
457	27.2	11.8	6.3	8.7	5.1	11.9	42.0	19.6	22.4	13.8	8.2	8.0	14.7	47.0	4
458	19.1	24.8	29.9	27.5	23.4	24.9	17.0	31.3	29.3	37.7	29.5	38.1	33.0	29.0	4
459	27.9	28.1	25.2	37.0	20.4	27.8	11.0	32.1	37.4	22.3	32.8	34.5	31.9	19.0	4
460	91.9	83.7	90.6	85.5	85.4	87.3	83.0	83.9	75.5	83.1	85.2	80.5	81.4	76.0	4
461	40.4	37.3	37.8	41.3	35.8	38.5	39.0	43.8	51.7	46.9	43.4	52.2	47.8	44.0	4
462	89.0	93.5	91.3	88.4	89.1	90.3	89.0	89.3	89.1	89.2	90.2	91.2	89.7	82.0	4
463	80.9	81.0	81.9	91.3	90.5	85.1	91.0	25.9	19.7	25.4	23.8	23.9	23.6	38.0	4
464	66.2	72.5	70.1	79.7	73.7	72.5	81.0	65.2	76.9	75.4	63.9	74.3	71.5	75.0	4
465	61.0	64.1	73.2	71.7	75.2	68.9	59.0	61.6	57.1	61.5	63.1	70.8	62.5	56.0	4
466	89.0	80.4	80.3	79.0	75.2	80.8	89.0	92.0	81.6	82.3	80.3	70.8	81.4	86.0	4
467	36.8	41.2	40.2	33.3	30.7	36.5	31.0	37.5	38.8	41.5	33.6	32.7	37.0	17.0	4
468	69.1	63.4	67.7	78.3	70.1	69.6	75.0	59.8	55.1	49.2	46.7	46.9	51.6	57.0	4

Percentage of Sample Responding True on Each MMPI Item

MMPI Item Number	Females, Age in Years					Total (N=691)	H and M (N=100)	Males, Age in Years					Total (N=624)	H and M (N=100)	MMPI Item Number
	13 (N=136)	14 (N=153)	15 (N=127)	16 (N=138)	17 (N=137)			13 (N=112)	14 (N=147)	15 (N=130)	16 (N=122)	17 (N=113)			
469	62.5	51.0	42.5	41.3	34.3	46.5	29.0	56.3	53.7	49.2	39.3	46.9	49.2	39.0	469
470	29.4	21.6	10.2	14.5	11.7	17.7	26.0	15.2	8.8	4.6	7.4	1.8	7.5	23.0	470
471	11.8	8.5	7.1	7.2	6.6	8.2	8.0	8.0	21.8	13.1	13.1	12.4	14.1	25.0	471
472	19.9	22.2	25.2	24.6	13.1	21.0	24.0	34.8	40.1	33.8	41.0	41.6	38.3	21.0	472
473	14.7	15.7	9.4	21.0	11.7	14.6	11.0	27.7	25.9	20.0	24.6	18.6	23.4	18.0	473
474	86.8	83.0	85.0	88.4	84.7	85.5	81.0	86.6	84.4	85.4	85.2	85.8	85.4	82.0	474
475	78.7	75.8	77.2	79.0	70.1	76.1	53.0	68.8	66.0	72.3	72.1	73.5	70.4	53.0	475
476	28.7	27.5	20.5	15.9	18.2	22.3	26.0	30.4	23.1	26.2	20.5	20.4	24.0	15.0	476
477	33.1	35.3	44.9	42.8	35.8	38.2	44.0	42.0	42.2	43.1	52.5	55.8	46.8	48.0	477
478	61.0	60.1	66.9	65.9	64.2	63.5	67.0	74.1	70.1	70.8	62.3	71.7	69.7	69.0	478
479	59.6	71.2	78.7	73.9	76.6	71.9	82.0	63.4	68.0	76.9	79.5	85.8	74.5	85.0	479
480	25.7	19.6	17.3	27.5	15.3	21.1	32.0	17.9	13.6	13.1	11.5	5.3	12.3	15.0	480
481	69.1	71.9	76.4	71.0	78.1	73.2	55.0	57.1	66.7	63.1	71.3	67.3	65.2	54.0	481
482	20.6	29.4	30.7	30.4	35.0	29.2	32.0	26.8	32.0	33.8	32.0	39.8	32.9	57.0	482
483	83.8	88.2	81.1	81.2	88.3	84.7	88.0	89.3	89.1	79.2	81.1	79.6	83.8	80.0	483
484	44.9	37.3	40.2	50.0	35.8	41.5	26.0	41.1	47.6	45.4	37.7	43.4	43.3	26.0	484
485	50.0	35.3	36.2	36.2	31.4	37.8	28.0	39.3	40.1	50.8	50.0	50.4	46.0	36.0	485
486	83.8	86.9	86.6	94.9	89.8	88.4	75.0	96.4	96.6	92.3	93.4	95.6	94.9	84.0	486
487	37.5	35.9	35.4	55.8	34.3	39.8	33.0	33.0	36.1	30.0	25.4	24.8	30.1	23.0	487
488	55.9	54.2	46.5	53.6	51.1	52.4	82.0	58.9	42.9	46.2	49.2	39.8	47.1	53.0	488
489	66.2	63.4	63.0	63.0	61.3	63.4	53.0	58.9	48.3	50.8	49.2	39.8	49.4	33.0	489
490	10.3	13.7	9.4	6.5	6.6	9.4	36.0	16.1	15.0	10.0	8.2	3.5	10.7	19.0	490
491	20.6	19.6	11.8	9.4	15.3	15.5	19.0	17.0	12.2	17.7	24.6	15.9	17.3	18.0	491
492	66.2	59.5	63.0	51.4	53.3	58.6	78.0	46.4	35.4	37.7	37.7	33.6	38.0	42.0	492
493	43.4	43.8	51.2	48.6	63.5	49.9	58.0	48.2	37.4	53.8	43.4	54.0	47.0	53.0	493
494	16.2	22.2	22.8	28.3	21.2	22.1	22.0	18.8	25.2	13.1	18.0	12.4	17.8	12.0	494
495	52.9	50.3	54.3	55.8	56.9	54.0	47.0	57.1	54.4	55.4	57.4	66.4	57.9	62.0	495
496	66.9	60.8	73.2	68.8	68.6	67.4	73.0	73.2	74.1	81.5	77.9	80.5	77.4	79.0	496
497	75.7	82.4	80.3	79.0	86.1	80.8	92.0	93.8	86.4	91.5	91.8	88.5	90.2	93.0	497
498	65.4	53.6	44.1	52.2	47.4	52.7	60.0	52.7	51.7	59.2	49.2	56.6	53.8	69.0	498
499	77.2	76.5	85.0	87.7	78.1	80.8	83.0	64.3	59.9	62.3	68.9	66.4	64.1	46.0	499
500	37.5	38.6	35.4	39.1	27.7	35.7	58.0	58.9	44.2	38.5	46.7	46.0	46.5	59.0	500
501	56.6	58.2	58.3	55.8	62.0	58.2	62.0	63.4	64.6	76.2	72.1	73.5	69.9	59.0	501
502	80.9	77.8	79.5	70.3	85.4	78.7	69.0	69.6	72.8	76.9	68.9	75.2	72.8	67.0	502
503	44.1	48.4	45.7	44.2	50.4	46.6	60.0	52.7	52.4	56.9	48.4	51.3	52.4	44.0	503
504	46.3	38.6	40.9	40.6	38.0	40.8	35.0	44.6	48.3	38.5	39.3	42.5	42.8	43.0	504
505	41.2	30.1	37.8	35.5	29.9	34.7	29.0	38.4	38.8	35.4	29.5	37.2	35.9	43.0	505
506	41.9	35.9	44.1	37.0	37.2	39.1	18.0	36.6	36.7	33.1	41.8	43.4	38.1	13.0	506
507	46.3	39.2	41.7	50.7	45.3	44.6	29.0	47.3	46.3	42.3	45.1	47.8	45.7	30.0	507
508	97.8	96.7	93.7	92.8	97.1	95.7	97.0	89.3	97.3	96.9	91.8	87.6	92.9	88.0	508
509	42.6	38.6	33.1	44.2	34.3	38.6	32.0	33.9	40.1	38.5	43.4	31.0	37.7	29.0	509
510	8.8	8.5	4.7	8.7	8.8	8.0	21.0	3.6	3.4	3.8	4.1	4.4	3.8	13.0	510
511	40.4	37.3	40.9	44.2	43.8	41.2	33.0	37.5	36.7	29.2	41.8	23.0	33.8	27.0	511
512	3.7	3.3	3.1	2.9	3.6	3.3	4.0	8.9	12.2	9.2	7.4	6.2	9.0	5.0	512
513	40.4	44.4	50.4	53.6	55.5	48.8	53.0	40.2	46.3	52.3	54.9	55.8	49.8	59.0	513
514	11.8	15.0	9.4	13.0	8.8	11.7	5.0	13.4	12.2	9.2	13.9	15.0	12.7	19.0	514
515	97.1	96.7	96.1	97.1	100.0	97.4	97.0	93.8	96.6	95.4	92.6	94.7	94.7	85.0	515
516	81.6	75.8	78.0	87.0	78.1	80.0	61.0	60.7	71.4	72.3	74.6	75.2	71.0	51.0	516
517	5.1	5.2	11.0	12.3	6.6	8.0	4.0	4.5	10.2	5.4	8.2	5.3	6.9	9.0	517
518	56.6	51.6	43.3	48.6	51.1	50.4	42.0	42.0	42.9	37.7	34.4	36.3	38.8	39.0	518
519	1.5	3.9	3.1	4.3	0.7	2.7	1.0	2.7	2.7	3.1	4.1	3.5	3.2	8.0	519
520	53.7	54.2	65.4	50.7	55.5	55.7	65.0	56.3	63.3	70.0	56.6	62.8	62.0	67.0	520

Percentage of Sample Responding True on Each MMPI Item

MMPI Item Number	Females, Age in Years							Males, Age in Years							MMPI Item Number
	13 (N=136)	14 (N=153)	15 (N=127)	16 (N=138)	17 (N=137)	Total (N=691)	H and M (N=100)	13 (N=112)	14 (N=147)	15 (N=130)	16 (N=122)	17 (N=113)	Total (N=624)	H and M (N=100)	
521	49.3	55.6	56.7	55.8	65.7	56.6	47.0	58.0	59.9	60.8	57.4	75.2	62.0	59.0	521
522	26.5	33.3	24.4	31.9	29.9	29.4	34.0	65.2	65.3	65.4	63.9	66.4	65.2	76.0	522
523	31.6	29.4	23.6	30.4	27.7	28.7	20.0	55.4	46.9	53.8	45.9	49.6	50.2	46.0	523
524	83.1	81.7	84.3	81.9	86.9	83.5	61.0	81.3	93.2	88.5	81.1	88.5	86.9	71.0	524
525	53.7	56.9	71.7	59.4	56.9	59.5	39.0	45.5	56.5	42.3	43.4	44.2	46.8	29.0	525
526	8.8	7.2	7.1	10.9	3.6	7.5	7.0	6.3	14.3	6.2	6.6	10.6	9.0	11.0	526
527	81.6	83.0	82.7	77.5	80.3	81.0	91.0	89.3	83.7	83.8	79.5	85.8	84.3	88.0	527
528	67.6	69.3	68.5	70.3	64.2	68.0	68.0	75.9	81.6	85.4	76.2	81.4	80.3	80.0	528
529	86.8	86.3	86.6	91.3	90.5	88.3	68.0	58.0	59.2	66.2	59.8	62.8	61.2	41.0	529
530	47.1	38.6	40.2	30.4	33.6	37.9	53.0	29.5	27.2	20.8	20.5	21.2	23.9	32.0	530
531	47.8	44.4	45.7	49.3	27.0	42.8	41.0	31.3	42.2	29.2	37.7	30.1	34.5	27.0	531
532	77.2	75.2	70.1	75.4	77.4	75.1	84.0	83.9	87.8	86.2	87.7	91.2	87.3	85.0	532
533	66.2	78.4	74.8	73.2	80.3	74.7	79.0	69.6	81.6	79.2	79.5	71.7	76.8	76.0	533
534	53.7	52.3	58.3	59.4	59.1	56.4	43.0	63.4	65.3	62.3	65.6	67.3	64.7	67.0	534
535	8.8	6.5	8.7	9.4	9.5	8.5	5.0	5.4	8.8	3.1	9.8	8.8	7.2	8.0	535
536	73.5	72.5	74.0	73.9	70.8	72.9	60.0	66.1	73.5	70.8	68.0	67.3	69.4	57.0	536
537	2.9	3.9	4.7	5.1	5.8	4.5	24.0	21.4	27.9	23.1	31.1	36.3	27.9	63.0	537
538	36.8	36.6	30.7	30.4	31.4	33.3	50.0	3.6	0.7	0.8	2.5	4.4	2.2	3.0	538
539	44.1	49.7	47.2	35.5	47.4	44.9	53.0	84.8	89.1	83.8	85.2	81.4	85.1	93.0	539
540	95.6	94.8	94.5	97.8	94.2	95.4	91.0	90.2	95.9	96.2	95.1	98.2	95.2	94.0	540
541	13.2	12.4	11.0	18.1	10.2	13.0	11.0	14.3	17.7	6.9	13.9	11.5	13.0	18.0	541
542	86.0	86.3	85.8	84.8	84.7	85.5	80.0	88.4	88.4	86.9	86.1	92.0	88.3	81.0	542
543	18.4	17.0	11.0	27.5	12.4	17.4	11.0	21.4	22.4	10.8	15.6	13.3	16.8	15.0	543
544	39.0	34.0	42.5	48.6	48.2	42.3	22.0	23.2	34.7	27.7	41.0	34.5	32.4	28.0	544
545	53.7	48.4	62.2	61.6	56.2	56.2	33.0	40.2	49.7	45.4	50.0	47.8	46.8	27.0	545
546	27.9	35.3	37.8	39.1	34.3	34.9	38.0	45.5	47.6	46.9	47.5	53.1	48.1	53.0	546
547	91.2	95.4	92.1	89.1	92.7	92.2	92.0	80.4	79.6	87.7	82.0	85.8	83.0	75.0	547
548	43.4	36.6	32.3	37.0	32.1	36.3	63.0	29.5	25.9	19.2	18.9	13.3	21.5	53.0	548
549	33.8	28.1	38.6	42.0	24.1	33.1	39.0	25.9	29.3	23.1	26.2	19.5	25.0	14.0	549
550	11.0	7.2	15.7	10.9	13.9	11.6	16.0	30.4	37.4	40.0	42.6	43.4	38.8	64.0	550
551	54.4	63.4	59.8	65.9	63.5	61.5	53.0	38.4	55.8	50.0	55.7	58.4	51.9	34.0	551
552	27.2	32.0	30.7	22.5	28.5	28.2	42.0	55.4	46.9	50.0	47.5	54.9	50.6	68.0	552
553	25.7	19.6	17.3	17.4	16.8	19.4	18.0	11.6	10.2	6.2	9.8	6.2	8.8	12.0	553
554	43.4	37.3	44.1	44.2	47.4	43.1	59.0	18.8	16.3	16.2	18.0	10.6	16.0	24.0	554
555	50.0	44.4	48.8	56.5	46.7	49.2	27.0	26.8	36.7	30.8	35.2	28.3	31.9	16.0	555
556	88.2	84.3	81.9	81.9	78.1	82.9	93.0	72.3	73.5	71.5	59.8	57.5	67.3	68.0	556
557	36.0	47.1	45.7	48.6	32.1	42.0	72.0	2.7	4.1	5.4	4.9	4.4	4.3	13.0	557
558	59.6	58.2	53.5	53.6	54.0	55.9	64.0	50.9	59.9	60.0	64.8	50.4	57.5	76.0	558
559	42.6	33.3	35.4	43.5	32.1	37.3	30.0	25.0	29.3	18.5	24.6	23.0	24.2	16.0	559
560	58.1	45.8	45.7	55.1	38.0	48.5	36.0	44.6	51.0	53.1	56.6	45.1	50.3	25.0	560
561	77.9	74.5	71.7	73.9	77.4	75.1	85.0	51.8	51.0	42.3	45.9	38.1	46.0	80.0	561
562	72.8	78.4	74.0	74.6	74.5	75.0	79.0	44.6	44.9	44.6	50.8	48.7	46.6	54.0	562
563	25.0	24.2	21.3	24.6	18.2	22.7	27.0	89.3	83.0	88.5	86.9	87.6	86.9	88.0	563
564	58.1	50.3	53.5	63.8	37.2	52.5	56.0	54.5	59.2	53.1	52.5	40.7	52.4	57.0	564
565	11.8	5.2	10.2	15.9	8.8	10.3	11.0	10.7	17.0	13.1	14.8	18.6	14.9	12.0	565
566	67.6	73.9	81.9	76.8	83.2	76.6	77.0	51.8	51.7	70.8	59.0	57.5	58.2	28.0	566

580

Comparison of Percentage Responding True, Between the Hathaway and Monachesi
Minnesota State Sample of Ninth Grade Students and Contemporary Normal Adolescents,
Listed Separately by Sex, in Order of Decreasing Endorsement Differences

Females

Item Number	Hathaway and Monachesi	Contemporary Adolescent Females	Difference (Absolute Value)	Item Number	Hathaway and Monachesi	Contemporary Adolescent Females	Difference (Absolute Value)
73	10.0	77.1	67.1	245	14.0	35.3	21.3
70	77.0	27.6	49.4	325	20.0	41.2	21.2
101	47.0	90.7	43.7	452	15.0	36.2	21.2
427	69.0	27.5	41.5	303	28.0	49.1	21.1
93	28.0	63.1	35.1	506	18.0	39.1	21.1
338	20.0	52.0	32.0	266	45.0	66.0	21.0
3	81.0	49.1	31.9	368	38.0	58.9	20.9
22	24.0	55.0	31.0	152	68.0	47.2	20.8
229	68.0	37.8	30.2	58	51.0	30.4	20.6
4	47.0	16.9	30.1	525	39.0	59.5	20.5
442	32.0	62.1	30.1	127	43.0	63.4	20.4
457	42.0	11.9	30.1	284	28.0	48.3	20.3
223	38.0	8.0	30.0	529	68.0	88.3	20.3
557	72.0	42.0	30.0	544	22.0	42.3	20.3
413	47.0	17.1	29.9	313	74.0	53.8	20.2
69	34.0	4.2	29.8	64	38.0	58.2	20.2
488	82.0	52.4	29.6	430	74.0	94.2	20.2
438	50.0	79.2	29.2	117	35.0	55.0	20.0
92	55.0	26.5	28.5	247	13.0	33.0	20.0
239	30.0	58.2	28.2	428	49.0	29.1	19.9
316	42.0	69.8	27.8	45	68.0	87.8	19.8
11	16.0	43.7	27.7	311	9.0	28.5	19.5
373	62.0	34.6	27.4	322	16.0	35.5	19.5
326	22.0	49.1	27.1	537	24.0	4.5	19.5
39	45.0	71.8	26.8	492	78.0	58.6	19.4
548	63.0	36.3	26.7	222	41.0	60.1	19.1
490	36.0	9.4	26.6	21	40.0	59.0	19.0
317	23.0	49.5	26.5	38	11.0	30.0	19.0
453	20.0	45.3	25.3	516	61.0	80.0	19.0
415	30.0	54.7	24.7	426	38.0	56.9	18.9
304	65.0	40.5	24.5	241	48.0	66.7	18.7
397	36.0	60.5	24.5	13	9.0	27.6	18.6
446	11.0	35.5	24.5	226	54.0	72.6	18.6
95	90.0	65.6	24.4	109	63.0	81.5	18.5
149	47.0	71.3	24.3	135	29.0	47.5	18.5
362	25.0	49.3	24.3	369	61.0	79.5	18.5
41	22.0	45.9	23.9	282	60.0	78.4	18.4
545	33.0	56.2	23.2	409	46.0	64.3	18.3
475	53.0	76.1	23.1	78	44.0	62.2	18.2
400	36.0	58.6	22.6	481	55.0	73.2	18.2
20	93.0	70.5	22.5	87	42.0	23.9	18.1
310	97.0	74.5	22.5	398	20.0	37.8	17.8
524	61.0	83.5	22.5	96	57.0	39.4	17.6
500	58.0	35.7	22.3	12	78.0	60.5	17.5
15	45.0	67.3	22.3	164	80.0	62.5	17.5
250	34.0	56.2	22.2	203	47.0	29.5	17.5
555	27.0	49.2	22.2	285	77.0	94.5	17.5
179	12.0	33.6	21.6	469	29.0	46.5	17.5
30	73.0	94.4	21.4	124	49.0	66.4	17.4
233	22.0	43.3	21.3	7	84.0	66.7	17.3

Comparison of Percentage Responding True, Between the Hathaway and Monachesi
Minnesota State Sample of Ninth Grade Students and Contemporary Normal Adolescents,
Listed Separately by Sex, in Order of Decreasing Endorsement Differences

Females

Item Number	Hathaway and Monachesi	Contemporary Adolescent Females	Difference (Absolute Value)	Item Number	Hathaway and Monachesi	Contemporary Adolescent Females	Difference (Absolute Value)
158	39.0	56.2	17.2	423	67.0	54.1	12.9
357	31.0	48.2	17.2	536	60.0	72.9	12.9
259	22.0	39.1	17.1	157	30.0	42.7	12.7
459	11.0	27.8	16.8	271	41.0	28.4	12.6
6	64.0	47.3	16.7	126	73.0	60.5	12.5
538	50.0	33.3	16.7	298	28.0	40.5	12.5
308	45.0	61.5	16.5	341	8.0	20.5	12.5
254	51.0	34.7	16.3	560	36.0	48.5	12.5
314	47.0	63.2	16.2	301	7.0	19.4	12.4
208	55.0	71.1	16.1	59	46.0	58.3	12.3
289	59.0	75.1	16.1	253	66.0	78.1	12.1
333	9.0	25.0	16.0	320	12.0	24.0	12.0
554	59.0	43.1	15.9	144	17.0	5.1	11.9
329	31.0	15.1	15.9	195	77.0	88.9	11.9
307	26.0	41.8	15.8	40	32.0	43.8	11.8
132	64.0	48.3	15.7	86	25.0	36.8	11.8
306	91.0	75.3	15.7	406	36.0	47.8	11.8
115	89.0	73.4	15.6	318	88.0	76.3	11.7
435	54.0	38.4	15.6	204	33.0	21.6	11.4
99	67.0	82.6	15.6	441	44.0	32.6	11.4
299	23.0	38.6	15.6	386	31.0	42.4	11.4
507	29.0	44.6	15.6	91	29.0	17.7	11.3
484	26.0	41.5	15.5	497	92.0	80.8	11.2
82	17.0	32.4	15.4	392	33.0	21.9	11.1
156	7.0	22.4	15.4	212	21.0	32.1	11.1
172	52.0	36.9	15.1	332	20.0	31.1	11.1
530	53.0	37.9	15.1	183	25.0	36.0	11.0
24	13.0	27.9	14.9	361	30.0	41.0	11.0
290	14.0	28.9	14.9	480	32.0	21.1	10.9
411	22.0	36.9	14.9	182	5.0	15.9	10.9
270	33.0	47.6	14.6	364	16.0	26.9	10.9
349	20.0	34.4	14.4	283	49.0	38.2	10.8
111	60.0	45.9	14.1	390	54.0	64.7	10.7
26	40.0	54.1	14.1	48	6.0	16.6	10.6
336	37.0	51.1	14.1	489	53.0	63.4	10.4
137	89.0	75.0	14.0	376	97.0	86.7	10.3
238	40.0	54.0	14.0	53	14.0	3.8	10.2
145	22.0	35.9	13.9	366	8.0	18.2	10.2
79	38.0	24.2	13.8	389	27.0	37.2	10.2
407	75.0	61.2	13.8	160	69.0	58.9	10.1
552	42.0	28.2	13.8	479	82.0	71.9	10.1
97	34.0	47.5	13.5	556	93.0	82.9	10.1
134	73.0	86.5	13.5	447	45.0	55.1	10.1
503	60.0	46.6	13.4	527	91.0	81.0	10.0
486	75.0	88.4	13.4	561	85.0	75.1	9.9
534	43.0	56.4	13.4	27	21.0	11.1	9.9
371	66.0	52.8	13.2	32	24.0	33.9	9.9
380	81.0	67.9	13.1	255	23.0	32.9	9.9
171	49.0	62.1	13.1	465	59.0	68.9	9.9
510	21.0	8.0	13.0	379	70.0	60.2	9.8

Comparison of Percentage Responding True, Between the Hathaway and Monachesi
Minnesota State Sample of Ninth Grade Students and Contemporary Normal Adolescents,
Listed Separately by Sex, in Order of Decreasing Endorsement Differences

Females

Item Number	Hathaway and Monachesi	Contemporary Adolescent Females	Difference (Absolute Value)	Item Number	Hathaway and Monachesi	Contemporary Adolescent Females	Difference (Absolute Value)
263	17.0	26.8	9.8	19	38.0	30.1	7.9
485	28.0	37.8	9.8	105	92.0	84.1	7.9
190	78.0	68.3	9.7	402	46.0	38.1	7.9
268	75.0	84.7	9.7	224	26.0	33.9	7.9
502	69.0	78.7	9.7	458	17.0	24.9	7.9
120	85.0	75.4	9.6	221	51.0	43.3	7.7
315	4.0	13.6	9.6	243	88.0	80.3	7.7
521	47.0	56.6	9.6	260	21.0	13.3	7.7
71	72.0	81.5	9.5	244	38.0	45.7	7.7
280	32.0	41.4	9.4	129	69.0	61.4	7.6
520	65.0	55.7	9.3	166	52.0	44.4	7.6
215	5.0	14.3	9.3	339	3.0	10.6	7.6
5	25.0	34.2	9.2	147	40.0	47.6	7.6
231	25.0	34.2	9.2	128	70.0	62.5	7.5
328	21.0	30.2	9.2	340	74.0	81.5	7.5
8	85.0	76.0	9.0	347	91.0	83.5	7.5
62	36.0	45.0	9.0	414	33.0	40.5	7.5
154	89.0	80.0	9.0	36	57.0	49.6	7.4
436	72.0	81.0	9.0	61	5.0	12.4	7.4
450	94.0	85.1	8.9	403	92.0	84.7	7.3
532	84.0	75.1	8.9	498	60.0	52.7	7.3
76	4.0	12.9	8.9	331	2.0	9.3	7.3
410	39.0	47.9	8.9	559	30.0	37.3	7.3
343	43.0	34.2	8.8	139	27.0	19.8	7.2
418	50.0	58.8	8.8	142	57.0	64.1	7.1
425	66.0	74.8	8.8	337	23.0	30.1	7.1
84	44.0	52.7	8.7	163	70.0	63.0	7.0
408	68.0	76.7	8.7	256	14.0	21.0	7.0
523	20.0	28.7	8.7	495	47.0	54.0	7.0
295	65.0	56.4	8.6	395	48.0	41.2	6.8
342	7.0	15.6	8.6	235	30.0	36.8	6.8
18	75.0	83.5	8.5	396	37.0	43.8	6.8
464	81.0	72.5	8.5	416	67.0	73.8	6.8
551	53.0	61.5	8.5	448	37.0	43.8	6.8
165	65.0	73.4	8.4	487	33.0	39.8	6.8
518	42.0	50.4	8.4	1	11.0	4.3	6.7
107	98.0	89.7	8.3	252	4.0	10.7	6.7
274	60.0	51.7	8.3	514	5.0	11.7	6.7
470	26.0	17.7	8.3	334	27.0	20.4	6.6
466	89.0	80.8	8.2	63	82.0	88.6	6.6
216	7.0	15.2	8.2	391	77.0	83.6	6.6
382	64.0	72.2	8.2	509	32.0	38.6	6.6
511	33.0	41.2	8.2	52	14.0	20.5	6.5
262	42.0	33.9	8.1	305	14.0	20.5	6.5
493	58.0	49.9	8.1	378	68.0	61.6	6.4
539	53.0	44.9	8.1	50	12.0	5.6	6.4
558	64.0	55.9	8.1	122	83.0	89.4	6.4
432	13.0	21.1	8.1	372	72.0	78.4	6.4
358	28.0	36.0	8.0	543	11.0	17.4	6.4
440	78.0	86.0	8.0	385	29.0	22.7	6.3

Comparison of Percentage Responding True, Between the Hathaway and Monachesi
Minnesota State Sample of Ninth Grade Students and Contemporary Normal Adolescents,
Listed Separately by Sex, in Order of Decreasing Endorsement Differences

Females

Item Number	Hathaway and Monachesi	Contemporary Adolescent Females	Difference (Absolute Value)	Item Number	Hathaway and Monachesi	Contemporary Adolescent Females	Difference (Absolute Value)
174	69.0	75.3	6.3	522	34.0	29.4	4.6
277	15.0	21.3	6.3	213	12.0	7.4	4.6
350	29.0	35.3	6.3	35	6.0	10.6	4.6
420	12.0	5.8	6.2	177	98.0	93.5	4.5
140	88.0	81.9	6.1	246	1.0	5.5	4.5
184	5.0	11.1	6.1	399	51.0	46.5	4.5
16	7.0	13.0	6.0	474	81.0	85.5	4.5
77	87.0	81.0	6.0	240	7.0	2.6	4.4
264	20.0	26.0	6.0	550	16.0	11.6	4.4
463	91.0	85.1	5.9	46	72.0	76.4	4.4
549	39.0	33.1	5.9	348	49.0	53.4	4.4
281	78.0	72.2	5.8	540	91.0	95.4	4.4
477	44.0	38.2	5.8	533	79.0	74.7	4.3
504	35.0	40.8	5.8	563	27.0	22.7	4.3
136	61.0	55.3	5.7	460	83.0	87.3	4.3
505	29.0	34.7	5.7	225	98.0	93.8	4.2
496	73.0	67.4	5.6	513	53.0	48.8	4.2
363	11.0	5.4	5.6	293	3.0	7.2	4.2
43	7.0	12.6	5.6	422	9.0	13.2	4.2
102	49.0	54.6	5.6	377	19.0	23.2	4.2
31	11.0	16.5	5.5	193	84.0	79.9	4.1
141	64.0	69.5	5.5	381	32.0	27.9	4.1
148	48.0	53.5	5.5	451	86.0	81.9	4.1
162	33.0	38.5	5.5	365	11.0	6.9	4.1
412	63.0	57.5	5.5	108	8.0	12.0	4.0
431	32.0	37.5	5.5	294	91.0	87.0	4.0
467	31.0	36.5	5.5	321	60.0	64.0	4.0
542	80.0	85.5	5.5	352	36.0	32.0	4.0
468	75.0	69.6	5.4	517	4.0	8.0	4.0
456	15.0	9.6	5.4	562	79.0	75.0	4.0
49	1.0	6.4	5.4	168	2.0	5.9	3.9
327	73.0	78.4	5.4	297	36.0	39.9	3.9
251	10.0	15.3	5.3	335	25.0	28.9	3.9
2	99.0	93.8	5.2	175	78.0	74.2	3.8
94	49.0	43.8	5.2	501	62.0	58.2	3.8
176	47.0	41.8	5.2	360	5.0	8.8	3.8
287	32.0	37.2	5.2	236	16.0	19.8	3.8
88	96.0	90.9	5.1	267	40.0	43.8	3.8
387	20.0	14.9	5.1	476	26.0	22.3	3.7
200	5.0	10.1	5.1	275	5.0	1.3	3.7
68	82.0	77.0	5.0	44	7.0	10.7	3.7
66	11.0	15.9	4.9	72	8.0	11.7	3.7
185	95.0	90.2	4.8	359	48.0	51.7	3.7
324	29.0	24.2	4.8	214	49.0	45.4	3.6
34	13.0	8.2	4.8	473	11.0	14.6	3.6
205	1.0	5.8	4.8	9	89.0	92.6	3.6
404	58.0	62.8	4.8	170	21.0	24.6	3.6
207	96.0	91.3	4.7	323	31.0	34.6	3.6
28	28.0	32.7	4.7	104	5.0	8.5	3.5
17	94.0	89.4	4.6	217	60.0	63.5	3.5

584

Comparison of Percentage Responding True, Between the Hathaway and Monachesi
Minnesota State Sample of Ninth Grade Students and Contemporary Normal Adolescents,
Listed Separately by Sex, in Order of Decreasing Endorsement Differences

Females

Item Number	Hathaway and Monachesi	Contemporary Adolescent Females	Difference (Absolute Value)		Item Number	Hathaway and Monachesi	Contemporary Adolescent Females	Difference (Absolute Value)
265	12.0	15.5	3.5		374	59.0	61.2	2.2
478	67.0	63.5	3.5		178	94.0	91.9	2.1
491	19.0	15.5	3.5		370	82.0	79.9	2.1
535	5.0	8.5	3.5		51	90.0	88.0	2.0
564	56.0	52.5	3.5		138	53.0	55.0	2.0
186	29.0	25.6	3.4		173	80.0	78.0	2.0
130	80.0	83.4	3.4		319	39.0	41.0	2.0
269	14.0	17.4	3.4		375	37.0	35.0	2.0
153	92.0	88.7	3.3		401	77.0	79.0	2.0
201	54.0	50.7	3.3		541	11.0	13.0	2.0
483	88.0	84.7	3.3		106	21.0	19.1	1.9
354	6.0	9.3	3.3		429	31.0	29.1	1.9
230	64.0	67.3	3.3		209	8.0	6.1	1.9
421	29.0	25.8	3.2		123	2.0	3.9	1.9
169	88.0	91.2	3.2		150	89.0	90.9	1.9
278	57.0	60.2	3.2		248	60.0	61.9	1.9
546	38.0	34.9	3.1		155	54.0	52.2	1.8
356	25.0	28.1	3.1		273	4.0	5.8	1.8
47	11.0	14.0	3.0		33	37.0	38.8	1.8
472	24.0	21.0	3.0		249	72.0	73.8	1.8
353	54.0	51.1	2.9		531	41.0	42.8	1.8
202	4.0	6.9	2.9		54	95.0	93.3	1.7
234	60.0	57.2	2.8		118	8.0	9.7	1.7
482	32.0	29.2	2.8		279	12.0	13.7	1.7
10	2.0	4.8	2.8		519	1.0	2.7	1.7
211	2.0	4.8	2.8		232	19.0	20.7	1.7
89	47.0	49.8	2.8		437	51.0	52.7	1.7
261	45.0	42.3	2.7		100	74.0	72.4	1.6
114	8.0	10.7	2.7		189	8.0	6.4	1.6
57	74.0	76.7	2.7		384	43.0	44.6	1.6
296	82.0	84.7	2.7		42	4.0	5.5	1.5
288	0.0	2.6	2.6		119	72.0	73.5	1.5
292	30.0	32.6	2.6		188	64.0	62.5	1.5
81	29.0	26.5	2.5		219	7.0	5.5	1.5
455	38.0	35.5	2.5		228	73.0	71.5	1.5
198	37.0	34.6	2.4		237	22.0	20.5	1.5
220	97.0	94.6	2.4		291	3.0	4.5	1.5
383	47.0	44.6	2.4		210	3.0	1.6	1.4
14	4.0	6.4	2.4		218	4.0	2.6	1.4
85	5.0	7.4	2.4		388	26.0	27.4	1.4
439	46.0	43.7	2.3		417	31.0	32.4	1.4
65	95.0	92.8	2.2		553	18.0	19.4	1.4
80	45.0	42.8	2.2		25	44.0	42.7	1.3
187	88.0	85.8	2.2		67	55.0	53.7	1.3
330	87.0	84.8	2.2		133	90.0	88.7	1.3
499	83.0	80.8	2.2		508	97.0	95.7	1.3
227	13.0	15.2	2.2		23	2.0	3.3	1.3
419	6.0	8.2	2.2		37	88.0	89.3	1.3
434	11.0	13.2	2.2		257	79.0	80.3	1.3
191	33.0	35.2	2.2		462	89.0	90.3	1.3

Comparison of Percentage Responding True, Between the Hathaway and Monachesi
Minnesota State Sample of Ninth Grade Students and Contemporary Normal Adolescents,
Listed Separately by Sex, in Order of Decreasing Endorsement Differences

Females

Item Number	Hathaway and Monachesi	Contemporary Adolescent Females	Difference (Absolute Value)	Item Number	Hathaway and Monachesi	Contemporary Adolescent Females	Difference (Absolute Value)
194	9.0	7.8	1.2	449	82.0	81.8	0.2
351	11.0	9.8	1.2	56	2.0	2.2	0.2
161	7.0	8.2	1.2	393	1.0	1.2	0.2
110	17.0	18.2	1.2	471	8.0	8.2	0.2
309	80.0	81.2	1.2	103	81.0	81.2	0.2
367	55.0	56.2	1.2	547	92.0	92.2	0.2
405	91.0	92.2	1.2	344	29.0	28.9	0.1
272	96.0	97.1	1.1	121	7.0	6.9	0.1
394	65.0	66.1	1.1	98	75.0	75.1	0.1
83	99.0	98.0	1.0	167	19.0	19.1	0.1
146	14.0	13.0	1.0	494	22.0	22.1	0.1
159	13.0	14.0	1.0	180	54.0	54.0	0.0
443	44.0	45.0	1.0	199	80.0	80.0	0.0
55	74.0	73.1	0.9	286	9.0	9.0	0.0
346	29.0	28.1	0.9	300	13.0	13.0	0.0
151	1.0	0.1	0.9	528	68.0	68.0	0.0
192	92.0	92.9	0.9				
29	6.0	6.8	0.8				
143	37.0	36.3	0.7				
445	93.0	92.3	0.7				
512	4.0	3.3	0.7				
565	11.0	10.3	0.7				
113	95.0	95.7	0.7				
433	21.0	20.4	0.6				
444	43.0	42.4	0.6				
454	24.0	23.4	0.6				
90	96.0	96.5	0.5				
125	6.0	6.5	0.5				
196	98.0	97.5	0.5				
276	95.0	94.5	0.5				
312	6.0	6.5	0.5				
345	32.0	31.5	0.5				
355	15.0	14.5	0.5				
461	39.0	38.5	0.5				
526	7.0	7.5	0.5				
74	70.0	69.6	0.4				
206	23.0	22.6	0.4				
302	91.0	90.6	0.4				
566	77.0	76.6	0.4				
116	16.0	15.6	0.4				
181	83.0	83.4	0.4				
258	97.0	97.4	0.4				
515	97.0	97.4	0.4				
424	31.0	30.7	0.3				
197	1.0	0.7	0.3				
75	99.0	99.3	0.3				
112	77.0	77.3	0.3				
131	57.0	57.3	0.3				
60	96.0	95.8	0.2				
242	76.0	75.8	0.2				

Comparison of Percentage Responding True, Between the Hathaway and Monachesi
Minnesota State Sample of Ninth Grade Students and Contemporary Normal Adolescents,
Listed Separately by Sex, in Order of Decreasing Endorsement Differences

Males

Item Number	Hathaway and Monachesi	Contemporary Adolescent Males	Difference (Absolute Value)	Item Number	Hathaway and Monachesi	Contemporary Adolescent Males	Difference (Absolute Value)
73	18.0	79.6	61.6	155	26.0	47.3	21.3
69	50.0	3.8	46.2	229	50.0	28.8	21.2
537	63.0	27.9	35.1	400	49.0	69.6	20.6
223	89.0	55.0	34.0	250	38.0	58.5	20.5
561	80.0	46.0	34.0	165	48.0	68.3	20.3
452	21.0	54.5	33.5	310	88.0	67.8	20.2
457	47.0	14.7	32.3	368	28.0	48.2	20.2
548	53.0	21.5	31.5	529	41.0	61.2	20.2
1	83.0	51.9	31.1	428	44.0	24.0	20.0
566	28.0	58.2	30.2	516	51.0	71.0	20.0
329	52.0	22.3	29.7	467	17.0	37.0	20.0
11	13.0	42.6	29.6	545	27.0	46.8	19.8
239	16.0	45.4	29.4	416	48.0	67.5	19.5
413	49.0	19.9	29.1	262	69.0	49.7	19.3
338	22.0	51.1	29.1	144	53.0	33.8	19.2
438	51.0	79.0	28.0	349	17.0	36.2	19.2
365	38.0	10.1	27.9	313	72.0	52.9	19.1
39	48.0	75.8	27.8	226	44.0	63.0	19.0
266	28.0	55.8	27.8	135	41.0	59.9	18.9
446	34.0	61.7	27.7	301	6.0	24.7	18.7
373	71.0	44.1	26.9	111	47.0	28.4	18.6
20	90.0	63.3	26.7	48	0.0	18.6	18.6
81	76.0	49.7	26.3	62	20.0	38.6	18.6
93	43.0	68.8	25.8	91	48.0	29.5	18.5
441	16.0	41.8	25.8	558	76.0	57.5	18.5
79	74.0	48.4	25.6	245	17.0	35.4	18.4
219	57.0	31.7	25.3	406	43.0	61.4	18.4
560	25.0	50.3	25.3	193	92.0	73.7	18.3
550	64.0	38.8	25.2	52	12.0	30.3	18.3
506	13.0	38.1	25.1	120	91.0	72.8	18.2
397	24.0	49.0	25.0	198	66.0	47.9	18.1
430	65.0	89.6	24.6	499	46.0	64.1	18.1
96	70.0	45.8	24.2	231	29.0	47.0	18.0
442	24.0	48.2	24.2	152	74.0	56.1	17.9
425	41.0	65.2	24.2	551	34.0	51.9	17.9
3	69.0	44.9	24.1	525	29.0	46.8	17.8
482	57.0	32.9	24.1	341	7.0	24.7	17.7
362	15.0	38.8	23.8	30	76.0	93.6	17.6
322	15.0	38.6	23.6	552	68.0	50.6	17.4
435	15.0	38.6	23.6	475	53.0	70.4	17.4
282	46.0	69.4	23.4	233	35.0	52.4	17.4
70	38.0	15.1	22.9	292	28.0	45.4	17.4
384	37.0	59.3	22.3	484	26.0	43.3	17.3
317	15.0	37.2	22.2	472	21.0	38.3	17.3
6	65.0	43.3	21.7	24	8.0	25.0	17.0
415	44.0	65.7	21.7	13	10.0	26.9	16.9
195	68.0	89.7	21.7	350	10.0	26.9	16.9
277	26.0	47.4	21.4	40	21.0	37.8	16.8
284	25.0	46.3	21.3	259	26.0	42.6	16.6
426	47.0	68.3	21.3	281	84.0	67.6	16.4

Comparison of Percentage Responding True, Between the Hathaway and Monachesi
Minnesota State Sample of Ninth Grade Students and Contemporary Normal Adolescents,
Listed Separately by Sex, in Order of Decreasing Endorsement Differences

Males

Item Number	Hathaway and Monachesi	Contemporary Adolescent Males	Difference (Absolute Value)	Item Number	Hathaway and Monachesi	Contemporary Adolescent Males	Difference (Absolute Value)
489	33.0	49.4	16.4	299	26.0	38.3	12.3
95	75.0	59.0	16.0	304	48.0	35.9	12.1
283	79.0	63.1	15.9	105	82.0	69.9	12.1
524	71.0	86.9	15.9	179	11.0	23.1	12.1
555	16.0	31.9	15.9	311	27.0	39.1	12.1
320	25.0	40.9	15.9	303	25.0	37.0	12.0
507	30.0	45.7	15.7	59	55.0	67.0	12.0
316	52.0	67.6	15.6	382	50.0	62.0	12.0
58	50.0	34.5	15.5	449	60.0	72.0	12.0
470	23.0	7.5	15.5	308	40.0	51.9	11.9
28	36.0	51.4	15.4	208	48.0	59.9	11.9
498	69.0	53.8	15.2	289	61.0	72.9	11.9
129	63.0	47.9	15.1	453	40.0	51.8	11.8
333	8.0	23.1	15.1	22	13.0	24.7	11.7
404	49.0	64.1	15.1	21	37.0	48.7	11.7
101	74.0	88.9	14.9	206	14.0	25.6	11.6
127	43.0	57.9	14.9	38	29.0	40.5	11.5
236	4.0	18.9	14.9	343	37.0	25.6	11.4
27	26.0	11.5	14.5	68	84.0	72.6	11.4
346	15.0	29.5	14.5	162	33.0	44.4	11.4
463	38.0	23.6	14.4	297	45.0	33.7	11.3
97	34.0	48.4	14.4	414	26.0	37.3	11.3
364	15.0	29.3	14.3	481	54.0	65.2	11.2
321	28.0	42.3	14.3	124	64.0	75.2	11.2
267	33.0	47.3	14.3	409	45.0	56.1	11.1
269	19.0	33.3	14.3	361	16.0	27.1	11.1
372	63.0	77.2	14.2	325	19.0	30.0	11.0
390	45.0	59.1	14.1	241	52.0	63.0	11.0
247	10.0	23.9	13.9	347	86.0	75.0	11.0
64	41.0	54.8	13.8	549	14.0	25.0	11.0
315	4.0	17.8	13.8	132	24.0	13.1	10.9
260	35.0	21.3	13.7	471	25.0	14.1	10.9
171	38.0	51.6	13.6	486	84.0	94.9	10.9
278	33.0	46.6	13.6	501	59.0	69.9	10.9
117	40.0	53.5	13.5	138	25.0	35.9	10.9
407	82.0	68.6	13.4	522	76.0	65.2	10.8
8	89.0	75.6	13.4	109	62.0	72.8	10.8
290	17.0	30.4	13.4	444	32.0	42.8	10.8
222	51.0	64.3	13.3	340	59.0	69.7	10.7
459	19.0	31.9	12.9	336	37.0	47.6	10.6
386	36.0	48.9	12.9	439	28.0	38.6	10.6
199	64.0	76.9	12.9	479	85.0	74.5	10.5
16	4.0	16.8	12.8	398	24.0	34.3	10.3
41	25.0	37.7	12.7	408	52.0	62.3	10.3
306	90.0	77.4	12.6	437	52.0	62.3	10.3
271	49.0	36.4	12.6	469	39.0	49.2	10.2
87	16.0	3.4	12.6	102	39.0	49.2	10.2
332	26.0	38.6	12.6	170	53.0	42.9	10.1
500	59.0	46.5	12.5	234	49.0	59.1	10.1
536	57.0	69.4	12.4	485	36.0	46.0	10.0

Comparison of Percentage Responding True, Between the Hathaway and Monachesi
Minnesota State Sample of Ninth Grade Students and Contemporary Normal Adolescents,
Listed Separately by Sex, in Order of Decreasing Endorsement Differences

Males

Item Number	Hathaway and Monachesi	Contemporary Adolescent Males	Difference (Absolute Value)	Item Number	Hathaway and Monachesi	Contemporary Adolescent Males	Difference (Absolute Value)
45	75.0	84.9	9.9	429	28.0	20.2	7.8
215	4.0	13.8	9.8	182	5.0	12.8	7.8
264	34.0	43.8	9.8	391	48.0	55.8	7.8
345	16.0	25.8	9.8	33	36.0	43.8	7.8
122	81.0	90.7	9.7	448	24.0	31.7	7.7
515	85.0	94.7	9.7	462	82.0	89.7	7.7
225	63.0	72.6	9.6	137	89.0	81.4	7.6
287	56.0	46.5	9.5	261	19.0	11.4	7.6
186	29.0	19.6	9.4	156	16.0	23.6	7.6
78	17.0	26.4	9.4	32	20.0	27.6	7.6
270	59.0	49.7	9.3	531	27.0	34.5	7.5
380	76.0	66.7	9.3	562	54.0	46.6	7.4
257	78.0	87.3	9.3	360	2.0	9.3	7.3
513	59.0	49.8	9.2	542	81.0	88.3	7.3
510	13.0	3.8	9.2	450	79.0	71.8	7.2
240	19.0	9.8	9.2	309	86.0	78.8	7.2
255	18.0	27.2	9.2	55	79.0	71.8	7.2
363	17.0	7.9	9.1	82	16.0	23.2	7.2
85	1.0	10.1	9.1	139	17.0	24.2	7.2
121	1.0	10.1	9.1	505	43.0	35.9	7.1
323	30.0	39.1	9.1	487	23.0	30.1	7.1
149	3.0	12.0	9.0	366	9.0	16.0	7.0
476	15.0	24.0	9.0	57	76.0	69.1	6.9
251	7.0	15.9	8.9	35	8.0	14.9	6.9
410	57.0	65.9	8.9	72	4.0	10.9	6.9
557	13.0	4.3	8.7	376	93.0	86.2	6.8
509	29.0	37.7	8.7	242	86.0	79.2	6.8
305	11.0	19.7	8.7	326	14.0	20.8	6.8
164	76.0	67.5	8.5	511	27.0	33.8	6.8
274	72.0	63.5	8.5	254	58.0	51.3	6.7
503	44.0	52.4	8.4	190	88.0	81.3	6.7
353	56.0	64.4	8.4	454	50.0	43.3	6.7
36	61.0	52.7	8.3	145	53.0	59.6	6.6
176	78.0	69.7	8.3	337	21.0	27.6	6.6
490	19.0	10.7	8.3	465	56.0	62.5	6.5
76	4.0	12.3	8.3	331	6.0	12.5	6.5
108	8.0	16.3	8.3	214	62.0	55.6	6.4
12	79.0	70.8	8.2	396	33.0	39.4	6.4
154	83.0	74.8	8.2	356	21.0	27.4	6.4
146	29.0	20.8	8.2	115	84.0	77.7	6.3
559	16.0	24.2	8.2	451	88.0	81.7	6.3
530	32.0	23.9	8.1	514	19.0	12.7	6.3
142	64.0	55.9	8.1	183	38.0	44.2	6.2
554	24.0	16.0	8.0	263	21.0	27.2	6.2
447	51.0	59.0	8.0	169	96.0	89.9	6.1
237	18.0	26.0	8.0	434	50.0	43.9	6.1
547	75.0	83.0	8.0	276	88.0	81.9	6.1
539	93.0	85.1	7.9	203	20.0	13.9	6.1
427	21.0	13.1	7.9	256	16.0	22.1	6.1
7	91.0	83.2	7.8	493	53.0	47.0	6.0

Comparison of Percentage Responding True, Between the Hathaway and Monachesi
Minnesota State Sample of Ninth Grade Students and Contemporary Normal Adolescents,
Listed Separately by Sex, in Order of Decreasing Endorsement Differences

Males

Item Number	Hathaway and Monachesi	Contemporary Adolescent Males	Difference (Absolute Value)	Item Number	Hathaway and Monachesi	Contemporary Adolescent Males	Difference (Absolute Value)
94	39.0	45.0	6.0	157	42.0	46.6	4.6
488	53.0	47.1	5.9	98	72.0	76.6	4.6
175	86.0	80.1	5.9	43	7.0	11.5	4.5
502	67.0	72.8	5.8	352	21.0	25.5	4.5
280	42.0	47.8	5.8	296	71.0	66.5	4.5
140	62.0	67.8	5.8	419	14.0	9.5	4.5
494	12.0	17.8	5.8	403	85.0	80.6	4.4
46	85.0	79.3	5.7	118	32.0	27.6	4.4
232	28.0	22.3	5.7	544	28.0	32.4	4.4
200	7.0	12.7	5.7	405	96.0	91.7	4.3
100	61.0	66.7	5.7	153	89.0	93.3	4.3
334	30.0	24.4	5.6	159	12.0	16.3	4.3
244	45.0	50.6	5.6	243	83.0	78.8	4.2
314	61.0	66.5	5.5	412	77.0	72.8	4.2
253	61.0	66.5	5.5	394	60.0	55.8	4.2
379	77.0	71.5	5.5	204	17.0	12.8	4.2
136	60.0	54.5	5.5	523	46.0	50.2	4.2
88	96.0	90.5	5.5	18	78.0	82.2	4.2
217	45.0	50.5	5.5	358	41.0	36.9	4.1
374	52.0	57.5	5.5	495	62.0	57.9	4.1
181	73.0	78.5	5.5	456	24.0	19.9	4.1
174	83.0	77.6	5.4	300	66.0	61.9	4.1
468	57.0	51.6	5.4	492	42.0	38.0	4.0
460	76.0	81.4	5.4	134	76.0	80.0	4.0
473	18.0	23.4	5.4	458	29.0	33.0	4.0
196	100	94.7	5.3	399	57.0	53.0	4.0
431	26.0	31.3	5.3	110	22.0	26.0	4.0
119	62.0	67.3	5.3	512	5.0	9.0	4.0
126	36.0	30.8	5.2	339	4.0	7.9	3.9
188	61.0	55.9	5.1	29	2.0	5.9	3.9
307	29.0	34.1	5.1	84	48.0	51.9	3.9
335	22.0	27.1	5.1	371	62.0	58.2	3.8
520	67.0	62.0	5.0	324	31.0	27.2	3.8
77	17.0	12.0	5.0	483	80.0	83.8	3.8
9	87.0	92.0	5.0	461	44.0	47.8	3.8
541	18.0	13.0	5.0	527	88.0	84.3	3.7
417	47.0	42.0	5.0	357	33.0	36.7	3.7
318	82.0	77.1	4.9	328	24.0	27.7	3.7
546	53.0	48.1	4.9	436	74.0	77.7	3.7
184	5.0	9.9	4.9	342	19.0	15.4	3.6
359	36.0	40.9	4.9	23	5.0	1.4	3.6
508	88.0	92.9	4.9	418	39.0	42.6	3.6
519	8.0	3.2	4.8	464	75.0	71.5	3.5
107	93.0	88.3	4.7	49	8.0	11.5	3.5
385	15.0	10.3	4.7	150	89.0	92.5	3.5
25	24.0	28.7	4.7	194	8.0	4.5	3.5
466	86.0	81.4	4.6	44	2.0	5.4	3.4
166	35.0	30.4	4.6	354	3.0	6.4	3.4
564	57.0	52.4	4.6	312	7.0	10.4	3.4
302	91.0	86.4	4.6	474	82.0	85.4	3.4

Comparison of Percentage Responding True, Between the Hathaway and Monachesi
Minnesota State Sample of Ninth Grade Students and Contemporary Normal Adolescents,
Listed Separately by Sex, in Order of Decreasing Endorsement Differences

Males

Item Number	Hathaway and Monachesi	Contemporary Adolescent Males	Difference (Absolute Value)	Item Number	Hathaway and Monachesi	Contemporary Adolescent Males	Difference (Absolute Value)
53	12.0	8.7	3.3	160	64.0	66.3	2.3
158	10.0	13.3	3.3	532	85.0	87.3	2.3
355	10.0	13.3	3.3	235	39.0	41.3	2.3
66	14.0	17.3	3.3	295	27.0	24.8	2.2
51	85.0	88.3	3.3	248	53.0	50.8	2.2
143	27.0	30.3	3.3	104	9.0	11.2	2.2
180	53.0	56.3	3.3	197	2.0	4.2	2.2
37	87.0	83.8	3.2	327	73.0	75.2	2.2
258	96.0	92.8	3.2	112	83.0	80.9	2.1
553	12.0	8.8	3.2	517	9.0	6.9	2.1
128	76.0	79.2	3.2	99	75.0	77.1	2.1
75	96.0	99.2	3.2	133	82.0	84.1	2.1
26	56.0	52.9	3.1	268	78.0	76.0	2.0
395	48.0	44.9	3.1	319	51.0	49.0	2.0
31	8.0	11.1	3.1	526	11.0	9.0	2.0
125	2.0	5.1	3.1	114	8.0	9.9	1.9
402	27.0	30.1	3.1	367	76.0	77.9	1.9
298	53.0	50.0	3.0	238	52.0	50.2	1.8
212	23.0	26.0	3.0	89	63.0	61.2	1.8
521	59.0	62.0	3.0	543	15.0	16.8	1.8
224	30.0	33.0	3.0	17	90.0	91.8	1.8
420	12.0	9.1	2.9	201	52.0	53.8	1.8
565	12.0	14.9	2.9	383	42.0	43.8	1.8
265	20.0	22.9	2.9	228	74.0	75.8	1.8
497	93.0	90.2	2.8	440	85.0	83.3	1.7
177	93.0	90.2	2.8	67	49.0	47.3	1.7
34	3.0	5.8	2.8	424	40.0	38.3	1.7
86	23.0	25.8	2.8	209	10.0	8.3	1.7
2	94.0	96.8	2.8	19	37.0	35.4	1.6
375	27.0	29.8	2.8	496	79.0	77.4	1.6
480	15.0	12.3	2.7	279	21.0	19.4	1.6
141	64.0	66.7	2.7	189	8.0	6.4	1.6
221	67.0	64.4	2.6	116	29.0	30.6	1.6
421	29.0	26.4	2.6	344	28.0	29.6	1.6
151	4.0	1.4	2.6	71	82.0	83.5	1.5
4	4.0	6.6	2.6	252	11.0	12.5	1.5
15	62.0	64.6	2.6	173	65.0	63.5	1.5
411	27.0	29.5	2.5	351	8.0	9.5	1.5
213	11.0	8.5	2.5	381	33.0	31.6	1.4
275	6.0	3.5	2.5	113	94.0	92.6	1.4
10	5.0	7.5	2.5	60	96.0	94.6	1.4
393	6.0	3.5	2.5	211	2.0	3.4	1.4
65	95.0	92.6	2.4	14	6.0	7.4	1.4
47	9.0	11.4	2.4	285	94.0	95.4	1.4
148	53.0	55.4	2.4	192	93.0	94.4	1.4
131	63.0	65.4	2.4	272	96.0	94.7	1.3
534	67.0	64.7	2.3	50	8.0	6.7	1.3
387	23.0	20.7	2.3	377	29.0	30.3	1.3
185	94.0	91.7	2.3	477	48.0	46.8	1.2
191	39.0	36.7	2.3	433	18.0	16.8	1.2

591

Comparison of Percentage Responding True, Between the Hathaway and Monachesi
Minnesota State Sample of Ninth Grade Students and Contemporary Normal Adolescents,
Listed Separately by Sex, in Order of Decreasing Endorsement Differences

Males

Item Number	Hathaway and Monachesi	Contemporary Adolescent Males	Difference (Absolute Value)		Item Number	Hathaway and Monachesi	Contemporary Adolescent Males	Difference (Absolute Value)
92	1.0	2.2	1.2		504	43.0	42.8	0.2
216	10.0	11.2	1.2		249	72.0	71.8	0.2
369	74.0	75.2	1.2		388	14.0	13.8	0.2
540	94.0	95.2	1.2		288	2.0	2.2	0.2
563	88.0	86.9	1.1		348	49.0	49.2	0.2
330	84.0	82.9	1.1		220	95.0	94.9	0.1
218	11.0	9.9	1.1		293	8.0	7.9	0.1
5	31.0	32.1	1.1		74	7.0	7.1	0.1
80	55.0	56.1	1.1		172	34.0	34.1	0.1
90	93.0	94.1	1.1		432	31.0	31.1	0.1
103	85.0	86.1	1.1		61	17.0	17.1	0.1
370	73.0	74.0	1.0		54	89.0	89.1	0.1
401	79.0	78.0	1.0		445	88.0	88.1	0.1
291	5.0	4.0	1.0		147	50.0	50.0	0.0
443	39.0	38.0	1.0		168	5.0	5.0	0.0
286	12.0	13.0	1.0		123	5.0	5.0	0.0
83	99.0	98.1	0.9					
273	7.0	6.1	0.9					
161	8.0	7.1	0.9					
205	10.0	10.9	0.9					
422	13.0	13.9	0.9					
389	38.0	38.9	0.9					
178	92.0	92.9	0.9					
207	91.0	90.2	0.8					
538	3.0	2.2	0.8					
535	8.0	7.2	0.8					
42	5.0	5.8	0.8					
533	76.0	76.8	0.8					
556	68.0	67.3	0.7					
491	18.0	17.3	0.7					
202	11.0	11.7	0.7					
227	15.0	15.7	0.7					
478	69.0	69.7	0.7					
392	11.0	10.4	0.6					
246	4.0	3.4	0.6					
423	79.0	78.5	0.5					
294	66.0	66.5	0.5					
167	29.0	28.5	0.5					
455	52.0	51.6	0.4					
210	3.0	2.6	0.4					
106	20.0	20.4	0.4					
230	70.0	69.7	0.3					
56	8.0	7.7	0.3					
163	79.0	79.3	0.3					
63	88.0	88.3	0.3					
130	84.0	84.3	0.3					
187	88.0	88.3	0.3					
528	80.0	80.3	0.3					
518	39.0	38.8	0.2					
378	71.0	70.8	0.2					

APPENDIX I

New Normalized T Scores for MMPI Raw Scores With K Correction for Adolescents Ages 13 to 17 Years

New Normalized T Scores for MMPI Raw Scores With K Correction for Contemporary Female Adolescents

K-corrected raw score	L	F	K	1(Hs) + 0.5K	2(D)	3(Hy)	4(Pd) + 0.4K	5(Mf)	6(Pa)	7(Pt) + 1K	8(Sc) + 1K	9(Ma) + 0.2K	0(Si)	K-corrected raw score
0	23	21	0	-34	-69	-35	-48	130	-9	-131	-93	-43	-16	0
1	40	32	15	-12	-41	-16	-27	128	9	-95	-64	-23	-4	1
2	48	38	21	2	-25	-9	-19	125	16	-73	-48	-15	2	2
3	53	42	26	11	-14	-3	-13	123	22	-58	-36	-9	6	3
4	58	46	30	18	-5	3	-7	121	27	-46	-26	-4	9	4
5	62	49	33	24	3	7	-2	119	31	-36	-19	1	12	5
6	66	51	36	29	9	11	2	117	35	-28	-12	5	14	6
7	70	53	39	34	14	15	6	114	38	-21	-7	9	17	7
8	73	55	42	38	19	18	10	112	42	-15	-2	13	19	8
9	76	57	45	41	23	22	13	110	45	-9	2	16	21	9
10	79	58	47	44	27	25	16	108	48	-4	6	19	23	10
11	82	59	49	47	30	28	19	106	50	1	10	22	25	11
12	84	61	51	50	33	30	22	103	53	5	13	25	27	12
13	87	62	54	52	36	33	25	101	55	9	16	28	29	13
14	89	63	56	54	39	36	28	99	58	12	19	30	30	14
15	91	64	58	56	41	38	31	97	60	16	22	33	32	15
16		65	59	58	44	40	33	94	62	19	24	36	34	16
17		66	61	60	46	43	36	92	65	22	27	38	35	17
18		67	63	62	48	45	38	90	67	25	29	40	37	18
19		67	65	64	50	47	40	88	69	28	31	43	38	19
20		68	66	65	52	49	43	86	71	30	33	45	40	20
21		69	68	67	54	52	45	83	73	33	35	47	41	21
22		69	70	68	56	54	47	81	75	35	37	49	42	22
23		70	71	70	58	56	49	79	77	37	39	51	44	23
24		71	73	71	59	58	51	77	78	39	40	53	45	24
25		71	74	72	61	59	53	75	80	42	42	55	46	25
26		72	76	73	62	61	55	72	82	44	44	57	47	26
27		73	77	75	64	63	57	70	84	45	45	59	48	27
28		73	79	76	65	65	59	68	85	47	47	61	50	28
29		74	80	77	66	67	61	66	87	49	48	63	51	29
30		74	81	78	68	68	63	63	89	51	49	64	52	30
31		75		79	69	70	65	61	90	53	51	66	53	31
32		75		80	70	72	67	59	92	54	52	68	54	32
33		76		81	71	74	68	57	94	56	53	70	55	33
34		76		82	73	75	70	55	95	57	54	71	56	34
35		76		83	74	77	72	52	97	59	56	73	57	35

594

New Normalized T Scores for MMPI Raw Scores With K Correction for Contemporary Female Adolescents

K-corrected raw score	L	F	K	1(Hs) + 0.5K	2(D)	3(Hy)	4(Pd) + 0.4K	5(Mf)	6(Pa)	7(Pt) + 1K	8(Sc) + 1K	9(Ma) + 0.2K	0(Si)	K-corrected raw score
36		77		84	75	78	74	50	98	60	57	75	58	36
37		77		85	76	80	75	48	100	62	58	76	60	37
38		78		86	77	82	77	46	101	63	59	78	61	38
39		78		86	78	83	79	43	102	64	60	79	62	39
40		78		87	79	85	80	41	104	66	61	81	63	40
41		79		88	80	86	82	39		67	62	83	63	41
42		79		89	81	88	83	37		68	63	84	64	42
43		79		89	82	89	85	35		69	64	86	65	43
44		80		90	83	90	86	32		71	65	87	66	44
45		80		91	83	92	88	30		72	66	88	67	45
46		81		92	84	93	89	28		73	67	90	68	46
47		81		92	85	95	91	26		74	68	91	69	47
48		81		93	86	96	92	24		75	68	93	70	48
49		81			87	97	94	21		76	69	94	71	49
50		82			88	99	95	19		77	70	96	72	50
51		82			88	100	97	17		78	71	97	73	51
52		82			89	101	98	15		79	72	98	74	52
53		83			90	103	100	12		80	72		74	53
54		83			91	104	101	10		81	73		75	54
55		83			91	105	102	8		82	74		76	55
56		83			92	107	104	6		83	75		77	56
57		84			93	108	105	4		84	75		78	57
58		84			93	109	106	1		85	76		79	58
59		84			94	110	108	-1		86	77		79	59
60		85			95	112	109	-3		87	78		80	60
61		85					110			88	78		81	61
62		85					112			89	79		82	62
63		85								89	80		83	63
64		86								90	80		83	64
65										91	81		84	65
66										92	81		85	66
67										93	82		86	67
68										93	83		86	68
69										94	83		87	69
70										95	84		88	70
71										96	84			71
72										96	85			72

New Normalized T Scores for MMPI Raw Scores With K Correction for Contemporary Female Adolescents

K-corrected raw score	L	F	K	1(Hs) + 0.5K	2(D)	3(Hy)	4(Pd) + 0.4K	5(Mf)	6(Pa)	7(Pt) + 1K	8(Sc) + 1K	9(Ma) + 0.2K	0(Si)	K-corrected raw score
73										97	86			73
74										98	86			74
75										98	87			75
76										99	87			76
77										100	88			77
78										101	88			78
79											89			79
80											89			80
81											90			81
82											90			82
83											91			83
84											91			84
85											92			85
86											92			86
87											93			87
88											93			88
89											94			89
90											94			90
91											95			91
92											95			92
93											95			93
94											96			94
95											96			95
96											97			96
97											97			97
98											98			98
99											98			99
100											98			100
101											99			101
102											99			102
103											100			103
104											100			104
105											100			105
106											101			106
107											101			107
108											102			108

Note. As an alternative to using a table look-up function, direct computer calculation of these T scores can be done with formulas available from the authors on request. From Colligan, R. C., Offord, K. P. (1991). Adolescents, the MMPI, and the issue of K correction: A contemporary normative study. *Journal of Clinical Psychology* 47:607–631. By permission of Clinical Psychology Publishing Company.

New Normalized T Scores for MMPI Raw Scores With K Correction for Contemporary Male Adolescents

K-corrected raw score	L	F	K	1(Hs) + 0.5K	2(D)	3(Hy)	4(Pd) + 0.4K	5(Mf)	6(Pa)	7(Pt) + 1K	8(Sc) + 1K	9(Ma) + 0.2K	0(Si)	K-corrected raw score
0	24	18	3	-39	-69	-30	-45	-47	-4	-126	-91	-51	-14	0
1	40	29	17	-15	-40	-11	-26	-27	12	-90	-62	-30	-2	1
2	47	35	23	-1	-24	-3	-17	-18	19	-68	-46	-21	3	2
3	52	40	27	9	-12	3	-11	-12	24	-53	-34	-15	7	3
4	56	44	·31	17	-3	8	-6	-7	29	-41	-25	-9	10	4
5	60	47	34	24	4	12	-1	-2	33	-32	-17	-4	13	5
6	63	49	37	29	11	16	3	2	36	-24	-11	1	16	6
7	66	51	40	34	16	20	7	6	39	-17	-6	5	18	7
8	69	53	42	38	21	23	10	10	42	-10	-1	9	20	8
9	72	55	45	42	25	26	14	13	45	-5	4	12	23	9
10	74	56	47	45	29	29	17	17	48	0	7	16	25	10
11	77	58	49	48	33	32	20	20	50	5	11	19	26	11
12	79	59	51	51	36	35	23	23	53	9	14	22	28	12
13	81	60	53	53	39	38	25	26	55	13	17	25	30	13
14	83	62	55	56	42	40	28	28	57	16	20	28	32	14
15	85	63	57	58	44	43	31	31	60	20	23	31	33	15
16		64	58	60	47	45	33	33	62	23	25	33	35	16
17		64	60	62	49	47	36	36	64	26	28	36	36	17
18		65	62	64	51	50	38	38	66	29	30	38	38	18
19		66	63	66	53	52	40	41	68	32	32	41	39	19
20		67	65	68	55	54	42	43	69	34	34	43	40	20
21		68	67	69	57	56	45	45	71	37	36	46	42	21
22		68	68	71	59	58	47	47	73	39	38	48	43	22
23		69	69	72	61	60	49	49	75	41	39	50	44	23
24		70	71	74	63	62	51	52	76	43	41	52	46	24
25		70	72	75	64	64	53	54	78	45	43	54	47	25
26		71	74	76	66	66	55	56	80	47	44	56	48	26
27		72	75	78	67	68	57	57	81	49	46	58	49	27
28		72	76	79	69	69	58	59	83	51	47	60	50	28
29		73	78	80	70	71	60	61	84	53	48	62	52	29
30		73	79	81	71	73	62	63	86	55	50	64	53	30
31		74		82	73	75	64	65	87	56	51	66	54	31
32		74		83	74	76	66	67	89	58	52	68	55	32
33		75		84	75	78	67	68	90	59	54	70	56	33
34		75		85	76	80	69	70	92	61	55	72	57	34
35		76		86	77	81	71	72	93	63	56	74	58	35
36		76		87	79	83	72	74	95	64	57	75	59	36
37		77		88	80	84	74	75	96	65	58	77	60	37
38		77		89	81	86	76	77	97	67	59	79	61	38

New Normalized T Scores for MMPI Raw Scores With K Correction for Contemporary Male Adolescents

K-corrected raw score	L	F	K	1(Hs) + 0.5K	2(D)	3(Hy)	4(Pd) + 0.4K	5(Mf)	6(Pa)	7(Pt) + 1K	8(Sc) + 1K	9(Ma) + 0.2K	0(Si)	K-corrected raw score
39		77		90	82	87	77	79	99	68	60	81	62	39
40		78		91	83	89	79	80	100	69	61	82	63	40
41		78		92	84	90	80	82		71	62	84	64	41
42		79		93	85	92	82	83		72	63	86	65	42
43		79		93	86	93	83	85		73	64	87	66	43
44		79		94	86	95	85	86		74	65	89	67	44
45		80		95	87	96	86	88		75	66	90	68	45
46		80		96	88	97	88	89		77	67	92	69	46
47		80		96	89	99	89	91		78	68	93	69	47
48		81		97	90	100	91	92		79	69	95	70	48
49		81			91	102	92	94		80	69	97	71	49
50		81			92	103	93	95		81	70	98	72	50
51		82			92	104	95	97		82	71	100	73	51
52		82			93	106	96	98		83	72	101	74	52
53		82			94	107	97	99		84	73		75	53
54		83			95	108	99	101		85	73		75	54
55		83			95	109	100	102		86	74		76	55
56		83			96	111	101	103		87	75		77	56
57		83			97	112	103	105		88	75		78	57
58		84			98	113	104	106		89	76		79	58
59		84			98	114	105	107		89	77		79	59
60		84			99	116	107	109		90	78		80	60
61		85					108			91	78		81	61
62		85					109			92	79		82	62
63		85								93	79		83	63
64		85								94	80		83	64
65										94	81		84	65
66										95	81		85	66
67										96	82		86	67
68										97	83		86	68
69										98	83		87	69
70										98	84		88	70
71										99	84			71
72										100	85			72
73										100	85			73
74										101	86			74
75										102	87			75
76										103	87			76
77										103	88			77
78										104	88			78

K-corrected raw score	L	F	K	1(Hs) + 0.5K	2(D)	3(Hy)	4(Pd) + 0.4K	5(Mf)	6(Pa)	7(Pt) + 1K	8(Sc) + 1K	9(Ma) + 0.2K	0(Si)	K-corrected raw score
79											89			79
80											89			80
81											90			81
82											90			82
83											91			83
84											91			84
85											92			85
86											92			86
87											93			87
88											93			88
89											93			89
90											94			90
91											94			91
92											95			92
93											95			93
94											96			94
95											96			95
96											96			96
97											97			97
98											97			98
99											98			99
100											98			100
101											99			101
102											99			102
103											99			103
104											100			104
105											100			105
106											101			106
107											101			107
108											101			108

Note. As an alternative to using a table look-up function, direct computer calculation of these T scores can be done with formulas available from the authors on request. From Colligan, R. C., Offord, K. P. (1991). Adolescents, the MMPI, and the issue of K correction: A contemporary normative study. *Journal of Clinical Psychology* 47:607–631. By permission of Clinical Psychology Publishing Company.

References

Ahles, T. A., & Martin, J. B. (1989). The relationship of electromyographic and vasomotor activity to MMPI subgroups in chronic headache patients: The use of the original and contemporary MMPI norms. *Headache, 29,* 584–587.

Ahles, T. A., Yunus, M. B., Gaulier, B., Riley, S. D., & Masi, A. T. (1986). The use of contemporary MMPI norms in the study of chronic pain patients. *Pain, 24,* 159–163.

Archer, R. P. (1984). Use of the MMPI with adolescents: A review of salient issues. *Clinical Psychology Review, 4,* 241–251.

Archer, R. P. (1987). *Using the MMPI with adolescents.* Hillsdale, NJ: Erlbaum.

Archer, R. P. (1990, October). *Using the MMPI/MMPI-2 with adolescents: Clinical applications and current research.* Workshop presented through the Section of Continuing Education by the Department of Psychiatry and Psychology, Mayo Clinic and Mayo Foundation, Siebens Education Building, Rochester, MN.

Bell, H. M. (1934). *Adjustment inventory.* Stanford, CA: Stanford University Press.

Ben-Porath, Y. S. (1990, March). MMPI-2 items. *MMPI-2 News and Profiles—A Newsletter of the MMPI-2 Workshops & Symposia, 1*(1), 8–9.

Bernreuter, R. G. (1933). The theory and construction of the personality inventory. *Journal of Social Psychology, 4,* 387–404.

Berry, D. F. (1971). Cited by Marks, P. A., Seeman, W., & Haller, D. L. (1974). *The acturial use of the MMPI with adolescents and adults.* Baltimore: Williams & Wilkins.

Berry, D. F., & Marks, P. A. (1972). Comparison of multivariate procedures for grouping MMPI profile data. *Proceedings of the 80th Annual Convention of the American Psychological Association,* Washington, D.C., American Psychological Association (pp. 387–388).

Binet, A., & Simon, T. (1916). *The development of intelligence in children (The Binet-Simon Scale).* Baltimore: Williams & Wilkins.

Bornstein, R. A., Rosenberger, P., Harkness-Kling, K., & Suga, L. (1989). Content bias of the MacAndrew's alcoholism scale in seizure disorder patients. *Journal of Clinical Psychology, 45,* 339–341.

Box, G. E. P., & Cox, D. R. (1964). An analysis of transformations. *Journal of the Royal Statistical Society, Series B, 26,* 211–243.

Burisch, M. (1984). Approaches to personality inventory construction: A comparison of merits. *American Psychologist, 39,* 214–227.

Butcher, J. N. (1990a, June). *Progress on the MMPI-2 for adolescents.* Paper presented at the 25th Annual Symposium on Recent Developments in the Use of the MMPI (MMPI-2), Minneapolis, MN.

Butcher, J. N. (1990b). *The MMPI-2 in psychological treatment.* New York: Oxford University Press.

Butcher, J. N., Dahlstrom, W. G., Graham, J. R., Tellegen, A., & Kaemmer, B. (1989). *Manual for administration and scoring—MMPI-2 Minnesota Multiphasic Personality Inventory-2.* Minneapolis: University of Minnesota Press.

Butcher, J. N., Graham, J. R., Williams, C. L., & Ben-Porath, Y. S. (1990). *Development and use of the MMPI-2 content scales.* Minneapolis: University of Minnesota Press.

Caldwell, A. B. (1988). *MMPI supplemental scale manual.* Los Angeles: Caldwell Report.

Chuong, C. J., Colligan, R. C., Coulam, C. B., & Bergstralh, E. J. (1988). The MMPI as an aid in evaluating patients with premenstrual syndrome. *Psychosomatics, 29,* 197–202.

Colligan, R. C., & Offord, K. P. (1989). The aging MMPI: Contemporary norms for contemporary teenagers. *Mayo Clinic Proceedings, 64,* 3–27.

Colligan, R. C., & Offord, K. P. (1991). Adolescents, the MMPI, and the issue of K correction: A contemporary normative study. *Journal of Clinical Psychology, 47,* 607–631.

Colligan, R. C., & Osborne, D. (1977). MMPI profiles from adolescent medical patients. *Journal of Clinical Psychology, 33,* 186–189.

Colligan, R. C., Osborne, D., & Offord, K. P. (1980). Linear transformation and the interpretation of MMPI T scores. *Journal of Clinical Psychology, 36,* 162–165.

Colligan, R. C., Osborne, D., & Offord, K. P. (1984a). Normalized transformations and the interpretation of MMPI T scores: A reply to Hsu. *Journal of Consulting and Clinical Psychology, 52,* 824–826.

Colligan, R. C., Osborne, D., Swenson, W. M., & Offord, K. P. (1983). *The MMPI: A contemporary normative study.* New York: Praeger Publishers.

Colligan, R. C., Osborne, D., Swenson, W. M., & Offord, K. P. (1984b). The aging MMPI: Development of contemporary norms. *Mayo Clinic Proceedings, 59,* 377–390.

Colligan, R. C., Osborne, D., Swenson, W. M., & Offord, K. P. (1984c). The MMPI: Development of contemporary norms. *Journal of Clinical Psychology, 40,* 100–107.

Colligan, R. C., Osborne, D., Swenson, W. M., & Offord, K. P. (1985). Using the 1983 norms for the MMPI: Code type frequencies in four clinical samples. *Journal of Clinical Psychology, 41,* 629–633.

Colligan, R. C., Osborne, D., Swenson, W. M., & Offord, K. P. (1989). *The MMPI: A contemporary normative study of adults* (2nd ed.). Odessa, FL: Psychological Assessment Resources.

Colligan, R. C., Osborne, D., Swenson, W. M., Offord, K. P., & Davis, L. J. (1984d, August). *Contemporary norms for the MMPI: Summarizing one year of clinical experience.* Symposium presented to the 93rd Annual National Convention of the American Psychological Association, Toronto, Ontario, Canada. (Discussant: Jan D. Duker, Ph.D., Executive Director, State Department of Mental Health, Jackson, MS.)

Dahlstrom, W. G., Diehl, L. A., & Lachar, D. (1986). MMPI correlates of the demographic characteristics of black and white normal adults. In W. G. Dahlstrom, D. Lachar, & L. E. Dahlstrom (Eds.), *MMPI patterns of American minorities* (pp. 104–138). Minneapolis: University of Minnesota Press.

Dahlstrom, W. G., & Welsh, G. S. (1960). *An MMPI handbook: A guide to use in clinical practice and research.* Minneapolis: University of Minnesota Press.

Dahlstrom, W. G., Welsh, G. S., & Dahlstrom, L. E. (1972). *An MMPI handbook. Volume I: Clinical interpretation.* Minneapolis: University of Minnesota Press.

Dahlstrom, W. G., Welsh, G. S., & Dahlstrom, L. E. (1975). *An MMPI handbook. Volume II: Research applications.* Minneapolis: University of Minnesota Press.

Diehl, L. A. (1977). The relationship between demographic factors, MMPI scores and the social readjustment rating scale (abstract). *Dissertation Abstracts International, 38*(5-B), 2360.

Drake, L. E. (1946). A social I.E. scale for the Minnesota Multiphasic Personality Inventory. *Journal of Applied Psychology, 30,* 51–54.

Drake, L. E., & Thiede, W. B. (1948). Further validation of the social I.E. scale for the Minnesota Multiphasic Personality Inventory. *Journal of Educational Research, 41,* 551–556.

Ellis, A. (1946). The validity of personality questionnaires. *Psychological Bulletin, 43,* 385–440.

Ellis, A., & Conrad, H. S. (1948). The validity of personality inventories in military practice. *Psychological Bulletin, 45,* 385–426.

Epstein, S. (1987). The relative value of theoretical and empirical approaches for establishing a psychological diagnostic system. *Journal of Personality Disorders, 1,* 100–109.

Evans, C., & McConnell, T. R. (1941). A new measure of introversion-extroversion. *Journal of Psychology, 12,* 111–124.

Friedman, A. F., Webb, J. T., & Lewak, R. (1989). *Psychological assessment with the MMPI.* Hillsdale, NJ: Erlbaum.

Glaros, A. G., & Kline, R. B. (1988). Understanding the accuracy of tests with cutting scores: The sensitivity, specificity, and predictive value model. *Journal of Clinical Psychology, 44,* 1013–1023.

Gottesman, I. I. (1963). Heritability of personality: A demonstration. *Psychological Monographs, 77*(9), 1–21.

Gottesman, I. I. (1966). Genetic variance in adaptive personality traits. *Journal of Child Psychology and Psychiatry, 7,* 199–208.

Gottesman, I. I., Hanson, D. R., Kroeker, T. A., & Briggs, P. F. (1987). New MMPI normative data and power-transformed T-score tables for the Hathaway-Monachesi Minnesota cohort of 14,019 15-year-olds and 3,674 18-year-olds. In R. P. Archer (Ed.), *Using the MMPI with adolescents* (Appendix C, pp. 241–297). Hillsdale, NJ: Erlbaum.

Gottesman, I. I., & Prescott, C. A. (1989). Abuses of the MacAndrew MMPI Alcoholism Scale: A critical review. *Clinical Psychology Review, 9,* 223–242.

Gough, H. G. (1947). Simulated patterns on the Minnesota Multiphasic Personality Inventory. *Journal of Abnormal and Social Psychology, 42,* 215–225.

Gough, H. G. (1949). A research note on the MMPI social I.E. scale. *Journal of Educational Research, 43,* 138–141.

Graham, J. R. (1987). *The MMPI: A practical guide* (2nd ed.). New York: Oxford University Press.

Graham, J. R. (1990). *MMPI-2: Assessing personality and psychopathology.* New York: Oxford University Press.

Graham, J. R., & Lilly, R. S. (March 1986). *Linear T-scores versus normalized T scores: An empirical study.* Paper presented at the 21st Annual Symposium on Recent Developments in the Use of the MMPI, Clearwater Beach, FL.

Greene, R. L. (1980). *The MMPI: An interpretive manual.* New York: Grune & Stratton.

Greene, R. L. (1988). *The MMPI: Use with specific populations.* Philadelphia: Grune & Stratton.

Greene, R. L. (1991). *The MMPI-2/MMPI: An interpretive manual.* Boston: Allyn and Bacon.

Guilmette, T. J., Faust, D., Hart, K., & Arkes, H. R. (1990). A national survey of psychologists who offer neuropsychological services. *Archives of Clinical Neuropsychology, 5,* 373–392.

Harris, R. E., & Lingoes, J. C. (1955). Subscales for the Minnesota Multiphasic Personality Inventory—An aid to profile interpretation. [Unpublished mimeographed data.] University of California, School of Medicine and the Langley-Porter Clinic, Department of Psychiatry, San Francisco, CA. (Available from J. C. Lingoes, Ph.D., Computing Center, University of Michigan, 1075 Beal Avenue, Ann Arbor, MI 48109–2112.)

Hathaway, S. R. (1956). Scales 5 (masculinity-femininity), 6 (paranoia), and 8 (schizophrenia). In G. S. Welsh & W. G. Dahlstrom (Eds.), *Basic readings on the MMPI in psychology and medicine* (pp. 104–111). Minneapolis: University of Minnesota Press.

Hathaway, S. R. (1964). MMPI: Professional use by professional people. *American Psychologist, 19,* 204–210.

Hathaway, S. R. (1965). Personality inventories. In B. B. Wolman (Ed.), *Handbook of clinical psychology* (pp. 451–476). New York: McGraw-Hill Book Company.

Hathaway, S. R. (1978). Through psychology my way. In T. S. Krawiec (Ed.), *The Psychologists: Autobiographies of distinguished living psychologists* (Vol. 3, pp. 105–123). Brandon, VT: Clinical Psychology Publishing Company.

Hathaway, S. R., & Briggs, P. F. (1957). Some normative data on the new MMPI scales. *Journal of Clinical Psychology, 13,* 364–368.

Hathaway, S. R., & McKinley, J. C. (1940). A multiphasic personality schedule (Minnesota): I. Construction of the schedule. *Journal of Psychology, 10,* 249–254.

Hathaway, S. R., & McKinley, J. C. (1942). A multiphasic personality schedule (Minnesota): III. The measurement of symptomatic depression. *Journal of Psychology, 14,* 73–84.

Hathaway, S. R., & McKinley, J. C. (1943). *Manual for the Minnesota Multiphasic Personality Inventory* (rev. ed.). Minneapolis: University of Minnesota Press.

Hathaway, S. R., & Meehl, P. E. (1951). Section IX. The Minnesota Multiphasic Personality Inventory. In *Military clinical psychology* (pp. 71–111). Washington, DC: United States Government Printing Office.

Hathaway, S. R., & Monachesi, E. D. (Eds.). (1953). *Analyzing and predicting juvenile delinquency with the MMPI.* Minneapolis: University of Minnesota Press.

Hathaway, S. R., & Monachesi, E. D. (1961). *An atlas of juvenile MMPI profiles.* Minneapolis: University of Minnesota Press.

Hathaway, S. R., & Monachesi, E. D. (1963). *Adolescent personality and behavior: MMPI patterns of normal, delinquent, dropout, and other outcomes.* Minneapolis: University of Minnesota Press.

Heilbrun, A. B., Jr. (1963). Revision of the MMPI K correction procedure for improved detection of maladjustment in a normal college population. *Journal of Consulting Psychology, 27,* 161–165.

Helmes, E., & Jackson, D. N. (1982). A comparison of methods of normalizing a discrete distribution. *Journal of Clinical Psychology, 38,* 581–587.

Hill, M. S., & Hill, R. N. (1973). Hereditary influence on the normal personality using the MMPI: I. Age-corrected parent-offspring resemblances. *Behavior Genetics, 3,* 133–144.

Hsu, L. M. (1984). MMPI T scores: Linear versus normalized. *Journal of Consulting and Clinical Psychology, 52,* 821–823.

Hsu, L. M. (1986). Implications of differences in elevations of K-corrected and non-K-corrected MMPI T scores. *Journal of Consulting and Clinical Psychology, 54,* 552–557.

Hsu, L. M., & Betman, J. A. (1986). Minnesota Multiphasic Personality Inventory T score conversion tables, 1957–1983. *Journal of Consulting and Clinical Psychology, 54,* 497–501.

Humm, D. G., & Wadsworth, G. W., Jr. (1933). A diagnostic inventory of temperament, preliminary report. *Psychological Bulletin, 30,* 602.

Humm, D. G., & Wadsworth, G. W., Jr. (1935). The Humm-Wadsworth temperament scale. *American Journal of Psychiatry, 92,* 163–200.

Landis, C., & Katz, S. E. (1934). The validity of certain questions which purport to measure neurotic tendencies. *Journal of Applied Psychology, 18,* 343–356.

Levitt, E. E. (1989). *The clinical application of MMPI special scales.* Hillsdale, NJ: Erlbaum.

Lewak, R. W., Marks, P. A., & Nelson, G. E. (1990). *Therapist guide to the MMPI & MMPI-2: Providing feedback and treatment.* Muncie, IN: Accelerated Development.

Loper, R., Robertson, J., & Swanson, E. (1968). College freshmen MMPI norms over a fourteen-year period. *Journal of College Student Personnel, 32,* 404–407.

Lubin, B., Larsen, R. M., & Matarazzo, J. D. (1984). Patterns of psychological test usage in the United States: 1935–1982. *American Psychologist, 39,* 451–454.

Lubin, B., Larsen, R. M., Matarazzo, J. D., & Seever, M. (1985). Psychological test usage patterns in five professional settings. *American Psychologist, 40,* 857–861.

Lyght, C. E. (Ed.). (1966). *The Merck manual of diagnosis and therapy* (11th ed.). West Point, PA: Merck Sharp and Dohme Research Laboratories.

MacAndrew, C. (1965). The differentiation of male alcoholic outpatients from nonalcoholic psychiatric outpatients by means of the MMPI. *Quarterly Journal of Studies on Alcohol, 26,* 238–246.

Marks, P. (1990, August). [Discussant remarks on "The MMPI and adolescents: Historical perspective, current research, future developments."] Symposium presented to the 99th Annual Convention of the American Psychological Association, Boston, MA.

Marks, P. A., & Briggs, P. F. (1967). Cited by Dahlstrom, W. G., Welsh, G. S., & Dahlstrom, L. E. (1972). *An MMPI handbook. Volume I: Clinical interpretation.* Minneapolis: University of Minnesota Press.

Marks, P. A ., & Briggs, P. F. (1987). Adolescent norms for males and females at ages 17, 16, 15, and 14 and below. In R. P. Archer (Ed.), *Using the MMPI with adolescents* (pp. 197–213). Hillsdale, NJ: Erlbaum.

Marks, P. A., & Seeman, W. (1962). Addendum to "an assessment of the diagnostic process in a child guidance setting." *Journal of Consulting Psychology, 26,* 485.

Marks, P. A., Seeman, W., & Haller, D. L. (1974). *The actuarial use of the MMPI with adolescents and adults.* Baltimore: Williams & Wilkins.

McKinley, J. C., & Hathaway, S. R. (1940). A multiphasic personality schedule (Minnesota): II. A differential study of hypochondriasis. *Journal of Psychology, 10,* 255–268.

McKinley, J. C., & Hathaway, S. R. (1942). A multiphasic personality schedule (Minnesota): IV. Psychasthenia. *Journal of Applied Psychology, 26,* 614–624.

McKinley, J. C., & Hathaway, S. R. (1943). The identification and measurement of the psychoneuroses in medical practice. *Journal of the American Medical Association, 122,* 161–167.

McKinley, J. C., & Hathaway, S. R. (1944). The Minnesota Multiphasic Personality Inventory: V. Hysteria, hypomania and psychopathic deviate. *Journal of Applied Psychology, 28,* 153–174.

McKinley, J. C., Hathaway, S. R., & Meehl, P. E. (1948). The Minnesota Multiphasic Personality Inventory: VI: The K scale. *Journal of Consulting Psychology, 12,* 20–31.

Meehl, P. E. (1945). An investigation of a general normality or control factor in personality testing. *Psychological Monographs, 59*(4), 1–62.

Meehl, P. E., & Hathaway, S. R. (1946). The K factor as a suppressor variable in the Minnesota Multiphasic Personality Inventory. *Journal of Applied Psychology, 30,* 525–564.

Miller, H. R., & Streiner, D. L. (1986). Difference in MMPI profiles with the norms of Colligan et al. *Journal of Consulting and Clinical Psychology, 54,* 843–845.

Monachesi, E. D. (1953). The personality patterns of juvenile delinquents as indicated by the MMPI (study 2). In S. R. Hathaway & E. D. Monachesi (Eds.), *Analyzing and predicting juvenile delinquency with the MMPI* (pp. 38–53). Minneapolis: University of Minnesota Press.

Moreland, K. L., & Dahlstrom, W. G. (1983). A survey of MMPI teaching in APA-approved clinical training programs. *Journal of Personality Assessment, 47,* 115–119.

Munley, P. H., & Zarantonello, M. M. (1989). A comparison of MMPI profile types across standard and contemporary norms. *Journal of Clinical Psychology, 45,* 229–239.

Nakamura, C. Y. (1960). Validity of the K scale (MMPI) in college counseling. *Journal of Counseling Psychology, 7,* 108–115.

Piotrowski, C., & Keller, J. W. (1984). Attitudes toward clinical assessment by members of the AABT [Association for Advancement of Behavior Therapy]. *Psychological Reports, 55,* 831–838.

Piotrowski, C., & Keller, J. W. (1989). Psychological testing in outpatient mental health facilities: A national study. *Professional Psychology: Research and Practice, 20,* 423–425.

Piotrowski, C., & Lubin, B. (1989). Assessment practices of Division 38 practitioners. *The Health Psychologist, 11*(1), 1–2.

Piotrowski, C., & Lubin, B. (1990). Assessment practices of health psychologists: Survey of APA Division 38 clinicians. *Professional Psychology: Research and Practice, 21,* 99–106.

Polley, H. F., Swenson, W. M., & Steinhilber, R. M. (1970). Personality characteristics of patients with rheumatoid arthritis. *Psychosomatics, 11,* 45–49.

Schneider, L. (1976). MMPI patterns of college males from 1969 to 1973. *Junior College Student Personnel, 17*(5), 417–419.

Schubert, D. S. P., & Wagner, M. E. (1975). A subcultural change of MMPI norms in the 1960s due to adolescent role confusion and glamorization of alienation. *Journal of Abnormal Psychology, 84,* 406–411.

Sellers, A. H., & Nadler, J. (1990, April). *A survey of current neuropsychological assessment procedures.* Paper presented at the 36th Annual Meeting of the Southeastern Psychological Association, Atlanta, GA.

Strong, E. K., Jr. (1927). Differentiation of certified public accountants from other occupational groups. *Journal of Educational Psychology, 18,* 227–238.

Strong, E. K., Jr. (1943). *Vocational interests of men and women.* Stanford, CA: Stanford University Press.

Swenson, W. M., Osborne, D., & Colligan, R. C. (1990). *A user's guide to the Mayo Clinic computerized scoring and interpretative system for the Minnesota Multiphasic Personality Inventory (MMPI)* (3rd ed.). Rochester, MN: Mayo Foundation.

Swenson, W. M., Pearson, J. S., & Osborne, D. (1973). *An MMPI source book: Basic item, scale, and pattern data on 50,000 medical patients.* Minneapolis: University of Minnesota Press.

Tellegen, A., & Ben-Porath, Y. S. (1990, June). *Adolescent norms for the MMPI-2.* Paper presented at the 25th Annual Symposium on Recent Developments in the Use of the MMPI (MMPI-2), Minneapolis, MN.

Terman, L. M., & Miles, C. C. (1936). *Sex and personality: Studies in masculinity and femininity.* New York: McGraw-Hill.

Tyler, F. T., & Michaelis, J. U. (1953). K-Scores applied to MMPI scales for college women. *Educational and Psychological Measurement, 13,* 459–466.

Watkins, C. E., Jr., Campbell, V. L., & McGregor, P. (1988). Counseling psychologists' uses of and opinions about psychological tests: A contemporary perspective. *The Counseling Psychologist, 16*(3), 476–486.

Watkins, C. E., Jr., Campbell, V. L., McGregor, P., & Godin, K. (1989). The MMPI: Does it have a place in counseling psychology training? *Journal of Personality Assessment, 53,* 413–417.

Weisgerber, C. A. (1965). Comparison of normalized and linear T scores in the MMPI. *Journal of Clinical Psychology, 21,* 412–415.

Welsh, G. S. (1956). Factor dimensions A and R. In G. S. Welsh & W. G. Dahlstrom (Eds.), *Basic readings on the MMPI in psychology and medicine* (pp. 264–281). Minneapolis: University of Minnesota Press.

Welsh, G. S. (1965). MMPI profiles and factor scales A and R. *Journal of Clinical Psychology, 21*, 43–47.

Welsh, G. S., & Dahlstrom, W. G. (1956). Cited by Marks, P. A., Seeman, W., & Haller, D. L. (1974). *The acturial use of the MMPI with adolescents and adults.* Baltimore: Williams & Wilkins.

Wiggins, J. S. (1966). Substantive dimensions of self-report in the MMPI item pool. *Psychological Monographs: General and Applied, 80*(22, Whole no. 630), 1–42.

Wiggins, J. S., Goldberg, L. R., & Appelbaum, M. (1971). MMPI content scales: Interpretative norms and correlations with other scales. *Journal of Consulting and Clinical Psychology, 37*, 403–410.

Williams, C. L. (1990a, March). Adolescents and the MMPI: Present and future. *MMPI-2 News and Profiles—A Newsletter of the MMPI-2 Workshops & Symposia, 1*(1), 5.

Williams, C. L. (1990b, June). *Developmental strategy for the adolescent MMPI content scales.* Paper presented at the 25th Annual Symposium on Recent Developments in the Use of the MMPI (MMPI-2), Minneapolis, MN.

Wiiliams, C. L., & Butcher, J. N. (1989a). An MMPI study of adolescents: I. Empirical validity of the standard scales. *Psychological Assessment: A Journal of Consulting and Clinical Psychology, 1*, 251–259.

Williams, C. L., & Butcher, J. N. (1989b). An MMPI study of adolescents: II. Verification and limitations of code type classification. *Psychological Assessment: A Journal of Consulting and Clinical Psychology, 1*, 260–265.

Wooten, A. J. (1984). Effective of the K correction in the detection of psychopathology and its impact on profile height and configuration among young adult men. *Journal of Consulting and Clinical Psychology, 52*, 468–473.

Yonge, G. D. (1966). Certain consequences of applying the K factor to MMPI scores. *Educational and Psychological Measurement, 26*, 887–893.

Information About the Authors

Robert C. Colligan was an elementary school, and later a junior high school math and science, teacher before he received his doctoral degree in school psychological services from the University of Minnesota under the direction of Dr. Jan Duker. He has been at the Mayo Clinic since 1969, where he currently is a Consultant in the Department of Psychiatry and Psychology, Head of the Section of Psychology, and Professor of Psychology in the Mayo Medical School. He earned diplomate status in school psychology from the American Board of Professional Psychology in 1976 and is a licensed school psychologist and licensed consulting psychologist in the state of Minnesota, licensed psychologist in the state of Florida, and certified psychologist in the state of Arizona.

Kenneth P. Offord is a Consultant in the Section of Biostatistics and Associate Professor of Biostatistics in the Mayo Medical School, is the founder and director of the Survey Research Center at Mayo Clinic, and has been an applied statistician at the Mayo Clinic since 1971. After high school, he spent 3 years as a flight engineer in the U.S. Navy. Concurrent with undergraduate studies, he was a foreign exchange student to India and also a senior scholar for the U.S. Agency of International Development in southern Brazil. He received a master's degree in statistics from Iowa State University in 1969. In addition to statistics and psychology, his research interests and more than 160 publications include topics in survey research, pulmonary physiology, allergy, anesthesiology, neurology, nephrology, pediatric cardiology, epidemiology, computer science, nicotine dependence, and smoking cessation.

AUTHOR INDEX

SUBJECT INDEX